Patterns in
American
History

Volume I

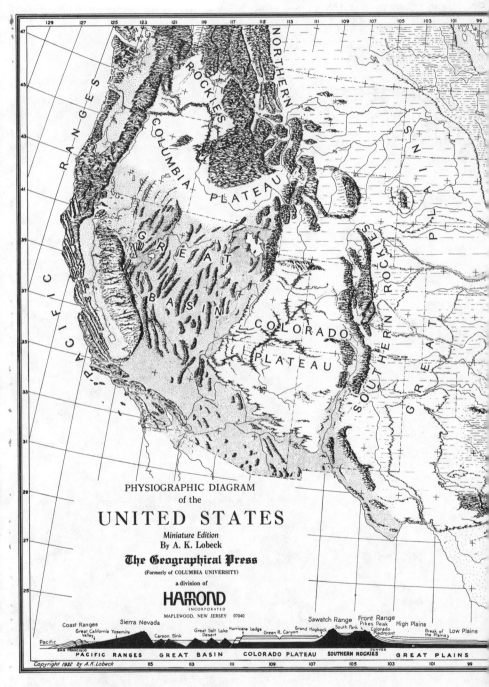

PHYSIOGRAPHIC DIAGRAM
of the

UNITED STATES

Miniature Edition
By A. K. Lobeck

𝕿𝖍𝖊 𝕲𝖊𝖔𝖌𝖗𝖆𝖕𝖍𝖎𝖈𝖆𝖑 𝕻𝖗𝖊𝖘𝖘
(Formerly of COLUMBIA UNIVERSITY)

a division of

HAMMOND
INCORPORATED
MAPLEWOOD, NEW JERSEY   07040

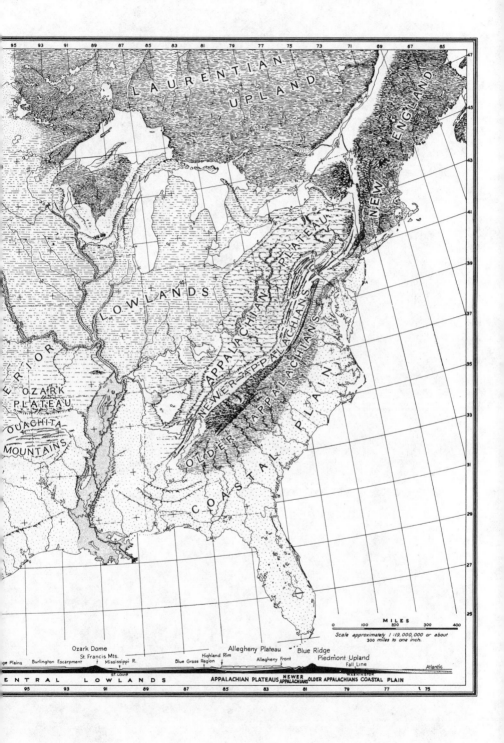

LAURENTIAN UPLAND

NEW ENGLAND

INTERIOR LOWLANDS

OZARK PLATEAU

OUACHITA MOUNTAINS

APPALACHIAN PLATEAU

NEWER APPALACHIANS

OLDER APPALACHIANS

COASTAL PLAIN

MILES
0   100   200   300   400

Scale approximately 1:19,000,000 or about
300 miles to one inch.

Ozark Dome
St. Francis Mts.
ge Plains   Burlington Escarpment   Mississippi R.

Allegheny Plateau   Blue Ridge

Highland Rim   Piedmont Upland
Blue Grass Region   Allegheny Front   Fall Line

ST. LOUIS   WASHINGTON   Atlantic

E N T R A L   L O W L A N D S   APPALACHIAN PLATEAUS   NEWER APPALACHIANS   OLDER APPALACHIANS   COASTAL PLAIN

Patterns in American History

Third Edition

Volume I

Alexander DeConde
University of California, Santa Barbara

Armin Rappaport
University of California, San Diego

William R. Steckel
The University of Wyoming

Wadsworth Publishing Company, Inc.
Belmont, California

© 1973 by Wadsworth Publishing Company, Inc.

© 1965, 1970 by Wadsworth Publishing Company, Inc., Belmont, California 94002. All rights reserved. No part of this book may be reproduced, stored in a retrieval system, or transcribed, in any form or by any means, electronic, mechanical, photocopying, recording, or otherwise, without the prior written permission of the publisher.

ISBN 0-534-00293-5

L. C. Cat. Card No. 72-95668

Printed in the United States of America

2 3 4 5 6 7 8 9 10 — 77 76 75 74

Preface

Written history won't stand still. The "facts" stay put, but which "facts" the historian chooses to look at and how he sees them are in a constant state of flux. To those who wish that historians would stand still, even if history will not, one may comment that the society of which historians are a part does not stand still either. The interests and attitudes of Americans have taken significant turns even in the eight years since the first edition of these volumes.

Historians are affected by and shape such turns in society. This third edition shows how historians, ourselves included, have changed our concerns and revised our interpretations. We assume that changes in concerns and interpretations will broaden and deepen our understanding of the American past.

Since our two volumes, which combine extensive editorial commentary with selected readings, differ noticeably from most anthologies of American history, an explanation of their structure and what we have sought to do may be helpful. The structure is basically thematic. We have tried to show that American history can be analyzed and understood by means of patterns, or topics, that have a measure of order and unity. We believe that there are significant themes which the college student should encounter on more intimate terms than is possible in the textbook, that these themes can provide a sound basis for teaching and for class discussion, and that they should be studied in depth through both interpretive and narrative literature—though we usually prefer the interpretive over the descriptive. With these ideas in mind, we have organized each chapter around a significant theme. Since there are thirty chapters and the usual course in American history covers an academic year of about thirty weeks, each chapter or topic offers material that can fit into one week's work in such a course.

Our introductions in each chapter, which are considerably longer than those found in most anthologies, constitute a unique feature of the book. These introductions show the unity in the topic; they help the reader by explaining significant themes, or by guiding him to a discovery of themes, of pervasive points of view, or of clashing interpretations; and they offer some insight on historical method and analysis. In the editorial commentaries preceding each selection, we have been guided by similar principles. In addition, we have stressed points that may serve as a departure for class discussion; and we have often included significant biographical data on the author of a selection, believing that this data will help the reader see historical writing in a context of scholarship.

We have sought to provide authoritative, stimulating, and enlightening selections, always with the view of introducing the reader to some of the best thinking in American historical literature. Although the main thread or unifying theme is the usual political one, we have tried to create variety and balance with readings that stress other aspects of American history, such as the economic, the diplomatic, the social, and the intellectual. We think that by treating such themes as war as a social institution and the intellectual problems in agrarianism and urbanism, we point up elements or connections in the mainstream of American development that have frequently been neglected in books of readings.

Since our purpose is to stimulate ideas and interpretations rather than to be concerned with the mechanics of scholarship, we have omitted the footnotes that frequently appear in the original selections. We do not consider the footnotes unimportant, however; we believe they are valuable, and hope that some readers will have their intellectual appetites whetted enough to go to the larger works from which many of the selections come.

The principles behind this edition are the same as those that guided the first, though we have been affected by the continuing ferment in academic life, especially by the revived concern for the quality of teaching. We are now more concerned than we were five years ago with producing a good teaching book. We have dropped some of the older descriptive selections, added a large number of new interpretive readings, introduced several new topics, modified our introductions in the light of recent scholarship, and generally brought the book up to date. More than in the first edition we have stressed interpretive themes, believing that the student should be kept abreast of new, provocative, and often controversial historical writing. The result is an extensively revised book that we feel is intellectually stimulating, readable, and teachable.

In Volume 1, Professor Steckel assumed the major responsibility for Chapters 1-10 and Professor DeConde for 11-15; in Volume 2, Professor DeConde for Chapters 1-5 and Professor Rappaport for 6-16.

Alexander DeConde
Armin Rappaport
William R. Steckel

Contents

Patterns in
American
History

Volume I

A pattern of hostility between red man and white arose early in Virginia. In the very year that the colony was planted, Captain John Smith was captured by the Indians (left). At first condemned to death, he was later pardoned, perhaps through the intercession of Pocahontas. The next year, he evened the score, capturing an Indian chief (right).

1 Patterns in Red, White, and Black

There are "patterns" in American history in several senses, one of which is well defined in *Webster's Third New International Dictionary*: "an established mode of behavior or cluster of mental attitudes, beliefs, and values held in common by the members of a group." This chapter is concerned with one of the oldest patterns (in this sense of the word) in American history, and one which is of central concern today: relations between the races.

In 1600 there had been virtually no direct contact between Englishmen and Indians and Africans. By the end of that century thousands of each race had encountered the others in a wide variety of ways, out of which had gradually arisen patterns of relationships which would persist for two centuries and more.

In 1600 the Englishmen who would come to America had only the fuzziest notions about Indians, largely distortions through a filter of romance and hearsay about Spain's century of experience in the West Indies and Latin America. By 1700 the descendants of those Englishmen, in a dozen continental colonies, had almost universally come to regard the red man as a "varmint" (to use a later term), to be shoved out of the way or, if he resisted, to be exterminated. Degradation of the Indian had become a matter of both attitude and policy.

In 1600 the Englishmen who would come to America had had no appreciable contact with Africans, in contrast to the long experience of Spaniards and Portuguese. Nor had they any experience with such slavery as had already developed in Latin America. By 1700 they·"knew" Africans well in the Chesapeake region and, indeed, to only a slightly lesser degree in the other continental colonies. Not only did they know them; they had evolved a pattern of relations with them, prejudicial in spirit and codified in laws, that would long continue.

Who were these peoples at the start, and how did they see themselves? How did the pattern of relations between them begin? How and why did it develop as it did? Why was it, as Winthrop D. Jordan has suggested in his recent and profound book, *White over Black: American Attitudes toward the Negro, 1550–1812* (Chapel Hill, N.C.: University of North Carolina Press, 1968), that "once the cycle of the debasement of slavery and prejudice in the mind was underway it was automatically self-reenforcing"? (The same principle applies to the degradation of the Indian.)

It is, of course, with the white person's attitudes and institutions that we must be concerned primarily, not only because it was he who brought on the confrontation by invading the red native's land and by introducing Africans for labor but also because they subdued both races, and in so doing set the stamp of their attitudes and institutions on the land. Only recently have we come to appreciate the richness of the heritage of black people and red; both have contributed to the heritage of America. But it was the Europeans, principally Englishmen, who by dominating the other two set the tone of relations and institutions that would long prevail.

By focusing on the Chesapeake Bay area (as the next chapter does on New England), we can discern significant attributes of the early English settlers. First, they were English and proud of it; they were heirs of the glories of the Age of Elizabeth, just ended. As such, they were contemptuous of Spaniards and other "lesser breeds," although this did not prevent them from envying the power and the riches that those people had found in the Americas; they wanted their "cut" of the loot of a whole New World. In a century when religion was all-important, they were Protestant (largely Puritans) and proud of that (even if they did erect a tavern in Jamestown before they built a church). Above all, they were venturesome, willing to risk all in a strange new world.

The risk was perhaps greater than they had realized; for those who survived it, the psychological shock was profound. First there was the voyage: 140 persons crammed aboard three vessels of one hundred, forty, and twenty tons with all the equipment and supplies to start a colony from scratch, tossed about for eighteen weeks. Following the shock of the voyage came the trauma of the new environment: the climate of coastal Virginia in summer, the strange natives, the unfamiliar flora and fauna on which to try to stay alive. And many of them failed; within six months more than half were dead, mostly from diseases like malaria and dysentery, and many of the rest were sick unto death.

Those who survived would never be the same. Almost totally cut off from England and their former sense of identity, physically they were on their own, and psychologically they were all alone. In the seventeenth century they moved steadily toward a new way of life and new institutions to fit it, and toward a new sense of identity—that understanding of who and what we are that is essential to any individual or group.

In setting out to build an empire on smoke, after John Rolfe began experimenting with West Indian tobacco plants, they solved their fundamental economic problem—a cash crop with which to pay for all that they needed to import—and they also thereby defined a whole new economic identity for themselves. By inventing the head-right system (awarding fifty acres for each person brought in), they not only made ingenious use of their greatest resource, land, to build up their weakest resource, people, but also defined who they were—independent landowners, not agricultural laborers locked into a manor or subservient to the Virginia Company. In the House of Burgesses they created a significant institution which defined them as a people with the right to and the capacity for self-government.

Thus groping to a new identity, they also found it meaningful to define who they were *not* and what they were determined *not* to become. Their own identity—their values and goals—was thrown into sharper perspective by ascribing to other peoples opposite values and goals. By defining the Spanish as saddled with autocratic government and ridden by a bigoted priesthood, they defined themselves and their institutions by contrast.

Their contacts with Spaniards were limited, however. Not so with the Indians of the Chesapeake Bay region, whom they encountered at once and with whom they had steady contact thereafter. That contact was characterized by misunderstanding from the start. Misunderstanding begot suspicion, and suspicion the conviction of treachery—on both sides. Defining themselves by opposites, the English in Virginia defined the red men as brutal and savage, disorderly and anarchic, lazy and without purpose, devoid of either religion or culture. To wrest a rich, "unused" land from such a people became not only reasonable but right.

Relations between red man and white usually began on a friendly footing. In his first contact with natives of the New World, Columbus found them friendly, helpful, and generous. "They are so ingenuous and free with all they have," he wrote, "that no one would believe it who has not seen it." How Squanto saved the Pilgrims from starvation in 1621 by teaching them how to plant and grow corn is an important part of the curriculum in American grade schools, at least at the Thanksgiving season. That Virginians had fared the same is not so well known. In the fall of 1607, when half their number had died and the rest were too weak to ward off an attack, the Indians could easily have wiped them out. Instead, the Indians saved them with gifts of corn.

The whites needed the reds' skills and foods and their furs for trade. The reds wanted the whites' superior technology: guns, blankets, and metal pots and pans. Exchange of such things continued throughout the century, providing the most important bond between the two races. But despite the fact that each needed the other, in the evolution of relations between red man and white, the forces causing distrust and violence proved greater than those working for friendship and cooperation. Embittering forces were constantly at work to undermine any bonds. Misunderstanding was deep-rooted among peoples whose cultures were so different. As one example, the Indian did not understand the white's theory of private *ownership* of land, from which others might be excluded; he understood only collective *use* of land, to which others might be invited. When he invited in the white, only to find the land soon fenced against him, he saw treachery. Such misunderstandings brought on individual clashes which soon escalated to mass violence in revenge.

In Virginia the turning point came in 1622. Distressed by the mounting numbers of English and their constant encroachment on the land in the pursuit of soil on which to grow the "sot-weed," tobacco, the Indians determined to wipe out the English. After a week of unusual friendliness, they suddenly fell on the various settlements along the James River, and within a few hours 347 settlers died. The survivors retaliated in kind; at one point 250 Indians seeking peace were lured to their death in a toast in poisoned wine. The negative forces had won. A pattern had been established that would be repeated elsewhere time and again.

As land had become the pivot in relations between red and white, so labor became the pivot in relations between black and white. Developing (or exploiting) the New World involved extracting from its soil the mineral and agricultural riches that Europeans sought: precious metals; tropical or semitropical products such as sugar, rice, and tobacco; and timber and naval stores. Such an extractive economy required vast amounts of labor in an age when muscle was virtually the sole source of energy.

Where to come by that labor? There were powerful lures in head-rights in land and indentures for service. Perhaps as many as three-quarters of all Europeans who came to Virginia in the seventeenth century came as indentured servants, but they simply were not enough. Nor were Indians a solution, either in numbers or interest. The Spanish had learned this, and the English perhaps learned from them. On the return from his second voyage, Columbus packed 500 Indians aboard his four little caravels for sale in the slave markets of Seville. Two hundred died at sea and were thrown overboard, and most of the rest were too sick to be of any use on arrival at Cadiz. On Hispaniola itself the Spanish soon nearly exhausted the native population, many of whom chose flight or death in starvation or punishment to work in the mines. Casting about for new sources of labor, two Spanish ships sailed to Florida. Hospitably received, they invited the Indians aboard, clapped 130 below decks, and set sail for Hispaniola. One ship went down at sea. Aboard the other all the Indians died of sorrow and starvation, "for being angry at the deception done them under the guise of friendship, they had refused to eat," in the words of the Spanish chronicler. But the Spanish learned slowly. In 1524 another expedition returned for the same purpose to the same place in Florida. Again the Indians received them hospitably, feasted the Spaniards royally for three or four days, and then one night slew them all. Indians were no solution.

Africans might be a solution. Spain had turned to enslaved Africans for her West Indies at least as early as 1502. By 1600 slavery was solidly established there, though it was yet outside the experience of most Englishmen (as were blacks of any status). Englishmen knew various kinds of servitude: that of people locked, so to speak, into an agricultural manor by long tradition; that of some kinds of convicted criminals or enemies defeated in war; that of persons voluntarily entering into a period of servitude to achieve a goal. But they did not know chattel slavery, in which humans are the personal property of other persons for life. Nor had any but a handful of them had any contact with Africans. They had virtually no trade with Africa in the sixteenth century, and only John Hawkins engaged in the slave trade from Africa to the Spanish

West Indies, in three expeditions during the 1560s. Neither introducing slavery nor importing Africans was in the minds of the Virginia Company or those who planted its colony in 1607. Nor was the introduction of blacks into the colony in 1619 either planned or deemed particularly significant at the time. Of that fateful day, John Rolfe recorded laconically: "About the last of August came in a dutch man of warre that sold us twenty Negars." Nothing more, though he wrote much more fully of other ships and their European immigrants.

After such chance beginnings, both the number of blacks and the status of slavery developed only gradually in the seventeenth century. From 1630 to 1660 an average of only twenty blacks arrived in the colony each year; from 1660 to 1700 less than ninety arrived per year. Such numerical precision is possible through analysis of land records, as Wesley F. Craven has shown in *White, Red, and Black: The Seventeenth-Century Virginian* (Charlottesville, Va.: University of Virginia Press, 1971), since a fifty-acre head-right was awarded for and recorded for each immigrant, black or white.

No such precision is possible in determining how and when the principles of and relationships in chattel slavery in Virginia developed. There is no evidence that they were present in 1619, but that they had been largely developed by about 1700 is clear. The stages in the process are traced in the selection from Jordan in this chapter. Suffice it to say here that a "pattern" emerged in the seventeenth century, that it was set by the dominant whites, that it was based on their demands for labor, that it involved a growing debasement of the black as prejudice and institutions were interwoven, and that debasement was one way in which whites achieved a sense of their own identity.

For relations between red and white and between black and white the seventeenth century was truly critical, because patterns established then prevailed into the mid-twentieth century. The story is also significant for the light it sheds on how human relationships develop, how attitudes and prejudices arise, how decisions are affected by misunderstandings, and how institutions arise gradually as answers to problems or needs. This was above all a gradual process in which many people were groping toward their own identity and well-being, were developing preferences and prejudices through countless individual decisions in a way strikingly uncoordinated, to end up where they had never expected to be.

Misconceptions and the Real Indian

Alvin M. Josephy, Jr.

It is somewhat misleading to think of North America on the eve of occupation by whites as a "virgin land." Between one and two million Indians lived north of Mexico, as had their ancestors for somewhere between fifteen and forty thousand years, according to most recent estimates. They had developed a wide variety of complex cultures which had left all sorts of marks on the land: fields and towns, trails and huge burial mounds. Indeed, even after a generation of English settlement in Virginia, it was the Indian who was the town-dweller, not the Englishman on his tobacco farm.

Most white men then (and since then) did not understand or appreciate the culture of the Indians. In the mid-eighteenth century Benjamin Franklin put the question with his usual clarity: "Savages we call them, because their Manners differ from ours, which we think the Perfection of Civility; they think the same of theirs."

The white man's "Manners" prevailed. First usually came a revolution in the Indian's way of life as he grasped for the white man's material things. The way in which the whole culture of the Plains Indians was revolutionized by the white man's horse is the most striking example, but there were many others. Also, there often came a revolution in the Indian's way of death, as he acquired the white man's weapons, alcohol, and diseases. Finally, the white man prevailed by pushing the red man out of his way all across the continent.

In thus prevailing, the white man did not come to understand or appreciate the Indian and his culture. On the contrary, Indianness, like the Indian himself, became more debased in the process. Misconceptions continued, prejudices grew. And in more recent times the myths and stereotypes instilled by countless "western" paperbacks, movies, and television shows have only added new dimensions to the strange image of the American Indian.

The images people have of each other powerfully affect their relationships. In the following selection, Alvin M. Josephy, Jr., discusses misconceptions that prevail today, the historical roots of those misconceptions and the stages in their development, and what are some of the realities, not the myths, about Indianness. [From The Indian Heritage of America, *by Alvin M. Josephy, Jr. Copyright© 1968 by Alvin M. Josephy, Jr. by permission of Bantam Books, Inc.]*

For almost five hundred years the American Indian has been one of the principal symbols of the New World. To many persons, the mention of Brazil, Peru, Bolivia, or almost any South American state evokes an image of its original native inhabitant, whether a river dweller in a dugout in the jungle basins of the Orinoco and Amazon, or a ponchoed descendant of the Incas tending llamas in the highlands of the Andes. Mexico, Guatemala, and the other countries of Cental America are still synonymous in the popular mind with visions of the Mayan, Aztec, and other glittering pre-Columbian civilizations and with the present-day arts and handicrafts of their inheritors. And in Washington, D.C., the United States Travel Service of the Department of Commerce, established to attract visitors from other countries to the modern, industrialized U.S. testifies to the great interest foreign tourists have to this day in the storied Iroquois, Apaches, and Sioux of other times by using the symbol of the warbonneted Plains Indian on much of its official travel literature. Even the Eskimo and his igloo and kayak come readily to mind at the thought of Alaska and parts of Canada.

In truth, the beliefs, ways of life, and roles of the American Indians are interwoven so intimately with the cultures and histories of all the modern nations of the Americas that no civilization of the Western Hemisphere can be fully understood without knowledge and appreciation of them. And yet, from the time of the Europeans' first meeting with the Indians in 1492 until today, the Indian has been a familiar but little known—and, indeed, often an unreal—person to the non-Indian. What has been known about him, moreover, frequently has been superficial, distorted, or false.

What the white man calls him is itself the result of an error. When Christopher Columbus reached the New World, he had no idea that a land mass lay between Europe and Asia; the islands at which he touched he thought were those known at the time as the Indies, which lay off the coast of Asia, and the people he found on them he called *los Indios,* the people of the Indies, or the Indians. Other early navigators and chroniclers used the same name mistakenly for the various peoples they met at the end of each westward voyage, and by the time the Europeans discovered their error and realized that they were still far from Asia, it was too late. The name had taken hold as a general term of reference for all the inhabitants of the newly found lands of the Western Hemisphere.

Errors of far greater significance—and seriousness—stemmed from fundamental cultural differences between Indians and non-Indians. Deeply imbedded in the cultural make-up of the white man with a European background were the accumulated experiences of the Judeo-Christian spiritual tradition, the heritages of the ancient civilizations of the Near East, Greece, and Rome, and the various political, social, and economic systems of western Europe. The Indians did not share any of these, but, on their part, were the inheritors of totally different traditions and ways of life, many of them rooted in Asia, some of them thousands of years old, and all as thoroughly a part of Indian societies as European ways were a part of the white man's culture.

Meeting peoples with such different backgrounds led white men to endless misconceptions. Beginning with Columbus, the whites, with rare exceptions, observed and judged natives of the Americas from their own European points of view, failing consistently to grasp the truths and realities of the Indians themselves or their backgrounds and cultures. In the early years of the sixteenth century educated whites, steeped in the theological teachings of Europe, argued learnedly about whether or not Indians were humans with souls, whether they, too, derived from Adam and Eve (and were therefore sinful like the rest of mankind), or whether they were a previously unknown subhuman species. Other Europeans spent long years puzzling on the origin of the Indians and developing evidence that they were Egyptians, Chinese, descendants of one of the Lost Tribes of Israel, Welshmen, or even the survivors of civilizations that had once flourished on lost continents in the Atlantic and Pacific oceans.

In the lands of the New World, white men who came in contact with Indians viewed Indian cultures solely in terms that were familiar to themselves, and ignored or condemned what they did not understand. Indian leaders were talked of as "princes" and "kings"; spiritual guides and curers were called wizards, witch doctors, and medicine men, and all were equated as practitioners of sorcery; Indian societies generally—refined and sophisticated though some of them might be—were termed savage and barbaric, often only because they were strange, different, and not understood by the whites.

Many of the differences brought friction and, on both continents, fierce, interracial war. Conflicts resulted from misconceptions of the nature of Indian societies, the limits of authority of Indian leaders, and the non-hostile motives of certain Indian traits. Differing concepts concerning individual and group use of land and the private ownership of land were at the heart of numerous struggles, as were misunderstandings over the intentions of Indians whose actions were judged according to the patterns of white men's behavior rather than those of the Indians.

Through the years, the white man's popular conception of the Indian often crystallized into unrealistic or unjust images. Sometimes they were based on the tales of adventurers and travelers, who wove myths freely into their accounts, and sometimes they were reflections of the passions and fears stirred by the conflicts between the two races. Described by early writers as a race of happy people who lived close to nature, the Indians of the New World were first envisioned by many Europeans as innocent, childlike persons, spending their time in dancing and equally pleasurable pursuits. From this image in time sprang Jean Jacques Rousseau's vision of the natural man, as well as arguments of liberal philosophers in Europe who influenced revolutionary movements, including those of the United States and France, with comparisons between the lot of Europeans "in chains" and Indians who lived lives of freedom.

This idealistic version of the Indian as a symbol of the naturally free man persisted into the nineteenth century, sometimes being advanced by admiring observers like the artist George Catlin who visited many tribes and found much to admire in their ways of life, but generally being accepted only by persons who had no firsthand contact with Indians. On each frontier, beginning along the Atlantic coast, settlers who locked in conflict with Indians quickly conceived of them as bloodthirsty savages, intent on murder, scalping, and pillage. As the frontier moved west, and the Indian menace vanished from the eastern seaboard, generations that did not know Indian conflict at firsthand again thought of the native American in more tolerant terms. James Fenimore Cooper's version of the Noble Red Man helped gain sympathy among easterners for Indians who were hard pressed by the whites elsewhere. Thus, throughout much of the nineteenth century people in the northeastern cities often gave support to movements for justice for the southern and western tribes.

But as long as conflicts continued, the border settlers regarded the Indians in terms that had been familiar to the New England colonists during King Philip's war in the seventeenth century, and echoed the sentiment that "the only good Indian is a dead Indian." Only with the defeat of tribes did that point of view change—and then, inevitably, it was succeeded by still another image, which also moved from one border to another as settlers took over lands from which they had dispossessed the natives. It was the cruel conception of the Whisky Indian, the destroyed and impoverished survivor who had lost his home, tribal life, means of sustenance, and cultural standards, and lacking motivation—and often even the will to live—sought escape in alcohol. Unfeeling whites, failing to recognize the causes of the Indians' degradation, forgot their past power, pride, and dignity, and regarded them as weak and contemptuous people. . . .

Despite vast study by scientists and a voluminous literature of modern knowledge about Indians, still common are ignorance and misconceptions, many of them resulting from the white man's continuing inability to regard Indians save from his own European-based point of view. Today most Indians on both continents have been conquered and enfolded within the conquerors' own cultures; but the span of time since the various phases of the conquest ended has been short, and numerous Indians still cling to traits that are centuries, if not millennia, old and cannot be quickly shed. Many Indians, for instance, still do not understand or cannot accept the concept of private ownership of land; many do not understand the need to save for the future, a fundamental requirement of the economies of their conquerors; many find it difficult, if not impossible so far, to substitute individual competitiveness for group feeling; many do not see the necessity for working the year-round if they can provide for their families by six months of work, or the reason for cutting the earth-mother with a plow and farming if they can still hunt, fish, and dig roots. Many yet feel a sacred attachment to the land and a reverence for nature that is incomprehensible to most whites. Many, though Christian, find repugnance in the idea that man possesses dominion over the birds and beasts, and believe still that man is brother to all else that is living.

Such ideas, among a multitude that continue to hold numerous Indians apart from non-Indians, are either unrecognized or frowned upon by most whites today. Those who are aware of them are more often than not irritated by their persistence, yet the stubbornness of the white critics' own culture to survive, if a totally alien way of life, like that of the Chinese Communists, were to be forced upon them, would be understood.

More common among most whites are the false understandings and images which they retain about Indians. For many, the moving pictures, television, and comic strips have firmly established a stereotype as the true portrait of all Indians: the dour, stoic, warbonneted Plains Indian. He is a warrior, he has no humor unless it is that of an incongruous and farcical type, and his language is full of "hows," "ughs," and words that end in "um." Only rarely in the popular media of communications is it hinted that Indians, too, were, and are, all kinds of real, living persons like any others and that they included peace-loving wise men, mothers who cried for the safety of their children, young men who sang songs of love and courted maidens, dullards, statesmen, cowards, and patriots. Today there are college-trained Indians, researchers, business and professional men and women, jurists, ranchers, teachers, and political office holders. Yet so enduring is the stereotype that many a non-Indian, especially if he lives in an area where Indians are not commonly seen, expects any American Indian he meets to wear a feathered headdress. When he sees the Indian in a conventional business suit instead, he is disappointed!

If Indians themselves are still about as real as wooden sticks to many non-Indians, the facts concerning their present-day status in the societies of the Americas are even less known. Again, stereotypes, like those of "the oil-rich Indian" or "the coddled ward of Uncle Sam" frequently obscure the truth. A few Indians have become wealthy, but most of them know poverty, ill health, and barren, wasted existences. Some have received higher education, but many are poorly educated or not educated at all. Some are happily assimilated in the white man's societies; others are in various stages of acculturation, and many are not assimilated and do not wish to be anything but Indian. In the United States, in addition, it often comes as a surprise to many otherwise well informed whites to learn that the Indians are citizens and have the right to vote; that reservations are not concentration camps but are all the lands that were left to the Indians, and that are still being guarded by them as homes from which they can come and go in freedom; that the special treaty rights that they possess and that make them a unique minority in the nation are payments and guarantees given them for land they sold to the non-Indian people of the United States; that Indians pay state and federal taxes like all other citizens, save where treaties, agreements, or statutes have exempted them; and that, far from being on the way to extinction, the Indian population is increasing rapidly.

Finally, there are facts that should be obvious to everyone after five hundred years but are not, possibly because Columbus's name for them, Indians, is to this day understood by many to refer to a single people.

Despite the still commonly asked question, "Do you speak Indian?" there is neither a single Indian people nor a single Indian language, but many different peoples, with different racial characteristics, different cultures, and different languages. From Alaska to Cape Horn, in fact, the Indians of the Americas are as different from each other as are Spaniards, Scots, and Poles—and, in many cases, as will be seen, they are even more different. . . .

As stated earlier, the outward manifestations of Indian cultures have been apparent to white observers since 1492, but not often have they been understood or accurately interpreted.

To a large extent, Indian cultures reflected the environments in which they were shaped. As the various peoples who preceded the white man to the Western Hemisphere spread through the Americas and occupied different portions of both continents, they adopted the traits and techniques necessary for their survival. There were local and regional adjustments to extremes in temperature and climate, to mountain, desert, jungle, woodland, grassland, and coastal topography, and to the availability of various kinds of food resources. According to the supply, men at different times hunted and trapped different species of large and small game, and adapted their weapons, methods of hunting, and even their manner of living and social customs and beliefs to the pursuit of food. Those who lived where game was scarce developed cultures based more on the gathering of wild plant foods or shellfish, or on fishing. With the rise of agriculture, farming spread into areas that could sustain it and changed many peoples' ways of life. Some lived almost entirely on agriculture, while others combined hunting, gathering, farming, and fishing. The different economies gave rise to diverse customs and to many different social, religious, and political systems. Many traits and patterns of existence, carried from group to group by migrations, intermarriage, fighting, or trade contacts, spread across large areas, often being adopted by people far distant from the originators. For instance, the idea of making pottery may have moved by steps from the coast of Ecuador to the coasts of Florida, Georgia, and South Carolina. But "borrowed" techniques and systems were frequently also modified and adapted to meet the specific needs of the "borrower," and throughout the hemisphere there came to exist a huge range and variety of Indian cultures.

This kaleidoscope of different—and often altering—native ways of life makes little more than a figure of speech the term "Indianness," which, more aptly, is a modern-day reference to traits by which Indians today retain recognition for themselves as Indians. But while it is difficult, if not impossible, to cite any cultural patterns that existed in every Indian society after the earliest stage of big-game hunters, some traits were common to many Indian cultures, and a number of generalizations can be made about many different groups. At the same time, it is well to begin with the realization that much of what the white man today often thinks of as peculiarly American Indian is not, in fact, exclusively Indian at all. Bows and arrows, the use of war paint, and so-called medicine men, or shamans, all existed among other peoples in the world; so did the mythical thunderbird, rain dances, and the practice of scalping.

Like numerous groups in Africa, Asia, and Oceania, the social organization of many American Indians was based on family and clan units. Small family units dominated the life of many of the more primitive bands, while in the more advanced groups people were organized frequently in clans composed of persons who traced themselves back through either the male or the female line alone to a common ancestor. The clans were sometimes named for animals known as *totems* (derived from an Algonquian word meaning approximately "brother"), which were regarded as their supernatural ancestors or spiritual guardians. Clan relationships and activities were usually important parts of a group's daily existence. A clan might share with the family the responsibility for the raising of children, overseeing the discipline of the youths when it was necessary—although rarely meting out physical punishment. Often clans had specific tribal or village rights and duties. Many supervised and conducted intricate ceremonies that attended the initiation of young people into adulthood. Among some tribes the clans were separated into two different encompassing bodies referred to by anthropologists as moieties (halves), which competed in games and divided between themselves the carrying out of various village functions and activities.

The life of almost all Indian societies was colored by a deep faith in supernatural forces that were believed to link human beings to all other living things. To many Indians, each animal, each tree, and each manifestation of nature had its own spirit with which the individual could establish supernatural contact through his own spirit or that of an intermediary. In some societies, the combined total of the people's spiritual powers was believed to be the unseen force that filled the world. It was a sum supernatural force that shaped and directed life. The Iroquois called it *orenda,* the Algonquians *manitou,* the Sioux *wakan,* and the South American Incas *huaca.* Various Indian groups believed in gods, ghosts, and demons. Some believed in personal guardian spirits and sought to establish contact with them through dreams and vision quests. Several tribes worshipped a single creator force, or Supreme Being, which white men taught them to call "The Great Spirit," but some groups, while acknowledging such a force or presence, regarded it as dead or disassociated from human affairs and dismissed it from consideration in daily life.

Common to most of Indian life were shamans, individuals with especially strong supernatural powers. Among many peoples, they were the "medicine men," but their functions often went far beyond curing the sick. Able to establish direct contact with the spirit world, they could call on aid from a supernatural helper or be possessed themselves by spirits. Sometimes they interceded for individuals, sometimes for the whole group. They could ensure good crops, a good hunt, or success in war. Or they could bring harm to an enemy or a rival. They occupied different roles and assumed different stations among different peoples, ranging from soothsayers, magicians, and hypnotists to members of hierarchies of trained priests who presided over formal cults and rituals. Some shamans exercised political power in bands or tribes; the Hunkpapa Sioux Sitting Bull was a notable example. Others, like the Mayan priest-rulers, dominated the total apparatus of statecraft of huge and complex civilizations. These differences reflected many diverse religious systems. Some peoples observed no formal religious practices. Others had small priesthoods that presided over carefully taught rites. Still others, like the Aztecs, were led by powerful religious hierarchies in paying homage to large pantheons of deities with specialized characteristics and functions.

Two mythical figures, the so-called culture hero and the trickster, were widespread in Indian lore, appearing in different guises among various tribes. The former figure was regarded as the person who had taught the members of the tribe their way of life in the distant past, while the latter, a fabulous jokester, was partly a sacred being and partly a humorous character who frequently managed to outsmart himself and get into trouble. Both figures, sometimes combined into one person, who might be an animal like the coyote, or a human, were the subjects of many tales told by grandmothers to children, and repeated from one generation to the next. Among the most common stories were those that related how mankind had been created. Typical of such tales was one told by the Achomawi, a group of Pit River Indians of northeastern California: One day Coyote watched Silver Fox gather some serviceberry sticks and start to whittle them down. Silver Fox told him he was going to make people. The finished sticks would be chiefs and warriors; the shavings would be common people. After a night and a day of whittling, Silver Fox turned the sticks and shavings into people. Coyote decided he would make people too. So, copying everything he had seen Silver Fox do, he gathered some serviceberry sticks and whittled them down. After a night and a day, he too turned the finished sticks and shavings into people. Then Coyote ran after some of the women he had created and at length caught them. But when he touched them, they all turned back into shavings.

Indian rituals and celebrations were often accompanied by dancing, drumming, and singing. Dances, many of them sacred but others done simply for pleasure, varied in all parts of both continents. Songs also differed greatly; some related people's experiences, extolled exploits, or merely expressed a thought, while others were sung to nonsense words or to sounds that had no meaning. The drum was used by almost all tribes. Two of the most common types were the double-headed drum and the water drum, the latter possessing a single head of skin and being filled with water. Some drums were held in the hand and beaten with a short stick; others, especially those used for dances in many parts of the present-day United States, were large round drums that rested on the ground, hung from sticks, or were held by chanters. Many drums could be heard for long distances and were used to transmit signals or messages. Among some tribes an eagle-bone whistle was also employed in ritualistic dances and ceremonies like the Sun Dance. The flute, blown at one end rather than at the side, was used by some peoples, often by young men who were courting maidens. Almost all tribes, also, employed rattles made either of gourds or turtle shells and various types of crude instruments, including notched sticks that were rubbed across each other to make rasping sounds.

Many Indians held in common certain fundamental ideas. A concept concerning the right of land ownership, basically different from that of the white man, was shared by most Indians. To them, land and its produce, like the air and water, were free to the use of the group. No man might own land as personal property and bar others from it. A tribe, band, or village might claim certain land as territory for farming, hunting, or dwelling, but land was held and used communally. No clash of concepts caused more friction than this one between Indians and white men in the United States, for Indians frequently found it difficult to accept an individual's right to own land and keep others from using it. Some tribes, moreover, regarded the earth as the mother of all life and thought it impossible to sell their mother. The concept is still strong among some Indians today. At Taos Pueblo in New Mexico, Indians may still be seen taking shoes off horses and walking about in soft-soled shoes themselves in the spring, for at that time of the year, they believe, the earth is pregnant and they must not harm her body. Taos Indians, also, are not alone among Indians who still resist or avoid the use of modern agricultural implements, such as steel-bladed plows, which would slice open the breast of their earth-mother.

Generally, most Indians had respect, if not reverence and awe, for the earth and for all of nature and, living close to nature and its forces, strove to exist in balance with them. If harmony with nature were disturbed, illness, pain, death, or other misfortunes would result. To most Indians, also, life after death was regarded as a continuation of existence in another world. Few thought of it, however, specifically as a hunter's paradise. The expression "happy hunting ground," a white man's invention, merely symbolized the belief of some Indians that it was a good land where everything, including the securing of food, was easier for people than it had been before.

Warfare was common on both continents and was a principal preoccupation among some Indian societies. But it is either false or exaggerated to conceive of all Indians as warriors or as war-motivated people. Certain groups like the Hopis were among the most peaceful on earth, and many Indians abhorred warfare and the misery and violent death that it brought. White men publicized images of the Indians as savage and "bestial" warriors, but Indian warfare was often no more savage than the type of war Europeans introduced to the hemisphere and waged against the natives. In fact, Indian warfare was often stimulated and intensified by the impact of the Europeans.

Few Indian groups, for example, were wealthy enough at any time to maintain a standing army. Warfare, even after the arrival of the whites, usually consisted of sporadic raids, conducted in defense of tribal lands and hunting grounds, or for honor, revenge, slaves, horses, or other booty. There were few sieges, protracted battles, or wars of conquest. Quite often an attacking side, believing that nothing was worth the loss of its own people, would break off fighting as soon as it had suffered casualties. Among various plains tribes in North America, counting coup, touching a live enemy and getting away unharmed, was the main goal of a warrior and the highlight of war, even more honorable an achievement to some than slaying an enemy.

Here and there on both continents, Indians indulged in cannibalism, although the reasons for its practice differed considerably among various tribes. Some groups in the Caribbean and South America, like the Brazilian Tupinambás, prized human flesh as a food and made war to obtain victims (the word itself comes from Carib Indians, among the first the Europeans observed practicing the custom). On the Northwest Pacific Coast, however, most Indians regarded cannibalism as a fearful and repellent act, to be indulged in only in rituals and while under the influence of supernatural powers. Elsewhere, some Indians ate the heart and other portions of enemies in the belief that they would thus acquire the courage or other qualities of the victim.

Many Indians could also be characterized in common by a number of implements and material objects that were associated with almost all of their cultures. Their weapons throughout the hemisphere included spears, spear throwers, and bows and arrows. Knives, scrapers, cordage, netting, and baskets were also in use almost everywhere. Some items, employed widely but not by everyone, included fishhooks, digging sticks, pottery, and canoes. Indians who became farmers developed corn, squash, and many varieties of beans, and these crops were cultivated in many different parts of the New World. In addition, Indians developed numerous other agricultural articles unknown to Europeans; grown in various regions, they included white and sweet potatoes, tobacco, peanuts, peppers, vanilla, tomatoes, pumpkins, cacao, avocados, and pineapples.

Indians are sometimes characterized, also, by what they did not possess, but even here there are many misconceptions. Most tribes made no effective use of metal. But metallurgy did exist among the higher Indian civilizations of Middle and South America; the Mexicans, Central American Indians, and Incas, among others, smelted gold and silver; and in various places groups made useful and decorative objects of beaten copper. No Indian group ever made practical use of the wheel; but some peoples were familiar with it, for in Middle America it was used on toys. The question of the domestication of animals also needs explanation. Although horses had existed in the New World for more than 60 million years, they became extinct in the Western Hemisphere after the Ice Age ended. Indians thus had neither horses nor cattle to domesticate until white men brought them over from Europe. Nevertheless, some Indians used domesticated dogs to drag or carry their burdens. People in Middle America and the Andes domesticated ducks, and the Andeans kept guinea pigs about their homes and employed the partly domesticated llama, alpaca, and vicuña for wool, food, and to carry loads. Turkeys were also domesticated for their feathers and for food in parts of the Southwest of the present-day United States and in Middle America, and honey and wax were harvested from bees by some Indian beekeepers.

Modern Pan-Indian movements in Latin America and organizations working toward unity among present-day United States and Canadian Indians have a tendency to list other qualities and characteristics as common attributes of "Indianness." Many of the traits cited, however, were typical only among some Indian groups. Democratic political institutions, an individual's freedom of choice, and the right to have a say in one's own affairs—frequently referred to as peculiarly "Indian"—were, indeed, a part of the pattern of life among some native peoples. But in many Indian societies authoritarianism prevailed, and the world perhaps never experienced a more totalitarian state than that of the Incas of Peru. Nevertheless, in the case of the United States particularly, there is some justification in citing these traits, for colonial records show that many of the Indian peoples of the Atlantic seaboard taught the European settlers much with regard to freedom, the dignity of the individual, democracy, representative government, and the right to participate in the settling of one's affairs.

The Pan-Indianism of today, particularly in the United States, has resulted from numerous forces, including relocation, education, government programs, social gatherings, and political strivings, that bring Indians of different tribes and backgrounds into contact with each other, and from the modern means of transportation which have encouraged and eased mobility. Youths from different tribes meet at schools and eventually marry; intertribal powwows, dances, and other social events attract participants from tribes in all parts of the country, and even from Canada and Latin America; religious convocations, nationalistic movements, and conferences on Indian economic and political problems bring together leaders from many tribes; and relocated Indians in urban areas find companionship and comfort at Indian centers in the cities. These associations have led gradually to an increasing feeling of unity among many Indians and an emphasis on recognition that they are Indians as well as members of particular tribes. Pan-Indianism has been felt strongly in parts of Oklahoma, where many tribes dwell, but it has grown also among Indians elsewhere. It is reflected at powwows where Indians of different tribes now dance the same dances and wear somewhat identical dance costumes; by the adoption by many Indians of such items as the Plains tribes' eagle-feather headdress as a symbolic article of garb for all Indians; by joint political action of many tribes in behalf of one or a few of them; and by efforts of relocated Indians, students, and others away from reservations to retain Indian identification in the midst of white society by finding new pride, dignity, and self-assuredness in their "Indianness." The forces of the world around the Indian have also had an effect: the ideals of the United Nations; the independence of countries that were formerly colonies in Africa and Asia; and the "war" on poverty and the Negroes' civil rights struggle in the United States have all tended to encourage the emergence of a unifying spirit among the Indians that transcends tribal affiliations or traditions.

Labor Problems in Early Jamestown

Edmund S. Morgan

With the arrival of 105 English colonists in the estuary of the James River in April 1607, the second of the three peoples with whom we are concerned appeared on the North American scene. We know a lot more about them than about the Indians they met, for the newcomers wrote amply and often of this strange new land—and their own marvelous exploits. Printed in London, their accounts were devoured by their stay-at-home contemporaries.

The intrepid and almost mythical Captain John Smith was among the first to break into print. Only a year after the landing, his A True Relation of such occurrences and accidents of noate as hath happened in Virginia since the first planting of that Collony was printed in London. His account included the following revealing picture of how a pattern of relations with the Indians was already developing:

For wronging a souldier but the value of a peny, I have caused Powhatam [to] send his owne men to Iames Towne to receiue their punishment at my discretion. It is true in our greatest extremitie they shot me, slue three of my men, and by the folly of them that fled tooke me prisoner; yet God made Pocahontas the Kings daughter the meanes to deliuer me; and thereby taught me to know their trecheries to preserue the rest.

Such accounts are very informative. They provide the basis for favorite historical stories, such as Pocahontas saving the "white knight" by throwing herself across him as he was about to have his skull crushed (as explained more fully, and probably embellished, in a new version by Captain Smith some fifteen years later, by which time, to the probable satisfaction of more romantic readers, she was portrayed as thirteen to fourteen years of age instead of the original ten). The accounts do more than form the basis for romantic stories, however. Escalating violence over petty, personal grievance; bad feelings; arrogance; display of power; and conviction of treachery—most of them on both sides—clearly come forth.

Much as they reveal, however, much remains concealed by the accounts. Why did Englishmen—and Indians—act that way? What were those Englishmen up to, or after, in Virginia? How did they see their mission? Why would they not even work when they were starving? (One desperate man murdered his wife and was apprehended only after he had consumed a good deal of the flesh he had salted to preserve it.)

We can never fully recover the past—too much is gone, even from what happened yesterday. But we can, and do, gain new insights when perceptive individuals pose new questions or probe old ones from different perspectives or imaginatively use new sciences or methods. The following selection, by one of the most distinguished contemporary historians of early America, Edmund S. Morgan, of Yale University, is an outstanding example of what can be done in this way to throw a whole new light on early Virginia. [From Edmund S. Morgan, "The Labor Problem at Jamestown, 1607–1618," American Historical Review, LXXVI, (1971), 595–611, footnotes omitted. Copyright by Edmund S. Morgan. Reprinted by permission.]

The story of Jamestown, the first permanent English settlement in America, has a familiar place in the history of the United States. We all know of the tribulations that kept the colony on the point of expiring: the shortage of supplies, the hostility of the Indians, the quarrels among the leaders, the reckless search for gold, the pathetic search for a passage to the Pacific, and the neglect of the crucial business of growing food to stay alive. Through the scene moves the figure of Captain John Smith, a little larger than life, trading for corn among the Indians and driving the feckless crew to work. His departure in October 1609 results in near disaster. The settlers fritter away their time and energy, squander their provisions, and starve. Sir Thomas Gates, arriving after the settlement's third winter, finds only sixty men out of six hundred still alive and those sixty scarcely able to walk.

In the summer of 1610 Gates and Lord La Warr get things moving again with a new supply of men and provisions, an absolute form of government, and a new set of laws designed to keep everybody at work. But when Gates and La Warr leave for a time, the settlers fall to their old ways. Sir Thomas Dale, upon his arrival in May 1611, finds them at "their daily and usuall workes, bowling in the streetes." But Dale brings order out of chaos. By enlarging and enforcing the colony's new law code (the famous Lawes Divine, Morall and Martiall) he starts the settlers working again and rescues them from starvation by making them plant corn. By 1618 the colony is getting on its feet and ready to carry on without the stern regimen of a Smith or a Dale. There are still evil days ahead, as the Virginia Company sends over men more rapidly than the infant colony can absorb them. But the settlers, having found in tobacco a valuable crop for export, have at last gone to work with a will, and Virginia's future is assured.

The story probably fits the facts insofar as they can be known. But it does not quite explain them. The colony's long period of starvation and failure may well be attributed to the idleness of the first settlers, but idleness is more an accusation than an explanation. Why did men spend their time bowling in the streets when their lives depended on work? Were they lunatics, preferring to play games rather than clear and plow and plant the crops that could have kept them alive?

The mystery only deepens if we look more closely at the efforts of Smith, Gates, La Warr, and Dale to set things right. In 1612 John Smith described his work program of 1608: "the company [being] divided into tennes, fifteenes, or as the businesse required, 4 hours each day was spent in worke, the rest in pastimes and merry exercise." Twelve years later Smith rewrote this passage and changed the figure of four hours to six hours. But even so, what are we to make of a six-hour day in a colony teetering on the verge of extinction?

The program of Gates and La Warr in the summer of 1610 was no more strenuous. William Strachey described it:

it is to be understood that such as labor are not yet so taxed but that easily they perform the same and ever by ten of the clock have done their morning's work: at what time they have their allowances [of food] set out ready for them, and until it be three of the clock again they take their own pleasure, and afterward, with the sunset, their day's labor is finished.

The Virginia Company offered much the same account of this period. According to a tract issued in 1610, "the setled times of working (to effect all themselves, or the Adventurers neede desire) [requires] no more pains than from sixe of clocke in the morning untill ten, and from two of the clocke in the afternoone till foure." The long lunch period described for 1610 was also a feature of the *Lawes Divine, Morall and Martiall* as enforced by Dale. The total working hours prescribed in the *Lawes* amounted to roughly five to eight hours a day in summer and three to six hours in winter.

It is difficult, then, to escape the conclusion that there was a great deal of unemployment or underemployment at Jamestown, whether it was the idleness of the undisciplined in the absence of strong government or the idleness of the disciplined in the presence of strong government. How are we to account for this fact? By our standards the situation at Jamestown demanded hard and continuous work. Why was the response so feeble?

One answer, given by the leaders of the colony, is that the settlers included too many ne'er-do-wells and too many gentlemen who "never did know what a dayes work was." Hard work had to wait until harder men were sent. Another answer may be that the Jamestown settlers were debilitated by hunger and disease. The victims of scurvy, malaria, typhoid, and diphtheria may have been left without the will or the energy to work. Still another answer, which has echoed through the pages of our history books, attributed the difficulty to the fact that the settlement was conducted on a communal basis: everybody worked for the Virginia Company and everybody was fed (while supplies lasted) by the company, regardless of how much he worked or failed to work. Once land was distributed to individuals and men were allowed to work for themselves, they gained the familiar incentives of private enterprise and bent their shoulders to the wheel. These explanations are surely all valid— they are all supported by the testimony of contemporaries—and they go far toward explaining the lazy pioneers of Jamestown. But they do not reach to a dimension of the problem that contemporaries would have overlooked because they would have taken it for granted. They do not tell us what ideas and attitudes about work, carried from England, would have led the first English settlers to expect so little of themselves in a situation that demanded so much. The Jamestown settlers did not leave us the kind of private papers that would enable us to examine directly their ideas and attitudes, as we can those of the Puritans who settled New England a few years later. But in the absence of direct evidence we may discover among the ideas current in late sixteenth- and early seventeenth-century England some clues to the probable state of mind of the first Virginians, clues to the way they felt about work, whether in the Old World or the New, clues to habits of thinking that may have conditioned their perceptions of what confronted them at Jamestown, clues even to the tangled web of motives that made later Virginians masters of slaves.

Englishmen's ideas about the New World at the opening of the seventeenth century were based on a century of European exploration and settlement. The Spanish, whose exploits surpassed all others, had not attempted to keep their success a secret, and by the middle of the sixteenth century Englishmen interested in America had begun translating Spanish histories and memoirs in an effort to rouse their countrymen to emulation. The land that emerged from these writings was, except in the Arctic regions, an Eden, teeming with gentle and generous people who, before the Spanish conquest, had lived without labor, or with very little, from the fruits of a bountiful nature. There were admittedly some unfriendly exceptions who made a habit of eating their more attractive neighbors; but they were a minority, confined to a few localities, and in spite of their ferocity were scarcely a match for Europeans armed with guns. Englishmen who visited the New World confirmed the reports of natural abundance. Arthur Barlowe, for example, reconnoitering the North Carolina coast for Walter Raleigh, observed that "the earth bringeth foorth all things in aboundance, as in the first creation, without toile or labour," while the people were "most gentle, loving, and faithfull, void of all guile, and treason, and such as lived after the manner of the golden age. . . ."

English and European readers may have discounted the more extravagant reports of American abundance, for the same authors who praised the land often gave contradictory accounts of the hardships they had suffered in it. But anyone who doubted that riches were waiting to be plucked from Virginia's trees had reason to expect that a good deal might be plucked from the people of the land. Spanish experience had shown that Europeans could thrive in the New World without undue effort by exploiting the natives. With a mere handful of men the Spanish had conquered an enormous population of Indians in the Caribbean, Mexico, and Peru and had put them to work. In the chronicles of Peter Martyr Englishmen learned how it was done. Apart from the fact that the Indians were naturally gentle, their division into a multitude of kingdoms, frequently at odds with one another, made it easy to play off one against another. By aiding one group against its enemies the Spaniards had made themselves masters of both. . . .

The settlers at Jamestown tried to follow the strategy, locating their settlement as the plan called for, near the mouth of a navigable river, so that they would have access to the interior tribes if the coastal ones were hostile. But as luck would have it, they picked an area with a more powerful, more extensive, and more effective Indian government than existed anywhere else on the Atlantic Coast. King Powhatan had his enemies, the Monacans of the interior, but he felt no great need of English assistance against them, and he rightly suspected that the English constituted a larger threat to his hegemony than the Monacans did. He submitted with ill grace and no evident comprehension to the coronation ceremony that the Virginia Company arranged for him, and he kept his distance from Jamestown. Those of his warriors who visited the settlement showed no disposition to work for the English. The Monacans, on the other hand, lived too far inland (beyond the falls) to serve as substitute allies, and the English were thus deprived of their anticipated native labor.

They did not, however, give up their expectations of getting it eventually. In 1615 Ralph Hamor still thought the Indians would come around "as they are easily taught and may be lenitie and faire usage . . . be brought, being naturally though ingenious, yet idly given, to be no lesse industrious, nay to exceed our English." Even after the massacre of 1622 Virginians continued to dream of an Indian labor supply, though there was no longer to be any gentleness in obtaining it. . . .

Although Englishmen long remained under the illusion that the Indians would eventually become useful English subjects, it became apparent fairly early that Indian labor was not going to sustain the founders of Jamestown. The company in England was convinced by 1609 that the settlers would have to grow at least part of their own food. Yet the settlers themselves had to be driven to that life-saving task. To understand their ineffectiveness in coping with a situation that their pioneering descendants would take in stride, it may be helpful next to inquire into some of the attitudes toward work that these first English pioneers took for granted. How much work and what kind of work did Englishmen at the opening of the seventeenth century consider normal?

The laboring population of England, by law at least, was required to work much harder than the regimen at Jamestown might lead us to expect. The famous Statute of Artificers of 1563 (re-enacting similar provisions from the Statute of Laborers of 1495) required all laborers to work from five in the morning to seven or eight at night from mid-March to mid-September, and during the remaining months of the year from daybreak to night. Time out for eating, drinking, and rest was not to exceed two and a half hours a day. But these were injunctions not descriptions. The Statute of Laborers of 1495 is preceded by the complaint that laborers "waste much part of the day . . . in late coming unto their work, early departing therefrom, long sitting at their breakfast, at their dinner and noon-meat, and long time of sleeping after noon." Whether this statute or that of 1563 (still in effect when Jamestown was founded) corrected the situation is doubtful. The records of local courts show varying efforts to enforce other provisions of the statute of 1563, but they are almost wholly silent about this provision, in spite of the often-expressed despair of masters over their lazy and negligent laborers.

It may be said that complaints of the laziness and irresponsibility of workmen can be met with in any century. Were such complaints in fact justified in sixteenth- and early seventeenth-century England? There is some reason to believe that they were, that life during those years was characterized by a large amount of idleness or underemployment. The outstanding economic fact of the sixteenth and early seventeenth century in England was a rapid and more or less steady rise in prices, followed at some distance by a much smaller rise in wages, both in industry and in agriculture. The price of provisions used by a laborer's family rose faster than wages during the whole period from 1500 to 1640. . . .

Wages were so inadequate that productivity was probably impaired by malnutrition. From a quarter to a half of the population lived below the level recognized at the time to constitute poverty. Few of the poor could count on regular meals at home, and in years when the wheat crop failed, they were close to starvation. It is not surprising that men living under these conditions showed no great energy for work and that much of the population was, by modern standards, idle much of the time. The health manuals of the day recognized that people normally slept after eating, and the laws even prescribed a siesta for laborers in the summer time. If they slept longer and more often than the laws allowed or the physicians recommended, if they loafed on the job and took unauthorized holidays, if they worked slowly and ineffectively when they did work, it may have been due at least in part to undernourishment and to the variety of chronic diseases that undernourishment brings in its train. . . .

Even the division of labor, which economists have customarily regarded as a means of increased productivity, could be a source of idleness. Plowing, for example, seems to have been a special skill—a plowman was paid at a higher rate than ordinary farm workers. But the ordinary laborer's work might have to be synchronized with the plowman's, and a whole crew of men might be kept idle by a plowman's failure to get his job done at the appropriate time. It is difficult to say whether this type of idleness, resulting from failure to synchronize the performance of related tasks, was rising or declining; but cheap, inefficient, irresponsible labor would be unlikely to generate pressures for the careful planning of time.

The government, while seeking to discourage idleness through laws requiring long hours of work, also passed laws that inadvertently discouraged industry. A policy that might be characterized as the conservation of employment frustrated those who wanted to do more work than others. English economic policy seems to have rested on the assumption that the total amount of work for which society could pay was strictly limited and must be rationed so that everyone could have a little, and those with family responsibilities could have a little more. It was against the law for a man to practice more than one trade or one craft. And although large numbers of farmers took up some handicraft on the side, this was to be discouraged, because "for one man to be both an husband-man and an Artificer is a gatheringe of divers mens livinges into one mans hand." So as not to take work away from his elders, a man could not independently practice most trades until he had become a master through seven years of apprenticeship. Even then, until he was thirty years old or married, he was supposed to serve some other master of the trade. . . .

Above and beyond the idleness and underemployment that we may blame on the lethargy and irresponsibility of underpaid labor, on the failure to synchronize the performance of related tasks, and on the policy of spreading work as thinly as possible, the very nature of the jobs to be done prevented the systematic use of time that characterizes modern industrialized economies. Men could seldom work steadily, because they could work only at the tasks that could be done at the moment; and in sixteenth- and seventeenth-century England the tasks to be done often depended on forces beyond human control: on the weather and the seasons, on the winds, on the tides, on the maturing of crops. In the countryside work from dawn to dusk with scarcely an intermission might be normal at harvest time, but there were bound to be times when there was very little to do. When it rained or snowed, most farming operations had to be stopped altogether (and so did some of the stages of cloth manufacture). As late as 1705 John Law, imagining a typical economy established on a newly discovered island, assumed that the persons en-gaged in agriculture would necessarily be idle, for one reason or another, half the time. . . .

Perhaps we may now view Jamestown with somewhat less surprise at the idle and hungry people occupying the place: idleness and hunger were the rule in much of England much of the time; they were facts of life to be taken for granted. And if we next ask what the settlers thought they had come to America to do, what they thought they were up to in Virginia, we can find several English enterprises comparable to their own that may have served as models and that would not have led them to think of hard, continuous disciplined work as a necessary ingredient in their undertaking.

If they thought of themselves as settling a wilderness, they could look for guidance to what was going on in the northern and western parts of England and in the high parts of the south and east. Here were the regions, mostly wooded, where wastelands still abounded, the goal of many in the large migrant population of England. Those who had settled down were scattered widely over the countryside in isolated hovels and hamlets and lived by pasture farming, that is, they cultivated only small plots of ground and ran a few sheep or cattle on the common land. Since the gardens required little attention and the cattle hardly any, they had most of their time to themselves. Some spent their spare hours on handi-crafts. In fact, they supplied the labor for most of England's minor indus-tries, which tended to locate in pasture-farming regions, where agriculture made fewer demands on the inhabitants, than in regions devoted to market crops. But the pasture farmers seem to have offered their labor sporadically and reluctantly. They had the reputation of being both idle and independent. They might travel to the richer arable farming regions to pick up a few shillings in field work at harvest time, but their own harvests were small. They did not even grow the wheat or rye for their own bread and made shift to live in hard times from the nuts and berries and herbs that they gathered in the woods.

Jamestown was mostly wooded, like the pasture-farming areas of England and Wales; and since Englishmen used the greater part of their own country for pasture farming, that was the obvious way to use the wasteland of the New World. If this was the Virginians' idea of what they were about, we should expect them to be idle much of the time and to get grain for bread by trading rather than planting (in this case not wheat or rye but maize from the Indians); we should even expect them to get a good deal of their food, as they did, by scouring the woods for nuts and berries.

As the colony developed, a pasture-farming population would have been quite in keeping with the company's expectation of profit from a variety of products. The Spaniards' phenomenal success with raising cattle in the West Indies was well known. And the proposed employment of the settlers of Virginia in a variety of industrial pursuits (iron works, silk works, glass works, shipbuilding) was entirely fitting for a pasture-farming community. The small gardens assigned for cultivation by Governor Dale in 1614 will also make sense: three acres would have been far too small a plot of land to occupy a farmer in the arable regions of England, where a single man could handle thirty acres without assistance. But it would be not at all inappropriate as the garden of a pasture farmer. In Virginia three acres would produce more than enough corn to sustain a man for a year and still leave him with time to make a profit for the company or himself at some other job—if he could be persuaded to work.

Apart from the movement of migrant workers into wastelands, the most obvious English analogy to the Jamestown settlement was that of a military expedition. The settlers may have had in mind not only the expeditions that subdued the Irish but also those dispatched to the European continent in England's wars. . . . Military expeditions were staffed from top to bottom with men unlikely to work. The nucleus of sixteenth-century English armies was the nobility and the gangs of genteel ruffians they kept in their service, in wartime to accompany them into the field (or to go in their stead), in peacetime to follow them about as living insignia of their rank. Work was not for the nobility nor for those who wore their livery. According to the keenest student of the aristocracy in this period, "the rich and well-born were idle almost by definition." Moreover they kept "a huge labor force . . . absorbed in slothful and parasitic personal service." Aside from the gentlemen retainers of the nobility and their slothful servants the military expeditions that England sent abroad were filled out by misfits and thieves whom the local constables wished to be rid of. It was, in fact, government policy to keep the able-bodied and upright at home and to send the lame, the halt, the blind, and the criminal abroad.

The combination of gentlemen and ne'er-do-wells of which the leaders at Jamestown complained may well have been the result of the company's using a military model for guidance. The Virginia Company was loaded with noblemen (32 present or future earls, 4 countesses, 3 viscounts, and 19 barons). Is it possible that the large number of Jamestown settlers listed as gentlemen and captains came from among the retainers of these lordly stockholders and that the rest of the settlers included some of the gentlemen's personal servants as well as a group of hapless vagabonds or migratory farm laborers who had been either impressed or lured into the enterprise by tales of the New World's abundance? We are told, at least, that persons designated in the colony's roster as "laborers" were "for most part footmen, and such as they that were Adventurers brought to attend them, or such as they could perswade to goe with them, that never did know what a dayes work was."

If these men thought they were engaged in a military expedition, military precedent pointed to idleness, hunger, and death, not to the effective organization of labor. Soldiers on campaign were not expected to grow their own food. On the other hand they *were* expected to go hungry often and to die like flies even if they never saw an enemy. The casualty rates on European expeditions resembled those at Jamestown and probably from the same causes: disease and undernourishment.

But the highest conception of the enterprise, often expressed by the leaders, was that of a new commonwealth on the model of England itself. Yet this, too, while it touched the heart, was not likely to turn men toward hard, effective, and continuous work. The England that Englishmen were saddled with as a model for new commonwealths abroad was a highly complex society in which the governing consideration in accomplishing a particular piece of work was not how to do it efficiently but who had the right or the duty to do it, by custom, law, or privilege. We know that the labor shortage in the New World quickly diminished considerations of custom, privilege, and specialization in the organization of labor. But the English model the settlers carried with them made them think initially of a society like the one at home, in which each of them would perform his own special task and not encroach on the rights of other men to do other tasks. We may grasp some of the assumptions about labor that went into the most intelligent planning of a new commonwealth by considering Richard Hakluyt's recommendation that settlers include both carpenters and joiners, tallow chandlers and wax chandlers, bowyers and fletchers, men to rough-hew pike staffs and other men to finish them. . . .

. . . Whatever idleness arose from the specialization of labor in English society was multiplied in the New World by the presence of unneeded skills and the absence or shortage of essential skills. Jamestown had an oversupply of glassmakers and not enough carpenters or black-smiths, an oversupply of gentlemen and not enough plowmen. These were Englishmen temporarily baffled by missing links in the economic structure of their primitive community. The later jack-of-all-trades American frontiersman was as yet unthought of. As late as 1618 Governor Argall complained that they lacked the men "to set their Ploughs on worke." Although they had the oxen to pull them, "they wanted men to bring them to labour, and Irons for the Ploughs, and harnesse for the Cattell." And the next year John Rolfe noted that they still needed "Carpenters to build and make Carts and Ploughs, and skilfull men that know how to use them, and traine up our cattell to draw them; which though we indeavour to effect, yet our want of experience brings but little to perfection but planting Tobacco."

Tobacco, as we know, was what they kept on planting. The first shipload of it, sent to England in 1617, brought such high prices that the Virginians stopped bowling in the streets and planted tobacco in them. They did it without benefit of plows, and somehow at the same time they managed to grow corn, probably also without plows. Seventeenth-century Englishmen, it turned out, could adapt themselves to hard and varied work if there was sufficient incentive.

But we may well ask whether the habits and attitudes we have been examining had suddenly expired altogether. Did tobacco really solve the labor problem in Virginia? Did the economy that developed after 1618 represent a totally new set of social and economic attitudes? Did greater opportunities for profit completely erase the old attitudes and furnish the incentives to labor that were needed to make Virginia a success? The study of labor in modern underdeveloped countries should make us pause before we say yes. The mere opportunity to earn high wages has not always proved adequate to recruit labor in underdeveloped countries. Something more in the way of expanded needs or political authority or national consciousness or ethical imperatives has been required. Surely Virginia, in some sense, became a success. But how did it succeed? What kind of success did it have? Without attempting to answer, I should like very diffidently to offer a suggestion, a way of looking ahead at what happened in the years after the settlement of Jamestown.

The founders of Virginia, having discovered in tobacco a substitute for the sugar of the West Indies and the silver of Peru, still felt the lack of a native labor force with which to exploit the new crop. At first they turned to their own overpopulated country for labor, but English indentured servants brought with them the same haphazard habits of work as their masters. Also like their masters, they were apt to be unruly if pressed. And when their terms of servitude expired—if they themselves had not expired in the "seasoning" that carried away most immigrants to Virginia—they could be persuaded to continue working for their betters only at exorbitant rates. Instead they struck out for themselves and joined the ranks of those demanding rather than supplying labor. But there was a way out. The Spanish and Portuguese had already demonstrated what could be done in the New World when a local labor force became inadequate: they brought in the natives of Africa.

For most of the seventeenth century Virginians were unable to compete for the limited supply of slaves hauled across the ocean to man the sugar plantations of the Americas. Sugar was a more profitable way to use slaves than tobacco. Moreover, the heavy mortality of newcomers to Virginia made an investment in Africans bound for a lifetime more risky than the same amount invested in a larger number of Englishmen, bound for a term that was likely to prove longer than a Virginia lifetime.

But Virginians continued to be Englishmen: the more enterprising continued to yearn for a cheaper, more docile, more stable supply of labor, while their servants loafed on the job, ran away, and claimed the traditional long lunch hour. As the century wore on, punctuated in Virginia by depression, discontent, and rebellion, Virginia's position in the market for men gradually improved: the price of sugar fell, making it less competitive with tobacco; the heavy mortality in the colony declined, making the initial outlay of capital on slaves less risky; and American and European traders expanded their infamous activities in Africa. The world supply of slaves, which had fallen off in the second quarter of the seventeenth century, rose sharply in the third quarter and continued to rise.

With these developments the Virginians at last were able to acquire substitute natives for the colony and begin, in their own English way, to Hispanize Virginia. By the middle of the eighteenth century Africans constituted the great majority of the colony's entire labor force. This is not to say that plantation slavery in Virginia or elsewhere can be understood simply as a result of inherited attitudes toward work confronting the economic opportunities of the New World. The forces that determined the character of plantation slavery were complex. But perhaps an institution so archaic and at the same time so modern as the plantation cannot be fully understood without taking into consideration the attitudes that helped to starve the first settlers of the colony where the southern plantation began.

Winthrop D. Jordan # Modern Tensions and the Origins of Slavery

The most striking example of the supreme relevance of early American history for today is in connection with the "Black Revolution" in mid-twentieth-century America. That movement has brought to the surface fundamental questions about race relations. Why does prejudice against

*blacks exist? Is it the result of slavery, or did it cause slavery? Is it
something innate or something culturally acquired?*

*Answers to such questions are important, not only for understanding
crucial current problems but also for what might be done about them,
and how. If, for instance, prejudice is somehow innate, how much can be
done about it? If, on the other hand, it is solely the product of two
centuries of slavery, very different prospects can be seen.*

*In every English colony from Canada through the Caribbean there was
a shortage of labor: so much to be done on the frontier and so few to do
it. The shortage was particularly acute where fertile land and long growing seasons encouraged large-scale production of sugar, rice, and tobacco
—crops which required much manual labor. That labor did not need to
be highly skilled, but it had to be numerous, cheap, and dependable over
the years.*

*The case was clearly presented as early as 1645 in a letter by Emanuel
Downing, a New Englander, not a Virginian:*

I doe not see how wee can thrive until wee get into a stock of slaves sufficient
to doe all our business, for our children's children will hardly see this great Continent filled with people, soe that our servants will still desire freedome to plant
for themselves, and not stay but for verie great wages. And I suppose you know
verie well how wee shall mayneteyne 20 Moores cheaper than one Englishe
servant.

*Enslaved and debased, "Moores" or "Negars" filled the bill. They had
no trouble learning the limited skills necessary, and the supply of them
seemed inexhaustible—one and a third million were brought to the New
World in the seventeenth century, according to the most recent scholarship. Compared to the labor of European immigrants, when it could be
hired at all, theirs was cheap. And compared to wage labor or indentured
servants, they were sure for the long pull since they were captives for
life.*

*They filled the bill, but how and when is not clear, although it is very
important. As slaves, they were clearly debased. But if they were not
always chattel slaves in America, how do we account for the appearance
of slavery and debasement? Once under way, slavery and debasement
were mutually reenforcing and progressive, but which came first, how,
and why have a great deal to do with how one sees the problems of
relations between the two races in America today.*

*Winthrop D. Jordan has made the most careful study of such questions
in his important book,* White over Black: American Attitudes toward the
Negro, 1550–1812. *In the following earlier article he suggested some of
the themes that would be developed more fully in the book. His article is
significant and provocative on several counts.*

*The past helps us understand the present. Historians live in their own
"present," and this present is always changing. Jordan traces how successive generations of historians have understood the origins of slavery
and racial prejudice, reacting to the mood and problems of their own
times. That "history" is no matter of cold, dead "facts" but rather a*

matter of constant reinterpretation, new perspectives, new "relevance" becomes abundantly clear.

By his examination of how black slavery arose, he makes equally clear the pattern in which relations between people develop, prejudices arise, and institutions are born. In the case of American slavery, that process meant that slavery, debasement, and prejudice were intertwined, each constantly reenforcing the others once the process was under way. [Winthrop D. Jordan, "Modern Tensions and the Origins of American Slavery," Journal of Southern History, XXVIII (February 1962), 18–30, footnotes omitted. Copyright 1962 by the Southern Historical Association. Reprinted by permission of the managing editor. A modified and much more complete description of the origin of American slavery is in Winthrop D. Jordan, White over Black: American Attitudes toward the Negro, 1550–1812 *(Chapel Hill, N.C.: University of North Carolina Press, 1968).]*

Thanks to John Smith we know that Negroes first came to the British continental colonies in 1619. What we do not know is exactly when Negroes were first enslaved there. This question has been debated by historians for the past seventy years, the critical point being whether Negroes were enslaved almost from their first importation or whether they were at first simply servants and only later reduced to the status of slaves. The long duration and vigor of the controversy suggest that more than a simple question of dating has been involved. In fact certain current tensions in American society have complicated the historical problem and greatly heightened its significance. Dating the origins of slavery has taken on a striking modern relevance.

During the nineteenth century historians assumed almost universally that the first Negroes came to Virginia as slaves. So close was their acquaintance with the problem of racial slavery that it did not occur to them that Negroes could ever have been anything but slaves. Philip A. Bruce, the first man to probe with some thoroughness into the early years of American slavery, adopted this view in 1896, although he emphasized that the original difference in treatment between white servants and Negroes was merely that Negroes served for life. Just six years later, however, came a challenge from a younger, professionally trained historian, James C. Ballagh. His *A History of Slavery in Virginia* appeared in the *Johns Hopkins Universtiy Studies in Historical and Political Science,* an aptly named series which was to usher in the new era of scholarly detachment in the writing of institutional history. Ballagh offered a new and different interpretation; he took the position that the first Negroes served merely as servants and that enslavement did not begin until around 1660, when statutes bearing on slavery were passed for the first time.

There has since been agreement on dating the statutory establishment of slavery, and differences of opinion have centered on when enslavement began in actual practice. Fortunately there has also been general agreement on slavery's distinguishing characteristics: service for life and inheritance of like obligation by any offspring. Writing on the free Negro in Virginia for the Johns Hopkins series, John H. Russell in 1913 tackled the central question and showed that some Negroes were indeed servants but concluded that "between 1640 and 1660 slavery was fast becoming an established fact. In this twenty years the colored population was divided, part being servants and part being slaves, and some who were servants defended themselves with increasing difficulty from the encroachments of slavery." Ulrich B. Phillips, though little interested in the matter, in 1918 accepted Russell's conclusion of early servitude and transition toward slavery after 1640. Helen T. Catterall took much the same position in 1926. On the other hand, in 1921 James M. Wright, discussing the free Negro in Maryland, implied that Negroes were slaves almost from the beginning, and in 1940 Susie M. Ames reviewed several cases in Virginia which seemed to indicate that genuine slavery had existed well before Ballagh's date of 1660.

All this was a very small academic gale, well insulated from the outside world. Yet despite disagreement on dating enslavement, the earlier writers—Bruce, Ballagh, and Russell—shared a common assumption which, though at the time seemingly irrelevant to the main question, has since proved of considerable importance. They assumed that prejudice against the Negro was natural and almost innate in the white man. It would be surprising if they had felt otherwise in this period of segregation statutes, overseas imperialism, immigration restriction, and full-throated Anglo-Saxonism. By the 1920's, however, with the easing of these tensions, the assumption of natural prejudice was dropped unnoticed. Yet only one historian explicitly contradicted that assumption: Ulrich Phillips of Georgia, impressed with the geniality of both slavery and twentieth-century race relations, found no natural prejudice in the white man and expressed his "conviction that Southern racial asperities are mainly superficial, and that the two great elements are fundamentally in accord."

Only when tensions over race relations intensified once more did the older assumption of natural prejudice crop up again. After World War II American Negroes found themselves beneficiaries of New Deal politics and reforms, wartime need for manpower, world-wide repulsion at racist excesses in Nazi Germany, and growingly successful colored anticolonialism. With new militancy Negroes mounted an attack on the citadel of separate but equal, and soon it became clear that America was in for a period of self-conscious reappraisal of its racial arrangements. Writing in this period of heightened tension (1949) a practiced and careful scholar, Wesley F. Craven, raised the old question of the Negro's original status, suggesting that Negroes had been enslaved at an early date. Craven also cautiously resuscitated the idea that white men may have had natural distaste for the Negro, an idea which fitted neatly with the suggestion of early enslavement. Original antipathy would mean rapid debasement.

In the next year (1950) came a sophisticated counterstatement, which contradicted both Craven's dating and implicitly any suggestion of early prejudice. Oscar and Mary F. Handlin in "Origins of the Southern Labor System" offered a case for late enslavement, with servitude as the status of Negroes before about 1660. Originally the status of both Negroes and white servants was far short of freedom, the Handlins maintained, but Negroes failed to benefit from increased freedom for servants in mid-century and became less free rather than more. Embedded in this description of diverging status were broader implications: Late and gradual enslavement undercut the possibility of natural, deep-seated antipathy toward Negroes. On the contrary, if whites and Negroes could share the same status of half freedom for forty years in the seventeenth century, why could they not share full freedom in the twentieth?

The same implications were rendered more explicit by Kenneth M. Stampp in a major reassessment of Southern slavery published two years after the Supreme Court's 1954 school decision. Reading physiology with the eye of faith, Stampp frankly stated his assumption "that innately Negroes *are,* after all, only white men with black skins, nothing more, nothing less." Closely following the Handlins' article on the origins of slavery itself, he almost directly denied any pattern of early and inherent racial antipathy: ". . . Negro and white servants of the seventeenth century seemed to be remarkably unconcerned about their visible physical differences." As for "the trend toward special treatment" of the Negro, "physical and cultural differences provided handy excuses to justify it." Distaste for the Negro, then, was in the beginning scarcely more than an appurtenance of slavery.

These views squared nicely with the hopes of those even more directly concerned with the problem of contemporary race relations, sociologists and social psychologists. Liberal on the race question almost to a man, they tended to see slavery as the initial cause of the Negro's current degradation. The modern Negro was the unhappy victim of long association with base status. Sociologists, though uninterested in tired questions of historical evidence, could not easily assume a natural prejudice in the white man as the cause of slavery. Natural or innate prejudice would not only violate their basic assumptions concerning the dominance of culture but would undermine the power of their new Baconian science. For if prejudice was natural there would be little one could do to wipe it out. Prejudice must have followed enslavement, not vice versa, else any liberal program of action would be badly compromised. One prominent social scientist suggested in a UNESCO pamphlet that racial prejudice in the United States commenced with the cotton gin!

Just how closely the question of dating had become tied to the practical matter of action against racial prejudice was made apparent by the suggestions of still another historian. Carl N. Degler grappled with the dating problem in an article frankly entitled "Slavery and the Genesis of American Race Prejudice." The article appeared in 1959, a time when Southern resistance to school desegregation seemed more adamant than ever and the North's hands none too clean, a period of discouragement for those hoping to end racial discrimination. Prejudice against the

Negro now appeared firm and deep-seated, less easily eradicated than had been supposed in, say, 1954. It was Degler's view that enslavement began early, as a result of white settlers' prejudice or antipathy toward the first Negroes. Thus not only were the sociologists contradicted but the dating problem was now overtly and consciously tied to the broader question of whether slavery caused prejudice or prejudice caused slavery. A new self-consciousness over the American racial dilemma had snatched an arid historical controversy from the hands of an unsuspecting earlier generation and had tossed it into the arena of current debate.

Ironically there might have been no historical controversy at all if every historian dealing with the subject had exercised greater care with facts and greater restraint in interpretation. Too often the debate entered the realm of inference and assumption. For the crucial early years after 1619 there is simply not enough evidence to indicate with any certainty whether Negroes were treated like white servants or not. No historian has found anything resembling proof one way or the other. The first Negroes were sold to the English settlers, yet so were other Englishmen. It can be said, however, that Negroes were set apart from white men by the word *Negroes,* and a distinct name is not attached to a group unless it is seen as different. The earliest Virginia census reports plainly distinguished Negroes from white men, sometimes giving Negroes no personal name; and in 1629 every commander of the several plantations was ordered to "take a generall muster of all the inhabitants men woemen and Children as well *Englishe* as Negroes." Difference, however, might or might not involve inferiority.

The first evidence as to the actual status of Negroes does not appear until about 1640. Then it becomes clear that *some* Negroes were serving for life and some children inheriting the same obligation. Here it is necessary to suggest with some candor that the Handlins' statement to the contrary rests on unsatisfactory documentation. That some Negroes were held as slaves after about 1640 is no indication, however, that American slavery popped into the world fully developed at that time. Many historians, most cogently the Handlins, have shown slavery to have been a gradual development, a process not completed until the eighteenth century. The complete deprivation of civil and personal rights, the legal conversion of the Negro into a chattel, in short slavery as Americans came to know it, was not accomplished overnight. Yet these developments practically and logically depended on the practice of hereditary lifetime service, and it is certainly possible to find in the 1640's and 1650's traces of slavery's most essential feature.

The first definite trace appears in 1640 when the Virginia General Court pronounced sentence on three servants who had been retaken after running away to Maryland. Two of them, a Dutchman and a Scot, were ordered to serve their masters for one additional year and then the colony for three more, but "the third being a negro named John Punch shall serve his said master or his assigns for the time of his natural life here or else where." No white servant in America, so far as is known, ever received a like sentence. Later the same month a Negro was again singled out from a group of recaptured runaways; six of the seven were assigned additional time while the Negro was given none, presumably because he was already serving for life. After 1640, too, county court records began to mention Negroes, in part because there were more of them than previously—about two per cent of the Virginia population in 1649. Sales for life, often including any future progeny, were recorded in unmistakable language. In 1646 Francis Pott sold a Negro woman and boy to Stephen Charlton "to the use of him . . . forever." Similarly, six years later William Whittington sold to John Pott "one Negro girle named Jowan; aged about Ten yeares and with her Issue and produce duringe her (or either of them) for their Life tyme. And their Successors forever"; and a Maryland man in 1649 deeded two Negro men and a woman "and all their issue both male and Female." The executors of a York County estate in 1647 disposed of eight Negroes—four men, two women, and two children—to Captain John Chisman "to have hold occupy posesse and inioy and every one of the afforementioned Negroes forever[.]" The will of Rowland Burnham of "Rapahanocke," made in 1657, dispensed his considerable number of Negroes and white servants in language which clearly differentiated between the two by specifying that the whites were to serve for their "full terme of tyme" and the Negroes "for ever." Nor did anything in the will indicate that this distinction was exceptional or novel.

In addition to these clear indications that some Negroes were owned for life, there were cases of Negroes held for terms far longer than the normal five or seven years. On the other hand, some Negroes served only the term usual for white servants, and others were completely free. One Negro freeman, Anthony Johnson, himself owned a Negro. Obviously the enslavement of some Negroes did not mean the immediate enslavement of all.

Further evidence of Negroes serving for life lies in the prices paid for them. In many instances the valuations placed on Negroes (in estate inventories and bills of sale) were far higher than for white servants, even those servants with full terms yet to serve. Since there was ordinarily no preference for Negroes as such, higher prices must have meant that Negroes were more highly valued because of their greater length of service. Negro women may have been especially prized, moreover, because their progeny could also be held perpetually. In 1645, for example, two Negro women and a boy were sold for 5,500 pounds of tobacco. Two years earlier William Burdett's inventory listed eight servants (with the time each had still to serve) at valuations ranging from 400 to 1,100 pounds, while a "very anntient" Negro was valued at 3,000 and an eight-year-old Negro girl at 2,000 pounds, with no time-remaining indicated for either. In the late 1650's an inventory of Thomas Ludlow's large estate evaluated a white servant with six years to serve at less than an elderly Negro man and only one half of a Negro woman. The labor owned by James Stone in 1648 was evaluated as follows:

	lb tobo
Thomas Groves, 4 yeares to serve	1300
Francis Bomley for 6 yeares	1500
John Thackstone for 3 yeares	1300
Susan Davis for 3 yeares	1000
Emaniell a Negro man	2000
Roger Stone 3 yeares	1300
Mingo a Negro man	2000

Besides setting a higher value on the two Negroes, Stone's inventory, like Burdett's, failed to indicate the number of years they had still to serve. It would seem safe to assume that the time remaining was omitted in this and similar documents simply because the Negroes were regarded as serving for an unlimited time.

The situation in Maryland was apparently the same. In 1643 Governor Leonard Calvert agreed with John Skinner, "mariner," to exchange certain estates for seventeen sound Negro "slaves," fourteen men and three women between sixteen and twenty-six years old. The total value of these was placed at 24,000 pounds of tobacco, which would work out to 1,000 pounds for the women and 1,500 for the men, prices considerably higher than those paid for white servants at the time.

Wherever Negro women were involved, however, higher valuations may have reflected the fact that they could be used for field work while white women generally were not. This discrimination between Negro and white women, of course, fell short of actual enslavement. It meant merely that Negroes were set apart in a way clearly not to their advantage. Yet this is not the only evidence that Negroes were subjected to degrading distinctions not directly related to slavery. In several ways Negroes were singled out for special treatment which suggested a generalized debasing of Negroes as a group. Significantly, the first indications of debasement appeared at about the same time as the first indications of actual enslavement.

The distinction concerning field work is a case in point. It first appeared on the written record in 1643, when Virginia pointedly recognized it in her taxation policy. Previously tithable persons had been defined (1629) as "all those that worke in the ground of what qualitie or condition soever." Now the law stated that all adult men and *Negro* women were to be tithable, and this distinction was made twice again before 1660. Maryland followed a similar course, beginning in 1654. John Hammond, in a 1656 tract defending the tobacco colonies, wrote that servant women were not put to work in the fields but in domestic employments, "yet som wenches that are nasty, and beastly and not fit to be so imployed are put into the ground." Since all Negro women were taxed as working in the fields, it would seem logical to conclude that Virginians found them "nasty" and "beastly." The essentially racial nature of this discrimination was bared by a 1668 law at the time slavery was crystallizing on the statue books:

Whereas some doubts, have arisen whether negro women set free were still to be accompted tithable according to a former act, *It is declared by this grand assembly* that negro women, though permitted to enjoy their ffreedome yet ought not in all respects to be admitted to a full fruition of the exemptions and impunities of the English, and are still lyable to payment of taxes.

Virginia law set Negroes apart in a second way by denying them the important right and obligation to bear arms. Few restraints could indicate more clearly the denial to Negroes of membership in the white community. This action, in a sense the first foreshadowing of the slave codes, came in 1640, at just the time when other indications first appear that Negroes were subject to special treatment.

Finally, an even more compelling sense of the separateness of Negroes was revealed in early distress concerning sexual union between the races. In 1630 a Virginia court pronounced a now famous sentence: "Hugh Davis to be soundly whipped, before an assembly of Negroes and others for abusing himself to the dishonor of God and shame of Christians, by defiling his body in lying with a negro." While there were other instances of punishment for interracial union in the ensuing years, fornication rather than miscegenation may well have been the primary offense, though in 1651 a Maryland man sued someone who he claimed had said "that he had a black bastard in Virginia." There may have been nothing racial about the 1640 case by which Robert Sweet was compelled "to do penance in church according to laws of England, for getting a negroe woman with child and the woman whipt." About 1650 a white man and a Negro woman were required to stand clad in white sheets before a congregation in Lower Norfolk County for having had relations, but this punishment was sometimes used in ordinary cases of fornication between two whites.

It is certain, however, that in the early 1660's when slavery was gaining statutory recognition, the colonial assemblies legislated with feeling against miscegenation. Nor was this merely a matter of avoiding confusion of status, as was suggested by the Handlins. In 1662 Virginia declared that "if any christian shall commit ffornication with a negro man or woman, hee or shee soe offending" should pay double the usual fine. Two years later Maryland prohibited interracial marriages:

forasmuch as divers freeborne English women forgettfull of their free Condicōn and to the disgrace of our Nation doe intermarry with Negro Slaves by which alsoe divers suites may arise touching the Issue of such woemen and a great damage doth befall the Masters of such Negros for prevention whereof for deterring such freeborne women from such shamefull Matches . . . ,

Strong language indeed if the problem had only been confusion of status. A Maryland act of 1681 described marriages of white women with Negroes as, among other things, "always to the Satisfaccōn of theire Lascivious & Lustfull desires, & to the disgrace not only of the English butt allso of many other Christian Nations." When Virginia finally prohibited all interracial liaisons in 1691, the assembly vigorously denounced miscegenation and its fruits as "that abominable mixture and spurious issue."

One is confronted, then, with the fact that the first evidences of enslavement and of other forms of debasement appeared at about the same time. Such coincidence comports poorly with both views on the causation of prejudice and slavery. If slavery caused prejudice, then invidious distinctions concerning working in the fields, bearing arms, and sexual union should have appeared only after slavery's firm establishment. If prejudice caused slavery, then one would expect to find such lesser discriminations preceding the greater discrimination of outright enslavement.

Perhaps a third explanation of the relationship between slavery and prejudice may be offered, one that might fit the pattern of events as revealed by existing evidence. Both current views share a common starting point: They predicate two factors, prejudice and slavery, and demand a distinct order of causality. No matter how qualified by recognition that the effect may in turn react upon the cause, each approach inevitably tends to deny the validity of its opposite. But what if one were to regard both slavery and prejudice as species of a general debasement of the Negro? Both may have been equally cause and effect, constantly reacting upon each other, dynamically joining hands to hustle the Negro down the road to complete degradation. Mutual causation is, of course, a highly useful concept for describing social situations in the modern world. Indeed it has been widely applied in only slightly altered fashion to the current racial situation: Racial prejudice and the Negro's lowly position are widely accepted as constantly reinforcing each other.

This way of looking at the facts might well fit better with what we know of slavery itself. Slavery was an organized pattern of human relationships. No matter what the law might say, it was of different character than cattle ownership. No matter how degrading, slavery involved human beings. No one seriously pretended otherwise. Slavery was not an isolated economic or institutional phenomenon; it was the practical facet of a general debasement without which slavery could have no rationality. (Prejudice, too, was a form of debasement, a kind of slavery in the mind.) Certainly the urgent need for labor in a virgin country guided the direction which debasement took, molded it, in fact, into an institutional framework. That economic practicalities shaped the external form of debasement should not tempt one to forget, however, that slavery was at bottom a social arrangement, a way of society's ordering its members in its own mind.

Cutaway view of the Mayflower II, *a modern reproduction of the Pilgrim vessel now docked at Plymouth, Massachusetts.* Mayflower II *weighs 181 tons and measures 78 feet, 8 inches at waterline, 21 feet, 6 inches in beam. Aboard the original* Mayflower *were crammed 102 passengers and 25 crew for 66 days, along with all supplies and necessities for planting a colony. (Courtesy of Plimoth Plantation)*

2 The Pattern of Puritanism

A child of Europe, America was conceived, born, and reared in an atmosphere of religiosity difficult to comprehend in the twentieth century. The peoples of Western Europe, whether Catholic or Protestant, found in Bible and church their explanations of the universe, their understanding of life and its meaning, their rules for personal conduct and for social order. Religion was the mold in which were cast all the cultural traits of early modern Europe.

The rulers who pushed exploration and colonization were cast in that mold. Their titles usually included phrases such as "Most Catholic Majesty" (Spain) and "Defender of the Faith" (England). Their wars were often wars of religion. Their interests in empire always included "inlarging the glory of the gospell." Those whom they sent out to explore the "inner space" of the world reflected the same spirit. Columbus was zealous to spread Christianity; he took literally and seriously his role as "Christopher": Christbearer. In New France, a century and a half later, Jesuits probed hundreds of miles into the interior of North America, striving to become Christian shepherds to savage flocks.

Kings and captains and priests did not monopolize the religious mood of the culture that spawned America; it was shared by people of all walks of life. Among seamen, for example, the daily routine aboard ship was set to religious ceremonies. Aboard Columbus' little fleet changes in the round were heralded by choruses of religious verses. Describing English shipboard practice a century later, Captain John Smith told how the crew marked the changing of the watch by singing a Psalm and saying a prayer. This does not mean that seamen were monks meditating in their cabins when not on watch or that Captain John Smith was not the driver of men and even the swashbuckler portrayed in his own story. It simply shows that the context or frame of reference in which men operated was religious.

That context had been the pattern of European culture for centuries. A new secular and scientific context was emerging in the sixteenth and seventeenth centuries, but it would not prevail until after the American colonies had come of age and asserted their independence. A half-dozen generations of colonists lived in that older framework. Their churches, as the Puritan one, may be long gone; their theology may seem strange; their influence nevertheless continues to be profound to this day. The first "pattern" in American history was a religious one.

In that era all western Europeans operated from fundamental assumptions about religion. Such fundamental assumptions naturally led to institutions that gave form and substance to the spirit of the age. A church, for instance, was universally accepted as essential; the importance of the community of believers was clear not only from Christ's example and admonition but also from the futile experience of those who had tried to go it alone. Hermits failed to show the vitality of the gospel, let alone to spread it. And, as far as Protestants were concerned, monastic orders were the same. Christ summoned men to live in the world, not apart from it.

To live in the world seemed to men of that age to require tying church to state in a strong "establishment." Religious faith was the absolute essential in life and the key to life after death. Heresy had to be avoided at any cost, because the heretic might lead others astray as well as dooming himself. Only the state could muster the force to prevent religious error. The "one" church must therefore not only be recognized by the state but "established" by it, that is, supported and enforced by it. For people operating from such profound convictions, religious toleration was obviously an absurd principle.

Like all ages, then, this one had its own faith and institutions to protect and promote it. By the sixteenth century, however, many were becoming convinced that the institution of the church had departed from the faith—emphasizing rituals instead of spirit, worldly power instead of divine, false doctrines instead of the original "true" ones. This, of course, was what the Protestant Reformation on the continent of Europe was all about. It was also what the Puritan Revolt in England was all about and the migration of more than 20,000 Englishmen to New England alone in the years from 1629 to 1640.

On the Continent, Protestant reformers such as Luther and Calvin asserted that the "church universal" had so deviated from the Christian ideal that only a complete re-formation would do, by which they meant a return to the "original church." They sought not something new but something old. In England, the break with the Roman Catholic church began in a different way. Unlike Luther's split with Rome in 1517, Henry VIII's break seventeen years later had nothing to do with fundamental matters of doctrine and little to do with practice, except as allegiance to Rome prevented his re-marriage and sapped his power as ruler of England. He established an English "Catholic" church, not a Protestant one; he and his heirs would be head of a national church, differing in no significant doctrinal way from the church of Rome.

For many in England this was not enough. Too much of the defective Roman institution was continued. After the death of Henry VIII in 1547, there followed a decade of hard political in-fighting between those who would restore Roman Catholicism and those who would carry the break further, to establish a more "Protestant" union of church and state.

In 1558 Elizabeth I, the third child of Henry VIII to rule, ascended the throne. An extraordinary monarch by any standard, in an extra-ordinarily long reign of forty-five years she bound up domestic wounds and warded off the external threat of the Spanish Armada. Her "Elizabethan Settlement" brought to England such unity, power, and glory as she had never known.

But that Settlement involved a compromise in religion completely unsatisfactory to an increasingly radical group of her subjects. For them, too much of the Roman corruption of the original Christian ideal and institution remained; too much, still, of the "Whore of Babylon," the church of Rome. Purify the English church of these fundamental taints they would. Those who put up with the "corrupt" Church of England, therefore, derisively called them "Puritans."

Perry Miller # The Perplexing Puritans

In a religious age, the Puritans were arch-religionists. With other Calvinists, they were the "shock troops" of the Protestant Revolution: deeply motivated, profoundly committed, sternly self-disciplined. Bitterly opposed to an "establishment" they saw as corrupt, thousands of them resolved the dilemma of what to do in such a society by migrating to New England in the 1630s. Those who stayed behind carried out a violent revolution in the 1640s.

Those who left did so primarily for religion's sake. To found a new Zion in the wilderness, as their great leader and Governor, John Winthrop, put it. Or, in the words of one who would become more famous, Roger Williams: "There is one commoditie for the sake of which most of God's children in N. England have run their mighty hazards, a commoditie marvellously scarce in former times. . . . It is a Libertie of searching after God's most holy mind and pleasure."

They knew what they were about. Others since then have presumed to know better. Some have asserted that the Puritans wanted to establish freedom of worship for all, an interpretation that could scarcely be further from their intent. Others, who see man as a creature dominated by economic self-interest, have held that the Puritans' real motive was economic self-improvement. Yet others have attributed to them almost all of the virtues and flaws that they see in the "American character." The historical reputation of the Puritans has had a wild career.

Most recently, historians have tried to recover the Puritans as they originally were, not what their descendants became or what many have assumed that they were. These scholars have tried to understand the Puritans in the light of the seventeenth century, not the twentieth, assuming that to study any age by the standards of another inevitably distorts it. Although Puritan theology may seem simply irrelevant or utterly incomprehensible today, in seventeenth-century Massachusetts it was logical, clear, and all-meaningful; it pervaded everything that the believer did.

One of the most perceptive historians dedicated to recovering the Puritans in their proper context was Perry Miller—the "best historical mind of his generation, perhaps of his century," in the estimation of a contemporary scholar, Edmund S. Morgan. As a young man, Miller was anything but an ivory-towered scholar. He wandered the United States from his native Chicago to Colorado to the New York City area, where he played Shakespearean roles on the stage. Then to sea, working his way from the Gulf of Mexico to the Mediterranean and the West Coast of Africa. He later recounted how, while supervising the unloading of oil drums in the Belgian Congo, "It was given to me . . . thrust upon me the mission of expounding what I took to be the innermost propulsion of the United States."

Miller pursued that mission to his death in 1963. In more than three decades of unusually fruitful work at Harvard, he recast much of our understanding about the Puritans and their role. In the following selection he suggests the importance of Puritanism, points out how and why it has often been misunderstood, and gives his own evaluation of it. Miller not only provides an introduction to perhaps the most important element in the making of the "American mind"; he also provocatively suggests the broader problem of reading the past aright, pointing out the pitfalls for the unwary and the ways in which history can become what Voltaire called "the playing of tricks upon the dead." [From The Puritans, *Perry Miller and Thomas H. Johnson, editors   (New York: American Book Company, 1938).]*

Puritanism may perhaps best be described as that point of view, that philosophy of life, that code of values, which was carried to New England by the first settlers in the early seventeenth century. Beginning thus, it has become one of the continuous factors in American life and American thought. Any inventory of the elements that have gone into the making of the "American mind" would have to commence with Puritanism. It is, indeed, only one among many: if we should attempt to enumerate these traditions, we should certainly have to mention such philosophies, such "isms," as the rational liberalism of Jeffersonian democracy, the Hamiltonian conception of conservatism and government, the Southern theory of racial aristocracy, the Transcendentalism of nineteenth-century New England, and what is generally spoken of as frontier individualism. Among these factors Puritanism has been perhaps the most conspicuous, the most sustained, and the most fecund. Its role in American thought has been almost the dominant one, for the descendants of Puritans have carried at least some habits of the Puritan mind into a variety of pursuits, have spread across the country, and in many fields of activity have played a leading part. The force of Puritanism, furthermore, has been accentuated because it was the first of these traditions to be fully articulated, and because it has inspired certain traits which have persisted long after the vanishing of the original creed. Without some understanding of Puritanism, it may safely be said, there is no understanding of America.

Yet important as Puritanism has undoubtedly been in shaping the nation, it is more easily described than defined. It figures frequently in controversy of the last decade, very seldom twice with exactly the same connotation. Particularly of recent years has it become a hazardous feat to run down its meaning. In the mood of revolt against the ideals of previous generations which has swept over our period, Puritanism has become a shining target for many sorts of marksmen. Confusion becomes worse confounded if we attempt to correlate modern usages with anything that can be proved pertinent to the original Puritans themselves. To seek no further, it was the habit of proponents for the repeal of the Eighteenth Amendment during the 1920's to dub Prohibitionists "Puritans," and cartoonists made the nation familiar with an image of the Puritan: a gaunt, lank-haired killjoy, wearing a black steeple hat and compounding for sins he was inclined to by damning those to which he had no mind. Yet any acquaintance with the Puritans of the seventeenth century will reveal at once, not only that they did not wear such hats, but also that they attired themselves in all the hues of the rainbow, and furthermore that in their daily life they imbibed what seem to us prodigious quantities of alcoholic beverages, with never the slightest inkling that they were doing anything sinful. True, they opposed drinking to excess, and ministers preached lengthy sermons condemning intoxication, but at such pious ceremonies as the ordination of new ministers the bill for rum, wine, and beer consumed by the congregation was often staggering. Increase Mather himself—who in popular imagination is apt to figure along with his son Cotton as the arch-embodiment of the Puritan—said in one of his sermons: "Drink is in it self a good creature of God, and to be received with thankfulness, but the abuse of drink is from Satan; the wine is from God, but the Drunkard is from the Devil." Or again, the Puritan has acquired the reputation of having been blind to all aesthetic enjoyment and starved of beauty; yet the architecture of the Puritan age grows in the esteem of critics and the household objects of Puritan manufacture, pewter and furniture, achieve prohibitive prices by their appeal to discriminating collectors. Examples of such discrepancies between the modern usage of the word and the historical fact could be multiplied indefinitely. It is not the purpose of this volume to engage in controversy, nor does it intend particularly to defend the Puritan against the bewildering variety of critics who on every side today find him an object of scorn or pity. In his life he neither asked nor gave mercy to his foes; he demanded only that conflicts be joined on real and explicit issues. By examining his own words it may become possible to establish, for better or for worse, the meaning of Puritanism as the Puritan himself believed and practiced it.

Just as soon as we endeavor to free ourselves from prevailing conceptions or misconceptions, and to ascertain the historical facts about seventeenth-century New Englanders, we become aware that we face still another difficulty: not only must we extricate ourselves from interpretations that have been read into Puritanism by the twentieth century, but still more from those that have been attached to it by the eighteenth and nineteenth. The Puritan philosophy, brought to New England highly elaborated and codified, remained a fairly rigid orthodoxy during the seventeenth century. In the next age, however, it proved to be anything but static; by the middle of the eighteenth century there had proceeded from it two distinct schools of thought, almost unalterably opposed to each other. Certain elements were carried into the creeds and practices of the evangelical religious revivals, but others were perpetuated by the rationalists and the forerunners of Unitarianism. Consequently our conception of Puritanism is all too apt to be colored by subsequent happenings; we read ideas into the seventeenth century which belong to the eighteenth, and the real nature of Puritanism can hardly be discovered at all, because Puritanism itself became two distinct and contending things to two sorts of men. The most prevalent error arising from this fact has been the identification of Puritanism with evangelicalism in many accounts, though in histories written by Unitarian scholars the original doctrine has been almost as much distorted in the opposite direction.

Among the evangelicals the original doctrines were transformed or twisted into the new versions of Protestantism that spawned in the Great Awakening of the 1740's, in the succeeding revivals along the frontier and through the back country, in the centrifugal speculations of enraptured prophets and rabid sects in the nineteenth century. All these movements retained something of the theology or revived something of the intensity of spirit, but at the same time they threw aside so much of authentic Puritanism that there can be no doubt the founding fathers would vigorously have repudiated such progeny. They would have had no use, for instance, for the camp meeting and the revivalist orgy; "hitting the sawdust trail" would have been an action exceedingly distasteful to the most ardent among them. What we know as "fundamentalism" would have been completely antipathetic to them, for they never for one moment dreamed that the truth of scripture was to be maintained in spite of or against the evidences of reason, science, and learning. The sects that have arisen out of Puritanism have most strikingly betrayed their rebellion against the true spirit of their source by their attack upon the ideal of a learned ministry; Puritans considered religion a very complex, subtle, and highly intellectualized affair, and they trained their experts in theology with all the care we would lavish upon preparing men to be engineers or chemists. For the same reasons, Puritans would object strenuously to almost all recent attempts to "humanize" religion, to smooth over hard doctrines, to introduce sweetness and light at the cost of hardheaded realism and invincible logic. From their point of view, to bring Christ down to earth in such a fashion as is implied in statements we sometimes encounter—that He was the "first humanitarian" or that He would certainly endorse this or that political party— would seem to them frightful blasphemy. Puritanism was not only a religious creed, it was a philosophy and a metaphysic; it was an organization of man's whole life, emotional and intellectual, to a degree which has not been sustained by any denomination stemming from it. Yet because such creeds have sprung from Puritanism, the Puritans are frequently praised or blamed for qualities which never belonged to them or for ideas which originated only among their successors and which they themselves would have disowned.

On the other hand, if the line of development from Puritanism tends in one direction to frontier revivalism and evangelicalism, another line leads as directly to a more philosophical, critical, and even skeptical point of view. Unitarianism is as much the child of Puritanism as Methodism. And if the one accretion has colored or distorted our conception of the original doctrine, the other has done so no less. Descendants of the Puritans who revolted against what they considered the tyranny and cruelty of Puritan theology, who substituted taste and reason for dogma and authority and found the emotional fervor of the evangelicals so much sound and fury, have been prone to idealize their ancestors into their own image. A few decades ago it had become very much the mode to praise the Puritans for virtues which they did not possess and which they would not have considered virtues at all. In the pages of liberal historians, and above all in the speeches of Fourth of July orators, the Puritans have been hymned as the pioneers of religious liberty, though nothing was ever farther from their designs; they have been hailed as the forerunners of democracy, though if they were, it was quite beside their intention; they have been invoked in justification for an economic philosophy of free competition and laissez-faire, though they themselves believed in government regulation of business, the fixing of just prices, and the curtailing of individual profits in the interests of the welfare of the whole.

The moral of these reflections may very well be that it is dangerous to read history backwards, to interpret something that was by what it ultimately became, particularly when it became several things. In order that the texts presented in this volume may be read for their proper meaning, it is necessary that the student divest himself as far as possible of those preconceptions which have been established only in later times, and approach the Puritans in terms of their own background. Only thus can we hope to understand what Puritanism was, or what it became and why. The Puritan had his defects, certainly, and he had his virtues, but the defects of one century may become the virtues of another, and what is considered commendable at one time may be viewed with horror by later generations. It is not easy to restrain one's own prejudices and to exercise the sort of historical imagination that is required for the understanding of a portion of the past according to its own intentions before we allow ourselves to judge it by our own standards. The Puritans were not a bashful race, they could speak out and did; in their own words they have painted their own portraits, their majestic strength and their dignity, their humanity and solidity, more accurately than any admirer has been able to do; and also they have betrayed the motes and beams in their own eyes more clearly than any enemy has been able to point them out. . . .

The Puritan attitude toward the Bible, to the extent that it was a preservation of intellectual values within the dogmatism, may elicit our hearty approbation. But when we come to the content of the dogma, to what the Puritan insisted the Bible did teach, and to what he expected the regenerate man to find reasonable, in short, when we come to Puritan theology, many persons encounter an insuperable stumbling block to an unqualified approval of Puritan thinking. Not only does the conventional picture of the Puritan creed seem exceedingly unattractive to twentieth-century taste, but the idea of theology in any form is almost equally objectionable. In most secondary accounts Puritans are called Calvinists, and then and there discussion of their intellectual life ceases. Dr. Holmes's "One-Hoss Shay" is deemed a sufficient description.

It is true, the Puritans were Calvinists, if we mean that they more or less agreed with the great theologian of Geneva. They held, that is, that men had fallen into a state of sin, that in order to be saved they must receive from God a special infusion of grace, that God gives the grace to some and not to others out of His own sovereign pleasure, and that therefore from the beginning of time certain souls were "predestined" to heaven and the others sentenced to damnation. But if the New Englanders were Calvinists, it was because they happened to agree with Calvin; they approved his doctrine not because he taught it, but because it seemed inescapably indicated when they studied scripture or observed the actions of men. The sinfulness of the average man was a fact that could be empirically verified, and in itself demonstrated that he needed divine grace in order to be lifted above himself; the men who did receive what they thought was an influx of grace learned by experience that only in such an ecstasy of illumination did truth become thoroughly evident and completely understandable. Obviously the experience was given to relatively few men; therefore God, who is outside time and who is omniscient, must have known from the beginning of time who would and who would not achieve it. This is the law of life; some men are born rich and some poor, some intelligent and some stupid, some are lucky and others unfortunate, some are happy and some melancholy, some are saved and some are not. There is no reason but that God so ordained it. . . .

Puritan theology, therefore, is simply a statement in dogmatic guise of a philosophy of life, wherein it is held on the one hand that men must act by reason and abide by justice, and strive for an inward communication with the force that controls the world, but on the other hand that they must not expect that force always to be cribbed and confined by their conceptions of what is reasonable and just. There is an eternal obligation upon men to be equitable, fair, and good, but who can say that any such morality is also binding on the universe? There are certain amenities which men must observe in their dealings with men, but who can say that they must also be respected by the tiger, by the raging storm, by the

lightning, or by the cancer? It is only when the theology of "predestination" is seen in these less technical terms that its vitality as a living faith
and its strength as a sustaining philosophy become comprehensible.

But the theology of New England was not simply Calvinism, it was not
a mere reduplication of the dogmas of the *Institutes*. What New Englanders believed was an outgrowth, as we have seen, of their background,
which was humanistic and English, and it was conditioned by their
particular controversy with the Church of England. Simon-pure Calvinism is a much more dogmatic, anti-rational creed than that of the
Congregational parsons in Massachusetts. The emigrants went to New
England to prove that a state and a church erected on the principles for
which they were agitating in England would be blessed by God and
prosper. The source of the New England ideology is not Calvin, but
England, or more accurately, the Bible as it was read in England, not in
Geneva.

Though, of course, the controversy in England was a political, social,
and economic one, it was also the intellectual dispute we have outlined.
We might summarize it at this point by saying that in order to harmonize
reason and scripture, the Anglican endeavored to reduce the doctrines
imposed by scripture to the barest minimum; the Puritan extended
scripture to cover the whole of existence and then set himself to prove the
content of all scripture essentially reasonable. Only with this definition of
origins and tendencies in mind can we read Puritan theology aright. In
order to demonstrate that the content of scripture was comprehensible to
reason, the Puritan theorists worked out a substantial addition to the
theology of Calvinism which in New England was quite as important as
the original doctrine. This addition or elaboration of the Calvinist
doctrine is generally called the "Covenant Theology," or the "Federal
Theology." There is no necessity here for examining it in detail. It was a
special way of reading scripture so that the books assembled in the Bible
could all be seen to make sense in the same way. The doctrine held that
after the fall of man, God voluntarily condescended to treat with man as
with an equal and to draw up a covenant or contract with His creature in
which He laid down the terms and conditions of salvation, and pledged
Himself to abide by them. The covenant did not alter the fact that those
only are saved upon whom God sheds His grace, but it made very clear
and reasonable how and why certain men are selected, and prescribed the
conditions under which they might reach a fair assurance of their own
standing. Above all, in the covenant God pledged Himself not to run
athwart human conceptions of right and justice; God was represented
while entering the compact as agreeing to abide by certain human ideas.
Not in all respects, not always, but in the main. . . .

To find equivalents in modern terms for the ideas we have been discussing is well-nigh impossible. To translate seventeenth-century issues
into twentieth-century phrases, when they cannot possibly mean the same
things, is to forego any accurate understanding of them. The results of
modern historical investigation and textual criticism have made fantastic,

even for those who believe the scripture to be the word of God, acceptance of it in anything like the spirit of the seventeenth century. But if we cannot find a common denominator for equating the ideas of the Puritans with ideas of today, we may possibly get at them by understanding the temperament, the mood, the psychology that underlay the theories. If Puritanism as a creed has crumbled, it can be of only antiquarian significance to us, but if Puritanism is also a state of mind, it may be something closer home. . . .

The strength of Puritanism was its realism. If we may borrow William James's frequently misleading division of the human race into the two types of the "tough-minded" and the "tender-minded," and apply it with caution, it may serve our purposes. Though there were undoubtedly men in the Church of England, such as John Donne, whom we would have to describe as "tough," and a number of Puritans who would fit the description of "tender," yet in the main Anglicans such as Hooker and Taylor are quite clearly on the side of the more tender-minded, while the Puritan mind was one of the toughest the world has ever had to deal with. It is impossible to conceive of a disillusioned Puritan; no matter what misfortune befell him, no matter how often or how tragically his fellowmen failed him, he would have been prepared for the worst, and would have expected no better. At the same time, there was nothing of the fatalist about him; as so often happens in the history of thought, the believers in a supreme determining power were the most energetic of soldiers and crusaders. The charge of Cromwell's Ironsides was, on that particular score, proof positive of the superiority of the Puritan over the Anglican, and the Indians of New England learned to their very great sorrow how vehement could be the onset of troops who fought for a predestined victory. There was nothing lukewarm, halfhearted, or flabby about the Puritan; whatever he did, he did with zest and gusto. In that sense we might say that though his life was full of anguish of spirit, he nevertheless enjoyed it hugely. Existence for him was completely dramatic, every minute was charged with meaning. And when we come to an end of this roll call of characteristics, the one which yet remains the most difficult to evoke was his peculiar balance of zeal and enthusiasm with control and wariness. In his inner life he was overwhelmingly preoccupied with achieving a union with the divine; in his external life he was predominantly concerned with self-restraint. . . .

No wonder the Puritan has been something of a puzzlement and a trial to the Gentiles. He was a visionary who never forgot that two plus two equals four; he was a soldier of Jehovah who never came out on the losing side of a bargain. He was a radical and a revolutionary, but not an anarchist; when he got into power he ruled with an iron hand, and also according to a fundamental law. He was a practical idealist with a strong dash of cynicism; he came to New England to found the perfect society and the kingdom of the elect—and never expected it to be perfect, but only the best that fallible men could make. His creed was the revealed word of God and his life was the rule of moderation; his beliefs were handed down from on high and his conduct was regulated by expediency. He was a doctrinaire and an opportunist. Truth for him had been written down once and for all in a definitive, immutable, complete volume, and the covers closed to any further additions; thereupon he devoted all the energies he could spare from more immediate tasks to scholarship and interpretation. He lived in the world according to the principles that must govern this world, with an ever-present sense that they were only for the time being and that his true home was elsewhere. "There is," said John Cotton, "another combination of vertues strangely mixed in every lively holy Christian, And that is, Diligence in worldly businesses, and yet deadnesse to the world; such a mystery as none can read, but they that know it." The Puritan ideal was the man who could take all opportunities, lose no occasions, "and bestir himselfe for profit," and at the same time "bee a man dead-hearted to the world." He might wrest New England from the Indians, trade in the seven seas, and speculate in lands; "yet his heart is not set upon these things, he can tell what to doe with his estate when he hath got it." . . .

When the historian thus attempts to consider Puritanism in all its ramifications, he finds himself at the end hesitating to deliver judgment upon it, or to be wholly satisfied that it has passed into the limbo of anthologies. Certainly we can look upon the disappearance of some features with no regrets, and only deplore some others where they still survive. We have had enough of the Puritan censoriousness, its tendency to make every man his brother's keeper. When the Puritan habit of probing into the soul has degenerated into the "New England conscience"—where it is apt to remain as a mere feeling that everything enjoyable is sinful—then the ridicule heaped upon Puritan inhibitions becomes a welcome antidote. Certainly many amenities of social life have increased in New England, and in America, in direct proportion as Puritanism has receded. But while we congratulate ourselves upon these ameliorations, we cannot resist a slight fear that much of what has taken the place of Puritanism in our philosophies is just so much failure of nerve. The successors of Puritanism, both the evangelicals and the rationalists, as we survey them today, seem to have been comparatively sentimental, to have lacked a stomach for reality. The optimism and cheerfulness to which the revolters against Puritanism turned now threaten to become rather a snare and a delusion than a liberation. "Science" tells us of a world of stark determinism, in which heredity and environmental conditioning usurp the function of the Puritan God in predestining men to ineluctable fates. It is, indeed, true that the sense of things being ordered by blind forces presents a different series of problems than does the conception of determination by a divine being; no matter how unintelligible the world might seem to the Puritan, he never lost confidence that ultimately it was directed by an intelligence. Yet even with this momentous difference in our imagination of the controlling power, the human problem today has more in common with the Puritan understanding of it than any time for two centuries: how can man live by the lights of humanity in a universe that appears indifferent or even hostile to them? We are terribly aware once more, thanks to the revelation of psychologists and the events of recent political history, that men are not perfect or essentially good. The Puritan description of them, we have been reluctantly compelled to admit, is closer to what we have witnessed than the description given in Jeffersonian democracy or in transcendentalism. The Puritan accounted for these qualities by the theory of original sin; he took the story of the fall of man in the Garden of Eden for a scientific, historical explanation of these observable facts. The value of his literature today cannot lie for us in his explanation; if there is any, it must rest in the accuracy of his observations.

Puritanism as a Whole, Rounded Approach to Life

Samuel Eliot Morison

In the preceding selection Perry Miller emphasized the importance of Puritanism, the difficulties in seeing it clearly, and the essence of its theological ideas. The need for exploring each of those themes arises from one fact, simple, but almost beyond the ken of more recent Americans.

For Puritans religion was no matter of an hour's comfort (or discomfort) of a Sunday morning. It provided all the answers to this life, as well as the keys to the next one. The Puritan emphasized the omnipotence and omniscience of God. Everything man did should be done to the glory of such a God; and the Bible, God's own revelation to man, told him how to do it. To the Puritan the term "non-religious" would simply have been non-meaningful.

From his religion the Puritan of seventeenth-century Massachusetts derived general principles for all of life: personal conduct, social relationships, political order, economic activity, educational theory. From those general principles he established specific laws which set prices and weights for bread, established public education, provided for town-meeting government, and even defined those who might wear certain kinds of finery.

Some of those principles and laws are deeply rooted in America, such as public education. Others, long gone after generations of calcification or decay, today seem either irrelevant or ludicrous; emphasis upon these has brought about some of the misunderstandings Perry Miller discussed above. In the words of Carl Degler in Out of Our Past: *"Simply because the word 'Puritan' has become encrusted with a good many barnacles, it is worth while to scrape them off if we wish to gain an understanding of the Puritan heritage."*

The encrustation of barnacles was proceeding rapidly until about 1930, when Samuel Eliot Morison began scraping away. He did not take up the task readily. As he put it in Builders of the Bay Colony: *"[It] is always easier to condemn an alien way of life than to understand it. My attitude toward seventeenth-century puritanism has passed through scorn and boredom to a warm interest and respect. The ways of the puritans are not my ways, and their faith is not my faith; nevertheless, they appear to me a courageous, humane, brave, and significant people."*

The voluminous works of Professor Morison have covered the whole spectrum of American history—from a biography of Columbus (Admiral of the Ocean Sea), *which won a Pulitzer Prize, to a many-volumed* History of United States Naval Operations in World War II, *which won him an admiralship. His works on Puritan New England, however, have had an especially profound influence on our understanding of the American heritage. In the following selection he shows how the Puritans' religious ideas shaped their whole outlook on aspects of life as diverse as politics, economics, love, education, and the arts.* [Samuel Eliot Morison, The Intellectual Life of Colonial New England, *copyright 1956, New York University Press. Reprinted by permission.*]

New England differed from the other English colonies in that it was founded largely for the purpose of trying an experiment in Christian living. This statement is self-evident to anyone who has read extensively in the literature of the times, both puritan writings and writings of their enemies. It has, of course, been challenged by people so superior in intellect that they can give you the essence of an era without the labor of reading the sources. We have all been told that the dynamic motive of settling New England was economic, though expressed in a religious jargon. Doubtless the idea of bettering their condition in life was present in a very large number of early New Englanders; the spirit of adventure must also claim a share; but no one who has delved deeply into the origin and history of the New England colonies can, by any fair application of the rules of evidence, deny that the dynamic force in settling New England was English puritanism desiring to realize itself. The leaders, whom the people followed, proposed like Milton to make over a portion of the earth in the spirit of Christian philosophy: a new church and state, family and school, ethic and conduct. They might and did differ among themselves as to the realization of these high and holy aims; but a new City of God was their aim.

Until 1630, New England was anybody's country; the little band of Pilgrims who landed at Plymouth Rock ten years earlier were too few and isolated to have leavened any large lump of people hostile or indifferent to their point of view. But once the Massachusetts Bay Colony was founded, the fate of New England was sealed. In ten years' time, fifteen or twenty thousand people came over under puritan leaders; and three new colonies, Connecticut, Rhode Island, and New Haven, had been founded to contest with Massachusetts Bay in rivalry for divine favor and godly living.

Who were these puritans, and what did they propose to do? They were a party in the Church of England that arose in Elizabeth's reign with the purpose of carrying out the Protestant reformation to its logical conclusion, to base the English Church both in doctrine and discipline on the firm foundation of Sacred Scripture; or in the words of Cartwright, to restore the primitive, apostolic church "pure and unspotted" by human accretions or inventions. Religion should permeate every phase of living. Man belonged to God alone: his only purpose in life was to enhance God's glory and do God's will, and every variety of human activity, every sort of human conduct, presumably unpleasing to God, must be discouraged if not suppressed.

English puritanism, though essentially a religious movement, had its political and economic aspects. In their search for the original pattern of the Christian church in the apostolic age, the puritan leaders did not agree. They were divided into the Presbyterians, who thought that the primitive church was governed by a series of representative assemblies or synods; and the Congregationalists, who insisted that there never had been a unified church, only churches: each individual congregation should be a democracy of the "visible saints," of those admitted to full communion upon satisfactory evidence that they were God's elect. New England was founded by Congregationalists, the more democratic wing; and the latent democratic principle in their polity proved, humorously enough, an exceptionally heavy cross for the autocratically inclined parsons to carry. But whether Congregational or Presbyterian in its polity, puritanism appealed to the average Englishman's anticlericalism. It gave the layman a larger part in the local church than he had enjoyed since the Roman emperors became Christian.

Puritanism also had its economic side. I do not hold to the thesis of Max Weber and Troeltsch, that puritanism arose as a justification for usury; i.e., for taking interest on loans. In New England, certainly, the Church was no respecter of persons, and the spectacle of Robert Keayne, the profiteering merchant of Boston, having to stand up in meeting and take a tongue-lashing from the Reverend John Cotton for infringing the puritan code of business ethics, would have warmed the heart of any modern radical. The Weber thesis, as restated by R. H. Tawney, accords better with the facts as observed in New England. Puritanism was unascetic; it came to terms with this world. Under the medieval church you could only approach perfection (short of Heaven) by withdrawing from this world and entering the priesthood or a monastic order. But puritanism taught that a man could serve God quite as effectually in his chosen calling as by entering the sacred ministry; that a farmer or merchant who conducted his business according to Christian ethics was more agreeable in the sight of God than one who withdrew from the world and escaped his social responsibilities by a celibate or monastic life. This doctrine of the calling, that you could serve God by nobly fulfilling a function determined by the conditions of this world, and thus prove your right to an easy place in the next world, was probably the main reason why puritanism appealed to the rising middle class, the nascent capitalists of the sixteenth and seventeenth centuries. Puritanism was essentially a middle-class movement. It was far too exigent in its moral demands ever to be popular with earthy-minded peasants, or with the nobility and the very rich, who saw no point in having money if you could not spend it as you liked.

In its attitude toward love, puritanism had more in common with Judaism than with medieval Christianity or Jesuit piety. Puritanism did not hold with asceticism or celibacy. The clergy married young and often; their church offered no monastic retreat for men who were too much troubled by women. Milton's invocation "Hail, wedded love!" in *Paradise Lost* expresses the puritan ideal very neatly; and William Ames, the puritan casuist, implies in his *de Conscientia* that women have a right to expect something more from their husbands than mere duty. "Increase and multiply," the oldest of God's commands, was one that the puritans particularly enjoyed obeying—or some of us would not be here. Continence was a moral ideal on which due weight was laid; abstinence was not a superior virtue confounded with chastity but was in conflict with the purpose of creation. Married men who came out to New England were bluntly told to send for their wives or return to them. It was easier to obtain a divorce in New England in the seventeenth century than in old England; for the puritans, having laid such store on wedded love, wished every marriage to be a success.

On its intellectual side, which mainly concerns us, puritanism was an enemy to that genial glorification of the natural man with all his instincts and appetites that characterized the Renaissance and the great Elizabethans. Shakespeare's

> What a piece of work is man! how noble in reason! how infinite in faculties! in form and moving how express and admirable! in action how like an angel! in apprehension how like a god!

is the antithesis of puritanism, which taught that natural man was wholly vile, corrupt, and prone to evil; that he could do no good without God's assistance; that he thoroughly deserved to broil in hell for all eternity, and would do so if he did not grasp the hand of grace proffered him by a merciful God through Jesus Christ.

Predestination, one of the cardinal doctrines of Calvinism, was not stressed by the New England puritans; Michael Wigglesworth does indeed touch on it when he consigns the *reprobate* infants (not the *unbap-*

tized infants as is commonly said) to the "easiest room in hell;" but after reading some hundreds of puritan sermons, English and New English, I feel qualified to deny that the New England puritans were predestinarian Calvinists. John Cotton indeed was wont to "sweeten his mouth with a bit of Calvin" before retiring (rather a sour bedtime confection, one would think), but in general the New England puritans quoted their revered Ames and Perkins and the church fathers much more than they did Calvin; and John Harvard had more volumes in his library by St. Thomas Aquinas than by St. John of Geneva. The puritan sermons assume (when they do not directly teach) that by virtue of the Covenant of Grace, and through the efforts of the churches, salvation lay within reach of every person who made an effort; Christ helped those who helped themselves. Fatalism is completely wanting in the New England view of religion or of life. The karma of Buddhism implied a blind, meaningless universe; a poor joke that God played on humanity in one of his idle or sardonic humors. But the puritans, like the Jews, regarded this earth and humanity as a divine enterprise, the management of which was God's major interest; they were God's people and their God was a living God, always thought of as intensely concerned with the actions and characters of people and nations. Each individual was a necessary item in a significant and divinely ordered cosmos. God has a personal interest in me, and has appointed work for me to do. If I am incapable of receiving his grace, it is unfortunate; but if that is God's will, who am I to complain? Yet while there's life, there's hope; and at any time before death my risen Lord may whisper in my heart that I am of the blessed ones elected by his Father to salvation.

It is generally supposed that puritanism hampered intellectual and artistic activity; and there is some truth in this charge. Puritanism banned three forms in which the English excelled: the drama, religious music, and erotic poetry. Just why it banned the drama is still a matter of debate among the professors. Was it that the drama was supposed to lead to immorality, or because it amused people too much? Or simply because a number of the church fathers, like Chrysostom, had thundered against the pagan drama of their day? Whatever the reason, the puritan war on the theatre was hideously successful. There is no stranger phenomenon in literature than the swift rise of the English drama to a high zenith between 1580 and 1611, with Marlowe and Shakespeare; and its equally swift decline a few years after the death of Shakespeare. But it was not the puritans alone who killed the theatre. Their theological enemies, Bishop Laud and the high churchmen, were equally responsible. James I liked a good show as much as anyone and, as long as he reigned, the English theatre had court patronage; but Bishop Laud took charge of the conscience of Charles I, and discouraged the King from patronizing the drama as an object unworthy of a Christian monarch's support. Deprived both of middle-class and court patronage, the English theatre had no audience left but the sort that attends burlesque shows today; and the

English theatre became not much better than burlesque shows. It was the puritans, to be sure, who closed the theatres; but one imagines that by 1642 the managers welcomed the closure, as it saved them from losing more money.

Although puritanism had nothing against music as such, the puritans injured music by taking it out of the churches. Religious exercises were stripped down to the bare rudiments of the days when early Christians met in secret, and would not have dared to play the organ, even if an organ had been available. Consequently instrumental music, like the other beautiful incidents with which the medieval church had enriched religious expression, was done away with for want of scriptural sanction, and because it was supposed to make the worshiper dreamy. To secular music (as Dr. Percy Scholes has shown in his recent work) the puritans had no objection; Oliver Cromwell kept an orchestra at his court, and the first Italian opera to be played in England was produced under his Protectorate, and by puritans. A few musical instruments were brought to New England, and more were ordered in the latter part of the century. There was "no law agin' it," but music was not a form of activity that the English puritans cared much about, or were willing to make an effort to maintain in the New World.

I do not propose to hide the puritans behind the excuse that there was no room or opportunity for these things in a pioneer community. The German Moravians who came to Pennsylvania in the early eighteenth century maintained high musical standards because they believed that music was worth making some effort to keep up. And the puritans transplanted high educational standards for the same reason. Hard as colonial Americans worked, they, or some of them, had a certain leisure and surplus to devote to things of the spirit; and it depended entirely on their set of values what things of the spirit, if any, they chose to cultivate.

While the puritan wrote off certain cultural activities such as the drama, and failed to do much for others, such as music, he was stimulated by his faith to an intellectual activity that was conspicuously absent in other English colonies. The alternative to a puritanically controlled intellectual life, in new settlements, was intellectual vacuity; the emphasis was on acquiring an estate. The "best people" were engaged in growing tobacco or sugar cane, or trading with the natives; there was no incentive to lead a life of the spirit, no market for books, or audience for a play. At about the same time as the founding of New England, four other important English colonies—Virginia, Bermuda, Maryland, Barbados—and some lesser island plantations were established. Virginia by 1660 had a population almost equal to that of the whole of New England, and for wealth, Barbados was not far behind; neither was a puritan colony. But both colonies were singularly barren in literary production, although it may be that some hitherto hidden corpus of poetry, like that of Edward Taylor, or some prose manuscript of great merit, like Robert Beverley's *History of Virginia* (1705), may turn up. And where is the devotional poetry we might expect from Maryland, a Catholic colony? Why did not the scenic beauties of "still-vext Bermoothes," which at second hand lend such grace to Shakespeare's *Tempest*, inspire some native Bermudian to song, or prose?

Even in Mexico and Peru, where an enormously wealthy governing class existed almost a century before New England was founded, and whither learned ecclesiastics were constantly emigrating, nearly a century elapsed before a native intellectual life developed. The seventeenth century was the great age of Mexican and Peruvian literature; Don Pedro de Peralta Rocha Barnuevo y Benavídes, the savant of Lima, was almost contemporary with Cotton Mather—and Don Pedro was very much the same sort of indiscriminate and omniscient pedant as Don Cotton. But New England, within ten years of the founding of Massachusetts Bay, had a vigorous intellectual life of its own, expressed institutionally in a college, a school system, and a printing press; applied in a native sermon literature, poetry, and history. What is more, this life did not perish with the founders: it deepened and quickened as the century grew older, developing a scientific side. For in puritanism, New England had a great emotional stimulus to certain forms of intellectual life.

A humanist New England would doubtless have provided a pleasanter dwelling place, and a more sweet and wholesome stream to swell the American flood than a puritan New England. But there was no such alternative. Humanism is a tender plant, depending on a stable and leisured society, and on a nice adjustment of human relations, that cannot bear transplanting. As already noted, in a new country the natural alternative to intellectual puritanism is intellectual vacuity; and for a very good reason, that the mere physical labor of getting a living in a virgin country is so great as to exhaust and stultify the human spirit unless it have some great emotional drive. That, I take it, explains why in the nonpuritan colonies the humanist tradition of Elizabethan England shriveled; and why those colonies had to wait a century or more before they had any intellectual life worthy of the name. In South Carolina, we are told, the French planters of the end of the seventeenth century brought their Montaignes, and Montaigne is perhaps the best representative in old-world literature of a kindly, reflective, and disciplined humanism; yet the soil was unpropitious, and the tradition perished. Puritanism, on the contrary, throve under conditions of vigor, hardship, and isolation; hence the New England colonies were able almost immediately to create and support a distinct way of life that showed an unexpected vigor and virility long after English puritanism had been diluted or overwhelmed. The intellectual alternatives for New England, then, were not puritanism *or* humanism, but puritanism *or* overwhelming materialism, such as we find in typical newly settled regions whether English, French, Dutch, or Spanish.

Again we have a paradox. Puritanism in New England preserved far more of the humanist tradition than did nonpuritanism in the other

English colonies. The grammar schools and the colleges fostered a love of *literae humaniores:* Cicero, Virgil, Terence, and Ovid; Homer, Hesiod, and Theocritus. It was no small feat to keep alive the traditions of classical antiquity in a region that had never known the grandeur that was Rome, the glory that was Greece. The New England schools and colleges did just that; and handed down a priceless classical tradition, which has been mangled and trampled under foot by the professional educators and progressive pedagogues of the last hundred years. The classics flourished in New England under puritanism, and began to decay when puritanism withered.

It is difficult to make a modern man appreciate the seventeenth-century interest in theology. Man's relation to God was a matter of great pith and moment to people in that era, and they needed no more compulsion to hear sermons than people now need compulsion to read newspapers. For one Englishman who had seen a play and for ten who had read one, there were literally hundreds who read theological literature, and thousands who listened intently to sermons. Theology was the leading topic of conversation around the campfires in Cromwell's army. Richard Baxter records that on a visit to the army in 1643 he found everyone talking about forms of prayer, infant baptism, free grace, free will, antinomianism, Arminianism, and liberty of conscience. The Reverend Mr. Baxter was so alarmed by the heterogeneity of religious opinion in the army that he gave up his quiet parish for an army chaplaincy in order to tell Cromwell's Ironsides what was what, and put the soldiers on the right track to salvation.

No subject of popular interest today, even economics, can compare in pervasiveness with the theology of the seventeenth century. Perhaps we can faintly grasp what theology meant to the people in those days if we imagine all parsons, priests, and rabbis turned out of our modern places of worship, and their places taken by economists who every Sabbath brought you the latest news from Washington, D.C., and told you just how you could escape taxes, or get a share of the divine (federal) bounty.

The puritans were the extreme wing of the Protestant party in the English universities, and the losing wing. They came to New England because they had lost every bout since 1570, when their great champion Cartwright was expelled from his chair of divinity at Cambridge. Until the reign of James I they thought that at least their theology was safe, since the Thirty-nine Articles of the Church of England were predominantly Calvinist; but James I discerned the antimonarchial implications of puritanism, high-church theologians began to interpret the Thirty-nine Articles in a reactionary manner, and through court influence puritans were expelled or excluded from posts of honor and emolument in the universities as in the government. This state of things, coming to a head in the years 1629–1634 with persecution, started the great puritan migration to New England. The educated men who organized and led this exodus brought with them a deep and lively interest in religion. The religious point of view dominated the intellectual life of New England for over a century, almost until the contest with England began. . . .

John Demos

Growing Up in Plymouth Colony

Puritanism was "a whole way of life." To understand the religious faith and how it set the content of convictions and tone of attitudes is essential. But how did Puritans actually live that life? To understand them we need to try to put flesh on the skeleton and warm blood in the veins.

Historians have long been interested in doing so but have often been limited by the kinds of materials they were accustomed to use: diaries and letters, early newspapers and histories, and the official records of governors and assemblies. In the tender letters of Governor John Winthrop to his wife we see a loving, considerate husband, not just one of the "great, grim men" who founded New England. William Bradford's journal tells us much of the problems and the cares, the joys and the satisfactions of the Pilgrims. Mistress Anne Bradstreet came to Boston in the "Great Migration" of 1630, at the age of eighteen, with her husband of two years. Of him she would write, in part of a remarkable collection of verse:

> *If ever two were one, then surely we.*
> *If ever man were loved by wife, then thee;*
> *If ever wife was happy in a man,*
> *Compare with me, ye women, if you can.*
> *I prize thy love more than whole Mines of gold,*
> *Or all the riches that the East doth hold.*
> *My love is such that Rivers cannot quench,*
> *Nor aught but love from thee, give recompense.*

They were warm-blooded individuals, not just "Puritans." They lived daily lives out of the baggage that they brought with them—cultural as well as material baggage—plus what they gradually fashioned in their new home. The traditional materials of historians, however, leave substantial gaps in recreating those daily lives. For one thing, those who left the records probably were not representative of the whole society, since they had to be persons of some formal education, property, and leadership. Moreover, they rarely wrote about things they took for granted. For instance, they did not find it necessary to describe the contents of their little frame houses or the tensions that had somehow to be coped with when a whole family was living in one or two rooms, into which were also crammed not only furniture but tools, utensils, and weapons. Could any-

one ever be alone? How could aggression be handled (there was no room to send Susie to when she had a tantrum)? How did young people court? In sum, how did people live?

In the past few years a number of historians have taken to new paths to try to answer such questions. From a variety of records heretofore largely ignored they have gained new insights. Applying modern statistical methods to birth, marriage, and death records, they have formed conclusions about things such as family size (large, though spread out over more childbearing years than today), age at marriage (older than generally thought), death in childbed (one women in five). From tax records, wills, and property transfers they have discovered principles of parental authority (as through control over gifts of property to the rising generation), how wealth was distributed, and the like.

By applying imagination and the insights of modern psychology to painstaking research in such materials, John Demos has opened up new vistas on family life in "The Old Colony," Plymouth. From a description of the house and its furnishings he moves to descriptions of the structure of the family and the relationships between the individuals in it. The following selection is taken from the concluding section of the book, in which he portrays the life cycle of an individual from birth to death. [Pp. 131–140, 145–164 of A Little Commonwealth: Family Life in Plymouth Colony *by John Demos. Copyright 1970 by Oxford University Press, by whose permission it is reprinted with footnotes omitted.]*

Surely no event in the life-cycle displays a greater difference between the conditions prevalent then and now than the first one—the crisis of birth itself. The usual setting, in its most general outlines, is easily imagined. Delivery would take place at home. Tradition has it that the "inner room" in the familiar house plan was also known as the "borning room," in reference to its special use in times of childbirth. There the mother was brought to bed, and there presumably she remained until she and her infant child were strong enough to venture forth into the household at large. Her attendants were older women experienced in such matters and acting in the role of midwives.

In our own culture childbirth normally presents few difficulties of any magnitude; but in the seventeenth century it was quite another story. We have noted already the evidence that in one out of thirty deliveries the mother would lose her life, or, stated another way, that every fifth woman in the Old Colony died from causes associated with childbirth. The mortality rate for newborn infants is more difficult to determine, but one in ten would seem a reasonable guess. These figures may seem surprisingly low when set alongside more traditional notions of life in the seventeenth century; but they nonetheless describe a very real danger. And this danger must have profoundly affected the perceptions of everyone directly involved in any given delivery.

When a baby was safely past the hazards of his first few days of life, he was doubtless incorporated quickly into the ongoing routine of his household. One major public event in which he took center stage was his baptism. Usually this occurred within six months of birth, and on some occasions, particularly in wintertime, it must have been quite an ordeal. Otherwise, he enjoyed a continuing round of sleep and nourishment. The matter of how and where he slept is uncertain. Wooden and wicker cradles are among the most appealing artifacts of the seventeenth century to have come down to us today; but they are not found often in the inventory lists. Perhaps some of them were too crude and of too little value to bother with in adding up a man's estate. Perhaps, too, some other kind of makeshift bed was contrived for the newborn; or possibly he would for a short period sleep alongside his parents. It does seem that within a few months he was moved elsewhere—most likely to a trundle bed, which he might share with some of his older siblings. One rather gruesome notation in the Court Records serves to illustrate this type of arrangement. A small child of "about halfe a yeer old" had been "found dead in the morning . . . lying in bed with Waitstill Elmes and Sarah Hatch, the childs sister." An official board of inquest studied the matter and concluded that "either it was stiffled by lying on its face or accedentally over layed in the bed."

The infant's clothing was probably quite simple. Previous studies of this subject have turned up no evidence of swaddling or otherwise binding the child so as to restrict his movement. Some type of linen smock seems to have been standard dress for seventeenth-century babies; and doubtless, too, they were frequently under several layers of woolen blankets.

The baby's nourishment consisted, it appears, entirely of breast milk. The subject is not much discussed in any documents extant today, but there are occasional, incidental references to it. There is also the indirect evidence which derives from the study of birth intervals. We touched on this matter briefly in an earlier section, but it deserves a more extended statement here. In the average family, we noted, children were spaced roughly two years apart (or a bit longer near the end of the wife's childbearing span). This pattern is consistent with a practice of breast feeding a child for about twelve months, since lactation normally presents a biological impediment to a new conception. The exceptions can nearly always be explained in the same terms. When one finds an interval of only twelve or fifteen months between two particular deliveries, one also finds that the older baby died at or soon after birth. (Here there would be no period of breast feeding, to speak of, and hence nothing to delay the start of another pregnancy.)

We can try to pull together these various bits of evidence bearing on infancy as customarily experienced in the Old Colony. And in doing so, we are left with the impression—no stronger word could be justified—that for his first year or so a baby had a relatively comfortable and tranquil time. The ebb and flow of domestic life must have been constantly around him: large families in small houses created an inevitable sense of intimacy. Often he must have been set close to the fireside for warmth. His clothing was light and not especially restrictive, yet the covers laid over him heightened his sense of protection. And most important, he had regular access to his mother's breast—with all that this implies in the way of emotional reassurance, quite apart from the matter of sound physical nourishment. Illness was, of course, a real danger; the death rate for infants under one year seems to have been substantially higher than for any later age. But this fact may well have encouraged an attitude of particular concern and tenderness towards infants.

All such statements are highly conjectural, and so too is any impression we may try to form of the subsequent phases of a child's life. Still, with this strong word of warning, it seems worth proceeding somewhat further. Let us return once again to the writings of John Robinson, for a most arresting pronouncement on the requirements of the child by way of discipline: "And surely there is in all children . . . a stubborness, and stoutness of mind arising from natural pride, which must, in the first place, be broken and beaten down; that so the foundation of their education being laid in humility and tractableness, other virtues may, in their time, be built thereon . . . For the beating, and keeping down of this stubborness parents must provide carefully . . . that the children's wills and wilfulness be restrained and repressed, and that, in time; lest sooner than they imagine, the tender sprigs grow to that stiffness, that they will rather break than bow. Children should not know, if it could be kept from them, that they have a will in their own, but in their parents' keeping; neither should these words be heard from them, save by way of consent 'I will' or 'I will not'. "

Translated into the language of modern psychology this statement amounts to a blanket indictment of the child's strivings toward self-assertion, and particularly of any impulses of direct aggression. The terms "break" and "beat down" ("destroy" is also used further on) seem to admit of no qualification. Robinson urged, moreover, that this sort of discipline be started very early. It had to be accorded "the first place" in a whole sequence of socialization, because until the child's inherent "stubborness" was thoroughly restrained training in the more positive virtues would not really take hold.

Precisely what age Robinson had in mind here is not clear; but we may suspect that it was somewhere between one and two years. This, at any rate, is the period when *every* child develops the ability to assert his own will far more directly and effectively than was possible earlier. His perceptions of himself as apart from other people grow progressively sharper; his world is for the first time explicitly organized in terms of "I" and "you," "mine" and "yours." He makes rapid progress with muscular control and coordination, and thus gains new power to express all his impulses. Even today, with our much more permissive style of child rearing, the second year is a time for establishing limits, and often for the direct clash of wills between parent and child. In all likelihood these first raw strivings of the infant self seemed to sincere Puritans a clear manifestation of original sin—the "fruit of natural corruption and root of actual rebellion against God and man," as Robinson himself put it. Such being the case, the only appropriate response from parents was a repressive one.

And there was more still. The second year of life was for many children bounded at either end by experiences of profound loss. Somewhere near its beginning, we have surmised, the child was likely to be weaned; and near its end the arrival of a new baby might be expected. All this would serve to heighten the crisis imposed by the crushing of the child's asser-tive and aggressive drives.

The pattern is striking in itself; but it gains added significance when set alongside an important theme in the *adult* life of the colonists—namely, the whole atmosphere of contention, of chronic and sometimes bitter enmity, to which we have already alluded. This point merits the strongest possible emphasis, because it serves to call in question some extremely venerable and widespread notions about Puritanism. It has long been assumed that the people of this time and culture were pecu-liarly concerned—were effectively "neurotic," if you will—about all as-pects of sex. But there is now a growing body of evidence to the contrary (some of which will be examined shortly) ; and it might even be argued that the Puritans took sex more nearly in their stride than most later generations of Americans. Perhaps, though, there was a *different* bugbear in their lives—and psyches—namely, a tight cluster of anxieties about aggression. To read the records of Plymouth, and also those of the other New England settlements, is to sense a very special sort of preoccupation with any overt acts of this character. Here, it seems, was the one area of emotional and interpersonal life about which the Puritans were most concerned, confused, conflicted.

John Robinson's thoughts are pertinent once again, right at this point. His *Works* contain a number of short essays dealing successively with each of the most basic human instincts and emotions; and the one en-titled "Of Anger" stands out in a very special way. Robinson could find nothing at all to say in favor of anger—no circumstance which could ever truly justify its expression, no perspective from which its appearance was less than totally repellent. The imagery which he summoned to describe it is intensely vivid. Anger, he wrote, "God so brands, as he scarce doth any created affection"; for it "hath always evil in it." The "wrathful man" is like a "hideous monster," with "his eyes burning, his lips fumbling, his face pale, his teeth gnashing, his mouth foaming, and other parts of his body trembling, and shaking."

But anger, of course, is not easily avoided: efforts to suppress it can succeed only partially and at a very considerable cost. This leads us back to the opening stages in the life of a Puritan child. If his experience was, first, a year or so of general indulgence, and then a radical turn towards severe discipline—if, in particular, his earliest efforts at self-assertion were met with a crushing counterforce—it should not be surprising to find that aggression was a theme of special potency in the culture at large. Patterns of this kind are usually mediated, to a great extent, by fundamental practices and commitments in the area of child-rearing. The latter create what psychologists call a "fixation." Some essential part of the child's personality becomes charged with strong feelings of guilt, anxiety, fear—and fascination. And later experiences cannot completely erase these trends.

The developmental theory of Erik Erikson, more directly applied, helps to fill out this picture: it suggests quite powerfully certain additional lines of connection between infant experience and Puritan character structure. The time between one and two years forms the second stage in Erikson's larger developmental sequence, and he joins its characteristic behaviors under the general theme of "autonomy." "This stage," he writes, "becomes decisive for the ratio between love and hate, for that between freedom of self-expression and its suppression." Further: while the goal of this stage is autonomy, its negative side—its specific vulnerability—is the possibility of lasting "shame and doubt." It is absolutely vital that the child receive support in "his wish to 'stand on his own feet' lest he be overcome by that sense of having exposed himself prematurely and foolishly which we call shame, or that secondary mistrust, that 'double-take,' which we call doubt." If a child does not get this type of support—if, indeed, his efforts to assert himself are firmly "beaten down"—then a considerable preoccupation with shame can be expected in later life as well. At just this point the evidence on the Puritans makes a striking fit; for considerations of shame (and of "face-saving"—its other side) loom very large in a number of areas of their culture. Such considerations are manifest, for example, throughout the legion of Court cases that had to do with personal disputes and rivalries. Many of these cases involved suits for slander or defamation—where the issue of public exposure, the risk of shame, was absolutely central. Moreover, when a conviction was obtained, the defendant was normally required to withdraw his slanderous statements, and to apologize for them, *in public*. Note, too, that a common punishment, for many different types of offense, was a sentence to "sit in the stocks." Presumably the bite here was the threat of general ridicule.

A second point, more briefly: Erikson contends that each of man's early stages can be fundamentally related to a particular institutional principle. And for the stage we are now discussing he cites "the principle of *law and order,* which in daily life as well as in the high courts of law apportions to each his privileges and his limitations, his obligations and his rights." Surely few people have shown as much concern for "law and order" as the Puritans.

Once established in the manner outlined above, the same style of parental discipline was probably maintained with little significant change for quite a number of years. The average child made his adjustments to it and became fully absorbed into the larger pattern of domestic life. With several older siblings on hand (or younger ones to come) he attracted no special attention. What concessions may have been made to his youth, what his playthings were, and what his games—if any—there is no way of knowing. All such details are hidden from us. As noted previously, however, the fact that children were dressed like adults does seem to imply a whole attitude of mind. The young boy appeared as a miniature of his father, and the young girl as a miniature of her mother. There was no idea that each generation required separate spheres of work or recreation. Children learned the behavior appropriate to their sex and station by sharing in the activities of their parents. Habits of worship provide a further case in point: the whole family went to the same Church service, and the young no less than the old were expected to digest the learned words that flowed from the pulpit. . . .

It is striking that the seventeenth century (indeed all centuries before our own) had no real word for the period of life between puberty and full manhood. The term "adolescence" is little more than seventy-five years old, at least in the sense of having a wide currency. Earlier the word "youth" might be used for many purposes, but its boundaries in time and its inner meaning were seemingly quite vague. These semantic details point to a very substantial area of contrast in the developmental process as experienced then and now. Our own view of adolescence as a time of "storm and stress," of deep inner conflict, of uncertainty and rebelliousness, needs no discussion here. But it does provide a convenient starting point from which to reconstruct the rather different set of assumptions that must have obtained among the people of the Old Colony.

The evidence on this matter is in a sense largely negative: one looks for signs of a difficult adolescence in the sources from the period, and looks in vain. For instance, nothing in the Court records suggests any particular problems of law enforcement connected with this stage of life. There was certainly no institution comparable to our own juvenile courts—and apparently no "juvenile delinquency." Moreover, the Church Records are equally uninformative. . . .

We might examine, also, another matter of some interest to recent scholars of Puritanism: the process whereby young people found a "calling" to a specific occupation. Perhaps *here* one can establish a firm link with adolescence? But several considerations stand in the way of this hypothesis. First, it is quite unclear what part of the total population was ever seriously preoccupied with the selection of a suitable calling. There are, for Massachusetts, literary materials (sermons, essays, and so forth) which bear directly on this subject, and which do argue a kind of intellectual concern among men of high social and economic status. But no similar evidence exists that would take in average people as well. . . . After all, the range of occupational possibilities confronting a young man in this period was quite limited—in dramatic contrast to the situation prevailing today. The professional and "artisan" classes were relatively small, and the vast majority of the populace was engaged simply in farming. In the typical case, therefore, the choice of a calling was scarcely a choice at all; instead it was something assumed, something everywhere implicit in the child's surroundings and in the whole process of growth. Finally, there is the matter of the age at which service or apprenticeship might begin. Even in those instances where the learning of a particular trade *was* specified, the child involved was often as young as six or seven.

In some cultures a crisis at adolescence is mediated by vivid symbolic observances. "Initiation rites," or other ceremonies of a less formal type, mark a certain point in time as the boundary between childhood and maturity, and help to smooth the transition. (In our own society graduation exercises might be regarded as a weak sort of functional equivalent.) But nothing of this kind can be traced for Plymouth. In fact, the extant materials imply a nearly opposite case—an understanding of growth which explicitly recognized a series of partial steps and changes. The pattern appears most clearly in the arrangement of legal privileges and responsibilities. Thus an orphaned child was allowed to make his own choice of "guardians" when he reached the age of fourteen. The laws against lying and slander were written so as to apply to all persons "of the age of discretion which is accounted sixteene yeares." Sixteen was also the age at which boys became liable for military duty. . . .

All of this is meant to suggest the fluidity, the range of gradations that the culture presented to children on their way to becoming adults. It may now be useful to introduce certain more theoretical considerations as a way of drawing the discussion together in one broad interpretive framework. Adolescence has, in every life, a real and important biological foundation: sexual maturation is only the most dramatic of a whole set of profound internal changes. But the matter of context—what a given society *does* with and about these changes—is highly variable. What appears as a crisis in one setting may wear a much more placid aspect in another. In cultures where a prolonged period of adolescent crisis *is,* more or less, a normal part of development two kinds of social factors seem broadly responsible: (1) There are major "discontinuities" between the generations; the common experiences of children and adults are radically different from one another. (2) The culture itself is enormously varied and complex. Thus the young person approaching adulthood confronts a bewildering array of alternatives as to career, values, life style, and so forth. In this overall context adolescence brings a deeply rooted cluster of fears and resentments, and a host of ominous questions: "Can I effectively bridge the gap?" "Will I be able to make the right basic choices?" "Or, for that matter, do I *want* to?"

In Plymouth, by contrast, and indeed in all communities of the seventeenth century, the environmental setting was much simpler—and the process of growth inherently less difficult. Once the child had begun to assume an adult role and style, around the age of six or seven, the way ahead was fairly straightforward. Development toward full maturity could be accomplished in a gradual, piecemeal, and largely automatic fashion. There were few substantial choices to be made; the boy's own father, or the girl's own mother, provided relatively clear models for the formation of a meaningful "identity." Here was no "awkward age"—but rather the steady lengthening of a young person's shadow, and the whole instinctive process through which one generation yielded imperceptibly to its successor. . . .

The average age at marriage in this period was, in fact, much higher than has usually been imagined. For men the figure ranged gradually downward from about twenty-seven years at the time of settlement to a little under twenty-five by the end of the Old Colony period. For women the average was just over twenty at the start, and rose during the same span to around twenty-two. These changes over time, and in particular the opposite trends of the sexes, reflected an important shift in the Colony's overall sex ratio. Men greatly outnumbered women among the first waves of settlers, but as the years passed this imbalance corrected itself. Thus for men it became progressively easier to find a spouse, and for women progressively more difficult. . . .

Let us try to construct a picture of the whole process of making a marriage, starting as far back as the evidence will allow. What basic steps and procedures were involved? And what did it all mean, how was it experienced, from the standpoint of the individuals directly concerned and of the community at large?

The initial phases of courtship must, unfortunately, be passed over with barely a word said, for they are nearly invisible from this distance in time. Probably they lacked much formal ceremony (no dating, dances, and so forth). Probably they showed close connections to other aspects of everyday life, to common patterns of work and leisure. Probably too they developed under the watchful eye of parents and siblings, or indeed of a whole neighborhood. (Sustained privacy is hard to imagine, in *any* part of the Old Colony setting.) But all this is very much in the realm of speculation.

It is worth noting, however, that some Plymouth courtships fell considerably short of "Puritanical" standards—and here the Court Records do supply certain pieces of concrete evidence. There was, throughout the century, a steady succession of trials and convictions for sexual offenses involving single persons. "Fornication," in particular, was a familiar problem. There is no way to measure its incidence in quantitative terms, but it happened, and happened with some regularity. The punishment for fornication was pretty standard—a fine of ten pounds, or a public whipping—and applied equally to both parties. When such acts became known and liable to prosecution, it was usually because a pregnancy had resulted. Occasionally the girl involved would refuse to reveal her lover's identity, but this decision laid her open to a particularly trying little ordeal. For when delivery was actually in progress and the girl's powers of resistance were presumed to be at their lowest ebb, the midwives were likely to "charge it upon her . . . to tell whose the child was." The authorities wished to discover the father in these cases, in order to punish him and to make him financially responsible for his child's maintenance. (Otherwise the community as a whole might be obliged to assume this expense, especially if the mother had few resources of her own.) Often, though, a woman who became pregnant out of wedlock was more than ready to name her partner: feelings of jealousy, or resentment at being abandoned, found an easy outlet in open testimony before the Court. But the man himself might contest such allegations, and the Court might eventually decide to let him off. There are numerous paternity cases in the Records, and some of them seem very complicated indeed.

When all of these materials are brought together it becomes difficult to sustain the traditional picture of seventeenth-century New England as being extremely strait-laced and repressive in anything pertaining to sex. . . .

Regardless how common or uncommon such episodes may have been, they clearly belonged to a category of behavior which the community opposed. But let us return now to the standard, *approved* procedures leading up to marriage. First of all, and most important: when a courtship had developed to a certain point of intensity, the parents became directly involved. An early order of the General Court directed that "none be allowed to marry that are under the covert of parents but by their consent and approbacon." Later on, the Court came to feel that a stronger statement was necessary and amended the law to read as follows: "If any shall make any motion of marriage to any mans daughter or mayde servant not haveing first obtayned leave and consent of the parents or master so to doe [he] shalbe punished either by fine or corporall punishment or both."

We cannot discover in any detail how parents and masters would evaluate a particular "motion of marriage," but some of the Court's own assumptions were explicitly stated. In a kind of preamble to the above legislation it deplored the actions of "divers persons unfitt for marriage both in regard of their yeong yeares as also in regard of theire weake estate" in "practising the enveagleing" of various "daughters & . . . mayde servants" in the Colony. Marriage by the very young or the very poor seemed a dubious proposition to men in authority. . . .

Court cases . . . were relatively infrequent, and it may be that informal sanctions and pressures were more important in the long run. The wills, for example, suggest that a parent's control of property and his power to dictate the terms of an inheritance gave him considerable leverage in these situations. One man left his daughter a handsome gift of household furnishings "att her marriage and if shee please her mother in her match." . . .

. . . Assume that a particular couple had recognized a mutual attraction, had courted for a reasonable interval, had shown at least outward conformance to the moral code of the community (no embarrassing pregnancy), had secured the approval of both sets of parents and reached a firm decision to marry. What next? In fact, a series of steps remained to be taken, some more and some less formal, but all of them absolutely necessary. There was, for example, the "betrothal" or "contract"—a simple ceremony which bears comparison to our own custom of "engagement." Its meaning was stated as follows in the Colony Records: "by a lawfull contract the Court understands the mutuall consent of two parties with the consent of parents or guardians if there be any to be had and a solemne promise of marriage in due tyme to eich other before two competent witnesses."

To be contracted in this way was a very serious undertaking, and it placed a person in quite a special position—not yet married, but no longer "single" either. Any failure to fulfill such a contract would create the likelihood of legal action, and a damage suit of very considerable proportions. The laws against adultery were written so as to cover married and "betrothed" people in exactly equal measure. On the other hand, sexual intimacies *between* the contracted parties fell into a category all their own. They could not be officially condoned, but the usual penalty was relatively light—only a fourth of what obtained for the same offense by those who were unequivocally single. The records are sprinkled through with cases of couples who had apparently "slipped" in this way—by being intimate during the period between the contract and the actual marriage. As with cases of ordinary fornication, the only way such misconduct could come to light was through a pregnancy. A pair of newlyweds who produced a child in substantially less than nine months after marriage were liable to immediate prosecution. Of course, there was always the possibility of a premature birth, and in this connection the opinion of midwives and other women present at the delivery was usually decisive. . . .

Once a contract had been solemnized in the manner described above, another formal step became necessary: the "publishing" of the banns. "For the prevention of unlawful Marriages"—the law stated—"it is ordered, That no person shall be joyned in Marriage, before the intention of the parties proceeding therein hath been published three times at some publick meeting, in the Towns where the parties or either of them do ordinarily reside; or by setting up in writing, upon some Post of their Meeting house door in publick view, there to stand as it may be easily read, by the space of fourteen dayes."

Another matter, less official but obviously of the greatest importance, was a set of transactions designed to underwrite the economic welfare of the contracted couple. Marriage was in this culture the usual occasion for the transfer from parent to child of a certain substantial "portion" of property. For many people, this represented most or all of the inheritance they would ever receive. There was no simple formula governing the content of a portion: a variety of special circumstances might prove decisive in any individual case. More often than not, however, a young man would receive the bulk of his portion in the form of land and housing, and a woman would be given a variety of domestic furnishings, cattle, and/or money. Usually these arrangements were very detailed. . . .

As noted already, fourteen days was the minimum interval allowable between the betrothal ceremony and the wedding itself—between "contract" and "covenant," in the language of the time. But in actual fact most couples waited considerably longer: two or three months seems to have been quite customary. Whether or not some contracts were given up by mutual agreement in the meantime we have no way of knowing, for such things would not turn up in any official records. But tradition has it that this was an occasion for sober reflection, and, if need be, for reconsideration—before the final step was taken.

With respect to the actual wedding ceremony the views of the Puritans, and the Pilgrims among them, were most distinctive. They regarded marriage "as being a civil thing" (the words are Bradford's), as an institution of this world that would find no place or parallel in the next.

It was, then, not a sacrament, but rather another type of contract between two individual persons, and centrally bound up with questions of ownership, inheritance, residence, and the like. None of this should be thought to imply that the Puritans took marriage lightly; surely, in some broader sense, they viewed it as having many vital interconnections with a whole Godly pattern of life. But still the ceremony was to them a *civil* ceremony, not a religious rite—and was therefore the responsibility of magistrates, not ministers. . . .

It is thought that the bride's home was the usual place for a wedding ceremony, and that no set prescriptions defined its content. Apparently any fitting words would do, and perhaps the whole affair was characterized by a kind of rough and ready spontaneity. Some evidence exists from eighteenth-century Massachusetts to connect weddings with a certain type of feasting and celebration, but there is nothing comparable for seventeenth-century Plymouth. Like so many other things in the Old Colony, weddings were probably short, simple, and very much to the point.

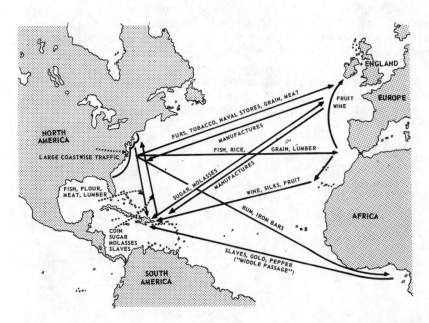

Principal colonial trade routes. Far from being restricted solely to trade with the mother country, the American colonists trafficked all around the world, for the most part quite legally under the Navigation Acts.

Capitalism and the Colonial Economy

3

America was born in an era of vast upheaval throughout the culture of Western Europe. "Renaissance," "Reformation," "Commercial Revolution," "Rise of the Nation State" are catch-words for different facets of a long period—at least two centuries—of radical change. The Puritans, both in their impulse to swarm overseas and in the society which they created in the New World, reflected various aspects of this change, only most noticeably religious ones. All who came, including Puritans, reflected economic ones. The rise of capitalism and the particular course that it took in the development of the English colonial economy is especially important as a pattern in American history.

Speaking of the century from 1550 to 1650, Lord John Maynard Keynes, the distinguished twentieth-century English economist, has written: "Never in the annals of the modern world has there existed so prolonged and so rich an opportunity for the businessman, the speculator, and the profiteer. In these golden years modern capitalism was born." So was America, and the two had a lot to do with each other. In the words of Carl Degler, "Capitalism came in the first ships."

The profit motive so essential to capitalism had not yet pervaded much of European society, as the first of the following selections shows, but it was strong in those who planted colonies: "merchant adventurers" organizing companies to profit from new trade; gentlemen adventurers searching vainly for gold in Virginia; and land-hungry yeomen farmers or agricultural laborers driven off their land by the enclosure movement in England. In varying ways, all were out to improve themselves economically. Puritans seeking a new "Zion in the wilderness" also sought a new economic start, as the fascinating journal of their first Governor, John Winthrop, clearly reflects. A half century later William Penn created another religious refuge in the wilderness, but he too had economic considerations in mind as well. The promotional literature which he had widely distributed in several languages stressed Pennsylvania's economic opportunities along with her religious and political freedoms.

For succeeding generations in the colonies the whole environment operated in such a way as to encourage hard work, frugality, individualism, competition, and involvement in a market economy—to stamp capitalism deeply on America and to give it distinctive attributes there. So much to be done, so few to do it; building a society in the wilderness, therefore, gave work a special importance. So much economic opportunity, so little restraint by society with its institutions and laws; individuals doing that work, therefore, were motivated primarily by the desire for profit, which of course becomes capital.

Profit and capital flowed primarily from the natural resources of the English settlements. Although no treasure-house of precious metals like Spanish America, the colonies had resources that would prove much more fruitful in the long run. The land was the base upon which the colonial economy rested, and the manner in which the colonists used it fundamentally affected their growth, their institutions, and their outlook. In the old country the agriculturist—whether a laborer on a manor or a small landowner in a village—still lived in a communal arrangement, working the outlying fields. In either case he was locked into a tight little community, dependent upon others and usually unable to move out of the community or up in it. His daily round was prescribed by the long tradition of a local society whose rules were as minutely defined as its limited arable land. The whole system had arisen in response to the fact that the amount of land was so limited and the pressures upon it were so great.

Coming to America, the individual found his situation completely altered. Seemingly limitless land made the traditional institutions of the Old World either impractical or irrelevant. There were no centuries-old communities to define his rights, limit his aspirations, and spell out his relations to others. He was on his own, with every incentive and opportunity to improve his own. He naturally came to think in terms of individualism, to act on the profit motive, and to engage in competition. Evolving as it was, his capitalism distinguished him from those he had left behind; it also distinguished him from some who would succeed him. Success in competition ordinarily did not need to be at the expense of someone else, as would often be the case in later and harsher stages of capitalism. With such untapped riches in forest, field, and sea, it was simpler to exploit nature than another individual in frontier America.

"America is the land of work," said Benjamin Franklin, and for long generations that work was fundamentally extractive. This was an economy in which the people were first of all engaged in taking from the soil and the sea: foods, furs, fish, forest products. In this way they could most readily tap the plenty that was America. Only gradually would they move out of this primary-stage, extractive economy into a secondary-stage one which emphasized industry and manufacturing. In the meantime they had to depend upon the Old World for the products of industry, for which they were avid. In making a new start in the New World, they had no desire to sacrifice the material standards they had known in the Old. If anything, they were more intent upon improving these standards than those who stayed behind.

Thus, the second fundamental economic activity of "the land of work" arose: overseas trade. Only in this way could members of a primary-stage economy procure the secondary-stage products they so needed and wanted, necessities and luxuries alike. Subsistence farming was not enough; they had to develop "cash crops," with which to pay for such imports. Having found and developed saleable crops, they then had to get them to European markets; and they found it both more sure and more profitable to get them there themselves. To this end those who had worked the land in old England turned to the sea in New England, building ships for trade all around the world. John Winthrop's vessel, *Building of the Bay*, was launched only a little over a year after he arrived in Massachusetts. Forty-five years later an English official estimated that 730 vessels had been built in Massachusetts alone. Thousands manned those ships, not only earning wages as seamen but also striking out on their own as capitalists, permitted to stow a few barrels of fish or salt meat or rum on board as their own "venture." The merchants who owned the ships were only the prime capitalists in the emerging colonial economy. The capitalism which came in the first ships burgeoned in the ships that the English colonies poured forth.

Robert L. Heilbroner # The Economic Revolution

The colonists were transplanted Englishmen who carried cultural baggage as well as material things. An understanding of the economy they developed logically starts with the economic luggage they brought with them: the ways in which they were accustomed to make a living, the attitudes they had toward the economic side of life, the economic and social institutions they knew.

In all these respects the seventeenth century was the crux of a long era of profound change from medieval to modern patterns. The old order was passing, but the outlines of what would replace it were only dimly visible. Those who migrated to America in that century were suspended between medieval and modern and often found that position precarious at best. The forty-two years John Winthrop lived in England before moving to the New World illustrate the times.

John Winthrop grew up an English country squire, taking over from his father the direction of Groton Manor in Suffolk in his early twenties. Lordship of such a manor still involved powers, rights, and duties that went back for centuries. The tenants on his lands owed him various dues and duties, had to grind their grain in his mills, brought various kinds of legal suits in the court over which he presided, worshipped in the church which he controlled. They, in turn, had rights that he could not violate; for instance, he could neither evict them nor change their rents, fixed by law. His life was full of the kinds of details necessary to run an extensive agricultural establishment—sowing, cultivating, reaping, threshing; cutting of wood, thatching of roofs, and erecting and maintaining all the numerous buildings on the estates; assigning rights to forests, pastures, fisheries, mills, and tolls. It had been thus for centuries in such a society: local, highly ordered and integrated, based upon the reciprocal rights and duties of clearly defined classes, agricultural, and to a considerable degree self-sufficient.

Times were changing, however, as Winthrop was well aware. Over several generations a textile industry had arisen in Suffolk. In the 1620s a deep depression hit the cottagers spinning and weaving in their homes for a capitalistic market. Out of work, they could not pay for country produce. Those raising that produce were hard pressed to pay their rents; and many tenants, for generations protected by law, faced eviction because of new Parliamentary acts that enclosed fields for sheep pastures.

Groton Manor was becoming inadequate. Winthrop considered making a new start in Ireland but turned instead to a part-time legal practice in London to bolster his income. During his visits to London, he encountered new evidence of decay in old institutions: rampant corruption in the courts; abuse of the weak by the powerful; public appointment of those who were often incompetent, cynical, lazy. But he also encountered there the enthusiasm, energy, and initiative of the rising class of merchant capitalists, building trade and planning colonies.

John Winthrop was a devout Puritan, and the familiar story of the government's suppression of his people impelled him to migrate. Also a man of warmth and compassion, he was deeply distressed by the social and moral conditions in England. And as a man of substance experiencing hardship in the changes sweeping England, he sought a new start.

Such was at least part of the cultural baggage brought to America in the seventeenth century, out of which several generations lived as they built anew. The full scope of the social and economic revolution in which they lived is the theme of the following selection. [From The Worldly Philosophers, *rev. ed., by Robert Heilbroner. Copyright © 1953 by Robert Heilbroner. Reprinted by permission of Simon & Schuster, Inc.]*

Since he came down from the trees, man has faced the problem of survival, not as an individual, but as a member of a social group. His continued existence is testimony to the fact that he has succeeded in solving the problem; but the continued existence of want and misery, even in the richest of nations, is evidence that his solution has been, at best, a partial one.

Yet man is not to be too severely censured for his failure to achieve a paradise on earth. It is hard to wring a livelihood from the surface of this planet. It staggers the imagination to think of the endless efforts which must have been expended in the first domestication of animals, in the discovery of planting seed, in the first working of surface ores. It is only because man is a socially cooperative creature that he has succeeded in perpetuating himself at all.

But the very fact that he has had to depend on his fellow man has made the problem of survival extraordinarily difficult. Man is not an ant, conveniently equipped with an inborn pattern of social instincts. On the contrary, he is pre-eminently the creature of his will-o'-the-wisp whims, his unpredictable impulses, his selfishness. He is torn between a need for gregariousness and a susceptibility to greediness.

In primitive society, the struggle between greed and gregariousness is taken care of by the environment; when the specter of starvation looks a community in the face every day—as with the Eskimos or the African hunting tribes—the pure need for self-preservation pushes society to the cooperative completion of its daily tasks. But in an advanced community, the pressure of the environment is lacking. In a community where half or more of the population never touches the tilled earth, enters the mines, keeps cattle, or builds with its hands, the perpetuation of the human animal becomes a remarkable social feat.

So remarkable, in fact, that society's existence hangs by a hair. A modern community is at the mercy of a thousand dangers: if its farmers should fail to plant enough crops, if its railroad men should take it into their heads to become bookkeepers or its bookkeepers should decide to become railroad men; if too few should offer their services as miners, puddlers of steel, candidates for engineering degrees—in a word, if any of a thousand intertwined tasks of society should fail to get done—industrial life would soon become hopelessly disorganized. Every day the community faces the possibility of breakdown—not from the forces of nature, but from sheer human unpredictability.

Over the centuries man has found only three ways of guarding against this calamity.

He has ensured his continuity by organizing his society around tradition, by handing down the varied and necessary tasks from generation to generation according to custom and usage: son follows father and a pattern is preserved. In ancient Egypt, says Adam Smith, "every man was bound by a principle of religion to follow the occupation of his father, and was supposed to commit the most horrible sacrilege if he changed it for another." Similarly, in India, until recently, certain occupations were traditionally assigned by caste; in fact, in much of the unindustrialized world, one is still born to one's métier.

Or society can solve the problem differently. It can use the whip of central authoritarian rule to see that its tasks get done. The pyramids of ancient Egypt did not get built because some enterprising contractor took it into his head to build them, nor do the Five Year Plans of the Soviet Union get carried out because they happen to accord with hand-me-down custom or individual self-interest. Both Russia and Egypt are authoritarian societies; politics aside, they have ensured their *economic survival* by the edict of one authority and by the penalties that supreme authority sees fit to issue.

For countless centuries man dealt with the problem of survival according to one or the other of these solutions. And as long as the problem of survival was handled by tradition or command, the economic problem never gave rise to that special field of study called economics. Although the societies of history have shown the most astonishing diversity, although they have exalted kings and commissars, used dried codfish for money and immovable stones, although they have distributed their goods in the simplest communistic patterns or in the most highly ritualistic fashion, so long as they ran by custom or command, they needed no economists to make them comprehensible. Technicians, statesmen, philosophers, historians, sociologists, yes—but, strange as it may seem, economists, no.

For economics waited upon the invention of a third solution to the problem of survival. It waited upon the development of an astonishing game in which society assured its own continuance by allowing each individual to do exactly as he saw fit provided he followed a central guiding rule. The game was called the "market system," and the rule was deceptively simple: each shall do what is to his best monetary advantage. In the market system the lure of gain, not the pull of tradition or the whip of authority, steers each man to his task. And yet, although each is free to go wherever his acquisitive nose directs him, the interplay of one man against another results in the necessary tasks of society getting done.

It was this paradoxical, subtle, and difficult solution to the problem of survival which called forth the economist. Unlike the simplicity of custom and command, it was not at all obvious that with each man out only for his immediate gain, society could in fact endure. It was by no means clear that all the jobs of society—the dirty ones as well as the plush ones—would be done if custom and command no longer ran the world. When society no longer obeyed one man's dictates, who was to say where it would end?

It was the economists who undertook to explain this puzzle. But until the idea of the market system itself had gained acceptance, there was no puzzle to explain. And until a very few centuries ago, men were not at all sure that the market system was not to be viewed with suspicion, distaste, and distrust. The world had gotten along for centuries in the comfortable rut of tradition and command; for it to abandon this security for the dubious and perplexing security of the market system, nothing short of a revolution was required.

It was the most important revolution, from the point of view of shaping modern society, that ever took place—fundamentally more disturbing by far than the French, American, or even the Russian Revolution. To appreciate its magnitude, to understand the wrenching which it gave society, we must immerse ourselves in that earlier and long-forgotten world from which our own society finally sprang. Only then will it be clear why the economists had so long to wait.

First stop: France. The year, 1305.

It is a fair we visit. The traveling merchants have arrived that morning with their armed guard, have set up their gaily striped tents, and are trading among themselves and with the local population. A variety of exotic goods are for sale: silks and taffetas, spices and perfumes, hides and furs. Some have been transported from the Levant, some from Scandinavia, some from only a few hundred miles away. Local lords and ladies frequent the stalls, eager to relieve the tedium of their boring, draughty, manorial lives; along with the strange goods from Araby they are eagerly acquiring new words from that incredibly distant land: divan, syrup, tariff, artichoke, spinach, jar.

But inside the tents we meet with a strange sight. Books of business, open on the table, are barely more than notebooks of transactions; a sample extract from one merchant reads: "Owed ten gulden by a man since Whitsuntide. I forgot his name." Calculations are made largely in Roman numerals and sums are often wrong; long division is reckoned as something of a mystery and the use of zero is not clearly understood. And for all the gaudiness of the display and the excitement of the people, the fair is a small thing. The total amount of goods which comes into France in a year over the Saint Gothard pass (on the first suspension bridge in history) would not fill a modern freight train; the total amount of merchandise carried in the great Venetian fleet would not fill one modern steel freighter.

Next stop: Germany. The year, 1550 odd.

Andreas Ryff, a merchant, bearded and fur-coated, is coming back to his home in Baden; he has visited thirty markets and is troubled with saddle-burn. As he travels he is stopped approximately once every six miles to pay a customs toll; between Basle and Cologne he pays thirty-one levies.

And that is not all. Each community he visits has its own money, its own rules and regulations, its own law and order. In the area around Baden alone there are 112 different measures of length, 92 different square measures, 65 different dry measures, 163 different measures for cereals and 123 for liquids, 63 special measures for liquor, and 80 different pound weights.

We move on: we are in Boston in the year 1644.

A trial is in progress; one Robert Keane, "an ancient professor of the gospel, a man of eminent parts, wealthy and having but one child, and having come over for conscience' sake and for the advancement of the gospel," is charged with a heinous crime: he has made over sixpence profit on the shilling, an outrageous gain. The court is debating whether to excommunicate him for his sin, but in view of his spotless past it finally relents and dismisses him with a fine of two hundred pounds. But poor Mr. Keane is so upset that before the elders of the Church he does "with tears acknowledge his covetous and corrupt heart." The minister of

Boston cannot resist this golden opportunity to profit from the living example of a wayward sinner and he uses the example of Keane's avarice to thunder forth in his Sunday sermon on some false principles of trade. Among them are these:

"I. That a man might sell as dear as he can, and buy as cheap as he can.

"II. If a man lose by casualty of sea, etc., in some of his commodities, he may raise the price of the rest.

"III. That he may sell as he bought, though he paid too dear. . . ."

All false, false, false, cries the minister; to seek riches for riches' sake is to fall into the sin of avarice.

We turn back to England and France.

In England a great trading organization, The Merchant Adventures Company, has drawn up its articles of incorporation; among them are these rules for the participating merchants: no indecent language, no quarrels among the brethren, no card playing, no keeping of hunting dogs. No one is to carry unsightly bundles in the streets. This is indeed an odd business firm; it sounds more nearly like a fraternal lodge.

In France there has been entirely too much initiative displayed of late by the weaving industry, and a *règlement* has been promulgated by Colbert in 1666 to get away from this dangerous and disruptive tendency. Henceforth the fabrics of Dijon and Selangey are to contain 1,408 threads including selvages, neither more nor less. At Auxerre, Avalon, and two other manufacturing towns, the threads are to number 1,376; at Chatillon, 1,216. Any cloth found to be objectionable is to be pilloried. If it is found three times to be objectionable, the merchant is to be pilloried instead.

There is something common to all these scattered fragments of bygone worlds. It is this: first, the idea of the propriety (not to say the necessity) of a system organized on the basis of *personal gain* has not yet taken root. Second, a separate, self-contained economic world has not yet lifted itself from its social context. The world of practical affairs is inextricably mixed up with the world of political, social, and religious life. Until the two worlds separate, there will be nothing that resembles the tempo and the feeling of modern life. And for the two to separate, a long and bitter struggle must take place.

It may strike us as odd that the idea of gain is a relatively modern one; we are schooled to believe that man is essentially an acquisitive creature and that left to himself he will behave as any self-respecting businessman would. The profit motive, we are constantly being told, is as old as man himself.

Nothing could be further from the truth. Not only is the notion of gain for gain's sake foreign to a large portion of the world's population today, but it has been conspicuous by its absence over most of recorded history. Sir William Petty, an astonishing seventeenth-century character (who was in his lifetime cabin boy, hawker, clothier, physician, professor of music and founder of a school named Political Arithmetick), claimed that when wages were good, labor was "scarce to be had at all, so licentious are they who labor only to eat, or rather to drink." And Sir William was not merely venting the bourgeois prejudices of his day. He was observing a fact which can still be remarked among the unindustrialized peoples of the world: a raw working force, unused to wagework, uncomfortable in factory life, unschooled to the idea of an ever-rising standard of living, will not work harder if wages rise; it will simply take more time off. The idea of gain, the idea that each man not only may but should constantly strive to better his material lot, is an idea which was quite foreign to the great lower and middle strata of Egyptian, Greek, Roman, and medieval cultures, only scattered throughout Renaissance and Reformation times, and largely absent in the majority of Eastern civilizations. It is as modern an invention as printing.

Not only is the idea of gain by no means as universal as we sometimes suppose, but the social sanction of gain is an even more modern and restricted development. In the Middle Ages the Church taught that "No Christian ought to be a merchant," and behind that dictum lay the thought that merchants were a disturbing yeast in the leaven of society. In Shakespeare's time the object of life for the ordinary citizen, for everybody, in fact, except the gentility, was not to advance his station in life, but to maintain it. Even to our Pilgrim forefathers, the idea that gain might be a tolerable—even a useful—goal in life would have appeared as nothing short of a doctrine of the devil.

Wealth, of course, there has always been, and covetousness is at least as old as the Biblical tales. But there is a vast deal of difference between the envy inspired by the wealth of a few mighty personages and a general struggle for wealth diffused throughout society. Merchant adventurers have existed as far back as the Phoenician sailors, and can be seen all through history, in the speculators of Rome, the trading Venetians, the Hanseatic League, and the great Portuguese and Spanish voyagers who sought a route to the Indies and to their personal fortunes. But the adventures of a few are a far different thing from an entire society moved by the venture spirit.

Take, for example, the fabulous family of the Fuggers, the great bankers of the sixteenth century. At their height, the Fuggers owned gold and silver mines, trade concessions, and even had the right to coin their own money; their credit was far greater than the wealth of the kings and emperors whose wars (and household expenses) they financed. But when old Anton Fugger died, his eldest nephew, Hans Jacob, refused to take over the banking empire on the ground that the business of the city and his own affairs gave him too much to do; Hans Jacob's brother, George, said he would rather live in peace; a third nephew, Christopher, was equally uninterested. None of the potential heirs apparent to a kingdom of wealth apparently thought it was worth the bother.

Apart from kings (those that were solvent) and a scattering of families like the Fuggers, the early capitalists were not the pillars of society, but the outcasts and the *déracinés*. Here and there an enterprising lad like St. Godric of Finchale would start as a beachcomber, gather enough wares from the wrecks of ships to become a merchant, save his money and eventually buy his own ship to trade as far afield as from Scotland to Flanders. But such men were few. As long as the paramount idea was that life on earth was only a trying preamble to Life Eternal, the business spirit was neither encouraged nor did it find spontaneous nourishment. Kings wanted treasure and for that they fought wars; the nobility wanted land and since no self-respecting nobleman would willingly sell his ancestral estates, that entailed conquest, too. But most people—serfs, village craftsmen, even the masters of the manufacturing guilds—wanted to be left alone to live as their fathers had and as their sons would in turn.

The absence of the idea of gain—in fact the positive disrepute with which the idea was held by the Church—constituted one enormous difference between the strange world of the tenth to sixteenth centuries and the world that began, a century or two before Adam Smith, to resemble our own. But there was an even more fundamental difference. The idea of "making a living" had not yet come into being. Economic life and social life were one and the same thing. Work was not yet a means to an end—the end being money and the things it buys. Work was an end in itself, encompassing, of course, money and commodities, but engaged in as a part of a tradition, as a natural way of life. In a word, the great social invention of "the market" had not yet been made.

Markets have existed as far back as history goes. The Tablets of Tell-el-Amarna tell of lively trade between the Pharaohs and the Levantine kings in 1400 B.C.: gold and war chariots were swapped for slaves and horses. But while the idea of exchange must be very nearly as old as man, as with the idea of gain, we must not make the mistake of assuming that all the world has the bargaining propensities of a twentieth-century American schoolboy. Purely by way of curious illustration, it is reported that among the New Zealand Maoris you cannot ask how much food a bonito-hook is worth, for such a trade is never made and the question would be regarded as ridiculous. By way of turnabout, however, in some African communities it is perfectly legitimate to inquire how many oxen a woman is worth—an exchange which we look upon as the Maoris do swapping food and fishhooks (although the delicate practice of dowries may somewhat narrow the gap between us and the savages).

But markets, whether they be exchanges between primitive tribes where objects are casually dropped on the ground or the exciting traveling fairs of the Middle Ages, are not the same as the market system. For the market system is not just a means of exchanging goods; it is a mechanism for sustaining and maintaining an entire society.

And that mechanism was far from clear to the minds of the médieval world. The concept of widespread gain was blasphemous enough, as we have seen. The broader notion that a general struggle for gain might actually bind together a community would have been held as little short of madness. . . .

We are back in France; the year, 1666.

The capitalists of the day face a disturbing challenge which the widening market mechanism has inevitably brought in its wake: change.

The question has come up whether a guild master of the weaving industry should be allowed to try an innovation in his product. The verdict: "If a cloth weaver intends to process a piece according to his own invention, he must not set it on the loom, but should obtain permission from the judges of the town to employ the number and length of threads that he desires, after the question has been considered by four of the oldest merchants and four of the oldest weavers of the guild." One can imagine how many suggestions for change were tolerated.

Shortly after the matter of cloth weaving has been disposed of, the button-makers guild raises a cry of outrage; the tailors are beginning to make buttons out of cloth, an unheard-of thing. The government, indignant that an innovation should threaten a settled industry, imposes a fine on the cloth button makers and even on those who wear cloth buttons. But the wardens of the button guild are not yet satisfied. They demand the right to search people's homes and wardrobes and even to arrest them on the streets if they are seen wearing these subversive goods.

And this dread of change and innovation is not just the comic resistance of a few frightened merchants. Capital is fighting in terror against change, and no holds are barred. In England a revolutionary patent for a stocking frame is not only denied in 1623, but the Privy Council orders the dangerous contraption abolished. In France the importation of printed calicoes is threatening to undermine the clothing industry. It is met with measures which cost the lives of sixteen thousand people! In Valence alone on one occasion 77 persons are sentenced to be hanged, 58 broken on the wheel, 631 sent to the galleys, and one lone and lucky individual set free for the crime of dealing in forbidden calico wares.

But capital is not the only agent of production which is frantically seeking to avoid the dangers of the market way of life. What is happening to labor is still more desperate.

Let us turn back to England.

It is the end of the sixteenth century, the great era of English expansion and adventure. Queen Elizabeth has made a triumphal tour of her kingdom. But she returns with a strange plaint. "Paupers are everywhere!" she cries. This is a strange observation, for only a hundred years before, the English countryside consisted in large part of peasant proprietors tilling their own lands, the yeomen, the pride of England, the largest body of independent, free, and prosperous citizens in the world. Now, "Paupers are everywhere!" What has happened in the interim?

What has happened has been an enormous movement of expropria-
tion. Wool has become a new, profitable commodity, and wool demands
grazing pastures for the wool producer. The pastures are made by enclosing the common land; the patchwork crazy quilt of small scattered holdings (unfenced and recognizable only by a tree here and a rock there
dividing one man's land from another) and the common lands on which
all might graze their cattle or gather peat are suddenly declared to be all
the property of the lord of the manor and no longer available to the
whole parish. Where before there was a kind of communality of ownership, now there is private property. Where there were yeomen, now there
are sheep. One John Hales in 1549 wrote: ". . . where XL persons had
their lyvings, now one man and his shepherd hath all. . . . Yes, those
shepe is the cause of all theise meschieves, for they have driven hus-
bandrie out of the countries, by the which was encreased before all kynde
of victuall, and now altogether shepe, shepe."

It is almost impossible to imagine the scope and impact of the process
of enclosure. In a single century, the greater part of the yeomanry was
converted into a demoralized mob of paupers who would haunt Britain
for two hundred years. Riots broke out: in a single uprising in the
middle of the sixteenth century 3,500 rioters were killed and their leader,
Robert Kett, hanged. In another instance a certain Duchess of Suther-
land dispossessed 15,000 tenants from 794,000 acres of land, replaced
them with 131,000 sheep, and by way of compensation rented her evicted
families an average of two acres of submarginal land apiece. And this
happened in 1820, at the tail end of the enclosure movement, nearly fifty
years after the American Revolution!

But it was not merely the wholesale land-grabbing which warrants
attention. The tragedy is what happened to the yeoman. Driven off the
land, he was at a total loss. He could not become a wage earner in the
modern sense, for there were no factories ready to receive him, and
nothing like large-scale industry available to absorb him. Deprived of his
independent farm, the yeoman became a robber, beggar, vagabond,
pauper, a miserable agricultural laborer, or a tenant. Terrified at the
flood of pauperism throughout the country, the English Parliament tried
to deal with the problem by localizing it. It tied paupers to their parishes
for a pittance of relief and dealt with wanderers by whipping, branding,
and mutilation. A social reformer of the time of Adam Smith seriously
proposed to deal with the migrant pauper by confining him to institutions for which he candidly suggested the name Houses of Terror. But
what was worst of all was that the very measures which the country took
to protect itself from the pauper—tying him to his local parish where he
could be kept alive on poor relief—prevented the only possible solution
to the problem. It was not that the English ruling classes were utterly
heartless and cruel. Rather, they failed to understand the concept of a
fluid, mobile labor force which would seek work wherever work was to be
found according to the dictates of the market. At every step, the com-

mercialization of labor, like the commercialization of capital, was feared, fought, and misconceived.

The market system with its essential components of land, labor, and capital was born in agony—an agony that began in the thirteenth century and did not run its course until well into the nineteenth. Never was a revolution less well understood, less welcomed, less planned. But the great market-making forces would not be denied. Insidiously they ripped apart the mold of custom, insolently they tore away the usages of tradition. For all the clamor of the button makers, cloth buttons won the day. For all the action of the Privy Council, the stocking frame became so valuable that in another seventy years the same Privy Council would forbid its exportation. For all the breakings on the wheel, the trade in calicoes increased apace. Over last-ditch opposition from the Old Guard, economic land was created out of ancestral estates, and over the wails of protest from employees and masters alike, economic labor was ground out of unemployed apprentices and dispossessed farm laborers.

The great chariot of society, which for so long had run by gravity down the gentle slope of tradition, now found itself powered by an internal combustion machine. Transactions, transactions, transactions and gain, gain, gain provided a new and startlingly powerful motive force.

Louis Hacker

The Economy of Colonial America: Agriculture

In Europe the "great chariot of society" had coasted for centuries down the slope of a static agricultural economy, based on strictly limited lands and therefore necessarily curbing the acquisitive instinct. To ship for America, emigrants dismounted from that chariot and then built a new one across the ocean. Although building upon familiar lines, they more readily accepted the new "internal combustion" engine of capitalism, which was more suited to the ups and downs of seemingly limitless land and a dynamic economy.

In America economic problems and pressures were reversed: not too many people to work the land, but too few even to clear it; not the task of enclosing it, but of opening it. To transplant into such an environment the closed manorial society typified by John Winthrop's Groton simply did not work, hard as some might try in Maryland, New Netherlands, and New France. John Winthrop II built a fort at the mouth of

*the Connecticut River, granted lands to those who would settle there,
and was elected Governor of the colony of Connecticut which grew from
this and similar efforts; but this was vastly different from inheriting the
lordship of a manor in Suffolk.*

*In the bounty of forest America, the man who worked with his hands
had from the start opportunities that he could never know in the Old
World. He was no less a "social animal" for his migration; he still sought
ties in church and community, but he was neither locked in by tradition
nor locked out by sheep in an enclosure movement. On his own as he
never could have been in England, he accepted the capitalistic revolution
as he could not have there. Certainly all who accepted it did not thereby
"make it," but the records tell repeatedly of penniless persons who got
passage only by binding themselves out as indentured servants, worked
themselves up to be freeholders after their servitude, and then moved
into speculation in lands. The capitalism which had "come in the first
ships" thrived in the new environment.*

*Above all, that environment was one of forested land. Those who came
into it were primarily land-starved Europeans, agriculturists in background, would-be landowners in prospect. If not free, land was within
the means of most people. Land and climate were remarkably similar to
what they had known in England, or Ireland or Germany, for that
matter. Thus encouraged by boundless good land, immigrant Europeans
set out to create a society in an unsettled, forest environment. The
manner in which they did it and some of the myths which have grown up
around them are the subjects of the following selection. [Reprinted by
permission of Columbia University Press from* The Triumph of American Capitalism *by Louis M. Hacker, copyright © 1940, 1947 by Columbia
University Press, New York and London.]*

The Farmer in the American Tradition.   At the outbreak of the American Revolution, the great majority of the American population—perhaps
nine tenths of it—was engaged on the land. It is a mistake to assume, as
has so frequently been done, that the colonial farmer in most areas
operated a self-sufficient farm. Indeed, virtually from the first years of
settlement, colonial agriculture to a great extent was conducted in a
commercial environment and the American farmer either produced
surpluses for sale in a market or sought to develop subsidiary activities
that would net him a cash return. Self-sufficiency is usually impossible
under capitalist organization. Ready cash is required for taxes, mortgage
payments, the improvement of wild and wet lands; and also for those
necessaries which no self-sufficing unit, no matter how completely
equipped, can hope to produce. Even the frontiersman needs cash and
therefore must produce goods or services that possess value in the market;
for the frontiersman must buy salt, rum, iron, and a gun and its ammuni-
tion. And even the most primitive farm plant occasionally will require
agricultural implements, "farm buildings, paint and glass for its houses,
chinaware and iron utensils for its table and kitchen, and sometimes feed

for its animals. This position the humblest backwoodsman and small farmer of the colonial period frequently occupied.

A brief digression is required here. The figure of the American farmer has been bathed in a soft glow of romance. It has been generally assumed that as a freeholder from the beginning and concerned quite completely with the feeding and sheltering of himself and his family, he has been impervious to the pullings and haulings of the market place. The freehold was an isle of safety and sanity distantly removed from the turbulences of the capitalist world. The American farmer and his numerous and sturdy sons, despite the alarms and excursions of the outside, occupied themselves exclusively with their simple and self-contained affairs: they plowed and harvested their broad acres for their own breadstuffs and the feed of their own herds and flocks; when they required timber for fencing and construction they repaired to the home wood lots; they dipped their own candles, tanned their own leather, made their own harness and even their work clothes. And the womenfolk delved and spun and wove; and churned and baked and sewed. Thus it continued until the free lands of the public domain were exhausted and the evil genius of capitalism came pounding on the door of the American freehold. It was not until the late 1880's—so runs the legend—that the American farmer fell on evil times: and then the conspiratorial railroads, the engrossing land companies, the monopolist industrialists, and the usurious bankers began to demand their pound of flesh. The farmer was caught in the capitalist relationship; and he had to become commercial in his attitudes in order to survive—or perish at the hands of his oppressors.

I believe that this analysis is a fiction in very considerable measure. I have said that the American farmer—not simply the grower of wheat or tobacco or cotton, but even the general farmer—virtually from the beginning could not escape the necessity for creating cash. This does not mean that he produced with an eye to making profits, as an ever-conscious process. Nor does it mean, on the other hand, that he became enmeshed in the tangled skein of the market relationship only when he sold a calf or a ham, a cheese or a bag of seed. He was an enterpriser in the real sense: for he labored to add to his capital plant (draining his wet meadows, buying the adjoining farm, erecting barns and silos), to fill his pastures with herds and flocks, and, later, to acquire machinery to increase the productivity of his own toil. To do so, he produced surpluses over and above his own home and farm needs; not, necessarily, single crops, but surpluses nevertheless that he sold in order to meet his debts and expanding requirements.

Some American farmers—but a smaller proportion than we have been led to assume—did obtain freeholds for the asking and taking or for the payment of nominal sums (under the later pre-emption system). Nevertheless, even these could never avoid debt. The moneylender was always to be found in the American Arcadia: and a momentary obligation perforce made even the humblest producer aware of the existence—and uncertainties—of the capitalist relationship. Even in early colonial times the American backcountry was preoccupied with the money question and the ever-existing presence of the mortgagee. And again, in the 1780's, the late 1830's, the late 1860's, the 1870's, the backcountry farming communities rang with the clamor of restless agrarians. At least these two staples, currency inflation and mortgage stay laws, have always been found at the center of farmer agitation. Under such banners, could one possibly see the farmer as a simple Arcadian?

The American farmer was aware of the pressures of his financial obligations: and that made his psychology essentially a capitalist one. He therefore produced agricultural surpluses or, what came to the same thing, he tried to find employment among a number of occupations that did not interfere with his agricultural activities. The colonial farmer, for example, was a trapper and a hunter; or he worked in logging camps; or he shipped with a fishing fleet. After the Revolution, when the English mercantilist ban was lifted off manufacturing, he and his family engaged in home industry: in the farmhouse, under the orders of the merchant-manufacturer, shoes were made, woolen cloth was woven, straw hats were plaited, brooms were fabricated. When railroads came, the farmer and his son worked on the maintenance and repair gangs.

Always, and this factor helps to explain why the agricultural community in America continued to be so large despite the fact that many farmers were never more than marginal producers, the American farmer was a land speculator. That is to say, because land values in the United States continued to mount, the farmer always could—and often did—sell his improved holding at a profit and buy a cheaper farm in the frontier areas, where the round of conquering the wilderness could be started once more. Thus, the American farmer was a dealer in land from the very dawn of settlement until 1920, a period of three centuries. The decline of land values after 1921 began to shake the basis of American agricultural well-being to its foundations. Now, for the first time, the marginal American farmer (and he was a vast company) began to approximate the position of the agriculturist of Europe and Asia: and there seemed small likelihood of real and lasting improvement in his economic status. Decline had set in.

Agriculture in the Northern Colonies.   The colonial farmer, then, was trying to develop a cash crop, something he could sell in the market. By the eighteenth century, even in rocky New England, staples had appeared: beef cattle and hogs, work animals, corn to be used for stall feeding. And a considerable portion of these products moved into the hands of Connecticut Valley merchants who shipped them directly to the West Indies. The middle colonies were the great granary where wheat was grown to be converted into flour for sale to the towns and also to the faraway West Indies. In the southern colonies, of course, commercial agriculture was the keystone of the whole economic structure. Virginia and Maryland planters grew tobacco for sale in England and Scotland. Interior farmers grew grains and raised cattle to be used in the West Indian trade. The tidewater planters of the Carolinas and Georgia cultivated and harvested rice, indigo, and some cotton. These crops were sent to seaports, sometimes processed, particularly in the case of cereals and meats, and then put on ships to be carried to distant places where they furnished those funds which were the basis of the commercial enterprise of the day.

Of the three regions, New England was able to develop agriculture least successfully. The reasons for this are not far to seek. The colonies, as we have seen, had been founded and were being maintained as commercial ventures within the framework of the Mercantile System. The export of goods and services to England, or the development of other commercial goods or services acceptable to England, was the key to the whole plan. England did not require foodstuffs; but it did need furs, the products of the forest, and iron. Occasionally it bought fish. Nor did it frown upon the establishment of a triangular trade with its own West Indian colonies as a result of which New Englanders might sell to the sugar planters of Barbados and Jamaica fish, lumber, and work animals, import sugar and molasses for manufacture into rum, and trade the heady liquor for Negro slaves on the African coast. The requirements of the Mercantile System, therefore, compelled New Englanders to create those goods and services with which they could pay most quickly their English balances—incurred by purchasing English manufactured goods. This meant they resorted to lumbering, fishing, trapping, shipbuilding, and the West Indian traffic.

The character of the New England soil and climate made the establishment of an intensive commercial agriculture difficult unless farmers were prepared to invest a heavy capital fund in it. Thus, it was not ignorance that prevented New England farmers from applying the lessons of scientific agriculture: they knew of the work of the English agriculturists Tull, Bakewell, Coke, and Townshend, who had demonstrated how easily animal stocks could be improved, forage crops raised, and the fertility of the soil renewed by rotation and natural and artificial manuring. It was simply that returns on investments could be obtained more readily from shipbuilding, the rum and slave trades, and from land speculation. When the West Indian market began to expand and opportunities for sizable profits began to present themselves in the production of beef cattle and work horses and oxen, many New England farmers turned to these activities. They could not, however, raise sheep because mercantilist bans on colonial manufactures prevented the growth of a market for wool. It is enough to note, in this connection, that New England today is a great agricultural region producing tobacco, dairy cattle, and a large variety of fruit and vegetable crops; and this indicates that no soil or climate is so stubborn or inhospitable that the enterprise of man cannot tame it.

New England farmers, therefore, grew for the market—largely the West Indian market—provisions and live animals. Complementary to their agriculture they also produced for the same market fish and lumbering goods. They caught and shot the wild creatures of the forest and sold the skins and peltries. And to a very considerable degree the smaller farmers of the interior valleys fed, clothed, and housed themselves. They produced their own flour, meatstuffs, lard, and maple sugar, sirup, and honey. But they had to buy, of course, salt, rum, and tea. They produced their own wool and woolcloth, flax and linen and leather. But they had to buy broadcloth when the goodman wanted a fine coat for prayer meetings. They produced their own dairy products. But they had to buy pedigreed cattle to improve and maintain the quality of their own herds. They made their own woodwork for the farm carts, plows, yokes, and tool handles. But they had to buy iron for the plowshares, chains, axes, billhooks, scythes, hoes, forks, and pitchforks; and they had to buy nails. In short, they never achieved complete self-sufficiency.

The middle colonies developed commercial agriculture on a more significant scale than did New England. Farms were greater in size; soil and climatic conditions were more favorable. The presence of a large landlord class and the existence of tenancy made necessary the development of cash crops. The local markets of New York, Philadelphia, and Baltimore gave spur to the production of foodstuffs. There existed a cheap and constantly renewable farm labor supply ·in the shape of the indentured servants; in Pennsylvania, notably, such servants were being employed as farmers and husbandmen. And proximity to the many excellent seaports encouraged the growth of agricultural products for the West Indian trade. As a result, during the eighteenth century, the middle colonies were producing large quantities of surplus grains which were being milled into flour and packed for export to New England, the West Indies, and occasionally to Great Britain and southern Europe. The middle colonies, like New England, also were raising beef and dairy cattle, hogs and work animals and entering them and their products into the foreign trade.

The importance of the West Indian sugar islands to the establishment and maintenance of a commercial agriculture in the mainland colonies has been commented on. In the year 1770 the following quantities of agricultural wares were shipped from the mainland to the sugar islands, chiefly from the middle colonies, though to a lesser extent New England also participated in the traffic: 559,000 bushels of Indian corn; 230,000 barrels of flour; 28,200 barrels of beef and pork; 55,400 pounds of cheese; 172,600 pounds of lard and tallow; 6000 horses; 3300 live oxen; and 18,500 hogs and sheep.

The Plantation System of the Southern Colonies. In the South, agriculture from the beginning operated on a commercial basis. The plantation form of economy prevailed, although many small independent farmers inhabited the interior. On the plantations, tobacco, rice, and indigo were being grown; in the backcountry the chief crops were tobacco, cereals, and cattle, which also by the eighteenth century were reaching markets. Tobacco was the great cash crop of colonial America just as cotton was to become that of the Middle Period. And because the economic fortunes of early America were so closely linked with the tobacco plant, it is important to examine closely all questions associated with its cultivation.

At the center of the tobacco cultivation stood the plantation—the customary farming organization. The plantation is not unique to colonial and slave America; it still exists as a significant form of agricultural economic organization and many of its characteristics remain today. What are these characteristics? Generally, they have been the following. The plantation is a large operating farm plant under unified direction and control. It produces staple crops for sale in a market and for this reason it is at the mercy of the price system and similar capitalist relations. It utilizes an unfree labor supply. The capital resources of the planter are not invested so much in the land and the improvement of its techniques (machine planting, cultivation and harvesting, irrigation, conservation of the soil) as they are in the maintenance of a permanent labor force. From this there flows either the institution of indenture or slavery or peonage or share cropping, and the distinguishing hallmark of all these systems is the fact that the capital fund is used to keep the agricultural laborer more or less permanently attached to the plantation.

Therefore, the plantation economy will spring up and flourish in those regions where land is relatively plentiful and cheap, where extensive rather than intensive operations can be carried on, and where a permanent labor supply can be collected and retained. There is nothing inherent in the crops themselves that accounts for the appearance of the system; tobacco and cotton can be grown successfully by small independent farmers. Nor have climate and the racial composition of the farm laborers anything to do with it. Plantation agriculture, essentially, is an exploitative activity that will appear in new countries where land is not restricted, where liquid funds are relatively scarce, and where surpluses can be invested in a growing laboring group.

It is not hard to see why the plantation system should take root almost immediately in colonial Virginia and Maryland. It furnished opportunities for the investment of capital in land, in the transportation of the labor supply, and in the carriage, financing, and processing of the crop. It worked in closely with the theory of mercantilism, for England looked to the southern colonies to produce many of those necessaries for which it was dependent upon the Near and Far East. Sugar and indigo were two products the New World grew for England; and when it also produced tobacco this gave additional cause for public encouragement. For as the taste for tobacco developed and began to spread into the European continent, England possessed a natural monopoly. Tobacco furnished an export in return for which large English stores of finished goods might be sent to the southern colonies. These colonies also provided an outlet to which might be sent, at the expense of the planter, those uprooted populations whose idleness at home was such a source of concern to seventeenth- and early eighteenth-century England. These persons became the indentured servants of the plantations.

Thus all the English mainland southern colonies and the British West Indies established the plantation system as a form of capitalist enterprise. And, as a rule, the planter-landlord came over to the mainland to manage personally his own undertaking. Because he was supplied with a capital fund, he quite frequently became interested at once also in furs, the raising of livestock, and the carrying on of a considerable trade with the Indians. Later, it was equally natural for the planter to utilize his capital fund and his surplus to enter into mercantile and financial activities and to buy up the wild lands of the western zones. In the eighteenth century, the southern planter was likely to be tobacco grower, retail storekeeper, merchant, Indian trader, banker, and land speculator all rolled into one. But the basis of his economic position was the fact that he grew a staple crop for sale in a market and had the greater part of his capital invested in his unfree labor supply, whether it happened to be indentured servants or Negro slaves.

Charles M. Andrews

The Economy of Colonial America: Commerce

"What would a man value ten thousand or an hundred thousand acres of excellent land, ready cultivated and well stocked, too, with cattle, in the middle of the inland parts of America, where he had no hope of commerce with other parts of the world, to draw money to him by the sale of the product? It would not be worth the enclosing, and we should see him give up again to the wild common of Nature whatever was more than would supply the conveniences of life . . . for him and his family." John Locke, the great English political philosopher whom the colonists would later adopt as their own apologist in the rebellion against England, thus described the colonial economic scene in his second treatise Of Civil Government. *Trade was absolutely essential if the colonists were not to succumb in the wilderness, let alone if they were to thrive and grow.*

As was the rule among colonies of all the imperial powers in that era, the mother country prescribed the principles of their trade according to the ideas of mercantilism. Those ideas, gradually evolving from the fourteenth century, came to dominate English convictions about political power and economic activity from 1550 to 1763. Several beliefs were at the root of mercantilism: (1) the nation-state is the institution through which a society achieves wealth, welfare, and safety; (2) such goals can be achieved only by good policies and strong actions by that state; (3) those policies and actions derive from concern for the well-being of the whole society, not just some parts of it. Thus, the state is not a mere policeman keeping order in society, but a father doing anything necessary to assure the health, well-being, and safety of the family. As junior members of the family, colonists were especially dependent upon and subject to the parent.

From those broad convictions derived more specific principles: (1) competition is inevitable between nation-states, each promoting the welfare of its own people; (2) that competition is focused most sharply on commerce, the economic activity by which national growth and power can most be developed; (3) the total possible volume of commerce in the world is fixed, not flexible, just like the total amount of land; (4) every nation therefore must scramble to control lands overseas and to take commerce away from other nations; (5) war is the likely outcome of this international race, so the nation-state must concentrate its policies above all on military strength.

For half a dozen generations American colonists lived in an empire based upon such principles. They were dependent upon it and happy in it, not thirteen independent units looking for a way out. They happily accepted military protection and willingly gave loyalty. Assured of protected markets, they submitted (with more grace than previously thought) to restraints upon their trade with competing empires. Except for those restraints, they traded where they willed all over the world. But above all, in a trading empire, they traded.

In the following selection one of the most perceptive recent colonial historians, Charles Andrews, suggests different perspectives for a better understanding of this long era in American history. He sees the colonies not as forerunners of the United States but as dependent units in a worldwide empire and, likewise, the colonists not simply as self-sufficient frontier farmers but also as cosmopolitan world-traders. Reading history backwards—knowing how the story comes out—we often read it awrong, to our own disadvantage. Professor Andrews suggests some correctives. [Charles M. Andrews, "Colonial Commerce," American Historical Review, *XX (October 1914). Reprinted by permission.]*

In the domain of history a shift in the angle of observation will often bring into view new and important vistas and will create such new impressions of old scenes as to alter our ideas of the whole landscape. In the case of colonial history this statement is peculiarly true. Viewing the colonies as isolated units of government and life, detached in the main from the larger world of England and the Continent, leads us to ignore those connections that constituted the colonial relationship in which commerce played a most important rôle. The older view is natural because it is easily taken and satisfies local interest and pride; the newer point of observation is more remote, less obvious, and more difficult of attainment. Yet it is the only view that enables us to preserve the integrity of our subject and so to comprehend the meaning of our history. The thirteen colonies were not isolated units; they were dependencies of the British crown and parts of a colonial empire extending from America to India. They were not a detached group of communities; on the contrary they were a group among other groups of settlements and plantations belonging colonially to five of the European nations, Portugal, Spain, Holland, France, and England, and their history was influenced at every point by the policies and rivalries of these maritime powers. The age in which they reached their maximum of strength as colonies was one in which the colonial relationship was highly developed and the feature of subordination to a higher authority an integral and dominant characteristic. Such an interpretation of colonial history is not a scholar's vagary, a matter of theory and hypothesis to be accepted or rejected as the writer on colonial history may please. It is historically sound, preserving the proper perspective, and preventing in no way the following out to the uttermost detail the local activities and interests of the colonists themselves.

The reason why this colonial relationship has been so persistently ignored in the past is not difficult to discover. The period of our history before 1783 has been construed as merely the ante-chamber to the great hall of our national development. In so doing writers have concerned themselves not with colonial history as such, but rather with the colonial antecedents of our national history. This form of treatment is common to all our histories, even the very best, because all limit their scope to the thirteen colonies, which formed but part of the colonial area and are segregated for no other reason than that they constituted the portion out of which the United States of America grew. In our text-books, not excepting the very latest, the colonial period is frankly presented as an era of beginnings, and stress is laid upon ideas and institutions that were destined to become dominant features of the nation's later career. With this mode of presenting the subject we may not quarrel, but it seems almost a pity, now that we are becoming such a nation of text-book writers, that the children of the country cannot be set upon the right way of understanding what the colonial period really means. Dealing with thirteen colonies, searching among them for the conditions under which were laid the foundations of the great republic, and treating those conditions as but preliminary to the history of the United States will never enable the writer to present an honest or complete picture of colonial life or to analyze successfully the causes that provoked revolution or rendered independence inevitable.

In one respect the colonial period is fundamentally different from that of our national history. For one hundred and seventy-five years, the people who inhabited the American seaboard were not members of an independent and sovereign state, free of all control except such as they exercised for themselves. Legally, they formed dependent and subordinate communities, subject to a will and authority higher than themselves and outside of themselves. This state of dependency was a reality and not a pretense. . . . Certainly the colonists deemed it so, when by their very restlessness under restraint they betrayed the reality of the ties that bound them. No act of the colonists, either individual or collective, can be traced to a conscious expectation of future citizenship in an independent republic. No aspect of colonial resistance to the royal authority was ever due to any definite belief that an independent nation was in the making. There is nothing to show that a colonist ever allowed visions of such a future to influence the course of his daily life. To the colonist there was no United States of America in anticipation, and there should be none to the student of colonial history to-day. The subject should be dealt with for its own sake and not for its manifestations of self-government and democracy; and the eye of the scholar should look no further ahead than to its legitimate end, the close of a period, the era of revolution, war, and independence.

To the colonists in America a commercial and trading life was the natural accompaniment of their geographical location. The colonists did not confine their interests, as do most of our historians, to the fringe of coast from Maine to Georgia. They ranged over a larger world, the world of the North Atlantic, a great ocean-lake, bounded on the east by the coast of two continents, Europe and Africa, and on the west by the coast of a third continent, America. On the northeast, the British Isles occupied a vantage-point of great commercial and strategic importance, while within the ocean area were scores of islands, massed chiefly along the southwestern border or off the coast of Africa, from the Bahamas to Curaçao and from the Azores to the Cape Verde Islands, which held positions of the highest importance for purposes of trade and naval warfare. It is an interesting fact that the British island colonies, and still more those of France, Holland, and Denmark, have been mere names to the students of our history; and it is equally significant that no atlas of American history displays in full upon any of its maps the entire field of colonial life. The American colonists were not landsmen only, they were seafarers also. They faced wide stretches of water, over which they looked, upon which hundreds of them spent their lives, and from which came in largest part their wealth and their profits. Though migration into the interior began early, nearly half the eighteenth century had spent its course before the American colonists turned their faces in serious earnest toward the region of the west. Though the lives of thousands were spent as frontiersmen and pioneers, as many crossed the sea as penetrated the land, for colonial interstate commerce was not by land but by water. In the shaping of colonial careers and colonial governments, sea-faring and trade were only second in importance to the physical conditions of the land upon which the colonist dwelt. No one can write of the history of Portsmouth, Salem, Boston, Newport, New Haven, New York, Philadelphia, or Charleston, or of the tidewater regions of Maryland, Virginia, and North Carolina, without realizing the conspicuous part that commerce played in the lives of those communities and regions. Even within the narrower confines of their own bays and rivers, the colonists of continental America, particularly of the northern part, spent much of their time upon the water. They travelled but rarely by land, unless compelled to do so; they engaged in coastwise trade that carried them from Newfoundland to South Carolina; they built, in all the colonies, but more particularly in New England, hundreds of small craft, which penetrated every harbor, bay, estuary, and navigable river along a coast remarkable for the natural advantages it offered for transit, transport, and traffic by water; and they devoted no small part of their time and energies as governors, councillors, and assemblymen to the furthering of a business which directly or indirectly concerned every individual, and which became more exigent and effective as the numbers of the colonists increased and their economic resources expanded.

With shipping we deal first of all with the actual extent of the ship-building industry. . . . All the leading towns of the North had dock-yards and built ships, and many of the smaller towns on sea-coast and navigable rivers laid the keels of lesser craft. So rapidly did the business increase that New England after 1700 was not only doing a large carrying trade on her own account, but was selling vessels in all parts of the Atlantic world—in the southern colonies and in the West Indies, Spain, Portugal, and England. The golden age of New England ship-building was during the first third of the eighteenth century, and so rapid was the growth of the business that in 1724 English shipwrights of the port of London would have had a law passed forbidding the New Englanders to build ships or compelling them to sell their ships after their arrival in England. But here the colonists scored, for, as the counsellor of the Board of Trade said, the English ship-builders had no remedy, since by the Acts of Navigation the shipping of the plantations was in all respects to be considered as English-built. Later, the business fell off, the centre of the ship-building activity moved north to north-eastern Massachusetts and New Hampshire, and the English builders ceased to be concerned. New York, too, had her ship-yards, as had northern New Jersey, that of Rip Van Dam occupying the water front on the North River in the rear of Trinity churchyard; and Philadelphia, the chief ship-building city in America, in the years between 1727 and 1766, built nearly half the entire number that were entered in the ship-registry of the port during those years. In the South ship-building was less of a negligible factor than has commonly been assumed. Maryland in 1700 had 161 ships, sloops, and shallops, built or building along the Chesapeake, and some of these were

large enough to engage in the English trade. Virginia built chiefly, but
. not entirely, for river and bay traffic, and North Carolina, though hampered by the want of good ports and harbors, made ship-building one
of the established industries of the colony. South Carolina carried on her
great trade with Europe chiefly in British bottoms and during the eighteenth century had scarcely a dozen ships at any one time that belonged
to the province. Among the island colonies only Bermuda and the Bahamas played any part as ship-builders; while the others, early denuded
of available timber, remained entirely dependent on outside carriers.

In size, the New England built vessels were mainly under 100 tons
with a large proportion of vessels of less than 20 tons, in which, however
ocean voyages were sometimes made. Occasionally vessels were built of
250 and 300 tons, and a few, monster ships for those days, reached 700
and 800 tons. Gabriel Thomas tells us that ships of 200 tons were built in
Philadelphia, but the largest ship entered in the register mentioned
above was of 150 tons, with others ranging all the way down to 4 tons.
The Maryland lists mention vessels of 300 and 400 tons built in that
colony, but the number could not have been large. In 1767 a vessel of 256
tons was offered for sale before launching in Virginia. . . .

Turning now to the complicated question of routes, which criss-crossed
so bewilderingly the waters of the Atlantic, we can, I think, group the
courses without difficulty, if we keep in mind the nature of supply and
demand and the requirements of the Navigation Acts.

The first determining factor was the requirement that all the enumerated commodities—tobacco, sugar, cotton, indigo, ginger, fustic and other
dye woods, and later cocoa, molasses, rice, naval stores, copper, beaver
and other skins—be carried directly to England, or from one British
plantation to another for the supply of local wants, whence, if re-exported, they were to go to England. This requirement gives us our first
set of trade routes. The chief staples of all the colonies from Maryland to
Barbadoes were carried to England in fleets of vessels provided by English merchants that during the days of convoys went out in the early
winter, about Christmas time, and returned to England in the spring.
The providing of naval protection in times of war was a matter of constant concern to the Admiralty, while the gathering of vessels and the
arranging of seasons was one of concern to the merchants. After 1713
when convoying became largely unnecessary except to the West Indies,
individual ships sailed at varying times, frequently returning from Maryland or Virginia as late as the end of August. We may call this route back
and forth across the ocean between England and her southern and West
Indian colonies the great thoroughfare of our colonial commerce. It was
regular, dignified, and substantial. Out of it grew two subsidiary routes,
one from New York and New England with re-exported commodities to
England, and one from South Carolina and Georgia to southern Europe
under the privilege allowed after 1730 and 1735 of exporting rice directly
to all points south of Cape Finisterre. Thus we have a series of direct

routes from nearly all of the American colonies converging upon England and one route from South Carolina and Georgia diverging to any point south of France, but generally confined to the Iberian Peninsula and the Straits. Along these routes were carried a definite series of commodities, raised, with the exception of naval stores and beaver, entirely in colonies south of Pennsylvania. To this commercial activity must be added the traffic in these same commodities among the colonists themselves, a service chiefly in the hands of the northerners, who carried tobacco, rice logwood, and sugar from the southern and West Indian colonies to their own ports and there either consumed them, re-exported them to England, or in the case of sugar and molasses worked them over into rum and shipped the latter where they pleased.

When we consider the export activities of the northern colonies, we find ourselves involved in a more varied and complicated series of voyages. First, all the colonies north of Maryland, except Pennsylvania, had a certain but not very extensive trade directly with England. They carried in greater or less quantities an assortment of furs, fish, rawhides, lumber, whale-fins and whale-oil, naval stores, wheat, wheat flour, hops, and a little iron, though the largest amount of exported iron came from Maryland and Virginia. They also re-exported tobacco, sugar, molasses, rum, cocoa, hard woods, and dye woods. All these they carried in their own ships as a rule, and because their own products were not sufficient to balance what they wished to buy, they frequently sold their ships also to English merchants. Salem, Newport, and New York were the chief centres of the English trade. Secondly, the northern colonies carried on a very large trade in non-enumerated commodities with the countries of Europe. To various ports, from the Baltic to the Mediterranean, they sent quantities of "merchantable" fish, lumber, flour, train oil, and rice and naval stores before they were enumerated, chiefly to Spain, Portugal, southern French ports, and Leghorn, the mart of the Mediterranean. A few ships appear to have crept through the Sound into the Baltic; others, very rarely, went up the Adriatic to Venice; and in the case of a few enterprising merchants, notably John Ross of Philadelphia, vessels were sent to India and the East, though in 1715 New England reported no trade there, only a few privateers having occasionally "strol'd that way and [taken] some rich prizes."

The bulk of the northern trade, however, was not with Europe but with the West Indies and with the other continental colonies. The ramifications of this branch of colonial commerce were almost endless, the routes followed were most diverse, and the commodities exported included almost every staple, native or foreign, that was current in the colonial world. Philadelphia and New York traded chiefly with the West Indies and concerned themselves less than did New England with the coastwise traffic; but the New Englanders, in their hundreds of vessels of small tonnage, went to Newfoundland and Annapolis Royal with provisions, salt, and rum, to New York, the Jerseys, Pennsylvania, Maryland,

Virginia, North Carolina, South Carolina, Bermuda, and the Caribbee Islands, peddling every known commodity that they could lay their hands on—meats, vegetables, fruits, flour, Indian meal, refuse fish, oil, candles, soap, butter, cider, beer, cranberries, horses, sheep, cows, and oxen, pipe-staves, deal boards, hoops, and shingles, earthenware and woodenware, and other similar commodities of their own; and tobacco, sugar, rum, and molasses, salt, naval stores, wines, and various manufactured goods which they imported from England. They went to Monte Cristi, Cape François, Surinam, and Curaçao, to the islands off the coast of Africa, commonly known as the Wine Islands, and there they trafficked and bargained as only the New Englander knew how to traffic and bargain. It was a peddling and huckstering business, involving an enormous amount of petty detail, frequent exchanges, and a constant lading and unlading as the captains and masters moved from port to port. Sometimes great rafts of lumber were floated down from Maine, New Hampshire, and the Delaware, and not infrequently New England ships went directly to Honduras for logwood and to Tortuga and Turks Island for salt.

Let us consider the return routes. With the southern and West Indian colonies the problem was a simple one. The merchant ships from England went as a rule directly to the colonies, generally laden with English and Continental manufactured goods that according to the act of 1663 could be obtained by the colonists only through England. They followed usually the same route coming and going, though occasionally a ship-captain would go from England to Guinea where he would take on a few negroes for the colonies. Maryland seems to have obtained nearly all her negroes in that way.

But with the northern colonies, where the vessel started in the first instance from the colony, the routes were rarely the same. A vessel might go to England, huckstering from port to port until the cargo was disposed of, and then return to America with manufactured goods. It might go to England with lumber, flour, furs, and naval stores, then back to Newfoundland for fish, then to Lisbon or the Straits, then to England with Continental articles, and thence back to the starting point. It might go directly to Spain, Portugal, or Italy, trying one port after another, Cadiz, Bilbao, Alicante, Carthagena, Marseilles, Toulon, Leghorn, and Genoa, thence to England, and thence to America. It might go directly to the Wine Islands and return by the same route with the wines of Madeira and Fayal and the Canaries, though it was a debatable question whether Canary wines were not to be classed with Continental commodities and so to be carried to America by way of England only. It might go to Spain or Portugal, thence to the Wine Islands, thence to Senegambia or Goree or the Guinea coast for beeswax, gums, and ivory, thence back to Lisbon and home by way of England; or, if it were a slave ship, it might go to the Guinea coast, thence to Barbadoes, and home, or as was probably common, to Barbadoes first, thence to Africa, thence back to the West Indies and home, with a mixed cargo of negroes, sugar, and cash. Frequently the captain sold his cargo and even his ship for cash, and if he did this in Europe, or in England to London or Bristol merchants, he would either return with the money or invest it in manufactured goods, which he would ship on some homeward-bound vessel, returning himself with his invoice. With the New Englander, and to a somewhat lesser degree with the New Yorker and Philadelphian, the variations were as great as were the opportunities for traffic. . . .

A useful addition to this paper would be a statement regarding our sources of information, in manuscript in England and America, and in print in a great number of accessible works. There is an immense amount of available material in the form of correspondence, accounts, registers, lists, reports, returns, log-books, port books, statements of claims, letter-books, and the like, which, though often difficult to use, are all workable and illuminating to the student who has organized his plan of treatment in a logical and not a haphazard fashion. The subject is a fascinating one, and the more one studies it, the more important and suggestive it becomes. I cannot believe that the future will show such a disregard of its significance as the past has done, for when its place is once recognized and its influence determined, colonial history will become not only fuller and richer, but also more picturesque, and the life of the colonists will appear as broader and more varied. And just as the local field will be enlarged and extended, so will the place of the colonies in the British and European systems of commercial empire be given its proper setting, and the balance between things imperial and things colonial will be restored. Only when such balance has been sought for and attained will the way be prepared for a history of the colonial period that is comprehensive in scope, scientific in conception, and thoroughly scholarly in its mode of treatment.

Recruiting poster for Washington's army. The manual of arms and the text under it convey the tone of the eighteenth century, appealing to patriotism, pride, and profit. (Historical Society of Pennsylvania)

4

The Road to Revolution, 1763-1776

For half-a-dozen generations transplanted Englishmen lived in colonies on the North American continent. For more than a century and a half they were proud to be English and on the whole were comfortable in the empire. The situation changed fairly suddenly. In the years from 1763 to 1775 mounting bitterness is apparent, especially in three crises brought on by laws of Parliament: Grenville's program of 1764 and 1765, the Townshend Acts of 1767, and the Coercive Acts of 1774. Hostilities began in 1775; eight years later it was all over.

As usual we have clear enough "facts," but they do not provide simple answers to the important questions. Why did this sharp reversal of long loyalty to England occur? Who decided to make it, and how, and when? What about those who did not go along? This kind of question is important in trying to understand a movement that not only brought the United States into being but also profoundly shook the late-eighteenth-century world and has provided inspiration and guides to numerous colonial revolutions in our own time.

Some other "facts" of 1775 and 1776 put such questions into sharper focus. Hostilities began in April 1775, although Washington still held that no reasonable person wanted independence. Yet two months later he accepted the commission of Commander-in-Chief from the Second Continental Congress. During that summer and fall the legislatures of five colonies went on record against independence. As late as January 1776, the officers of Washington's army, besieging the British bottled up in Boston, nightly toasted the king's health when sitting down to mess.

Americans, even when fighting, seem to have been remarkably reluctant about breaking with England. Many of them could not bring themselves to do it. John Adams estimated that the Loyalists formed one-third of the population. Recent studies put the figure at closer to one-fifth, still a large fraction. In addition, an even greater number declined to play an active role on either side—somewhere between a third and a half of the entire population. Out of a population of more than two million, Washington never had more than 22,000 under his command at any one time, and on occasion he could not muster one-tenth that number.

All of which emphasizes the importance of questions about the road to revolution: Who took it? For what reasons? With what qualms? And what about those who did not take it: Who were they? Why were they either opposed or disinterested? The Loyalists, modern studies conclude,

103

were a fairly typical cross-section of American society. They perhaps included more than their share of people of education, property, and demonstrated capacity for leadership. And they held fast to a virtue—loyalty—which the twentieth century prizes highly, just as it condemns treason.

The focus of this chapter is on the revolution, not the War for Independence. As John Adams said in a letter to Thomas Jefferson long after the war:

What do we mean by the revolution? The war? That was no part of the revolution; it was only an effect and consequence of it. The revolution was in the minds of the people, and this was effected from 1760 to 1775, in the course of fifteen years, before a drop of blood was shed at Lexington.

Charles M. Andrews   # Roadblocks to Understanding

One of the most perceptive of American historians penned the following selection half a century ago. His message, however, is as relevant today as it was then, perhaps more so as worldwide attention is drawn toward the occasion of the bicentennial of American independence.

The past is meaningful of and for itself. We also need it to understand ourselves. However, there are pitfalls along the path to understanding self by looking to the past. Some people fall into glorifying themselves by inflating their ancestors; others topple into glorifying themselves by demeaning their ancestors, "debunking" (taking the "bunk" out), often in reaction against the inflaters.

Such a truly important, dramatic movement as the path toward the American Revolution is particularly riddled with such pitfalls, simply because it was so significant, so dramatic, and so full of "ancestors." The pitfalls are there, but they can be avoided. In the following selection Charles M. Andrews marks out clearly where some of those pitfalls lie and how inviting they might appear, even to persons of good vision. He further suggests how they can be avoided by keeping a steady eye on the events leading to the Revolution. Above all, however, it is his plea for "honesty, charity, openmindedness and growing intelligence for the past" that merits constant reiteration and awareness. Only through such an approach can we hope to understand the past, and through it, ourselves. For an era as potent, as puzzling, and as provocative as that of the American Revolution, such an approach is especially required. [Reprinted by permission of Yale University Press from The Colonial Background of the American Revolution *by Charles M. Andrews. Copyright 1924 by Yale University Press.]*

Before passing to a consideration of the American Revolution and its causes, it is necessary to comment briefly upon the influences, subjective and otherwise, which in the past have governed much writing upon these topics and which continue to characterize the attitude of many people toward them at the present time. The scholar's approach to the study of these critical years of our history is beset with many a pitfall and impeded by many a tangled obstruction in the form of myths and legends which have grown up about the principal events and characters. He who is accustomed to the open door of opportunity in nearly all other fields of historical investigation is always disconcerted by the half-truths that often pass current for history in this country, and by the opposition aroused and the criticism excited, when in all honesty he tries to discover the truth for himself. Perhaps he is discouraged chiefly by the lack of interest which prevails very widely among the American people in that reinterpretation of our history which is very greatly needed and which is bound to take place as historical knowledge increases, historical standards improve, and a better understanding is reached of the problems involved. In some instances this lack of interest is due to sheer apathy, in others to a complacent satisfaction with our history as it is now written, and in still others to a deliberate attempt to block revision of judgments by those whose interest it is that the older version be preserved.

Among the chief obstructions that one meets in the attempt to popularize accurate interpretations of our pre-Revolutionary and Revolutionary periods is propaganda, harmless in a way because only temporary and certain to lose its force with the disappearance of the cause that provoked it, but constantly reappearing in new guises. As new issues arise, propagandists find in our revolutionary movement precedents and parallels available for their arguments, while others use it to keep alive the ancient grudge against Great Britain. . . . Almost every religious body, conservative or liberal party, or radical group misuses history in its appeal to precedent; and among the advocates of many popular movements are always some who cleverly manipulate the history of the past in their desire to give an air of ancientry to their ideas and to find a precedent furnishing a warrant for action.

The second obstacle is the fondness of our American people for the worship of their ancestors and the cult of their heroes and their tendency to envelop men and events connected with our colonial past in an atmosphere of piety, patriotism, and perfection. In our desire to exalt local personages and to raise those of older days above the level of ordinary mortals, we are apt to forget that the men and women of our Revolution were little better or little worse than those who walk the earth to-day, and that their conduct must be judged by the conditions of their own times and not by the circumstances and ideas of a century and a half later. . . . People . . . convinced of the sacrosanct character of any part of their past history are sure to resent the intrusion of the truth seeker and to make at least a show of indignation whenever the historian questions judgments already accepted as divine truths. Fortunately the

American public is more receptive to-day to the truth of its own history than it was twenty-five years ago and will come in time and in increasing numbers to realize that the facts of its history, whether colonial, revolutionary, or national, are more inspiring and enlightening than are the exaggerations and fictions built up and defended by propagandist and hero-worshiper.

The third obstacle lies in the partisanship always exhibited by those who interpret history along patriotic lines. In the past, writers have endeavored to justify rather than to explain our Revolution, and in so doing have demonstrated the truth of the historical axiom that those who are seeking mere justification will never deal accurately with any subject. Such writers study but part of the evidence and fail to see that there are two sides to the story; or else prefer the kind of history which glorifies their country's past, and deem it less than one hundred per cent Americanism to dim in any way their country's achievements. The number of those who write this American brand of history or who demand that it shall be written for their children, is greater than one would readily suppose, and some striking instances of such human obliquity could be given. It is impossible to be fair and impartial if we study, as is usually done, only the American or revolutionary side of the story; or if we persist in extolling without discrimination all who supported the revolution, often glorifying as "patriots" lawless men who were nothing more than agitators and demagogues. The American sense of fair play and a square deal is not going to deny forever a hearing to the conservative side and to condemn almost unheard the cause that was lost. The established order, then as to-day, has a right to defend itself; and, in harmony with the prevailing attitude among historians, which moves them to look for truth on both sides of a controversy, it is the duty of the scholar in history to present its claims. There is ample evidence to show that an increasing number of those to-day who are interested in our early history are willing to view the case impartially, for though the summing up of the judge always lacks the excitement and picturesqueness of the plea of the advocate, it is equally true that a picture of embodied perfection is distasteful to the majority of mankind.

The fourth and most serious obstacle is the disinclination of the average American reader to take any interest in phases of our history that will have to be thoroughly and comprehensively examined before the causes of our Revolution can be understood. As a rule the hero-worshiper is repelled by the laborious methods of scientific investigation, and it has been well said that "hero-worship is always impatient of effort expended on the study of institutional, economic, or psychological phenomena, and its votaries are unfitted by temperament to measure the value of any other influences than those that are expressed in terms of biography." To interpret and reconstruct the life of the past one must have a lively imagination and the ability to sift and check up critically all evidence, of whatsoever kind it may be. To the average reader scientific history makes no appeal. He distrusts the critical scholar much as the politician distrusts the expert, and objects to high thinking and mental overstrain. He seeks in history mental relaxation rather than mental effort and gathers his impressions as he runs. His judgments are frequently inaccurate because based on secondary and often trivial evidence. General readers rarely go to the root of a matter or seek to discover the deeper purposes or principles involved, and are usually without that inquisitive scepticism which drives the scholar on and on in the search for truth. There are times when one fears that the public at large does not care for any other version of our history than that which already exists and is content to continue reading the same old story, provided it be salted and savored to taste. . . . There are those who see in our history nothing but dramatic episodes and soul-stirring actions; who view our colonial era as a tangled mass of genealogical tree roots; who search in our past, as one would in a junk pile, for historical trivialities about which to dispute; or who have no higher concern than to demonstrate the superiority of a particular individual, event, or colony over all the others. Such people, whether writers or readers, are certain to generalize from insufficient data and to be satisfied with explanations and conclusions which in their ignorant disregard of vital forces at work in the fields of industry, commerce, and finance, seem to the scholar glaringly inaccurate. . . .

. . . Nothing is easier than to endow our ancestors with the minds and manners that we would like them to have had and that some people think they ought to have had. Excessive devotion to biography leads almost inevitably to panegyric or abuse, and to the ascription of motives that are frequently purely imaginary. I have read school children's essays in which George III is pictured as a monster of wickedness, responsible for the Revolution and the loss to Great Britain of her colonies; and I have wondered whether even a child might not be taught that single individuals, no matter how important, do not create or stop revolutions at well, however much they may influence them, and that to charge a single man or even a group of men with responsibility for a great uprising like the American Revolution is to accept a trivial explanation for what in reality is a mighty cosmic event.

The American Revolution was a world movement far more important than the Revolution of 1689 in England and only equaled as a factor in the world's progress by the French Revolution of 1789. Its causes must be sought for deep down in the hearts and minds of a people, and not of one people only, but of two, for there are always two sides to a revolution. In studying the revolt of the American colonies we are dealing with two different types or states of political and social development, which were the results of environment and historical evolution and exhibit differences not merely of external conditions but of frames of mind and ways of living as well. In our Revolution, as in all revolutions, two great and powerful influences came into conflict, the conservative and the radical, each with its habits, impulses, and principles, and there can be no real comprehension of causes and results unless each is studied with equal thoroughness and care. No matter with which side we happen to be in sympathy, we are in all justice bound to try, at least, to understand the other. I am never quite sure that those who are loudest in their approval of the Declaration of Independence would be among the revolutionists were they to face a similar issue to-day, or that those who talk most insistently about patriotism would have been among those whom they love to call the "patriots of '76." Are we consistent in glorifying revolution in the past and abhorring it in the present or in ennobling many of those who committed acts that to-day we would execrate as offenses against law and order? "Dead radicals," says a recent writer, "are eulogized because the issues for which they fought are as dead as the men who advocated them. Belief in them has become traditional and therefore eminently respectable." To this truism may be added the further one, that a revolutionist who is unsuccessful is likely to be condemned as a criminal, whereas he who succeeds is sure to be dubbed a patriot, a statesman, a hero, or a saint. It is always too much for human nature to glorify the losing side.

In the preceding essays we have already discussed the historical antecedents of our Revolution. We have seen how for a hundred years before that event the colonies and the mother country were moving in exactly opposite directions, each in obedience to historical tendencies that could not be resisted, the former toward intensive self-government, the latter toward empire. We have seen how the colonies, self-absorbed and preoccupied with their domestic problems, were gradually and almost insensibly outgrowing their status as dependencies and becoming self-conscious independent communities. Just because they were the most important and most advanced of all Great Britain's overseas territories, they were fully competent to have a separate life of their own, even though they remained bound politically and legally to the mother country. In these hundred years they had passed through a silent revolution with so little outward evidence of the fact as to make it sometimes difficult for us to follow it in all its bearings. Their inhabitants knew very little of the world outside themselves or of the interests of the mother country across the sea, and among them were very few who understood at all the difficulties of Great Britain's position after 1763 or realized any better than did the Britons themselves the new status of the British empire. So little did they comprehend it that in 1778, during a momentary lull in what has been called the second hundred years' war with France, they entered into an alliance with the French against their own mother country, and later won their independence through the aid of England's greatest colonial and commercial rival. It is not always easy to feel satisfied with the thought that we won our independence through the aid of a power that was using us for its own ends; and despite the fact that events of the Great War have thrown a glamour of romance about our relations with France in colonial times, it is difficult not to become a little cynical regarding that early alliance. Individuals like Lafayette undoubtedly had genuine sympathy for the American colonists and the issues they were facing; but the French government had no such interest in American independence. What France saw was an excellent opportunity to resume the war with Great Britain and, by aiding the colonies to obtain their freedom, to cripple her traditional enemy who had beaten her in the Seven Years' War.

On the other hand, Great Britain, with no clear-cut comprehension of where she was going, was moving toward territorial expansion and the establishment of an imperial policy and system. After 1763 the ministers were endeavoring, often with bewilderment and unconcealed dismay, to meet heavy demands for the defense and administration of large additions of territory, without adequate resources except through increased taxation. The British ruling classes, comprising less than one in fifty of the people of England—or if we take those actually in office, less than one in ten thousand—were concerned chiefly with external problems, and were paying very little attention to the domestic needs of the British people. Thus in England the period of our Revolution is one barren of internal reforms either in government or social life. Prominent Englishmen of the day were not burdening their minds with perplexing domestic questions any more than they could help, for in that selfish and scheming age the conscience of the English aristocracy and well-to-do gentry had not been awakened to the inequalities, the miseries, and the low standards of living that existed among the masses of England.

Here were divergent and antagonistic groups of interests, one of the colonies and the other of Great Britain, and the greatest problem facing men of the day was, as we see it now, that of reconciling the two. Would British statesmen prove themselves big enough to solve this problem of adjusting the colonial demand for greater freedom and independence to the equally imperative need of preserving the integrity of the empire, or would the differences go on widening and deepening until all hope of reconciliation was past and war only could decide the issue? We know the answer, for the War of the American Revolution shows the failure of the British policy, and proves also that the British ministries of the period after 1763, with their minds set on the value of the colonies from the point of view of profit, were wholly incapable of grasping that higher solution of the colonial problem, whereby these first self-governing dominions of Great Britain—the predecessors of Canada and Australia—might have been retained as part of the British empire. Evolution works as slowly in the world of ideas as in the physical world and it is not surprising that in the eighteenth century men did not conceive as a practical solution of the problem a union based on liberty and equality and cemented by ties of loyalty and affection. That was an idea which only another century of circumstance and experience, of a widening franchise and a growing democratic sympathy, could bring to birth in the British official mind. . . .

Even so, the failure to solve the colonial problem in the way it has been solved to-day does not explain why reconciliation was not effected and some working form of adjustment arrived at. There can be no doubt but that at first the vast majority of the colonists did not want revolution. They looked on the connection with Great Britain as necessary and beneficial and preferred to maintain it as long as it was possible to do so. They would have been content with moderate concessions, and had such been made, it seems more than likely that the conservative majority in America would have been able to prevent the radical minority from going to extremes and committing the country to war. Over and over again, in studying the period from 1764 to 1774, we are driven to believe that a little more yielding, a little more of the spirit of friendliness and compromise, and a little less of British ignorance, stubbornness, and prejudice, would have calmed the troubled waters and stilled the storm that was brewing. Why a dispute about trade, which could have been ended with satisfaction to both parties, and a dispute about taxation, which in large part was quieted by the repeal of the acts that provoked it, should have been followed by defiance, coercion, and war, is one of the questions that cannot be answered except by a close examination of conditions not observable on the surface. . . .

Lawrence H. Gipson   # The Starting Point: 1763

Explaining causes lies at the very heart of history. It is also the bane of historians because it does not have the kind of precision that is so much a part of the modern scientific world. One valid principle nevertheless was laid down at the very start of the writing of what might be called "scientific" history, as opposed to mere chronicles of events or the recording of stories. In his classic History of the Peloponnesian War, *the long and climactic struggle between Athens and Sparta that shook Greek culture to its very roots in the fifth century* B.C., *Thucydides undertook to explain the causes of the war, not just to record its battles. He held that it was necessary to distinguish between the long, profound, underlying causes and the immediate ones, between the powder keg and the match that touches it off.*

To look at the coming of the American Revolution in such a way is at least a start on the problem of its causes. Thinking of the underlying causes, one of its leaders suggested that the American Revolution began in 1620 (New Englanders did not make much of Jamestown, 1607!). He was obviously thinking of the effects of migration across a whole ocean, the awareness of physical separation from England, and the inherently diverse interests of such colonists from mother country.

If that was the powder keg, the match was the Great War for the Empire. The conclusion in 1763 of this last and greatest of what used to be called, not very meaningfully, the French and Indian Wars brought critical new problems for England, and attempts to solve them would touch off rebellion in America. The British victory over France was overwhelming. The man most responsible for it, William Pitt, could call upon the English people in justifiable pride, if something less than British understatement, to "throw away your history books—the Greeks and Romans were little people."

The very scope of that victory, ironically, had destructive consequences. The expense of running such a new empire, in addition to the debt incurred in winning, were unprecedentedly high. How to run such an empire—to integrate and rationalize it—was a problem of similar order. What to do about the conquered New France, for example, with its Catholic religion and French culture, a thorn in New England's side.

Those were only a few of a host of new problems that resulted from the war. The following selection comes from the masterful fifteen-volume work, The British Empire before the American, *completed in 1971 after a lifetime of work by Lawrence H. Gipson. His point of view is basically sympathetic toward Great Britain as she sought to solve those problems, but his identification of the problems and the difficulties in the way of solutions is clear and pertinent to understanding the revolution that was under way in the hearts and minds of Americans before the War of the Revolution began. [From* The British Empire before the American Revolution, *Vol. X, by Lawrence H. Gipson. Copyright © 1961 by Alfred A. Knopf, Inc. Reprinted by permission of the publisher.]*

The termination of the war that was waged for nine years from 1754 to 1763 between Great Britain and France and their respective allies brought many profound changes to the British Empire. Some of these were visible, such as the geopolitical revisions. Others, of equal if not greater importance, were psychological and could only be sensed. It is our purpose to examine some of the changes in both categories in order to make clear why the British Empire after 1763 was, in certain respects, quite different from the Empire that had existed for over a century before 1754, and why a crisis in the relations of Great Britain with her North American colonies soon developed after the Peace of Paris.

First of all, the ascertainable boundaries of the Old British Empire, or at least those that had been generally recognized, were vastly increased in 1763 over those that had existed in 1754, as has been developed in the preceding volume of this series. Indeed, new territories embraced within the limits so defined had tripled its size, at the most conservative calculation. Moreover, beyond these accepted boundaries were other areas that could now be called potential British territory—the undefined western sweep both of Canada and of the possessions of the Hudson's Bay Company. There was the expanding sphere of influence of the United East India Company with its setting up of factories in the Far East that must be included as lying within the British imperial orbit by 1763. The world, in fact, had never before witnessed so vast an accumulation of exploitable material resources by any single power as had resulted from processes of expansion which, beginning with the attempt to colonize Newfoundland by Sir Humphrey Gilbert in the days of Queen Elizabeth I, culminated in the Peace of Paris of 1763. It may properly be called in that year the *great* Empire—an empire with which the Spanish, Russian, and Dutch empires, extensive as they were, could in no respect be compared for dynamic quality, wide-spread enlightenment and freedom of expression, political maturity, industrial development, and accumulated wealth. Further, it possessed the ability to protect itself by means of a navy that dominated the high seas and was unchallengeable even by the combined navies of the other three great powers.

So huge an enlargement of the Empire inevitably brought with it particular problems. Among others was the difficulty involved in establishing within the new possessions a type of government that would reflect the spirit and genius of the British people and would thus be in harmony with the fundamental principles on which was based the control of the much more contracted Empire of the pre-war period. . . . consistent with peculiar local conditions, the form of government decided upon was patterned roughly after that of the royal colony. The expectation was that all those things characteristic of a royal colony—for example, the setting-up of a lawmaking body representative of its freemen—would be realized at the earliest possible moment.

Another problem, presented by the manner in which the war was terminated in North America, had to do with the establishment of policies that would guarantee fair treatment of those western Indians, whose guardianship the British government had felt impelled to assume because of the solemn commitments made in such treaties as that concluded at Easton, Pennsylvania, in 1758. These commitments involved not only the recognition of the superior rights of the natives to trans-Appalachian lands and the safeguarding of these rights in the face of pressure by white men eager to acquire these same lands, but also the obligation to seek to protect the red men from the unfair practices of white traders and from the exclusive domination of the Indian trade by merchants of any one colony.

A third, and also a post-war, problem was the provision of adequate means for guaranteeing the security of North America, the eastern part of which, from Hudson Bay to the southern tip of Florida, was now wholly embodied within the Empire. Should or could this great responsibility be turned over to the older continental colonies, whose welfare and safety were obviously most immediately and vitally at stake? Or should this be the exclusive responsibility of the mother country? Or should it be in the nature of a joint responsibility, as had been the case in waging the New World phase of the Great War for the Empire between 1754 and 1763? If so, after what manner? One thing at least seemed to be quite clear in light of the experience of the late war: those security forces that must be employed for routine garrison duty in critical areas—such as the new Province of Quebec, the scattered forts and posts in the Indian country, and certain strategic seaboard points . . . —must be regular troops held to their duty by military discipline.

Granted this to be the case, it brings us to a fourth problem. Who should be expected to assume the burden of the very considerable expense involved in these strictly North American security measures, as well as other charges upon the tax-payers, that altered conditions in the New World seemed to require? In this connection it should be pointed out that the war had brought unprecedented prosperity to countless people and even great fortunes to many in the older colonies. This was the result of shipments of vast sums of Spanish and Portuguese specie from England to America, not only as pay for the soldiers, teamsters, army pioneers, *bateau-men,* and others, but also for the purchase at good prices of enormous quantities of food supplies and many other things needed for carrying on the war. Indeed, almost everyone, at least along the Atlantic seaboard and the interior that was tributary to its ports and chief towns, seems to have shared directly or indirectly in this lavish distribution over a period of nine years, resulting in the elevation of standards of living. But could this potential source of revenue be tapped?

A fifth problem presented itself at the termination of the war. In addition to the costs of policing all critical points in North America as well as the high seas, there was the necessity of honouring the great British public debt left by the war. From the point of view of every person responsible for making the vital decisions that brought Great Britain into a state of hostilities with France, this war debt was incurred chiefly for the protection of the most vital interests of the British North American colonies. Parliament reimbursed most of these colonies for much of their war expenditures; so that by 1763 they were rapidly and easily getting rid of the public debts resulting from the hostilities and were enjoying the progressive lightening of the burden of wartime taxation. The questions therefore inevitably arose: To what extent could the people of Great Britain, who had assumed such heavy financial obligations during the war years and who were now called upon to carry the public debt, also be expected to continue, for an indefinite period, the payment of taxes at war rates to provide for the defence of North America? And to what extent was the British government, in order to afford some relief to British taxpayers and maintain public credit, now justified in tightening up the enforcement outside the British Isles of trade and navigation regulations which, although designed to apply to all parts of the Empire, had not been at all strictly observed? This, it is obvious, would increase public revenues to service the war debt and to provide funds for the defence of North America—clearly matters of utmost importance. But, could it be done without creating great bitterness and dangerous unrest within the older colonies?

The effects of the Great War for the Empire and the remarkable manner of its termination went beyond the creation of the above-enumerated colonial problems that faced British statesmen. The war had hastened the conversion of an immature British North America into a group of mature and increasingly self-confident commonwealths. Moreover, the colonials of Massachusetts Bay, New York, Virginia, and those of the other older so-called plantations had been led to think of themselves during the war years as "American" colonials to a degree that had never previously been the case, with an outlook for the first time that was continental rather than local and with a new sense of intercolonial solidarity. Among the factors that contributed to this changed outlook were the bald facts of the war itself with its direct menace to the lives and property of all British North America. This threat served to break down much of the older isolation and exclusiveness of the colonies in relation to one another. North Carolina troops had been recruited to fight side by side with Virginians in the valley of the Ohio; North Carolina troops also had been sent by their government into South Carolina to meet an expected attack upon Charleston. New Hampshire, Massachusetts Bay, Rhode Island, Connecticut, New York, and New Jersey regiments had fought together, had been brigaded together, and had mixed freely with one another in the campaigns in upper New York about Lake George and against Fort Ticonderoga. . . . In close association in this war they had fought, bled, suffered captivity—as at the surrender of Fort William Henry—and died together. . . .

It is of equal significance that, as the result of the protracted war, for the first time British North America possessed thousands of battle-hardened veterans, men whose courage had been put to the test and who had attained some knowledge of warfare as practised among civilized peoples. But it should also be pointed out that these veterans could not, by and large, be depended upon to settle down to the dull, unambitious routine of garrison duty—they were not professional soldiers. With the end of hostilities, most of them eagerly returned to the farm, plantation, shop, fishery, or other peaceful pursuits. Nevertheless, in any future crisis that seemed to imperil them, their families, and their near neighbours, most of them could be relied upon to respond with alacrity. The importance of this fact in shaping the attitude of Americans in the post-war years, it would appear, can hardly be overestimated.

This lessening of isolation among the people of the older colonies and the creation of a certain consciousness of being fellow Americans, rather than simply subjects of the British King, was powerfully aided by the expansion of settlements and gradual development during the preceding half-century or more of improved means of intercommunication which had come with the expansion of post-roads, postal service, and coastal trade along the Atlantic seaboard. This was accompanied by a steady growth in emphasis on intercolonial business and cultural relations, all of which was intensified by the movement of thousands of people from one colony to another over well-travelled highways, such as the Valley Road of Virginia, as well as by the ties, created by religious denominations and educational institutions, that tended to forget colonial boundary lines. Nor should one ignore the contribution of the American press through the printing and circulation of newspapers, pamphlets, and books in bringing into existence an American community feeling. Indeed, so potent was the influence exerted by the press that we must stress the unique place held by the British colonial newspaper in the New World. . . .

Between 1763 and 1775 there were some forty-three newspapers in existence for brief or fairly long periods in the older British North American colonies. . . . As was to be expected, most of these newspapers reflected local, popular feeling on public issues and helped mightily—as Professor Schlesinger, in his recent book, *Prelude to Independence,* has so strikingly brought out—to create after 1763 a common American public opinion.

Nor does this tell the full story of the significance of the free American press toward that end. During the period from the beginning of 1763 to the end of 1774 there appeared some 4,467 distinct publications. Besides the newspapers, counting each year's issue only by title, there were many books, including those printed by authority as well as privately, pamphlets, and broadsides, making an average of 372 each year, with 239 issuing from the press in 1763, and 694 in 1774.

Although little criticism of the government of Great Britain was voiced in the American publications before, or even in 1763, since they were concerned with other and in most cases more local things, by 1774 the situation was quite reversed, with a majority of writers devoting their chief efforts to denouncing that government. Indeed, one is amply justified in raising the question as to whether there would have been an American Revolution in the course of the eighteenth century had there been no press and particularly, no free press. . . .

If the vast power wielded by the colonial press differentiates the British America of 1763 onward to the end of the period of colonial dependence from the America of the earlier decades of the eighteenth century, factors other than those already given consideration also played a large part. For example, the inhabitants of the older colonies, instead of being hemmed in by the military forces and Indian allies of powerful and generally hostile nations, were now at last free of this brooding menace. Thus the feeling of insecurity that had hovered over them for generations, and had caused them in times of international emergency, when their very existence was threatened, to place a high value on their connections with the mother country, now tended to disappear.

It seemed in 1763 that as the result of the fortunes of war they themselves, as British colonials, would inevitably fall heir to most of a vast continent. For with France all but eliminated from North America, who now feared Spain, so disastrously defeated in the recent war and occupying, outside of Mexico, only the western part of old French Louisiana?

Instead, visions began to take shape of an ever-westward expansion through what was still the seemingly endless North American western wilderness. With those visions developed a sense of mission and high destiny that was not to be thwarted by any temporal, outside interference. Had they not already achieved greatly? Could they not point to hundreds of towns and villages and thousands of farms and plantations that they had planted along the Atlantic seaboard and well into the interior east of the Appalachians?

To understand why the feeling of self-sufficiency on the part of American colonials was so manifest in 1763 it is necessary to take into consideration the fact that they had now become a numerous, rather highly cultivated and wealthy people, who had developed to a point where they were beginning to feel themselves capable of managing their own affairs without much further guidance from the mother country.

Take, for example, the growth of population. In 1700 the number of inhabitants settled in the English North American colonies was probably not more than 250,000. While no figures are available that may be relied upon, it is fair to assume, upon the basis of various contemporary estimates, that there were probably little short of 2,000,000 people, both whites and blacks, living in these same colonies in 1763.

Carl Becker The Spirit of '76

How English actions and colonial reactions evolved in the dozen years after 1763 is the subject of noted historian Carl Becker's "reconstruction" of history below. It is an example of how important a creative imagination is in trying to reconstruct the past, for its characters are fictitious and their words only fancied. The events to which they refer are factual, but the ways in which they react are imaginary. The "diarist" in the selection, although his political views are merely implied, apparently came early and readily to the "Patriot" position. For his friend Jeremiah Wynkoop—the principal figure in his diary—the course to that position was vastly different. For him the spirit of '76 is a matter of doubt, even torment, and of wondering how in a short span of years he has come to such a position. He stands fast in that position, but his is hardly the conviction of a zealot. The third figure, Nicholas Van Schoickendinck, is yet different. Loyalty, even to a country not really his own, is a burden he cannot unload, especially in the hands of a "democratical mob" that seems to him as much concerned with who should rule at home as with home rule. For him, loyalty and security go hand in hand, and he prizes both. What will come with liberty he doesn't know, but it smacks of mobs and destruction of property.

All three are men of property, education, and station in society—men of integrity and honor. Yet they have in common no "spirit of '76" as they had had what might be called a "spirit of '63." The selection thus gives one reason to pause before attributing to the signers of the Declaration of Independence that unanimity and depth of conviction too often imputed to them. The records of the Second Continental Congress bear out Becker's characterization; there was a significant number of "Wynkoops" in that body. [From The Spirit of '76 and Other Essays *by Carl Becker, J. M. Clark, and William E. Dodd (Washington, D.C.: The Brookings Institution, 1927).]*

[Last October Mr. Lyon asked me to come down to the Brookings School and tell you about the spirit of '76. I suspected that he hadn't any clear notion of what was meant by the phrase "spirit of '76," and I was positive I hadn't. I was therefore about to decline the invitation when, rummaging among my papers, I came upon an old and imperfect manuscript which seemed providentially designed to throw some light on this obscure subject. The manuscript bore the date of 1792, but who may have written it I was unable to determine. There are obviously some pages missing, and the tale ends suddenly as if never quite finished. But such as it is I have transcribed it, and I give it to you for what it may be worth. The title of the manuscript is "Jeremiah Wynkoop."]

During the war of independence I not infrequently heard zealous patriots say that Mr. Wynkoop was not as warm in the cause as he should be. The charge has lately been revived by those who had no great liking for Mr. Wynkoop's Federalist principles. Mr. Wynkoop was of course not alone in being thus distinguished. It is now said of many men who were never suspected of being Tory that they look back with regret to the old days before the breach with Britain. It is said of them, to employ a phrase now becoming current, that they were never really inspired by the true spirit of '76. For my part, I suspect that, in recalling the desperate days of the war, we are likely to invest the so-called spirit of '76 with a glamor which it did not have at the time. Be that as it may, I knew Jeremiah Wynkoop as an honest man and a genuine patriot. I was his closest friend, intimate enough to know better than most the difficulties that confronted him and the sentiments that determined his conduct. And so I think it worth while, now that the man is dead, to set down a plain tale of his activities and opinions from the beginning of the quarrel in 1763 to the final breach in 1776. This I do, not only for old friendship's sake and as a justification of Mr. Wynkoop, but as a contribution to the history of those troubled times; for Jeremiah Wynkoop was fairly representative, both in his station in life and in his opinions, of that considerable class of substantial men who did as much as any other class, and I think more than any other class, to enable these states to maintain their liberties against British tyranny.

Born of rich middle class parents of genuine Dutch-American stock, Jeremiah was educated at Kings College, then recently established. In fact we both entered the College the year it was founded, and graduated with the first class in 1758. Jeremiah then spent two years in the office of William Moore reading law, a profession which he nevertheless abandoned for the trade. Taking over a profitable business upon the sudden death of his father, he rapidly achieved a notable success in commerce, chiefly in West Indian ventures, and was already known, in 1765, as a leading merchant in New York, where he had offices near the wharves, and a town house, inherited from his father, on the Bowling Green. But Jeremiah, being much given to study and the reading of books, preferred to live away from the distractions of the city, and had in fact for some years resided in the country, out Greenwich Village way, where he possessed a fine estate which had come to him as part of the generous dowry of his wife, the daughter of old Nicholas Van Schoickendinck, a great landowner in the province. . . .

[A break in the manuscript here.]

In the year 1765 Mr. Wynkoop shared the general feeling of apprehension which for two years had been steadily increasing on account of the measures, as unprecedented as they were unfortunate, of the king's minister, Mr. George Grenville The chief of these measures were undoubtedly the Sugar Act of the last, and the Stamp Act of the then present year. On the nature and effects of these measures Mr. Wynkoop had read and reflected as much as a busy man well could do. The Sugar Act, obviously designed to placate the British West Indian sugar planters, was certain, as indeed it was intended, to put obstacles in the way of the island trade with New York and New England. In that trade Mr. Wynkoop was personally interested. It is true, as indeed he was careful to tell me, that his profits for the last year were much as usual; but it had been abundantly demonstrated in pamphlets that the Sugar duties were bound to have a disastrous effect on American trade in general; would, for example, undermine the New England rum industry and thereby depress the fisheries and the African trade; would diminish the exports of lumber and grain from New York and Pennsylvania; would above all, since the new duties were to be paid in silver, drain the colonies of their small store of hard money and thereby make it difficult for American merchants to settle their balances due in London on account of imported British manufactures.

No one doubted, at least no one in America, that the Sugar Act was unwise in point of policy, calculated to defeat the very end intended. Yet there it was, an act of Parliament imposing duties for the regulation of trade, and we could not deny that Parliament had long exercised without opposition the right to regulate trade. . . . I knew Mr. Wynkoop well enough to know that he harbored the firm conviction that Americans were not only as free as Englishmen but even a little freer, a degree less subservient to aristocrats and kings, a degree more emancipated from custom and the dead hand of the past. I often heard him compare the Assembly of New York, chosen by the free suffrages of the people, with the British Parliament in which so often the members were chosen by irresponsible Peers and Boroughmongers—compare them of course to the disadvantage of the latter. To suppose that Parliament was now bent upon restricting the dearly bought and well deserved liberties of America was to Jeremiah, as indeed it was to all of us, an alien and distressing thought.

We could scarcely therefore avoid asking the question: "What constitutional right has the British Parliament to legislate in restraint of American liberties?" We never doubted that we were possessed of liberties, and no American, certainly no American as well informed as Mr. Wynkoop, needed to be told that there was a British Constitution which guaranteed the rights of Englishmen. Yet, as I recall those early years, I must confess that we were somewhat perplexed, had a little the air of groping about in the dark for the precise provisions of the British Constitution. The spirit of the British Constitution we knew was to be found in the Magna Charta and the Bill of Rights. Rights were indeed of its very essence; and to Mr. Wynkoop at least it was incredible that there was not to be found in it an adequate guarantee of the rights which Americans ought to enjoy. I remember his reading to me certain passages from the pamphlets of Stephen Hopkins and Governor Hutchinson— pamphlets which he thought expressed the American view very adequately. "What motive," Mr. Hopkins asked, "can remain to induce the Parliament to hedge the principles and lessen the rights of the most dutiful and loyal subjects—subjects justly entitled to ample freedom, who have long enjoyed and not abused, their liberties?" This passage I think expressed Mr. Wynkoop's state of mind very well in the year of the Sugar Act. His state of mind was one of amazement, the state of mind of a man who is still at the point of asking questions—Why? For what reason?

Meantime the Stamp Act, presenting the question more clearly, did much to clarify our ideas on the matter of American taxation; and certainly Mr. Wynkoop was never in doubt as to the unconstitutionality of that famous measure. In those days I was much at Mr. Wynkoop's house, and I remember one day in November, 1765, sitting with him and his father-in-law, old Nicholas Van Schoickendinck, discussing the state of the nation. Even old Nicholas had been startled out of his customary complacency by the furious excitement occasioned by the Stamp Act.

"The Act is unconstitutional, sir," Mr. Wynkoop had just declared, somewhat dogmatically it must be confessed, and for perhaps the third time. "There can be no question about that I think. It is not only contrary to precedent, but is destructive of British liberty, the fundamental principle of which is that Englishmen may not be taxed without their own consent. We certainly never gave our assent to the Stamp Act."

"I won't say no to that," old Nicholas remarked. "And if we had done no more than to protest the measure I should be well content."

"Little good protests would have done, sir. We protested before the bill was passed, and without effect. Mr. Grenville would not hear our protests, and now he finds the act virtually nullified. I can't say I regret it."

"Nullified!" Old Nicholas exclaimed with some asperity. "A soft word for a nasty business. Mr. Grenville finds his law 'nullified,' you say. But in getting the law nullified we get half the windows of the Broad Way smashed too, and Governor Colden gets his chariot burned. For my part I don't know what Mr. Colden's chariot had to do with the devilish stamps —it wasn't designed to carry them."

"Very true, sir, I admit. And regrettable enough, all this parading and disturbance. But if Ministers will play with oppression the people will play with violence. Similar incidents occurred in England itself in the last century. Let Mr. Grenville beware of playing the role of Strafford. God knows I am no friend of rioting. I have windows too. But a little rioting may be necessary on occasion to warn ministers that legislative lawlessness is likely to be met by popular violence."

Mr. Wynkoop had perhaps a little the air of talking to convince himself rather than old Nicholas. Old Nicholas at least was not convinced.

"Tush!" he exclaimed irritably. "That's a new word, 'popular.' You young fellows have picked up a lot of precious democratical phrases, I must say. Who are 'the people' you talk so loosely about? Another word for 'populace' or I miss my guess. Don't delude yourself by supposing that it was hatred of the Stamps that made them break Mr. Livingston's windows and burn Mr. Colden's chariot. They hate Mr. Livingston and Mr. Colden because they are men of substance and standing. It is not windows they aim at but class privileges; the privileges of my class and yours, the class that always has, and I trust always will, govern this province. The bald fact is that a mob of mechanics and ne'er-do-wells, led by obscure fellows like John Lamb and Isaac Sears who have hitherto doffed their caps and known their places, are now aiming to control the city through their self constituted committees. Sons of Liberty, they call themselves; sons of anarchy, in fact. I wish as much as you to preserve our liberties. But I warn you that liberty is a sword that cuts two ways, and if you can't defend your rights against ministerial oppression without stirring the 'people,' you will soon be confronted with the necessity of defending your privileges against the encroachments of the mob on the Bowling Green."

Old Nicholas stopped to light his pipe, and after a few puffs added:

"You don't associate with *Mr.* John Lamb, do you? You ain't one of the Liberty Boys who erect poles and break windows, I hope."

Mr. Wynkoop laughed off the sarcasm.

"Certainly not, sir. I don't know the fellow Lamb, never saw him in fact, although I am told, and believe, that he is an honest, worthy man. The danger you mention has of course occurred to me, but I think you probably exaggerate it. Let Britain repeal the Stamp Act, as she must do, and the populace will be quiet enough."

We sat until a late hour. I took but little part in the discussion, enjoying nothing better than to listen to the good natured wrangling of these two friends. During the course of the evening each repeated, many times over, his former argument, all without rancor, but all equally without effect. Except in opinion, they were not divided; and at last, pledging one another courteously in a glass of stiff toddy, we separated for the night.

During the following months Mr. Wynkoop continued firm in the defence of American rights. He agreed, as all the substantial merchants did, not to use the stamps, which was indeed not possible since none were to be had. Yet he would do no business without them. Let the courts close, he said. Let his ships stand idle in the harbor, a year, two years, let them rot there rather than submit to an unconstitutional measure. So I often heard him declare roundly, sitting at dinner sipping his madeira. . . .

[Again something missing from the manuscript.]

. . . secret misgivings, during the long cold winter, by the continued disturbances in the streets, and by the clamor of those, mostly of the common sort, who demanded that the courts should open and denounced the merchants for timidly refusing to do business without stamps. The Sons of Liberty were saying that the stopping of business was all very well for gentlemen of fortune, but that it was ruining the people who must starve unless business went on as usual. The Sons of Liberty were grown more hostile to the merchants than they were to ministers, and they even hinted that the better sort were by their timidity betraying the cause. Meantime Old Nicholas appeared to enjoy the situation, and never lost an opportunity of asking him, Jeremiah Wynkoop, whether he hadn't yet joined the Liberty Boys, and why after all he didn't send his ships out, clearance papers or no clearance papers.

Mr. Wynkoop was therefore immensely relieved when the British Parliament finally repealed the hateful measure, thus at once justifying his conduct and restoring his confidence in the essential justice of Britain. He had now, I recall, rather the better of the argument with Old Nicholas (the two were forever disputing) and pointed out to him ever so often that a little firmness on America's part was all that was needful to the preservation of her liberties. For two years he went about his business and pleasure with immense content. I dare say he easily forgot, as men will do, the distasteful incidents of the Stamp Act struggle, and allowed his mind to dwell chiefly on its satisfactions. He often spoke of the principle, "No taxation without representation," as being now fully established; often expressed his gratification that, by taking a firm and sensible stand, he and his substantial friends had brought Britain to recognize this principle; so that by the mere passing of time as it were these ideas acquired for Jeremiah a certain axiomatic character. I was never so sure of all this, and sometimes called his attention to the Declaratory Act as evidence that Britain still claimed the right of binding the colonies in all matters whatsoever. Needless to say, old Nicholas called his attention to the Declaratory Act oftener than I did. But Mr. Wynkoop would not take the Declaratory Act seriously. It was, he said, no more than a bravely flying banner designed to cover a dignified retreat from an untenable position; and he had no fear that Britain, having confessed its error by repealing the Stamp Act, would ever again repeat it.

It presently appeared that the British government could commit errors without repeating itself. In 1767, following the mysterious retirement and delphic silences of Mr. Pitt, Mr. Charles Townshend had come forward, no one knew on whose authority, and promised the House to obtain a revenue from America without doing violence to her alleged rights. The Americans, he said, had drawn a distinction between "internal" and "external" taxes, denying the former but admitting the latter. This distinction Mr. Townshend thought "perfect nonsense," but was willing to humor Americans in it; which he would do by laying an external tax on the importation of glass, lead, paper, and tea. These duties, which would bring into the Exchequer about £40,000, the Americans must on their own principles, Mr. Townshend thought, admit to be constitutional.

It may strike my readers as odd that any one could have been surprised by anything Mr. Townshend took a notion to; but we were indeed not then as well aware of the man's essential frivolity as we have since become. I recall at all events that Mr. Wynkoop followed the proceedings in the House with amazement; and when he learned, one day in 1768, that Mr. Townshend had actually blarneyed the House into passing the Tea Act, the whole business struck Jeremiah as preposterous—"doubtless one of those deplorable jokes," I remember his saying, "which Mr. Townshend is fond of perpetrating when half drunk." I had some recollection that in the time of the Stamp Act troubles certain writers had hinted at a distinction between "internal" and "external" taxes; and Mr. Wynkoop admitted that some such distinction may have been made. But he said that for his part he thought little of such subtle distinctions, agreeing rather with Mr. Pitt that the real question was whether Parliament could "take money out of our pockets without our consent" by any tax whatsoever. There was, however, a difficulty in taking so advanced a position at that time, and as usual it was old Nicholas, always quick to perceive difficulties, who pointed it out.

"I fancy," old Nicholas had said, "that every act in regulation of trade takes money out of our pockets, but I don't imagine you have yet become so ardent a Son of Liberty as to deny Parliament the right of regulating our trade."

At that time we were all reading Mr. Dickinson's Letters of A Pennsylvania Farmer, and Mr. Wynkoop, who read everything, was able to meet that objection.

"The essential question," he said, "is whether an act of Parliament is laid primarily for the regulation of trade or for the raising of a revenue. If for the latter, it is a tax. The intention of the framers must decide, and there can be no question that the Tea Act is a tax since the framers expressly declare its purpose to be the raising of a revenue."

"A fine distinction, that! But it would be easy for the framers of an act to levy duties on imports with the real intention of raising a revenue, all the while professing loudly their intention of regulating trade. What then?"

"Americans would not be so easily deceived, sir. The nature of the Act would reveal the real intention clearly enough."

"Ha! You would determine the nature of an act by the intention of the framers, and the intention of the framers by the nature of the act. Excellent! That is the logic of your Pennsylvania Farmer. The New Englanders are still more advanced, I see. They are now saying that our rights are founded on a law of Nature, and God only knows what that is. God and Mr. Adams—it's the same thing, I dare say."

"The New Englanders are likely to be a little rash, sir, I think," Mr. Wynkoop admitted. "The argument of their Mr. Adams is complicated, and I 'fear too subtle to be easily followed. I'm not sure I understand it."

"Well, never mind. You will all understand it soon enough. First you say that Britain has no right to lay internal taxes. Then that she has no right to levy taxes of any sort. Next you will be saying that Parliament has no right of legislation for the colonies on any matter whatsoever. And as you can't derive that from precedent you will derive it from the law of nature."

Mr. Wynkoop smiled at this outburst.

"I have no fear of its coming to that," he said. "The Tea Act is not really an act of Britain; it is Mr. Townshend's foolish hobby. A firm and sensible resistance on our part will effect its repeal. But if one could conceive Britain to be so blind as to push matters to extremes—well, I don't know. If it were really a choice between admitting that Parliament has a right of making all laws for us or denying that she has a right of making any laws for us, it would be a hard choice, but should we not be forced to choose the latter alternative? What other answer could we make?"

"You may well ask! What answer will you make when your precious Adams comes out with a declaration of independency from Great Britain?"

"Independence!" Mr. Wynkoop exclaimed. "Good God, sir, what an idea!"

And indeed, at that time, the idea of separation from Great Britain struck us all as fantastic.

A firm and sensible resistance, Jeremiah had maintained, would bring a repeal of the Townshend duties, as it had formerly brought a repeal of the Stamp Act. When it was learned that Lord North, on March 5, 1770, had moved the repeal of all the Townshend duties save that on tea, Mr. Wynkoop could with some reason say, and did say, that events had proved the justice of his view. . . .

The years of '71 and '72 were quiet years—ominously so as it proved. But in those days we all nourished the conviction that the controversy with Britain was definitely closed. Nothing occurred to remind us of it even, unless it would be the annual celebrations of the repeal of the Stamp Act, or the faint reverberations, always to be heard in any case, of political squabbles in the Massachusetts Bay. Then, out of a clear sky as it seemed, the storm burst—the landing of the tea ships, the destruction of the tea in Boston harbor, and the subsequent meeting of the Philadelphia Congress. These events, all occurring in rapid succession, seemed to fall like so many blows on Mr. Wynkoop's head, and I recall his saying to me . . .

[Here the manuscript breaks off again, and there are evidently some pages missing.]

. . . return from Philadelphia, I met him at his father's house where we were to take dinner, as often happened. Arriving early, we had a long talk while waiting for old Nicholas to come down. I found Mr. Wynkoop in low spirits, an unusual thing for him. It may have been no more than a natural weakness after the excitement of attending the Congress, but to my accustomed eyes his low spirits seemed rather due to the uncomfortable feeling that he had been elbowed by circumstances into a position which he never intended to occupy. I was eager for the details of the Congress, but he seemed unwilling to talk of that, preferring rather to dwell upon the events leading up to it—matters which we had threshed out many times before. It was as if Mr. Wynkoop wished to revive the events of the last year and his own part in them, as if, feeling that he might and perhaps should have followed a different line of conduct, his mind was eagerly engaged in finding some good reasons for the line of conduct which he had followed in fact. What first gave me this notion was his saying, *apropos* of nothing,

"I will confess to you, what I would not to another, that if I could twelve months ago have foreseen the present situation I should probably not have attended the Congress." . . .

"No man can foresee the future," I remarked, somewhat sententiously.

"That is true," he said. "And even could I have foreseen the future, I fail to see how I could have acted differently, at least not honorably and with any satisfaction to myself. It is past a doubt that Britain, in authorizing the India Company to sell its teas in America, deliberately sought to raise the issue with America once more. It was a challenge, and so insidiously contrived that America had no choice but submission or a resort to a certain amount of violence. Once landed the teas were bound to be sold, since even with the 3d duty they were offered at a less price than the Holland teas. The issue could not be met by commercial agreements, still less by argument. Well, we sent the teas back to London. The Massachusetts people threw theirs into the harbor. Violence, undoubtedly. I had no part in it, but what could be done? Who after all was responsible for the violence? Let ministers who revived an issue happily settled answer that."

"There is no doubt in my mind," I said, "that Britain welcomed the violence in Boston harbor as a pretext for strong measures."

"It seems incredible," Mr. Wynkoop resumed, "but what else can we think? Hitherto it might be said of ministers that they blundered, that they did not know the consequences of their acts. But not on this occasion. They knew perfectly the temper of America; and in any case the destruction of a little tea was surely a mild offense compared with the abrogation of the Massachusetts Charter and the closing of Boston harbor. To subject a loyal province to military despotism, and then deliberately to set about starving the people into submission reveals a vindictiveness foreign to the British character. I can't think the Coercive Acts represent the will of the English people, and I am confident, always have been, that the sober second thought of the nation will repudiate these acts of ministerial despotism."

It was not the first time I had heard Mr. Wynkoop express that sentiment.

"I trust it may prove so," I said. "At least we have done our part. No one can say that the Congress has countenanced rash measures. It has merely adopted a commercial agreement, a measure which we have frequently resorted to before. I don't see how it could have done less."

Mr. Wynkoop seemed a little uncertain of that.

"Yes," he said. "I suppose we could not have done less; Heaven knows we have shown a proper restraint. And I may say that what little influence I have had has always been exerted to that end.". . .

"I am very glad you went to Philadelphia," I said.

What else could I have done?" he exclaimed. "I have asked myself that a dozen times without finding any answer. But about the Association I don't know. You say it is a moderate measure, but after all it was the measure of the New Englanders, and among the moderates of Philadelphia it was commonly thought to be perhaps too vigorous. I was opposed to it. I voted against it. And having done so perhaps I was ill advised to sign it. I don't know."

I was about to make some reply, when old Nicholas came into the room, and I fancied I could see Mr. Wynkoop stiffen to defend his conduct against inevitable sarcasms.

"Fine doings!" Old Nicholas growled. "The New Englanders had their way, as I expected. I warned you against meddling with treason."

"Treason's a strong word, sir."

"The Association smells of it."

"I cannot think so, sir. The Association is a voluntary agreement not to do certain things; not to import or to export certain goods after a certain date. No law that I know of compels me to import or to export."

"No law requires you to import or to export, very true. But does any law require *me not* to import or export? Certainly no law of the British Parliament or of New York Province obliges me. But suppose I exercise my lawful privilege of importing after the date fixed? What then? Will not your Association compel me not to import, or try to do so? Are not your committees pledged to inspect the customs, to seize my goods, and sell them at public auction for the benefit of the starving mechanics of Boston? I tell you your Association erects a government unknown to the law; a government which aims to exert compulsion on all citizens. When I am given a coat of tar for violating the Association, will you still say it is a *voluntary* Association?"

"I think little compulsion will be necessary," Mr. Wynkoop replied. "The continent is united as never before; and when the British people realize that, and when British merchants find markets wanting, ministers will be made to see reason."

"You signed the Association, I hear."

"I did, sir. I was opposed to it as Mr. Jay was, but when it was finally carried we both signed it. Once adopted as expressing the policy of Congress, it seemed useless to advertise our divisions, and so weaken the effect of the measures taken. Congress has decided. The important thing now is not what policy Congress should have adopted; the important thing now is for all to unite in support of the policy which it has in fact adopted. If the Colonies present a united front to Britain, as they will do, Britain must yield."

"My advice," old Nicholas said as we went into dinner, "is to drop it. And don't say I didn't warn you." . . .

When in April the news came from Lexington I was not much surprised. It meant war to a certainty, and my first thought was to learn what Mr. Wynkoop would make of it. Curiously enough, with that faculty he had for moulding the world close to the heart's desire, Mr. Wynkoop found some satisfaction in this untoward event. War with Great Britain—no, he would not pronounce the word prematurely. He spoke of the Lexington affair as a repetition of the Boston Massacre, seemingly more serious only because America was now prepared to defend its liberties with arms in its hands. I was delighted that he could take it so; for it convinced me that we might still carry him along with us. The Assembly of New York was too lukewarm to be depended on, half the members or more being frankly Tory, so that we found it convenient to organize a Provincial Congress, composed of delegates elected under the supervision of the Committees, in order to take charge of affairs and keep New York in line with the continent. The most adavanced party was already suspicious of Mr. Wynkoop's loyalty; but the moderate men saw the wisdom of winning his support if possible. Mr. Jay and Mr. Alsop were especially keen to have Mr. Wynkoop serve in the Provincial Congress, and they asked me to do what I could to obtain his consent to stand as a candidate.

I did what I could, and I flatter myself that my representations had some influence with him. Knowing his admiration for Mr. Jay, I put it to him as a thing strongly urged by that gentleman.

"Mr. Jay thinks it the more necessary," I said to Mr. Wynkoop, "for men of your sound and moderate views to serve, since the Mechanics are every day gaining headway, and at the same time many men of standing are withdrawing altogether. There is a twofold danger to meet; we must keep the province loyal to the cause, and we must prevent the levelling ideas of the New Englanders from gaining the ascendancy here. If men of your standing refuse to direct the affairs of the colony in these crucial times we shall surely succumb to one or the other of these evils."

"I understand that very well," Mr. Wynkoop replied, "but the decision is not, as you know, an easy one for me."

"Your difficulties are appreciated, and by no one more than by Mr. Jay and all his friends. But it is precisely for that reason, as they point out, that we need your support. Old Nicholas is known to be Tory, and it is much commented on that the Van Schoickendinck Interest is largely lukewarm if not actually hostile. The family Interest is a powerful one, and if you are cordially with us it will do much to bring over many who are hesitating. Your responsibility is the greater, as Mr. Jay rightly says, because of the fact that you will carry with you, one way or another, a great number."

"It is very flattering of Mr. Jay to say so."

Mr. Wynkoop had a great respect for Mr. Jay's judgment—had always had. He consented to stand, and was elected. Throughout the summer of 1775 he attended the sessions of the Provincial Congress faithfully, giving his support to those who were endeavoring to hold the province to a sane middle course—enforcing the Association; raising a militia for defense; keeping the door carefully open for conciliation. Old Nicholas charged him with being too much led about by Mr. Jay. Mr. Wynkoop naturally replied that the notion was ridiculous. What kept him to the mark I feel sure was the feeling that his views and his conduct had been hitherto justified by events, and were now justified by Lord North's Resolution on Conciliation. On this he placed all his hopes. Unacceptable Lord North's Resolution was, he told me on one occasion; but he regretted that the Congress at Philadelphia had seen fit to pronounce it "unseasonable and insidious." When bargains are to be struck, Mr. Wynkoop said, politicians do not offer everything at the first approach. The Resolution proved, he thought, that Lord North was preparing to retreat, as gracefully as possible no doubt. Meantime the policy adopted by the Philadelphia Congress Mr. Wynkoop thought eminently satisfactory; the Resolution on Taking up Arms was admirably phrased to convince Britain that America would defend her rights; the Petition to the King admirably phrased to prove her loyalty. Throughout the summer and autumn Mr. Wynkoop therefore held the same language to men of extreme views—to the over timid and to the over zealous: the Petition's the thing, he said; it will surely effect the end desired.

Hope delayed makes the heart sick, it has been said. But I think this was not the effect on Mr. Wynkoop. On the contrary, I am sure that for four months he found peace of mind by looking forward to the happy day when the king would graciously make concessions. I had little expectation of any concessions, and it was no great shock to me when the news arrived in November that the king had not even deigned to receive the Petition, much less to answer it. But I knew it would be a heavy blow to Mr. Wynkoop; and when the British government, placing an embargo on American trade, proclaimed America to be in a state of rebellion, it is not too much to say that Mr. Wynkoop's little world of opinion and conduct, held together by recollection of the past and hope for the future, was completely shattered. For a month I saw him scarcely at all. He rarely went abroad, even to attend the Provincial Congress. He must have sat at home in seclusion, endeavoring to adjust his thought to the grim reality, gathering together as best he could the scattered fragments of a broken faith.

During the winter of '76 I saw him more frequently. We often discussed the situation at length. The time for discussion, for discussion of the past that is, seemed to me to be over. But Mr. Wynkoop was seemingly more interested in discussing what had happened than in discussing what ought now to be done. At first this puzzled me; but I soon found the explanation, which was that he knew very well what had to be done; or at least what he had to do, and was only engaged in convincing himself that it had been from the first inevitable, that the situation that now confronted him was not of his making. His one aim from the first, he said, and he said it many times, was to prevent the calamity now impending. I know not how many times he reviewed his past conduct. Short of tamely submitting to the domination of Parliament, he was forever asking, what other course could America have followed but the one she had followed? What other course could he have followed? If America had appealed, not to force but to reason, was this not due to the efforts of men of substance and standing, men of Mr. Wynkoop's class? If Mr. Wynkoop and all his kind had washed their hands of the affair, would not the populace and their hot headed leaders long since have rushed America into violence, and so have given Britain's measures the very justification which they now lacked?

In all this I quite agreed with Mr. Wynkoop. I assured him that his conduct had always been that of a wise and prudent man, and that if events had disappointed the expectations of prudent men, the fault was clearly not his. . . .

War with Great Britain! Mr. Wynkoop was forced to pronounce the word at last. But independence! That was the hardest word of all. Yet the word was in the air, passing from mouth to mouth behind closed doors and in the open streets. I had long since accustomed myself to the idea, but Mr. Wynkoop hated the thought of it, said he had never desired it, did not now desire it—"unless," he admitted as a kind of after thought, "the Britain I have always been loyal to proves an illusion." It was this notion, I think, that enabled Mr. Wynkoop to reconcile himself to the policy of separation. The Britain of his dreams was an illusion. The Britain he had known did not exist. In those days we were all reading the fiery papers of Mr. Paine entitled *Common Sense*. I know that Mr. Wynkoop read them, and I fancy that they helped him to see Britain in her true colors.

"I like neither the impudence of the man's manner nor the uncompromising harshness of his matter," Mr. Wynkoop once said to me. "Yet it seems that events give only too much foundation for his assertion that we have deluded ourselves in proclaiming the advantages of the connection with Britain. I can't agree with him that the loyal and respectful tone of our pamphlets and petitions is no more than mawkish sentiment; but I do wonder if the alleged benefits of the union with Britain are but figments of the imagination. It is hard to think so. And yet what now are those benefits? We must surely ask that."

Thus in the long winter of '76 Mr. Wynkoop repaired the illusions by which he lived, reconciling himself to the inevitable step. At this time he saw little of Mr. Van Schoickendinck—it was too painful for both of them, I dare say. At least their last conversation I know (it was by Jeremiah's express invitation that I was present) was a trying one. It was on the 30th of May that we found old Nicholas in the hall of his house, standing, leaning on his cane, evidently much moved.

"I asked you to come," old Nicholas said after greeting us a little stiffly, "because I must know what you purpose to do. General Howe is about to take New York. The Philadelphia Congress is about to declare a separation from Great Britain. The so-called Provincial Congress of New York will hesitate, but it will probably support the measure. Am I to understand that you will burn your bridges and side with the rebels?"

With great seriousness and gravity, Mr. Wynkoop replied:

"I wish you to believe, sir, that I have given the matter every consideration in my power; and it seems to me that I can't do other than go with America. America is my country, and yours too, sir."

"America *is* my country." The voice of old Nicholas was shrill. "I have no great love for Britishers, as you know. Damn them all, I say! But I am too old to meddle with treason. Especially when it can't come to any good. Either we shall be crushed, in which case our last state will be worse than our first; or we shall succeed, in which case we shall be ruled by the mob. Which is better, God knows. What I can't see is why you have allowed the fanatics to run away with the cart. Fight if you must, but why close the door to reconciliation by declaring an independency?"

"We can't fight without it, sir. That's the whole truth of the matter. I was much against it, and so were most. But the necessity is clear. First we refused to trade, hoping that Britain would make terms as she had formerly done. Instead of making terms Britain closed our ports and prepared to make war. To fight we must have supplies and munitions. We must have money. We can get none of these things without reviving trade; and to revive trade we must have allies, we must have the support of France. But will France aid us so long as we profess our loyalty to Britain? France will give money and troops to disrupt the British empire, but none to consolidate it. The act of separation will be the price of a French alliance."

"Am I to understand that the act of separation is not to be seriously made, except to buy French assistance? That you will let France go by the board as soon as Britain is willing to negotiate?"

Mr. Wynkoop did not at once reply. After a moment he said,

"No, I would not say that, sir. The act of separation is intended for Britain's benefit too. It will make it plain that we mean what we say—that we mean to defend our liberties to the last ditch if necessary. Yet I hope, and believe, in spite of all, that it will not come to that."

For a long moment old Nicholas stood stiff and silent. Suddenly extending his hand, but turning his face away, he said, "Well, good bye. Our ways part then."

"Don't say that, sir."

"I must say it. I must remain as I began—a loyal British subject. You have ceased to be one. I am sorry to have seen this day. But I must submit to necessity, and you must too."

Slowly old Nicholas ascended the stairs, tapping each tread with his cane. Half way up, he cried out, as if in anger, "Good bye, I say!"

"God keep you, sir," was all Mr. Wynkoop could find to reply.

Mr. Wynkoop afterwards told me that he spent a sleepless night in his half-abandoned house. In anticipation of General Howe's arrival he had already begun to move his effects out of the city, into Westchester County, near White Plains, where the Provincial Congress was adjourned to meet on July 2. With the business of settling his personal affairs to the best advantage he was so fully occupied that he did not attend the Congress on the opening days. But on the afternoon of the 9th of July he took his place, a little late. Slipping quietly into a vacant chair just in front of me, he was handed a copy of "A Declaration by the Representatives of the United States of America, in Congress Assembled." The chairman of a committee, appointed to report on the validity of the reasons given for separation from Great Britain, was reading the document. We listened to the felicitous and now familiar phrases—"hold these truths to be self-evident"—"just powers from the consent of the governed"—"right of the people to alter or abolish it"—

"Who are the people?" I heard Mr. Wynkoop murmur to his neighbor.

His neighbor, not hearing or not understanding him, whispered behind his hand,

"This is not an easy time for you, I dare say. Mr. Van Schoickendinck can't be induced to join us." The last a statement rather than a question.

"No," Mr. Wynkoop said. "He will go Tory. He will not oppose us. His sympathies are with us really, I think. He is thoroughly American, with no great love for Britain. But he is old—he will go Tory."

"The Declaration will carry, I think."

"Yes."

"It seems well phrased. Jefferson's pen, I understand."

Presently the chairman, having finished the reading of the Declaration, read the report of the committee. "While we lament the cruel necessity which has made that measure unavoidable, we approve the same, and will, at the risk of our lives and fortunes, join with the other colonies in supporting it."

The report of the committee was carried, unanimously, a bare majority being present.

Whereupon a member begged leave, before proceeding to other routine business, to make a few remarks. Permission being granted, the member spoke of the decisive step which had just been taken; of the solemn crisis which confronted all America; of the duty of meeting that crisis with high courage, with the indomitable perseverance of freemen fighting for their liberties. "The time for discussion is over," he said. "The time for action has come. Once thoroughly united, we cannot fail, and if we triumph, as we shall, a grateful posterity will recall these days, and do honor to the patriotic men whose conduct was inspired by the spirit of freedom. God grant we may so act that the spirit of freedom will ever be synonymous with the spirit of '76!"

In the perfunctory applause which greeted these remarks, Mr. Wynkoop joined, as heartily I think, as . . .

[Here, most unfortunately, the manuscript ends. What the conclusion of the story may have been, if indeed it ever was concluded, will probably never be known.]

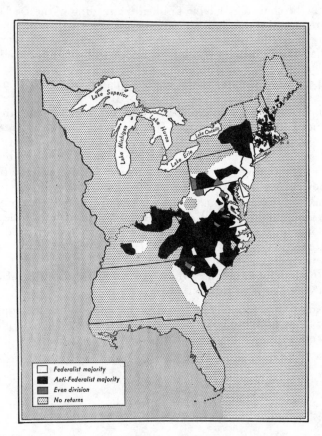

Federalist majority
Anti-Federalist majority
Even division
No returns

Ratification of the Constitution, 1787–1790. Opposition to adopting the Constitution was widespread in the new nation. (From Historical Atlas of the United States *by Clifford L. Lord and Elizabeth H. Lord. Copyright, 1944, by Clifford L. Lord. Reprinted by permission of Holt, Rinehart and Winston, Inc.*)

5 The New Nation

The reverse side of destroying old allegiances and institutions is that of constructing new ones. Rejecting colonial dependence was one thing; establishing national independence was quite another.

The Americans of the Revolutionary generation had a great deal of experience with local self-government. At the level of the town and the colony it seems probable that people in British North America exercised the right to run their own affairs to a greater degree than any people in the Western world at that time. Their experience on a broad level of government, however, was extremely limited, since this had been the sphere in which England had operated. On a few occasions the colonists had tried to work out intercolonial cooperation for better military defense or for more effective opposition to the policies of the mother country. These experiences, however, fell considerably short of great success even in their limited areas. The New England Confederation of 1643, although it lasted until the 1680s, was never really effective in either of its main goals—resolving conflicting interests among the member colonies or providing common defense against French, Dutch, and Indians. The Albany Conference of 1754 adopted Franklin's "Plan of Union," proposing an intercolonial government with limited powers in a few areas. Urgent as such cooperation appeared to be because of the expected war with the French, this plan was nevertheless unanimously rejected by the colonial legislatures. In 1765, nine colonies sent representatives to the Stamp Act Congress. The delegates formulated a bill of rights, a statement of grievances, and petitions and memorials to King and Parliament, but undertook no governmental organization. Meeting briefly and for the sole purpose of collective remonstrance against an act of Parliament, they neither intended nor achieved more than that.

These were the major examples of intercolonial political and military cooperation before 1774, when the First Continental Congress was organized. The fact that these instances were few, their purposes limited, and their successes slight shows that the colonies were local and particularistic in their outlook, as well as suspicious of each other. In the affairs ordinarily associated with central government, they were happy, until the 1760s at least, to "let George do it"—King George, that is.

By rejecting King George, the colonists did not solve the problems of government; they merely inherited them. Not only that; they assumed these problems when they were putting forth all their energy to win the war. For a people who had no significant experience either with mounting a common military effort or with establishing or running a national government, these were Herculean tasks.

The Second Continental Congress assumed those tasks. When it convened in the spring of 1775, the remonstrances of the First Continental Congress to England had failed and hostilities had begun. The Second

Congress therefore seized and exercised supreme powers: the directing of the war, the raising of men and money, the opening of diplomatic relations with foreign governments, and, after a year, the declaring of independence.

Politically, this was an extraordinarily creative era. At the level of state government, Americans were not so much breaking new ground as reworking old; the colony was a long-familiar political unit, and, among the colonies, the structure of offices and institutions was remarkably uniform. The national government, however, presented different problems. Experience provided no blueprints here. On the contrary, the experience of a strong central government as represented by England made Americans fearful and distrustful of it, and the first effort to create a central government, under the Articles of Confederation, reflected that fear. The weaknesses of the federal government from 1781 to 1788 thus flowed not from ignorance but from choice.

During those years, however, more and more men became convinced that such a weak central government might well undo the new nation completely. George Washington was among them, and his reaction to the Shays Rebellion of 1786 in Massachusetts was typical: "I predict," he wrote, "the worst consequences from a half-starved, limping government, always moving upon crutches and tottering at every step." From such convictions grew the movement for a new constitution, one that would involve a different kind of answer to the federal problem. In the Constitution of 1787, Americans established a new balance of power in their federal republic. To the federal government they now gave the powers whose assertion by the English central government they had opposed so bitterly, such as the powers to tax and to regulate commerce. Indeed, they gave to it broad powers that England had never exercised.

Acceptance of the new Constitution was by no means universal. But enough Americans were convinced of the need for a radical change to win ratification. A large number of the people thus came full circle in approximately a decade: from warring for freedom against a central government deemed oppressive, through trial of a weak central government of their own, to acceptance of a new central government with powers greater than those of the rule they had overthrown. This is striking testimony to the political creativity, the experimental spirit, and the maturity of this raw nation.

The Constitution of 1787 was the culmination of this era. Through a century and three quarters under it the American nation has thrived and prospered as no other people in history. But the principles of the Articles of Confederation are by no means dead. In every generation, assertion of "states' rights" against the federal government recurs. Over the generations, one sees that a desire to swing the balance of power back to the states is the private possession of no section, economic group, or social class. Fear of too much government is part of the American heritage. There are, thus, two continuing streams of political thought in the

United States. The Articles of Confederation exemplify one, as the Constitution does the other. In every generation many Americans are drawn into whichever current seems to mirror their dreams, run with their interests, or follow their beliefs. Even the Founding Fathers, extraordinarily wise as they were, could not balance powers in a republic well enough to solve the federal problem once and for all.

Merrill Jensen

The 1780s: Momentous and Misunderstood

The Articles of Confederation, the first written constitution for the new nation, was the result of long and careful deliberation. Even before declaring independence of Great Britain, the Second Continental Congress appointed a committee to draft a frame of government. When that committee made its report, the Congress weighed, debated, and amended its recommendations for sixteen months. Ratification by all the states of the Congress' proposals then took three years and five months more. In March 1781, almost five years after the committee had first gone to work and two long years before the Revolutionary War would end, the Articles of Confederation went into effect.

The title of the constitution was both clear and revealing; this was to be a confederation of sovereign states, not a centralized nation-state. The second and third articles spelled this out specifically: "Each state retains its sovereignty, freedom, and independence"; and "The said states hereby severally enter into a firm league of friendship with each other." Only sharply limited and clearly defined powers were given to the federal government.

Although the lengthy deliberation and the eventual acceptance by all thirteen states would seem to reflect widespread conviction about these political principles, the Articles of Confederation prevailed for only eight years—to the ratification of the Constitution in 1789. That short period, however, was of extraordinary importance. It was an era of hard economic and diplomatic adjustment, as the newly independent nation groped toward solutions of the political problems inherent in that independence. The people of the time did not agree on the answers, nor have people ever since. In the Articles of Confederation and the Constitution they tried two different approaches. They came to try each only after such cogent and heated (and often fulsome) debate as has hardly been seen since.

This was not simply a question of the mechanics of government, for, as the author of the following selection suggests, "men have ever interpreted

the two constitutions of the United States in terms of their hopes, inter-
ests, and beliefs rather than in terms of knowable facts." It is no wonder
that there was division then, as now, about the meaning of that decade
and about the relative merits of each political system.

Having thrived for half-a-dozen generations under the Constitution,
Americans have come to accord its principles something like reverence.
The Articles of Confederation, therefore, is often considered an unwork-
able if not a foolish system. Its emphasis on the state as the basic political
unit in our system, however, is still very much alive. In every generation
the cry of states·rights is raised whenever any region or substantial group
of people feels unfairly treated by the federal government.

During the past thirty years, Merrill Jensen of the University of
Wisconsin has been the most prolific and most provocative author on the
1780s. In the following selection, he demonstrates how the issues of that
decade are still vital and summarizes his interpretation of the period as a
"critical era"—an interpretation which challenges many traditionally
accepted ideas about it.   [From The New Nation, *by Merrill Jensen.*
Copyright 1950 by Alfred A. Knopf, Inc. Reprinted by permission of the
publisher.]

This book is an account of the first years of the new nation that was born
of the American Revolution. Like every other segment of time, the history of the United States from 1781 to 1789 was an integral part of the
past in which it was rooted and of the future into which it was growing.
It was a time when men believed they could shape the future of the new
nation, and since it was also a time in which they disagreed as to what
that future should be, they discussed great issues with a forthrightness
and realism seldom equalled in political debates. The history of the
Confederation is therefore one of great inherent importance for the study
of human society if for no other reason than that during it men debated
publicly and even violently the question of whether or not people could
govern themselves.

Aside from its inherent importance, the history of the Confederation
has been of enormous significance to one generation of Americans after
another in the years since then. Repeatedly Americans have turned to
that history in the course of innumerable social and political struggles.
They have done so because it was during those years that the Articles of
Confederation were replaced by the Constitution of 1787. In order to
explain their Constitution, Americans have appealed to the history of the
period out of which it came. In the course of such appeals, sometimes
honestly for light and guidance and sometimes only for support of partisan arguments, Americans have usually found what they sought. As a
result the "history" has been obscured in a haze of ideas, quotations, and
assumptions torn bodily from the context of fact that alone gives them
meaning. Again and again political opponents have asserted that the

founding fathers stood for this or that, while their writings have stood idly and helplessly in volumes on shelves or have lain buried in yellowed manuscripts and newspapers.

Since the founding fathers themselves disagreed as to the nature of the history of the period and as to the best kind of government for the new nation, it is possible to find arguments to support almost any interpretation one chooses. It is not surprising therefore that conflicting interpretations have filled thousands of pages and that all this effort has never produced any final answers and probably never will, for men have ever interpreted the two constitutions of the United States in terms of their hopes, interests, and beliefs rather than in terms of knowable facts.

The conflict of interpretation has been continuous ever since the first debates over the Articles of Confederation in the summer of 1776. Men then differed as to the kind of government which should be created for the new nation. They continued to debate the issue during the 1780's. The members of the Convention of 1787 differed as to the need for and the amount of constitutional change. When the Constitution was submitted to the public in October 1787 the controversy rose to new heights. Men talked in public meetings and wrote private letters and public essays in an effort to explain, justify, or denounce what the Convention had done. They disagreed as to what had happened since the war. Some said there had been chaos; others said there had been peace and prosperity. Some said there would be chaos without the new Constitution; others that there would be chaos if it were adopted.

Once it was adopted Thomas Jefferson and Alexander Hamilton, with two opposed ideals of what the United States should be, laid down two classic and contradictory opinions of the nature of the Constitution. These two basic interpretations may be simply stated. Jefferson held that the central government was sharply limited by the letter of the Constitution; that in effect the states retained their sovereign powers except where they were specifically delegated. Hamilton argued in effect that the central government was a national government which could not be restrained by a strict interpretation of the Constitution or by ideas of state sovereignty. These rival interpretations did not originate with Hamilton and Jefferson, for they had been the very core of constitutional debate ever since the Declaration of Independence, and even before it, for that matter.

Jefferson and his followers used the states rights idea to oppose the plans of the Federalists when they passed the Alien and Sedition Acts in 1798. But when Jefferson became president and purchased Louisiana, he justified his actions by constitutional theories that even Hamilton hardly dared use. Meanwhile Jefferson's opponents seized upon his earlier theories in a vain attempt to block the expansion of the United States. They did so again during the War of 1812 when the Federalists of New England became out-and-out exponents of "states rights" and threatened secession because they were opposed to the war.

In the decades before the Civil War, Daniel Webster and John C. Calhoun carried on the dispute, each having changed sides since his youthful years in politics. Webster, who had been a states rights spokesman during the War of 1812, became the high priest of nationalism, while Calhoun, a leading nationalist in 1812, became the high priest of the states rights idea which he elaborated to defend the slave-owning aristocracy of the South.

The Civil War itself was the bloody climax of a social conflict in which the ultimate nature of the Constitution was argued again and again in seeking support for and arguments against antagonistic programs. But even the Civil War did not finally settle the constitutional issue. The stresses and strains that came with the rise of industrial and finance capitalism produced demands for social and regulatory legislation. The passage of such legislation by the states involved the interpretation of the nature of the Constitution, for business interests regulated by state governments denied their authority and appealed to the national courts. Those courts soon denied the power of regulation to state legislatures. Then, when regulatory laws were passed by the national government, the regulated interests evolved a "states rights" theory that limited the power of the central government, and the national courts once more agreed.

Throughout American history the courts have drawn boundary lines between state and national authority. The pose of judicial impartiality and finality assumed by the courts cannot hide the fact that they have shifted those boundary lines with the shifting winds of politics, and always with sufficient precedents, if not with adequate grace. As a result they had created by 1900 a legal and constitutional no man's land in which all sorts of activity could be carried on without effective regulation by either state or national governments.

The crash of American economy in 1929 once more posed in imperative terms the problem of the nature of the Constitution. How should it, how could it deal with the potentiality of chaos inherent in unemployment, starvation, and bankruptcy, and ultimately, the loss of faith in the utility of the economic and political foundation of the society itself?

As the national government began to act where, plainly, state and local governments had failed to or were unable to act, the question of constitutionality was raised. For a time the courts once more listened to and heeded states rights constitutional theories which were expounded by opponents of the New Deal. New Deal lawyers, in turn, adopted as weapons John Marshall's nationalistic interpretations of the Constitution for ends which Marshall himself would have fought to the death. President Roosevelt, in his fight on the Supreme Court, declared that the Constitution was not a lawyer's document; yet some of the ablest lawyers who ever lived in America wrote it. New Deal publicists wrote tracts in the guise of history to prove that there had been a "national sovereignty" in the United States from the beginning of the Revolution. Therefore, they argued, the courts could not stop the New Deal from doing what needed doing by following a strict interpretation of the Constitution. Both the New Dealers and the Republicans insisted that they were the sole heirs of the legacy of Thomas Jefferson, while Alexander Hamilton went into an eclipse from which he has not yet emerged.

The most recent appeal to the history of the Confederation Period has come from those who support some form of world government. Adequate arguments for such a government can be found in twentieth-century experience, but, like most men, its backers turn to history for analogies and lessons.

When the League of Nations was set up at the end of the First World War men turned to American history after the American Revolution as a parallel experience. At that time books were written to show the "chaos" of the Confederation Period and the happy solution that came with the Constitution of 1787. Among them was a book by a great authority on international law with the title *James Madison's Notes of Debates in the Federal Convention of 1787 and their Relation to a More Perfect Society of Nations.* The book was widely distributed by the Carnegie Endowment for International Peace. This and other books like it had little relation to the realities of world politics in the 1920's and 1930's, but despite this supporters of the United Nations and of various plans of world government have again turned to the history of the American states after the American Revolution.

The most notable appeal has been that of Clarence Streit. In his book *Union Now* he analyzes the history of our past as he sees it. He calls the Articles of Confederation a "league of friendship." He says, paraphrasing John Fiske, that by 1786 there was universal depression, trade had wellnigh stopped, and political quackery with cheap and dirty remedies had full control of the field. Trade disputes promised to end in war between states. Territorial disputes led to bloodshed. War with Spain threatened. The "league" could not coerce its members. Secession was threatened by some states. Congress had no money and could borrow none. Courts were broken up by armed mobs. When Shays's Rebellion came, state sovereignty was so strong that Massachusetts would not allow "league" troops to enter the state, even to guard the "league's" own arsenal. Streit goes on to say that the idea of turning a league into a union was not even seriously proposed until the Convention opened in May 1787. And then, he says, within two years the freedom-loving American democracies decided to try out this invention for themselves. Streit goes on to argue that it would be just as easy to secure union of the democracies now as it was for the American democracies to achieve a union then. Some things made it difficult then; some make it so now. Some made it easy then; some make it easy now. . . .

Even if it can be granted that most appeals to the history of the Confederation have been sincere, let it also be said that they have seldom been infused with any knowledge of the period or its problems. The result has been the drawing of lessons the past does not have to teach.

This is a luxury too expensive in an age when men have discovered how to unhinge the very force that holds matter itself together but have advanced very little beyond cave men in their notions of how to live peacefully with one another.

Yet it is little wonder that such false lessons have been drawn in the twentieth century because most of them have come from John Fiske's *The Critical Period of American History,* a book of vast influence but of no value as either history or example. Fiske, a philosopher and popular lecturer, wrote the book "without fear and without research," to use the words of Charles A. Beard. As long ago as 1905, Andrew C. McLaughlin, an impeccably conservative historian of the Constitution who wrote a far better book on the same period, said that Fiske's book was "altogether without scientific standing, because it is little more than a remarkably skilful adaptation of a very few secondary authorities showing almost no evidence of first hand acquaintance with the sources."

The story told by Fiske and repeated by publicists and scholars who have not worked in the field—and some who have, for that matter—is based on the assumption that this was *the* "critical period" of American history during which unselfish patriots rescued the new nation from impending anarchy, if not from chaos itself. The picture is one of stagnation, ineptitude, backruptcy, corruption, and disintegration. Such a picture is at worst false and at best grossly distorted. It is therefore important to attempt a history which makes an effort to examine the sources, which is concerned with the nature of political and economic problems rather than with proving that one side or another in the innumerable political battles of the period was "right" or "wrong." Nothing is to be gained by following a "chaos and patriots to the rescue" interpretation. We have too long ignored the fact that thoroughly patriotic Americans during the 1780's did not believe there was chaos and emphatically denied that their supposed rescuers were patriotic. The point is that there were patriots on both sides of the issue, but that they differed as to desirable goals for the new nation. At the same time, of course, there were men as narrow and selfish on both sides as their political enemies said they were.

If one approaches the history of the Confederation in this way, if one tries to see it as men who lived in it saw it and to write of it in their terms, one may achieve some semblance of reality. It is not the task of the historian to defend or attack the various groups of men whose conflicts were the essence of the period, but to set forth what they believed and what they tried to achieve. This can be illustrated no better than in the definition of terms. Throughout this book the words "federalist" and "nationalist" are used to describe two opposed bodies of opinion as to the best kind of central government for the United States. In so doing I have followed the members of the Convention of 1787. Those men believed that the Articles of Confederation provided for a "federal" government and the majority of them wanted to replace it with a "national" government. The fact that the men who wanted a national government called themselves Federalists after their work was submitted to the public is relevant to the history of politics after 1787, not to the discussion of the nature of the central government prior to and during the Convention of 1787.

Whatever the confusion since then, there was none at the time. Gouverneur Morris stated the issue concisely in the Convention when he "explained the distinction between a federal and a national, supreme government; the former being a mere compact resting on the good faith of the parties; the latter having a complete and compulsive operation." This explanation was in answer to those members of the Convention who wanted to know what Edmund Randolph meant in his opening speech when he spoke of the "defects of the federal system, the necessity of transforming it into a national efficient government. . . ."

The issue was not, as has been argued from time to time, whether there was a "nation" before the adoption of the Constitution of 1787. That was not the question at all during the 1780's. There was a new nation, as the men of the time agreed: they disagreed as to whether the new nation should have a federal or a national government. They did so from the outset of the Revolution and men have continued to do so ever since. The Constitution of 1787 was, as Madison said, both national and federal. And while this fact has led to innumerable conflicts of interpretation, it has also been a source of strength; for as one political group after another has gotten control of the central government it has been able to shape the Constitution to its needs and desires. Thus with the single exception of the Civil War, peaceful change has always been possible, and as long as Americans are willing to accept the decisions of ballot boxes, legislatures, and courts, the Constitution will continue to change with changing needs and pressures. . . .

The foregoing pages indicate that the Confederation Period was one of great significance, but not of the kind that tradition has led us to believe. The "critical period" idea was the result of an uncritical acceptance of the arguments of the victorious party in a long political battle, of a failure to face the fact that partisan propaganda is not history but only historical evidence. What emerges instead is a much more complex and important story in which several themes are interwoven. It was a period of what we would call post-war demobilization, of sudden economic change, dislocation, and expansion, and of fundamental conflict over the nature of the Constitution of the United States. Each of these themes is so interwoven with the others that any separation is arbitrary but, taken separately or together, they are better keys to an understanding of the period than the traditional one.

At the end of the war Americans faced innumerable problems arising from it. What should be done with war veterans? Should the Loyalists return to their homes? What should be our relations with foreign friends and foes? Should commerce be free or should there be discrimination, and if so, against whom and for whose benefit? How would peace affect the economy? How should the war debt be paid? What kind of taxes should be levied to pay it, and who should pay them? When the war-boom collapsed, why did it? What should the state or central governments, or both, do about it? Should government encourage one form of economic enterprise over another or should it keep hands off? What about discontented groups: should government ignore them, cater to them, or forcibly suppress those who might revolt?

Such questions or others like them have probably been asked after every great war in history. They were asked, debated, and given various solutions during the 1780's. The significance of those debates and solutions has often been misunderstood. This is no better illustrated than in the case of the national debt during the 1780's which is usually discussed only in terms of depreciation and nonpayment of interest. Actually much more was involved than this. The debt was fantastically low compared with the national debt of today—about twelve dollars per capita as compared with seventeen hundred—and the nation had vast untouched natural resources with which to pay it. Multitudes of accounts had to be reduced to simple forms so that they could be paid, and this the Confederation government managed to do. But even more important than the economics of the national debt was its politics: should it be paid by the states or the central government? A fundamental assumption of every political leader was that the political agency which paid the debt would hold the balance of power in the new nation. Hence, the supporters of a strong central government insisted that the national debt must be paid by Congress while their opponents insisted that it should be divided among the states and paid by them. The latter group was on the way to victory by the end of the 1780's, for they were supported by clamoring creditors. The result was that one state after another assumed portions of the national debt owing to its citizens. Thus the traditional story is so out of context as to be virtually meaningless. This is true of other traditions as well. Most of the ports of the world were open, not closed, to American citizens. Reciprocity and equal treatment of all United States citizens was the rule in the tonnage and tariff acts of the states, not trade barriers.

To say that many of the pessimistic traditions are false is not to say that all Americans were peaceful and satisfied. The holders of national and state debts wanted bigger payments than they got. The merchants wanted more government aid than was given them. The farmers, hit by high taxes and rigid collection of both taxes and private debts, demanded relief in the form of lower taxes and government loans from state legislatures. Such demands kept state politics in an uproar during the 1780's. However, the often violent expression of such discontents in politics should not blind us to the fact that the period was one of extraordinary economic growth. Merchants owned more ships at the end of the 1780's than they had at the beginning of the Revolution, and they carried a greater share of American produce. By 1790 the export of agricultural produce was double what it had been before the war. American cities grew rapidly, with the result that housing was scarce and building booms produced a labor shortage. Tens of thousands of farmers spread outwards to the frontiers. There can be no question but that freedom from the British Empire resulted in a surge of activity in all phases of American life. Of course not all the problems of the new nation were solved by 1789—all have not yet been solved—but there is no evidence of stagnation and decay in the 1780's. Instead the story is one of a newly free people who seized upon every means to improve and enrich themselves in a nation which they believed had a golden destiny.

Politically the dominating fact of the Confederation Period was the struggle between two groups of leaders to shape the character of the state and central governments. The revolutionary constitutions of the states placed final power in the legislatures and made the executive and judicial branches subservient to them. The members of the colonial aristocracy who became Patriots, and new men who gained economic power during the Revolution deplored this fact, but they were unable to alter the state constitutions during the 1780's. Meanwhile they tried persistently to strengthen the central government. These men were the nationalists of the 1780's.

On the other hand the men who were the true federalists believed that the greatest gain of the Revolution was the independence of the several states and the creation of a central government subservient to them. The leaders of this group from the Declaration of Independence to the Convention of 1787 were Samuel Adams, Patrick Henry, Richard Henry Lee, George Clinton, James Warren, Samuel Bryan, George Bryan, Elbridge Gerry, George Mason and a host of less well known but no less important men in each of the states. Most of these men believed, as a result of their experience with Great Britain before 1776 and of their reading of history, that the states could be best governed without the intervention of a powerful central government. Some of them had programs of political and social reform; others had none at all. Some had a vision of democracy; others had no desire except to control their states for whatever satisfactions such control might offer. Some were in fact as narrow and provincial as their opponents said they were. However, the best of them agreed that the central government needed more power, but they wanted that power given so as not to alter the basic character of the Articles of Confederation. Here is where they were in fundamental disagreement with the nationalists who wanted to remove the central government from the control of the state legislatures.

The nationalist leaders from the Declaration of Independence to the Philadelphia convention were men like Robert Morris, John Jay, Gouverneur Morris, James Wilson, Alexander Hamilton, Henry Knox, James Duane, George Washington, James Madison, and many lesser men. Most of these men were by temperament or economic interest believers in executive and judicial rather than legislative control of state and central governments, in the rigorous collection of taxes, and, as creditors, in strict payment of public and private debts. They declared that national honor and prestige could be maintained only by a powerful central government. Naturally, not all men who used such language used it sincerely, for some were as selfish and greedy as their opponents said they were. The nationalists frankly disliked the political heritage of the Revolution. They deplored the fact there was no check upon the actions of majorities in state legislatures; that there was no central government to which minorities could appeal from the decisions of such majorities, as they had done before the Revolution.

There were men who veered from side to side, but their number is relatively small and their veering is of little significance as compared with the fact that from the outset of the Revolution there were two consistently opposed bodies of opinion as to the nature of the central government. There was, of course, a wide variation of belief among adherents of both points of view. There were extremists who wanted no central government at all and others who wanted to wipe out the states entirely. There were some who wanted a monarchy and others who would have welcomed dictatorship. But such extremists are not representative of the two great bodies of men whose conflict was the essence of the years both before and after 1789.

While the federalist leaders gradually moved to a position where they were willing to add specific powers to the Articles of Confederation, the nationalist leaders campaigned steadily for the kind of government they wanted. During the war they argued that it could not be won without creating a powerful central government. After the war they insisted that such a government was necessary to do justice to public creditors, solve the problems of post-war trade, bring about recovery from depression, and win the respect of the world for the new nation. Meanwhile their experience with majorities in state legislatures merely intensified their desire. They became desperate as state after state in 1785 and 1786 adopted some form of paper money that could be loaned on farm mortgages and be used to pay taxes, and in some cases private debts as well. When they were able to hold off such demands and farmers revolted, as in Massachusetts, they were thoroughly frightened.

They looked upon such events as evidence of the horrors of unchecked democracy and they said so in poetry, private letters, newspaper essays, and public speeches. The problem, they said, was to find some refuge from democracy. They worked hard to control state legislatures and they were often successful, but such control was uncertain at best, for annual elections meant a constant threat of overturn and the threat was realized repeatedly.

We may not call it democracy, but they did. Edmund Randolph put their case bluntly in his opening speech in the Convention of 1787. He said, "our chief danger arises from the democratic parts of our constitutions . . . None of the [state] constitutions have provided a sufficient check against the democracy. The feeble senate of Virginia is a phantom. Maryland has a more powerful senate, but the late distractions in that state, have discovered that it is not powerful enough. The check established in the constitutions of New York and Massachusetts is yet a stronger barrier against democracy, but they all seem insufficient." Outside the Convention General Knox was saying that a "mad democracy sweeps away every moral trait from the human character" and that the Convention would "clip the wings of a mad democracy." James Madison in the *Federalist Papers* argued that the new Constitution should be adopted because a "republican" form of government was better than a "democracy."

The debate was white-hot and was carried on with utter frankness. It was white-hot because for a moment in history self-government by majorities within particular political boundaries was possible. Those majorities could do what they wanted, and some of them knew what they wanted. Democracy was no vague ideal, but a concrete program: it meant definite things in politics, economics, and religion. Whatever side of the controversy we take, whether we think the majorities in state legislatures governed badly or well—the fact to face is that men of the 1780's believed that the issue was democracy as a way of government for the United States of those days.

They faced the issue squarely. They thought hard and realistically about the problems of government. They understood that society is complex and that the truth about it is multifold rather than simple. James Madison summed it up as well as it has ever been done. There are, he said, many passions and interests in society and these will ever clash for control of government and will ever interpret their own desires as the good of the whole. Men like Madison and John Adams believed, as Madison said, that the "great desideratum which has not yet been found for Republican governments seems to be some disinterested and dispassionate umpire in disputes between different passions and interests in the state." In the tenth number of *The Federalist,* after citing various origins of political parties, Madison said that "the most durable source of factions [parties] has been the various and unequal distribution of property. Those who hold and those who are without property have ever formed distinct interests in society. Those who are creditors and those who are debtors, fall under a like discrimination. A landed interest, a manufacturing interest, a mercantile interest, a monied interest, with many lesser interests, grow up of necessity in civilized nations, and divide them into different classes, actuated by different sentiments and views. The regulation of these various and interfering interests forms the principal task of modern legislation, and involves the spirit of party and faction in the necessary and ordinary operations of the government."

The constitutional debate of the 1780's was thus carried on by men with a realistic appreciation of the social forces lying behind constitutional forms and theories, by men who were aware of the relationship between economic and political power. This realistic approach was lost sight of in the nineteenth century by romantic democrats who believed that once every man had the right to vote the problems of society could be solved. It was lost sight of too by those who came to believe in an oversimplified economic interpretation of history. In a sense they were as romantic as the democrats, for they assumed a rationality in the historic process that is not always supported by the evidence.

If the history of the Confederation has anything to offer us it is the realistic approach to politics so widely held by the political leaders of the time, however much they might differ as to forms of government and desirable goals for the new nation. Throughout the Confederation men with rival goals pushed two programs simultaneously. The federalists tried to strengthen the Articles of Confederation; the nationalists tried to create a new constitution by means of a convention, and thus avoid the method of change prescribed by the Articles of Confederation. The movement to strengthen the Articles failed on the verge of success; the movement to call a convention succeeded on the verge of failure. The failure of one movement and the success of the other, however we may interpret them, is one of the dramatic stories in the history of politics.

The Founding Fathers: Young Men of the Revolution

Stanley Elkins
and Eric McKitrick

In May 1787, 55 men assembled in Philadelphia to propose changes in the national government. They deliberated and debated for nearly four months, gradually hammering out not modifications in the Articles of Confederation but a new Constitution—a different answer to the problem of how political power should be divided between state and national government. What that answer was is not our concern here, but rather how and why they arrived at it. Not the content and meaning of the Constitution, but the intent and motivation of those who made it. In the twentieth century the "Founding Fathers" have come under sharp scrutiny, with profound consequences for Americans, even down to the grade school level.

In the following selection, Elkins and McKitrick first trace the way in which the interpretation of the framing of the Constitution has evolved and then suggest a new dimension. The name "Founding Fathers" im-

plies a paternal, conservative image that the authors assert is misleading. They hold that a more meaningful image would stress the Constitution-makers' youth (especially as contrasted with their opponents), energy, and nationalistic "radicalism."

But how did the other image arise, and why did it go without question or modification for more than a century? Why did it come under such sharp attack in the early 1900s, and why has that reversal of interpreta-tion been so convincing to two generations of Americans? And why has it, in turn, come under such devastating attack in the past decade? The "facts" of the past do not change. The "history" of it certainly does. Why will it not stand still?

Trying to answer such questions is part of what can make the study of history provocative instead of provoking, fascinating instead of frustrat-ing. In analyzing an issue of profound significance for Americans' under-standing of themselves, Elkins and McKitrick provide an unusually clear focus upon just such questions. [Stanley Elkins and Eric McKitrick, "The Founding Fathers: Young Men of the Revolution," Political Sci-ence Quarterly, Vol. LXXVI, No. 2 (June 1961).]

The intelligent American of today may know a great deal about his history, but the chances are that he feels none too secure about the Founding Fathers and the framing and ratification of the Federal Consti-tution. He is no longer certain what the "enlightened" version of that story is, or even whether there is one. This is because, in the century and three quarters since the Constitution was written, our best thinking on that subject has gone through two dramatically different phases and is at this moment about to enter a third.

Americans in the nineteenth century, whenever they reviewed the events of the founding, made reference to an Olympian gathering of wise and virtuous men who stood splendidly above all faction, ignored petty self-interest, and concerned themselves only with the freedom and well-being of their fellow-countrymen. This attitude toward the Fathers has actually never died out; it still tends to prevail in American history curricula right up through most of the secondary schools. But bright young people arriving at college have been regularly discovering, for nearly the last fifty years, that in the innermost circle this was regarded as an old-fashioned, immensely oversimplified, and rather dewy-eyed view of the Founding Fathers and their work. Ever since J. Allen Smith and Charles Beard wrote in the early years of the twentieth century, the "educated" picture of the Fathers has been that of a group not of dis-interested patriots but of hard-fisted conservatives who were looking out for their own interests and those of their class. According to this worldlier view, the document which they wrote—and in which they embodied these interests—was hardly intended as a thrust toward popular and democratic government. On the contrary, its centralizing tendencies all reflected the Fathers' distrust of the local and popular rule which had been too little restrained under the Articles of Confederation. The authors of the Constitution represented the privileged part of society. Naturally, then, their desire for a strong central government was, among other things, an effort to achieve solid national guarantees for the rights of property—rights not adequately protected under the Articles—and to obtain for the propertied class (their own) a favored position under the new government.

This "revisionist" point of view—that of the Founding Fathers as self-interested conservatives—has had immeasurable influence in the upper reaches of American historical thought. Much of what at first seemed audacious to the point of lèse majesté came ultimately to be taken as commonplace. The Tory-like, almost backward-turning quality which this approach has imparted to the picture of constitution-making even renders it plausible to think of the Philadelphia Convention of 1787 as a counter-revolutionary conspiracy, which is just the way a number of writers have actually described it. That is, since the Articles of Confederation were the product of the Revolution, to overthrow the Articles was—at least symbolically—to repudiate the Revolution. The Declaration of Independence and the Constitution represented two very different, and in some ways opposing, sets of aspirations; and (so the reasoning goes) the Philadelphia Convention was thus a significant turning-away from, rather than an adherence to, the spirit of the Declaration.

In very recent years, however, a whole new cycle of writing and thinking and research has been under way; the revisionists of the previous generation are themselves being revised. The economic ideas of the late Professor Beard, which dominated this field for so long, have been partially if not wholly discredited. And yet many of the old impressions, intermingled with still older ones, persist. Much of the new work, moreover, though excellent and systematic, is still in progress. Consequently the entire subject of the Constitution and its creation has become a little murky; new notions having the clarity and assuredness of the old have not as yet fully emerged; and meanwhile one is not altogether certain what to think.

Before the significance of all this new work can be justly assessed, and before consistent themes in it may be identified with any assurance, an effort should be made to retrace somewhat the psychology of previous conceptions. At the same time, it should be recognized that any amount of fresh writing on this subject will continue to lack something until it can present us with a clear new symbolic image of the Fathers themselves. The importance of this point lies in the function that symbols have for organizing the historical imagination, and the old ones are a little tired. The "father" image is well and good, and so also in certain respects is the "conservative" one. But we may suppose that these men saw themselves at the time as playing other rôles too, rôles that did not partake so much of retrospection, age, and restraint as those which would come to be assigned to them in after years. The Republic is now very old, as republics go, yet it *was* young once, and so were its founders. With youth goes energy, and the "energy" principle may be more suggestive now, in reviewing the experience of the founding, than the principle of paternal conservatism.

Charles A. Beard, who in 1913 published *An Economic Interpretation of the Constitution of the United States,* did more than any single figure to make of the Constitution something other than a topic for ceremonial praise. By calling it a product of economic forces, Beard established an alternative position and enabled the entire subject to become one for serious historical debate. He thus created the first real dialectic on the Constitution and Founding Fathers, and for that reason Beard's work must still be taken as the point of departure for any historical treatment of that subject.

For Beard, the reality behind the movement for a constitution in the 1780's was economic interest. The animating surge came from holders of depreciated Continental securities who were demanding that their bonds be paid at par, and from conservative elements throughout the Confederation who wanted a national bulwark against agrarian-debtor radicalism. Beard thus identified the Federalists as those who wanted protection for property, especially personal property. The Anti-Federalists, on the other hand, were the great mass of agrarian debtors agitating for schemes of confiscation and paper money inflation in the state legislatures. Their hard-earned taxes would go to support any new bonds that a stronger United States government might issue; conversely, further fiscal experimentation on their part would be checked by national power. The Anti-Federalists, those who opposed a new constitution, were therefore the radicals; the Federalists, who favored it, were the conservatives.

Beard's argument was immediately challenged and kept on being challenged, which helped it to retain the fresh attractiveness of an avant-garde position for many years. But the man's influence grew, and his work played a vital part in historical thinking until well after the Second World War. Historical thinking, however, has its own historical setting. Why should such a statement as Beard's not have been made until the twentieth century, more than 125 years after the event?

In the nineteenth century the American Constitution had operated as the central myth of an entire political culture. While that culture was still in the tentative stages of its growth, still subject to all manner of unforeseen menaces, and with very little that was nationally sacred, there reigned everywhere the tacit understanding that here was the one unifying abstraction, the one symbol that might command all loyalties and survive all strife. The Constitution thus served multiple functions for a society that lacked tradition, folk-memory, a sovereign, and a body of legend. The need to keep the symbol inviolate seems to have been felt more instinctively during its earlier history than later on. Public controversy of the bitterest kind might occur over the charter's true meaning;

enemies might accuse each other of misconstruing the document; but one did not challenge the myth itself. Americans even fought a civil war with both sides claiming to be the true upholders of the Constitution. Thus it was natural that when the historians of the nineteenth century—Bancroft, Hildreth, Frothingham, Fiske, McMaster—came to describe the origins of the Constitution, they should reach for the non-controversial idiom and imagery of a Golden Age. The Supreme Law had been fashioned and given to the people by a race of classic heroes.

America's veneration for its Constitution became steadily more intense in the years that followed the Civil War. Now it was the symbol not only of the Union, for which that generation had made such heavy sacrifices, but also of the unfettered capitalism which was turning the United States into one of the richest and most powerful nations in the world. The new material order—wasteful, disorderly, already acquainted with labor disturbances, yet immensely productive—was watched over by the benevolent solicitous eye of the Constitution. . . .

By the opening of the twentieth century, the state of mind in which men could uncritically ascribe a sort of immaculateness to their political and legal arrangements had altered sharply. By then a profound economic and social crisis had been met and overcome, but with remnants of psychological crisis left unresolved in its wake. The ending of the depression and hard times of the 1890's, the defeat of Populism and Bryanism, the election of McKinley and return of Republican rule—these things were not enough to restore the old complacent innocence. The American public, now full of guilty misgivings, had begun to ask itself searching questions about the evils of the existing order and about the price it had allowed itself to pay for material progress. The answer which was hit upon by publicists and civic spokesmen was *vested interest*. The formula was not exactly new, but after the experience of the 1890's, when public rhetoric had abounded in sinister allusions to "Wall Street" and "the monopolies," it was no more than natural that the "vested interest" concept should have taken on an immensely new and widened range of application. The "interests" were the shadowy powers that manipulated things and made them run the way they did. Thus vested interest came to be seen in the Progressive Era—those years roughly from the turn of the century through the First World War—as the ultimate reality behind the life of affairs. . . .

In view of this mounting preoccupation with "interests," one might be led to conclude that significant numbers of intelligent people were approaching a "class" theory of society not unlike that of Marx—a theory in which classes and class interests contended more or less frankly with each other for advantage. Yet by and large this did not happen; these were not the terms in which most people thought about society. For one reason, there was very little evidence to support such a theory. But a more important reason was that, to a people saturated in democratic prejudices, "class" habits of thought were fantastically difficult to understand, let alone imitate. To the Progressive mind, the way vested interest worked was not so much through class as through *conspiracy*.

Vested interest and conspiracy were concepts so closely related that they were almost synonymous. The interests worked in secret; their power rested on stealthy understandings and was exercised through the pulling of invisible strings. Hidden from view, they might freely circumvent the law and gain their ends by corrupting and manipulating the agencies of government. . . . Such a mode of conceiving reality would even be brought to bear upon the origins of the United States Constitution. . . .

It was Charles A. Beard, taking up the "class interest" formula in his famous *Economic Interpretation* the following year, who succeeded to all intents and purposes in making it stick. . . . Early in his book Beard insisted that it was not his purpose "to show that the Constitution was made for the personal benefit of the members of the Convention," but merely to determine whether the Fathers represented "distinct groups whose economic interests they understood and felt in concrete, definite form, through their own personal experience with identical property rights. . . ." Then, setting in motion an impressive system of scholarly apparatus, he proceeded to answer his own questions.

. . . At any rate, the reason he was able to create his sensation was that the things he showed the Fathers doing were of exactly the sort that the muckraking magazines had, in other connections, made all too familiar.

Beard's basic research materials were a batch of old Treasury records which had never previously been opened ("reality"), and in them he found the names of a number of the Federalist leaders, members of the Philadelphia Convention as well as delegates to ratifying conventions in the various states. These men held substantial amounts of Continental securities which—Beard reasoned from later developments—would rise sharply in value with the establishment of a strong central government. This seemed to explain the energy with which they worked to bring such a government into being, and this was just the sort of evidence that impressed Beard's contemporaries most. Beard himself, for all his disclaimers, sums up his argument in language whose dominant theme is *direct personal interest*. Here, three of his thirteen conclusions are quite explicit:

1. The first firm steps toward the formation of the Constitution were taken by a small and active group of men immediately interested through their personal possessions in the outcome of their labors.

2. The members of the Philadelphia Convention who drafted the Constitution were, with a few exceptions, immediately, directly, and personally interested in, and derived economic advantages from, the establishment of the new system.

3. The leaders who supported the Constitution in the ratifying conventions represented the same economic groups as the members of the Philadelphia Convention; and in a large number of instances they were also directly and personally interested in the outcome of their efforts.

Accompanying the principal theme of personal interest were several sub-themes:

1. The Constitution was essentially an economic document based upon the concept that the fundamental private rights of property are anterior to government and morally beyond the reach of popular majorities.

2. [The entire process, from the calling of the Philadelphia Convention to the ratifying of the Constitution, was unrepresentative and undemocratic; there was no popular vote on calling the convention; a large propertyless (and therefore disfranchised) mass was not represented at Philadelphia; and only a small minority in each state voted for delegates to the ratifying conventions.]

3. [Where battles did occur over ratification], the line of cleavage . . . was between substantial personalty interests on the one hand and the small farmers and debtor interests on the other.

. . . Beard himself was nothing if not a Progressive, fully immersed in his times. It was the interests and their inside doings that caught the Progressive imagination; it was this that the Progressives longed to befool and discomfit by public exposure. If Beard was to show that the Federal Constitution was not a product of abstract political theory but of concrete economic drives, there was no happier way of doing it than to paint the Founding Fathers in the familiar image of the vested interests —the small group of wealthy conspirators hostile to, even contemptuous of, the majority will, and acting for clear, "practical" reasons such as rigging the value of public securities.

Despite the bursts of pained protests which *An Economic Interpretation* initially drew from many older academics (who either thought that Beard could comprehend no motives other than base ones, or else concluded that he must be a socialist), it also drew plenty of praise from academic as well as non-academic quarters. Not only did the book do well for a scholarly monograph, it did better and better as time went on. . . .

. . . At the same time Beard had bequeathed to American historical method something far more pervasive, a technique of explanation which could take "class" interpretations or leave them alone. This was the "reality" technique, which assumes that the most significant aspects of any event are those concealed from the eye. Men's true intentions are to be judged neither from the words we hear them speak nor the deeds we see them do, and the "real" forces behind historical change will turn out, more often than not, to be those of conspiracy.

In 1940 certain new and interesting corollaries were added to the mode of approach which, due so largely to Beard's example, had come to influence historical thinking on the formation of the Constitution. In that year Merrill Jensen published *The Articles of Confederation: An Interpretation of the Social-Constitutional History of the American Revolution, 1774–1781.* Jensen's own approach was consistent with most of the general principles which had been laid down by Beard. . . .

In a second book, *The New Nation* (1950), Jensen considered the accomplishments of the Confederation, together with the social and economic conditions of the period from 1781 to 1789. He concluded that the "critical period" was really not so critical after all. American ships were not excluded from many foreign ports; tariff wars between states were the exception rather than the rule; the Confederation government had solved the problem of western lands and was well on the way to settling the outstanding boundary disputes. By 1786 the economic depression which had struck the country in 1784 was coming to an end. Even the problem of national credit was not so serious as the Federalists wanted people to believe, since a number of the states had assumed responsibility for portions of the Continental debt held by their own citizens. Had the states been brought to accept a national impost—a tariff duty on incoming foreign goods levied solely and exclusively by Congress, the revenue of which would be reserved for the support of the government—the Confederation would have been fully capable of surviving and functioning as a true federal establishment.

The collapse of the Confederation, Jensen argued, was not the logical outcome of weakness or inefficiency. It was the result of a determined effort by a small but tightly-organized group of nationalists to impose a centralized government upon the entire country despite the contrary desires of great majorities everywhere . . . These were the men who conspired to overthrow the Confederation and who masterminded the triumph of the Constitution.

There were points at which Jensen had not seen eye to eye with Beard. He was more impressed, for instance, by the Fathers' general outlook and ideology than by their property holdings; unlike Beard, moreover, he denied that the Confederation era was a time of serious economic difficulty. Yet he had actually strengthened the Beardian logic at more than one point, and the differences were minor in the light of the convictions which united the two in spirit and intention. The work of Merrill Jensen, like that of Beard and Parrington and J. Allen Smith before him, still balanced on the assumption that the energy behind the American Constitution was conspiratorial energy, and that the Constitution came into being by means of a coup d'état—through the plotting of a well-disciplined Toryish few against the interests of an unvigilant democratic majority.

Indeed, Merrill Jensen's *The New Nation*—published two years after the death of Charles Beard—was the last major piece of Constitution scholarship to be done in the Progressive tradition, and represented the end of an era. By that time, 1950, Beard's own notions had begun to arouse not the admiration, but the suspicion, of a new generation of postwar intellectuals.

. . . By 1956, Beard's *Economic Interpretation* had been set up for the *coup de grâce*. The executioner was Robert E. Brown, a professor at

Michigan State who had been at work for some time implacably compil-
ing a catalogue of the Master's offenses. In his *Charles Beard and the
Constitution,* published that year, Brown tracked Beard through every
page of the latter's masterpiece and laid the ax to virtually every statement of importance that Beard had made in it. There was absolutely no
correlation between the Philadelphia delegates' property holdings and
the way they behaved on the question of a constitution. It was not true
that large numbers of adult males were disfranchised; the suffrage was
remarkably liberal everywhere. Farmers as a class were by no means
chronically debtors; many were creditors and many others were both.
The supporters of Shays' Rebellion (the debtors' uprising in western
Massachusetts which occurred during the fall and winter of 1786–1787)
were certainly not united against the Constitution; if they had been, it
could never have been ratified, since the Shaysites had a clear majority at
the time of the Massachusetts convention. . . .

Not only was Beard's evidence inconclusive at all points, Brown insisted, but there were even occasions when the Master had not been
above doctoring it. He edited Madison's Federalist No. 10 to eliminate
all but its economic emphasis; he quoted only those passages of the
Philadelphia debates that made the Fathers look least democratic; he
arranged his treatment of the ratification process in an order that violated chronology, centered unjustified attention on states where hard
struggles did occur, overlooked the ease with which ratification was
achieved in other states, and thus created a wildly exaggerated picture of
the opposition at large.

Brown's book was respectfully received; there was little inclination to
dispute his arguments; no champions arose to do serious battle for the
departed Beard. . . .

The first effort in recent years to view the Constitution all over again
in a major way, shaking off the Beardian categories and starting as it
were from scratch, has been undertaken by Forrest McDonald. *We The
People,* published in 1958, was the first of a planned trilogy whose design
was to survey anew the entire story of how the Constitution was brought
into existence. Although McDonald, like Brown, felt it necessary to show
the inadequacy of Beard's conclusions, his strategy was quite different
from Brown's; it was undertaken less to discredit Beard than to clear the
way for his own projected treatment of the great subject. In the *Economic Interpretation,* Beard had made a number of proposals for research which he himself had not performed—and never did perform—
but which would, Beard felt, further corroborate his own "frankly fragmentary" work. McDonald began by undertaking the very research which
Beard had suggested, and its results convinced him that Beard had
simply asked all the wrong questions.

One of the things McDonald investigated in *We The People* was an
assumption upon which Beard had put a great deal of stress, the notion
of a fundamental antagonism between "personalty" and "realty" interests at the time of the Philadelphia Convention. ("Personalty" was

wealth based on securities, money, commerce, or manufacturing; "realty" was landed property whose owners' outlook tended to be primarily agrarian.) He found that there was no such split in the Convention. The seven men who either walked out of the Convention or else refused to sign the completed document were among the heaviest security-holders there, and represented "an all-star team of personalty interests." In state after state, moreover, there was no appreciable difference between the property holdings of Federalists and Anti-Federalists. Finally, the three states that ratified the Constitution unanimously—Delaware, New Jersey, and Georgia—were overwhelmingly dominated by agrarian interests.

Unlike Brown, McDonald was quite unwilling to write off the possibility of an economic analysis (his book's subtitle was *The Economic Origins of the Constitution*) ; it was just that Beard's particular economic categories led nowhere. Beard's sweeping "personalty" and "realty" classifications were meaningless, and he had deceived himself profoundly in supposing that the Federalists' property interests "knew no state boundaries" but were "truly national in scope." On these two points of difference McDonald set up an entirely new and original research scheme, and in so doing effected a really impressive conceptual maneuver. He was quite ready, in the first place, to find "economic forces" behind the movement for a constitution, but these must be sought not in "classes" or in broad categories of property but rather in the specific business interests of specific groups in specific places. The other organizing category would be the individual states themselves. The political framework within which any group had to operate was still that imposed by the state; the states were, after all, still sovereign units, and the precise relationship between economic forces and political action depended almost entirely on the special conditions within those states, conditions which varied from one to the other.

By abandoning Beard's "national" framework and recasting the entire problem on a state-by-state basis, McDonald made it possible to see with a sudden clarity things which ought to have been obvious all along. The states where ratification was achieved most readily were those that were convinced, for one reason or another, that they could not survive and prosper as independent entities; those holding out the longest were the ones most convinced that they could go it alone. The reasons for supporting ratification might vary considerably from state to state. For Georgia, an impending Indian war and the need for military protection could transcend any possible economic issue; New York, at one time imagining for itself an independent political and economic future, would finally ratify for fear of being isolated from a system which already included ten states and which might soon be joined by a seceded New York City. . . .

Recognizing the importance of specific location made it also easier and more natural to appreciate the way in which particular interests in particular places might be affected by the question of a stronger national government. Boston shipping interests, for example, seem to have been less concerned in the 1780's over class ideology or general economic philosophy than over those conditions of the times which were especially bad for business. The British would not let them into the West Indies, the French were excluding their fish, and their large vessels were no longer profitable. A strong national government could create a navy whose very existence would reduce high insurance rates; it could guarantee an orderly tariff system that would remove all pressure for higher and higher state tariffs; and it could counter British and French discrimination by means of an effective navigation act. . . .

Forrest McDonald's work, according to him, has only just begun; years of it still lie ahead. But already a remarkable precision of detail has been brought to the subject, together with a degree of sophistication which makes the older economic approach—"tough-minded" as it once imagined itself—seem now a little wan and misty. The special internal conditions of the several states now seem fully valid as clues to the ratification policies of those states, each in its separate turn. And there is a credibility about the immediate needs and aspirations of particular groups, and the way they varied from place to place, that Beard's "interests" never quite possessed—or if they did, they had long since lost their hold on the modern mind.

And yet there are overtones in McDonald's work—for all its precise excellence, perhaps partly because of it—that have already succeeded in creating a new kind of "reality" spell. McDonald is very open-minded about all the manifold and complex and contradictory forces that converged upon the movement for a constitution. But somehow the ones he takes most seriously—the "real" forces behind the movement—were specific, particular, circumscribed, hard, and immediate. They were to be looked for mostly on the local level, because that is where one really finds things. A state—the largest permissible "reality" unit—was an agglomeration of specific, particular, immediate localities. There were interests to be served, political or economic, and they were *hard*. They were pursued rationally and without sentimentality; men came down where they did because their hard, immediate, specific interests brought them there. But are we prepared to say that the final result was just the sum—or extension—of these interests? . . .

The new approach is extremely enlightening and useful. But has it yet taken on life? When will it fully engage the question of initiative and energy? How do we account for the dedication, the force and éclat, of Federalist leadership? When all is said and done, we do not exactly refer to the "interests" of a James Madison. We wonder, instead, about the terms in which he conceives of personal fulfillment, which is not at all the same. What animates him? The nationalist movement *did* have a mystique that somehow transfigured a substantial number of its leaders. What was it like, what were its origins?

The work of Merrill Jensen, done in the 1930's and 1940's, has suffered somewhat in reputation due to the sweep and vehemence of the anti-Beardian reaction. Yet that work contains perceptions which ought not to be written off in the general shuffle. They derive not so much from the over-all Beardian traditions and influences amid which Jensen wrote, as from that particular sector of the subject which he marked off and pre-ëmpted for his own. Simply by committing himself—alone among Beardians and non-Beardians—to presenting the Confederation era as a legitimate phase of American history, entitled to be taken seriously like any other and having a positive side as well as a negative one, he has forced upon us a peculiar point of view which, by the same token, yields its own special budget of insights. For example, Jensen has been profoundly impressed by the sheer force, determination, and drive of such nationalist leaders as Hamilton, Madison, Jay, Knox, and the Morrises. This energy, he feels, created the central problem of the Confederation and was the major cause of its collapse. He deplores this, seeing in the Confederation "democratic" virtues which it probably never had, finding in the Federalists an "aristocratic" character which in actual fact was as much or more to be found in the Anti-Federalists, smelling plots everywhere, and in general shaping his nomenclature to fit his own values and preferences. But if Professor Jensen seems to have called everything by the wrong name, it is well to remember that nomenclature is not everything. The important thing—what does ring true—is that this driving "nationalist" energy was, in all probability, central to the movement that gave the United States a new government.

The other side of the picture, which does not seem to have engaged Jensen's mind half so much, was the peculiar sloth and inertia of the Anti-Federalists. Cecelia Kenyon, in a brilliant essay on these men, has shown them as an amazingly reactionary lot. They were transfixed by the specter of power. It was not the power of the aristocracy that they feared, but power of any kind, democratic or otherwise, that they could not control for themselves. Their chief concern was to keep governments as limited and as closely tied to local interests as possible. Their minds could not embrace the concept of a national interest which they themselves might share and which could transcend their own parochial concerns. Republican government that went beyond the compass of state boundaries was something they could not imagine. Thus the chief difference between Federalists and Anti-Federalists had little to do with "democracy" (George Clinton and Patrick Henry were no more willing than Gouverneur Morris to trust the innate virtue of the people), but rather with the Federalists' conviction that there was such a thing as national interest and that a government could be established to care for it which was fully in keeping with republican principles. To the Federalists this was not only possible but absolutely necessary, if the nation was to avoid a future of political impotence, internal discord, and in the end foreign intervention. So far so good. But still, exactly how did such convictions get themselves generated? . . .

Much depends here on the way one pictures the Revolution. In the beginning it simply consisted of a number of state revolts loosely directed by the Continental Congress; and for many men, absorbed in their effort to preserve the independence of their own states, it never progressed much beyond that stage even in the face of invasion. But the Revolution had another aspect, one which developed with time and left a deep imprint on those connected with it, and this was its character as a continental war effort. If there is any one feature that most unites the future leading supporters of the Constitution, it was their close engagement with this continental aspect of the Revolution. A remarkably large number of these someday Federalists were in the Continental Army, served as diplomats or key administrative officers of the Confederation government, or, as members of Congress, played leading roles on those committees primarily responsible for the conduct of the war.

Merrill Jensen has compiled two lists, with nine names in each, of the men whom he considers to have been the leading spirits of the Federalists and Anti-Federalists respectively. It would be well to have a good look at this sample. The Federalists—Jensen calls them "nationalists"—were Robert Morris, John Jay, James Wilson, Alexander Hamilton, Henry Knox, James Duane, George Washington, James Madison, and Gouverneur Morris. Washington, Knox, and Hamilton were deeply involved in Continental military affairs; Robert Morris was Superintendent of Finance; Jay was president of the Continental Congress and minister plenipotentiary to Spain (he would later be appointed Secretary for Foreign Affairs); Wilson, Duane, and Gouverneur Morris were members of Congress, all three being active members of the war committees. The Anti-Federalist group presents a very different picture. It consisted of Samuel Adams, Patrick Henry, Richard Henry Lee, George Clinton, James Warren, Samuel Bryan, George Bryan, George Mason, and Elbridge Gerry. Only three of these—Gerry, Lee, and Adams—served in Congress, and the latter two fought consistently against any effort to give Congress executive powers. Their constant preoccupation was state sovereignty rather than national efficiency. Henry and Clinton were active war governors, concerned primarily with state rather than national problems, while Warren, Mason, and the two Bryans were essentially state politicians.

The age difference between these two groups is especially striking. The Federalists were on the average ten to twelve years younger than the Anti-Federalists. At the outbreak of the Revolution George Washington, at 44, was the oldest of the lot; six were under 35 and four were in their twenties. Of the Anti-Federalists, only three were under 40 in 1776, and one of these, Samuel Bryan, the son of George Bryan, was a boy of 16.

This age differential takes on a special significance when it is related to the career profiles of the men concerned. Nearly half of the Federalist group—Gouverneur Morris, Madison, Hamilton, and Knox—quite literally saw their careers launched in the Revolution. The remaining five—Washington, Jay, Duane, Wilson, and Robert Morris—though established in public affairs beforehand, became nationally known after 1776 and the wide public recognition which they subsequently achieved came first and foremost through their identification with the continental war effort. All of them had been united in an experience, and had formed commitments, which dissolved provincial boundaries; they had come to full public maturity in a setting which enabled ambition, public service, leadership, and self-fulfillment to be conceived, for each in his way, with a grandeur of scope unknown to any previous generation. The careers of the Anti-Federalists, on the other hand, were not only state-centered but—aside from those of Clinton, Gerry, and the young Bryan—rested heavily on events that preceded rather than followed 1776. . . .

. . . A significant proportion of relative newcomers, with prospects initially modest, happened to have their careers opened up at a particular time and in such a way that their very public personalities came to be staked upon the national quality of the experience which had formed them. In a number of outstanding cases energy, initiative, talent, and ambition had combined with a conception of affairs which had grown immense in scope and promise by the close of the Revolution. There is every reason to think that a contraction of this scope, in the years that immediately followed, operated as a powerful challenge.

The stages through which the constitutional movement proceeded in the 1780's add up to a fascinating story in political management, marked by no little élan and dash. That movement, viewed in the light of the Federalist leaders' commitment to the Revolution, raises some nice points as to who were the "conservatives" and who were the "radicals." The spirit of unity generated by the struggle for independence had, in the eyes of those most closely involved in coördinating the effort, lapsed; provincial factions were reverting to the old provincial ways. The impulse to arrest disorder and to revive the flame of revolutionary unity may be pictured in "conservative" terms, but this becomes quite awkward when we look for terms with which to picture the other impulse, so different in nature: the urge to rest, to drift, to turn back the clock. . . .

The revolutionary verve and ardor of the Federalists, their resources of will and energy, their willingness to scheme tirelessly, campaign everywhere, and sweat and agonize over every vote meant in effect that despite all the hairbreadth squeezes and rigors of the struggle, the Anti-Federalists would lose every crucial test. There was, to be sure, an Anti-Federalist effort. But with no program, no really viable commitments, and little purposeful organization, the Anti-Federalists somehow always managed to move too late and with too little. They would sit and watch their great stronghold, New York, being snatched away from them despite a two-to-one Anti-Federalist majority in a convention presided over by their own chief, George Clinton. . . . By the time the New York convention was ready to act, ten others had ratified, and at the final moment Hamilton and his allies spread the chilling rumor that New York City was about to secede from the state. The Anti-Federalists, who had had enough, directed a chosen number of their delegates to cross over, and solemnly capitulated.

In the end, of course, everyone "crossed over." The speed with which this occurred once the continental revolutionists had made their point, and the ease with which the Constitution so soon became an object of universal veneration, still stands as one of the minor marvels of American history. But the document did contain certain implications, of a quasi-philosophical nature, that make the reasons for this ready consensus not so very difficult to find. It established a national government whose basic outlines were sufficiently congenial to the underlying commitments of the whole culture—republicanism and capitalism—that the likelihood of its being the subject of a true ideological clash was never very real. That the Constitution should mount guard over the rights of property—"realty," "personalty," or any other kind—was questioned by nobody. There had certainly been a struggle, a long and exhausting one, but we should not be deceived as to its nature. It was not fought on economic grounds; it was not a matter of ideology; it was not, in the fullest and most fundamental sense, even a struggle between nationalism and localism. The key struggle was between inertia and energy; with inertia overcome, everything changed.

There were, of course, lingering objections and misgivings; many of the problems involved had been genuinely puzzling and difficult; and there remained doubters who had to be converted. But then the perfect bridge whereby all could become Federalists within a year was the addition of a Bill of Rights. After the French Revolution, anti-constitutionalism in France would be a burning issue for generations; in America, an anti-constitutional party was undreamed of after 1789. With the Bill of Rights, the remaining opponents of the new system could say that, ever watchful of tyranny, they had now got what they wanted. Moreover, the Young Men of the Revolution might at last imagine, after a dozen years of anxiety, that *their* Revolution had been a success.

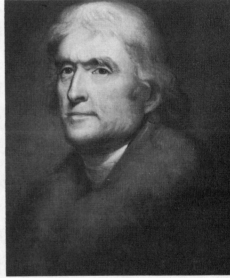

Opponents of the 1790s. Jefferson: "All men are created equal." Hamilton: "In every community where industry is encouraged, there will be a division of it into the few and the many." (Jefferson Memorial Foundation and Historical Society of Pennsylvania)

6

The 1790s: Hamiltonianism versus Jeffersonianism

The adoption of the Constitution in 1789 marked the end of Act II in the drama of establishing a new nation. Act I had seen the struggle for independence; and Act II focused on the evolution of the fundamental political pattern for the new nation, first in the Articles of Confederation and then in the Constitution. The Constitution, however, was only a skeleton—a brief six thousand words. Now came the problems of putting flesh on it and infusing it with life, of setting policies, of setting up offices and agencies, of building institutions. This process was certainly as important and creative as those involved in breaking with England and establishing a constitution. The war would have been for nought, and the constitution-making too, if these problems could not be resolved. There was high drama, then, in this third and final act, which held the stage during the decade of the 1790s.

The cast of characters was the same: the "Young Men of the Revolution," now at the peak of their political development and careers. We usually think of them in their roles in Act I, in the glory and romance of fighting for independence. It is only by the third act, however, that they had developed into full-blown characters, just as, in the style of any good play, the whole action comes to a climax—and a resolution.

The action in this third act involves tension, conflict, and rancor. There had been friction during the War of the Revolution and the years of adjustment which followed, but the fundamental mood was one of cooperation, concession, compromise. By contrast, the mood now becomes one of dissension and bitterness. It is simple to read this as petty bickering or mere personality clash or haggling over the spoils of a new government and a new continent. To read it cynically is to misread it, however. The basic issues were very big, concerning the entire direction that the nation would take. The answers were by no means obvious; men agreed upon them no more than they do now. And the times were perilous, as both England and France pressured the United States fiercely for support in the titanic struggle that began with the French Revolution.

Americans have often misread this era. Since each of today's two major political parties traces its origins to Hamilton or Jefferson, their political oratory somtimes confuses the times, the issues, the leaders. Hamilton, for instance, becomes a twentieth-century capitalist rather than an eigh-

163

teenth-century mercantilist, while Jefferson becomes the progenitor of the New Deal. If taking them out of their times is one source of misunderstanding, another, perhaps more common one is to oversimplify them. They were extraordinarily complex personalities. The more recent biographies of both Hamilton and Jefferson emphasize this theme. John C. Miller subtitles his life of Hamilton *Portrait in Paradox* (1959), while in *The Jefferson Image in the American Mind* (1962), Merrill D. Peterson finds Jefferson "a baffling series of contradictions." Hamilton and Jefferson have become the mythic giants, and the popular explanation of such heroes does not run to paradox and contradictions.

Their times were critical. As others of that generation, they saw the importance of the issues, which accounts in part for the bitternesses that developed. They saw themselves as "fixing the national character," or, in James Madison's words, "deciding forever the fate of Republican government." And, in a very real sense, they were doing just that. As John Fiske put it when he first popularized American history several generations ago:

All American history has since run along the lines marked out by the antagonism of Jefferson and Hamilton. Our history is sometimes charged with a lack of picturesqueness because it does not deal with the belted knight and the moated grange. But to one who considers the moral import of events, it is hard to see how anything can be more picturesque than the spectacle of these two giant antagonists contending for political measures which were so profoundly to affect the lives of millions of human beings yet unborn.

Historians after Fiske have generally agreed with his interpretation of the great confrontation of the 1790s, concerning both the primary roles of Hamilton and Jefferson and the long-range consequences. A note of caution should be introduced, however. To focus upon their differences may obscure very fundamental similarities. Above all, both operated from the same general philosophy of liberty. Both were determined to protect the rights of individuals and minorities. As "Young Men of the Revolution," both were concerned with achieving national security and national growth along the lines blocked out in that struggle. Like the parties which arose around them—indeed all the major American parties ever since—they stood on a common ground that they never left, even when moving in opposite directions.

John C. Miller   # Alexander Hamilton

The framers of the Constitution expected most of the contention and strife in the new government to come from self-seeking groups whose members had some particular interest in common—factions such as shippers, slaveholders, or small states in a power struggle against the large ones. The First Congress, however, saw accord not discord. Neither parties nor factions predominated, and the former opponents of the Constitution seemed to accept defeat in good grace.

Within a few years all that had changed. Profound differences did arise. But the institutions that reflected them were not factional but partisan—not a number of small, special-interest groups but two broad-based parties, really bundles of factions. Such a two-party system has of course been the pattern of American politics ever since. That pattern had deep roots in colonial political practice; but it emerged in the new nation only in the 1790s and then with a suddenness and an asperity that raises fascinating questions. How and why did it come about? What divided the two parties? How significant was (and is) the basis for that division? What were the roles of the two party leaders, Thomas Jefferson and Alexander Hamilton? Do men such as they make the times, or do the times cast up leaders?

The differences between the two individuals and the groups that clustered around them can be traced to divergent convictions about human nature and possibilities for the "human condition." Basically optimistic about both, Jefferson emphasized man's equality and perfectibility, as in this simple assertion from the Declaration of Independence: "All men are created equal." Hamilton, in contrast, was essentially pessimistic, emphasizing man's inequality and imperfectibility: "In every community where industry is encouraged, there will be a division of it into the few and the many. Hence, separate interests will arise. . . . Give all power to the many, they will oppress the few. Give all power to the few, they will oppress the many."

Jefferson's optimism led to a conviction that both individualism and national growth would flow from mild institutions, minimal government, and maximal education to release the vast potential in man. Hamilton's pessimism is equally clear in his belief that the same goals demanded strong institutions to prevent oppression by either the few or the many and to protect and encourage the talents of the few in building the nation.

Such philosophical differences produced conflicts on key political questions: how much government and where should its power be concentrated, in state or nation; how broad the base of American self-government; how far can the governed be trusted to choose their leaders wisely; with how much power can the governors be trusted? In sum, the whole direction that the United States would take was involved; this was not just some political game.

In the 1790s these issues came to a sharp focus on questions of economic policy, specifically fiscal policy. As Hamilton saw it, the government under the Articles of Confederation had been destroyed by fiscal incapacity and irresponsibility. He was determined not only to prevent a recurrence of such disaster but also to establish by law a powerful financial and economic "engine" to propel the development of the nation.

Those who opposed him feared that the federal "engine" would become a juggernaut, crushing everything (like states rights) and everybody (at least the little people) in its path. As they saw it, his proposals for the federal government to pay off its debts at par (no matter how depreciated and no matter what speculators now held them), to take over state debts (no matter that some states would thus be saddled with paying part of the debts of those less responsible), to levy federal internal taxes and import duties, and to establish a national bank (a "moneyed monster") would take money out of the pockets of those who could least afford it and would create a centralized authority that would endanger liberty.

The lines were clearly drawn. As Joseph Charles has put it in The Origins of the American Party System, *"Nowhere do we draw nearer to the central issue of the 1790's, the question of what kind of government and society we were to have in this country, than in the study of Hamilton's economic policy" (emphasis added).*

Hamilton's engine had several moving parts, described above. As the designer saw it, all were essential and interrelated. One, however, was the basis for all: his solutions to the debt problems. The following selection suggests why this was so and how his solutions were designed to promote the stability and order that he and his followers have emphasized. As a figure study and character sketch of Alexander Hamilton, it also provides a vivid picture of a true "giant" of the early days of the republic. [John C. Miller, Alexander Hamilton: Portrait in Paradox *(Harper & Bros., Publishers, 1959), pp. 226–237, footnotes omitted. Copyright by John C. Miller, by whose permission it is reprinted.]*

With Hamilton on the threshold of his career as Secretary of the Treasury, the American people would have been well advised to take a close look at this young man who was so relentlessly bent upon doing them good. They would have seen a smallish man—he was about five feet seven inches—whose deficiency in height was compensated by his slenderness and his erect military bearing. He had a fine presence: always elegantly dressed in the height of fashion—and this was an age in which the male came closest to resembling the peacock—he stood out in all companies by the bold colors he affected in waistcoats and the dashing air with which he wore his lace and ruffles. In the eighteenth century, women affected to admire "a well-turned leg" in men; and Hamilton's legs, decked out in the finest stockings, were the envy of the beaux. Certainly there has never been a more sartorially resplendent Secretary of the Treasury—or one more calculated to set female hearts fluttering. Here was no dry-as-dust statistician, spouting facts and figures like a walking encyclopedia, but a figure of romance whose impeccable manners would have won approval from Lord Chesterfield himself.

Hamilton's features, if not exactly handsome, were strong and well-defined; the angle of his jaw denoted a purposeful nature and his eyes were deep-set and piercing. Certainly he was not a man to suffer fools gladly or to defer to men less well endowed intellectually than himself. He impressed not a few people as vain and arrogant—there was a certain stiffness and formality in his manner, it was observed, which reduced his effectiveness as a political leader. Certainly there was nothing of the hail-fellow-well-met about him. On the other hand, among his friends, Hamilton seemed to be the most generous, eloquent, charitable, patriotic, forceful and charming of men. They could not say enough in praise of his "lively imagination—a quick and almost intuitive perception—profound and comprehensive views, a ready invention of expedients in cases of difficulty, with a solid & correct judgment." He ruled by virtue of his intellectual pre-eminence and the ardor and conviction with which he propounded his ideas. In the select circles of his intimates, it was remarked that Hamilton was "so much trusted, admired, beloved, and adored, that his power over their affections was entire."

While Hamilton disdained the arts of popularity and the more commonly accepted methods of influencing the mass mind, his best qualities were displayed in a small group of his peers. Here the very characteristics that alienated popular support—his candor, his contempt for the low shifts of politics, his partiality for the company of the rich, the well-born and the educated—were seen to best advantage. As a political leader, Hamilton conducted himself like a general of an army: instead of dealing directly with the rank and file, he operated through hand-picked subordinates; he was primarily a policy maker and leader of leaders. Holding demagoguery in abhorrence, Hamilton leaned so far in the opposite direction that he almost succeeded in disqualifying himself from becoming an effective popular leader.

Some of Hamilton's friends found him too inflexible in his ideas: Gouverneur Morris, for example, traced most of Hamilton's difficulties to "the pertinacious adherence to opinions he had once formed." It is true that Hamilton's convictions were strongly held and that he seldom changed his mind; but, at the same time, he was capable of moving slowly and patiently toward his objective, and he possessed a sense of timing that, at least in the early and most constructive period of his career, did not play him false. And yet it remained true that while Hamilton was capable of compromise, he could not conciliate: it was not for him to hold a party together by bridging differences between divergent groups or sections. By temperament as well as by the intensity with which he sought to realize his objectives, Hamilton was best fitted to be the leader of a small group of devoted followers.

If the American people did not already know it, they were soon to be made acutely aware of the fact that Hamilton's credo was audacity and yet more audacity. Where others temporized, calculated the risks and paused in indecision, Hamilton acted; he was above all a man of action, not a philosopher seeking some elusive abstract truth. Whether consciously or not, he based his life upon a maxim of Machiavelli: "I certainly think that it is better to be impetuous than cautious," said the Florentine statesman, "for fortune is a woman, and it is necessary, if you wish to master her, to conquer her by force; and it can be seen that she lets herself be overcome by the bold rather than by those who proceed coldly. And, therefore, like a woman, she is always a friend to the young, because they are less cautious, fiercer, and master her with greater audacity." But as Hamilton perhaps insufficiently recognized, this goddess, after lavishing favors upon her worshipers, was also capable of destroying them utterly.

An even less sanguine man than Hamilton might have been forgiven for imagining that he was a favorite of fortune. He had repeatedly made audacity pay off richly: when he assumed the post of Secretary of the Treasury, if experience could be trusted, there was nothing to which he might not aspire. Hamilton had come a long way by pushing his luck, and he thought that the United States ought to act upon the principle that had guided him in the conduct of his own life. Certainly he believed that the United States was the last place in the world where caution ought to be accounted a virtue; and, almost to the last, the events of his career vindicated his philosophy of risking, venturing and striving.

Despite his keen appreciation of the part played by economic forces in the shaping of men's destiny, Hamilton held the "great man" view of history. He tended to glorify the hero, the great state builders, the daring and farsighted who had brought order out of chaos and raised nations to the pinnacle of power. He did not think that the people had leadership, political wisdom and initiative in themselves—leadership came from the exceptional individuals, the "natural aristocrats" and the rich and educated. Leadership, he held, could not wait for the pressures of public opinion: the impulse must be communicated from the government to the masses. In short, it was incumbent upon a statesman to act for the national welfare, and he could not evade this responsibility by thrusting it upon the people or their representatives.

During the Revolutionary War, Hamilton recorded in his Artillery Company Account Book a quotation from Demosthenes' orations that might be regarded as the guiding principle of his career: "As a general marches at the head of his troops, so ought wise politicians, if I dare use the expression, to march at the head of affairs. . . . They ought not to wait the event, to know what measures to take; but the measures which they have taken, ought to produce the *event*." In the writings of Plutarch and Machiavelli he found a wealth of examples of leaders who, dedicating themselves to a great cause, had triumphed over adversity. Hamilton, too, had found his cause—the creation of a nation—and he was sustained by the conviction that all the obstacles to its realization could be overcome by the exercise of wisdom and resolution on the part of a determined man.

With a new and untried Constitution, a crushing burden of debt, and two states still out of the union, it might well have seemed advisable for the government to feel its way cautiously toward the "more perfect union" envisaged by the framers of the Constitution. James Madison, for one, believed that in order to establish the government firmly in the affections of the people, it was essential that the administration adopt a mild and conciliatory policy. The Bill of Rights represented his contribution to the spirit of amity.

In *The Federalist,* Hamilton had given the impression that he, too, was resigned to moving slowly toward his objectives. Acknowledging that the union was fundamentally federal in nature, he declared that " 'tis time only that can mature and perfect so compound a system, can liquidate the meaning of all the parts, and can adjust them to each other in a harmonious and consistent WHOLE." He had frequently made light of the fear that the federal government would aggress upon the states: content with its powers of commerce, finance, peace and war, he contended, it would be under no temptation to invade the powers reserved to the states, because such powers "would contribute nothing to the dignity, to the importance, or the splendor of the national government."

And yet Hamilton was not a man to wait for time to effect the consummation he devoutly wished—the triumph of the national government over the states. He had observed that the Constitution was "a fabric which can hardly be stationary, and which will retrograde if it cannot be made to advance." Neither the national government nor the states could afford to stand still, for a constitutional equilibrium was unthinkable between sovereign powers engaged in a life-and-death struggle for power.

Some nationalists took comfort in the thought that the Constitution had created "a great Oak which is to reduce them [the states] to paltry shrubs," but Hamilton feared that for this very reason the states would not rest until they had hewn down the monarch of the forest. He was certain in his own mind that the only way to prevent them from doing so was to lay the ax to the root of state sovereignty. Nothing that had occurred in the United States since the adoption of the Constitution had altered his opinion that "the centrifugal is much stronger than the centripetal force in these States—the seeds of disunion much more numerous than those of union." All the passions which governed men—ambition, avarice and self-interest—appeared to him to attach the people to the states, thereby ensuring that they would always be an overmatch for the general government. Not until there had been established "such a compleat sovereignty in the general Government as will turn all the strong principles & passions" to its side was Hamilton disposed to pronounce the union out of danger.

Of all the problems confronting the Washington administration, none was more complex, more urgent and less understood than was the national debt. And yet the success of the Constitution and the very existence of the republic depended upon the skill with which the financial obligations of the government were handled. Hamilton had always contended that the government could not endure without credit "commensurate with the utmost extent of the lending faculties of the community"; but credit could not be established until provision had been made for the existing debt. Little could be done toward disposing of the existing debt, however, until the government had regained its ability to borrow. Truly, the finances of the United States were a dilemma wrapped in a paradox.

If Hamilton was impelled by some inner compulsion to reduce chaos to order, the finances of the United States offered ample scope for that propensity. The domestic debt consisted of a chaos of virtually worthless paper money; loan-office certificates; IOU's signed by the Quartermaster and commissary generals; lottery prizes (the government had conducted lotteries but had been unable to pay the winners in cash); certificates given to soldiers and officers in lieu of pay; indents (paper certificates representing interest paid on the debt); Treasury certificates; and various other evidences of debt. Hardly a means of going into debt known to the governments of the eighteenth century had been omitted by the Continental Congress: and it enjoyed the unenviable distinction of having more creditors than any other government in the world.

When Hamilton came to the Treasury, the foreign debt of the United States was about $10 million, plus $1,600,000 in arrears of interest. The domestic debt Hamilton estimated to be slightly over $27 million, not including $13 million in accrued interest. The total debt therefore stood at slightly over $50 million. But there was no certainty in these figures: how much debt in the form of certificates had been contracted by the various agencies of the government—the commissary and quartermaster accounts were especially confused—was known, as one congressman observed, only to the Supreme Being. Although commissioners had been appointed by the Continental Congress to settle the accounts of individuals holding claims against the government, their work had not been completed. Nor had the claims of the states against the general government been ascertained: here was a terra incognita, an impenetrable wasteland of unliquidated debt.

To a less sanguine and resolute man than Hamilton, the national debt might well have appeared more like an albatross hung about the neck of the federal government than a sword with which to vanquish the states. For this mass of paper seemed to lie like a dead weight upon the national economy, stifling governmental credit and diverting into speculation capital which might have been more profitably employed in business enterprise. And, despite all that the government could do, the debt was constantly increasing: revenue was inadequate to meet even the interest which the government had pledged itself to pay.

Under these circumstances, some Americans were of the opinion that the government ought to repudiate the national debt and start out with a clean financial slate. Why, they asked, should the federal government bankrupt itself in order to repay money that had served its purpose and from which everyone had profited in the form of independence of Great Britain? It seemed to them perfectly proper for the government to inform its creditors that, through no fault of its own, the debt was cancelled.

As an exponent of strong government, Hamilton did not deny that under some conditions the government was privileged to repudiate its debts. The highest law of the state, he admitted, was self-preservation; when its existence was at stake, a government could alter the terms of contracts, discriminate between various groups of creditors and declare its obligations null and void. But he emphatically did not agree that this right ought to be applied to the existing debt. In his opinion, the federal government was capable of fulfilling in all essentials the terms of the contract it had made with its creditors and was therefore debarred from entering a plea of abatement.

Besides the purely legal aspect, every consideration—morality, justice and expediency—seemed to Hamilton to require that the government dealt honestly with its creditors. "Establish that a government may decline a provision for its debts, though able to make it," he said, "and you overthrow all public morality. . . . You have anarchy, despotism, or what you please, but you have no *just* or *regular* government." For governments, the first commandment was: honor thy financial obligations. According to the gospel preached by Hamilton, if "the dead corpse of the public credit" was to be resurrected, it would not be by a miracle but by the observance of probity and sound bookkeeping.

In October, 1789, Hamilton was given an opportunity to put these ideas to the test. Having received petitions from the public creditors asking that funds be set aside for the payment of the national debt, Congress requested the Secretary of the Treasury to submit a plan for "the adequate support of the public credit." Hamilton gave full latitude to this directive: in his Report on Public Credit he undertook to show how the debt could be paid, to whom it should be paid and what was to be done with the state debts dating from the Revolutionary War.

Displaying an optimism to which nothing in the previous financial experience of the United States gave warrant, Hamilton took the position that the tariff could be made to furnish the government with sufficient revenue to liquidate the national debt and at the same time pay the operating expenses of the government. He admitted of no doubt that the foreign debt must be paid in full, accrued interest and all, but at the same time he declared his determination to stretch every resource of the government in order to do justice to the domestic creditors. Everything he had said and done up to the time of his appointment as Secretary of the Treasury indicated that he held the satisfaction of these claims to be a prerequisite to the success of the Federal Constitution.

If the domestic creditors were to be paid, the question inevitably arose: which creditors? For in 1789, the securities of the United States government were for the most part not in the possession of the original holders:

they had been transferred—often at a fraction of their nominal value—to purchasers who bought them for speculative or investment purposes. As a result, the evidences of governmental debt had gravitated into the hands of a few, most of whom were residents of the northern states. A class and a section therefore stood to profit from the payment of the debt. In view of this change of ownership, Hamilton was confronted with the question whether the original holders or their assignees ought to receive the windfall that would descend when the government redeemed its securities at face value.

Hamilton had long since made up his mind that the possessors of these securities, whether original holders or purchasers, were entitled to the full usufruct. The certificates themselves stated that the amount thereon specified should be paid to the bearer, thereby creating, said Hamilton, a contractual relationship that made them as much the property of bona fide purchasers "as their houses or their lands, their hats or their coats." Moreover, the Continental Congress had assured foreign capitalists that there would be no discrimination between original holders and assignees—and upon the strength of this promise, Dutch bankers had purchased securities worth many thousands of dollars. If the federal government now attempted to discriminate in the name of equity between different types of creditors, Hamilton was prepared to renounce all hope that foreigners would ever again trust their money to the perfidious republicans across the Atlantic.

All Hamilton's plans for the financial and economic development of the United States were founded upon the assumption that government bonds would be freely transferrable—otherwise they could not serve as a supplementary circulating medium, nor could they be used to stimulate capitalistic enterprise. If discrimination were adopted, Hamilton saw an end to this prospect: the pledges of the government would carry no weight with men who had learned from experience that it broke its promises to suit its convenience; and no man could buy a certificate in the confidence that he was acquiring a good title. . . .

Even conceding that equity required that something be done for the original holders, Hamilton took the position in his Report on Public Credit that it was wholly impracticable inasmuch as many of the original records had disappeared or, in some instances, had never existed. He therefore felt justified in saying that any attempt to ascertain and reimburse the original holders would produce endless fraud and perjury and, "beyond all powers of calculation, multiply the evils of speculation.". . .

Besides the mass of depreciated securities and paper money issued by the Continental Congress, the people of the United States labored under a heavy load of state debts. Like the national debt, the evidences of state indebtedness had followed the well-worn course from original holders to speculators and investors. Hamilton's constant objective was to bind these men to the national government by the durable ties of *"Ambition and Avarice";* but as matters stood in 1789, ambition and avarice tended to attach the state creditors to the state governments. As long as the states possessed their debts, they were certain to compete with the federal government for the allegiance of the creditor class and for the citizens' tax dollar. The result, Hamilton feared, would be that the states would attempt to pre-empt (as the Constitution, by recognizing concurrent taxation, permitted them to do) the remaining objects of taxation and that the affluent citizens of the United States would be divided against themselves, the state creditors seeking to strengthen the states while the holders of federal securities endeavored to aggrandize the powers and the revenues of the national government.

It can be said of Hamilton that whenever he saw a Gordian knot, he attempted to cut it forthwith. In this instance, he called in his Report on Public Credit for the assumption by the federal government of $25 million of state debts incurred in the prosecution of the War of Independence. Here he acted upon the principle that "if all the public creditors receive their dues from one source, distributed by an equal hand, their interest will be the same. And, having the same interests, they will unite in the support of the fiscal arrangements of the Government." Thus the most valuable members of the community—valuable because they were the most liberally endowed with the goods of this world—would bestow their affections and, Hamilton hoped, their money upon the federal government. With all the creditors, state and national, gathered into the fold of the federal government, Hamilton's vision of a powerful national government, supreme over the states, would begin to assume concrete reality.

But was not the federal government inviting financial ruin by taking upon itself $25 million of the debts of the states? If Hamilton's plan were adopted, the debt of the United States government would soar to $80 million or more. At one time, Americans had been in the habit of talking in terms of hundreds of millions of dollars, but that was in the piping days of paper money when, as a member of Congress remarked, a million dollars was like a sprat in a whale's belly. Hamilton was clearly not thinking of the kind of money that was fed whales, or, as was more often the case, used as wallpaper. Furthermore, only a confirmed optimist could have struck the rock of national resources in the expectation that streams of revenue would gush forth: when tapped previously, it had given forth only a hollow sound, as of a great void. Even Hamilton went through a long and painful period of doubt before he could bring himself to cast the die. His state of mind was that of a soldier resolved at all costs to storm the enemy's entrenchments. "In a personal view," he remarked, "it would have been pusillanimity and weakness to have stopped short of a provision for the aggregate debt of the country." It remained to be seen whether he had not overreached himself in his anxiety to consolidate the debt and the political power it connoted in the federal government. . . .

To anyone acquainted with the working of British government and economy, Hamilton's report had a familiar ring. Great Britain bore witness how a funded national debt could be converted into a national blessing by binding men of wealth to the government, stimulating capitalistic development and promoting financial stability. The ability of the British government to pay its debts had become "in the British mind," Hamilton marveled, "an article of faith, and is no longer an article of reason." He was now prepared to believe that the credit of that government was immortal. His task was to confer a similar immortality upon the credit of the United States government without, he lamented, the benefit of the British constitution and British capital.

Marshall Smelser   # Mr. Jefferson in 1801

Thus, early in our national history, Hamilton introduced the whole question of the relation of government to the economy. In order to protect individual liberty (especially by securing property rights) and to promote national development (especially by encouraging the mercantile, manufacturing, and financial interests), he believed in a strong role for government. This of course is closer to mercantilism than to capitalism or "laissez-faire"—government hands off.

Jefferson approached the same basic goals, individual liberty and national development, from the opposite direction. Fearing anarchy above all, Hamilton wanted strong government, centralized in the nation. Fearing tyranny above all, Jefferson wanted weak government, decentralized in the states. Hamilton feared the mob. Jefferson feared the man on horseback. Hamilton saw order and security as necessary antecedents to civil liberty. Jefferson put civil liberty ahead of order and security, because, without it, only the order and security of a police state would remain.

Some historians have seen the entire history of the Western world as a kind of pendulum action between these goals of liberty and security, which are to some degree mutually exclusive. American history can be meaningfully interpreted in these terms, moving in the Revolutionary era toward liberty (the colonists having experienced a strong measure of security in the British Empire) and then in the 1790s swinging back toward security. Hamilton and Jefferson thus become especially meaningful, because each so clearly personified one of the poles toward which the pendulum swings.

Jefferson's Declaration of Independence, of course, called liberty an "unalienable right," this being a "self-evident truth." For him it was not just a "right" but a kind of star by which he navigated, on which he set his course. Above all, he emphasized the freedom of the mind. Through freedom of thought and belief would come the progress in the human condition he so believed in—a progress that, like the liberty upon which it was based, was for all, not just Hamilton's few. "The sheep are happier of themselves," wrote Jefferson, "than under the care of the wolves." Further, both liberty and progress were best entrusted to the many: "The people are the only sure reliance for the preservation of our liberty."

While Hamilton's principles tended to divide Americans, Jefferson's ideas encouraged unity. They appeal especially to the young in any generation and to peoples all around the world today. Hamilton set the course for the American ship of state, but those aboard repeatedly return to Jefferson's star. [Pages 1–15 of "Mr. Jefferson in 1801" in The Democratic Republic 1801–1815 *by Marshall Smelser. Copyright © 1968 by Marshall Smelser. Reprinted by permission of Harper & Row, Publishers, Inc.]*

At least we know what he looked like. He was tall and slender, framed of large, loosely shackled bones. His clothes, including a cherished scarlet vest and a pair of run-over slippers, never seemed quite to fit. He struck one observer as a man who was all ends and angles. A Federalist senator, William Plumer of New Hampshire, on calling at the White House, mistook him for "a servant" and carefully noted that he wore a dirty shirt. The senator was fair-minded enough to record the wearing of a clean shirt at a dinner some time later.

Mr. Jefferson's usual manner was good-humored, even sunny, although occasionally abstracted or cynical. His disposition fitted a country squire whose excellent health and enviable digestion gave him a lifelong euphoria, interrupted only by periodic headaches and occasional rheumatic twinges. He had the typical complexion of the freckled gray-eyed Celt. His hair was cut short and powdered. Its color we know, because a correspondent saluted him in a letter, carefully preserved by the recipient, as "You red-headed son of a bitch."

His small talk was built as loosely as his lounging body. Although often brilliant, his conversation was usually rambling and diffuse. It might range from weather and crops to the ingenuity of the Senate in finding excuses to recess during the local race meetings. Following the ponies was a lesser vice than dice; it gave the gentlemen "time for reflection," as he put it, between investments of their risk capital.

That was the exterior Jefferson as seen by the casual caller, but his personality had layers like an onion. His intimate friends knew the next layer, his family knew the third, but no one except God and Thomas Jefferson knew what lay farther inside this sensitive, unsentimental violinist, bird watcher, and horticulturist. We do know that forgiveness of his enemies did not come to him easily.

He broke the precedent of delivering messages orally to the Congress, which was set by George Washington and carried on by John Adams. Jefferson sent his messages to Capitol Hill to be read by a clerk. He said it was to save time, but we know he hated to speak in public, and he was only entirely at ease in the company of kinfolk, artists, savants, and a few Republican leaders. Margaret Bayard Smith, daughter of a warm Federalist and wife of the Republican editor of the new *National Intelligencer*, expected to meet a fanatical boor. To her surprise he was "so meek and mild, yet dignified in his manners, with a voice so soft and low, with a countenance so benignant and intelligent. . . ." But Anthony Merry, the British minister, and his wife did not think the President so dignified and benignant. When Jefferson, lacking a hostess, disregarded all protocol at state dinners, saying "pele-mele is our law," they felt literally degraded and quit coming to the White House. The Spanish minister joined the banquet boycott.

The absence of the diplomatic corps was not of first importance. To Jefferson the dinner party—particularly the stag dinner party—was a principal domestic political tool. Inviting not more than a dozen legislators at a time, he managed to get through the whole list more than once a session. The groups were chosen for compatibility. He seated them at a round table where he would be only first among equals and where private conversations would be difficult. He served his guests himself from a dumb-waiter to preclude the presence of eavesdropping servants. His French chef has been rated highly and his cellar must have been superb. Never dominating the conversation, he guided it away from the shoptalk in which congressmen found themselves already too much immersed, and planted the seeds of his political philosophy by indirection, letting his charm and his menu carry things along. The diplomatic corps knew well enough what he was doing, since it was the customary procedure of European courts, but to the political community in the raw new capital it seems to have been dazzling, and it showed Thomas Jefferson at his guileful best in the tactics of politics.

The contrast between his manner with Mrs. Smith across a tea table and his treatment of the diplomatic corps makes clear the split between his private life and his public bearing as the chief of state of a democratic republic. In private, the gentle introvert; in public matters, the incarnation of a stormy nation of freemen, willing to provide contention, even though he found controversy painful. When relaxed with friends or family, his simple carriage was obviously not the way of a clod, but was more the manner of a negligent, self-assured nobleman, correctly confident of his status and of his own good taste. Yet, in a conference on the public's business, a senator could notice his "stiff gentility or lofty gravity."

It seems very unlikely that such an undramatic and diffident man, whose charm was felt only in private, could have reached the White House in any later generation. His merits were publicized only by his friends. Not for him was the alley fighting of ballot politics. Once he warned his grandson to avoid two kinds of disputants: self-assured young intellectuals with more confidence than knowledge, and bad-tempered, passionate politicians—these latter needed "medical more than moral counsel."

Now peel down to the third layer. There one sees a homesick widower with chronic money troubles, yearning for his children and his grandchildren. His was a great career but rarely a happy life. Between 1772 and 1782, four of his six children died. In 1781 a British army devastated his farm, and the difficulties of his term as governor of Virginia left a faint smear on his reputation. Then in 1782 Mrs. Jefferson died. At the age of forty his life had become a vacuum. It is almost enough to explain his later career to say that political, scientific, and intellectual projects rushed into his vacant soul to fill that vacuum and to make him the man we remember instead of the reclusive squire he wished to be. His two surviving daughters married young. One, Polly Jefferson Eppes, died in childbirth. He had a brief hope of something approaching normal family life when both of his sons-in-law were elected to the House of Representatives, but each of the girls was advanced in pregnancy and dared not risk the rigors of travel to Washington.

After assuming the debts of his father-in-law, his personal finances were forever out of control. In old age he owed $107,000. When his daughters married, there was nothing left for him to take pleasure in except the talk of his intellectual friends, and the forty years of building and rebuilding Palladian Monticello. What he liked about Washington was that it lay between Monticello and "The American Philosophical Society Held at Philadelphia for the Diffusion of Useful Knowledge."

All men claim to be Jeffersonians today. It is doubtful whether the study of any other public man in our national story has been equally absorbing to so many minds. Jefferson's popularity has reached its zenith since 1920. The published evaluations differ so widely that they tell us more about their writers than about Jefferson. There is so much to see, so much to understand about this man of many flashing facets that it requires more self-discipline than most students have been willing to exercise in order to get the emphases in the right places. He would, perhaps, be easier to understand except for the monument of literary evidence he left us—fifty thousand items, dated from 1760 to 1826, one of the richest left by any man. It has not yet been completely mastered.

Thomas Jefferson's work has been scrutinized and searched not so much for understanding as to justify positions which often contradict each other. As the pendulum of public favor swings from generation to generation, he and Alexander Hamilton exchange the roles of Saint Michael and Lucifer. Laissez faire, states' rights, isolationism, agrarianism, rationalism, civil liberty, and constitutional democracy have all been fiercely defended by the use of quotations from Jefferson's writings, regardless of context. On a more sophisticated level of scholarship, professors drub each other with Jeffersonian tags to prove mutually exclusive generalizations. To get all of the academic theorizers under Jefferson's roof, we must label him the Agrarian Commercial Industrial Democratic Federalist. Fortunately for the history of the republic, the Jeffersonian administration, because of its optimistic evaluation of the public's common sense, was keen on explaining everything to the people. The wholly public business, despite the inner personal subtleties and complexities of the leaders, was very well documented, although one must read the public statements with the usual disciplined skepticism.

Nothing that promised the ultimate physical or moral improvement of mankind was alien to the polygonal mind of Thomas Jefferson. With the Adamses and Woodrow Wilson he was one of the four most intellectual of the Presidents of the United States, and he and Wilson are still the objects of hero worship by some Americans. His own heroes were Francis Bacon, Isaac Newton, and John Locke, a "trinity of the three greatest men the world had ever produced." His nominal occupations were farmer and lawyer. He was close to being a true scientist of agriculture, and he was a much more active and successful lawyer, at least up to 1771, when public affairs began to take more and more of his time, than has been generally known.

He mastered Greek and Latin before he was eighteen. Thereafter his reading revolved around the classical authors like a wheel around its hub. Because so few of us nowadays know the classics, we miss much in his mind. He not only knew Greek but he tried to reform its pronunciation by an essay in which he leaned more toward eighteenth-century Greek pronunciation than toward the Italian style then in vogue. He spoke French and Italian, although not fluently, and he had looked into, and had some acquaintance with, forty Indian languages. He also tried to reform the spelling of English. Although he was surely a first-rate writer of his own language, he thought of himself only as a discriminating reader. Omnivorous would be as good an adjective as discriminating. By 1794 he could honestly say he had the best library in the United States. Its 6,500 volumes, all of them collected since a fire destroyed his first library in 1770, formed the nucleus of the Library of Congress.

He must have been a pretty fair violinist or he could not have endured to practice as much as he did, and he certainly has won praise as an architect, but his attitude toward the arts was the attitude of his age. Artists were craftsmen who succeeded if their works pleasantly filled the leisure of the connoisseur by giving him something animating, interesting, attractive to contemplate. Jefferson would not have understood the phrase "art for art's sake," nor could he have approved of the self-appointed Great Tormented Souls who floridly dominated the next generation's lush romanticism.

Thomas Jefferson was more inclined toward science than toward politics. He knew more of applied science, and he knew more scientists, than any of his American contemporaries. He was *the* American agricultural student of his day. For forty-seven years he belonged to the American Philosophical Society; for nearly twenty years he was its president and may have contributed more to its greatness than Benjamin Franklin. Not only was his *Notes on the State of Virginia* (1784–85) a respectable contribution, but his stimulation of the researches of other men, for example, Lewis and Clark, is an influence still felt. His scientific methods will still pass close scrutiny. If the Revolution had failed, and if he had escaped the gallows, he would probably have been barred from public life; in the seclusion of Albemarle County, Virginia, he likely would have become the father of American agricultural chemistry.

Early in life he lost his faith, but not his morals; nevertheless, he had his children baptized in the Anglican Church, attended Anglican services, and had all of his relatives buried according to the Anglican rites. In Pennsylvania, he was Unitarian; in Virginia, Episcopalian; and in the District of Columbia, who-knows-what. He ended as a deist after enduring a lifetime of fierce, intemperate, even slanderous attacks on his infidelity from many who became Unitarians, that is, deists, themselves. According to his home-made theology, Saint Paul corrupted Christianity to prove Christ divine. Better, he said, that men should apply reason to the Book of Nature in order to discover the laws of God.

This remarkable virtuoso, nationally honored for the virtues of the intellect before the time of the establishment of the federal government, was a talented connoisseur of all the arts. In some he had a taste and dexterity which approached professional standards. He was neither pure scientist nor pure philosopher.

Thomas Jefferson's prefederal political career was the career of a man who hated contention, who was better at counsel than at execution, who was better in committee than on the floor. As the scribe of Independence he had drawn together the feelings of his fellow countrymen into superb but prudently circumscribed prose. He gained no glory as revolutionary governor of Virginia and, indeed, barely escaped the censure of the Virginia legislature at the end of his term. The famous legislative reforms in Virginia, which were enacted under his leadership, were merely reforms of the squirearchy.

His mild and conversationally uncontentious liberalism, and his diplomatic experience as minister to France, made him seem the natural choice for Secretary of State in President George Washington's new administration. Jefferson accepted the appointment reluctantly and assumed the office in March, 1790. At that moment in the story, the President and the Secretary were cordial friends, but their relations chilled in the late 1790's. When the new Secretary of State came to New York, he was walking on to a political battlefield. He did not take a place in the array immediately. Indeed, as late as 1792, he still recoiled from direct political action.

An opposition had emerged in the Congress, led by Representative James Madison of Virginia. It was hotly opposed to the Treasury policies of Alexander Hamilton. Madison and John Beckley, the Clerk of the House, carried the antiadministration banner. From early 1791 they had Jefferson's sympathy, but he did not create their faction. It recognized and claimed him as its leader. Not until 1796, during the fierce wrangle over the Jay Treaty, did Jefferson become the public partisan head of antifederalism. The notion that Jefferson founded the opposition was an invention of the Hamiltonians, to suit their short-range vote-getting purposes.

True, Jefferson disapproved of Hamilton's policies because Hamilton influenced the Congress to favor finance and commerce over farming. By late 1792 he was so stirred that he could describe Hamilton's career to the uneasy Washington as "a tissue of machinations against the liberty of the country," but the explanation of the history of the Federalist period as a struggle between Jefferson and Hamilton is useful only as what Broadus Mitchell called "a sociological shorthand." It was Madison and Beckley who organized the group that later made Jefferson its idol. The squire of Monticello has been sketched as a shadowy *provocateur* from 1790 to 1795, holding other men's coats while they smote the enemy in the public prints, but this picture too is a Hamiltonian caricature. Only twice did Jefferson urge men to take up their quills and stab Hamilton, and in each instance it was in a public debate on a question of deep importance. Jefferson was always available at the elbows of the front-rank anti-Hamiltonians, but he did not march in public. The famous liberal sentiments which are so venerated by modern democrats were—after 1776—all written in private letters, not for publication. Even during the campaign of 1800 he stayed at Monticello to supervise the baking of bricks, while letting his political views filter out to the public through letters to his friends.

Thomas Jefferson was never a flaming radical. His environment made it impossible, although there is a monumental Jeffersonian mythology which makes him out a doctrinaire democrat. In truth, he believed in getting what seemed best for the public good with as little painful acrimony and criticism as possible. He had no oratorical talent as a crowd pleaser and he never made a speech that brought cheers. The energy and admiration of his friends, not his own qualities of leadership, put him in the White House.

If the French Revolution had not caused a recanvass of fundamental libertarian principles, he and his supporters probably could not have pulled off the electoral coup of 1800. Nor was his election a victory for infidel rationalism. It was the counterattack of theologically conservative farmers against the Federalists' aristocratic contempt for America's sunburned agricultural drudges. They thought they were voting for electors, or assemblymen who would choose electors, who would favor Thomas Jefferson, a Whiggish moderate, whose only controversial publications had been the Declaration of Independence and the Virginia Statute for Religious Freedom long, long before. And they were right.

Thomas Jefferson never wrote a formal comprehensive treatise of political philosophy. His views were expressed in parts—in the Declaration of Independence, in his *Notes on Virginia,* his arguments for legal reform in Virginia, the Kentucky Resolutions of 1798 (the authorship of which was unknown when he was elected), inaugural addresses, messages to the Congress, and, most of all, in private correspondence and conversation. Friends and enemies, with little public help from him, pushed him forward to accept the Federalists' label which tagged him as the chief symbol of opposition to Hamiltonian Federalism. Liberty, not democracy, was the key word in his sometimes inconsistent political talk and correspondence.

When faced by a political problem, he went to printed classical and modern sources for solutions which harmonized with his broad political experience and observation. He can properly be called a professional scholar of legal history and of the political history of the seventeenth century, but his historical method was utilitarian and servile. It was not used for pure understanding and liberal learning. Theoretical treatises which could not be applied immediately to concrete and present questions had little appeal for him. His intellectual pedigree included the Epicureans; the Stoics; a purely human Jesus Christ; John Locke; the Scottish commonsense philosophers; Adam Smith; Henry St. John, Viscount Bolingbroke; Henry Home, Lord Kames; and Dugald Stewart. Because the French *philosophes* venerated some of the same masters, Jefferson was at ease when he talked with them in France. In a sense, Jefferson's outlook in 1801 was reactionary. He consistently pressed for a return to the pure republicanism of the years of the American Revolution.

How much his mind owed to France is a fair question. His *Commonplace Book* shows his views were pretty well formed long before the French Revolution. The only French author who was extensively quoted in it was Charles Secondat de Montesquieu, but Jefferson only copied out the parts he already agreed with. No doubt his residence in France broadened his political outlook and, at the same time, stiffened his repugnance to monarchy, aristocracy, land monopoly, and urbanism. What he saw in France alerted him to the necessity for certain political safeguards to guarantee and to preserve agrarian republicanism. But he remained more Whig than *philosophe.*

Jefferson's faith in reason, education, and the future of America was fixed, but his procedures were adjustable. Unlike most of his contemporaries, he had a constitutional theory of change—"the earth," he said, "always belongs to the living." His political thought was a search for intellectual props for the democratic republican state. Such thinking is the method of an eclectic utilitarian rather than the method of a political philosopher. Because he was optimistically working for something new in the world's limitless future, his philosophical affirmations were necessarily a little indefinite. But certainly he was no doctrinaire. He studied history to learn the traps into which Great Britain had fallen. From his study he concluded that all had gone wrong since the Norman Conquest. Studying the age before the Norman Conquest, he thought he discovered an Anglo-Saxon utopia, an antifeudal utopia, which might be re-established in North America by directed progress toward the perfection of the past. Although he was a materialist in science, he accepted the notion of moral responsibility in man. Because he erroneously assumed that all men were as interested in public concerns as he was, he believed the United States could be as perfect as King Alfred's England, if every child were taught history as Thomas Jefferson understood it.

By a careful selection of his most liberal remarks, a specious case can be constructed to support a Jeffersonian anarchism, or something near it. The people, he said, if they had the proper education and the correct public information, were the only sure reliance for the preservation of liberty. A rebellion every twenty years might be a good thing. Constitutions and laws should periodically expire. "The tree of liberty must be refreshed from time to time with the blood of patriots and tyrants. It is it's [*sic*] natural manure." No men were congenitally of the governing or the governed classes. The Constitution must be changed only by amendment, not by interpretation. He even exceeded Locke in toleration, because he believed ridicule would kill opinions which were morally harmful to society. And, finally, there is the classic, much-quoted, but not authentic aphorism, "that government is best which governs least."

All of these politically relaxed apothegms can be matched by seemingly antagonistic opinions and legislative proposals: tax-supported schools, public libraries, and dispensaries, subsidized newspaper circulation, subdivision of great landholdings and the legal frustration of land speculators by geometrically proportional taxation, a literacy test for voting, a national transport system. He did not believe in simple, direct government, but wished for a sharp separation of powers and difficult methods of amending constitutions. Some of his views on the vigor of the powers of the President, written or spoken privately to George Washington during the 1790's, would have surprised his followers if they had been published.

The apparent paradox can be reconciled by remembering that liberty was his navigating star, even though there were cloudy nights in his career when he steered in another direction. He did not fear any act of the state except encroachment on civil liberty. Civil liberty comprised those rights guaranteed in the several American bills of rights which were drawn and ratified between 1776 and 1791. He would support any other use of that political power and authority which had been *delegated* by constitutional compact, if it seemed for the common good, and if it did not limit civil liberty. This liberalism had a strong agrarian color, which limits its relevance to the problems of a later industrial society. When he spoke of the people as the guardians of liberty, he meant farmers, who comprised nearly the whole people of the United States. City mobs were easily corruptible by largesse from the public funds. Landowning farmers were unlikely to tax themselves in order to corrupt themselves. Like the several varieties of physiocrats, he opposed mercantilism, and his high opinion of Adam Smith's *Wealth of Nations*—"of money and commerce . . . the best book . . ."—suggests Smith as the source of his opposition. In sum, he thought if land were fairly distributed, and the business community (meaning the Federalists) could be prevented from manipulating the economy in its own interest, liberty was safe.

His thinking had already contributed to the form of the United States. His pamphlet *A Summary View* (1774) was among the first by a native American to forecast sharply the division of power and authority now found in our federal arrangement. By interpretation or misinterpretation, the implicit theory of state nullification of federal law, as written in his then anonymous "Kentucky Resolutions" of 1798, was to have catastrophic consequences long after his death. As a social-contract theorist, he believed the state of nature to be a state of peace. Applying this theory to international relations, he concluded that war was unnatural, peace natural. Therefore, he had sought and would continue to seek peace by every means possible.

Jefferson would have been more than human if he had always practiced what he preached. In private life he showed a certain meanness of spirit by carefully recording much of the derogatory gossip he heard about his political rivals and enemies, and having the manuscript bound as a literary monument to the difficulties of his cause. He also privately slandered his opponents by ungrounded accusations of monarchism. As a public official, at one time or other he supported or countenanced loyalty oaths for those of doubtful fidelity to the Revolution and internment camps for political suspects, drafted a bill of attainder, championed a peace process of outlawry (there being no process of extradition of fugitives), urged prosecutions for seditious libel, left himself open to charges of unconstitutional search and seizure, censored reading, and rated prospective professors according to their political orthodoxy. Of these lapses it can be said that they were in character for a man who so admired seventeenth-century Whiggery. He was never committed to the tyrannical side of his opponents, he aided the victory of liberty, and his abstract and formal teachings became the enduring positions while his concrete departures from his own principles were temporary.

On the immediate problems facing the union in the year of his inauguration as President, he appears to have joined with Edmund Pendleton and John Taylor of Caroline in a proposal to amend the federal Constitution (published in Richmond in October, 1801) which would have prohibited the re-election of the President, have given the Congress the appointment of judges and ambassadors, have shortened the terms of senators or have made them removable by their constituents, have prevented the appointment of judges and members of the Congress to other offices, have made judges removable by vote of the Congress, and have limited the federal borrowing power.

The proposals to "reform" the Constitution were not the proposals of the library politician. They were the reactions of Virginia Republicans as they looked back in anger at the Federalist policies which enacted the Hamiltonian fiscal program and the Alien and Sedition Acts. If the Republicans had remained in the minority for another decade or so, we would have heard more about these propositions.

Macdonough's victory on Lake Champlain, 1814. The decisive battle of the War of 1812 occurred neither on land nor on the high seas. England's hope for victory were dashed when her invasion from Canada was turned back on Lake Champlain. (Library of Congress)

7 The Second War with England

The position of the United States in the 1790s was in some respects like that of new nations emerging today. In the Revolution it had cut the apron strings tying it to the mother country, but this assertion of independence meant no estrangement from the family of Western civilization. The attachment was too deep for anything like that, and political independence had virtually nothing to do with economic independence. With a primary-stage, extractive, expanding economy, the United States depended on other members of the Atlantic community for capital and manufactures and for outlets of its own marketable surplus. In addition, the new nation was vitally concerned with the events taking place in Europe—principally the French Revolution and the upheaval it caused. Having begun in 1789—the same year, coincidentally, that the United States launched its government under the Constitution—the French Revolution had evolved into a general European war by 1792, when the other monarchs of Europe sought to restore the crown in France and thus prevent the possible spread of the revolutionary virus. For the next 23 years Europe was racked by what amounted to a world war, and Americans were affected by this struggle in both convictions and cash. Jeffersonians saw the French Revolution as a great battle against entrenched privilege; Hamiltonians saw it as an irresponsible and destructive uprising by a rabble who would gut a great civilization. Americans have never been more deeply divided over a foreign issue.

That issue had profound consequences for the American economy. The patterns of international trade were reshuffled; alternative trade routes had to be plotted, new markets developed, and domestic manufactures created to replace imported ones cut off by blockades. Extraordinary profits were made in trading with both England and France, but at the same time hundreds of American vessels were captured or sunk by both nations, and thousands of seamen were stranded in foreign ports, imprisoned, or even killed. Thus foreign policy became a question of first priority for the new government, and skillful diplomacy was essential.

Another area in which foreign policy was critical was on the American continent itself. As the United States expanded westward, increased contacts with the empires of European powers brought complications and conflicts. Until Jay's Treaty in 1795, England controlled thousands of square miles of American territory along the frontier to the northwest. Spain controlled the mouth of the Mississippi and the area along the southwestern frontier. Frontiersmen were convinced that both nations sought to maintain their control over the Indians by inciting them against American settlers.

For almost 20 years the United States avoided entry into the world war. Such a stand of neutrality was always difficult, because the American people were involved in the emotions and interests of that conflict, and because the actions of the belligerents bit deeply into their freedoms. Why then the change of heart in 1812? Abuses on the high seas were no greater in 1812 than before; if anything, they were fewer. Nor were there any new developments in the West in the weeks or even months prior to the decision for war. The battle of Tippecanoe had been won seven months before, and there had been no major incidents since then. Some historians maintain, therefore, that the United States went to war in 1812 because there had developed a national psychology different from that of earlier years. Perhaps the "long train of abuses," as others had been called in the Declaration of Independence, had had their cumulative effect.

History is concerned with cause and effect relationships in time. Without that it is nothing but antiquarianism or genealogy or a meaningless chronicle of events. Causation, however, is tricky business, humans being as complex as they are; and the record is often either fractional or "loaded." It seems especially important to understand how nations get into wars and at the same time especially difficult, because so much emotion becomes involved as the war progresses. For reasons such as those suggested in the preceding paragraph, the War of 1812 is a particularly knotty example of this problem.

We can never fully recover the past; the record of yesterday is already dim and fragmentary. The historian therefore always works partly in the dark, groping to understand cause and effect relationships. On the other hand, we can never fully understand the significance of events even while they are happening. Statesmen act, and peoples go to war, according to what they *think* is reality. In 1812 many frontiersmen were hot for war because they believed England was inciting Indians. That they thought so is more important in understanding the coming of war than whether England was actually doing so. The following selections show how the realities of 1812 look to two recent historians, in contrast to how they looked to the President who summoned the nation to war and to the principal leader of the "War-Hawks" in Congress.

Robert G. Albion and Jennie B. Pope   # The Maritime Problem

The American shipping industry, which had wallowed after the winning of independence from Great Britain, took on new life when the French Revolution became an international war in the 1790s. Pouring their own energies into the war, both France and England paid handsomely for

cargo carriage in neutral ships. For two decades, both sides used—and abused—the American merchant marine. Each of them seized hundreds of American vessels bound for enemy ports, and only the constantly increasing profits made the Americans' risks worthwhile. After 1795, however, French seizures of American ships became so frequent and often so brutal that the United States came to the verge of war. In the years 1798 to early 1800, there was undeclared naval war with France, complete with frigate duels. A nominal peace between England and France in 1802 caused a temporary lull in both losses and profits, but the martial storm returned the following year. Albion and Pope describe the maritime strains of the ensuing decade in the following selection. [Reprinted from Sea Lanes in Wartime: The American Experience, 1775–1942 *by Robert Greenhalgh Albion and Jennie Barnes Pope by permission of W. W. Norton & Company, Inc. Copyright 1942 by W. W. Norton & Company, Inc. Copyright Renewed. © 1970 by Robert Greenhalgh Albion and Jennie Barnes Pope.]*

But the second round of the Anglo-French conflict, recommencing in 1803, was a more serious matter for the Americans as well as for the belligerents. Napoleon gave France a more stable government, increased its naval strength, and sent its victorious armies into almost every nation of the Continent. England, between the threat of invasion and the loss of its European markets, was in no mood to be complaisant about the role of neutrals. With sea power its most potent weapon, Britain used it vigorously and effectively.

During the first phase, our chief troubles had come from undisciplined swarms of British and French privateers; now we were to encounter sweeping national policies carried out in a more orderly but, at the same time, more ruthlessly thorough manner. For a while, American seaborne trade flourished as never before; then came the series of violent interruptions, when it was caught between the rival belligerent measures.

One distinctive new feature was Britain's wholesale and very successful use of blockades. Instead of relying simply upon cruising at large to catch the enemy or neutrals at sea, warships were kept on constant vigil off scores of ports. On the grand scale, powerful fleets of ships of the line held continual watch to prevent any concentration of the rapidly increasing French forces, which might gain control of the Channel long enough for Napoleon's Grand Army to be ferried over to England in flatboats. As Mahan expressed it, "Those far distant, storm-beaten ships, upon which the Grand Army never looked, stood between it and dominion of the world." The Americans were more concerned with the lesser cruiser forces stationed off neutral ports, which in time meant American as well as European. Day in and day out, they waited to check the comings and goings of merchantmen as well as of stray French cruisers.

This expanded role of the Royal Navy called for more ships, and that, in turn, meant more sailors. Many Englishmen were deserting the "floating hell" of their naval service for the freer life aboard the American merchant marine, which, too, was growing rapidly and offered higher wages. To England, American naturalization did not count; "once an Englishman, always an Englishman." Britain claimed the right to recover its seagoing subjects wherever it might find them, in port or even on the high seas. It was not always easy to recognize bona fide Englishmen in an American crew, but the Royal Navy generally allowed itself the benefit of any doubts. Such was the galling practice of impressment that eventually helped to goad the United States into war in 1812.

Impressment was no novelty, though it became acute about 1803. For more than a century, the Royal Navy had relied upon abductors and press gangs, who had long spread terror through all the seacoast towns. Its service was so unpopular that most men in their right minds refused to join voluntarily. The American colonists, protected by an act of Queen Anne's time, had opposed any attempts violently. John Adams in 1769 had secured a verdict of "justifiable homicide" for a Marblehead sailor who had killed a British frigate lieutenant while resisting impressment. Even before the current war began, the United States was protesting the snatching of men from its vessels in British ports. The outcry grew when early in 1796 officers from H.M.S. *Regulus* removed five men from the crew of an American ship by force, not in port, but on the high seas. That precedent rapidly spread into general practice.

Congress, contending that a nation's merchantmen under its flag were an extension of its territory, tried to mitigate a situation which it lacked the power to check. Among other things, it provided American seamen with certificates of citizenship, which the British scorned as often being forged and too easily negotiable. According to a senator's later comment, if a sailor had a "protection," the British called it a forgery; if not, they considered the lack as proof of noncitizenship.

The dispute missed a satisfactory settlement early in 1803, when the American minister at London took tactful advantage of a temporary lull in the fighting to promise to bar British seamen from American merchantmen if impressment were stopped. Only the consent of Lord St. Vincent, a tough old sea dog in charge of the Admiralty, was needed, but his quibbling balked the solution; and in a short time England was in the thick of war again. Later, a bill was introduced in Congress to declare impressment piracy, with the death penalty, and with a bounty of two hundred dollars offered to any American seaman for killing anyone trying to impress him; but action was postponed.

Meanwhile, the seizures did not stop. By 1806, American seamen were being taken within sight of Sandy Hook. A little tragedy was re-enacted hundreds of times during these years. An American vessel would be forced to lay to, with topsails helplessly backed, while a boat came over from a British cruiser. Even the toughest foremast hand must have had his moment of terror when the boarding naval lieutenant came over the side. If his visit meant the seizure of ship or cargo, that was a matter for the captain and owners to worry about; at least the case would go through the forms of legal trial at some Vice-Admiralty Court. But if the lieutenant called for a line-up of the crew, the future liberty and happiness of any one in that group might depend upon the snap judgment of that haughty young man of twenty, inspecting the anxious line of sailors. Even a Maine twang or a Georgia drawl might not save a likely looking topmast hand if the officer pronounced him an Englishman. Off he went for forced service in His Majesty's fleet, where enlistments never terminated save through disability or death. . . .

American cargoes, as well as seamen, were running afoul of the Royal Navy. . . . England's reasons for the change of policy were strongly set forth in a book, *War in Disguise; or The Frauds of the Neutral Flags,* written during the anxious months when invasion scares put England in no mood to humor even its best customer. The author, James Stephens, who had had ample experience in the prize courts of the West Indies and London, argued that England was letting slip through its fingers one of the main advantages of sea power by letting its enemies trade with their sugar islands in neutral bottoms. Not a single enemy merchantman dared appear on the high seas, yet France received its sugar from Guadeloupe more cheaply than England could bring it from Jamaica. He charged that the Americans did not really own those sugar cargoes but simply gave neutral coverage for a consideration. . . .

The ubiquitous cruisers of the Royal Navy, along with British privateers, were soon snapping up American merchantmen all over the seven seas. . . . By 1804 American vessels did not have to travel beyond their own coast to meet British cruisers exercising control of the seas. They were beginning to haunt the immediate approaches to the major American ports. The *Guerrière,* which in due time would receive her punishment, stood watch near Boston Light. A squadron was posted to check the comings and goings in Chesapeake Bay. Most conspicuous were several cruisers patrolling the waters around Sandy Hook. The frigate *Leander,* the most persistent of this last exasperating group, made herself particularly obnoxious. As one of her midshipmen later described her annoying routine:

> Every morning at daybreak, we set about arresting the progress of all vessels we saw, firing off guns to the right and left to make every ship that was running in heave to, or wait until we had leisure to send a boat on board "to see" in our lingo, "what she was made of." I have frequently known a dozen, and sometimes a couple of dozen, ships lying a league or two off the port, losing their fair wind, their tide, and worse than all their market, for many hours, sometimes the whole day, before our search was completed.

Inward bound New York vessels from the West Indies and abroad were boarded within sight of Sandy Hook light and sent to Halifax under prize crews. Seamen were impressed by the dozen from British as well as from American merchantmen.

The climax was the attack by the *Leander* on the little sloop *Richard* as she came up the Jersey coast about a quarter of a mile off Sandy Hook on April 24, 1806. The *Leander* started firing without warning; one shot landed forty feet ahead; another flew directly over the sloop; and as she obediently started to heave to, a third shot struck the quarter rail. A splinter carried off the head of the helmsman, John Pierce, brother of the master. His headless body was viewed by angry crowds on the New York water front before being laid in state at the City Hall. A huge mass meeting passed vigorous resolutions against the "repeated outrages committed by foreign ships of war at the mouths of our harbors." Within ten days, President Jefferson issued a proclamation calling for the arrest of the *Leander's* captain, forbidding the captains of all three men-of-war from ever again entering United States waters, commanding the ships to leave, and barring any shore assistance in the form of food, pilotage, or repairs. The squadron did not depart at once; incoming vessels continued to be seized.

During all this, American shipping and commerce were both flourishing as never before. Even if a few hundred vessels were seized, thousands successfully completed their highly profitable voyages. Combined imports and exports, which had been only $52,000,000 in 1792, had risen to $205,000,000 by 1801. With the peace interval, they slumped to $110,-000,000 in 1803. Then they started up again; $162,000,000 in 1804, $215,000,000 in 1805, $221,000,000 in 1806, and finally hit the high-water mark of $246,000,000 in 1807, a level not touched again until 1835.

All along the coast from Maine to Georgia every maritime community was still enjoying the rush of the thriving business boom, blissfully unconscious of the blight that was about to descend. As one traveler recorded his impressions of the bustling activity of New York harbor:

The port was filled with shipping and the wharves were crowded with commodities of every description. Bales of cotton, wool,. and merchandize; barrels of pot-ash, rice, flour, and salt provisions; hogsheads of sugar, chests of tea, puncheons of rum, and pipes of wine; boxes, cases, packs and packages of all sizes and denominations, were strewed upon the wharves and landing places, or upon the decks of the shipping. All was noise and bustle. The carters were driving in every direction; and the sailors and labourers upon the wharves, and on board the vessels, were moving their ponderous burthens from place to place.

Two months later, all that was changed. With its commerce at flood tide, America suddenly withdrew from the sea. In the dislocations and readjustments of the next seven years, that exuberant atmosphere of 1807 would never be recaptured. Every schoolboy knows why—Berlin and Milan decrees, Orders in Council, Embargo, Nonintercourse, Macon Act, and War of 1812.

John Lambert, the traveler who described the rushed and thriving port scenes in November, returned in April to find a hopeless inertia along the water front:

The coffee-house slip, the wharves and quays along South-street, presented no longer the bustle and activity that had prevailed there five months before.

The port, indeed, was full of shipping; but they were dismantled and laid up. Their decks were cleared, their hatches fastened down, and scarcely a sailor was to be found on board. Not a box, bale, cask, barrel or package, was to be seen upon the wharves. Many of the counting houses were shut up, or advertised to be let, and the few solitary merchants, clerks, porters, and labourers, that were to be seen, were walking about with their hands in their pockets . . . a few coasting sloops, and schooners, which were clearing out for some ports in the United States, were all that remained of that immense business which was carried on a few months before. . . . In fact, everything presented a melancholy appearance. The streets near the waterside were almost deserted, grass had begun to grow upon the wharves.

The same stagnation would have been found in a dozen other ports, from Portland to Savannah and around to New Orleans. Soup kitchens and other relief agencies alone found plenty of customers. Unemployed seamen, who had not found their way to Canada, were "on the town." But plenty of other people were in a similar fix; shipwrights, longshoremen, and clerks were also suffering from the sudden dislocation of their livelihood. Insolvent debtors by the hundreds crowded the jails, with now and then a suicide. Farmers felt the drop in the price of wheat from $1.45 to $1.00 a bushel and of flour from $7.13 to $5.25 a barrel. Southern planters did not escape, with cotton at thirteen instead of twenty cents a pound.

This puncturing of the balloon of merchant shipping did not come from a clear sky. Even in those booming summer months of 1807, dark clouds were gathering on the distant horizon, while nearer home the British cruisers were increasingly insolent. No longer content with overhauling merchantmen, they were now highhandedly insulting American government armed vessels, even warships. A revenue cutter, for example, with Vice-President Tompkins aboard, was fired upon as she left Chesapeake Bay for New York. A naval gunboat, approaching New York, also came under British naval fire and was forced to send a midshipman over to the two waylaying cruisers. The customhouse barge was sent to warn them off, only to be boarded and searched in insolent fashion. A deeper humiliation awaited the frigate *Chesapeake* off the Virginia Capes in June. Halted on the high seas by the fire of the British *Leopard*, which killed and wounded several men, she was forced to bow to the seizure of four deserters aboard her. This was the last straw for the aroused nation, particularly when England postponed immediate disavowal of the affront and replied instead with orders for increased impressment.

Far more significant in ultimate effects was the use to which Napoleon was putting those same summer months of 1807. His recent smashing victories had made him master of much of the Continent, but in those preaircraft days, a few miles of salt water kept England safe from his armies. Attempts to defeat it through Ireland, Egypt, and direct invasion had all failed; its gold was still financing the Europeans, who kept on fighting him. Now he had found a grandiose project to bring his most persistent enemy to its knees. This was nothing less than drying up the source of its gold by closing all the ports of Europe to its manufactures and products from beyond the seas, whether borne in British or in neutral vessels. Napoleon had announced this program in the Berlin Decree of December, 1806, but he had been too busy to act until he stopped fighting the Russians on the same June day that the *Leopard* overhauled the *Chesapeake*. Four weeks later he secured the co-operation of the Czar at their famous conference on a raft in the Niemen; and soon afterwards, most of the Continent had been persuaded or compelled to close all ports from the Baltic to the Mediterranean.

England, faced with the loss of its valuable Continental markets, countered vigorously with new Orders in Council in November. By these, no vessel might trade with the ports involved in Napoleon's Continental system without first stopping at a British port to unload her cargo and pay duties upon it, before being allowed to reload and proceed. In December, Napoleon struck back from Milan with another decree; any vessel, which submitted by entering a British port or was visited by a cruiser of the Royal Navy, was to be a fair prize. . . .

Obviously, if such rival decrees were enforced at their face value, neutrals would be getting no more profits from their carrying trade. Their vessels faced a quandary: If they submitted to the British regulations, they risked seizure in any European port, but if they tried evasion, they were fair game for the ever present cruisers of the Royal Navy. According to Mahan:

> The imperial soldiers were turned into coastguardmen to shut out Great Britain from her markets; the British ships became revenue cutters to prohibit the trade of France. The neutral carrier, pocketing his pride, offered his services to either for pay, and the other then regarded him as taking part in hostilities.

All this put Yankee shipping and its rich profits in such jeopardy that the government worked strenuously to obtain a relaxation of either or both of these belligerent measures. Jefferson's solution was the negation of "freedom of the seas." By withdrawing American vessels from foreign trade, he hoped not only to avoid war and prevent seizures, but also to show Britain and Napoleon that those neutral bottoms filled an indispensable need. In that way he expected to find that the harsh regulations would soon be relaxed.

Three days before Christmas, Congress embodied this new withdrawal policy of Jefferson's in the celebrated Embargo Act that was to become effective immediately. It forbade any American vessel to clear from an American port for a foreign destination. Except for certain British goods prohibited by another act just going into effect, American vessels already abroad might bring in cargoes, but once in, could not legally clear for foreign ports again. Messengers were rushed up and down the coast to instruct the customs collectors to put the law into operation immediately. Congress knew that if a week's advance notice were given, scarcely an American vessel would be found still in port at the end of that time.

The northbound courier, by dint of hard riding, reached New York before dawn on the fourth day to give the city one of the liveliest Christmas days in its history. By seven that morning, printed handbills with the text of the act were being distributed. As McMaster described the ensuing excitement:

On a sudden the streets were full of merchants, ship-owners, ship-captains, supercargoes, and sailors hurrying toward the water-front. Astonished at this unusual commotion, men of all sorts followed and by eight o'clock the wharves were crowded with spectators, cheering the little fleet of half-laden ships which, with all sail spread, was beating down the harbor. None of them had clearances. Many were half-manned. Few had more than part of a cargo. One which had just come in, rather than be embargoed, went off without breaking bulk. At the sight of the headings on the handbills, the captains made crews of the first seamen they met, and, with a few hurried instructions from the owners, pushed into the stream.

In spite of this scramble, hundreds of vessels failed to get away. By one estimate 537 were left in port, 666 by another. Several arrivals were given in the *Evening Post* the day after Christmas, but their announcement was followed by the ominous statement, "No Clearances in the Future." . . .

In March, 1809, during the last week of Jefferson's presidency, Congress finally repealed the Embargo. Then and since, men have been divided in their estimates of its wisdom. It had at least accomplished what Jefferson had had in mind when he wrote, "This exuberant commerce brings us into collision with other powers in every sea, and will force us into every war with European powers." The wholesale seizures that would otherwise have probably resulted from the belligerent decrees were radically reduced. Few seamen were impressed, and dangerous "incidents" were safely avoided. That aspect of the voluntary abandonment of "freedom of the seas" was enough to encourage similar legislation in neutrality acts in later years. On the other hand, the Embargo did not succeed in forcing any concessions from either Britain or Napoleon. American shipping services and markets proved to be less indispensable than Jefferson had hoped. The mills of Lancashire suffered from short rations; the West Indies worried about their food supply; and England seemed almost entirely cut off from foreign markets when the Act went into effect. By an unfortunate coincidence, from the American point of view, Spain and Portugal with their extensive colonies became available as British markets a few months later. Napoleon, too, found that he could get along without American shipping. Both his decrees and the Orders in Council remained in full force.

The end of the Embargo did not bring complete freedom of action; in its place Congress substituted Nonintercourse. Altogether, trade with England was permitted for only fifteen months between the enactment of the Embargo and the end of the war in 1815. Still expecting its restrictive measures to cause the belligerents to modify their decrees, Congress continued to forbid trade with British and French territories as long as the oppressive measures remained in force, but elsewhere it now permitted American shipping to go freely. This Nonintercourse lasted from March, 1809, to May, 1810; and for a few months in the summer of 1809 trade was permitted with England through negotiations with the British minister, but his work was disavowed at London.

Nonintercourse was superseded by Macon's Act, which allowed free trade with the proviso that if either France or Britain ended its obnoxious regulations, the United States would co-operate by renewing Nonintercourse against the other. Napoleon duped the Americans into believing he had suspended his decrees, and consequently trade with British territories was again prohibited in May, 1811, and was not resumed before war was declared in 1812.

The Western Problem

Bradford Perkins

Foreign policy was just as critical a problem in the West as on the seas—with a significant difference: France was not involved, only England. When Spain ceded Louisiana to France in 1802, Westerners were more fearful than ever that their artery, the Mississippi, might be choked off, because the control was now in the hands of Napoleon instead of the feeble grasp of Spain. But the threat of a Napoleonic Louisiana was never fulfilled; the American purchase of Louisiana in 1803 removed Western concern about France. England, however, was a different story. Frontiersmen were convinced that the English were behind Indian uprisings and economic slumps caused by blockades. The Englishman was the traditional enemy, and he was increasingly resented along the northwest frontier.

Only in the twentieth century have historians come to appreciate the role of the West in the international tensions between 1790 and 1812. With that appreciation has also come perplexity and disagreement concerning the real nature and importance of that role. In the following selection, Bradford Perkins describes and analyzes the events in the West and the mood of its people in the two years before the start of the war. [Bradford Perkins, Prologue to War: England and the United States, 1805–1812 *(Berkeley, California: University of California Press, 1961). Reprinted by permission.]*

While Foster, Madison, and Monroe vacationed, news of an impending Indian war flowed through the Appalachians. In October, 1809, Governor William Henry Harrison of the Indiana Territory inveigled Indians assembled at Fort Wayne into a cession of nearly 3 million acres. The Madison administration, while ratifying this treaty, directed Harrison not to occupy the ceded territory immediately. The weak warnings of Secretary of War Eustis, however, deterred the governor far less than threats delivered to him in the summer of 1810 and again in 1811 by Tecumseh, speaking for a new Indian league organized by Tecumseh himself and his brother, the Prophet. Harrison's provocative statements to the legislature, accounts of increased subsidies to tribes that visited Canada, and, in 1811, news that Tecumseh had gone southward to attempt to add other tribes to his confederacy ignited a real fear of Indian hostilities all along the Western frontier. . . .

In July, 1811, responding to Harrison's reports of approaching war, Secretary Eustis ordered a detachment of regulars to the governor's aid. Three days later the Secretary wrote that Madison still hoped for peace and trusted that Harrison would follow a pacific policy. As Madison and Eustis should have known, peremptory orders alone could restrain the aggressive governor. Harrison gathered together an expedition of regulars and volunteers, construed in his own fashion directives from Eustis, and plunged northward to break up the Indian forces and establish white possession of the Fort Wayne cession. At dawn on November 7, 1811, Indians from the Prophet's Town attacked Harrison's army. At the cost of about 200 men, Harrison narrowly held his position, then burned the Indian settlement and retired precipitately to the Ohio. News of this encounter, called the battle of Tippecanoe, ran swiftly across the nation.

Americans blamed the British for the Indian troubles. During the crisis preceding the Jay treaty and again after the *Chesapeake* affair, friction with the Western tribes had accompanied difficulties with England. Few Americans accepted as coincidental a recurrence of this friction in 1810 and 1811. As early as 1810, calling for the conquest of Canada, Henry Clay demanded: "Is it nothing to us to extinguish the torch that lights up savage warfare?" Newspapers in Clay's part of the country took up the cry. One called for decisive action to wipe out the threat of "the tomahawk and scalping knife, which for many years past and at this very moment the inhuman blood-thirsty cabinet of St. James had incessantly endeavored to bring on the *women* and *children* of our western frontiers." Another sanctimoniously bewailed the fact that "British intrigue and British gold . . . has greater influence with them [the Indians] of late than American justice and benevolence."

After Tippecanoe such complaints multiplied. Andrew Jackson denounced "Secret agents of Great Britain" as catalysts of the attack. The Lexington *Reporter* asked if Congress intended to "treat the citizens of the *Western country* as they have treated the [impressed] seamen" for eighteen years, then added, "The *whole* body of Western citizens call for the probing of this British villiny to the bottom." Back East, Duane's *Aurora* proclaimed that "war has been begun with British arms and by the Indians instigated by British emissaries. The blood of American citizens have already been shed in actual war, begun undeclared." . . .

The easiest way to end the Indian threat, many agreed, was to drive the British from Canada. Jefferson considered the conquest of Canada, at least as far as the walls of Quebec, an almost costless corollary of war with England. During the war scare of 1807 one of his young supporters even argued for enlistment for the duration rather than for a twelve-month period, on the ground the former would actually be shorter. Five years later Andrew Jackson appealed to the youth of Tennessee to seize the opportunity of "performing a military *promenade*" by joining him in a visit to Niagara Falls and Quebec. "That which pleases me most in these people, Monseigneur," the French minister reported to his chief, "Is the tranquil confidence they have in their means of aggression and of resistance." Sérurier intended no sarcasm.

In 1811 and 1812 few Americans stopped to ask for a real "probing of . . . British villiny to the bottom." After all, the *Independent Chronicle* argued, "it is not rational to conclude that the Indians would have taken up arms against us, had they not been instigated by British mercenaries." Time did not provide evidence to back up this logic. In his war message the President merely stated that it would be difficult to account for Indian hostilities unless they had been inspired by the British. A House committee report on the message, presented by John C. Calhoun, admitted the evidence was uncertain but added, "your committee are not disposed to occupy much time in investigating."

British policy was not what most Americans assumed it to be. Canadian agents maintained close connections with Indians living in American territory and sometimes encouraged the Indians to think Britain would support an offensive war against the United States. At the top level, however, British policy was essentially precautionary, based, as Castlereagh put it, on the principle that "we are to consider not so much their Use as Allies, as their Destructiveness if Enemies." Indian neutrality in an Anglo-American war, although desired by Bathurst even after hostilities began in 1812, was felt to be unattainably utopian. Britain therefore tried to make sure that if war came the Indians would side with her. Both to husband Indian strength and to avoid a flare-up against Britain precisely like that which arose in 1811, the Cabinet tried to prevent war between Indians and frontiersmen.

Sir James Craig and Isaac Brock, the principal Canadian executors of this policy, loyally attemped to implement it. Craig once even informed Washington of Indian plans he was attempting to check, and in 1811 Brock specifically stated to the Indians that British supplies would cease if they fought the United States. Brock warned his superiors that the distinction between encouraging Indians and simply preserving their friendship was a difficult one, and after Tippecanoe he added that the existing policy would eventually destroy British influence among the tribes. However, only a month before the American declaration of war he wrote, "The utmost attention is continued to be paid that no just cause of umbrage is given, in our intercourse with the western tribes, to the United States Government." Policy was one thing, execution another; from time to time subordinate officials and Brock himself stepped over the line sketched by London. But no responsible Englishman desired the clash of arms which began along Harrison's perimeter, knowing full well that this could only strengthen America's sense of grievance.

History is often influenced as much by erroneous conviction as by truth. Believing that the tendrils of Indian war wound back to Canada, many Westerners desired to apply their axes to the root. In addition, some Americans doubtless wanted to conquer Canada to gain for their country a monopoly of the fur trade. John Randolph, who ascribed every conceivable evil motive to the War Hawks, alleged that the Western farmer and his spokesmen wanted to plunder the British Empire of fertile agricultural land in Upper Canada. But millions of acres of desirable land were still available south of the border, and on the other hand British possession of Canada did not prevent frontiersmen from settling there. Four of every five settlers in Upper Canada were American by either birth or descent, only a small proportion of them Loyalist refugees. Any Westerner troubled by a land shortage could follow a well-worn path to Canada. National loyalties did not yet have binding force, at least among impoverished or marginal farmers.

A more convincing economic explanation of rising Western discontent emphasizes fluctuations in the price level. The West, particularly the southerly cotton and tobacco areas, overexpanded production after 1805. For a short period farmers got extraordinary profits, but low quality, high costs, and feeble marketing and credit structures made the West really "a sort of marginal area in relation to world markets." When prices collapsed in 1808, Westerners blamed foreign restrictions on trade, ultimately concentrating on the Orders in Council. The West supported commercial warfare until it was proved ineffective, then demanded more vigorous measures. In the summer of 1811, when the price level of goods exported from New Orleans stood 30 per cent below the peak of 1807, many thought war might reopen foreign markets and restore prosperity.

Such reasoning owed more to emotion than to rational thought, for a war with the mistress of the seas was certainly unlikely to bring an immediate increase in foreign commerce. Nevertheless, perhaps from frustration, many Westerners adopted it. Andrew Jackson asked volunteers to join him in a fight to secure, among other things, "a market for the productions of our soil, now perishing on our hands because the mistress of the ocean has forbid us to carry them to any foreign nation." Some Westerners found such naked self-interest embarrassing or perhaps doubted that war would open blocked channels of trade. Although strongly for war, the Lexington *Reporter* at first regretted that it was to be fought for a market rather than to free impressed seamen. Later, attacking Congress for delay, the *Reporter* combined the Indian and economic arguments for war: "The *Scalping knife* and *Tomahawk* of *British savages, is now again devastating our frontiers. Hemp* at three dollars. *Cotton* at twelve dollars. *Tobacco* at nine shillings. Thus will our farmers, and wives and children, continue to be *ruined* and *murdered*, whilst those half-way, *quid,* execrable measures and delays preponderate." The *Reporter's* columns probably fairly accurately reflected Western feelings, placing on an almost equal level of importance the rights of seamen (and through them the nation), Indian warfare, and economic depression.

An emphasis on Western war spirit can distort the national picture. The frontiersman certainly was more volatile, more directly subject to pressure, and perhaps also more sensitive to the imperatives of honor. However, at least during the summer and fall of 1811, well after the congressional elections, feelings of frustration and even bellicosity temporarily influenced the entire nation, not merely the sparsely populated West. The *Little Belt* affair aroused all sections. Economic pressure fell upon the nation fairly generally, although not so heavily on food growers in the Middle States. South Carolina, for example, suffered seriously when the price of cotton fell by two-thirds from 1808 to 1811. During the war session her congressmen served in the front ranks of the war men, often frankly admitting that commercial motives placed them there. At Boston prices fell substantially, although not so sharply as at New Orleans, and, according to Senator Smith, Baltimore's commerce was in "a deplorable situation." Port towns, even in New England, became increasingly bellicose. Huge segments of Northern opinion steadily resisted the ultimate remedy, partly because they saw that war with England would not cure commercial ills, but the greatest opposition to war developed only after hostilities proved to be neither a certain nor a quick solution. In 1811–1812, unlike 1808–1809, most New England Republicans stayed loyal. Finally, while the outbreak of hostilities on the Wabash most directly threatened transappalachia, virtually the entire country believed that the conflict had revealed Britain as an inveterate, jealous, intriguing enemy. The anti-British trend did not unite the East or even the South, nor was it long-lived. Temporarily, it affected the entire nation.

Thus the cry for Canada. Doubtless there were sectional reasons for urging its conquest: Westerners sought to end the Indian menace, Southerners conceivably hoped to purchase support for their Florida aims by backing war against Canada, some Northerners believed annexation would shift the center of power within the Union to the free states. The central, universal theme was far simpler: strike at Canada, the most vulnerable British target, the easiest way to inflict punishment and extort concession. "The great advantage to be derived from the acquisition of these possessions," a Richmond paper declared, "will not accrue so much from the tenure of them as a conquest, . . . but from the very important consequences which their loss will occasion to the British." In Cincinnati the *Liberty Hall* warned Britain that unless she rescinded the Orders in Council and abandoned impressment (Indian intrigues were not mentioned), "the most valuable of all her colonies, will be torn from her grasp, & thus she will accelerate her own destruction." This view found steady expression in newspapers and in the halls of Congress. "What," asked a leading War Hawk in January, 1812, ". . . is the object of all our military preparations? The object has been repeatedly avowed to be to retaliate on Great Britain the injuries which she has inflicted upon our maritime rights, by an invasion of her provinces, as the only quarter in which she is vulnerable." On such a program alone could supporters of war from all parts of the nation unite. . . .

All these things—war on the Wabash, naval arrogance, and even the temporarily overlooked continuation of impressment—seemed to show mounting British scorn for the United States. Thomas Jefferson might argue, as he did in September, that America's reputation would rise if she showed her wisdom by remaining immune from Europe's madness. But more and more of his countrymen felt that only direct action could vindicate the nation's character. Of course, to disentangle honor and self-interest is often difficult, and editors and congressmen frequently cloaked material appeals in the rhetoric of honor, sovereignty, and independence. Still, materially the United States was little if any worse off than in previous years. It seems reasonable to believe that the psychological consequences of British assaults, and the accumulating embarrassment over the cowardly policy followed since 1806, were the chief influences stirring the American people in 1811.

James Madison   # The War Message

In 1793 President Washington issued a proclamation of American neutrality in the storm of international war blown up by the French Revolution. In June, 1812, the United States declared war on England. After maintaining neutrality for 19 years, how and why did President Madison and a majority of both houses of Congress come to accept war as necessary? Part of the answer to this question is to be found in the new political leaders, especially in Congress. The "War-Hawks," as they were derisively dubbed by John Randolph of Virginia, were influential after 1812. Henry Clay typified them in his youth, vigor, and frontier background. President Madison, too, acted differently than had his predecessors. In 1811 he summoned Congress into session a month ahead of the usual time because of the state of foreign affairs. His message to that Congress stressed the many hostile acts by Britain and her contempt for American rights; he urged Congress to build up American military forces. Whatever their justification, such words hardly promoted the spirit of neutrality. Congress responded in kind. Henry Clay and others, on the floors of both houses, spoke with patriotism and truculence of American rights, British dishonor, and Canadian menace. They assumed war was coming and they said so openly in those speeches. Congress voted to increase the armed forces even more than the President had intended. In the following year, President Madison again spoke strongly to Congress. Excerpts from that message follow. [A Compilation of the Messages and Papers of the Presidents, James D. Richardson, ed. (New York: Bureau of National Literature, Inc., 1897).]

WASHINGTON, *June 1, 1812. To the Senate and House of Representatives of the United States:* I communicate to Congress certain documents, being a continuation of those heretofore laid before them on the subject of our affairs with Great Britain.

Without going back beyond the renewal in 1803 of the war in which Great Britain is engaged, and omitting unrepaired wrongs of inferior magnitude, the conduct of her Government presents a series of acts hostile to the United States as an independent and neutral nation.

British cruisers have been in the continued practice of violating the American flag on the great highway of nations, and of seizing and carrying off persons sailing under it, not in the exercise of a belligerent right founded on the law of nations against an enemy, but of a municipal prerogative over British subjects. British jurisdiction is thus extended to neutral vessels in a situation where no laws can operate but the law of nations and the laws of the country to which the vessels belong, and a self-redress is assumed which, if British subjects were wrongfully detained and alone concerned, is that substitution of force for a resort to the responsible sovereign which falls within the definition of war. . . .

The practice, hence, is so far from affecting British subjects alone that, under the pretext of searching for these, thousands of American citizens, under the safeguard of public law and of their national flag, have been torn from their country and from everything dear to them; have been dragged on board ships of war of a foreign nation and exposed, under the severities of their discipline, to be exiled to the most distant and deadly climes, to risk their lives in the battles of their oppressors, and to be the melancholy instruments of taking away those of their own brethren.

Against this crying enormity, which Great Britain would be so prompt to avenge if committed against herself, the United States have in vain exhausted remonstrances and expostulations, and that no proof might be wanting of their conciliatory dispositions, and no pretext left for a continuance of the practice, the British Government was formally assured of the readiness of the United States to enter into arrangements such as could not be rejected if the recovery of British subjects were the real and the sole object. The communication passed without effect.

British cruisers have been in the practice also of violating the rights and the peace of our coasts. They hover over and harass our entering and departing commerce. To the most insulting pretensions they have added the most lawless proceedings in our very harbors, and have wantonly spilt American blood within the sanctuary of our territorial jurisdiction. . . .

Under pretended blockades, without the presence of an adequate force and sometimes without the practicability of applying one, our commerce has been plundered in every sea, the great staples of our country have been cut off from their legitimate markets, and a destructive blow aimed at our agricultural and maritime interests. In aggravation of these predatory measures they have been considered as in force from the dates of their notification, a retrospective effect being thus added, as has been done in other important cases, to the unlawfulness of the course pursued. And to render the outrage the more signal these mock blockades have been reiterated and enforced in the face of official communications from the British Government declaring as the true definition of a legal blockade "that particular ports must be actually invested and previous warning given to vessels bound to them not to enter."

Not content with these occasional expedients for laying waste our neutral trade, the cabinet of Britain resorted at length to the sweeping system of blockades, under the name of orders in council, which has been molded and managed as might best suit its political views, its commercial jealousies, or the avidity of British cruisers. . . .

Abandoning still more all respect for the neutral rights of the United States and for its own consistency, the British Government now demands as prerequisites to a repeal of its orders as they relate to the United States that a formality should be observed in the repeal of the French decrees nowise necessary to their termination nor exemplified by British usage, and that the French repeal, besides including that portion of the decrees which operates within a territorial jurisdiction, as well as that which operates on the high seas, against the commerce of the United States should not be a single and special repeal in relation to the United States, but should be extended to whatever other neutral nations unconnected with them may be affected by those decrees. . . .

It has become, indeed, sufficiently certain that the commerce of the United States is to be sacrificed, not as interfering with the belligerent rights of Great Britain; not as supplying the wants of her enemies, which she herself supplies; but as interfering with the monopoly which she covets for her own commerce and navigation. She carries on a war against the lawful commerce of a friend that she may the better carry on a commerce with an enemy—a commerce polluted by the forgeries and perjuries which are for the most part the only passports by which it can succeed. . . .

In reviewing the conduct of Great Britain toward the United States our attention is necessarily drawn to the warfare just renewed by the savages on one of our extensive frontiers—a warfare which is known to spare neither age nor sex and to be distinguished by features peculiarly shocking to humanity. It is difficult to account for the activity and combinations which have for some time been developing themselves among tribes in constant intercourse with British traders and garrisons without connecting their hostility with that influence and without recollecting the authenticated examples of such interpositions heretofore furnished by the officers and agents of that Government.

Such is the spectacle of injuries and indignities which have been heaped on our country, and such the crisis which its unexampled forbearance and conciliatory efforts have not been able to avert. . . .

Our moderation and conciliation have had no other effect than to encourage perseverance and to enlarge pretensions. We behold our seafaring citizens still the daily victims of lawless violence, committed on the great common and highway of nations, even within sight of the country which owes them protection. We behold our vessels, freighted with the products of our soil and industry, or returning with the honest proceeds of them, wrested from their lawful destinations, confiscated by prize courts no longer the organs of public law but the instruments of arbitrary edicts, and their unfortunate crews dispersed and lost, or forced or inveigled in British ports into British fleets, whilst arguments are employed in support of these aggressions which have no foundation but in a principle equally supporting a claim to regulate our external commerce in all cases whatsoever.

We behold, in fine, on the side of Great Britain a state of war against the United States, and on the side of the United States a state of peace toward Great Britain.

Whether the United States shall continue passive under these progressive usurpations and these accumulating wrongs, or, opposing force to force in defense of their national rights, shall commit a just cause into the hands of the Almighty Disposer of Events, avoiding all connections which might entangle it in the contest or views of other powers, and preserving a constant readiness to concur in an honorable reëstablishment of peace and friendship, is a solemn question which the Constitution wisely confides to the legislative department of the Government. In recommending it to their early deliberations I am happy in the assurance that the decision will be worthy the enlightened and patriotic councils of a virtuous, a free, and a powerful nation. . . .

Henry Clay   # The New Army Bill

Only three days after President Madison's war message, the House of Representatives voted, 79 to 49, that a state of war in fact existed between the United States and Great Britain. The Senate was more deliberate. Only on June 17 did it vote, 19 to 13, the same way. Had only three Senators voted differently the war might have been avoided. In a speech in the House of Representatives in 1813, Henry Clay—perhaps the leading "War-Hawk" in that body—looked back over the "causes" for the war and analyzed them as follows. [Abridgement of the Debates of Congress from 1789 to 1856 (New York: Appleton & Co., 1857–1861).]

Considering the situation in which this country is now placed—a state of actual war with one of the most powerful nations on the earth—it may not be useless to take a view of the past, and of the various parties which have at different times appeared in this country, and to attend to the manner by which we have been driven from a peaceful posture to our present warlike attitude. Such an inquiry may assist in guiding us to that result, an honorable peace, which must be the sincere desire of every friend to America. . . .

The war was declared, because Great Britain arrogated to herself the pretension of regulating our foreign trade, under the delusive name of retaliatory orders in council—a pretension by which she undertook to proclaim to American enterprise, "thus far shalt thou go, and no further" —orders which she refused to revoke, after the alleged cause of their enactment had ceased; because she persisted in the practice of impressing American seamen; because she had instigated the Indians to commit hostilities against us; and because she refused indemnity for her past injuries upon our commerce. I throw out of the question other wrongs. The war in fact was announced, on our part, to meet the war which she was waging on her part. So undeniable were the causes of the war, so powerfully did they address themselves to the feeling of the whole American people, that when the bill was pending before this House, gentlemen in the opposition, although provoked to debate, would not, or could not, utter one syllable against it. It is true, they wrapped themselves up in sullen silence, pretending they did not choose to debate such a question in secret session. . . .

I am far from acknowledging that, had the orders in council been repealed, as they have been, before the war was declared, the declaration of hostilities would of course have been prevented. In a body so numerous as this is, from which the declaration emanated, it is impossible to say, with any degree of certainty, what would have been the effect of such a repeal. Each member must answer for himself. As to myself, I have no hesitation in saying, that I have always considered the impressment of American seamen as much the most serious aggression. . . .

It requires a strong and powerful effort in a nation, prone to peace as this is, to burst through its habits, and encounter the difficulties and privations of war. Such a nation ought but seldom to embark in a belligerent contest; but when it does, it should be for obvious and essential rights alone, and should firmly resolve to extort, at all hazards their recognition. The war of the Revolution is an example of a war begun for one object and prosecuted for another. It was waged, in its commencement, against the right asserted by the parent country to tax the colonies. Then no one thought of absolute independence. The idea of independence was repelled. But the British government would have relinquished the principle of taxation. The founders of our liberties saw, however, that there was no security short of independence, and they achieved that independence. When nations are engaged in war, those rights in controversy, which are not acknowledged by the treaty of peace, are abandoned. And who is prepared to say, that American seamen shall be surrendered as victims to the English principle of impressment? And, sir, what is this principle? She contends, that she has a right to the services of her own subjects; and that, in the exercise of this right, she may lawfully impress them, even although she finds them in American vessels, upon the high seas, without her jurisdiction. Now I deny that she has any right, beyond her jurisdiction, to come on board our vessels, upon the high seas, for any other purpose than in the pursuit of enemies, or their goods, or contraband of war. But she further contends, that her subjects can not renounce their allegiance to her, and contract a new obligation to other sovereigns. I do not mean to go into the general question of the right of expatriation. If, as is contended, all nations deny it, all nations at the same time admit and practice the right of naturalization. Great Britain herself does this. Great Britain, in the very case of foreign seamen, imposes, perhaps, fewer restraints upon naturalization than any other nation. Then, if subjects can not break their original allegiance, they may, according to universal usage, contract a new allegiance. . . .

The honorable gentleman from New York [Mr. Bleeker], in the very sensible speech with which he favored the committee, made one observation which did not comport with his usual liberal and enlarged views. It was, that those who are most interested against the practice of impressment, did not desire a continuance of the war on account of it; while those (the southern and western members) who had no interest in it, were the zealous advocates of American seamen. It was a provincial sentiment unworthy of that gentleman. It was one which, in a change of condition, he would not express, because I know he could not feel it. Does not that gentleman feel for the unhappy victims of the tomahawk in the western wilds, although his quarter of the Union may be exempted from similar barbarities? I am sure he does. If there be a description of rights which, more than any other, should unite all parties in all quarters of the Union, it is unquestionably the rights of the person. No matter what his vocation; whether he seeks subsistence amid the dangers of the deep, or draws them from the bowels of the earth, or from the humblest occupations of mechanic life; wherever the sacred rights of an American freeman are assailed, all hearts ought to unite, and every arm should be braced to vindicate his cause.

The gentleman from Delaware sees in Canada no object worthy of conquest. According to him it is a cold, sterile, and inhospitable region. And yet such are the allurements which it offers, that the same gentleman apprehends that if it be annexed to the United States, already too much weakened by the extension of territory, the people of New England will rush over the line and depopulate that section of the Union! That gentleman considers it honest to hold Canada as a kind of hostage, to regard it as a sort of bond for the good behavior of the enemy. But he will not enforce that bond. The actual conquest of that country would, according to him, make no impression upon the enemy; and yet the very apprehension only of such a conquest would, at all times, have a powerful operation upon him! Other gentlemen consider the invasion of that country as wicked and unjustifiable. Its inhabitants are represented as harmless and unoffending; as connected with those of the bordering States by a thousand tender ties, interchanging acts of kindness, and all the offices of good neighborhood. Canada . . . innocent! Canada unoffending! Is it not in Canada that the tomahawk of the savage has been molded into its death-like form? Has it not been from Canadian magazines, Malden and others, that those supplies have been issued which nourish and continue the Indian hostilities—supplies which have enabled the savage hordes to butcher the garrison of Chicago, and to commit other horrible excesses and murders? Was it not by the joint cooperation of Canadians and Indians that a remote American fort, Michilimackinac, was assailed and reduced while in ignorance of a state of war? . . .

An honorable peace is attainable only by an efficient war. My plan would be to call out the ample resources of the country, give them a judicious direction, prosecute the war with the utmost vigor, strike wherever we can reach the enemy, at sea or on land, and negotiate the terms of a peace at Quebec or at Halifax. We are told that England is a proud and lofty nation, which, disdaining to wait for danger, meets it half way. Haughty as she is, we once triumphed over her, and, if we do not listen to the counsels of timidity and despair, we shall again prevail. In such a cause, with the aid of Providence, we must come out crowned with success; but if we fail, let us fail like men, lash ourselves against our gallant tars, and expire together in one common struggle, fighting for *free trade and seamen's rights.*

"Junction of the Erie & Northern Canals," John Hill *(ca. 1830–1832)*. *A pastoral but very busy America is depicted in this scene on the most important of the canals that changed the United States in the 1820s. (New York Historical Society)*

8 One Nation— Indivisible?

By the end of the War of 1812, a pattern was clearly emerging that would dominate American history for half a century: nationalism vs. sectionalism. The tension between these conflicting loyalties would mount until it caused the most destructive war in American history. The development of each of these loyalties was gradual. Each arose out of the rapid growth of the United States in numbers, area, and power. Ironically, two diametrically opposed forces flowed from the success story of the early United States.

Winning the Revolutionary War against England meant a new nation but hardly deep nationalism, the emotion of profound loyalty to the nation-state. The "Young Men of the Revolution" thought "continentally," as Hamilton put it, but they were exceptional. Most Americans still thought in terms of their state. Soldiers mustering out at the end of the Revolutionary War went home to pick up their lives as Virginians or New Yorkers or Massachusetts-men.

Wars usually have a way of uniting a people as almost nothing else. The roots of American nationalism were in the first war with England. Twenty years of teetering on the brink of a world war, then finally becoming involved in hostilities against England in 1812, brought that sentiment to flower. No matter that the war was somewhat less than glorious or even truly victorious. No matter that many were opposed to it. Americans felt a new sense of unity and of pride in their nation as they again fought the British.

Accompanying this sense of community, however, was a new disunity in an emerging sectionalism. Opposition to the war was widespread and bitter in New England. It culminated in late 1814 with a meeting at Hartford, Connecticut, where men pondered regional action against national policies. A Southern sectional awareness was growing, too. As Eli Whitney's cotton gin made the raising of short-staple cotton in vast areas economically profitable, a new "South" arose. Virginia was left behind as "King Cotton" established a new dynasty in the "Deep South." In the West, a third section of vast potential was rapidly emerging. There were no states across the Alleghenies to ratify the new Constitution in 1788. By 1821 one-third of the states were trans-Allegheny, and frontier settlements had jumped the Mississippi River.

As the United States expanded rapidly to the west and the southwest, it became a country of very different geographical regions. As those regions were more densely settled, they developed distinctive cultural patterns, only most clearly seen in the cotton and slavery culture of the South. Thus "region" became "section," with profound consequences. As Stuart Chase put it in *Rich Land, Poor Land:* "A *region* may be defined as an area where nature acts in a roughly uniform manner, a *section* as an area where men think in a uniform manner. . . . A region provides a major basis for economic planning, a section a basis for political uproar." The idea of regions thus implies geographic areas whose differences complement each other and promote cooperation and integration. The concept of sections, on the other hand, connotes geographic areas whose peculiar economic and cultural characteristics beget division and conflict.

The United States was doubling in population every generation. Geographically, that population was on the move as no other people in history. The consequence of this success was that Americans were being pulled in two different directions at the same time: together in national pride but apart in sectional differentiation, toward unity and toward disunity. Tension was the inevitable consequence, a tension which mounted with each passing decade. The "political uproar" between sections grew through one crisis after another—only to end in a catastrophic clash.

Daniel J. Boorstin

The "Know-How Revolution" in New England

The United States was changing rapidly in the years following the War of 1812. A new West was emerging in the valleys of the Ohio and Upper Mississippi, a region of mixed farming. A new South was coming to life as well, one which left Virginia and tobacco behind as masters and slaves moved southwest across the mountains to the new cotton lands of Georgia, Alabama, and Mississippi. A new New England was also evolving, not through people moving out but in, into factory communities.

The facts about the inventions and the rise of factories have long been familiar: Samuel Slater carrying in his head the secrets of English spinning machinery to New York in 1789; Eli Whitney's invention of the cotton gin in 1793; the first real factory at Waltham, Massachusetts, in 1814. In terms of technology, inventions are dramatic and easily comprehended, and the function of the factory is similarly clear. The broader and deeper significance of these changes is not so apparent.

In two volumes Daniel J. Boorstin has sought to interpret afresh various themes in American history. One he examines in his usual thoughtful and provocative way is that of the rise of the factory system that transformed New England, what was distinctive about it, and what were its consequences. He finds that there was little that was completely new in the system. Its basic elements had been conceived and even tried in Europe, but there the power of tradition and entrenched interests was too strong for ready acceptance. In America there were no such elements—no guilds to stifle change and experiment, no vested interests in long-established firms. On the contrary, he suggests, New England, poor

*in resources, needed industry. Rich in shipping, she had capital to invest
and bottoms in which to bring in volumes of raw materials and to carry
away vastly larger amounts of finished goods than she could consume.*

*The heart of the New England manufacturing system, in his opinion,
lay in bringing together some processes heretofore done separately (as
spinning and weaving) and separating others heretofore done together
(as a Pennsylvania German gunsmith performing all the operations to
make a "Kentucky rifle"). In the Waltham factory of the Boston Manufacturing Company the "bringing together" was first fully worked out.
Cotton fibers went in at one end, finished cloth came out at the other
end. This, however, was not so profound in its consequences as the
second innovation: separating processes heretofore united, making the
intricate and varied skills of a gunsmith into a chain of simple, unskilled
operations.*

*This second innovation is set forth in the following selection, with all
of its profound consequences for relations between capital and labor, for
the look of towns and countryside, for the position of women, and for the
role of the family. In addition, of course, the flood of things which typify
modern America would be impossible without this innovation.* [From The
Americans: The National Experience *by Daniel J. Boorstin, pp. 26–34.
Copyright © 1967 by Daniel J. Boorstin. Reprinted by permission of
Random House, Inc.*]

The men who made the new factory at Waltham—Francis Cabot Lowell,
Nathan Appleton, and Patrick Tracy Jackson—had never before been in
a textile venture, nor in any other manufacturing project. It was less
their technical knowledge than their boldness, energy, enterprise, versatility, and, above all, their organizing ability that made their epochal
innovations possible. In fact, their lack of strong craft traditions actually
helps explain why new-style factories first appeared in New England.

During the colonial period, the center of American craftsmanship had
been Philadelphia. There one found the best tailors, the best hatmakers,
the best shoemakers, the best finished-metal workers, and the best cabinet
makers. It was around Philadelphia that the largest number of 18th-
century immigrant artisans, especially those from Germany and central
Europe, had settled. The two most distinctively "American" craft products—the Pennsylvania rifle (later called the "Kentucky rifle") and the
Conestoga wagon (named after Conestoga Township, in Lancaster
County; later called the "covered wagon")—were actually the work of
Swiss and German craftsmen who had only recently settled in Pennsylvania. In the Philadelphia area were concentrated the skilled textile-
craftsmen, the spinners and weavers who turned out fine goods, elegant
plaids, and hand-woven fancy designs in small shops.

These traditions of fine craftsmanship seem to have been more a
hindrance than an encouragement to innovation. Just as the European
industrial revolution did not come first to France, with its great artisan

traditions in luxury products, but to England; so the revolutionary American factory first came not to Philadelphia but to New England.

The "American System of Manufacturing" from its very beginning was no triumph of American inventive genius. Almost all the basic inventions that mechanized textile manufacturing came from England. And they had reached America slowly. Take, for example, the machinery for spinning raw cotton into cotton thread. Fully twenty years passed after Richard Arkwright began operating his first cotton-spinning machinery in England before Americans succeeded in copying it—and that was actually a feat of smuggling!

The evidence of American technical backwardness would be less impressive had there not been such strenuous efforts here to devise machinery similar to that used in England. State lotteries had actually been organized to collect prize money for the first inventor; the Massachusetts legislature even offered a subsidy. Despite many such incentives, American efforts failed repeatedly.

Unable to invent their own, Americans made desperate efforts to import or copy samples of English machines. But English laws forbade the export of manufacturing machinery, including models or drawings of them; even the emigration of any skilled workman who might reproduce such machinery abroad was prohibited. And New Englanders seemed to have lost that skill at smuggling which had helped build their economy in colonial days. Tench Coxe, a public-spirited Philadelphian, persuaded some London workmen to make him a set of brass models of Arkwright's patent machinery, but when the models were all crated and ready to leave England, British customs officers discovered them on the dock.

The crucial feat was finally accomplished by an adventurous young Englishman, Samuel Slater, who, at the age of fourteen, had been luckily apprenticed to Jedediah Strutt, partner of Richard Arkwright. Attracted here by American newspaper advertisements for improved cotton machinery, he was only twenty-one when he arrived in New York in 1789. Because of his knowledge of the Arkwright machinery his departure was forbidden by English law, but he left secretly, without even telling his mother. Not daring to take along plans or models, he had committed all the necessary information to his phenomenal memory. Dissatisfied with the unenterprising business methods and the meager sources of waterpower he found in New York, he accepted an invitation from Moses Brown, the Providence merchant–philanthropist after whom Brown University was named, to set up a cotton mill in Rhode Island. Brown and his son-in-law William Almy saw the opening Slater's skill gave them. They put up the initial capital and gave Slater a half interest in the business. Slater built, entirely from memory, a cotton-spinning frame of twenty-four spindles, which he put into operation. The firm of Brown & Almy prospered from the beginning.

In England itself employers could draw on the large pool of able-bodied paupers and unemployed. From crowded poorhouses they took workers who could not afford to be choosy about their employment. But in New England there were few poorhouses; laborers had more alternatives; land was plentiful, people scarce. As early as 1791, Alexander Hamilton had noted this as an obstacle to American manufacturing. Forty years later, some European travelers like the Frenchman Chevalier still expressed their surprise that American laborers were not forcing down wages by competing against one another for the chance to work. In America, therefore, manufacturing could secure a labor force only by attracting hands from other work or by drawing new workers into the labor market.

Such advocates of manufacturing as Alexander Hamilton had long been concerned lest the new factories disrupt American farm life by attracting away its essential labor. Hamilton himself noted that women and children were the only workers who could be spared from American farms. Brown & Almy's pioneer cotton-spinning factory at Providence, as Moses Brown himself boasted, did not at first take able-bodied men from other work. On the contrary, by drawing on a new source, it produced "near a total saving of labor to the country." The factory's first labor force consisted of seven boys and two girls, all between seven and twelve years of age. Not for long, however, could enough women and children be found to operate even this first cotton-spinning factory at Providence. Slater turned to the familiar English pattern. He attracted whole families to live in tenements or in company houses; under this "family" system every member of a family over seven years of age was employed in the factory. Such arrangements came to prevail in Rhode Island, Connecticut, and southern Massachusetts, where one began to see a factory working-class similar to that whose condition in England in 1844 Friedrich Engels painted so luridly.

In a few places appeared a more peculiarly American way of recruiting a factory work force, a way that fired the American imagination and shaped American notions of social class: perhaps America could have factories without a "factory class." Such a possibility, pure fantasy in England, seemed real enough in America because of the many alternative opportunities for employment, the well-being of the American populace, the cheapness of farming land, and the relative newness and lack of squalor of American cities.

When Francis Cabot Lowell visited England in 1810–12, he admired the Lancashire textile machinery but was horrified by the condition of the new factory class. He and his partners were determined that New England should not pay this price for industrial progress. Nathan Appleton recalled:

The operatives in the manufacturing cities of Europe, were notoriously of the lowest character, for intelligence and morals. The question therefore arose, and was deeply considered, whether this degradation was the result of the peculiar occupation, or of other and distinct causes. We could not perceive why this peculiar description of labor should vary in its effects upon character from all other occupation.

There was little demand for female labor, as household manufacture was superseded by the improvements in machinery. There was in New England a fund of labor, well educated and virtuous. It was not perceived how a profitable employment has any tendency to deteriorate the character. The most efficient guards were adopted in establishing boarding houses, at the cost of the Company, under the charge of respectable women, with every provision for religious worship. Under these circumstances, the daughters of respectable farmers were readily induced to come into these mills for a temporary period.

This was the "Waltham" or "Lowell" system, sometimes called the Boarding-House System. It had originated in the belief that there would not, and should not, be a permanent factory class in New England. The Waltham and Lowell communities became show places to support the New England businessman's boast that his new system had "rendered our manufacturing population the wonder of the world." When Harriet Martineau, herself the daughter of a Norwich manufacturer, visited them in 1835, she feared that any accurate description would tempt most of England's workers to the New World. Charles Dickens, not known for his sympathy to anything American, toured New England in 1842 and could not restrain his enthusiasm, describing the contrast with the English mill towns as "between the Good and Evil, the living light and deepest shadow."

Happy communities of well-dressed young ladies, living in spacious houses with piazzas and green venetian blinds, spending their spare time in churches, libraries, and lecture halls, were by no means representative of the new industrial life. Not even in America. New England, of course, had its share of callous factory-owners who considered their workpeople part of the machinery, but the hope of establishing factories without a permanent factory class was widespread and vivid.

As late as 1856, Francis Cabot Lowell's nephew, John Amory Lowell, boasted that American factory life was something new under the sun. The factory girl, he said, was not pursuing a lifetime vocation. She was simply spending a few years in a mill to help earn her dower or to provide for the professional education of a brother. "The business could thus be conducted without any permanent manufacturing population. The operatives no longer form a separate caste, pursuing a sedentary employment, from parent to child, in the heated rooms of a factory, but recruited in a circulating current from the healthy and virtuous population of the country." The ideal of a "circulating current" rather than a static class—of men on the move rather than in the groove—grew naturally. It flourished in this world of the undifferentiated man, where the unexpected was usual. The Old World vision of the industrious poor had dissolved. Even more characteristic than the ideal of equality, the vagueness of social classes became an ideal in America.

In the early 19th century, labor was generally better paid in America than in England. But the unskilled laborers profited most from their

American situation: in the 1820's, for example, they commanded a wage a third or a half higher here than in England, while the highly skilled were only slightly better off than in England, if at all. Thus the wage premium on artisan skills was much less in America than in England in the decades before the Civil War. The general labor shortage seems, as usual, to have operated most in favor of the least skilled, as did other factors: abundant land, wide geographic and social mobility, general literacy, and the lack of organized guilds. All these factors tended to reduce the social and monetary premium on the acquisition of artisan skills. Why train yourself for a task you hoped and expected soon to leave? American working men and women, already known the world over for literacy and intelligence, were not noted for specialized skills.

The purpose of the Interchangeable System, Eli Whitney himself explained, was "to substitute correct and effective operations of machinery for that skill of the artist which is acquired only by long practice and experience; a species of skill which is not possessed in this country to any considerable extent." The unheralded Know-how Revolution produced a new way, not only of making things, but of making the machines that make things. It was a simple but far-reaching change, not feasible in a Europe rich in traditions, institutions, and vested skills.

What happened in America in manufacturing was comparable to what had happened here in other fields. The scarcity of legal learning did not lead to a scarcity of laws or lawyers (we soon became the most lawyered and most legislated country in the world), but instead to a new kind of legal profession and a new concept of law; the scarcity of specialized medical learning soon led to a new kind of doctor and a new concept of medicine; and a scarcity of theological learning led to a new kind of minister and a new concept of religion. Similarly, the scarcity of craft skills set the stage for a new nearly craftless way of making things. And this prepared a new concept of material plenitude and of the use and expendability of things which would be called the American Standard of Living.

The Know-how Revolution brought an unexpected new power to make everything, and for nearly everybody! Oddly enough, the finer and more complex the machine to be manufactured, the more effective and more economical would be the new method. With a momentum of its own, this new American way of making things led people to want more and more things, in kinds and quantities never known before.

For all this New England was the center. The system would first be called the "Uniformity System" or the "Whitney System," for the key man was Eli Whitney. Though Europeans called it the "American System," it had not been invented in America nor by Whitney. Jefferson had seen it in France over a decade before, but there, when difficulties were encountered, Frenchmen preferred time-honored skills to uncertain experiments. In England, too, Jeremy Bentham, his brother Samuel, and the ingenious Marc Isambard Brunel had contrived a way of mass-producing wooden pulley blocks for the navy in an effort to employ the idle hands of prisoners and dockyard workers. But in England, too, little changed for decades.

The Uniformity System was simplicity itself, yet to imagine it one again had to leave time-honored ruts. The American factory organization described in the last chapter had merely drawn together separate manufacturing processes under a single roof. Whitney's Uniformity System was more novel: it transformed the role of the worker and changed the very meaning of skill. In Europe the making of a complex machine, such as a gun or a clock, had remained wholly in the hands of a single highly skilled craftsman. The gunsmith or clockmaker himself fashioned and put together all the parts of each gun or clock. By immemorial practice, each gun or clock was a distinctive hand-crafted object, bearing the hallmark of its maker. When it needed repair it was returned to its maker or to another gunsmith or clockmaker who shaped and fitted the required piece. Nothing was more obvious than that the production of guns or clocks depended directly on the numbers of qualified gunsmiths or clockmakers.

The new Uniformity System broke down the manufacture of a gun or of any other complicated machine into the separate manufacture of each of its component pieces. Each piece could then be made independently and in large quantities, by workers who lacked the skill to make a whole machine. The numerous copies of each part would be so nearly alike that any one would serve in any machine. If one piece broke, another of its type could be substituted without shaping or fitting.

How Whitney himself came upon so simple and so revolutionary a notion, the greatest skill-saving innovation in human history, we do not know. Perhaps he had first happened on it in his search for a way of mass-producing his cotton gin. The first successful application of the idea on a large scale was in the making of muskets. The occasion was the new nation's need for firearms in the turbulent era of Europe's Napoleonic Wars. In 1798 France, under a revolutionary dictatorship, threatened war against an unprepared United States. Most of the muskets with which Americans had won their Revolution fifteen years before had been made in France or elsewhere in Europe. Since military firearms had not been manufactured in quantity in this country, the nation was, in effect, unarmed. A tightened Naturalization Act and the infamous Alien and Sedition Acts were symptoms of its hysterical insecurity.

In March of 1798, President John Adams warned that diplomacy had failed. Soon thereafter, on May 1, Eli Whitney of Connecticut wrote the Secretary of the Treasury offering his machinery, water power, and workmen (originally collected for manufacturing cotton gins) for the manufacture of muskets. Whitney signed a contract for ten thousand muskets, a fantastic number in those days, to be delivered within twenty-eight months. He was to be paid $134,000, which would have made the average cost per musket only a few dollars above that paid for imports.

This was probably the first contract for mass production in the American manner.

It is significant that Whitney was inexperienced in making guns. He had probably never carefully examined the particular Charleville musket he contracted to reproduce. Had he been a skilled gunsmith, had he loved the feel and look of a beautifully crafted and ornamented piece, he might never have dared violate traditional craft standards by agreeing to mass-produce muskets by the thousands. What Whitney had to offer, he well knew, was not skill but know-how: a general organizing competence to make anything.

Whitney used up his time in perfecting his new production method. Fully twenty-eight months, the contract term for delivery of the whole ten thousand, expired without his delivering even one musket. All the while Whitney was building and equipping his new musket factory at Mill Rock outside New Haven. In January, 1801, desperate for cash and in need of moral support against influential people who were writing him off as a charlatan, he went to Washington and there gave a dramatic demonstration that proved to President John Adams, Vice-President Jefferson, and members of the cabinet that his "interchangeable system" really worked. He spread out before them the musket and a supply of its parts. Then he asked them to select any example of each part at random from its pile and to try with their own hands whether any one would fit with any other into a complete working musket lock. The proof was overwhelming. "He had invented moulds and machines for making all the pieces of his lock so exactly equal," Jefferson reported, "that take 100 locks to pieces and mingle their parts and the hundred locks may be put together as well by taking the first pieces which come to hand. . . . good locks may be put together without employing a Smith."

Now Whitney asked for another six months' grace for delivery of the first 500 muskets of his original contract and for two years beyond that to deliver the remainder. He secured everything he asked for, including another $10,000 advance, an agreement by the government to advance an additional $5000 in three months, and a further $5000 upon delivery of each 500 muskets. Although the new agreement trebled the money he received in advance and doubled the time allowed to perform his contract, Whitney was unable—by a large margin—to meet the revised terms. Not until January, 1809, ten years after the date of the first contract, did Whitney deliver the last musket of the agreed ten thousand. He had made a profit of only $2500 on a job which consumed a decade.

But Whitney had finally proved and successfully applied the basic idea of American mass production, without which the American Standard of Living would have been inconceivable. His was a triumph of organization. The original conception was perhaps not his own; other New Englanders were at the same time experimenting along similar lines. Only twenty miles away, at Middletown, Simeon North, whose main business had been manufacturing scythes, signed his first contract with the War Department in 1799 for 500 horse pistols to be delivered within one year. One of his later contracts (in 1813, for 20,000 pistols) provided that "The component parts of pistols are to correspond so exactly that any limb or part of one Pistol may be fitted to any other Pistol of the twenty thousand." Simeon's son, Selah North, is traditionally credited with inventing the filing jig, the matching concave mold which holds the metal so that any workman then necessarily follows the required shape.

Another feature of this story is worth noting. Government subsidy was crucial. The government's great power to invest and to wait for a return on its investment enabled Whitney to build his factory and tool up for mass production. This first great triumph of the American businessman was a government-sponsored and government-aided (but not government-run) venture.

America was already on its way to becoming the land of human salvation and of material waste. New England versatility now shaped at least two great and lasting tendencies in American civilization.

Machines, not men, became specialized. Where labor was scarce, where a man was expected to turn easily from one task to another, his machines had to possess the competence he lacked. Whitney's Interchangeable System, as he himself explained, was "a plan which is unknown in Europe & the great leading object of which is to substitute correct & effective operations of machinery for that skill of the artist which is acquired only by long practice & experience, a species of skill which is not possessed in this country to any considerable extent." Specialized machinery was required for an unspecialized people. "One of my primary objects," wrote Whitney, "is to form the tools so the tools themselves shall fashion the work and give to every part its just proportion." American technology would be an accessory of the undifferentiated man: the versatile, mobile American. New England had led the way.

A premium on general intelligence. In the Old World, to say a worker was unskilled was to say he was unspecialized, which meant his work had little value. In America, the new system of manufacturing destroyed the antithesis between skilled and unskilled. Lack of artisan skill no longer prevented a man from making complex products. Old crafts became obsolete. In America, too, a "liberal"—that is, an unspecialized—education was no longer proof of gentility; it no longer showed its possessor to be liberated from the need for gainful employment. Unspecialized education was useful to all.

English observers in the mid-19th century admired the ease with which American laborers moved about the country, from one job to another. They were amazed at the general freedom from fear of unemployment, at the vagueness of social classes, at the facility of moving up from one class to another. These facts, among others, they said, explained the absence of trade unions and strikes and the willingness of American workers to try new methods. Even the skilled immigrant sooner or later found it hard to stay in his old groove. While neighboring nations in Europe had jealously guarded their techniques from one another, here individual laborers from England, France, and Germany learned from one another and freely mingled their techniques.

The New England system of manufacturing, destined to become the American system, prized generalized intelligence, literacy, adaptability, and willingness to learn. As the machinery of production became larger, more complicated, more tightly integrated, more expensive, and more rigid, working men were expected to be more alert and more teachable. Open minds were more valuable than trained hands. Technicians and industrialists from England noted a new type of workman being created in the United States. The most skilled English mechanics, they regretfully confessed, showed such "timidity resulting from traditional notions, and attachment to old systems, even among the most talented persons, that they keep considerably behind." In the American system, they said, "you do not depend on dexterity—all you want is intellect." Needing a versatile as well as intelligent populace, New Englanders now reshaped the system of education they had founded two centuries earlier to instil dogmatism and singleness of purpose. They were working a similar transformation in their attitude toward law, and through that, toward all the problems of social change.

Wilbur J. Cash # The Mind of the South

A new South was arising, centered in South Carolina and the Gulf Coast region rather than in Virginia. This was the "Cotton South," rising on a new economy now that tobacco soils were becoming exhausted from long cultivation. The cotton industry brought not only a new geographic center but a new stake in slavery, which had appeared to many in the preceding era to be a dying institution. In the words of Frederick Jackson Turner, "Never in history, perhaps, was an economic force more influential upon the life of a people." Wilbur J. Cash, in the following excerpt, uses his creative imagination to reconstruct the rise of this new South and its society. [Copyright 1941 by Alfred A. Knopf, Inc., and renewed 1969 by Mary R. Maury. Condensed from The Mind of the South by Wilbur J. Cash, by permission of the publisher.]

How account for the ruling class, then? Manifestly, for the great part, by the strong, the pushing, the ambitious, among the old coon-hunting population of the backcountry. The frontier was their predestined inheritance. They possessed precisely the qualities necessary to the taming of the land and the building of the cotton kingdom. The process of their rise to power was simplicity itself. Take a concrete case.

A stout young Irishman brought his bride into the Carolina up-country about 1800. He cleared a bit of land, built a log cabin of two rooms, and sat down to the pioneer life. One winter, with several of his neighbors, he loaded a boat with whisky and the coarse woolen cloth woven by the women, and drifted down to Charleston to trade. There, remembering the fondness of his woman for a bit of beauty, he bought a handful of cotton seed, which she planted about the cabin with the wild rose and the honeysuckle—as a flower. Afterward she learned, under the tutelage of a new neighbor, to pick the seed from the fiber with her fingers and to spin it into yarn. Another winter the man drifted down the river, this time to find the half-way station of Columbia in a strange ferment. There was a new wonder in the world—the cotton gin—and the forest which had lined the banks of the stream for a thousand centuries was beginning to go down. Fires flared red and portentous in the night—to set off an answering fire in the breast of the Irishman.

Land in his neighborhood was to be had for fifty cents an acre. With twenty dollars, the savings of his lifetime, he bought forty acres and set himself to clear it. Rising long before day, he toiled deep into the night, with his wife holding a pine torch for him to see by. Aided by his neighbors, he piled the trunks of the trees into great heaps and burned them, grubbed up the stumps, hacked away the tangle of underbrush and vine, stamped out the poison ivy and the snakes. A wandering trader sold him a horse, bony and half-starved, for a knife, a dollar, and a gallon of whisky. Every day now—Sundays not excepted—when the heavens allowed, and every night that the moon came, he drove the plow into the earth, with uptorn roots bruising his shanks at every step. Behind him came his wife with a hoe. In a few years the land was beginning to yield cotton—richly, for the soil was fecund with the accumulated mold of centuries. Another trip down the river, and he brought home a mangy black slave—an old and lazy fellow reckoned of no account in the rice-lands, but with plenty of life in him still if you knew how to get it out. Next year the Irishman bought fifty acres more, and the year after another black. Five years more and he had two hundred acres and ten Negroes. Cotton prices swung up and down sharply, but always, whatever the return, it was almost pure velvet. For the fertility of the soil seemed inexhaustible.

When he was forty-five, he quit work, abandoned the log house, which had grown to six rooms, and built himself a wide-spreading frame cottage. When he was fifty, he became a magistrate, acquired a carriage, and built a cotton gin and a third house—a "big house" this time. It was not, to be truthful, a very grand house really. Built of lumber sawn on the place, it was a little crude and had not cost above a thousand dollars, even when the marble mantel was counted in. Essentially, it was just a box, with four rooms, bisected by a hallway, set on four more rooms bisected by another hallway, and a detached kitchen at the back. Windswept in winter, it was difficult to keep clean of vermin in summer. But it was huge, it had great columns in front, and it was eventually painted white, and so, in this land of wide fields and pinewoods it seemed very imposing.

Meantime the country around had been growing up. Other "big houses" had been built. There was a county seat now, a cluster of frame houses, stores, and "doggeries" about a red brick courthouse. A Presbyterian parson had drifted in and started an academy, as Presbyterian parsons had a habit of doing everywhere in the South—and Pompeys and Cæsars and Ciceros and Platos were multiplying both among the pickaninnies in the slave quarters and among the white children of the "big houses." The Irishman had a piano in his house, on which his daughters, taught by a vagabond German, played as well as young ladies could be expected to. One of the Irishman's sons went to the College of South Carolina, came back to grow into the chief lawyer in the county, got to be a judge, and would have been Governor if he had not died at the head of his regiment at Chancellorsville.

As a crown on his career, the old man went to the Legislature, where he was accepted by the Charleston gentlemen tolerantly and with genuine liking. He grew extremely mellow in age and liked to pass his time in company, arguing about predestination and infant damnation, proving conclusively that cotton was king and that the damyankee didn't dare do anything about it, and developing a notable taste in the local liquors. Tall and well-made, he grew whiskers after the Galway fashion—the well-kept whiteness of which contrasted very agreeably with the brick red of his complexion—donned the long-tailed coat, stove-pipe hat, and string tie of the statesmen of his period, waxed innocently pompous, and, in short, became a really striking figure of a man.

Once, going down to Columbia for the inauguration of a new Governor, he took his youngest daughter along. There she met a Charleston gentleman who was pestering her father for a loan. Her manner, formed by the Presbyterian parson, was plain but not bad, and she was very pretty. Moreover, the Charleston gentleman was decidedly in hard lines. So he married her.

When the old man finally died in 1854, he left two thousand acres, a hundred and fourteen slaves, and four cotton gins. The little newspaper which had recently set up in the county seat spoke of him as "a gentleman of the old school" and "a noble specimen of the chivalry at its best"; the Charleston papers each gave him a column; and a lordly Legaré introduced resolutions of respect into the Legislature. His wife outlived him by ten years—by her portrait a beautifully fragile old woman, and, as I have heard it said, with lovely hands, knotted and twisted just enough to give them character, and a finely transparent skin through which the blue veins showed most aristocratically.

The Tyranny
of King Cotton

The South of Wilbur Cash's Irishman was a society wearing blinders; it could see nothing but cotton. The new industry created a society with an aristocracy paying homage to it and a slave caste serving it, and it prescribed a way of life and a set of ideas from which none might deviate. How tyrannical was this rule, and how tiresome to an outsider, was indicated by an anonymous traveler in 1827, as quoted in the Georgia Courier *(Augusta) for October 11, 1827. [Reprinted by permission of the publishers, The Arthur H. Clark Company, from* Plantation and Frontier Documents, 1649–1863, *by Ulrich B. Phillips, editor.]*

'A Plague o' this Cotton.' A traveller from Charleston to St. Louis on the Missouri, in a letter to a friend in the former city, thus describes the manner in which he was bored with the eternal sight and sound of this staple produce of the country:

When I took my last walk along the wharves in Charleston, and saw them piled up with mountains of Cotton, and all your stores, ships, steam and canal boats, crammed with and groaning under, the weight of Cotton, I returned to the Planters' Hotel, where I found the four daily papers, as well as the conversation of the boarders, teeming with Cotton! Cotton!! Cotton!!! Thinks I to myself 'I'll soon change this scene of cotton.' But, alas! How easily deceived is short-sighted man! Well, I got into my gig and wormed my way up through Queen, Meeting, King, and St. Philip's-streets, dodging from side to side, to steer clear of the cotton waggons, and came to the New Bridge Ferry. —Here I crossed over in the Horse-boat, with several empty cotton waggons, and found a number on the other side, loaded with cotton, going to town. From this I continued on, meeting with little else than cotton fields, cotton gins, cotton waggons—but 'the wide, the unbounded prospect lay before me!' I arrived in Augusta; and when I saw cotton waggons in Broad-street, I whistled! but said nothing!!! But this was not all; there was more than a dozen tow boats in the river, with more than a thousand bales of cotton on each; and several steam boats with still more. And you must know, that they have cotton warehouses there covering whole squares, all full of cotton; and some of the knowing ones told me, that there were then in the place from 40,000 to 50,000 bales. And Hamburg (as a negro said) was worser, according to its size; for it puzzled me to tell which was the largest, the piles of cotton or the houses. I now left Augusta; and overtook hordes of cotton planters from North Carolina, South Carolina, and Georgia, with large gangs of negroes, bound to Alabama, Mississippi and Louisiana; 'where the cotton land is not worn out.' Besides these, I overtook a number of empty cotton waggons, returning home, and a great many loaded with cotton going to Augusta. Two of these waggons meeting one day, directly opposite me, the following dialogue took place between the drivers—'What's cotton in Augusta?' says the one with a load. —'Cotton! says the other. The enquirer supposing himself not to be understood, repeats 'What's cotton in Augusta?' 'Its cotton,' says the other. 'I know that,' says the first, 'but what is it?'—'Why,' says the other, 'I tell you its cotton! cotton is cotton! in Augusta, and every where else, that ever I heard of.' 'I know that as well as you,' says the first, 'but what does cotton bring in Augusta?' 'Why, it brings nothing there, but everybody brings cotton.' 'Look here,' says the first waggoner, with an oath, 'you had better leave the State; for I'll be d——d if you don't know too much for Georgia.'

I continued my journey passing cotton fields; till I arrived at Holt's Ferry, on the Oconee, where I saw three large pole boats loaded with bales of cotton, twelve tier in height. From thence I went to Milledgeville, where I found the prevailing topic of the place, "what an infernal shame it was, that such a quantity of virgin cotton land should be suffered to remain in the possession of the infernal Creek Indians." From Milledgeville, I went to Macon, which they say is surrounded with most excellent cotton land; but the town it is supposed, will grow much faster when it becomes the seat of Government, and has more banks. From thence, I moved on to the westward, crossing Flint River, and from thence to the Chattahoochie found cotton land speculators thicker than locusts in Egypt. But from Line Creek to Montgomery (14 miles) the land is nearly level; the fields of one plantation joining by a fence those of another; and all extending back from the road farther than you can distinctly see; and the cotton pretty even, and about as high as the fences, and has the appearance (as Riley says of Zahara) of a complete horison of cotton. They have, almost all of them, over-planted; and had not more than one-half their cotton picked in; each plantation has a cotton gin. I next came to Montgomery, which I found over stocked with cotton, and no boats to take it away. From Montgomery I went to Blakely, and on my way, saw many cotton plantations, and met, and over-took, nearly one hundred cotton waggons, traveling over a road so bad, that a State Prisoner could hardly walk through it to make his escape. And although people say that Blakely is done over, there was not a little cotton in it. From there I crossed over to Mobile, in a small steam boat loaded up to the top of the smoke-pipe with cotton. This place is a receptacle monstrous for the article. Look which way you will you see it; and see it moving; keel boats, steam boats, ships, brigs, schooners, wharves, stores, and presshouses, all appeared to be full; and I believe that in the three days that I was there, boarding with about one hundred cotton factors, cotton merchants, and cotton planters, I must have heard the word cotton pronounced more than 3000 times.

From Mobile I went to New Orleans in a schooner, and she was stuffed full of cotton. I arrived at New Orleans on the 8th of February, on the night on which Miss Kelly was to make her first appearance there; and I went to the Theatre. I was directed to go up a certain street in the upper Faubourg and turn into the first conspicuous brick building, lighted up on the right. I did so; and lo and behold! I found myself in a steam cotton-press house, where they work, watch and watch by candle-light, screwing cotton. After an examination, however, I went to the play: and after that was out, I enquired the way to a licensed Pharo Bank, and was told that I would find one at the Louisiana Coffeehouse, just below the cotton-press, opposite to a cotton ware-house. I don't know how many hundred thousand bales of cotton there were in New Orleans; but I was there only six days, in which time there arrived upwards of 20,000 bales,—and when we dropped out into the stream in a steam-boat, to ascend the river, the levee for a mile up and down, opposite the shipping, where they were walking bales on end, looked as if it was alive. A Kentuckian who was on board, swore the cotton had rose upon the town: 'don't you see' says he, 'the bales marching up the levy.' Coming up the river, I saw many cotton plantations, and many boats at Baton Rouge, Bayou Sarah, and other intermediate places, loading with cotton. And in passing the mouth of Red River, we took on board five more passengers, who live near Natchitoches. They say that they cannot get boats enough in the river to bring the cotton down that is made there, that they make the best cotton they ever saw; that they have the best cotton lands of all the cotton countries; and that if they continue to settle up there as fast for the next five years, as they have for the last, they will be able to inundate the world with cotton!! At the mouth of Arkansas River, we took on board about fifty negroes and two overseers, who had made a very excellent crop of cotton in the Territory, but found it too unhealthy a place to remain, and were going back to North Alabama. From New Orleans to the mouth of Tennessee River, we passed about thirty steamboats, and more than half of them laden with cotton; also about twenty flat boats a day, for ten days, and about half of them were loaded with cotton. When we got up to the Muscle Shoals there was more cotton in waiting than would fill a dozen steam-boats. I went by land from Florence and Tuscumbia, to Huntsville. There is a vast deal of cotton made about the Shoals, in North Alabama; and they go all for quantity, and not for quality. Ginned cotton was selling there for about six cents; and most of the lesser planters have sold theirs, in the seed, at one and a half. After leaving Huntsville, I passed to Nashville; and on my way, saw an abundance of cotton and cotton fields. The Tennesseans think that no other State is of any account but their own; Kentuck, they say, would be, if it could grow cotton; but, as it is, it is good for nothing. They calculate on 40 or 50,000 bales of cotton going from Nashville this season; that is, if they can get boats to carry it all.

From Nashville, I descended the Cumberland river in a steam-boat, between two keelboats, the Cherokee and Tecumseh, (poor Indian names, that have rang from Nickajack to Michilimackinac! now doomed to bear the burthen of the whites!) all three piled up with cotton; and after getting below the Shoals, to Clarksville, they stopped and took in 30 bales more. I left this boat at Smithfield, at the mouth of Cumberland, where, there was another large steam boat loaded with cotton for New Orleans. After seeing, hearing, and dreaming of nothing but cotton for seventy days and seventy nights, I began to anticipate relief. For on the route I took, whether by night or by day or by stage or by steam boat, wake up when or where you would, you were sure to hear a dissertation on cotton. One night, in Mobile I was waked up about two o'clock, by two merchant's clerks, who slept in the same room, and were just going to bed. They were talking of Lottery Tickets; and says one to the other, 'If you were to draw the 50,000 dollars Prize, what would you do with it?' 'Do with it?' says the other, 'why I would take 25,000 dollars of it and build a large fire proof brick store; and with the other 25,000 dollars I would fill it with cotton at 8½ cents, the present prices, and keep it till it rose to 17, and then I would sell.' But this is only one item of a thousand. On the 16th of March, there came along a steam boat from Louisville, bound to St. Louis, and I took my passage in her. She had not a bale of cotton on board, nor did I hear it named more than twice in 36 hours. We ran down the Ohio to its mouth, thence up the Mississippi, and I had a pretty tolerable night's sleep; though I dreamed of cotton.

Frederick Jackson Turner   # The New West

From the earliest days of the American colonies there had always been a *"West"—the frontier a few miles from the beach at Jamestown or the rock at Plymouth, moving ever west as the density of settlement increased. From early days, too, the "West" was a region apart, with interests different from the "East" and an awareness of the difference. When the West moved across the Alleghenies, in the era of the American Revolution, it became a more distinctive region. West was cut off from East everywhere by at least a hundred miles of mountainous country. As this new West boomed in the early decades of the nineteenth century, its special interests and problems loomed increasingly larger on the national scene. The following selection is from the work of Frederick Jackson Turner, a distinguished historian of the American West—or better, "Wests." In it he shows what was the economic basis of the trans-Allegheny West, how dependent it was upon commerce and upon arteries such as roads and canals to carry commerce, and how its political principles as a region flowed from those factors.* [Frederick J. Turner, The Rise of the New West, 1819–1829 (*New York: Harper & Bros., 1906*).]

By 1820 the west had developed the beginnings of many of the cities which have since ruled over the region. Buffalo and Detroit were hardly more than villages until the close of this period. They waited for the rise of steam navigation on the Great Lakes and for the opening of the prairies. Cleveland, also, was but a hamlet during most of the decade; but by 1830 the construction of the canal connecting the Cuyahoga with the Scioto increased its prosperity, and its harbor began to profit by its natural advantages. Chicago and Milwaukee were mere fur-trading stations in the Indian country. Pittsburgh, at the head of the Ohio, was losing its old pre-eminence as the gateway to the west, but was finding recompense in the development of its manufactures. By 1830 its population was about twelve thousand. Foundries, rolling-mills, nail-factories, steam-engine shops, and distilleries were busily at work, and the city, dingy with the smoke of soft coal, was already dubbed the "young Manchester" or the "Birmingham" of America. By 1830 Wheeling had intercepted much of the overland trade and travel to the Ohio, profiting by the old National Road and the wagon trade from Baltimore.

Cincinnati was rapidly rising to the position of the "Queen City of the West." Situated where the river reached with a great bend towards the interior of the northwest, in the rich farming country between the two Miamis, and opposite the Licking River, it was the commercial centre of a vast and fertile region of Ohio and Kentucky; and by 1830, with a population of nearly twenty-five thousand souls, it was the largest city of the west, with the exception of New Orleans. The centre of steamboat-building, it also received extensive imports of goods from the east and exported the surplus crops of Ohio and adjacent parts of Kentucky. Its principal industry, however, was pork-packing, from which it won the name of "Porkopolis." Louisville, at the falls of the Ohio, was an important place of trans-shipment, and the export centre for large quantities of tobacco. There were considerable manufactures of rope and bagging, products of the Kentucky hemp-fields; and new cotton and woollen factories were struggling for existence. St. Louis occupied a unique position, as the entrepôt of the important fur-trade of the upper Mississippi and the vast water system of the Missouri, as well as the outfitting-point for the Missouri settlements. It was the capital of the far west, and the commercial centre for Illinois. Its population at the close of the decade was about six thousand.

Only a few villages lay along the Mississippi below St. Louis until the traveller reached New Orleans, the emporium of the whole Mississippi Valley. As yet the direct effect of the Erie Canal was chiefly limited to the state of New York. The great bulk of western exports passed down the tributaries of the Mississippi to this city, which was, therefore, the centre of foreign exports for the valley, as well as the port from which the coastwise trade in the products of the whole interior departed. In 1830 its population was nearly fifty thousand.

The rise of an agricultural surplus was transforming the west and preparing a new influence in the nation. It was this surplus and the demand for markets that developed the cities just mentioned. As they grew, the price of land in their neighborhood increased; roads radiated into the surrounding country; and farmers, whose crops had been almost worthless from the lack of transportation facilities, now found it possible to market their surplus at a small profit. While the west was thus learning the advantages of a home market, the extension of cotton and sugar cultivation in the south and southwest gave it a new and valuable market. More and more, the planters came to rely upon the northwest for their food supplies and for the mules and horses for their fields. Cotton became the engrossing interest of the plantation belt, and, while the full effects of this differentiation of industry did not appear in the decade of this volume, the beginnings were already visible. In 1835, Pitkin reckoned the value of the domestic and foreign exports of the interior as far in excess of the whole exports of the United States in 1790. Within forty years the development of the interior had brought about the economic independence of the United States.

During most of the decade the merchandise to supply the interior was brought laboriously across the mountains by the Pennsylvania turnpikes and the old National Road; or, in the case of especially heavy freight, was carried along the Atlantic coast into the gulf and up the Mississippi and Ohio by steamboats. The cost of transportation in the wagon trade from Philadelphia to Pittsburg and Baltimore to Wheeling placed a heavy tax upon the consumer. In 1817 the freight charge from Philadelphia to Pittsburg was sometimes as high as seven to ten dollars a hundredweight; a few years later it became from four to six dollars; and in 1823 it had fallen to three dollars. It took a month to wagon merchandise from Baltimore to central Ohio. Transportation companies, running four-horse freight wagons, conducted a regular business on these turnpikes between the eastern and western states. In 1820 over three thousand wagons ran between Philadelphia and Pittsburg, transporting merchandise valued at about eighteen million dollars annually.

The construction of the National Road reduced freight rates to nearly one-half what they were at the close of the War of 1812; and the introduction of steam navigation from New Orleans up the Mississippi cut water-rates by that route to one-third of the former charge. Nevertheless, there was a crying need for internal improvements, and particularly for canals, to provide an outlet for the increasing products of the west. "Even in the country where I reside, not eighty miles from tidewater," said Tucker, of Virginia, in 1818, "it takes the farmer one bushel of wheat to pay the expense of carrying two to a seaport town."

The bulk of the crop, as compared with its value, practically prevented transportation by land farther than a hundred miles. It is this that helps to explain the attention which the interior first gave to making whiskey and raising live-stock; the former carried the crop in a small bulk with high value, while the live-stock could walk to a market. Until after the War of 1812, the cattle of the Ohio Valley were driven to the seaboard, chiefly to Philadelphia or Baltimore. Travellers were astonished to see on the highway droves of four or five thousand hogs, going to an eastern market. It was estimated that over a hundred thousand hogs were driven east annually from Kentucky alone. Kentucky hog-drivers also passed into Tennessee, Virginia, and the Carolinas with their droves. The swine lived on the nuts and acorns of the forest; thus they were peculiarly suited to pioneer conditions. At first the cattle were taken to the plantations of the Potomac to fatten for Baltimore and Philadelphia, much in the same way that, in recent times, the cattle of the Great Plains are brought to the feeding-grounds in the corn belt of Kansas, Nebraska, and Iowa. Towards the close of the decade, however, the feeding-grounds shifted into Ohio, and the pork-packing industry, as we have seen, found its centre at Cincinnati, the most important source of supply for the hams and bacon and salt pork which passed down the Mississippi to furnish a large share of the plantation food. From Kentucky and the rest of the Ohio Valley droves of mules and horses passed through the Tennessee Valley to the south to supply the plantations. Statistics at Cumberland Gap for 1828 gave the value of livestock passing the turnpike gate there at $1,167,000. Senator Hayne, of South Carolina, declared that in 1824 the south was supplied from the west, through Saluda Gap, with livestock, horses, cattle, and hogs to the amount of over a million dollars a year.

But the outlet from the west over the roads to the east and south was but a subordinate element in the internal commerce. Down the Mississippi floated a multitude of heavily freighted craft: lumber rafts from the Allegheny, the old-time arks, with cattle, flour, and bacon, hay-boats, keel-boats, and skiffs, all mingled with the steamboats which plied the western waters. Flatboatmen, raftsmen, and deck-hands constituted a turbulent and reckless population, living on the country through which they passed, fighting and drinking in true "half-horse, half-alligator" style. Prior to the steamboat, all of the commerce from New Orleans to the upper country was carried on in about twenty barges, averaging a hundred tons each, and making one trip a year. Although the steamboat did not drive out the other craft, it revolutionized the commerce of the river. Whereas it had taken the keel-boats thirty to forty days to descend from Louisville to New Orleans, and about ninety days to ascend the fifteen hundred miles of navigation by poling and warping up-stream, the steamboat had shortened the time, by 1822, to seven days down and sixteen days up. As the steamboats ascended the various tributaries of the Mississippi to gather the products of the growing west, the pioneers came more and more to realize the importance of the invention. They resented the idea of the monopoly which Fulton and Livingston wished to enforce prior to the decision of Chief-Justice Marshall, in the case of Gibbons *vs.* Ogden—a decision of vital interest to the whole interior. . . .

By 1830 the produce which reached New Orleans from the Mississippi Valley amounted to about twenty-six million dollars. In 1822 three million dollars' worth of goods was estimated to have passed the Falls of the

Ohio on the way to market, representing much of the surplus of the Ohio Valley. Of this, pork amounted to $1,000,000 in value; flour to $900,000; tobacco to $600,000; and whiskey to $500,000. The inventory of products reveals the Mississippi Valley as a vast colonial society, producing the raw materials of a simple and primitive agriculture. The beginnings of manufacture in the cities, however, promised to bring about a movement for industrial independence in the west. In spite of evidences of growing wealth, there was such a decline in agricultural prices that, for the farmer who did not live on the highways of commerce, it was almost unprofitable to raise wheat for the market.

An Ohio pioneer of this time relates that at the beginning of the decade fifty cents a bushel was a great price for wheat at the river; and as two horses and a man were required for four days to make the journey of thirty-five miles to the Ohio, in good weather, with thirty-five or forty bushels of wheat, and a great deal longer if the roads were bad, it was not to be expected that the farmer could realize more than twenty-five cents in cash for it. But there was no sale for it in cash. The nominal price for it in trade was usually thirty cents. When wheat brought twenty-five cents a bushel in Illinois in 1825, it sold at over eighty cents in Petersburg, Virginia, and flour was six dollars a barrel at Charleston, South Carolina.

These are the economic conditions that assist in understanding the political attitude of western leaders like Henry Clay and Andrew Jackson. The cry of the east for protection to infant industries was swelled by the little cities of the west, and the demand for a home market found its strongest support beyond the Alleghanies. Internal improvements and lower rates of transportation were essential to the prosperity of the westerners. Largely a debtor class, in need of capital, credit, and an expansion of the currency, they resented attempts to restrain the reckless state banking which their optimism fostered.

But the political ideals and actions of the west are explained by social quite as much as by economic forces. It was certain that this society, where equality and individualism flourished, where assertive democracy was supreme, where impatience with the old order of things was a ruling passion, would demand control of the government, would resent the rule of the trained statesmen and official classes, and would fight nominations by congressional caucus and the continuance of presidential dynasties. Besides its susceptibility to change, the west had generated, from its Indian fighting, forest-felling, and expansion, a belligerency and a largeness of outlook with regard to the nation's territorial destiny. As the pioneer, widening the ring-wall of his clearing in the midst of the stumps and marshes of the wilderness, had a vision of the lofty buildings and crowded streets of a future city, so the west as a whole developed ideals of the future of the common man, and of the grandeur and expansion of the nation. . . .

Thus this society beyond the mountains, recruited from all the older states and bound together by the Mississippi, constituted a region swayed for the most part by common impulses. By the march of the westerners away from their native states to the public domain of the nation, and by their organization as territories of the United States, they lost that state particularism which distinguished many of the old commonwealths of the coast. The section was nationalistic and democratic to the core. The west admired the self-made man and was ready to follow its hero with the enthusiasm of a section more responsive to personality than to the programmes of trained statesmen. It was a self-confident section, believing in its right to share in government, and troubled by no doubts of its capacity to rule.

"The County Election" by George Caleb Bingham. A typical election scene in Missouri about 1850 shows open campaigning at the polling place, open (not secret) balloting, liquor flowing freely, and money changing hands just as freely. (Reproduced by courtesy of the Boatmen's National Bank of St. Louis)

9 Jacksonian Democracy

A true folk-hero moved into the White House in 1829. Andrew Jackson was the first President from across the mountains, thus reflecting the changing nation. His image was that of the frontiersman: self-made and self-reliant, energetic, aggressive, egalitarian. In the last year of the War of 1812, he made himself a national idol by smashing three different enemies in one campaign: the Creek Indians at Horseshoe Bend in what is now Alabama, the Spanish at Pensacola, Florida, and the English at New Orleans. Jackson demonstrated twice and for all just how politically important the image of military prowess could be: in 1824 he got more popular votes than any other candidate for the presidency, although he did not have a majority and lost the run-off in the House of Representatives; in 1828 he was swept into the White House on a wave of popular votes larger in percentage than any President would receive for three-quarters of a century.

Thus began the "Age of Jackson," which both fascinated and puzzled Americans then and has continued to do so ever since. The fascination flows from the changes, tensions, and clashes as a new, more democratic America emerged. The puzzlement stems from the difficulties in finding the roots and explaining the meaning of the changes that were taking place. Any era of rapid change, of course, provides such interest and presents such problems. The age of Jackson, however, does these things to an unusual degree because of the personality and role of the man, "Old Hickory," and because of the profound consequences of the changes that he typified, if he did not cause.

The first attempt at an impartial biography of Andrew Jackson was undertaken by James Parton fifteen years after Jackson's death. Both a journalist and a skilled biographer, Parton had lived through the age, and he knew the man through careful scrutiny of a mountain of materials. From such background he set forth in the introduction to his three-volume biography his summary of the paradox of Jackson: "[He] was a patriot and a traitor. He was one of the greatest of generals, and wholly ignorant of the art of war. A writer brilliant, elegant, eloquent, without being able to compose a correct sentence, or spell words of four syllables. The first of statesmen, he never devised, he never framed a measure. He was the most candid of men, and was capable of the profoundest dissimulation. A most law-defying, law-obeying citizen. A stickler for discipline, he never hesitated to disobey his superior. A democratic autocrat. An urbane savage. An atrocious saint." One need but read a little way into Parton's fascinating life of Jackson, or any other, for that matter, to recognize that such anomalies did run through his career. This may be a devil or a hero, or almost anything in between, according to one's outlook and values.

Even more a question of outlook and values is one's judgment on the changes that swept America in the age of Jackson. This "age"—the era from about 1829 to 1841, since it is usually thought of as including the single term of his hand-picked successor, Martin Van Buren—was one in which the United States took a long step toward democracy. The "era of the common man," as it has been called, saw the extension of social equality, of political democracy, and of capitalistic opportunity to degrees that the Founding Fathers neither foresaw nor would have appreciated. These changes were neither simple nor sudden, and they were not the work of one man. They evolved gradually over the years preceding the inauguration of 1829. They flowed from the rise of Eastern urban craftsmen as well as Western frontier farmers. They created an age in which interest in economic opportunity moved many. Jacksonian democracy meant the extension of such opportunity. The stirrings in America were not from oppressed factory workers or from peasants on manorial farming estates; they were from middling and lesser free men, who perceived their possibilities in an "open" society. It is only in this perspective that "common man" can be understood in the phrase "age of the common man."

The consequences of this democratization of American culture were profound and sweeping. It was a gradual process, of which the end even yet seems not in sight. Its consequences were to be worldwide, as, linked with nationalism and industrialism, it transformed Western civilization.

Charles G. Sellers, Jr. # Jacksonian Democracy

Few people feel neutral about any strong President, in his own day or in later times. Attitudes toward President Jackson and his policies, for instance, were largely responsible for the changing and hardening of party lines that took place during his two administrations, as men of like mind aligned anew as Democrats and Whigs. The names "pro-Jackson men" and "anti-Jackson men" were commonly used in his own day, and the principles that those names reflected have continued to divide men ever since. Historians have by no means agreed in their interpretation and evaluation of Jackson—partly because of those principles, and partly because their attitudes toward their own times have influenced their interpretation of the past, and, sometimes, have provided incentive for their interest in the past. How these attitudes have operated to give successive generations of Americans different pictures of "Old Hickory" is set forth in Charles Sellers' selection. [Charles G. Sellers, Jr., Jacksonian Democracy, Publication 9, Service Center for Teachers of History (Washington, D.C.: American Historical Association, 1958). Reprinted by permission.]

Few phases of American history should appeal more strongly to both teachers and students than Jacksonian Democracy. The hatchet-faced old Indian fighter and military hero who dominated the American scene in the 1830's was one of the most colorful figures in our history. But more important, the 1830's saw the triumph in American politics of that democracy which has remained pre-eminently the distinguishing feature of our society. Today we take democracy so much for granted that we might have a hard time explaining precisely what it is, how it originated, or under what conditions it can flourish. What, then, could be more valuable to the student of American history than a real understanding of the period when democracy finally emerged as a dominant influence?

No sooner do we dig beneath the surface of Jacksonian Democracy, however, than we discover that its characteristics are elusive and that historians disagree widely about it. Old Hickory's masterful personality and aggressive policies, we find, made him one of the most controversial figures ever to occupy the White House. To his contemporaries Andrew Jackson was either the wise, patriotic Old Hero, or a rash, despotic King Andrew, while later historians have likewise found it difficult to achieve neutrality or detachment about him. Yet even without Jackson's personality, the democratic triumph he symbolized would still be controversial. For as long as democracy remains pervasive in American life, its historical characteristics will remain elusive, and historians will continue to argue about the period and symbol of its triumph.

The past, after all, interests us not so much for its own sake as for its relevance to our present concerns. It follows from this that the historian's approach to any particular past must inevitably be influenced by the forces and problems that are of greatest concern in his own day. Because historians writing in different periods have different "frames of reference," each generation sees the events of the past in a somewhat different light. Similarly two historians writing at the same time may see the same segment of the past differently because they make different assumptions about the nature of man and society or have different values and loyalties. It is easy to understand why German historians take a different view of Bismarck from French historians; and we should be no more surprised to find, for example, that American historians who are enthusiastic about democracy's possibilities describe the democratic upsurge of Jackson's day in rather more favorable terms than other historians who are more concerned with democracy's shortcomings.

In recent years historians have come to realize how greatly their evaluations of the past are influenced by their frames of reference, and this awareness has made them better able to recognize and avoid the more obvious distortions that result from the various ways of looking at things which they inevitably carry to the past. They have come to realize, too, that frames of reference may prove fruitful if critically employed, that they may furnish hypotheses and reveal features of the past which might otherwise be overlooked. Thus in order to understand the current state of

Jacksonian historiography, it is essential to understand the various frames of reference that various groups of historians have brought to this aspect of the American past and the various "schools of interpretation" that have resulted.

While American democracy emerged victorious on the plane of political ideology around 1776 or 1800, and on the plane of political practice around 1828, it did not achieve respectability in American historical writing until about 1900. From the Jacksonian era to the end of the nineteenth century historians of Jacksonian Democracy echoed the views of the Whig politicians who had opposed Old Hickory so vehemently in his own day. This "Whig" school of Jacksonian historiography included the first two important Jackson biographers, James Parton and William Graham Sumner; the authors of the first two detailed American histories extending to the Civil War, Hermann von Holst and James Schouler; and M. I. Ostrogorski, who wrote an enormously influential study of *Democracy and the Organization of Political Parties.*

All these authors were extremely critical of Jackson personally. Sumner thought him a "barbarian" who "acted from spite, pique, instinct, prejudice or emotion"; von Holst was appalled at the "ingenuous coarseness" of this "arrogant general"; Schouler flatly declared him "illiterate"; Ostrogorski expatiated on his "autocratic policy"; and Parton, despite a grudging admiration for some aspects of Old Hickory's character, lamented "the elevation to the presidency of a man whose ignorance, whose good intentions, and whose passions combined to render him, of all conceivable human beings, the most unfit for the office."

Yet it was not fundamentally Jackson's personality that turned the Whig historians against him, nor was it the general policies he pursued as president. These writers were all liberals of the nineteenth-century stripe and actually approved the laissez-faire tendencies of most of the Jacksonian measures. How, then, could Parton say that "notwithstanding the good done by General Jackson during his presidency, his election to power was a mistake"? How could von Holst speak of "the frightful influence . . . which he exercised during the eight years of his presidency"?

A clue may be found in the horror with which the Whig historians uniformly treated Jackson's policy of removing his political enemies from federal office to make way for his friends. Indeed, for these writers, the institution of the spoils system on a large scale became almost the distinguishing feature of Jackson's administration. "If all his other public acts had been perfectly wise and right," said Parton, "this single feature of his administration would suffice to render it deplorable."

Yet the spoils system was only a symptom of the real disease—the new system of democratic politics that both Jackson and the spoils system symbolized. "Popular sovereignty," said von Holst, would be "a dreadful condition of things"; while Schouler lamented the fact that, all too often, "the great body of our American democracy . . . slips back unconsciously into the mire whence the poverty-stricken millions emerge and falls too easy a prey to vice and ignorance." Ostrogorski got to the heart of the Whig historians' case against Jacksonian Democracy when he complained that it "excluded men of sterling worth and high principles from public life." Von Holst similarly argued that since Jackson "the people have begun to exchange the leadership of a small number of statesmen and politicians of a higher order for the rule of an ever increasing crowd of politicians of high and low degree, down even to the pothouse politician and the common thief, in the protecting mantle of demagogism." And as a result, said Parton, "the public affairs of the United States have been conducted with a stupidity which has excited the wonder of mankind."

It is important to remember that the Whig historians all came from eastern or European middle-class or upper-middle-class families with traditions of education, social prestige, and public service, the kind of families that had claimed social and political leadership as their natural right during the early days of the republic. By the time these men began to write the history of Jacksonian Democacy, however, their kind had been largely ousted from political leadership by the professional politicians and new-style parties that had arisen as the institutional embodiments of the Jacksonian democratic revolution. At the same time, this older elite was losing its superior social status to the vulgar *nouveaux riches* spawned by the Industrial Revolution. The Whig historians were writing, moreover, in the era of Grantism in national politics and Tweedism in local politics, when the least lovely aspects of both democracy and plutocracy were most conspicuous.

The Whig school of Jacksonian historiography can be viewed, in fact, as one phase of the significant movement in late nineteenth-century America that historians have called "patrician liberalism," a movement that sought to restore the pristine purity of American politics by eliminating the spoils system, destroying the unholy alliance between government and business, breaking the power of the political bosses, and placing gentlemen in public office. What could be more natural, then, than for the Whig historians to find in Jacksonian Democracy the origin of the features of American life they most deplored? These scholars displayed, in short, the class bias of an elite displaced from leadership by a vulgar and frequently corrupt democracy.

By the 1890's patrician liberalism was giving way to the broader movement of Progressivism, which was soon to effect a profound shift in the mood and direction of American life. A corresponding shift in the mood of American historiography was signalled in 1893 when the young Wisconsin historian, Frederick Jackson Turner, read his famous paper emphasizing "The Significance of the Frontier in American History." Yet Turner's real significance lies less in his controversial frontier thesis than in his influence as leader of the massive shift of American historiography to a pro-democratic orientation. For a whole new generation of young historians—men like Woodrow Wilson, John Spencer Bassett, William E. Dodd, Charles A. Beard, and Vernon L. Parrington—stood ready to echo Turner's vibrantly sympathetic description of democracy emerging, "stark and strong and full of life, from the American forest."

Two facts should be especially noted about these young scholars who were to transform the writing of American history. One is that nearly all of them came from rural or small-town backgrounds in the West or South, and this in itself brought a new point of view into a field previously dominated by the urban Northeast. The second significant fact is that though they came from substantial middle-class families, they lived in a period when middle-class Americans, and particularly middle-class intellectuals, were being swept into the current of reform. The Progressive campaign to preserve the traditional values of American society in the threatening new context of industrialism and urbanism was made possible by a revival of faith in the possibilities of the Whole People, and the Progressives characteristically devoted much of their energy to making the democratic process work more effectively. Small wonder, then, that the young scholars of the Progressive era responded enthusiastically to Turner's reaffirmation of the long tarnished democratic faith of an earlier day.

Andrew Jackson and his democracy were naturally among the leading beneficiaries of the new pro-democratic orientation of American historiography. Out of the "frontier democratic society" of the West, said Turner, "where the freedom and abundance of land in the great Valley opened a refuge to the oppressed in all regions, came the Jacksonian democracy which governed the nation after the downfall of the party of John Quincy Adams." This Jacksonian Democracy was "strong in the faith of the intrinsic excellence of the common man, in his right to make his own place in the world, and in his capacity to share in government."

Turner's contemporaries quickly took up the refrain. William E. Dodd pictured the "brave and generous" Old Hickory as "a second Jefferson," whose mission it was "to arouse the people to a sense of their responsibility"; while John Spencer Bassett published in 1911 a distinguished biography describing Jackson as "a man who was great, spite of many limitations." Though Jackson had ample faults, said Bassett, "all lose some of their infelicity in the face of his brave, frank, masterly leadership of the democratic movement which then established itself in our life." The new orientation was pushed furthest perhaps by another young scholar, Carl Russell Fish, who almost made a Jacksonian virtue of the spoils system. "The spoils system paid for the party organization . . . which established a 'government of the people' in the United States in 1829," he declared, and in so doing, "it served a purpose that could probably have been performed in no other way, and that was fully worth the cost."

The pro-democratic orientation that transformed Jacksonian historiography at the turn of the century has continued to be the dominant influence on writings about the Jackson period ever since. It permeated

Marquis James's impressive Jackson biography of the 1930's as well as the extensive studies of the Jackson period by Claude Bowers in the 1920's and Arthur M. Schlesinger, Jr., in the 1940's. More significantly it has controlled the interpretations of Jacksonian Democracy to be found in nearly all general works on American history written in the twentieth century, from the widely influential accounts by Vernon L. Parrington and Charles and Mary Beard to the most obscure textbooks. Political scientists have joined in the chorus of approval, with such writers as John W. Burgess, Wilfred E. Binkley, and Leonard D. White praising Jackson and his followers for strengthening the presidency and developing the new-style political party as an indispensable democratic institution.

Despite this widespread acceptance, the twentieth-century democratic school of Jacksonian historiography has attained neither the unchallenged hegemony nor the unity of outlook that the Whig school enjoyed in the nineteenth century. For one thing, the Whig interpretation refused to play dead. Most embarrassing to the democratic view of Andrew Jackson has been the interpretation of Old Hickory's role in early Tennessee politics advanced by Thomas P. Abernethy. Abernethy presents Jackson as a frontier nabob who took sides against the democratic movement in his own state; actually this leader of the democratic movement in national politics was a demagogic aristocrat, says Abernethy, an "opportunist" for whom "Democracy was good talk with which to win the favor. of the people and thereby accomplish ulterior objectives."

The Whig interpretation has received its fullest modern application to the Jackson movement as a whole, however, in Charles M. Wiltse's distinguished biography of Calhoun. Wiltse sees the reality of Jacksonian politics as a selfish struggle for office and federal subsidy. Jackson was in many respects "a frontier bully," and "in a growing, expanding, gambling, ebullient country like the United States of the 1820's and 30's, the frontier bully was a national hero."

Yet the democratic historians have suffered less from these dissenting views than from their own inability to make clear just what they mean by "democracy." The men of Turner's generation who originated democratic historiography conceived of the democratic process in a characteristically middle-class, Progressive way. Hating monopoly and plutocracy, they rejoiced in the egalitarian, anti-monopolistic tradition that stemmed from Jacksonian Democracy. But hating the class consciousness of Populism and Socialism as much or more, they shrunk from any interpretation of the American past that smacked of social conflict. Their enthusiasm for democracy rested on an essentially romantic faith in the Whole People, whom they saw as an undifferentiated mass, virtually free of inequalities and conflicts. Democracy, in the view which informed both Progressive politics and Turnerean historiography, was the process by which the Whole People's fundamentally virtuous impulses were translated into public policy.

Thus Turner was careful to assert that "classes and inequalities of fortune played little part" in frontier democracy. It "did not demand equality of condition," he insisted, for it believed that the "self-made man had a right to his success in the free competition which western life afforded." Mere inequality of condition was a negligible consideration to Turner alongside the more spiritual brand of equality that frontier process had guaranteed. "Mere success in the game . . . gave to the successful ones no right to look down upon their neighbors," he insisted, and he clung passionately to his conviction that the abundance of free land made it impossible for "the successful ones . . . to harden their triumphs into the rule of a privileged class."

However plausible this view of democracy may have been for the early nineteenth century, the free land was undeniably gone by Turner's day, while inequality of condition had become so gross that its danger to democracy could no longer be ignored. The successful ones now threatened either to harden their triumphs into the rule of a privileged class, or to provoke a bitter class struggle, and both alternatives horrified middle-class Americans.

It was this apparent crisis of democracy that produced both the Progressive movement and the democratic school of historians. Turner mirrored one mood of Progressivism in his desperate efforts to believe that there was no crisis, that the great monopolists themselves were products of the democratic West and "still profess its principles." But the more typical response of both Progressivism and democratic historiography was to rely upon a revival of democracy, a movement of the Whole People. The democratic historians were in effect supplying a historical tradition for Progressivism when they described the democratic upheaval of Jackson's day as an amorphous force, arising with no specific cause or particular program from the creative western forest, and spreading over the East by contagion.

The democratic historians' aversion to social conflict was a major factor in causing them to supplement the frontier thesis with a heavy emphasis on sectionalism. Conflict was simply too obvious in the Jackson era to be ignored, but Turner and his followers muted the discordant note of class struggle by transposing it into conflict among distinct geographical sections. Thus, alongside the Jacksonian rise of the Whole People, we find in their writings a three-way contest among the democratic West (epitomized by Jackson), the capitalist Northeast, and the planting and increasingly aristocratic South. Beard and Parrington, to be sure, made social conflict central to their interpretations. But even their dramas of struggle against privileged minorities were grounded on the same Rousseauistic concept of the Whole People as the conventional democratic interpretation; and more often than not they, too, fell back upon oversimplified sectional categories.

This vague conception of democracy remained prevalent in Jacksonian historiography until 1945, when Arthur M. Schlesinger, Jr., published

The Age of Jackson. Schlesinger's thesis was that "more can be understood about Jacksonian democracy if it is regarded as a problem not of sections but of classes." Defining the central theme of American political history to be the efforts "on the part of the other sections of society to restrain the power of the business community," he interpreted Jacksonian Democracy as a movement "to control the power of the capitalistic groups, mainly Eastern, for the benefit of noncapitalist groups, farmers and laboring men, East, West, and South." Schlesinger traced the movement to the economic hardships of the 1820's, and he saw the East and the workingmen as playing the crucial roles in the Jacksonian coalition.

Schlesinger not only provided a sharper definition of the democratic movement and a clearer explanation of its origins, but he stirred up a warm debate, which prompted other historians to offer alternative definitions. The attack on *The Age of Jackson* was launched by a scholarly official of the New York Federal Reserve Board, Bray Hammond, who insisted that the real animus of Jacksonian Democracy was not against business but against the exclusion of new entrepreneurs from business opportunities.

Hammond was quickly joined in his criticism of Schlesinger by a group of historians at Columbia University who argued that Jackson was anti-labor rather than pro-labor and that workingmen opposed him at the polls more often than they supported him. These historians showed a considerable affinity for the Whig view of Jackson personally, especially in the version advanced by Thomas B. Abernethy. Their own interpretation of the Jackson movement was expressed best, perhaps, by Richard Hofstadter, who described it as "a phase in the expansion of liberated capitalism," and as "closely linked to the ambitions of the small capitalist."

Thus the recent historiography of Jacksonian Democracy has been dominated by the debate over Schlesinger's "class-conflict" or "labor" thesis on the one hand, and the "entrepreneurial" thesis put forward by Schlesinger's critics on the other. Schlesinger and his supporters picture the democratic impulse as essentially a movement of protest against the unfair privileges claimed by an exploitative business elite, while the Columbia historians defend the diametrically opposed view that the democratic movement was itself strongly capitalist in spirit and objected only to any limitation on free entry into the game of capitalist exploitation.

Yet closer examination reveals some significant affinities between the two interpretations. For one thing, both were first worked out fully by the same man, the socialist publicist Algie Simons. In various articles and tracts around 1905 and then in a book published in 1920, Simons argued that the labor movement was not only an important part of the democratic upsurge of Jackson's day, but "measured by the impress it left, was the most important event in American history." At the same time Simons was too impressed by Turner's thesis to deny the frontier an important role in Jacksonian Democracy. But the frontier that he described was "distinctly individualistic and small capitalistic in its instincts." Jacksonian Democracy, in Simons' view, was "neither frontier, nor wageworking, or even purely capitalist in its mental make-up." It was the "democracy of expectant capitalists."

The striking fact that both the labor thesis and the entrepreneurial thesis found their first full development in Simons invites a further examination of their affinities. Both, it is clear, are indebted to Marxian analysis and represent a "realistic" approach to history, the Columbia historians maintaining a detached, analytical attitude, which occasionally betrays an implicit distaste for the middle-class norms of American democratic capitalism, and Schlesinger viewing democratic liberalism as being perennially sustained and advanced by anti-business elements, class-conscious and organized for social and political struggle. This "realism" explains the hostility of both to the diffuse Turnerean concept of democracy, but it does not account for the fact that writers of both schools are consistently critical of agrarian elements and seek to de-emphasize their importance in our history. These latter facts, when correlated with the personal origins and sympathies of the writers involved, suggest the belated emergence of the city as a major influence on American historical scholarship.

Thus we are brought sharply back to a final consideration of the profound influence of frames of reference. Indeed the historians of Jacksonian Democracy might best be classified by the social and intellectual environments that seem so largely to control their interpretations. In place of the simple categories of a Whig school and a democratic school, we might distinguish three main groups.

First, a "patrician" school of historians, drawn from eastern middle or upper-middle-class backgrounds, dominated Jacksonian historiography until the end of the nineteenth century. Resenting the vulgar democracy and the equally vulgar plutocracy that were displacing their kind of social and intellectual elite from leadership, these men spoke for the conservative, semiaristocratic, Mugwumpish liberalism of the Gilded Age.

Around 1900 the patrician historians were displaced by an "agrarian democratic" school, drawn from western and southern middle-class backgrounds and reflecting the revival of old-fashioned democratic dogmas in the Progressive era. Fearful of both class antagonism and monopoly capitalism, these men effected a reorientation of American historiography around the concept of an agrarian-derived democracy of the Whole People.

Finally, in recent years, we have seen the emergence of a school of "urban" historians, drawn from eastern cities, who find the agrarian democratic theme naive or otherwise unsatisfactory. Most of these urban historians came to maturity during the New Deal years, and they manifest a greater sympathy for industrial labor than for farmers and middle-class businessmen. Their stance seems to be that of self-conscious intellectuals and critics, expressing through their detached, "scientific," faintly ironic, "realistic" analysis an alienation from the middle-class mainstream of American life that is reminiscent of the patrician school. The entrepreneurial thesis is the most characteristic product of this group, though the labor thesis grows out of many of the same influences.

Actually, Arthur M. Schlesinger, Jr., the leading proponent of the labor thesis, emphasizes entrepreneurial elements in Jacksonian Democracy far more than his critics appear to realize; indeed he sees the western Jacksonians as almost wholly entrepreneurial in spirit. Basically, however, his *Age of Jackson* seems to represent a marriage of the agrarian democratic and the urban points of view. Schlesinger's "realistic" emphasis on class conflict is solidly urban, but the democratic idealism with which he combines it is clearly in the tradition of Turner. Of course, the three schools as defined here represent central positions, leaving some historians on the fringes. Parrington and the Beards, for example, reveal urban tendencies in a context that is mainly agrarian democratic.

But what of Old Hickory himself and Jacksonian Democracy? What are we to conclude when, after a century of scholarship, historians still squarely contradict each other about the essential nature of both man and movement? Has the frame of reference cut us off from the past as it was? Do historical writings tell us more about their authors than they do about their purported subjects?

Before accepting these disheartening conclusions, it may be well to remind ourselves that an interpretation is not necessarily wrong merely because a writer seems to have been impelled toward that interpretation by a particular frame of reference. The conclusions of honest men, working within limits set by an abundance of reliable and relatively unmalleable evidence, must have some basis in the reality of the past they seek to interpret. This may suggest that each school of Jacksonian historiography has been correct up to a point, and that the real problem of interpreting Jacksonian Democracy is to define the proper relationship among the various elements emphasized by the different schools.

Several recent writers, in attempting to do just this, have concluded that the Jacksonian movement was essentially paradoxical. Louis Hartz describes the American democrat of the Jackson era as a hybrid personality—both a class-conscious democrat and an incipient entrepreneur—at once the "man of the land, the factory and the forge . . . who has all the proletarian virtues that Marx was forever contrasting with the pettiness of the petit-bourgeois," and "an aggressive entrepreneur, buying 'on speculation,' combining 'some trade with agriculture,' making 'agriculture itself a trade.' " He had "a certain smallness of entrepreneurial preoccupation which has never been glamorous in Western thought," Hartz concludes, but at the same time he was involved in "two heroic dramas, the covered wagon drama of the American frontier and the strike-ridden drama of a rising labor movement, so that when we come to men like Jackson and Leggett we are never quite sure whether we are dealing with a petty hope or a glorious dream."

Another scholar has defined the paradox of Jacksonian Democracy somewhat differently. Judging from Jackson's own public papers, says Marvin Meyers, the Jacksonians appealed "not to some workingmen's yearning for a brave new world; not to the possibilities of a fresh creation at the western limits of civilization; not to the ambitions of a rising laissez-faire capitalism—not to any of these so much as to a *restoration* of old virtues and a (perhaps imaginary) old republican way of life." Meyers states the paradox thus: "the movement which in many ways cleared the path for the triumph of laissez-faire capitalism and its culture in America, and the public which in its daily life acted out that victory, held nevertheless in their conscience an image of a chaste republican order, resisting the seductions of risk and novelty, greed and extravagance, rapid motion and complex dealings." Still another scholar, John W. Ward, has found confirmation for this mood of Old Republican restorationism in the symbolic uses to which Jackson was put by his generation.

If these scholars are right about the paradoxical character of the Jacksonian democratic impulse, then it is easy to see why historians, in emphasizing different elements of the paradox, have reached such different interpretations. Viewed in this light, the frame of reference has served a valuable purpose after all, by leading historians to the different elements of the complex Jacksonian past out of which an overall synthesis must eventually be constructed.

Few phases of American history currently offer scholars a greater challenge to research and synthesis. Much digging in the sources will be required to establish the relative importance of the various factors already singled out, and new factors will be discovered. Historians know that they will never altogether reach the "objective reality" of the past—Jacksonian or any other—but they need not apologize for assuming it is there, or for believing that their zig-zag course brings them swinging in on a circle of ever closer vantage points for discerning its salient features.

Marvin Meyers

The Jacksonian "Persuasion": Politics and Belief

In the years since Charles G. Sellers, Jr., wrote the preceding article the interest of historians in Jackson and his age has continued. In part, at least, this seems to reflect a new frame of reference, to use Sellers' phrase.

In the 1960s and early 1970s Americans in general have been looking at their democracy and its problems from some different perspectives, especially those stemming from a new awareness of minorities, a new emphasis on the role of women, and a new concern for ecology. This is a very different context from those of the New Deal years, the Second World War, and the "bland" 1950s and it has brought a new relevance for the Age of Jackson..

That age saw America changing rapidly. In a sense it was America's "awkward age," in the phrase of Samuel Eliot Morison. America was growing up, moving west, flexing new economic muscles, and feeling some rather sharp growing pains, as well as experiencing the psychological problems associated with a youth's finding himself. With "King Cotton" now firmly on the throne in the South, slavery became even more entrenched there, whereas a cry against it was growing in the North. With Americans moving into the rich lands of the upper and lower Midwest, the tempo of dispossessing (and degrading) the Indians mounted. With factories, canals, railroads, and a new thrust in trade and shipping in the North, capitalistic theory and practice was moving into a new stage; there was a new and different emphasis on economic individualism, or economic liberalism (i.e., economic freedom for the individual, from the Latin liberalis, *"free") .*

This was an era of rapid and profound change. For generations "the Age of Jackson" has been the name attached to it, at least to the central years in it. Why is this so? Why his age? Is the name just a convenience, if not a misnomer? What was the meaning of the age, by any name?

In the following selection a distinguished historian who has been analyzing such problems recently poses some relevant questions and suggests some new answers. Marvin Meyers finds that the second quarter of the nineteenth century truly was the Age of Jackson, and that the message of Jacksonian democracy touched off powerful political emotions. What that message was and why it was so potent is the theme of his book, The Jacksonian Persuasion. *Using "persuasion" not in the sense of the act of persuading but of the things to which one is persuaded ("a matched set of attitudes, beliefs, projected actions," in his words) , he finds this an important key to understanding an age which was seminal for America, deeply divisive for those living in it, and controversial for Americans ever since. [Reprinted from* The Jacksonian Persuasion: Politics and Belief *by Marvin Meyers, pp. 3–15 with the permission of the publishers, Stanford University Press. © 1957 by the Board of Trustees of the Leland Stanford Junior University.]*

James Parton, that excellent popular biographer of his eminent countrymen, consulted a map in 1859 to discover which notables had given their names most frequently to American places. I doubt that one can find a brief guide to relative popularity, and to relative political significance for the people, than Parton's simple finding:

Washington	198 times
Jackson	191
Franklin	136
Jefferson	110
Clay	42

Washington the founder; Jackson the defender; Franklin the practical preceptor; Jefferson the republican sage; and far below, Clay the adjuster and promoter.

To have routed British veterans at New Orleans and cleared a region for settlement in the Indian campaigns gave Andrew Jackson a strong initial claim to national attention; and the military style which made him Old Hickory, Old Hero, put the claim in its strongest terms. Yet there had to be more to account for the passionate involvement of men's loyalties with Jacksonian politics: there had been other generals, other battles, other colorful personalities. At first, the battlefield reputation was enough: the unfailingly acute Governor Ford of Illinois, an uneasy late Jacksonian, observed how eager politicians had flocked to the banner of "a popular and fortunate leader" in the early days. But Ford saw too, in the perspective of 1850, that Jackson had been the master figure of American political life during his two administrations and the eight years of his retirement, and that he "has since continued to govern, even after his death."

Jackson entered the presidency a national hero out of the West; he became the great partisan protagonist of his generation. No man of his time was at once so widely loved and so deeply hated. His blunt words and acts assumed the character of moral gestures which forced men to declare themselves, for or against. The movement we have come to call Jacksonian Democracy borrowed more than a powerful name; it projected into politics a fighting image of the man who would save the republic from its enemies. Exactly where and how Andrew Jackson and his party met is a question for biographers; but once joined, they excited and focused the concerns of a political generation. George Bancroft's memorial panegyric, for all its Transcendental claptrap, comes to a truth about Jackson's political significance:

Before the nation, before the world, before coming ages, he stands forth the representative, for his generation, of the American mind. And the secret of his greatness is this: by intuitive conception, he shared and possessed all the creative ideas of his country and his time; he expressed them with dauntless intrepidity; he enforced them with an immovable will; he executed them with an electric power that attracted and swayed the American people.

From contemporary commentators to recent scholars there has been agreement upon initial facts: that politics substantially engaged the interest and feelings of American society; that Jacksonian Democracy was a large, divisive cause which shaped the themes of political controversy;

that the second quarter of the nineteenth century is properly remembered as the age of Jackson. Here agreement ends. The limits of the subject are in dispute: Is Jacksonian Democracy to be considered primarily as an affair of party politics, or as a broad political, social, and intellectual movement? What message did Jacksonian Democracy carry to society, whom did it reach, what did it signify in the setting of the times? These are yet unsettled questions, for all the wealth of industry and talent spent upon them.

In one view of the subject, urban masses rise against a business aristocracy; in another, simple farming folk strike out at capitalist trickery; in still another, fresh forest democracy seeks liberation from an effete East. Some recent works discover at the heart of the movement hungry men on the make invading the positions of chartered monopoly. Some stress the strengthening of the presidency, or the heightening of nationalist sentiment. An older emphasis upon King Andrew, master demagogue, exploiting the gullibility of the masses for the sake of his own power, reappears in altered form—the shrewd politicos behind a popular hero learning to manage a new mass electorate by perfecting the organization and tactics of machine politics. Woven into many accounts are elements of the official Jacksonian version: the friends of limited and frugal government, equal rights and equal laws, strict construction and dispersed power, taking up from Jefferson the defense of the republic.

These are not all the theses; and each is, of course, far more formidable in its author's custody than I have made it out in quick review. My object is simply to suggest the variety of plausible interpretations, and to suggest further the gaps and conflicts that invite a new effort to order our knowledge of Jacksonian Democracy. Much remains to be learned from precise and limited studies of the movement and the period; but now, I think, the need is to keep the focus wide: to ask the small questions with constant reference to the large.

Accepting the conclusions of Jacksonian scholarship as so many diverse hints to be considered when occasion gives them relevance, I have undertaken a new reading of some familiar sources. Somehow Jacksonian Democracy communicated a message which touched off powerful political emotions. What was this message, and what conditions gave it force? The questions are not easily answered.

When the Jacksonian movement formed in the late 1820's America was far out upon a democratic course: political democracy was the medium more than the achievement of the Jacksonian party. The Jacksonians proclaimed popular principles with but little more insistence than the Whig supporters of Harry of the West or Old Tip. For most of the country the Federalist conservatism of Hamilton or John Adams was stone dead: its ghost walked only in the speeches of Jacksonians trying to frighten honest citizens out of their opposition. Government by the people was largely a matter of consensus and of wont. Basic principles and institutions were firmly settled; only their legal elaboration—for example, in suffrage extension and the increase of elective offices—was recent and still in progress. There was some party conflict over details, none over the general democratic direction. The completion of a popular regime seemed to follow an unquestionable logic.

Indeed the most consequential political changes entered silently, without formal consideration or enactment: changes in the organization and conduct of parties. The winning of elections became to an unprecedented degree the business of professionals who managed powerful machines. On the surface such developments might suggest a bureaucratization of political life; in main effect, however, they brought a novel intimacy to the relation between the people and politics. The political machine reached into every neighborhood, inducted ordinary citizens of all sorts into active service. Parties tended to become lively two-way channels of influence. Public opinion was heard with a new sensitivity and addressed with anxious respect. The bureaucratic science of machine operation was effective only in association with the popular art of pleasing the many. As never before, the parties spoke directly, knowingly, to the interests and feelings of the public. The Jacksonians initiated much of the change in the instruments and methods of popular democracy; they adopted new party ways with a natural ease and competence which earned them some electoral advantage; the Whigs understandably resented their success, and quickly followed their example. Thus the new party democracy, like democracy in the abstract, was a common element of politics and raised no substantial public issues between Jacksonians and their rivals. At most, the less successful partisans carped at the more successful.

Under the new political conditions parties were alert to interests everywhere in society. One is tempted to think that Jacksonian Democracy found a major class constituency, identified its concrete needs, catered to them in its program, won the interested vote, and so became a great political force; and that the Whigs did much the same thing with opposite interests and policies. Unfortunately, the scheme breaks down at critical points. The chief Jacksonian policies—opposition to special corporate charters, hostility toward paper money, suspicion of public enterprise and public debt—do not patently contribute to the needs of a distinctive class following. The parties show some interesting marginal variations in their sources of support; nonetheless—given the relatively loose class structure, the heavy concentration in the middle social ranks as then identified (farmers, mechanics, shopkeepers), the flexibility of careers and the mixture of interests—it seems clear that both parties must have reached broadly similar class constituencies to gain, as they did, only a little more or less than half the popular vote. In sum: social differences were subtly shaded and unstable; party policies were ambiguous in their probable effects upon group interests; and so no general and simple class difference appears in party preferences.

The flaws in this class-interest approach have provoked a reaction toward the view that the Jacksonian movement had no great insurgent mission. In this view, the parties were fraternal twins, devoted to the advancement of slightly varying business interests in a free economy, their essential similarity disguised by a series of practical quarrels which windy party leaders dressed up in a conventional grand rhetoric; the essential meaning of Jacksonian politics is found in the objective import of legal and institutional changes. But why did political language go so far beyond practical objects? Why did men respond out of all proportion to their manifest interests? How were they convinced that party differences were profound, persistent—mattered greatly? Why did some kinds of rhetoric touch the quick, others not? Here, as elsewhere, the revisionist temper seems too impatient with the impalpable motives, feelings, perceptions, which lie between external act and external consequences.

I have spoken of the sensitive relationship which developed between parties and people: not only interests but attitudes and feelings reached the receptive eye of politicians. And politics took on what might be called an expressive role, along with its traditional task of conducting the business of the state. Here one enters a region of elusive psychological fact buried in a fragmentary record of words and acts. But here I think the vital transaction between Jacksonians and their generation must be found.

The appeals of the Democracy were carried by ideas and rhetoric, by policies and public gestures. Taken singly, these elements point this way and that, and no one of them conveys a full notion of the party message that worked such large effects. Taken together, I think, they converge to form an urgent political message with a central theme. It will be my purpose to identify that theme and the nature of its appeal. "Ideology" is a conventional term for one aspect of my subject, "ethos" for another, but I have chosen the less formal "persuasion" to fit my emphasis upon a matched set of attitudes, beliefs, projected actions: a half-formulated moral perspective involving emotional commitment. The community shares many values; at a given social moment some of these acquire a compelling importance. The political expression given to such values forms a persuasion.

In Jacksonian political appeals I have found—as might be expected—distinct traces of every theme used by historians to explain the nature and import of Jacksonian Democracy. Jacksonian spokesmen drew upon an exhaustive repertory of the moral plots which might engage the political attention of nineteenth-century Americans: equality against privilege, liberty against domination; honest work against idle exploit; natural dignity against factitious superiority; patriotic conservatism against alien innovation; progress against dead precedent. A first ungraded inventory shows only a troubled mind groping for names to fit its discontent.

The great specific mission of Jacksonian Democracy was the war against the Monster Bank. Here the party formed, or found, its character. Here was the issue which stood for all issues. Broad popular fear and hatred of the Second Bank, evoked by Jacksonian appeals, cannot be understood simply as a matter-of-fact reaction to material injuries. The economic operations of the institution conferred some manifest general benefits, directly crossed the interests of only a limited group: its hand was not found upon men's throats or in their pockets. The Bank was called a Monster by Jacksonians. A monster is an unnatural thing, its acts are out of reason, and its threat cannot be estimated in ordinary practical terms. The effort to destroy the Monster Bank and its vicious brood—privileged corporations, paper money—enlisted moral passions in a drama of social justice and self-justification.

Broadly speaking, the Jacksonians blamed the Bank for the transgressions committed by the people of their era against the political, social, and economic values of the Old Republic. The Bank carried the bad seed of Hamilton's first Monster, matured all the old evils, and created some new ones. To the Bank's influence Jacksonians traced constitutional impiety, consolidated national power, aristocratic privilege, and plutocratic corruption. Social inequality, impersonal and intangible business relations, economic instability, perpetual debt and taxes, all issued from the same source.

Jefferson had brought into temporary equilibrium the formal ideal of a dynamic liberal society and the concrete image of a stable, virtuous yeoman republic. "It is," he wrote, "the manners and spirit of a people which preserve a republic in vigor." And God had made the independent citizen farmer "His peculiar deposit for substantial and genuine virtue." Nothing is more revealing than Jefferson's later concession of the need for domestic manufacturing, under the pressures of war: "Our enemy has indeed the consolation of Satan on removing our first parents from Paradise: from a peaceful agricultural nation he makes us a military and manufacturing one." Now Jacksonian society was caught between the elements—the liberal principle and the yeoman image—and tried again to harmonize them. Americans were boldly liberal in economic affairs, out of conviction and appetite combined, and moved their world in the direction of modern capitalism. But they were not inwardly prepared for the grinding uncertainties, the shocking changes, the complexity and indirection of the new economic ways. Their image of the good life had not altered: somehow, as men and as a society, they hoped to have their brave adventures, their provocative rewards, their open-ended progress, and remain essentially the same. The practical outcomes of the free pursuit of economic interest had never been legitimated, or even fully associated with the abstract liberal principle. Yet the ideological and material attachment to the liberal code was too deep to be severed, even in considerable distress.

Thus many found in the anti-Bank crusade, and in the Jacksonian appeal generally, a way to damn the unfamiliar, threatening, sometimes punishing elements in the changing order by fixing guilt upon a single protean agent. A laissez-faire society with this source of corruptions cut out would re-establish continuity with that golden age in which liberty and progress were joined inseparably with simple yeoman virtues. Under the Jacksonian persuasion men could follow their desires, protest their injuries, affirm their innocence. In this direction one can begin to meet the Jacksonian paradox: the fact that the movement which helped to clear the path for laissez-faire capitalism and its culture in America, and the public which in its daily life eagerly entered on that path, held nevertheless in their political conscience an ideal of a chaste republican order, resisting the seductions of risk and novelty, greed and extravagance, rapid motion and complex dealings.

The Jacksonian movement was forged in the Bank War. Its new machine carried its influence throughout American society; its Old Hero, at once the voice and the exemplar of Jacksonian values, linked the machine to the essential cause. However far Jacksonians went in adapting policies to the practical requirements of local conditions, special interests, and effective party operation, the movement continually returned to its core appeal: death to the Monster; life and health to the old republican virtues. However carefully the knowledgeable voter looked to his immediate interests—when they could be linked plausibly to party policies—he would always see the moral choice proposed by Jacksonian Democracy.

If the Jacksonian persuasion gained relevance and force from common social experience, common tradition, how then did the Whigs develop a distinct voice and a substantial following? Reducing a complex matter to the utmost simplicity: the Whig party spoke to the explicit hopes of Americans as Jacksonians addressed their diffuse fears and resentments. To say this is to reverse a common historical appraisal. The Federalists had been, at the end, a party of fear and resentment. There is some loose justice in deriving Whiggery from Federalism; but only if one recognizes that the language of mob terror and elite guidance had gone out of general use before Jacksonians and Whigs assumed political leadership. Some unregenerate Federalists who worried openly about the dangers of extreme democracy still survived; Whig party leaders tapped them for campaign funds and otherwise wished them out of sight.

What the Whigs deliberately maintained in the inheritance was the ambitious scheme for economic progress through banks, tariffs, and public promotion of internal improvements. Clay's American System, the nearest approach to a coherent Whig policy, was a popularization of Hamiltonian economic designs and John Marshall's flexible interpretation of national authority. Whigs, too, fully associated themselves with the Old Republican idyll—Webster wept in memory of his father's forest hut; zealous clerks helped to clutter city streets with Harrison log cabins—but they felt no serious tension between past and present. Their cabin was a nostalgic prop, a publicity gimmick without focused moral content. The fulfillment of liberal premises in capitalist progress was for them entirely natural and unproblematic.

The Whigs distinctively affirmed the material promise of American life as it was going; and they promised to make it go faster. They were inclined to see the corporation not as a nameless monster but as an engine of progress; public debt not as a curse on honest labor but as a sound gamble on a richer future. Ironically, depression gave them their greatest popular success; yet they did not take depression as an omen of profound social maladjustment. They could see only that an imperious demagogue with primitive economic notions had thrown society into crisis by his spiteful war against the Bank. Indeed the Whigs were so markedly an anti-Jackson coalition that often their positive message was obscured in mere personal invective. To some degree, perhaps, the Whigs did succeed in spreading the conviction that Jacksonian dictatorship menaced the integrity of the republic. Principally, however, the party appealed to interested hopes, offering concrete advantages to groups and sections, and a quickening of economic progress for society as a whole.

Succeeding chapters will present a series of related commentaries on the appeal Jacksonian Democrats made to their generation, and on the changing social situation which lent relevance and force to that appeal. Perhaps they can convey the effort of Jacksonian Democracy to recall agrarian republican innocence to a society drawn fatally to the main chance and the long chance, to the revolutionizing ways of acquisition, emulative consumption, promotion, and speculation—the Jacksonian struggle to reconcile again the simple yeoman values with the free pursuit of economic interest, just as the two were splitting hopelessly apart.

John William Ward # Jackson: Symbol for an Age

"Democracy" (like "persuasion") is an abstraction, an intellectual construct for a set of attitudes or beliefs. As generalizations for such sets, abstractions are invaluable; we all deal constantly with such abstractions as democracy, totalitarianism, capitalism, communism, and Protestantism.

Among other things, such abstractions summarize the clutches of values and attitudes for which (or against which) people live. Those by which they live is another matter. For this the abstract needs to be made concrete: visible, tangible representations of the abstractions. Symbols are needed to make abstractions understandable and socially effective. George Washington is such a symbol for selfless patriotism in times of crisis; the cross is a symbol for the role of Jesus in Christianity. Symbols are essential and universal.

The story was told of one backwoods preacher in the middle of the nineteenth century who, groping for words to try to explain to his untutored congregation the meaning of Jesus, finally came up with: "He's just like Andrew Jackson." Both were symbols, though some might

*boggle at lumping them together. Another contemporary put it thus in a
eulogy on the death of Jackson, recorded in the volume from which the
following selection is taken:*

What was he? He was the imbodiment [sic] of the true spirit of the nation in
which he lived. . . . Run the eye across the history of the world. You observe
that there are certain cycles, or ages, or periods of time, which have their peculiar spirit, their ruling passion, their great, characterizing, distinctive movements. He, who imbodies in its greatest fulness, the spirit of such an age, and
enters with most earnestness into its movements, received the admiration of his
contemporaries. . . . And why? because they see in him their own image.

It is this theme, Andrew Jackson: Symbol for an Age, *that John William
Ward develops in his provocative book of that title. Americans of his
time made of him a symbol because they saw in him their own image, in
the phrase of the eulogist above. What was that image, and how did he
symbolize it?*

*Ward, historian and President of Amherst College, develops three
themes (abstractions) as particularly significant in the way that Americans then saw themselves. The first he calls simply "Nature": the yeoman
farmer, industriously working the fruitful earth, but capable and energetic enough that he can put aside his plow, take up his gun, and defeat
the best that Europe can throw against him. Next, "Providence": God
smiles on the Americans, not only as shown by their success in battle but
also by the rich bounty of the land He has given them. Finally, "Will":
God's beneficence is not enough; Americans must act, and they can and
do.*

*Ward shows how these were the convictions and the faith of Americans
of that era and how, above all, Jackson himself seemed to them to personify, to symbolize them. In the selection which follows he shows clearly
how Jackson symbolized one dimension of "Will": the man who is
"self-made," through character, industry, and competence—"Will."*

[From Andrew Jackson: Symbol for an Age *by John William Ward, pp.
162–180. Copyright © 1955 by John William Ward. Reprinted by permission of Oxford University Press.*]

In 1845 when Andrew Jackson died, Andrew Stevenson pointed out for
the benefit of the citizens of Richmond, Virginia, the moral implicit in
Jackson's life.

I shall say nothing [asserted Stevenson] of his ancestors. Virtue and greatness
have no need of birth. Born a simple citizen, of poor but respectable parents,
he became great by no other means than the energy of his own character, and
being, as he seems to have been, the favourite of nature and Heaven! Had he
been born to wealth and influence, he might probably have lived and died, an
obscure and ordinary man!
Severe discipline and poverty, inured him, in early life, to great hardship
and industry, and it has been justly said of him that he seems to have been an
orphan from the plough to the presidency. He must, therefore, be regarded as
the architect of his own fortunes!

Andrew Jackson's rise from humble circumstances gave substance to the idea that man is the master of his own fate. 'Of all the men I have known,' Francis P. Blair told James Parton, 'Andrew Jackson was the one most entirely sufficient for himself.' To Blair's remark Parton added that 'not only had [Jackson] no such word as *fail,* but no belief, not the slightest, that he could fail in anything seriously undertaken by him. And he never did.' Thus, after more than 2000 pages of narrative, James Parton found Jackson's life to illustrate the fact that 'what man supremely admires in man is manhood.'

> Every great career [wrote Parton], whether of a nation or of an individual, dates from an heroic action, and every downfall from a cowardly one. To dare, to dare again, and always to dare, is the inexorable condition of every signal and worthy success, from founding a cobbler's stall to promulgating a nobler faith.
>
> It is not for nothing that nature has implanted in her darling the instinct of honoring courage before all other qualities. What a delicate creature was man to be tossed upon this planet . . . compelled instantly to to [sic] begin the 'struggle for life.'

The phrase, 'struggle for life,' leads one's imagination to the period after Jackson, to the end of the nineteenth century rather than to its beginning. This only reminds us that history is a development. In the social situation of the late nineteenth century, it may have seemed that the great man needed only 'the energy of his own character,' but as Stevenson's eulogy reminds us, in the America of Andrew Jackson, he needed more than daring. It helped to be the 'favourite of nature and Heaven!'

The idea that every man is the architect of his own fortunes has its roots deep in the American past, although the years of Jacksonian democracy, according to one student, contain the first important enunciation of the cult of the self-made man. One thinks immediately of Franklin in connection with the theme of self-help and contemporaries of Jackson linked their Hero with the sage of Philadelphia in order to state explicitly what Jackson's whole career was held to demonstrate implicitly: 'He had, like Franklin, to establish his name without the patronage of a single relative or friend; if he had not talents and virtues, would he not have remained in obscurity?' Franklin suggests the long history which belongs to the idea of success. The same pattern which one discovers in examining the concepts of nature and providence emerges when one scrutinizes Jackson's relation to the idea of the self-made man. The concept of will, which is at the base of the idea of self-help, did not suddenly come to be valued because of Andrew Jackson's career. The idea that man is the architect of his own fortunes had long been present in the society. Jackson simply lent further support to an article of faith already subscribed to in America.

Central to the idea that man is the master of his own fate is the belief in the efficacy of the human will. If one is believed to succeed through personal determination, the will must be exalted and the limitations of

environment and heredity must be denied. As a social type the man of
efficient will power, the man capable of self-direction, comes to be valued
when society, because of social and economic fluidity, presents its members with a variety of choices and demands a great amount of initiative.
Such a social period is, of course, a period of change, a period of transition. Transition is a pallid word for what was happening to America in
the period 1815 to 1845. Change was the ruling characteristic. Movement
was not only westward geographically, it was upward socially. Expansion
was extensive, measured by land mass, and intensive, measured by economic development. But as America faced its future, less attention was
paid to the material basis which made that future seem so promising than
to the quality of American character. The material endowment of the
new continent was not denied; it was asserted to be secondary. 'The
character of the American people,' said a Fourth of July orator, 'has been
the sole cause of their growth and prosperity. Natural advantages have
been elsewhere wasted.' This speech echoes that of Representative Troup
with which we began. America has been given its opportunity to succeed,
but it must have the will power to seize and improve that opportunity.
Sixteen years after Troup, the Fourth of July orator arrives at the same
conclusion as the Congressman from Georgia: 'A nation that wills to be
free, is free.'

The idea that character is more important than extrinsic advantage
received full development by another Fourth of July orator for the edifi-
cation of the mechanics of Troy, New York.

> It too often happens [said O. L. Holley] . . . that the practical value of charac-
> ter, even in private life is underrated, and an undue importance is attached to
> external condition. . . . But, though external circumstances and the accidents
> of birth and connexion, are not to be disregarded. . . . It is plainly character
> alone, that can lift a man above accident—it is that alone, which, if based
> upon good principles and cultivated with care, can render him triumphant over
> vicissitudes and prosperous even in adversity; and it is that alone, which, if
> neglected and suffered to degenerate, will defeat the most benevolent designs of
> Providence; will render a man weak, though surrounded by wealth, and unsuc-
> cessful, though backed by numbers. The Almighty may, indeed, if it so please
> him, give the race to the slow and the victory to the feeble; but he has indi-
> cated by the ordinary course of his dispensations to mankind, that he does not
> often choose to do so; that he prefers, as an enticement to exertion and for the
> reward of prudence, to permit effects to follow their appropriate causes—to give
> the race to the swift and the battle to the strong.

The importance of character was insisted upon throughout the period.
In 1817, 'Decision of Character' was offered as the key to the future
success of the individual and the nation: 'And what is this great secret
which we are anxious to be put in possession of, this talisman that dis-
solves difficulties into air, this magic wand which disperses every opposing
obstacle, and seems to command surrounding events? Nothing more nor
less than a firm, decisive mind.' A newspaper urged in 1828 that 'it was
the great duty of man to be active. . . It is that firmness of purpose—

that ardour of soul, which shrinks at no discouragement, startles at no false alarm, but with an eye steadily fixed on the object of pursuit, makes its way with resistless energy to attainment. It is *this* that elevates the character of man.' And at the end of the period, in 1842, it was pronounced as obvious that every great man is marked by a 'hearty self-reliance' and that every failure is due to self-distrust.

From beginning to end, the period 1815 to 1845 is dominated by the belief that the cause of man's success lies within himself. It was no accident that the people attributed Andrew Jackson's victory over the British to his superior will power, or that they selected as their leader a man in whom they saw living proof that success inevitably awaits the man of iron will.

Andrew Stevenson, in the quotation with which this chapter began, said of Jackson that 'he seems to have been an orphan from the plough to the presidency.' For another, who was trying to get Jackson into the world without any parents at all, the sentiment seemed so hackneyed that he apologetically enclosed it in quotation marks: 'he was almost born an orphan, and won his way "from the plough to the presidency." ' Jackson's father died before Andrew was born; when Jackson was fourteen his mother went to an unknown grave, from a disease contracted while caring for prisoners of the Revolutionary army aboard a British prison ship in Charles Town harbor.

Jackson's orphaned youth made various appeals to the American imagination. First, of course, was the one of simple sentiment. It was also suggested that because he had no personal family Jackson took for his family the democracy, that is, the people of the country. But the most persistent attitude derived from the circumstances of Jackson's childhood was the one stressed by Stevenson: 'He must, therefore, be regarded as the architect of his own fortunes.' Jackson was the self-made man *par excellence* because, alone in the world from the very beginning, he must have created his own future beyond any possible doubt.

A highly fluid society, such as the United States in the early years of the nineteenth century, faces the problem of insuring social conformity and establishing social direction without the aid of traditional institutions which implement such purposes. The most obvious institution which makes for conformity and direction is the family. Jackson, without a family almost from birth, is the epitome of the self-directed man. As one of his many admirers said, 'There was no one to counsel or guide him; no one to inculcate lessons of prudence; no one to lead him into the paths of useful industry and of restored tranquility—but Jackson wanted no one. At this, perhaps the most critical period of his life, the "iron will" subsequently attributed to his treatment of others, was nobly exercised in governing himself.'

A society in flux solves the problem of social direction by the development of a new character type. Instead of relying upon tradition, which would be impossible since tradition is what is changing, an expanding society internalizes its goals within each of its members, creating what the sociologist, David Riesman, calls the 'inner-directed' character. 'Inner-directed' more precisely describes the type I have been calling 'self-directed.' 'Self-directed' has honorific overtones; it suggests that one creates one's own standards of conduct from within, it creates a sharp antithesis between the individual and the society. What actually seems to happen is that the individual incorporates society's demands into his own consciousness and thereby is led to strive even harder because the demands of the society seem to be the demands of one's own self. The wide horizon of possibilities before the member of a society which is economically and socially open requires the goals of society to be defined in generalized terms. Thus, 'work,' or 'power,' or 'wealth' are designated as goals, goals which are by their nature almost infinitely expansive.

But abstractions are not generally effective instruments of persuasion. It is for this reason that society creates its symbols. Symbols make abstract ideals concrete. One of the functions of the popular image of Andrew Jackson was to give substance to the abstraction, will. For the early nineteenth century Jackson objectified the belief that man was not the creature of circumstance but the master of his own destiny. As President, he seemed to prove that man could overcome all obstacles and rise from obscurity to greatness. As an orphan he underlined the moral implicit in the myth of the self-made man: man is 'self-supported by the innate energy of his own master-spirit.' The history of Andrew Jackson, it was said, established 'beyond disputation . . . that true merit, sooner or later, meets a suitable reward. . . Connected with his life history, there is a moral lesson, imposing as it is grand. To the youth of the country, it is a volume written in letters of gold, and establishes a precedent for imitation, that is beyond price. . . In this land of equal rights, the humblest youth, with honesty, talents and perseverance to recommend him, enjoys the same opportunities with the high-born and wealthy. . . An orphan child, unprotected, without friends, without influence [became President]. . . The American presidents were all "self-made men." '

The statement that all American Presidents were 'self-made' discloses the psychological rather than the factual basis of the myth of the self-made man. It also reminds us that Jackson was only one among a number of men whose careers were interpreted to support the myth. An essay, 'Representative Men,' in the *Southern Literary Messenger* maintained that the two men who stood for the political divisions of the nation, Andrew Jackson and Henry Clay, also represented the basic unity of the nation: 'Both were denied the advantage of education. . . Both were dependent only upon their own exertions and equally independent of adventitious aid. Both were the architects of their own fortunes . . . Both displayed from the start the same enterprizing spirit—the same obduracy and vehemence of will—the same almost arrogant defiance of opposition—the same tenacity and continuity of purpose.' There is a certain ironic appropriateness that Henry Clay, the proponent of Whig economics, should be credited with coining the phrase, 'self-made man,' in a speech on behalf of a paternalistic tariff. But the fact testifies to the universal acceptance of the cult of self-help in America. Clay may have found the phrase that described the belief that man succeeds to the degree of his own will power; Andrew Jackson embodied that belief.

After the Revolution 'our orphan hero,' as Bancroft called Jackson, 'was alone in the world, with no kindred to cherish him, and little inheritance but his own untried powers.' This was sufficient to support the assertion, in the words of still another, that Jackson 'owed to himself, and himself alone, both his education and his fortune.' However, Jackson's youth was not outstanding for the exemplification of 'labour, temperance, and perseverance and virtue,' which was ascribed to it by one biographer. On the contrary, he gambled away what little inheritance he had from his family and was remembered by those who knew him in his early years as a cock-fighting, horse-racing, swaggering young blade. Rather than a depressant, however, Jackson's wastrel youth provided a stimulus to those who were intent on objectifying through him the myth of the self-made man.

Bereft of the guardianship of father or mother, or friends, with the idle and dissolute habits contracted in times of confusion and civil war, he soon squandered the little patrimony that was left him. And to all discerning eyes, the lad, Andrew Jackson, was destined to wander a vagabond through the world, and doomed to a life of want and profligacy. But the divine fire that burned in his bosom, kindled up an energy that enabled him to make his greatest conquest —the conquest of himself. He fled from the country in which he was born—forsook the companions that led him astray; and in a strange land threw away his habits and commenced a new life.

Although this admirer of Jackson has to invoke the divine fire of God (who as we shall see has an important role in the myth of the self-made man) and transport Jackson to a new environment before he can find success, the sense of the statement is that self-control is the final requisite of a man of strong will.

Only to one who assumes that myth-making is a logical process will it seem strange that Jackson's youth could support the belief that the deserving alone find success. The reason such awkward material suited the myth of self-reliance lies in a sentence quoted before. When Jackson was compared to Franklin, it was said that he had 'to establish his name without the patronage of a single relative or friend.' The next clause is the important one: 'if he had not talents and virtues, would he not have remained in obscurity?' Behind that 'if' lies the assumption that the world is a world of justice, an ordered world in which, as we have seen another maintain, God permits 'effects to follow their appropriate causes.' Because they did not doubt that virtue does receive its own reward, believers in the myth of the self-made man were not arguing from cause to effect, they were arguing from effect back to cause; if

Jackson succeeded he *had* to deserve success, particularly since 'he entered the stage of life entirely alone . . . [and] received no aid but what he commanded by his own energy.' In taking Jackson as the example of the self-made man, the popular mind was not arguing from his youth to his success; it was arguing from his success to his youth. If the youth were dissolute, it made little difference. The fact only proved he must have been doubly victorious; he must have conquered himself as well as adverse circumstances.

The orator who was quoted before as saying that 'the character of the American people has been the sole cause of their growth and prosperity,' also observed that the early settlers 'built no alms-houses; (for they tolerated no paupers) .' One who tolerates no paupers can justify his lack of charity only on the grounds that paupers deserve their poverty. This is the obverse of the belief that man succeeds because of himself; he also fails because of himself. When, under the guidance of Robert Hartley, the New York Association for Improving the Condition of the Poor attempted in 1843 a city-wide plan of social service it sent volunteers into the homes of the poor. The function of each social service worker was to combine material aid with exhortations to thrift, diligence, and temperance, and to help the needy to 'discover those hidden springs of virtue within themselves from which *alone* their prosperity might flow.' One patriot put it succinctly: "Plenty overspreads the land. There may be, it is true, much poverty and even suffering; but these, to some extent, spring necessarily from the condition of human society, from the dispensations of Providence, and in no small degree from the vices of mankind.' The tentative tone, 'there may be' and 'to some extent,' vanishes when it comes to the vices of mankind.

When the editor of the *Democratic Review* reviewed 'The Course of Civilization' he felt that the culmination of progress would come when 'all ranks of men would begin life on a fair field, "the world before them where to choose, and Providence their guide." Inclination and sagacity would select the sphere, and dictate the mode and measure of exertion. Frugality and vigilance would compel success, and defeat and ruin be felt only as the requital of ill-desert; or, if such things be, as vicissitudes inflicted by Heaven among its inscrutable designs.' The uneasy qualification at the end is lessened first by the doubt that such things as unmerited adversity do exist, and then dismissed with the assurance that vicissitudes are incorporated in the divine scheme, anyway, and not to be questioned by man.

Andrew Jackson was felt to symbolize the fact that the time had already come when all Americans could begin life on a fair field. The first lesson for posterity that Levi Woodbury found in Jackson's life was the fact that 'without wealth or powerful connections, which even in republics are sometimes passports to fame, he first appeared on the theatre of public action as an orphan . . . he soon displayed an energy and perseverance . . . which are full of encouragement to the most lowly and unfriended.' Another observed that 'when we see the humble orphan boy become a mighty ruler, we feel increased attachment to our form of government, which secures alike to high and low its blessings and its honours.' The success of the self-made man in the United States was due to 'the actions of institutions . . . which throw open to the humblest individual the avenues to wealth and distinction.'

Belief in the self-made man was a source of national pride to Americans, since the American system was supposed to establish conditions which made individual worthiness the only means to success. In the United States an inauspicious beginning in life was a boon; it proved that one deserved whatever success one achieved. 'The greatest merit of our system is that it cooperates with providence to execute the primeval curse, "In the sweat of thy face shalt thou eat bread, till thou return unto the ground." No individual among us can arrive at any high degree of respectability and influence, except by his own efforts.' The primeval curse is transmuted in America into a blessing. As Andrew Stevenson observed in the quotation which began this chapter, 'had [Jackson] been born to wealth and influence, he might probably have lived and died, an obscure and ordinary man.' Although wealth and powerful connections might sometimes, even in republics, bring success, they more often brought the impotence of indolence; poverty is the breeding ground of success. By a geological rather than a biological metaphor, a contemporary admirer ascribed Jackson's success to poverty.

His origin was humble; and the poorest may learn from his career, that poverty is no insuperable bar to the soarings and triumphs of the free spirit. Nay! Let us rather say as we remember how the soil of poverty has sent up its harvest of great men, our Franklin, our Adams, our Henry, and our Jackson; let us rather say, that, as in *the kingdom of geology* the everlasting granite, the underlying basis of all other formations is found in the deepest gulf, yet ever bursting upward from the abyss, towering aloft into highest hills, and crowning the very pinnacles of the world; so in *the kingdom of man,* the primitive rock, the granite formation, is poverty; found deepest in the abyss, borne down, buried thousand-fathom deep, overlaid, crushed to the very centre, yet everywhere forcing its way upward, towering aloft and claiming kindred with the sky!

Although nearly obscured, there was always present in the worship of success the dogma that America *is* an open field. Otherwise it made little sense to compliment the dispossessed of society on their high good fortune.

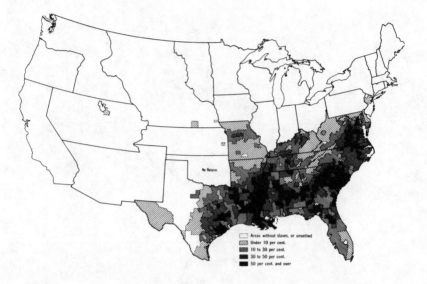

Percent of slaves in total population, 1860. *(Courtesy of Carnegie Institution)*

10 Reform at High Tide, 1830–1860

Reform, a main theme in America's social history, is imbedded in and runs through that history like a vein of common quartz. Seldom has the idea of reform been as much a part of American life as it was in the middle of the nineteenth century, or from about 1830 to 1860. According to Ralph Waldo Emerson, a contemporary observer of the movement, the reformers wished to revise the entire social structure—the state, the school, religion, marriage, trade, science—and explore the very foundation of man's nature. Reform, in other words, was universal in its concern, touching almost every aspect of American life. This universality was wedded to a fundamental moral concern, a fusion that gave the reform movement of this period a unique quality, one that set it off from later reforming crusades.

The basic ideas in this nineteenth-century reform movement were neither new nor peculiar to the United States; they were rooted in the Enlightenment of the preceding century—in the traditions of natural rights, human equality, and the perfectibility of man. In the United States those ideas of the eighteenth century were to a large degree transmitted to the reformers through philosophy—especially through a way of thinking called *transcendentalism,* which assumed the existence of great moral truths that transcend mere proof. If ideas stressing that God is benevolent and man divine and perfectible are unchallengeable truths, it follows that any departure from them violates God's purpose. It was wrong, therefore, for man to be enslaved, or crippled by disease, or shrouded in ignorance, or chained by superstition.

Accepting these conclusions, the reformers held that Christianity guarantees men the right to live as brothers, that as children of God men must be restored to the divinity with which they had been endowed. The reformers wanted to bring freedom to the slave, knowledge to the ignorant, and more humane treatment to the sick, the insane, and the criminal; they wanted to abolish imprisonment for debt and to improve the unfortunate classes in general. As Emerson explained it, the motivation behind all efforts of reform is "the conviction that there is an infinite worthiness in man, which appears at the call of worth, and that all particular reforms are the removing of some impediment." Faith in the perfectibility of man and of society through the reconstruction of social institutions thus formed a philosophical foundation of the movement.

This yearning to bring man to God's perfection also gave the movement the fervor of a crusade. This is, in fact, one of the few American reform movements to take on the characteristics of a moral crusade, and the only major one in which the clergy gave consistent leadership as well as inspiration.

In contrast to most other waves of reform, the crusade of the nineteenth was individualistic—a characteristic that grew logically from transcendentalism's emphasis on private truth and private salvation. Henry D. Thoreau's retreat to Walden Pond, for instance, may be considered a symbol of this untrammeled individualism. Even though the reformers had a passion for all kinds of organizations and collectivistic utopian communities, they would not subordinate the individual mind to the common will.

Even though reformers such as Horace Mann and Dorothea Dix sought government aid for education and the insane, the nineteenth-century crusade also differed from twentieth-century reform movements in that it was, in its essentials at least, nonpolitical. Although some sought to reform the state through political action, the crusaders generally distrusted the state—which, after all, supported social inequities such as slavery, war, and the exploitation of women and children. They were usually indifferent to organized political activity, and the politics of the period were not reformist.

Another distinctive facet of the movement was its leadership. The social reformers were not prominent politicians; they were dignified agitators, men who generally shunned violence, fanatics who were not revolutionary. They usually fought with words, with weapons of the mind and heart. The leaders who were not clergymen were men of letters, men and women we would today call intellectuals.

These reformers and their ideas, despite their nonviolence, inspired a deep distrust of the whole reform movement in the South. In other words, regardless of its universal concern and broad impact on American life, this reform crusade was sectional, mainly a product of New England and the North. The South was practically untouched by its currents, in part at least because the South's ruling class had committed itself to a defense of slavery—an institution that practically all reformers considered indefensible. As a result of the reformers' attitude toward slavery, Southerners felt that whatever the Northern reformers espoused was obnoxious; Southerners considered all reforms tainted because of their association with abolitionism. Thus the South did not experience even the educational and humanitarian reforms of the movement.

The reform movement was also cosmopolitan, enjoying a common climate in Great Britain, Western Europe, and the United States. Europe, in fact, provided models, inspiration, and theory for American reformers. Throughout the Western world there were reformers who demanded recognition of human rights and improvement in the plight of the oppressed and unfortunate. Organized philanthropists in England and on the continent strove to cure all kinds of social ills through humanitarian efforts. For instance, the antislavery crusade had its origins in England; educational reform, in Switzerland and Germany; the utopian movement, in England and France; and penal reform, in Italy.

Another international aspect of the reform movement was romanticism, with its emphasis on the dignity of the individual, on his capacity to perceive his own problems and solve them, and on brotherhood and utopianism. Romanticism imbued the whole crusade. Its influence can be seen in the frequently sentimental and philosophical attitude of the reformers toward women and children, and toward primitive peoples. Romanticism strengthened the concern for "natural rights" and gave vigor to the new humanitarianism—as, for instance, in the attack on capital punishment.

We should note, however, that romanticism was not everywhere humanitarian and did not of itself always inspire reform. In the South it had a contrary effect, being used there to support the myth that slavery was a blessing for the Negro.

In summary, the goal of the nineteenth-century reformers was the full flowering of man's capacities. This goal could be achieved by removing the obstacles in every institution or tradition that stood in the way of an individual's realization of his own powers. "I believe," one of them wrote, "that man becomes more and more endowed with divinity; and as he does he becomes more Godlike in his character and more capable of governing himself. Let us go on elevating our people, perfecting our institutions, until democracy shall reach such a point of perfection that we can acclaim with truth that the voice of the people is the voice of God."

Americans of the mid-nineteenth century thus did see an ultimate connection between social reform and government. They identified nationalism and democracy with social progress and perfectibility. For them reform had both a practical and a supernatural basis.

The reformers failed to wipe out such broad social evils as poverty, disease, vice, and crime. They did succeed, however, in winning many specific objectives in whole or in part, such as women's rights. Yet even in victory, reform did not often lead to the bright, uncorrupted world that its leaders envisioned. Negro slavery came to an end with the adoption of the Thirteenth Amendment in 1865; but recent events have demonstrated that this was only a beginning in "removing the impediments," as Emerson put it, which block the self-fulfillment of this large group in our society.

Nonetheless, the reformers of the mid-nineteenth century performed an important service for the nation. Their crusade made the public aware of basic social ills—many of them stemming from the disruptions of a continuing industrial revolution—and it accelerated changes necessary to cope with new as well as old social problems. That crusade, moreover, has a special place in American history; there has never been another like it. Since their day, furthermore, liberal and humanitarian reform has been in the mainstream of American life.

Merle Curti

New Goals for Democracy

The Growth of American Thought, Merle Curti's classic intellectual history, includes a perceptive analysis of the origins, character, and consequences of the reform movement a generation before the Civil War. The following excerpts have been selected to illuminate one important facet of each of these themes.

The origins of the movement were manifold: American and European; religious, intellectual, and social; reflecting both the optimism of the frontier and the pessimism of the emerging industrial city. Ralph Waldo Emerson, the greatest spokesman for the era, emphasized one source above all: the simple conviction that reform was a law of nature. Curti explains how Emerson arrived at this belief and what its consequences were. The second theme in the selection is the drive for women's rights as an example of the reform movement. This was particularly significant because it involved not a small segment of society, as the blind or insane, but one-half of it, demeaned simply because of their sex. Finally, Curti takes up criticisms of the reform movement as one of its "consequences." His analysis of contemporary attacks on reformers and the principle of reform adds perspective to an important picture. [From "New Goals for Democracy" in The Growth of American Thought, *3rd ed., by Merle Curti. Copyright 1943, 1951 by Harper & Row, Publishers, Inc. Copyright © 1964 by Merle Curti.]*

"What is a man born for," asked Emerson, "but to be a Reformer, a Remaker of what man has made . . . imitating that great Nature which embosoms us all, and which sleeps no moment on an old past, but every hour repairs herself, yielding us every morning a new day, and with every pulsation a new life?" In these words the popular lyceum lecturer from Concord expressed a central tenet in the reform philosophy which inspired men and women in their efforts to reform dress and diet in the interest of universal health, to uproot capital punishment and imprisonment for debt, slavery, intemperance, war, and prostitution, and to agitate for the full rights of women, the humane treatment of the insane and the criminal, and even for the overthrow of such venerable institutions as the family, private property, and the state itself. In another mood, to be sure, Emerson half-whimsically, half-seriously, laid at the door of the reformers many an idiosyncrasy; and in no mood did he ever, like the whole-hearted reformer, surrender his very self to any cause; he was too much an individualist for that, as his criticism of Brook Farm implied. "Spoons and skimmers," he remarked in connection with that idealistic effort to build a better society in microcosm, "you can lay indiscriminately together, but vases and statues require each a pedestal for itself."

Nevertheless, Emerson put his finger on the essential faith of the reformer when he assumed that institutions exist to be improved, that man can improve them along with himself, that the law of human society, like that of physical nature, is one of change. It was this faith that gave a sense of fellowship to reformers even when they vied with each other in celebrating the merits of the particular cause to which they had given the largest place in their hearts. It was this faith in reform as a law of nature that preserved some bond between the most doctrinaire reformers and those of milder temperaments and more pragmatic attitudes. The essential faith Emerson expressed remained even after reformers were bitterly separated on the basic issue of "immediatism" (faith in the possibility of realizing the desired objective in the near future) and "gradualism" (doubt concerning such optimism). Not even the condemnation of powerful and respectable voices or the general indifference of the plain people discouraged the zeal of the true reformer.

Democracy: Women's Rights. The wave of reforms which enlisted so much enthusiasm and so much condemnation in part reflected the advancing force of democracy and in part extended this force into the field of social relationships. Although American democracy in many ways was related to comparable patterns of thought in the Old World, especially to humanitarianism and Romanticism, in some ways it was a unique creed and program of action.

With much plausibility Ralph Gabriel has argued that the American democratic faith which had emerged by the mid-century included both a naturalistic and a supernaturalistic base. On the one hand it rested on the eighteenth-century faith in an orderly, law-governed universe in which both man and his institutions, the more these were harmonized with natural law, improved. On the other hand American democracy merged these concepts with a religiously fervent, transcendental faith in the dignity and potentiality and power of the individual, including the common man. The thoroughly consistent exponents of democracy widened the circle to include women and emphasized the individual not only as a final end but as a means of achieving that end. That end was the full growth and power of the individual, of every individual; the means by which this was to be achieved was individual effort, combined with that of others, to break down all the barriers, be they tradition, law, or interest, that stood in the way of elevating every individual in the most depressed ranks to full power and glory.

It was the merging of the rational doctrine of perfectibility and progress on the one hand with the religious emotion of individualism on the other that came to be identified with America both as a symbol and as an actuality. This complex of democracy and Americanism further implied an inexorable faith in the eternal and universal superiority of America's republican and democratic institutions, of their fitness for all people, at all times, in all places, and of the duty of furthering their final triumph.

The relation of the democratic philosophy to the reform movements could easily be illustrated by an analysis of almost any one of them. Yet for several reasons the agitation against "women's wrongs" is an especially appropriate movement for detailed consideration. For one thing, this crusade was aimed to elevate one-half of the entire population rather than a mere minority of unfortunates. Again, the increasing participation of women in the larger world of ideas, itself of course the result of complex economic and social changes, has so affected the character of American intellectual life in the past three-quarters of a century that the early feminist agitation becomes, in an intellectual history, an obvious illustration to choose for bringing out the democratic implications of the whole humanitarian movement.

The revolt of the feminists—it must never be forgotten that they represented a small fragment of their sex—was in large part a protest in the name of democracy against the subordinate role of females, to use the word most common to the mid-century. Every argument that men had ever employed for their rights as citizens and human beings women crusaders now used. Henceforth, they insisted, the relations between the sexes must be governed by the doctrine of equality, of democracy. And the equality and democracy they had in mind and made explicit in stirring manifestoes was that of mid-century America; its foundation was the natural rights philosophy, its framework was the religious faith that God had created all human beings equal, that He intended each individual to achieve the full realization of every potentiality.

To appreciate the vigor of the demand for the redress of women's wrongs the inferior status of women at that time must be visualized as concretely as possible. In spite of the early interest in Mary Wollstonecraft's *Vindication of the Rights of Women* (1792) on the part of a handful of democratic idealists, and in spite of the example of sex equality among the Shakers, opinion almost universally continued to regard women as unfitted by nature for exercise of the higher mental processes. In consequence they were barred from opportunities for any education beyond the elementary or, at best, the secondary branches. The more usual course was for girls of the farming and lower middle classes to acquire practical skills at home, and for those of better-off families to be polished at boarding schools in the social amenities and the esthetic arts of fancy embroidery and painting on velvet. In general, women did not discuss politics or the larger social issues. According to common law, husbands and fathers not only controlled the property of their wives and daughters but were entitled to complete submissiveness. Even the churches—the Quakers alone excepted—subordinated women by excluding them not only from the ministry but from any public participation in church affairs. Even in what presumably was woman's own sphere, the home, she was bound to be submissive to her husband's will in theory if not in practice. . . .

The first clear-cut and dramatic protest against such ideas came when Frances Wright, a Scottish friend of Lafayette, took up residence in the United States in 1824. Her championship of labor, of public education, and of gradual emancipation of the slave was no less ardent than her devotion to woman's rights. Undeterred by ridicule and venomous threats of physical violence for daring to support greater freedom in marriage relationships, birth control, and what was almost as shocking, the appearance of the delicate sex on the public platform, Frances Wright continued her agitation. Except in Quaker circles, where women had traditionally taken part in "meeting" and in ministration, her campaign met only with rebuffs. Nevertheless, the subsequent feminist campaign owed much to the clear, logical, and forceful arguments by which this courageous crusader denounced the subjection of women by law and custom and pleaded for their emancipation on every level—economic, social, and cultural.

What really launched the feminist crusade was the desire on the part of a small group of women to participate in the movement for the abolition of slaves. The refusal to admit women to the existing antislavery societies or even to permit them to speak in public for the cause led to defiance on the part of such women as Lucretia Mott, the Philadelphia Quakeress, and Angelina and Sarah Grimké, South Carolina aristocrats who had become converted to Quakerism and abolitionism. Barred from existing organizations, women abolitionists formed a national organization of their own in 1834. So great was the opposition that in 1838 a Philadelphia mob burned the hall in which they were meeting. The next year the issue of admitting women to the existing national antislavery society of men broke up the organization into two movements, one composed of men alone, and one in which women cooperated with men on equal terms.

The refusal of the World's Antislavery Convention in London in 1841 to admit the American women delegates led two of them, Lucretia Mott and Elizabeth Cady Stanton, to launch a formal women's rights movement on their return to America. Their program was set forth in the Declaration of Sentiments issued in 1848 at the Seneca Falls Convention. This declaration paraphrased the Declaration of Independence in indicting men for their tyrannies over women. Notwithstanding great opposition, the advocates of women's rights continued to hold conventions, to agitate for the revision of state laws affecting their rights over property, and, in addition, to demand full political, economic, and cultural rights.

It was necessary for the champions of women's rights to shift the arguments that both religion and the natural rights philosophy provided. In spite of Garrison's firm statement, "We *know* that man and woman are equal in the sight of God," the Bible could be and was used with much effectiveness by the conservatives. The Bible apparently made God a male and woman responsible for man's woes. Besides, many specific texts seemed clearly to consign women to a role of inferiority. Gradually the most logical among the crusaders were forced to put greater relative emphasis on natural rights. Women, the argument went, were human beings; all human beings possessed the same inalienable rights to life, liberty, property, and the pursuit of happiness. But able conservative foes were quick to point out that nature meant that which had always existed; women had been eternal inferiors, *ergo* they were so by nature's dictate. Thus it became necessary for feminists to insist that nature included not alone what had been but that which might come. However inferior and degraded women might be as a result of their immemorial thralldom, God and nature alike ordained the necessity of growth.

But the foes of women's wrongs did not stop with reinterpretations of Christianity and of natural law in the interest of an all-inclusive democracy. In the course of time more and more emphasis was put on the argument of utility. The full emancipation of women would, in the words of Elizabeth Oakes Smith, not only enable women to achieve that individuality which was their due; it would also make "the world the better for it." Once free women from the slavery that welded them, regardless of their true individuality, into one stereotype, and they would raise to new heights every cause dear to the best of men: justice, religion, freedom, democracy. The subordination of women, concluded Mrs. Smith, had made them a retarding force in civilization; their emancipation would convert them into a dynamic agent for its progress.

The most profound treatise on women's rights was Margaret Fuller's *Woman in the Nineteenth Century*. In this remarkable book the New England Transcendentalist critic brought together virtually all the arguments in behalf of the full development of women as individuals, and to these she added certain psychological insights and social visions of her own. Sex, she contended, is a relative, not an absolute, matter: "There is no wholly masculine man, no purely feminine woman." Thus all nature cried out against the hard and fast barrier society had drawn between the two. Once this truth was recognized, women would cease living so entirely for men and begin to live for themselves as well. And in so doing they would, in truth, help men to become what had been promised, the sons of God. For men's interests were not contrary to those of women; they were identical by the law of their common being, a law which, if observed, would make them the pillars of one porch, the priests of one worship, the bass and contralto of one song. Man had educated woman more as a servant than as a daughter and had found himself a king without a queen. Stripped of its occasionally vague mysticism and its Transcendentalist verbiage, *Woman in the Nineteenth Century* is seen to demand, on the score of reason, religion, and beauty, the elevation of sex relationships to a new and thoroughly democratic level. . . .

Reform and Democracy Criticized. If in general reformers were too greatly blinded by their zeal for the cause to which they gave unstinted labor, a few at least did occasionally analyze both the motives of many of their colleagues and the shortcomings of the group as a whole. No conservative critic, for example, ever wrote a more witty and penetrating account of "the lunatic fringe" than Thomas Wentworth Higginson, a devoted abolitionist and advocate of other "causes." William Ellery Channing, friend of peace and of the slave, on more than one occasion warned fellow reformers to let their genius have full play, to avoid too narrow modes of action, to give a wide range to thought, imagination, taste, and the affections. In much the same spirit Lydia M. Child, an intense abolitionist, warned her coworkers against permitting "the din of the noisy Present to drown the Music of the Past." Horace Greeley approached some of the conservative critics in analyzing reformers' motives in terms of personal factors. In his essay, "Reforms and Reformers," the crusading editor of the *New York Tribune* wrote that a great number of persons in a democratic society, believing themselves to be underrated in the world's opinion, promoted some reform not because of any genuine quarrel with the actual structure of society but solely because of their own place in it. According to this reformer the desire to be someone, the frustration of being unable to do with impunity much that desires promoted, led many a restless soul into the reform camp. . . .

It remained for conservative intellectuals to criticize the reformer for what they termed his "dyspeptic zeal," inflexible commitment to an oversimplified formula, and indifference to the niceties of social convention. In a bright but mordant essay James Russell Lowell, once of the breed himself, declared that every reformer had a mission (with a capital M) to attend to everybody else's business and to reform, at a moment's notice, everything but himself. Other critics, pushing to an extreme the idea that Greeley expressed, charged that reformers were reformers by reason of mental dyspepsia. One of New York City's four hundred, a scion of the Astor family, facetiously had it that Mr. So-and-So took up with Fourieristic socialism because, being the most henpecked of men, he hoped that in the general distribution of women and goods incident to the triumph of the Cause someone else might get his wife!

That personal motives, psychological maladjustments, the unconscious drive to compensate for feelings of inadequacy and frustration did motivate many a reformer to take up the cudgels for the still more unfortunate Negro or inebriate or criminal is probably as true as it is undemonstrable. In any case the suspicion is at least present, to cite one or two from a score of possible examples, that Joshua Giddings found it easier to turn his back on orthodox Whiggery and take up with reforms after he had lost heavily in land speculations and been generally defeated by hard times. Nor can anyone read of the sorrows and frustrations of such a high-strung child and young girl as Dorothea Dix without sensing some connection between them and her subsequent devotion to the cause of the ill-treated, even tortured victims of insanity.

On the other hand, certain considerations suggest the need of caution in attributing zeal for reform to personal maladjustment. It is open to question whether any one geographical area, such as the northeastern states, was marked by a disproportionate number of psychologically maladjusted persons. Nor is there available evidence to prove that social and economic conservatives included a higher proportion of well-adjusted men and women.

However much conservatives belittled reformers for their personal idiosyncrasies, the wisest admitted, at least in times of crisis when reform views became popular, as abolitionism did after the Emancipation Proclamation, that these men and women were not without a social function. Oliver Wendell Holmes observed that reformers, interfering as they did with vested rights and time-hallowed interests, must needs perform an office comparable to that of nature's sanitary commission for the removal of material nuisances. . . .

The jibes against the reformer on the score that he was a fanatic, a misfit, or a scavenger did not exhaust the onslaughts of the opposition. If Lydia Maria Child may be taken as an authority on the antiabolitionists, the major contingent among the critics of reform, the root of the trouble lay not with the farmers and mechanics. "Manufacturers who supply the South, . . . ministers settled at the South, and editors patronized by the South, are the ones who really promote the mobs," declared this able lady in 1835. "Withdraw the aristocratic influence, and I should be perfectly ready to trust the cause to the good feeling of the people." Mrs. Child no doubt oversimplified the relationship between the opposition to abolitionism on the one hand and personal interest and the aristocratic spirit on the other. Yet an analysis of the arguments of critics of reform and of the democracy to which it was related suggests that much truth lies in the words of this penetrating crusader for the black man's freedom. . . .

To those to whom the present seemed best to the degree that it preserved the past in customs and institutions, reform was a ruthless scythe. In urging the female graduates of an Alabama seminary to cling to the old, the ministerial orator declared that the Amazons of the age who raised a hurricane 'over such harebrained notions and speculations as women's rights and abolitionism were "no co-laborers with the mighty spirits of the past, who have bequeathed to us this good land, and the glorious institutions that we inherit." They were rather, he went on, "the disorganizers of civilization, the foes of liberty, the vampires of high-toned morals and chivalrous deeds." In the words of a critic of the movement for the abolition of capital punishment, reformers had better "recollect that all movement is not progress, and that 'to innovate is not to reform.' "

But reverence for the past was no more important a sentiment in the antireform literature than patriotism. Again and again feminism, abolitionism, and Utopian socialism were condemned as imported European vagaries that had no place at all in America. Even the British-born and British-trained scholar, George Frederick Holmes of the University of Virginia, himself a friendly correspondent of Auguste Comte, Europe's great philosophical innovator, began a critical review of Greeley's *Hints*

Toward Reforms by stigmatizing the proposals under discussion as European importations and therefore un-American. More logical was the deeply felt fear that reform might disturb the traditional love of laissez faire, that it might augment the powers of centralized government and "the seductive embrace of power." Equally frequent was the argument in discussions of Utopian socialism that least of all countries should America permit it, inasmuch as here men of wealth had generally earned their fortunes and treated the industrious poor with as much courtesy as a rich neighbor. In attacks on the peace crusade patriotism was appealed to in support of war and in criticism of the men who would abolish the institution by which our independence had been won and our liberty preserved and extended. Even the temperance cause aroused patriotic denunciation. In opposing it Alexander S. Davis of Hanover, Pennsylvania, declared that the temperance agitation repudiated the principles of 1776—the right to life, liberty, property, and happiness!

Recognizing the importance of a small but active group of the clergy in almost every reform cause, certain critics tried to mobilize anticlerical and free thought sentiment in their denunciations of reform. Thus Alexander Davis, to whom temperance was an un-American crusade, went on, in his *A Loud Call to the Citizens of this Nation,* to defend the constitutional right of manufacturing and selling spiritous liquor without consulting any "bastardly priest in existence . . . and without worshiping, kneeling, cringing to the army of wicked, aristocratic, kingly, haughty, lounging and dissipated priests who are ever engaging in seducing, gulling and blind-folding the people, that the people can be more easily wheedled to support their humbuggery, blackguardism, scoundrelism and beelzibubism."

On the whole the religious interest was more frequently regarded as an anchor to the past than a propeller to the future. If the reformers relied on Scripture, the antireformers did so no less. Indeed, Biblical texts were hurled like David's stones in the counterattacks against the movements for the abolition of capital punishment, Negro slavery, and the alleged wrongs of women. In his criticism of Utopian socialism George Frederick Holmes did not, to be sure, quote Scripture, but he did remind his readers that God, not man, had decreed the curse of labor. He spoke for many gentlemen of the cloth in attributing "the lust for equality in material goods" to a want of earnest religious faith.

Nor did these arguments exhaust the weapons of those who spoke against reform in the name of religion. The old Calvinistic theory of human nature continued to be urged as an impassable barrier in the way of the most philanthropic reforms. Moved by tender sympathy for the sufferings of mankind, the reformer, according to the Reverend James W. Massie, forgot that "men are incurably fallible, that absolution from pain and woe is impossible." But no churchman represented this position so engagingly as the layman Nathaniel Hawthorne. It is true that this faithful follower of the Jackson men in politics had no illusions about American aristocrats, and that his sympathy with the exploited, whether on the plantation or in the mill, found expression. At the same time he was unable to pin his faith to mere reform. "Earth's Holocaust" allegorically pictured the reformers relentlessly heaping into a huge bonfire all that stood in the way of their object, only to find in the end that by neglecting to throw the human heart into the flames they had burned all but the earth itself to a cinder in vain! . . .

All these sources of special interest, patriotism, and religion bulked large in the pressure of public opinion against reform. This despotic and intolerable restraint of conventional forms, Lydia Maria Child urged, led men and women to check their best impulses, suppress their noblest feelings, conceal their highest thoughts. "Each longs," she commented, "for full communion with other souls, but dares not give utterance to such yearnings." What hindered chiefly was the fear of what Mrs. Smith or Mrs. Clark would say, "or the frown of some sect; or the anathema of some synod; or the fashion of some clique; or the laugh of some club; or the misrepresentation of some political party. Oh, thou foolish soul! Thou art afraid of thy neighbor, and knowest not that he is equally afraid of thee. He has bound thy hands, and thou has fettered his feet. It were wise for both to snap the imaginary bonds, and walk onward unshackled."

Reformers never lost faith in their ability sooner or later to make the common man see eye to eye with them on all the matters which to the active humanitarians so vitally affected the well-being of the masses. Humble folk did, to be sure, take active parts in the reforms immediately affecting their own status, such as the movement for the abolition of imprisonment for debt, manhood suffrage, and the onslaught against monopolies. Temperance also enlisted fairly widespread support. But in general it seems clear, from present knowledge of the reform causes, that the majority of the people in the ordinary walks of life were either indifferent or hostile to the reform movements that did not seem to touch their own interests in some fairly immediate or obvious way. The industrial workers for the most part were apparently indifferent to the antislavery argument that linked the advance of the wage earner with the freedom of the slave. Artisans and farmers were represented in the Fourierist communities, but in many instances at least they were outnumbered by the small business and professional men and their wives who provided the leadership. By and large, neither the plain man nor the plain woman had much except contempt for the democratic doctrines of the feminists.

The doctrine of democracy, which did indeed arouse the enthusiasm of the common man, also felt the sting of critics. The sympathetic account of America by Tocqueville, perhaps the most profound and original of the European commentators on American institutions in this period, was nevertheless qualified by a basic reservation. Equalitarianism, according to this French aristocrat, on the whole tended to promote despotism, the despotism of the masses. Once the leveling of individuals had progressed far enough, the historical and conventional barriers which protected individuals from invasions of state power by the masses no longer held. This position was probably publicized in greater measure by Francis Lieber, the German-American scholar whose writings in political science were widely read among scholars. Lieber never tired of denouncing the tendency of democracy to jeopardize individual liberties, especially property rights. His attacks on the social contract theory, similar to those of Story and other legal conservatives, were as vigorous as his demands for the restraint of the people by fundamental laws, the best buttresses, he thought, for individual liberties.

Among the literary critics of democracy James Fenimore Cooper and Herman Melville may be taken as representative. Cooper, it will be recalled, quarreled with democracy not from any theoretical concern—he approved of democratic theory—but because of the everyday churlishness of ordinary people with their disrespect for the aristocratic values of decorum and dignity. As a large landowner he found additional reason to vent his spleen when the New York antirent agitation demanded the abolition of tenantry; equalitarian agrarianism was in his jaundiced eyes the worst possible of the evils born of democracy. Herman Melville's distrust of democracy was both more theoretical and more profound. He observed in one of his allegorical novels, *Mardi* (1849), that, after all, political freedom was not a prime and chief blessing; it was good only as a means to personal freedom, uprightness, justice, and felicity. These, continued the adventuresome and mystical sailor of the Southern Seas, were qualities not to be shared or to be won by sharing. On the contrary, they were virtues either born with the individual, civilized or barbarian, flesh of his flesh, blood of his blood, or to be won and held by him and by him alone. However loudly the thrall yelled out his liberty, he still remained a slave. In a universe in which chronic malady was a fact, the individual was more likely to be free, upright, just, and happy under a single monarch than if he were exposed to the violence and whims of twenty million monarchs, though he be one of them. . . .

Cooper with his whining thrusts at men in shirtsleeves and Melville with his dislike of mankind in the mass spoke largely for themselves, though in a sense they also voiced the misgivings of the older Calvinist and Episcopalian mercantile and landed classes toward democracy. The most systematic attacks, however, came not from these quarters in the North or, certainly, from the rising industrialists, but from the southern planting aristocracy. . . .

Toward a
Reconsideration
of Abolitionists

David Donald

Although concerned mainly with one aspect of the reform movement—abolitionism—the following essay raises questions pertinent to the whole humanitarian crusade. Not satisfied with traditional explanations, David Donald, one of the more perceptive historians writing on the era of the Civil War, asks why humanitarian reform emerged with such vigor when it did, why Americans were more conscious of social evils in the 1830s than in any earlier decade. In offering his own interpretation, Donald analyzes the leadership of the abolitionist cause, using techniques of the social scientist as well as of the historian. His conclusions confirm the identification of reform with New England, but he questions the basic humanitarian impulses of the reformers—especially the abolitionists—and he places the origin of reform in the disruptions in Northern society rather than in the ideas from abroad. [Reprinted from Lincoln Reconsidered *by David Donald. Copyright 1956 by David Donald. Reprinted by permission of Alfred A. Knopf, Inc.]*

Abraham Lincoln was not an abolitionist. He believed that slavery was a moral wrong, but he was not sure how to right it. When elected President, he was pledged to contain, not to extirpate, the South's peculiar institution. Only after offers of compensation to slaveholders had failed and after military necessities had become desperate did he issue his Emancipation Proclamation. Even then his action affected only a portion of the Negroes, and the President himself seemed at times unsure of the constitutionality of his proclamation.

It is easy to see, then, why earnest antislavery men were suspicious of Lincoln. Unburdened with the responsibilities of power, unaware of the larger implications of actions, they criticized the President's slowness, doubted his good faith, and hoped for his replacement by a more vigorous emancipationist. Such murmurings and discontents are normal in American political life; in every village over the land there is always at least one man who can tell the President how the government ought to be run.

But a small group of extreme antislavery men, doctrinaire advocates of immediate and uncompensated abolition, assailed the wartime President with a virulence beyond normal expectation. It was one thing to worry about the fixity of Lincoln's principles, but quite another to denounce him, as did Wendell Phillips, as "the slave-hound of Illinois." Many Republicans might reasonably have wanted another candidate in 1864, but there was something almost paranoid in the declaration by a group of Iowa abolitionists that "Lincoln, . . . a Kentuckian by birth, and his brothers-in-law being in the rebel army, is evidently, by his sympathies with the owners of slaves, checked in crushing the rebellion by severe measures against slaveholders." A man might properly be troubled by Lincoln's reconstruction plans, but surely it was excessive for a Parker Pillsbury to pledge that, "by the grace of God and the Saxon Tongue," he would expose the "hypocrisy and cruelty" of Lincoln and of "whatever other President dares tread in his bloody footsteps."

The striking thing here is the disproportion between cause and effect— between Lincoln's actions, which were, after all, against slavery, and the abuse with which abolitionists greeted them. When a patient reacts with excessive vehemence to a mild stimulus, a doctor at once becomes suspicious of some deep-seated malaise. Similarly, the historian should be alert to see in extraordinary and unprovoked violence of expression the symptom of some profound social or psychological dislocation. In this instance, he must ask what produced in these abolitionists their attitude of frozen hostility toward the President.

These abolitionist leaders who so excessively berated Lincoln belonged to a distinct phase of American antislavery agitation. Their demand for an unconditional and immediate end of slavery, which first became articulate around 1830, was different from earlier antislavery sentiment, which had focused on gradual emancipation with colonization of the freed Negroes. And the abolitionist movement, with its Garrisonian deprecation of political action, was also distinct from political antislavery, which became dominant in the 1840's. The abolitionist, then, was a special type of antislavery agitator, and his crusade was part of that remarkable American social phenomenon which erupted in the 1830's, "freedom's ferment," the effervescence of kindred humanitarian reform movements—prohibition; prison reform; education for the blind, deaf, dumb; world peace; penny postage; women's rights; and a score of lesser and more eccentric drives.

Historians have been so absorbed in chronicling what these movements did, in allocating praise or blame among squabbling factions in each, and in making moral judgments on the desirability of various reforms that they have paid surprisingly little attention to the movement as a whole. Few serious attempts have been made to explain why humanitarian reform appeared in America when it did, and more specifically why immediate abolitionism, so different in tone, method, and membership from its predecessors and its successor, emerged in the 1830's.

The participants in such movements naturally give no adequate explanation for such a causal problem. According to their voluminous memoirs and autobiographies, they were simply convinced by religion, by reading, by reflection that slavery was evil, and they pledged their lives and their sacred honor to destroy it. Seeing slavery in a Southern state, reading an editorial by William Lloyd Garrison, hearing a sermon by Theodore Dwight Weld—such events precipitated a decision made on the highest moral and ethical planes. No one who has studied the abolitionist literature can doubt the absolute sincerity of these accounts. Abolitionism was a dangerous creed of devotion, and no fair-minded person can believe that men joined the movement for personal gain or for conscious self-glorification. In all truth, the decision to become an antislavery crusader was a decision of conscience.

But when all this is admitted, there are still fundamental problems. Social evils are always present; vice is always in the saddle while virtue trudges on afoot. Not merely the existence of evil but the recognition of it is the prerequisite for reform. Were there more men of integrity, were there more women of sensitive conscience in the 1830's than in any previous decade? A generation of giants these reformers were indeed, but why was there such a concentration of genius in those ten years from 1830 to 1840? If the individual's decision to join the abolitionist movement was a matter of personality or religion or philosophy, is it not necessary to inquire why so many similar personalities or religions or philosophies appeared in America simultaneously? In short, we need to know why so many Americans in the 1830's were predisposed toward a certain kind of reform movement.

Many students have felt, somewhat vaguely, this need for a social interpretation of reform. Little precise analysis has been attempted, but the general histories of antislavery attribute the abolitionist movement to the Christian tradition, to the spirit of the Declaration of Independence, to the ferment of Jacksonian democracy, or to the growth of romanticism. That some or all of these factors may have relation to abolitionism can be granted, but this helps little. Why did the "spirit of Puritanism," to which one writer attributes the movement, become manifest as militant abolitionism in the 1830's although it had no such effect on the previous generation? Why did the Declaration of Independence find fulfillment in abolition during the sixth decade after its promulgation, and not in the fourth or the third?

In their elaborate studies of the antislavery movement, Gilbert H. Barnes and Dwight L. Dumond have pointed up some of the more immediate reasons for the rise of American abolitionism. Many of the most important antislavery leaders fell under the influence of Charles Grandison Finney, whose revivalism set rural New York and the Western Reserve ablaze with religious fervor and evoked "Wonderful outpourings of the Holy Spirit" throughout the North. Not merely did Finney's invocation of the fear of hell and the promise of heaven rouse sluggish souls to renewed religious zeal, but his emphasis upon good works and pious endeavor as steps toward salvation freed men's minds from the bonds of arid theological controversies. One of Finney's most famous converts was Theodore Dwight Weld, the greatest of the Western abolitionists, "eloquent as an angel and powerful as thunder," who recruited a band of seventy antislavery apostles, trained them in Finney's revivalistic techniques, and sent them forth to consolidate the emancipation movement in the North. Their greatest successes were reaped in precisely those communities where Finney's preaching had prepared the soil.

Barnes and Dumond also recognized the importance of British influence upon the American antislavery movement. The connection is clear and easily traced: British antislavery leaders fought for immediate emancipation in the West Indies; reading the tracts of Wilberforce and Clarkson converted William Lloyd Garrison to immediate abolitionism at about the same time that Theodore Weld was won over to the cause by his English friend Charles Stuart; and Weld in turn gained for the movement the support of the Tappan brothers, the wealthy New York merchants and philanthropists who contributed so much in money and time to the antislavery crusade. Thus, abolition had in British precedent a model, in Garrison and Weld leaders, and in the Tappans financial backers.

Historians are deeply indebted to Professors Barnes and Dumond, for the importance of their studies on the antislavery movement is very great. But perhaps they have raised as many questions as they have answered. Both religious revivalism and British antislavery theories had a selective influence in America. Many men heard Finney and Weld, but only certain communities were converted. Hundreds of Americans read Wilberforce, Clarkson, and the other British abolitionists, but only the Garrisons and the Welds were convinced. The question remains: Whether they received the idea through the revivalism of Finney or through the publications of British antislavery spokesmen, why were some Americans in the 1830's for the first time moved to advocate immediate abolition? Why was this particular seed bed ready at this precise time?

I believe that the best way to answer this difficult question is to analyze the leadership of the abolitionist movement. There is, unfortunately, no complete list of American abolitionists, and I have had to use a good deal of subjective judgment in drawing up a roster of leading reformers. From the classified indexes of the *Dictionary of American Biography* and the old Appleton's *Cyclopaedia of American Biography* and from important primary and secondary works on the reform generation, I made a list of about two hundred and fifty persons who seemed to be identified with the antislavery cause. This obviously is not a definitive enumeration of all the important abolitionists; had someone else compiled it, other names doubtless would have been included. Nevertheless, even if one or two major spokesmen have accidentally been omitted, this is a good deal more than a representative sampling of antislavery leadership.

After preliminary work I eliminated nearly one hundred of these names. Some proved not to be genuine abolitionists but advocates of colonizing the freed Negroes in Africa; others had only incidental interest or sympathy for emancipation. I ruthlessly excluded those who joined the abolitionists after 1840, because the political antislavery movement clearly poses a different set of causal problems. After this weeding out, I had reluctantly to drop other names because I was unable to secure more than random bits of information about them. Some of Weld's band of seventy agitators, for instance, were so obscure that even Barnes and Dumond were unable to identify them. There remained the names of one hundred and six abolitionists, the hard core of active antislavery leadership in the 1830's.

Most of these abolitionists were born between 1790 and 1810, and when the first number of the *Liberator* was published in 1831, their median age was twenty-nine. Abolitionism was thus a revolt of the young.

My analysis confirms the traditional identification of radical antislavery with New England. Although I made every effort to include Southern and Western leaders, eighty-five per cent of these abolitionists came from Northeastern states, sixty per cent from New England, thirty per cent from Massachusetts alone. Many of the others were descended from New England families. Only four of the leaders were born abroad or were second-generation immigrants.

The ancestors of these abolitionists are in some ways as interesting as the antislavery leaders themselves. In the biographies of their more famous descendants certain standard phrases recur: "of the best New England stock," "of Pilgrim descent," "of a serious, pious household." The parents of the leaders generally belonged to a clearly defined stratum of society. Many were preachers, doctors, or teachers; some were farmers and a few were merchants; but only three were manufacturers (and two of these on a very small scale), none was a banker, and only one was an ordinary day laborer. Virtually all the parents were staunch Federalists.

These families were neither rich nor poor, and it is worth remembering that among neither extreme did abolitionism flourish. The abolitionist could best appeal to "the substantial men" of the community, thought Weld, and not to "the *aristocracy* and fashionable worldliness" that remained aloof from reform. In *The Burned-Over District,* an important analysis of reform drives in western New York, Whitney R. Cross has confirmed Weld's social analysis. In New York, antislavery was strongest in those counties which had once been economically dominant but which by the 1830's, though still prosperous, had relatively fallen behind their more advantageously situated neighbors. As young men the fathers of abolitionists had been leaders of their communities and states; in their old age they were elbowed aside by the merchant prince, the manufacturing tycoon, the corporation lawyer. The bustling democracy of the 1830's passed them by; as the Reverend Ludovicus Weld lamented to his famous son Theodore: "I have . . . felt like a stranger in a strange land."

If the abolitionists were descendants of old and distinguished New England families, it is scarcely surprising to find among them an enthusiasm for higher education. The women in the movement could not, of course, have much formal education, nor could the three Negroes here included, but of the eighty-nine white male leaders, at least fifty-three attended college, university, or theological seminary. In the East, Harvard and Yale were the favored schools; in the West, Oberlin; but in any case the training was usually of the traditional liberal-arts variety.

For an age of chivalry and repression there was an extraordinary proportion of women in the abolitionist movement. Fourteen of these leaders were women who defied the convention that the female's place was at the fireside, not in the forum, and appeared publicly as antislavery apostles. The Grimké sisters of South Carolina were the most famous of these, but most of the antislavery heroines came from New England.

It is difficult to tabulate the religious affiliations of antislavery leaders. Most were troubled by spiritual discontent, and they wandered from one sect to another seeking salvation. It is quite clear, however, that there was a heavy Congregational-Presbyterian and Quaker preponderance. There were many Methodists, some Baptists, but very few Unitarians, Episcopalians, or Catholics. Recent admirable dissertations on the antislavery movement in each of the Western states, prepared at the University of Michigan under Professor Dumond's supervision, confirm the conclusion that, except in Pennsylvania, it is correct to consider humanitarian reform and Congregational-Presbyterianism as causally interrelated.

Only one of these abolitionist leaders seems to have had much connection with the rising industrialism of the 1830's, and only thirteen of the entire group were born in any of the principal cities of the United States. Abolition was distinctly a rural movement, and throughout the crusade many of the antislavery leaders seemed to feel an instinctive antipathy toward the city. Weld urged his following: "Let the great cities *alone;* they must be burned down by *back fires*. The springs to touch in order to move them *lie in the country*."

In general the abolitionists had little sympathy or understanding for the problems of an urban society. Reformers though they were, they were men of conservative economic views. Living in an age of growing industrialization, of tenement congestion, of sweatshop oppression, not one of them can properly be identified with the labor movement of the 1830's. Most would agree with Garrison, who denounced labor leaders for trying "to inflame the minds of our working classes against the more opulent, and to persuade men that they are contemned and oppressed by a wealthy aristocracy." After all, Wendell Phillips assured the laborers, the American factory operative could be "neither wronged nor oppressed" so long as he had the ballot. William Ellery Channing, gentle high priest of the Boston area, told dissatisfied miners that moral self-improvement was a more potent weapon than strikes, and he urged that they take advantage of the leisure afforded by unemployment for mental and spiritual self-cultivation. A Massachusetts attempt to limit the hours of factory operatives to ten a day was denounced by Samuel Gridley Howe, veteran of a score of humanitarian wars, as "emasculating the people" because it took from them their free right to choose their conditions of employment.

The suffering of laborers during periodic depressions aroused little sympathy among abolitionists. As Emerson remarked tartly, "Do not tell me . . . of my obligation to put all poor men in good situations. Are they *my* poor? I tell thee, thou foolish philanthropist, that I grudge the dollar, the dime, the cent I give to such men."

Actually it is clear that abolitionists were not so much hostile to labor as indifferent to it. The factory worker represented an alien and unfamiliar system toward which the antislavery leaders felt no kinship or responsibility. Sons of the old New England of Federalism, farming, and foreign commerce, the reformers did not fit into a society that was beginning to be dominated by a bourgeoisie based on manufacturing and trade. Thoreau's bitter comment, "We do not ride on the railroads; they ride on us," was more than the acid aside of a man whose privacy at Walden had been invaded; it was the reaction of a class whose leadership had been discarded. The bitterest attacks in the journals of Ralph Waldo Emerson, the most pointed denunciations in the sermons of Theodore Parker, the harshest philippics in the orations of Charles Sumner were directed against the "Lords of the Loom," not so much for exploiting their labor as for changing the character and undermining the morality of old New England.

As Lewis Tappan pointed out in a pamphlet suggestively titled *Is It Right to Be Rich?*, reformers did not object to ordinary acquisition of money. It was instead that "eagerness to amass property" which made a man "selfish, unsocial, mean, tyrannical, and but a nominal Christian" that seemed so wrong. It is worth noting that Tappan, in his numerous examples of the vice of excessive accumulation, found this evil stemming from manufacturing and banking, and never from farming or foreign trade—in which last occupation Tappan himself flourished.

Tappan, like Emerson, was trying to uphold the old standards and to protest against the easy morality of the new age. "This invasion of Nature by Trade with its Money, its Credit, its Steam, its Railroads," complained Emerson, "threatens to upset the balance of man, and establish a new universal monarchy more tyrannical than Babylon or Rome." Calmly Emerson welcomed the panic of 1837 as a wholesome lesson to the new monarchs of manufacturing: "I see good in such emphatic and universal calamity."

Jacksonian democracy, whether considered a labor movement or a triumph of laissez-faire capitalism, obviously had little appeal for the abolitionist conservative. As far as can be determined, only one of these abolitionist leaders was a Jacksonian; nearly all were strong Whigs. William Lloyd Garrison made his first public appearance in Boston to endorse the arch-Whig Harrison Gray Otis; James G. Birney campaigned throughout Alabama to defeat Jackson newspapers. Not merely the leaders but their followers as well seem to have been hostile to Jacksonian democracy, for it is estimated that fifty-nine out of sixty Massachusetts abolitionists belonged to the Whig party.

Jacksonian Democrats recognized the opposition of the abolitionists and accused the leaders of using slavery to distract public attention from more immediate economic problems at home. "The abolitionists of the North have mistaken the color of the American slaves," Theophilus Fisk wrote tartly; "all the real Slaves in the United States have pale faces. . . . I will venture to affirm that there are more slaves in Lowell and Nashua alone than can be found South of the Potomac."

Here, then, is a composite portrait of abolitionist leadership. Descended from old and socially dominant Northeastern families, reared in a faith of aggressive piety and moral endeavor, educated for conservative leadership, these young men and women who reached maturity in the 1830's faced a strange and hostile world. Social and economic leadership was being transferred from the country to the city, from the farmer to the manufacturer, from the preacher to the corporation attorney. Too distinguished a family, too gentle an education, too nice a morality were handicaps in a bustling world of business. Expecting to lead, these young people found no followers. They were an elite without function, a displaced class in American society.

Some—like Daniel Webster—made their terms with the new order and lent their talents and their family names to the greater glorification of the god of trade. But many of the young men were unable to overcome their traditional disdain for the new money-grubbing class that was beginning to rule. In these plebeian days they could not be successful in politics; family tradition and education prohibited idleness; and agitation allowed the only chance for personal and social self-fulfillment.

If the young men were aliens in the new industrial society, the young women felt equally lost. Their mothers had married preachers, doctors, teachers, and had become dominant moral forces in their communities. But in rural New England of the 1830's the westward exodus had thinned the ranks of eligible suitors, and because girls of distinguished family hesitated to work in the cotton mills, more and more turned to schoolteaching and nursing and other socially useful but unrewarding spinster tasks. The women, like the men, were ripe for reform.

They did not support radical economic reforms because fundamentally these young men and women had no serious quarrel with the capitalistic system of private ownership and control of property. What they did question, and what they did rue, was the transfer of leadership to the wrong groups in society, and their appeal for reform was a strident call for their own class to re-exert its former social dominance. Some fought for prison reform; some for women's rights; some for world peace; but ultimately most came to make that natural identification between moneyed aristocracy, textile-manufacturing, and Southern slave-grown cotton. An attack on slavery was their best, if quite unconscious, attack upon the new industrial system. As Richard Henry Dana, Jr., avowed: "I am a Free Soiler, because I am . . . of the stock of the old Northern gentry, and have a particular dislike to any subserviency on the part of our people to the slave-holding oligarchy"—and, he might have added, to their Northern manufacturing allies.

With all its dangers and all its sacrifices, membership in a movement like abolitionism offered these young people a chance for a reassertion of their traditional values, an opportunity for association with others of their kind, and a possibility of achieving that self-fulfillment which should traditionally have been theirs as social leaders. Reform gave meaning to the lives of this displaced social elite. "My life, what has it been?" queried one young seeker; "the panting of a soul after eternity— the feeling that there was nothing here to fill the aching void, to provide enjoyment and occupation such as my spirit panted for. The world, what has it been? a howling wilderness. I seem to be just now awakened . . . to a true perception of the end of my being, my duties, my responsibilities, the rich and perpetual pleasures which God has provided for us in the fulfillment of duty to Him and to our fellow creatures. Thanks to the antislavery cause, it first gave an impetus to my palsied intellect."

Viewed against the backgrounds and common ideas of its leaders, abolitionism appears to have been a double crusade. Seeking freedom for the Negro in the South, these reformers were also attempting a restoration of the traditional values of their class at home. Leadership of humanitarian reform may have been influenced by revivalism or by British precedent, but its true origin lay in the drastic dislocation of Northern society. Basically, abolitionism should be considered the anguished protest of an aggrieved class against a world they never made.

Such an interpretation helps explain the abolitionists' excessive suspicion of Abraham Lincoln. Not merely did the President, with his plebeian origins, his lack of Calvinistic zeal, his success in corporate law practice, and his skill in practical politics, personify the very forces that they thought most threatening in Northern society, but by his effective actions against slavery he left the abolitionists without a cause. The freeing of the slaves ended the great crusade that had brought purpose and joy to the abolitionists. For them Abraham Lincoln was not the Great Emancipator; he was the killer of the dream.

*As shown above, both presidential candidates in 1848 were attacked for their associa-
tion with the Mexican War. General Zachary Taylor, the war hero and Whig candidate,
sits in triumph on a mound of skulls. (Courtesy of the New York Historical Society)
His Democratic opponent, Lewis Cass of Michigan, waves a "Manifest Destiny" sword
and is depicted as a cannon belching "gas"—since the Whigs deemed him a bag of
wind. (Houghton Library, Harvard University)*

11 Manifest Destiny

No theme is more prominent in the history of nineteenth-century America than that of expansion. From the beginning, Americans were an expanding people who pushed westward from the Atlantic seaboard, pierced the Appalachians, spanned the Mississippi, challenged the Rockies, and in the 1840s coveted the coastal lands washed by the Pacific. Historians have usually attempted to explain this expansion—especially the feverish, ruthless burst of the 1840s that added over 1,200,000 square miles to the national domain, an increase of more than 65 per cent—with a mystic concept called *manifest destiny*. In other words, by bringing most of the Oregon country, California, Texas, and the lands of the Southwest into the Union, Americans were merely doing what was "manifestly destined."

Despite the bumptious self-confidence implicit in the very idea of manifest destiny, definitions of the term—or the characteristics attributed to it—are often vague and contradictory. One characteristic most often considered a part of the manifest destiny of the 1840s was democracy. According to those who have advanced this idea, Americans had a mission, a mandate, a special gift from heaven, to spread their democratic faith and institutions over all of North America, and perhaps beyond. It was their duty to "extend the area of freedom," for they were destined to transmit to posterity their sublime capacity for self-government.

Linked closely to democracy, according to some interpretations, was nationalism. Americans had to increase their nation's power and territory, nationalists insisted, to exercise their civilizing mandate properly. They had to expand, it has been said, to release "the pent-up forces of the developing national spirit." "I suppose," a congressional expansionist announced, "the right of a manifest destiny to spread will not be admitted to exist in any nation except the universal Yankee." Despite sentiments such as these, Frederick Merk, a careful student of expansion, has denied that manifest destiny was an expression of nationalism. The era of the 1840s, he asserts, exhibited little nationalism. Powerful among the forces constituting manifest destiny was the doctrine of states' rights, for which expansionists had a strong taste. Because manifest destiny did not reflect the national spirit, he argues, it never acquired national, sectional, or party following commensurate with its bigness.

Nonetheless, some of those who believed in national destiny claimed that the nation's expansion had the sanction of higher law, because Americans' claims were based on moral principles, and God preferred to be on the side of morality even though secular law might say that those lands belonged to others. The American conviction also had Newtonian law on its side. The law of political gravitation, John Quincy Adams said, would inevitably pull outlying territory to the United States. This view was allied to the theory of geographical predestination, or contiguity. Geography, it was maintained, had ordained that the stars and stripes should fly over all of North America. From this it was easy to advance to the idea of the destined use of the soil: Americans would till the soil more efficiently than could the Mexicans, and hence were destined to have it. "To replenish the earth and subdue it," the New York Democrats said in 1848, "was man's ordained mission and destiny."

Another characteristic stressed by some historians is that of *peaceful* expansion. These historians allege that manifest destiny, unlike European imperialism, was not based on force, on militarism. Americans spread over what was practically an empty continent. Their action might even be called, according to one analyst, manifest opportunity. If this explanation is contradicted by pointing to American action in the Mexican War, one might still argue that manifest destiny was in essence peaceful because the thrust against Mexico was a defensive maneuver designed to forestall British encroachments in North America. Moreover, the Mexican people would be regenerated by the superior democratic institutions from the north and by "purer blood."

This last rationalization touches on another element within the folklore of manifest destiny—racism. The Mexicans and Indians, the racial argument goes, were as manifestly incapable of self-government as Americans were capable. These "backward" peoples had no right to question destiny; they must accept it. Justin H. Smith, an historian of the Mexican War, has said that providence called upon Americans to regenerate Mexico's "decadent population," and a congressman of the 1840s saw democracy and racism committed to the same mission. He was convinced that "this continent was intended by Providence as a vast theatre on which to work out the grand experiment of Republican government, under the auspices of the Anglo-Saxon race."

Although historians have not agreed upon these characteristics or upon any precise definition of manifest destiny as a rationale for mid-century expansion, the origins of the term and the circumstances of its use are clear enough. Whatever zeal there was for manifest destiny seems to have reached a high point in 1844. In that year, expansionists gained key positions in the Democratic party, and at its Baltimore convention the party accepted their demands by resolving "that our title to the whole territory of Oregon is clear and unquestionable; that no portion of the same ought to be ceded to England or any other power; and that the reoccupation of Oregon and the re-annexation of Texas at the earliest practicable period are great American measures." That resolution implied what was not so—that all of Oregon and Texas rightfully belonged to the United States.

Since the resolution linked the Oregon question with that of Texas and hence balanced the objectives of Southern and Western expansionists, it has been referred to as the "Bargain of 1844." While it may not have resulted from a formal bargain, that part of the platform certainly expressed the sentiments of expansionists from the South and West. Texas and Oregon—and hence, in one sense of the term, manifest destiny—became primary issues in the presidential campaign.

Although James K. Polk, the Democratic candidate, won only a narrow victory, he took it as a mandate to press for as much of Oregon as he could get, to settle the Texas issue with Mexico, and to acquire California and Mexico's lands in the Southwest. In other words, he identified himself fully with his party's platform and was prepared to carry out its expansionist demands.

When Polk's demands for all of Oregon led to a crisis with Great Britain, excitement in the United States rose to feverish intensity. Those who supported him advanced arguments explaining why Oregon should belong to the United States. One of them, John L. O'Sullivan, editor of the New York *Morning News,* apparently coined the phrase "manifest destiny." The "true title" to Oregon, he wrote in December 1845, comes from "our manifest destiny to overspread and to possess the whole of the continent which Providence has given us." A week later a member of Congress picked up O'Sullivan's phrase and told the House that the American title to Oregon was founded on *"the right of manifest destiny to spread over the whole continent."* Opponents of Polk's policy, however, called this the "robber's title."

This criticism was particularly cutting when applied to Polk's policy that led to the war with Mexico, and to his policy during the war. Polk insisted that he had tried to avoid war, yet his actions prior to the outbreak of hostilities give the impression that he was determined to force war upon Mexico to satisfy territorial ambitions—mainly to acquire California and the Southwest. His Whig opponents thus charged that he provoked war with the intent of despoiling his neighbor. Scholars, too, have questioned the sincerity of his desire to avoid war, pointing out that entries in his diary reveal that he anticipated the conflict.

Historians have also questioned the rationale of manifest destiny itself, especially the contradictions in the arguments of the expansionists. If it was in fact the national destiny to expand, they ask, why was the Mexican War unpopular? Why did so many Americans question destiny itself?

To some historians, manifest destiny was nothing more than a form of imperialism, the use of force to acquire other people's territory. The war against Mexico, they point out, was a war of conquest, and manifest destiny merely a self-righteous attempt to justify it—an effort to make a weak case look good through the use of pious phrases. Regardless of the American emphasis on the sense of mission, it is clear that destiny did not manifest itself to the Mexicans. They could not understand why the American mandate had to be carried out at their expense. Nonetheless, defenders of manifest destiny still insist that it was essentially a peaceful development, an expansion that despoiled no nation unjustly.

The expansionist fervor of the 1840s ended with the Civil War, but the idea of manifest destiny did not die, nor did the debate over the meaning of the concept. In the selections that follow, one historian explains the nature of the opposition to the Mexican War and why manifest destiny, in effect, was involved in politics, and the other two probe the general theme of manifest destiny.

Julius W. Pratt   # The Ideology of American Expansion

In this essay a distinguished diplomatic historian and careful student of American territorial expansion places manifest destiny in an ideological and historical context. Some historians have seen manifest destiny as a flowering of American idealism, as a fever in the blood, as evidence of a Southern plot to expand the power of slaveholders, as a feeling that Americans must spread the benefits of democracy throughout North America, or as the expression of an unquenchable nationalism. Pratt accepts none of these interpretations at face value. In tracing the course of American expansionism in the nineteenth century, he points out that the character of manifest destiny has never been defined in any precise way and that Americans have always resorted to divine sanction to rationalize the taking of other peoples' territory. If manifest destiny had any distinctive qualities, according to Pratt's analysis, they were its racism and its close ties to the Democratic party. Manifest destiny, in his judgment, "became a justification for almost any addition of territory which the United States had the will and the power to obtain." Does your own analysis of the evidence suggest a similar conclusion? [From Julius Pratt, "The Ideology of American Expansion," in Essays in Honor of William E. Dodd, *ed. Avery Craven (Chicago: University of Chicago Press, 1935), pp. 335–353.]*

Lincoln Steffens has observed that Americans have never learned to do wrong knowingly; that whenever they compromise with principle or abandon it, they invariably find a pious justification for their action. One is reminded of this observation in reviewing the history of American territorial expansion. For every step in that process, ingenious minds have found the best of reasons. From the year 1620, when King James the First granted to the Council for New England certain "large and goodlye Territoryes' in order "to second and followe God's sacred Will," to the year 1898, when William McKinley alleged that he had divine sanction for taking the Philippine Islands, it has been found possible to fit each successive acquisition of territory into the pattern of things decreed by divine will or inescapable destiny. The avowal of need or greed, coupled with power to take, has never satisfied our national conscience. We needed Florida and the mouth of the Mississippi; we thought we needed Canada, Texas, Oregon, California. But when we took, or attempted to take, that which we needed, we persuaded ourselves that we were but fulfilling the designs of Providence or the laws of Nature. If some of the apologists for later ventures in expansion were more frank in avowing motives of "national interest," the pious or fatalistic justification was none the less present.

The idea of a destiny which presides over and guides American expansion has rarely, if ever, been absent from the national consciousness. The precise character of that destiny, however, as well as the ultimate goal to which it points, has varied with changing ideas and circumstances. One of its earliest forms was geographical determinism. Certain contiguous areas were thought of as surely destined for annexation because their location made them naturally part of the United States. This idea seems to have been the basis for Thomas Jefferson's sure conviction that Florida would inevitably become American territory. In this expectation his mind never wavered; he questioned only the time and the means. The settling of Americans in Florida, he wrote in 1791, "will be the means of delivering to us peaceably, what may otherwise cost us a war." The failure of his own efforts to secure it did not shake his faith. In 1820, when it appeared likely that Spain would not ratify the Florida-purchase treaty, he wrote Monroe that this was not to be regretted. "Florida," he said, ". . . is ours. Every nation in Europe considers it such a right. We need not care for its occupation in time of peace, and, in war, the first cannon makes it ours without offence to anybody." Jefferson's belief was widely shared. Florida, said *Niles' Register* in 1819, "will just as naturally come into our possession as the waters of the Mississippi seek the sea; . . . . We believe this is the universal conclusion of the United States. . . . " The young expansionists who led the country into war in 1812 in the hope of conquering Canada and Florida appealed to the God of Nature in behalf of their plans. "In point of territorial limit, the map will prove its importance," one of them proclaimed. "The waters of the St. Lawrence and the Mississippi interlock in a number of places, and the great Disposer of Human Events intended those two rivers should belong to the same people"; while to another it appeared that "the Author of Nature has marked our limits in the south, by the Gulf of Mexico; and on the north, by the regions of eternal frost." If neither of these Congressmen was able to discern the westward limits set by the Author of

Nature, this task was performed by a writer for a southwestern paper, who asked rhetorically: "Where is it written in the book of fate that the American republic shall not stretch her limits from the capes of the Chesapeake to Nootka sound, from the isthmus of Panama to Hudson Bay?" Even Cuba was thought of by some as drawn inevitably by geographic laws toward union with the United States. Upon this idea two men as dissimilar as Thomas H. Benton and John Quincy Adams could agree. The island, thought Benton, was "the geographical appurtenance of the valley of the Mississippi and eventually to become its political appurtenance." Adams, as Secretary of State, likened Cuba to an apple which, when detached from the parent tree, would be drawn by a law of political gravitation to the United States.

What were the "natural boundaries" of the young republic? One mode of determining them was defined by Jefferson. Writing to Madison in 1809 of the hope of acquiring Cuba, he said: "Cuba can be defended by us without a navy, and this develops the principle which ought to limit our views. Nothing should ever be accepted which would require a navy to defend it." Northwardly, Jefferson visioned Canada as eventually to be drawn under the American flag; southwardly, Florida, Cuba, and probably Texas. On the west he apparently thought of the Rocky Mountains as forming the natural boundary. The West Coast would be peopled "with free and independent Americans, unconnected with us but by the ties of blood and interest, and employing like us the rights of self-government." Sheer distance seemed an insuperable barrier to the incorporation of the Oregon country in the American Union. A representative from Oregon, it was asserted in 1825, if he visited his constituency once a year, would have but two weeks annually to spend in Washington; the remainder of the year would be spent in the journey to and fro. Even Senator Benton, who predicted that the future route to Asia would follow the Missouri and Columbia rivers, and who in 1825 argued in favor of military occupation of Oregon by the United States, believed that in settling that territory Americans would be planting the seed of a new republic. The natural western limit of the United States was "the ridge of the Rocky Mountains. . . . Along the back of this ridge, the Western limit of this republic should be drawn, and the statue of the fabled god, Terminus, should be raised upon its highest peak, never to be thrown down."

Such restricted ideas of the nation's natural boundaries were not to survive for many years. Indeed, some three years before Benton made this speech, the conservative weekly, *Niles' Register,* made an interesting prophecy. News had been received of the successful arrival at Santa Fe of one of the first parties of traders from Missouri. Commenting on this exploit, the *Register* predicted that crossing the Rockies would soon be as familiar to the western people as was the voyage to China to the easterners. "It was very possible that the citizens of St. Louis, on the *Mississippi,* may eat fresh salmon from the waters of the *Columbia!*—for

distance seems as if annihilated by science and the spirit of adventure."
On July 4, 1828, the people of Baltimore, amid elaborate ceremony,
watched Charles Carroll, of Carrollton, lay the cornerstone that marked
the beginning of the Baltimore and Ohio Railroad. In his address from
the president and directors of the company, Mr. John B. Morris assumed
the rôle of prophet. "We are," he said, "about affording facilities of intercourse between the east and the west, which will bind the one more
closely to the other, beyond the power of an increased population or
sectional difficulties to disunite. We are in fact commencing a new era in
our history." It was inevitable that the coming of the railroad and, later,
of the telegraph should result in an expanding conception of the nation's
natural boundaries. Daniel Webster could still maintain in 1845 that
there would arise an independent "Pacific republic" on the west coast,
but for many others the "throne of Terminus" had moved on from the
Rockies to the shores of the Pacific. The *Democratic Review*, leading
organ of the expansionists of the Mexican War era, predicted in 1845
that a railroad to the Pacific would soon be a reality, and that "the day
cannot be far distant which shall witness the conveyance of the representatives from Oregon and California to Washington within less time
than a few years ago was devoted to a similar journey by those from
Ohio." The telegraph, furthermore, would soon enable Pacific coast
newspapers "to set up in type the first half of the President's Inaugural,
before the echoes of the latter half shall have died away beneath the lofty
porch of the Capitol, as spoken from his lips." In the debate on the
Oregon question in the House of Representatives in January, 1846, the
significance of the Pacific as a natural boundary was repeatedly stressed.
From the Atlantic to the Pacific, said Bowlin of Missouri, "we were by
nature, ay, we were stamped by the hand of God himself, as one nation of
men." Similarly, in the debate of 1844 and 1845 over the annexation of
Texas, the Rio Grande with the neighboring strips of desert country had
been portrayed as the divinely fixed natural boundary of the United
States on the southwest.

If a divine hand had shaped the outlines of the North American continent with a view to its attaining political unity, the divine mind was
thought to be by no means indifferent to the type of political organism
which should dominate it. The American god of the early nineteenth
century was the God of Democracy, and his followers had no doubt that
he had reserved the continent for a democratic nation. Jefferson may not
have regarded this consummation as a divinely appointed destiny, but he
certainly contemplated as probable and desirable the spread of democratic institutions throughout the continent. The true flowering of this
idea, however, belongs properly to the Jacksonian era, and its most
enthusiastic exponent was the *Democratic Review*, a monthly magazine
founded and for many years edited by Mr. John O'Sullivan. This
exuberant Irish-American, whose faith in the institutions of his adopted
country was irrepressible, not only coined the phrase "manifest destiny"

but for years expounded in the pages of the *Review* the idea which it embodied.

The *Democratic Review* was founded in 1837. In the issue for November, 1839, appeared an article, presumably by O'Sullivan, entitled "The Great Nation of Futurity." This rôle was to be America's, it was argued,

> because the principle upon which a nation is organized fixes its destiny, and that of equality is perfect, is universal. . . . Besides, the truthful annals of any nation furnish abundant evidence, that its happiness, its greatness, its duration, were always proportionate to the democratic equality in its system of government. . . . We point to the everlasting truth on the first page of our national declaration, and we proclaim to the millions of other lands, that "the gates of hell"—the powers of aristocracy and monarchy—"shall not prevail against it."

Thus happily founded upon the perfect principle of equality, the United States was destined to a unique success. Her shining example should "smite unto death the tyranny of kings, hierarchs, and oligarchs." What all this portended for the future boundaries of the United States the writer did not state except in poetic language. "Its floor shall be a hemisphere," he wrote, "its roof the firmament of the star-studded heavens, and its congregation an Union of many Republics, comprising hundreds of happy millions, . . . governed by God's natural and moral law of equality. . . ." Within a few years, however, the *Democratic Review* became sufficiently concrete in its ideas of the extent of the democratizing mission of the United States. Texas, Oregon, California, Canada, and much or all of Mexico, were to receive the blessings of American principles. The American continent had been reserved by Providence for the dawn of a new era, when men should be ready to throw off the antique systems of Europe and live in the light of equality and reason. The time was now at hand, and no American should shrink from the task of spreading the principles of liberty over all the continent. Cuba, too, had been left by Providence in the hands of a weak power until the United States was ready for it. Now it, like the rest, was "about to be annexed to the model republic."

The ideas so fervently reached in the *Democratic Review* were echoed in Congress and elsewhere. With reference to the Oregon controversy, James Buchanan asserted in 1844 that Providence had given to the American people the mission of "extending the blessings of Christianity and of civil and religious liberty over the whole North American continent." Breese of Illinois declared that "the impartial and the just" would see in the occupation of Oregon "a desire only to extend more widely the area of human freedom, ... as an extension, sir, of that grand theatre, on which God, in his providence, and in his own appointed time, intends to work out that high destiny he has assigned for the whole human race." California was not forgotten. A letter from an American in that Mexican state, published in the *Baltimore Patriot,* commented on the way in which "our people, like a sure heavy and sullen tide, are overflowing the country"; and the writer declared that, while not himself an advocate of territorial aggression, he thought he could "foresee in the inevitable destiny of this territory, one of the most efficient fortresses from which new and liberal are to combat old and despotic institutions." Kaufman of Texas was sure the day was near "when not one atom of kingly power will disgrace the North American continent." Apologists for the war with Mexico were apt at urging its providential character and beneficent results. B. F. Porter, of Alabama, in an article on "The Mission of America," intimated that the war was a divine instrument for spreading American institutions and ideals to the Pacific; and Robert J. Walker, Secretary of the Treasury, inserted in his report for December, 1847, a paragraph gratefully acknowledging the aid of a "higher than any earthly power" which had guided American expansion in the past and which "still guards and directs our destiny, impels us onward, and has selected our great and happy country as a model and ultimate centre of attraction of all the nations of the world."

Neither natural boundaries nor divinely favored institutions were in themselves sufficient to insure the peopling of the continent by the favored race. The third essential factor was seen in what more than one Congressman termed "the American multiplication table." "Go to the West," said Kennedy of Indiana in 1846, "and see a young man with his mate of eighteen; after the lapse of thirty years, visit him again and instead of two, you will find twenty-two. This is what I call the American multiplication table." Apparently Jefferson had in mind this same fecundity of the Anglo-Saxon race in America when he predicted in 1786 that "our confederacy must be viewed as the nest from which all America, North & South is to be peopled," and when in 1803 he expressed full confidence in the growth of such an American population on the Mississippi "as will be able to do their own business" in securing control of New Orleans. On the same principle, Barbour of Virginia foretold in 1825 the peopling of the Oregon country by Americans.

It was partly, too, upon the basis of this unexampled growth in numbers that the editor of the *Democratic Review* founded his doctrine of "manifest destiny." It was in an unsigned article in the number for July–August, 1845, that the phrase first appeared. The writer charged foreign nations with attempting to impede the annexation of Texas, with the object of "checking the fulfilment of our manifest destiny to overspread the continent allotted by Providence for the free development of our yearly multiplying millions." Texas, he said, had been

absorbed into the Union in the inevitable fulfilment of the general law which is rolling our population westward; the connexion of which with that ratio of growth in population which is destined within a hundred years to swell our numbers to the enormous population of *two hundred and fifty millions* (if not more), is too evident to leave us in doubt of the manifest design of Providence in regard to the occupation of this continent.

When war with Mexico came, and the more rabid expansionists were seeking excuses for annexing large portions of Mexican territory, a different side of the idea of racial superiority was advanced. The Mexicans, it seemed, had a destiny too—how different from that of their northern neighbors! "The Mexican race," said the *Democratic Review*, "now see, in the fate of the aborigines of the north, their own inevitable destiny. They must amalgamate and be lost, in the superior vigor of the Anglo-Saxon race, or they must utterly perish." The *New York Evening Post* indorsed the idea, sanctifying it in the name of Providence. "Providence has so ordained it; and it is folly not to recognize the fact. The Mexicans are *aboriginal Indians,* and they must share the destiny of their race."

This pre-Darwinian version of the "survival of the fittest" was branded by the aged Albert Gallatin, an opponent of the war, as "a most extraordinary assertion." That it persisted, that it constituted, in the 1850's, an integral part of the concept of manifest destiny is clear from the remarks of both friends and foes. John L. O'Sullivan was serving in 1855 as United States minister to Portugal. He reported to Secretary Marcy a conversation with some French imperialists in which he had said:

I should be as glad to see our common race and blood overspread all Africa under the French flag and all India under the British, as they ought to be to see it overspread all the Western hemisphere under ours;—and that probably enough that was the plan of Providence; to which we in America were accustomed to give the name of "manifest destiny."

On the other hand, George Fitzhugh of Virginia, who believed in institutions (such as slavery) for the protection of weaker races, charged the members of the "Young American" party in Congress with boasting "that the Anglo-Saxon race is manifestly destined to eat out all the other races, as the wire-grass destroys and takes the place of other grasses," and with inviting admiration for "this war of nature"—admiration which Fitzhugh, for one, refused to concede.

Thus manifest destiny, which must be thought of as embracing all the ideas hitherto considered—geographical determinism, the superiority of democratic institutions, the superior fecundity, stamina, and ability of the white race—became a justification for almost any addition of territory which the United States had the will and the power to obtain.

Such ideas were not, as has been rather generally assumed, peculiarly southern. In their extreme form, at least, both the ideas and the imperialistic program which they were used to justify were repudiated by southern Whig leaders, and even by John C. Calhoun himself. The southerner most closely associated with the program, Robert J. Walker, was of northern birth, was by no means an unwavering supporter of slavery, and was presently to sever entirely his connections with the South. The inventor of the phrase "manifest destiny" and one of the most persevering advocates of expansion was, as has been said, John L. O'Sullivan, who described himself in a letter to Calhoun as a "New York Free Soiler";

and he had the friendship and sympathy of prominent northern Democrats like Buchanan, Marcy, and Pierce. Indeed, if the manifest destiny of the 1840's and 1850's must be classified, it should be described as Democratic rather than sectional. Yet, even this generalization will not bear too close scrutiny, for William H. Seward, an antislavery Whig and Republican, was scarcely less intrigued by the idea than O'Sullivan himself. As early as 1846 he was predicting that the population of the United States was "destined to roll its resistless waves to the icy barriers of the North, and to encounter oriental civilization on the shores of the Pacific"; and in a speech at St. Paul, Minnesota, in 1860, he asserted with assurance that Russian, Canadian, and Latin on the American continents were but laying the foundations for future states of the American republic, whose ultimate capital would be the City of Mexico.

Seward, in fact, supplies the chief link between the manifest destiny of the pre–Civil War years and the expansionist schemes of the decade following the war. As Secretary of State he had an opportunity to try his hand at a program of expansion; and though of all his plans the purchase of Alaska alone was carried through, the discussions of that and of other proposed acquisitions—the Danish West Indies, the Dominican Republic, the Hawaiian Islands, and Canada—demonstrated the continuity of ideas from 1850 to 1870. Professor T. C. Smith, who made an analysis of the expansionist arguments used in this period, found annexations urged on four principal grounds: economic value, strategic value to the navy, extension of republican institutions, and geographic determinism. Only the second of these—the naval base argument—was at all new. It owed its vogue at the time to the navy's difficulties during the war. The first was always to be met with, and the third and fourth were carry-overs from the days of manifest destiny.

The collapse of the expansionist program of Seward and Grant was followed by a general loss of interest in such enterprises, which did not recover their one-time popularity until the era of the Spanish-American War. In the meantime, however, new arguments were taking shape which would eventually impinge on the popular consciousness and raise almost as keen an interest in expansion as that which had elected Polk in 1844. But while manifest destiny was a product indigenous to the United States, some of the new doctrines owed their origin to European trends of thought.

In 1859 Charles Darwin published his *Origin of Species,* setting forth the hypothesis that the evolution of the higher forms of life had come about through the preservation and perpetuation of chance variations by the "survival of the fittest" in the never ending struggle for existence. The authoritativeness of this work, and the stir which it made in the scientific world, gave a scientific sanction to the idea that perpetual struggle in the political and social world would lead upward along the evolutionary path. Many were the applications that might be made of such a principle—especially by nations and peoples considering themselves highly "fit." A nation with a faith in its political, moral, or racial

superiority might take pleasure in the thought that in crushing its inferior neighbors it was at once obeying the law of destiny and contributing to the perfection of the species.

What did Darwinism signify for the future of the United States? One
of the first to attempt an answer to that riddle was the historian, John
Fiske, who spoke with double authority as a student of American institutions and a follower and popularizer of Darwin. Fiske's conclusion was
sufficiently gratifying. Anglo-Saxons in the United States had evolved the
"fittest" of all political principles—federalism—upon which all the world
would at some future day be organized. Anglo-Saxons, moreover, excelled
not only in institutions but in growth of numbers and economic power.
So evident was the superior "fitness" of this race that its expansion was
certain to go on "until every land on the earth's surface that is not
already the seat of an old civilization shall become English in its language, in its religion, in its political habits and traditions, and to a
predominant extent in the blood of its people." "The day is at hand,"
said Fiske, "when four-fifths of the human race will trace its pedigree to
English forefathers, as four-fifths of the white people of the United States
trace their pedigree today." This was surely encouraging doctrine to
Americans or British who wanted an excuse to go a-conquering.

Conclusions very similar to Fiske's were reached by Josiah Strong, a
Congregational clergyman, who in 1885 published what became a popular and widely read book entitled *Our Country: Its Possible Future and
Its Present Crisis.* The Anglo-Saxon, thought Strong, as the chief representative of the two most valuable civilizing forces—civil liberty and "a
pure *spiritual* Christianity"—was being divinely schooled for *"the final
competition of races. . . . "* "If I read not amiss," he said, "this powerful
race will move down upon Mexico, down upon Central and South
America, out upon the islands of the sea, over upon Africa and beyond.
And can any one doubt that the result of this competition of races will be
the 'survival of the fittest'?" The extinction of inferior races before the
conquering Anglo-Saxon might appear sad to some; but Strong knew of
nothing likely to prevent it, and he accepted it as part of the divine plan.
His doctrine was a curious blending of religious and scientific dogma.

If Fiske and Strong could show that expansion was a matter of destiny,
another scholar of the day preached it as a duty. In his *Political Science
and Comparative Constitutional Law,* published in 1890, John W.
Burgess, of Columbia University, surveyed the political careers of the
principal civilized races and concluded that, of them all, only the Teutonic group had talent of the highest order. Greek and Roman, Slav and
Celt, had exhibited their various abilities. Some had excelled in building
city-states; others, in planning world-empires. Only Teutons had learned
the secret of the national state, the form fittest to survive. The Teutonic
nations—German and Anglo-Saxon—were "the political nations *par
excellence,"* and this pre-eminence gave them the right "in the economy
of the world to assume the leadership in the establishment and adminis-

tration of states." Especially were they called "to carry the political civilization of the modern world into those parts of the world inhabited by unpolitical and barbaric races; i.e. they must have a colonial policy." There was "no human right to the status of barbarism." If barbaric peoples resisted the civilizing efforts of the political nations, the latter might rightly reduce them to subjection or clear their territory of their presence. If a population were not barbaric but merely incompetent politically, then too the Teutonic nations might "righteously assume sovereignty over, and undertake to create state order for, such a politically incompetent population."

There is in these pages of Burgess such a complete justification not only for British and German imperialism but also for the course of acquiring colonies and protectorates upon which the United States was to embark in 1898 that one learns with surprise from his rather naïve autobiography that Burgess was profoundly shocked by the war with Spain and felt that the adoption of an imperialistic career was a colossal blunder. One would have supposed that he would have rejoiced that his country was assuming its share of world-responsibility as one of the Teutonic nations.

To Fiske and Strong, expansion was destiny; to Burgess, it was duty, though he apparently excused his own country from any share in its performance. To Alfred Thayer Mahan, the historian and prophet who frankly assumed the rôle of propagandist, it was both duty and opportunity. Mahan's *Influence of Sea Power upon History,* the result of a series of lectures at the Naval War College at Newport, Rhode Island, was published in 1890. Other books on naval history followed, but it is likely that Mahan reached a wider American public through the many magazine articles which he published at frequent intervals during the ensuing decade. History, as Mahan wrote it, was no mere academic exercise. Searching the past for lessons applicable to the here and now, he found them in full measure. Rather, he found *one,* which he never tired of driving home: Sea power was essential to national greatness. Sea power embraced commerce, merchant marine, navy, naval bases whence commerce might be protected, and colonies where it might find its farther terminals. One nation, Great Britain, had learned this lesson by heart and practiced it faithfully, with results that Mahan thought admirable. One other nation, he hoped, might walk in her footsteps.

Certain specific needs, beside the obvious one of a stronger navy and better coast defenses, Mahan urged upon his countrymen. If an Isthmian canal were to be built, the United States ought to build and control it, or, failing this, to control completely the approaches to it. This involved a willingness to accept islands in the Caribbean whenever they could be had by righteous means; sheer acts of conquest Mahan repudiated. It involved also a willingness to accept the Hawaiian Islands, partly as an outpost to the Pacific end of the canal, partly for another reason which weighed heavily with Mahan. The Pacific, he believed, was to be the theater of a vast conflict between Occident and Orient, with the United States holding the van of the Western forces. His deep religious sense assured him that the Deity was preparing the Christian powers for that coming cataclysm, but he was equally sure that mere human agents must keep their powder dry. The United States must be ready, with a navy, a canal, and as many island outposts as she could righteously acquire, for her share in the great struggle between civilizations and religions. Even the practical-minded naval officer must have a cosmic justification for the policy of national imperialism which he advocated.

It was such ideas as these of Fiske, Strong, Burgess, and Mahan which created a public opinion receptive to expansion overseas in 1898. Theodore Roosevelt and Henry Cabot Lodge, whose influence upon the events of that year was large indeed, were under the spell of Mahan's writings. Roosevelt had been a pupil of Burgess while studying law at Columbia. In the debate over imperialism which ensued, the argument from Anglo-Saxon or Teutonic superiority and the divinely appointed mission of the race was probably as influential as the more practical strategic and economic arguments. Kipling's contribution, "The White Man's Burden," which appeared in 1898, fitted in well with the American temper. In the United States Senate, young Albert J. Beveridge, using language that might almost have been taken bodily from Burgess' treatise, declared that God "has made us [Anglo-Saxons and Teutons] the master organizers of the world to establish system where chaos reigns. . . . He has made us adepts in government that we may administer government among savage and senile peoples." William Allen White, in the *Emporia Gazette*, proclaimed: "Only Anglo-Saxons can govern themselves. . . . It is the Anglo-Saxon's manifest destiny to go forth as a world conqueror. He will take possession of the islands of the sea. . . . This is what fate holds for the chosen people." Senator O. H. Platt wrote President McKinley that in Connecticut "those who believe in Providence, see, or think they see, that God has placed upon this Government the solemn duty of providing for the people of these islands [the Philippines] a government based upon the principle of liberty no matter how many difficulties the problem may present." A missionary from China was quoted as saying: "You will find that all American missionaries are in favor of expansion."

Even those who stressed the economic value of new possessions could not refrain from claiming the special interest of Providence. That the war with Spain and the victory in the Philippines should have come just as the European powers were attempting to partition China and monopolize its markets, seemed to the *American Banker* of New York "a coincidence which has a providential air." Familiar to all students of the period is McKinley's story of how he prayed for divine guidance as to the disposition of the Philippines, and of how "one night it came to me this way—I don't know how it was but it came: . . . that we could not turn them over to France or Germany—our commercial rivals in the Orient— that would be bad business and discreditable." Reasons of a more ideal character were vouchsafed to William McKinley on the same occasion, but McKinley's God did not hesitate to converse with him in terms that might better have befitted Mark Hanna. Perhaps McKinley did not misunderstand. Josiah Strong was a clergyman and hence in a better position than McKinley to interpret the wishes of the Deity; yet he found in Providence a concern for American business similar to that which McKinley detected. Strong, too, had in mind the Philippines and especially their relation to China and to the maintenance of the Open Door in the markets of that developing empire.

And when we remember [he wrote] that our new necessities [markets for our manufactures] are precisely complementary to China's new needs, it is not difficult to see a providential meaning in the fact that, with no design of our own, we have become an Asiatic power, close to the Yellow Sea, and we find it easy to believe that

> "There's a divinity that shapes our ends,
> Rough-hew them how we will."

Expansionists of different periods had invoked a God of Nature, a God of Democracy, a God of Evolution. It seems appropriate enough that those who inaugurated the last phase of territorial expansion, at the close of the nineteenth century, should have proclaimed their faith in a God of Business.

Frederick Merk

Dissent in the Mexican War

Frederick Merk, for many years professor of history at Harvard University, is one of the foremost students of American expansion. In the course of a lifetime of research on nineteenth-century expansionism he has published a number of works that reinterpret the concept of manifest destiny in a political context. In the following essay Merk analyzes how President James K. Polk and his supporters forced war on Mexico. Although Whigs and antislavery Democrats disputed Polk's version of who started hostilities and held him to be the aggressor who coveted the land of a helpless neighbor, they were unable to prevent or stop what they considered an immoral and unconstitutional war. Merk shows how the opponents of war were stifled and Congress was stampeded into voting for war. Note how he reveals in his phrases, adjectives, and general analysis where his own sympathies lie. Note also the dissenters' inconsistencies in accepting war measures and voting supplies for the armed forces even though they attacked the war itself as unjust. Did the dissent have any effect on the war and its outcome? Merk's analysis has meaning for democratic governments beyond the Mexican War and is pertinent to our own time. [Reprinted by permission of the publishers from Samuel Eliot Morison, Frederick Merk and Frank Freidel, Dissent in Three American Wars, *pp. 35–63. Cambridge, Mass.: Harvard University Press, Copyright, 1970, by the Massachusetts Historical Society.]*

On a Monday morning—May 11, 1846—President James K. Polk sent to Congress a special message announcing war with Mexico. He declared in the message that Mexican troops had crossed the boundary of the United States, had invaded American territory, and had shed American blood on American soil. He ended the message with the words "War exists, and, notwithstanding all our efforts to avoid it, exists by the act of Mexico herself." He asked Congress to fulfill a requirement of the Constitution by formally declaring a war that was in progress. This was the first instance in American history when a president informed Congress of the existence of a war before a declaration of war had been made by Congress.

The boundary crossed by the Mexican force was the Rio Grande River. If the Rio Grande was truly the boundary, it had only recently become so, as recently as December 1845 when Texas was formally annexed to the Union by act of Congress. The alleged invasion occurred five and a half months after the annexation.

The Rio Grande had not been the boundary of Texas in earlier history. In 1816 the boundary had been set by the Spanish government at the Nueces River, which lies 130 miles north and east of the Rio Grande. The Nueces appeared on all reliable maps and atlases of the period as the boundary and had been accepted as such by many sturdy Americans, among them Stephen F. Austin, Andrew Jackson, Thomas Hart Benton, Martin Van Buren, and John C. Calhoun.

But in 1836, after Texas declared her independence and her army under Sam Houston won the smashing victory of San Jacinto, she claimed the Rio Grande as her line. In the battle, Santa Anna, the President of Mexico, was captured. In order to obtain release he signed, as a prisoner of war, an agreement that in a treaty later to be made, Texas might be permitted to extend as far as the Rio Grande. That agreement was repudiated at once by the Mexican Congress, which, under the Mexican Constitution, was the sole treaty-making body of the government. But Polk considered the agreement a treaty, and before Texas was formally admitted, he undertook to make the Rio Grande the boundary.

Another issue dividing the two governments was the damage claims of American citizens against Mexico. These had been advanced by persons who had suffered losses in Mexico in the course of the recurring Mexican revolutions. A mixed commission in 1840 had heard the claims, amounting to $8,500,000. It had found that the valid ones amounted to about a quarter of this sum. The rest were found fraudulent or heavily padded. The Mexican government agreed to pay the valid claims in installments, but after three had been paid it went bankrupt and defaulted on the remainder. The defaulted payments seemed to Polk a major American grievance. The total was afterward set by the American government at $3,250,000, not an enormous sum. American states and corporations were in default at this time on bonds in British possession to a total estimated at $200,000,000, as critics of the war pointed out.

Another grievance of the Polk government was that Mexico refused to receive an American minister, John C. Slidell, to settle these issues. Slidell had been sent by Polk in great secrecy to Mexico City in November 1845. He carried instructions that leaked out to the press—instructions to combine the issue of the unpaid damage claims with the issue of Mexican recognition of the Rio Grande boundary and, in addition, the sale of California and New Mexico to the United States. The Mexican government did not dare to receive Slidell, because it feared a revolt by an army under a military chieftain which lay outside the capital. It based its refusal on the ground that it had agreed only to discuss the issue of the annexation of Texas.

When news of the refusal reached Washington, Polk ordered the army of General Zachary Taylor to march to the Rio Grande. On reaching the river Taylor planted his cannon so as to command Matamoras, on the other side, and blockaded the river. This kept the Mexican army from receiving supplies by sea. The commander of the Mexican army sent a cavalry force across the river above Taylor's camp. This intercepted and surrounded a reconnoitering party of Taylor's, which tried to fight its way out. Several Americans were killed and the rest were taken prisoner. That was the American blood shed on American soil.

Accompanying Polk's special message came a bill to the House of Representatives drawn up by the Military Affairs Committee over the Sabbath. This authorized the President to accept militia and volunteers for military duty. The bill did not actually declare war. But a preamble was added to it on the floor by a Democratic war hawk, Representative William H. Brockenbrough of Florida, which was said to be needed to give formal recognition to a state of war. In final form it read: "Whereas, by the act of . . . Mexico, a state of war exists between that government and the United States," the President is authorized to employ the militia and military forces to bring the war to a successful conclusion.

That preamble, like the President's message, was greeted with instant denunciation. It was declared to be so bold a falsehood as to defile at the outset the whole bill. It was said to have been framed to commit everyone voting for the bill to the President's position that the war was defensive when patently it was aggressive—forced on Mexico by Polk. This initial reaction, immediately echoed by the Whig press, became the platform of the opposition during the remainder of the war.

Debate on the war bill was limited, by order of the majority, to two hours. Whig members asked for time to read the documents sent with the message. This was denied, though selected parts were read by the Clerk of the House. Protestors who rose to speak were not seen by the Speaker. Two of them succeeded in getting recognized by resorting to a parliamentary trick. They demanded permission to explain why they wanted to be excused from voting—a right that could not be denied. Both explained before they were cut off that the preamble was an utter falsehood.

Administration spokesmen upheld the stifling of debate on the ground of need to promptly rescue Taylor's army. The army was outnumbered and might be destroyed. The answer of the Whigs was that "Old Rough and Ready" was more than able to take care of himself, especially since he would be aided by militia from neighboring states. They also pointed out that, if Taylor was really in peril, aid from Washington could not reach him on time.

The war bill was passed two hours after it was received—by a vote that was overwhelming, 174 to 14. This was a victory for stampede tactics. The negative votes were nearly all from New England and from centers of New England influence in the West. At the head of the dissenters was John Quincy Adams. Five of the dissenters came from Massachusetts. Five more came from Ohio.

The Senate acted on the bill the next day. The tactics of stampede were there repeated. One day only was allowed for debate. Minority Senators protested, particularly at the denial of an opportunity to study the documents before voting. They thought the ordering of Taylor to the Rio Grande and his blocking off the river was as much an aggression as pointing a pistol at a man's breast. All the Whig speakers urged striking from the war bill the false and offensive preamble. Among the protestors a Southern Democrat—John C. Calhoun—was especially vehement. He said he would find it more impossible to vote that preamble than to plunge a dagger into his own heart. He went beyond the question who had been the aggressor, though he clearly thought Polk had been. He raised the more basic issue whether a local skirmish between parts of armies on the Rio Grande constituted war. War, he declared, required a declaration by Congress in both republics and he would not make war on Mexico by making war on our Constitution.

The Senate's vote on the war bill was as lopsided as that of the House. It was 40 to 2. The courageous nays were both Whigs—John Davis of Massachusetts and John M. Clayton of Delaware. A number of Whigs voted "aye except the preamble." Calhoun refused to vote. Daniel Webster was absent. Calhoun said later that not 10 percent of Congress would have voted for the war bill if time had been given to examine the documents.

In the Boston press the same criticism was made of the war bill as had been made in Congress. The Boston *Whig*, an anti-slavery paper, which Charles Francis Adams and John G. Palfrey were soon to acquire, contained a letter from Charles Francis Adams in which he pronounced the preamble "one of the grossest national lies that was ever deliberately told." He singled out for special attack Robert C. Winthrop, Boston's representative in Congress, who had voted for the war bill. He wrote that Winthrop by his vote had signed his name to a "national lie." Charles Sumner assailed Winthrop in the press with even greater bitterness. He wrote that Winthrop's hands were covered with blood, and by this language he broke up an old friendship. Palfrey, a notable clergyman and historian, was equally wrathful. These protestors all held that Polk was the aggressor and that his aggression was for the purpose of expansion over a helpless neighbor.

In the *New York Tribune* Horace Greeley expressed the same dissent. He wrote in an editorial sarcastically: "Grant the Father of Lies his premises, and he will prove himself a truth-teller and a saint by faultless logic. Shut your eyes to the whole course of events through the last twelve years . . . and it will become easy to prove that we are a meek, unoffending, ill used people, and that Mexico has kicked, cuffed and grossly imposed upon us. Only assume premises enough, as Polk does, and you may prove that it is New Orleans which has just been threatened with a cannonade instead of Matamoras, and that it is the Mississippi which has been formally blockaded by a stranger fleet and army instead of the Rio del Norte [Rio Grande]."

In Washington the *National Intelligencer*, another of the nation's great Whig dailies, used similar language.

After the initial excitement at the war's opening the political parties of the country settled down to positions that became fixed. The Whigs, North and South, were highly critical of the war. The administration Democrats supported the war. In both parties, however, there were variations of criticism and of support.

The Northern Whigs became divided into conservatives and radicals. The conservatives emphasized the fraud and the aggressiveness of the war. They wished to avoid the added charge, made by the radicals, that the primary aim of the administration was the extension of slavery. Such a charge offended Southern Whigs, who, though opposed to the war, were slaveholders and were sensitive about attacks on slavery. Moreover, conservative Northern Whigs were not wholly persuaded that slavery extension was a primary aim of the administration.

In Massachusetts, Whigs upholding the moderate view included such politicians as Webster and Winthrop and such wealthy businessmen as Abbott Lawrence and Nathan Appleton, who were connected with the cotton belt by business ties. They were known as the Cotton Whigs. In Boston and in the North as a whole the conservatives outnumbered the radicals.

What were the facts which supported the conservative view that the war was not primarily for the extension of slavery? One fact, already mentioned, is that the Southern Whig leaders (slaveholders in every case) strenuously opposed the war. Henry Clay and John J. Crittenden, both from Kentucky, Alexander H. Stephens, George M. Berrien, Robert A. Toombs, all of Georgia, and many others, took that stand. Northern conservative Whigs, eager to retain this support, were fearful that if, in opposing the war, they added an anti-slavery stand to the anti-aggression stand, the unity of the party would be imperiled, and probably even the Union in the end. They recognized another obvious fact, militating against the radical explanation of the war, namely that many of the most rabid of the war hawks in the country were Northerners.

But radical Whigs were sure that the extension of slavery was a primary objective of the war. They were sure the ambition of the administration was to spread slavery over all Mexico and Central America. In Massachusetts those of such convictions included John Quincy Adams, Charles Francis Adams, Charles Sumner, Henry Wilson, and John G. Palfrey. These men and their followers were the Conscience Whigs— Whigs with a conscience not only regarding the iniquity of the aggression but the iniquity of its purpose—the spread of slavery.

The Democrats were also divided. They had come into power as a result of victory in the presidential campaign of 1844, in which the platform had emphasized expansionism—the immediate annexation of Texas and reoccupation of Oregon. That platform was a reflection of a belief recently come into prominence—the belief that it was the Manifest Destiny of the United States to expand over the entire continent of North America, from "the arctic to the tropic," as the slogan ran. . . . During the Mexican War the belief in Manifest Destiny became focused on a demand to absorb All Mexico.

The conspicuous expansionists and war hawks were the administration Democrats—George Bancroft, Caleb Cushing, Lewis Cass, James Buchanan, Vice-president George M. Dallas, and Stephen A. Douglas. All were believers in Manifest Destiny. They had no very strong objections to slavery extension. They were willing to postpone the solution of the slavery problem to some future day. Their immediate ambition was territory. They were described contemptuously by the anti-slavery radicals as "doughfaces.". . .

But the Democratic party included others. It embraced a large minority of anti-slavery radicals, personified by John P. Hale of New Hampshire, David Wilmot of Pennsylvania, and Preston King of New York. It also included old-fashioned Jeffersonians, personified by an elder statesman of the party, Albert Gallatin. And, finally, it included Calhoun Democrats.

In view of all this diversity in both parties, how does the historian explain the overwhelming vote by which Congress declared the war? The explanation is found in a momentary hysteria on the part of the public which Polk converted into a stampede. Horace Greeley in an editorial explained the vote as a normal public response to an attack on the flag. The editorial was entitled "Our Country, Right or Wrong!" It ran:

"This is the spirit in which a portion of the Press, which admits that our treatment of Mexico has been ruffianly and piratical, and that the invasion of her territory by Gen. Taylor is a flagrant outrage, now exhorts our People to rally in all their strength, to lavish their blood and treasure in the vindictive prosecution of War on Mexico. We protest against such counsel. . . .

"We can easily defeat the armies of Mexico, slaughter them by thousands, and pursue them perhaps to their capital; we can conquer and 'annex' their territory; but what then? Have the histories of the ruin of Greek and Roman liberty consequent on such extensions of empire by the sword no lesson for us? Who believes that a score of victories over Mexico, the 'annexation' of half her provinces, will give us more Liberty, a purer Morality, a more prosperous Industry, than we now have? . . . Is not Life miserable enough, comes not Death soon enough, without resort to the hideous enginery of War?

"People of the United States! Your Rulers are precipitating you into a fathomless abyss of crime and calamity! Why sleep you thoughtless on its verge, as though this was not your business, or Murder could be hid from the sight of God by a few flimsy rags called banners? Awake and arrest the work of butchery ere it shall be too late to preserve your souls from the guilt of wholesale slaughter!"

This editorial contained hard truth. An attack on the flag had been used by Polk to stampede the country into war. Such tactics were precisely what the framers of the Constitution had sought to prevent. They had sought to do it by writing the principle of checks and balances into the war provisions of the Constitution. A war-minded president was to be controlled by vesting in Congress the power to declare war and the power to provide supplies. The framers had faith in Congress because Congress represented diverse interests and because its minorities would keep a rein on majorities. All those precautions of the framers failed in the crisis of May 11 and 12, 1846. They failed because Polk had stampeded Congress and because minorities had failed to function.

The minorities failed in both parties. The Whigs did not function because they feared that if they voted against the war declaration they would meet the fate which had overtaken their predecessors, the Federalists, who had destroyed themselves by opposition in the War of 1812. Hesitant Democrats were equally quiet because their leaders had sponsored the joint resolution annexing Texas, a resolution which, by reason of its vague boundary provision, had produced the war.

Once the war declaration was approved by Whigs the party was committed to further support of the war. Most Whigs regularly voted supplies and men for the fighting, though they still denounced the war as iniquitous and unconstitutional. Even John Quincy Adams did this. Toward the end of 1847 he wrote Albert Gallatin, who was a fellow objector to the war: "The most remarkable circumstance of these transactions is that the war thus [unconstitutionally] made has been sanctioned by an overwhelming majority of both Houses . . . and is now sustained by similar majorities professing to disapprove its existence and pronouncing it unnecessary and unjust." Abraham Lincoln, who entered Congress in 1847 and registered his protest against the war, regularly voted supplies for it.

The defense for voting supplies was set forth in the House by such Whigs as Winthrop, and, in the Senate, by John J. Crittenden. Congress, they pointed out, cannot abandon armies it has called into the field. Soldiers at the front cannot question orders on moral grounds. To do so would be subversive of all discipline. A war, right or wrong, which Congress has voted must be upheld.

In the House a radical anti-slavery Whig, Joshua R. Giddings from the Western Reserve of Ohio, challenged the worth of that reasoning. He cited the great British Whigs of the era of the American Revolution who announced in Parliament in 1776 their refusal to vote supplies for an unjust and oppressive war against America. Giddings proposed that similar means be used by American Whigs to force Polk out of Mexico. But Winthrop frowned on this revolutionary procedure and thought British precedent inapplicable in any case, for whereas in England the defeat of a supply measure brought down an administration and forced the creation of a new one, in the United States it would merely paralyze an administration which would still hang on.

As the war progressed the conservative Whigs made further adjustments of expediency to its demands. While always denouncing Polk they not only voted the supplies and men but lauded the gallantry of the front-line troops and the achievements of the generals leading them, especially the glory-covered Whig generals. On a number of occasions they voted resolutions of thanks to Generals Zachary Taylor and Winfield Scott.

These tactics were excellent politics and they paid high dividends. In the congressional election of 1846, which came half a year after the war declaration, the Whig party reversed the Democratic control of the House. The party acquired, in the next session of Congress, the control of the purse.

The loss of control of Congress in the midst of a highly successful war was to the Polk administration an unusual and humiliating experience. It was a clear measure of the moral protest which had developed against the war. What was equally significant was that the Whigs gained strength in all sections of the nation except in the interior of the South, and even there they stayed even.

The President sent his annual message to Congress soon after this rebuke. It was the message of December 8, 1846. In it he took a defensive stand. He devoted two thirds of the message to an elaboration of his earlier argument as to the origins of the war. He insisted that the boundary really was the Rio Grande and that the Mexican force, in crossing it, had invaded American soil and shed American blood there. He deplored Whig charges that he had been the aggressor. He thought those who made such charges were giving "aid and comfort to the enemy," which was saying that they were traitors.

The message was greeted by a new explosion of wrath on the part of the Whigs. In Congress a Whig from the President's own state called the message "an artful perversion of the truth . . . to make the people believe a lie." The challenge of "lie" was thrown at the President again and again in Congress and in the press. The President's assurance that the Whig opposition was giving aid and comfort to the enemy was denounced as a "foul imputation" for purposes of intimidation, which would have the opposite effect of the one intended.

In New England the President's review of the war's origins was met with biting sarcasm. An example is an editorial in the *Boston Whig*, written by Charles Francis Adams. It was addressed especially to the President's assertion that the war was supported by the great body of the American people. Adams observed:

"It is somewhat uncommon for a president who feels very sure that he is right, and also that the justice of his policy is understood by 'the great body of the people' to devote 2/3 of an annual message . . . to an effort to remove the scruples of a small minority of dissentients. It betrays a fatherly care of the stray sheep in his flock . . . [Moreover] the President does not . . . in December rest his justification of the war *solely* upon the ground selected by himself in May. That 'American blood should have been shed on American soil' was deemed in the spring ample cause for the call . . . to arms. It is now held not quite defense enough . . . without bringing in a long array of old offenses committed by Mexico."

In April 1847 the Massachusetts legislature adopted a set of resolutions still more condemnatory. The resolutions lifted the slavery issue into prominence. They read:

"Resolved that the present war with Mexico . . . was unconstitutionally commenced by the order of the President to General Taylor to take military possession of territory in dispute . . . and that it is now waged by a powerful nation against a weak neighbor . . . at immense cost of treasure and life, for the dismemberment of Mexico, and for the conquest of . . . territory from which slavery has been . . . excluded, with the triple object of extending slavery, of strengthening the slave power, and of obtaining the control of the Free States. . . . That such a war of conquest, so hateful in its objects, so wanton, unjust and unconstitutional in its origin and character, must be regarded as a war against freedom, against humanity, against justice, against the Union, . . . and against the free states. . . ."

These resolutions were approved by overwhelming majorities in both houses. They were based to a large extent on a report Charles Sumner had written for a committee of the legislature. In the report Sumner had taken the radical stand that Congress should withhold supplies from the armed forces. But the state legislature refused to go that far.

The growing bitterness of the radicals against the war appeared in a startling speech delivered in the United States Senate on February 11, 1847, by Thomas Corwin, a Whig of Ohio. He denounced the war as "flagrant," "a usurpation of authority," "a senseless quest for more room," a quest he would, if he were a Mexican, respond to with the words: "Have you not room in your own country to bury your dead men? If you come into mine we will greet you with bloody hands and welcome you to hospitable graves." He predicted that the war would generate a sectional clash over slavery and plunge the sister states of the Union into the bottomless gulf of civil conflict. The speech seemed traitorous to conservative Whigs and to conservative Democrats. But to such radical Whigs as Charles Francis Adams and Joshua Giddings it seemed admirable. They thought hopefully of Corwin as a candidate in 1848 for the presidency.

In December 1847 the Congress chosen the preceding year convened in Washington and took the necessary measures to organize itself. One step was the election of a Whig speaker of the House. A contest developed in this process between the conservative Whigs and the Conscience Whigs, which brought to the surface all the bitterness that had developed between them. Robert C. Winthrop was the leading conservative candidate, but on the first ballot he was short three votes of a House majority necessary for election. The three holdouts were Palfrey, Giddings, and Amos Tuck of New Hampshire, all of them radical anti-slavery men. They held out because Winthrop had shown half-heartedness in opposing the war and because, as speaker, he would appoint committees that would support war measures. In the end he won the speakership, but only after several conservative Whigs, who had been voting for other candidates, switched to him and canceled his deficit of votes. . . .

While the anti-war feeling in the North was intensifying, the armies of the United States were battering down Mexican resistance. One army under Taylor held the north; the other, under Scott, moved toward Mexico City from Vera Cruz. Both armies were winning spectacular victories against great odds.

The appetite of the All Mexico men was thus stimulated. The All Mexico movement and the related Manifest Destiny movement reached a climax during the second half of the war. Those ideas were especially attractive to the great urban masses of the northeastern seaboard: the city Democrats, in considerable part immigrants, the "unterrified Democracy" of New York City and Tammany Hall. The penny press of New York fed these ideas to its readers. So did the penny press of Philadelphia, Baltimore, and Boston. In Boston, the *Boston Times* was the great expansionist teacher. In the interior, Illinois was an outstanding center of All Mexico feeling.

The South was hesitant about accepting the program of All Mexico. Absorption would mean extending citizenship to colored and mixed races. Extending citizenship to colored and mixed races ran counter to all Southern instincts. It clashed especially with the instincts of Calhoun, who was the voice of Southern racism. His speeches in Congress were a bitter assault on the All Mexico movement on this ground. He felt that if any Mexican territory were to be taken, it should be only the sparsely populated northern parts—California and New Mexico. Even these areas he hesitated to accept because he doubted they were suitable for slavery. He wanted no territory that would spawn free states.

The great military successes in Mexico were most frightening to the radicals. They seemed to open a growing opportunity for slavery expansion. That foreboding had been reflected early in the war in a rider attached to a bill desired by Polk for two million dollars with which to negotiate a peace with Mexico. The rider was the famous Wilmot proviso of August 1846, declaring that none of the territory acquired from Mexico should ever be open to slavery or involuntary servitude. This represented an evolution from mere protest to an attempt to restrict the administration. It created tremendous excitement in Congress and in the country. It failed on the last day of the session but was attached again and again to war bills thereafter. It was never adopted. It was defeated always by a Southern opposition that was unanimous, aided by the votes of Northern "doughfaces."

The Wilmot proviso was the most ominous of the protests generated by the war. It was ominous because it so sharply divided the nation into quarreling sections. It did just what conservative Whigs had feared the most. Its support in Congress was exclusively Northern. Outside of Congress ten Northern state legislatures, by resolutions in one form or another, voted for it. It represented a Northern coalition of anti-slavery radicals. It was what Thomas Corwin had prophesied in his radical speech. It led Calhoun to despair of the Union.

What was the answer given by Whig conservatives to the growing Wilmotism of the North? It was as simple as the omission of one word from the Wilmot prescription of "No more slave territory." The new prescription was "No more territory." The omission of the word "slave" was designed to quiet the disruptive moral overtones of the Wilmot proviso, and to draw the sting that offended the Southern slaveholding society. "No more territory" was neutral on slavery and held Northern and Southern Whigs together. It spurned as immoral only the Polk program of brutal territorial conquest. For just this reason it was not enough for Northern moralists. These distinctions were explained with care by Horace Greeley in his editorials.

Some conservative Whigs and even some radicals were willing to compromise, however, about taking territory if it was territory that would not support slavery. Also they insisted that the territory be obtained only in exchange for our assuming the claims of American citizens or by purchase from Mexico. Whigs were attracted especially by Upper California with its magnificent harbor of San Francisco. Northern commercial Whigs would particularly have liked to obtain part or all of Upper California. Webster considered the port of San Francisco alone to be twenty times as valuable as the whole of Texas.

While these party responses to the war were being made, Scott's army irresistibly pounded its way to the heart of Mexico. By the early autumn of 1847 it had taken Mexico City by storm and the American flag flew over the Halls of the Montezumas. That thrilled expansionists and opened the prospect of obtaining the kind of peace they wanted.

Before discussing the efforts at peace, I should like to put aside politics for a moment and refer to dissent in American literary circles. Ralph Waldo Emerson was disgusted with the war, predicting that the United States would absorb Mexico "as the man swallows the arsenic, which brings him down in turn." But he was too engrossed in his own pursuits to actively enter the anti-war ranks. His friend, Henry Thoreau, became an activist when he delivered his famous lecture in which he urged "The Duty of Civil Disobedience" against any government that condoned slavery and engaged in unjust war. James Russell Lowell denounced the war and Manifest Destiny in his satirical *Biglow Papers*. William Ellery Channing, the poet, condemned the war in verse in the Whig press. Samuel Gridley Howe, Theodore Parker, and Wendell Phillips eloquently denounced the war. . . .

As for the efforts at peace, they were pressed by Polk even in an early stage of the fighting. He had learned indirectly from Santa Anna, who was then in Cuba as an exile wanting to get back home, that if he were allowed as a former leader to return, he would overthrow the Mexican government and would negotiate a treaty of peace with the United States that would include a cession of territory. This prospect attracted Polk, and orders were given the American navy to let Santa Anna slip through the blockade. Santa Anna did slip through, and he did effect a successful overthrow of the Mexican government. But instead of entering into peace negotiations he reorganized the Mexican resistance; and the only result of the maneuver was more strenuous fighting for the rest of the war.

That story was made known to Congress and to the press late in 1846 by the opposition Whigs. Polk's tactics were described as contemptible for a great state to use in fighting a weak one. A Southern Whig summed up the sentiments of many others in Congress. He did it in the form of rhetorical questions: "Does history furnish an example of more abhorrent perfidy? Was any government through its chief magistrate ever more vilely prostituted?"

Polk continued for another year his efforts to bring Santa Anna into peace negotiations. He entrusted negotiations to Nicholas P. Trist, Chief Clerk of the State Department. Trist operated under the wing of Scott's army while it was advancing on Mexico City. Late in August 1847 an armistice was arranged and a Mexican peace offer was obtained, which was not, however, very genuine. The Mexicans proposed among other things that a buffer state—a kind of neutral zone—be erected in the disputed area between the Nueces and the Rio Grande. This was a throwback to the old boundary dispute. Trist rejected it, but was incautious enough to send it, with the other proposals, for reference to his government. Polk was infuriated with his agent for showing weakness regarding the sensitive issue of the origins of the war. He canceled Trist's powers, rebuked him, and ordered him home. These orders were late in arriving. By the time they reached Trist, Mexico City had been captured, Santa Anna was in disgrace, and the new government was ready to negotiate in earnest. With this government Trist, in defiance of his orders, but supported by Scott, negotiated the treaty of Guadalupe Hidalgo of February 2, 1848. The treaty took from Mexico more than a third of her territory. Yet it was the most lenient treaty Trist could sign under Polk's instructions.

Trist reckoned that the President would be compelled to accept the treaty in spite of its irregular negotiation. And he was right. For the nation was utterly weary of the war, was suspicious of the ever-promised peace that like a mirage was never reached, and was dangerously divided over the issue of the extension of slavery. The House of Representatives was controlled by the peace party. If the President were to spurn the treaty giving the United States the sparsely populated northern part of Mexico, the Whigs would declare this to be proof of their charge that the war had been begun to seize All Mexico. The House might refuse further supplies, in which case even California and New Mexico might be lost. Dissenters such as Gallatin and Calhoun were deploring the fiscal burdens of the war. The press was charging that while the war was draining the nation's resources, urgent domestic needs were not being met. Polk decided, therefore, to submit the treaty to the Senate, where it was promptly ratified, with alterations not affecting the boundary provisions. The vote to ratify was 38 to 14.

This big affirmative vote reflected a universal demand for peace. Even Horace Greeley desired ratification in order to end the slaughter in Mexico. The big vote reflected also a wide tolerance for acquisitions which were thought unsuitable for slavery.

The fourteen negative votes reflected dissatisfaction with the treaty on diverse grounds. Six were from expansionists who felt defrauded because the treaty did not take enough. Seven were from Whigs who thought the treaty took too much. Thomas Hart Benton, a Democrat, voted nay, probably because he felt as the Whigs did.

A question arises in conclusion. How effective was dissent in the war? The question necessitates asking another. What would the treaty have been except for the dissent? The answer is that it would have been even harsher. Much more of Mexico would have been taken. Dissent moderated the treaty by revealing the dangers of the programs of All Mexico and Manifest Destiny.

On the other hand, the war and the dissent left behind sectional strains that began the process of breaking the old bonds of union, especially the national political parties, and replacing them with sectionalized parties. In the fierce struggles occurring over the organization of the Mexican cession, the Free Soil party was born, the crisis of 1850 occurred, and the Republican party was foreshadowed, which, when it triumphed in 1860, led to the secession of the Southern states. These effects illustrate an old truth: that moral issues are not easily quieted when they are as basic as those raised by Polk in 1846. They remain in the earth like dragon's teeth to grow into future armed conflict.

Norman A. Graebner
Empire on the Pacific

In the following selection Norman A. Graebner, a provocative contemporary historian, analyzes the concept of manifest destiny and concludes that it does not stand up under close scrutiny. He argues that "manifest destiny is an inadequate description of American expansionism in the forties," explains why he believes historians have tended to exaggerate the urge of the American people to expand in that decade, and offers his own interpretation of the expansion into Oregon and California. His thesis plays down the traditional emphasis on pioneers and their hunger for land, on public opinion, and on destiny's call to spread democratic institutions, as causes for that expansion. Instead, it stresses the desire for commerce and harbors on the Pacific Coast as primary motives. This interpretation, expressed in stimulating prose, is a fine example of how a historian can take an old theme, analyze and challenge it, and advance new ideas to replace the traditional ones. [From Norman A. Graebner, Empire on the Pacific: A Study in American Continental Expansion. Copyright 1955, The Ronald Press Company. Reprinted by permission.]

Manifest destiny persists as a popular term in American historical literature to explain the expansion of the United States to continent-wide dimensions in the 1840's. Like most broad generalizations, it does not bear close scrutiny. Undoubtedly, the vigor of the American people in that decade, their restless and sometimes uncontrollable energy, their idealism and faith in their democratic institutions convinced them of a peculiar American mission. Perhaps for many expansionists the American purpose remained that of spreading democracy over the land from ocean to ocean.

Public sentiment in 1844 seemed to favor the extension of the United States into Oregon. But lands along the Pacific were not for the taking, and public opinion is never simply defined or casually conveyed into specific proposals by a national administration. This was especially true in the forties when political leaders at no time were in agreement on precise objectives on the Pacific. There was, in fact, sufficient disagreement over expansionist purpose that the territorial gains of the Polk administration were achieved amid vigorous political opposition. Nor did these acquisitions prevent the American people from voting from power the party that gave them their immense foothold on the distant sea. Diverse are the elements which shape the course of history.

The concept of manifest destiny, as a democratic expression, represented an expanding, not a confining or limiting, force. As an ideal, it was not easily defined in terms of precise territorial limits. In 1844, when the claims of the ideal had fully taken hold, American expansionism looked far beyond Texas and Oregon. Indeed, it had no visible limit. The New York *Herald* prophesied that the American Republic would in due course embrace all the land from the Isthmus of Panama to the polar regions and from the Atlantic to the Pacific. One Texas correspondent wrote that "the fact must be no longer disguised, that we, the people of the United States must hold, and govern, under free and harmonious institutions, the continent we inhabit."

Some suggested that American laws be extended to include the downtrodden peons of South America. "And who does not wish to have them finally reach Cape Horn if their democratic character can be preserved?" demanded one expansionist. "Certainly no friend of the largest liberty of oppressed humanity." In their enthusiasm to extend the "area of freedom," many even looked beyond the continental limits to Cuba, the Sandwich Islands, the far-flung regions of the Pacific, and even to the Old World itself. This was a magnificent vision for a democratic purpose, but it hardly explains the sweep of the United States across the continent.

For American expansion to the Pacific was always a precise and calculated movement. It was ever limited in its objectives. American diplomatic and military policy that secured the acquisition of both Oregon and California was in the possession of men who never defined their expansionist purposes in terms of a democratic ideal. The vistas of all from Jackson to Polk were maritime and they were always anchored to specific waterways along the Pacific Coast. Land was necessary to them merely as a right of way to ocean ports—a barrier to be spanned by improved avenues of commerce. Any interpretation of westward extension beyond Texas is meaningless unless defined in terms of commerce and harbors.

Travelers during the decade before 1845 had created a precise vision of the western coasts of North America. It was a vision born of the sea. With the exception of Fremont, every noted voyager who recorded his impressions of Oregon and California had approached these regions via the Pacific. Some traders had sailed these coasts directly from Boston; others had first traversed the broad Pacific world as captains of merchant vessels or as explorers. But whatever their mission on the great ocean, they were without exception struck by the excellent quality of the Strait of Juan de Fuca, San Francisco Bay, and the harbor of San Diego, as well as the possible role of these ports in the development of Pacific commerce.

Charles Wilkes, as the commander of the United States exploring expedition to the Pacific, studied minutely not only the islands and sea lanes of the entire area, but also the important harbors and bays along the North American coast from Fuca Strait to San Francisco. Wilkes was not certain that these coastal regions, separated as they were in the early forties by almost two thousand miles of wilderness from the settled portions of the Midwest, would become other than a prosperous and independent maritime republic. Eminently qualified, however, to speculate on these Western harbors as stations in a Pacific commerce, he predicted a sizable stream of traffic emanating from them:

This future state is admirably situated to become a powerful maritime nation, with two of the finest ports in the world,—that within the straits of Juan de Fuca, and San Francisco. These two regions have, in fact, within themselves every thing to make them increase, and keep up an intercourse with the whole of Polynesia, as well as the countries of South America on the one side, and China, the Philippines, New Holland, and New Zealand, on the other. Among the latter, before many years, may be included Japan. Such various climates will furnish the materials for a beneficial exchange of products, and an intercourse that must, in time, become immense; while this western coast, enjoying a climate in many respects superior to any other in the Pacific, possessed as it must be by the Anglo-Norman race, and having none to enter into rivalry with it but the indolent inhabitants of warm climates, is evidently destined to fill a large space in the world's future history.

American officials and expansionists refused to accept his prediction of a separate commercial nation across the mountains. The threat of European encroachment convinced them that the grandeur of the Pacific Coast must accrue to the wealth, prosperity, and commercial eminence of the United States. By 1845 the American press accepted the dreams of Webster and Calhoun who had anticipated an American Boston or New York situated on some distant harbor. For those who perpetuated the expansionist program after Polk's inaugural, ports of call in Oregon and California were as vital as had been land empires in Texas during the preceding year. Except for what remained of the whole-of-Oregon fever, American expansionism had lost its broad nationalism and had become anchored to the mercantile interests of the United States.

After California entered the American consciousness, the expansionist purpose increasingly embraced both Oregon and California as two halves of a single ambition. Thereafter the complete vision of empire on the Pacific included the harbors from Puget Sound to San Diego. It called for a peaceful settlement of the Oregon controversy at 49° and the acquisition of Upper California. Writing to President Polk in July, 1845, Charles Fletcher pictured an American Union stretching from the Atlantic to the Pacific and from the thirtieth to the forty-ninth degree of north latitude. The St. Louis *Missourian* demanded both the Strait of Fuca and San Francisco harbor to fulfill the maritime destiny of the United States. Quite typically William Field, a Texan, advised the President to accept the parallel of 49° and then purchase California for as much as fifty million if necessary. He wrote, "I will only remark that if you can settle the Oregon difficulty without war and obtain California of

Mexico, to the Gulf of California and the river Gila for a boundary, you will have achieved enough to enroll your name *highèst* among those of the benefactors of the American people."

By 1846 this unitary but limited view of the Pacific Coast had penetrated the halls of Congress, where Meredith P. Gentry, of Tennessee, observed: "Oregon up to the 49th parallel of latitude, and the province of Upper California, when it can be fairly acquired, is the utmost limit to which this nation ought to go in the acquisition of territory."

With the Oregon treaty of 1846 the United States had reached the Pacific. Its frontage along the sea from 42° to Fuca Strait and Puget Sound fulfilled half the expansionist dream. On those shores the onward progress of the American pioneer would stop, but commercial expansionists looked beyond to the impetus that the possession of Oregon would give to American trade in the Pacific. "Commercially," predicted Benton, "the advantages of Oregon will be great—far greater than any equal portion of the Atlantic States." This Missourian believed that Oriental markets and export items would better complement the mercantile requirements of the United States than would those of Europe.

Through Fuca Strait, moreover, lay the new passage to the East which would bring to America the wealth and splendor which had always gone to those who commanded the trade of the Orient. The editor of the Baltimore *American* declared that

The commerce of the world is to be ours, and both oceans are to be subject to us. The splendors of Eastern cities which grew into greatness by the trade between the Valley of the Nile and the Valley of the Ganges, will shine but dimly, even in the enhanced illumination of fancy and tradition, when compared with the stately magnificence and colossal structure of the cities which are to concentrate the rich elements of the Valley of the Mississippi. The ruins of Thebes and Memphis, of Palmyra and Balbee remain still to attest a wonderful degree of former greatness; but they grew up by means of a caravan trade on camels, or by a commerce of galleys on the Red Sea and the Persian Gulf. From such a traffic let the eye turn to the rivers, canals, and railroads of this continent of ours, to the mighty agency of steam, propelling innumerable vessels and cars, and the immense expanse of alluvial soil, fertile in products under the culture of a people who for enterprise, energy and invention have no superiors—we may say no equals.

For decades after 1846 British travelers in the Far Northwest recognized the magnitude of this American diplomatic achievement. With a Columbia River boundary, complained one British observer in 1872, Canadian shipping in the north Pacific might have competed with that of the United States. Upon viewing the waters of Puget Sound, another English traveler acknowledged dejectedly the significance of the American triumph in Oregon: "It is not easy to conceive what reasons for claiming the country north of the Columbia could be urged by the United States Government. But they knew the prospective value of the magnificent inland waters of Puget Sound, and acted upon that knowledge. With the possession of that grand inlet, British Columbia could easily compete with California and Oregon; without it, it becomes a difficult matter to do so." British observers in western Canada agreed that the American negotiators knew the value of the waterways they sought, whereas the British did not.

Following the outbreak of the Mexican War in May, 1846, metropolitan editorialists soon regarded that conflict as the agency whereby the United States might consummate her westward movement and annex the harbors of California. To them the Oregon settlement had been made particularly acceptable by the anticipation of adding certain Mexican ports to the American Union. In May the New York *Herald* urged the Polk administration to seize San Francisco Bay so that men would forget the whole of Oregon. One California correspondent predicted the result of the speedy occupation of the Pacific ports by the American naval squadron: "We shall have then a country, bounded at the North latitude by 49 degrees, to the Pacific—and the South on the same ocean by 32 degrees—and the western and eastern boundaries, being what Nature intended them, the Pacific, with China in the outline, and the Atlantic with Europe in the background."

Such prospects pleased the editor of the New York *Herald*. He noted that the proposed boundaries gave the United States 1,300 miles of coast on the Pacific, several magnificent harbors, and "squared off our South-Western possessions." One writer for the New York *Journal of Commerce* in December, 1846, rejoiced that with the acquisition of New Mexico and California the territory of the United States would "spread out in one broad square belt from one ocean to the other, giving us nearly as much coast on the Pacific as we possess on the Atlantic." The imaginary line of 42° meant little to these commercial expansionists of a century ago.

This vision was not lost on the Midwest. The Mississippi Valley responded eagerly to the call to arms, stimulated perhaps by the prospect of conquering Mexican soil. Such enthusiasm was not misplaced, for future trade routes through the great valley lay in the direction of California as well as Oregon. During the Oregon debates Andrew Kennedy and John McClernand had revealed the significance of the Strait of Fuca to the grain regions of the Midwest. Now this agrarian concept of commercial empire in the Pacific encompassed also the harbors of California. It was the editor of the Baltimore *American* who analyzed cogently in September, 1847, the possible mercantile relationships between this Mexican province and the broad prairies of the Mississippi Valley:

The Mississippi River . . . stretches out its arms east and west to lay hold of both oceans. That vast alluvial region, the garden of the civilized world . . . is to be, and that before many generations shall have passed, the centre of the world's commerce and its most prolific source. It must have access to the sea coast on both shores, and along the whole extent, communicating freely with the Atlantic sea board, which we already possess, entire, and with the Pacific which we must possess, entire. . . . Besides, it is clear that California must have its connections with the Mississippi Valley. . . . Without these connections California would be insulated. Confined to her own resources . . . her fine harbors without the materials of commerce would not avail her much. But once drawn into the embrace of the great valley and suffused with the rich currents of its ample products, California, from her position alone, becomes important, and her commercial greatness stands revealed.

American expansion over contiguous territory was complete with the Treaty of Guadalupe Hidalgo. Thereafter United States frontage on the Pacific remained unchanged. In 1848, it is true, some did not believe that American continental expansion had run its course. Tom Corwin anticipated demands for even greater annexations in the future. He wrote to William Greene in March, 1848, that the treaty gave to the United States a third of Mexico immediately "with the implied understanding that the ballance is to be swallowed when our anglo-saxon gastric juices shall clamor for another Cannibal breakfast." The New York *Herald* recognized the same feeling but with considerably more pleasure: "We will take a large portion now, and the balance at a more convenient season." Both were wrong, for American expansion was a deliberate movement, and the United States had achieved what two decades of observers had thought essential for this nation's future development.

Polk alone could fulfill the expansionist goals of the forties. Although he was an advocate of agrarian democracy, his expansionist outlook as President was as narrowly mercantile as that of Webster or Winthrop. He accepted the wisdom of compromise in Oregon for the precise reasons that the Whigs and the metropolitan press called for a settlement along the forty-ninth parallel. His wartime expansionist policy was aimed primarily at San Francisco and San Diego, and as the war neared completion Polk acknowledged no other objectives to Congress. In his message of December, 1847, he declared that the bay of San Francisco and other harbors on the California coast "would afford shelter for our navy, for our numerous whale ships, and other merchant vessels employed in the Pacific ocean, [and] would in a short period become the marts of an extensive and profitable commerce with China, and other countries of the East."

With the ratification of the Treaty of Guadalupe Hidalgo, the weary President could at last contemplate the success of his arduous foreign policy. In July he delivered to Congress a personal appraisal of his success in expanding the boundaries of the United States. Again his eyes were focused solely on the ports of San Diego, Monterey, and San Francisco. These, he declared, "will enable the United States to command the already valuable and rapidly increasing commerce of the Pacific." Under the American flag they would "afford security and repose to our commercial marine; and American mechanics will soon furnish ready means of ship-building and repair, which are now so much wanted in that distant sea." The President prophesied the growth of great commercial cities on these capacious harbors which would secure "the rich commerce of the East, and shall thus obtain for our products new and increased markets, and greatly enlarge our coasting and foreign trade, as well as augment our tonnage and revenue."

Democratic spokesmen in 1848 likewise measured the diplomatic settlements of the Polk administration in terms of harbors and trade. Lucien Chase of Tennessee limited the important acquisitions of the United States to Puget Sound, Monterey, San Diego, and San Francisco. His particularism focused his attention even more narrowly. "In the Bay of San Francisco," he wrote, "will converge the commerce of Asia and the model Republic. It possesses advantages over every other harbor upon the western coast of North or South America. . . . The vast and increasing commerce of Asia, and the islands of the East, is now open to our adventurous seamen. . . .

Similarly a Democratic electioneering pamphlet singled out the California ports as the key acquisition of recent United States expansionist policy which had placed the American nation firmly on the distant coast. "From our cities on the Pacific," it predicted, "a speedy communication will be opened with China, and a profitable trade enjoyed, which must soon pour the wealth of that nation into our laps." For Whigs who had flayed Polk's Mexican policy, San Francisco Bay possibly made somewhat more palatable the huge swallow of territory acquired by the war.

During the succeeding years observers at San Francisco continued to appraise the acquisition of California in commercial terms. The French consul at this port viewed the region as the controlling element in the development of Pacific trade. He concluded in 1852 that "all the archipelagoes of the Pacific Ocean, the entire American continent from Sitka to the Straits of Magellan, China, Japan, are destined to submit to the influence of this state [and] to be attracted into the sphere of its commercial activity." One Californian in the fifties revealed the importance of that region's waterways to the total commercial growth of the United States in the following words:

The commerce of the Pacific is in the hands of New York, Boston, New Bedford, Bangor, Cape Cod, and all-along-shore to New Orleans, and whatever benefits commerce derives hereby, is felt throughout the whole country. Neither are other portions of the sunny south, or the rich valleys of the west unrepresented there. Though the ships may be of Eastern construction, and commanded by the indomitable and enterprising Yankee skipper, yet he and his hardy crew are but the carriers for the products of the East and South.

Historians have tended to exaggerate the natural urge of the American people to expand in the forties. For that reason they have attributed an unrealistic importance to the impact of pioneers, public sentiment, and war on American continental expansion. None of these had any direct bearing on the determination of United States boundaries along the Pacific. American frontiersmen never repeated the role they played in the annexation of Texas. In time they might have secured possession of California, but in 1845 hardly a thousand had reached that province. More numerous in Oregon, American pioneers were still limited to regions south of the Columbia. If they prompted the British to retreat from that line, they hardly explain why the United States insisted on that British retreat.

What mattered far more in the definition of American purpose were the travelers who toured the Pacific coasts and recorded the location and significance of waterways. These men, not pioneers, formulated the objectives of American officials from Adams to Polk. For two decades the official analysis of United States needs on the Pacific changed imperceptibly. Pioneers undoubtedly strengthened the American urge to expand westward, but they had little effect on the extent to which the nation would expand.

Public opinion as reflected in the spirit of manifest destiny played no greater role in the determination of United States ocean frontage than did the pressure of pioneers. Politicians had aroused sufficient interest in Oregon by 1844 to turn it into a popular issue. But to the extent that the Oregon settlement was a mandate, the American people voted for 54° 40', a boundary which they never acquired.

California was never a campaign issue at all. Its annexation was never the result of popular demand. After the metropolitan press turned its attention to that region in 1845, the Mexican province undoubtedly became a coveted objective for thousands of Americans. Yet for the mass of citizens it remained a remote, unknown region. California persisted probably as an area of vital concern for those relatively few merchants, politicians, travelers, and officials who appreciated its commercial significance. Whig success in attacking Democratic expansionist policy during 1848 reveals an extensive lack of interest in Polk's diplomatic achievement. The Washington *National Intelligencer* interpreted the Whig victory as proof that the American people had rejected the seductive visions of manifest destiny.

American triumphs in Mexico were essential to the success of the expansionist program, but they had no bearing on administration goals. These had been defined by Polk and his cabinet before the war was hardly under way. Manifest destiny revealed itself in the Mexican War only when it clamored for the whole of Mexico, but even that final burst of agrarian nationalism was effectively killed by the Treaty of Guadalupe Hidalgo. Polk's objectives, clear and precise, were ever limited to two ocean ports. Victories along the road to Mexico City were important only in that they eventually brought to the President the opportunity to secure what he had once hoped to achieve by diplomacy alone.

Nor can Nicholas P. Trist be overlooked in the fulfillent of United States territorial growth, for in the final analysis it was he, lonely and unobserved, who secured the southern boundary of California. If the nation achieved all this through the dictates of manifest destiny, that destiny revealed itself through some exceedingly devious patterns.

Particularism had its way in both the Oregon and Mexican treaties. Administration goals, therefore, had to be achieved through private diplomacy, England assuming the leadership in the former negotiations. This was essential, for only thus could the President defy that public opinion and avoid those pressures of American politics that sought to prevent both the peaceful settlement of the Oregon question and the acquisition of California.

Indeed, manifest destiny is an inadequate description of American expansionism in the forties. The mere urge to expand or even the acceptance of a destiny to occupy new areas on the continent does not create specific geographical objectives. Nor do these factors take into account the role of chance or the careful formulation and execution of policy. It was not by accident that the United States spread as a broad belt across the continent in the forties. It was rather through clearly conceived policies relentlessly pursued that the United States achieved its empire on the Pacific.

Sitting Bull, one of the victorious Indian leaders at the battle of the Little Big Horn in Montana, 1876. (Library of Congress)

12 Social Cross Currents

Until recent years historians usually examined American society from the point of view of those who were at the top, the leaders who set standards for others to follow. The history surveys told a great deal about politicians, diplomats, successful industrialists, and others who formed the ruling elites but seldom explored the attitudes or way of life of those who were in the middle or at the bottom. Now scholars are beginning to overcome their ethnocentric bias and are examining the heritage of minorities and others who have not been allowed to participate in the mainstream of American history.

One minority that has only recently been treated fairly or with understanding in our histories is the American Indian. In the past the Indian appeared merely as the losing antagonist in the long Indian-white conflict. The whites wrote the histories and in doing so glorified their ancestors as heroic frontiersmen, as civilizers who tamed the wilderness and conquered the savage natives. More often than not, these writers ignored or brushed aside careful examination of the Indians' long, futile struggle to preserve their way of life. Rarely did historians approach the story from the Indians' point of view.

Of course, much depended on the attitude of the individual who wrote about Indian-white relations. Some white writers portrayed the Indian as a noble savage or saw in him virtuous qualities such as a peaceful temperament in harmony with nature and fellow humans. Other writers depicted the Indian as brutish, cruel, and treacherous, an image that persisted in the minds of nineteenth-century Americans.

White Americans considered the Indians stupid, subhuman savages who had no culture worth preserving. These savages had to be subdued or exterminated or they would hold up the westward march of white progress. To justify the taking of Indian lands, whites—including such Presidents as John Adams and Theodore Roosevelt—early took the position that these natives were nomads who roamed the wilderness and had no fixed habitation. This concept ignored the evidence. A number of tribes lived in towns and villages that were well organized and capably run, and many Indians farmed and practiced other occupations that kept them in one place.

Although documents that recorded the Indians' side of the confrontation with whites are scarce and often unreliable, we know that they complained continuously of white ingratitude and injustice. Lenape, a Mohican, said of Europeans: "They at first asked only for a little land on which to raise bread for themselves and their families, and pasture for their cattle, which we freely gave them. They soon wanted more, which we also gave them." When we refused to give land, "they took it from us by force, and drove us to a great distance from our ancient homes."

These words describe the basic pattern of Indian-white relations through the first half of the nineteenth century. Unwilling, reluctant, or incapable of adapting themselves to white civilization, the Indians resisted. In virtually every instance the Indians came out losers, and their way of life virtually disappeared.

Now the culture and life style of the Indians, not just their lost battles, are being studied and appreciated on their own terms. Historians are reinterpreting the long confrontation from the Indian as well as from the white side. Scholars are also reinterpreting other aspects of the social and intellectual life of America in the middle years of the nineteenth century, a period in historical writing usually dominated by accounts of territorial expansion and sectional conflict. Racial conflict, as in the Indian-white confrontation and in the slave-master relationship, has always been important in America's history. So has conflict between ethnic, religious, and other radically distinctive groups.

Freemasons did not differ from other Americans except in their commitment to a secret organization. In the 1820s and 1830s an antipathy to all kinds of secret societies spread through various parts of the country, expressing itself strongly in New York as opposition to Freemasonry. Churches fell in with this sentiment and attacked the Masons in what appeared to be a small religious crusade. This feeling spilled over into politics; in New York citizens vowed not to support Masons for public office. From New York the anti-Masonic movement spread to other states, so in 1831 its leaders launched a national organization that held a convention in Baltimore and nominated its own presidential candidate. Within a few years the movement spent itself. It had served as a vehicle for various discontented and disturbed elements of the population, who turned to other agitation after the anti-Masonic politicians concentrated on national politics rather than on alleged Masonic conspiracies.

Like the Masons, Mormons did not differ from other Americans in color or in cultural traits, only in religious belief and in a few social practices. The Mormons, or Latter-Day Saints, founded their religious society in New York in 1830. Forced out of the state the following year, they moved to Ohio and Missouri. Mob violence, stirred by differences in religion, social issues, and politics, drove them out of Missouri to Illinois, where they built the settlement of Nauvoo. Again violence, stimulated by such Mormon practices as plural marriages and by the fears of the populace that Mormons posed a threat to social stability, forced the group to migrate. A mob with blackened faces assaulted a jail and lynched their leader, Joseph Smith. Finally, in 1848 they settled in the Valley of the Great Salt Lake in Utah. Problems with the federal government, mainly over polygamy, and clashes with gentiles kept anti-Mormon agitation alive, however, for more than a decade. Only when the larger society no longer saw in the Mormons a threat, real or imagined, to its way of life did the hostility against them subside.

Anti-Catholic and antiforeign feelings had deeper roots than either anti-Masonry or anti-Mormonism, for almost all societies distrust strangers. From the earliest days of the republic most Americans had disliked Catholics and foreigners; all kinds of conspiracies and plots were attributed to Jesuits, to priests in general, and to undefined foreign influences. When Catholics and foreigners speaking their own language and practicing their own customs became visible in large numbers in American cities, mainly as a result of heavy Irish and German immigration in the 1830s, nativism blossomed, and the word itself entered American vocabulary. In 1837 nativists formed the Native American Association, and in 1843 in New York they established the American Republican party, which wanted to keep Catholics and foreigners from voting and holding office. Clashes between Catholics and Protestant nativists became common. Some of the worst took place in Philadelphia in 1844, where twenty people were killed and a hundred injured.

In 1845 the nativists organized the Native American party and became a potent political force. Four years later the Protestant nativists in New York founded the secret Order of the Star-Spangled Banner, and with its successor, the American party, popularly known as the Know-Nothing party, moved into national politics. Proclaiming themselves the true standard-bearers of Americanism, the nativists demanded restriction of immigration and agitated for an America homogeneous in blood, religion, and ideals. They attracted a large following and elected a number of men to state and local offices. Although the Civil War overshadowed the concerns of the nativists, their fears did not vanish. Antiforeignism, anti-Catholicism, demands for immigration restriction, and uncompromising Americanism remained popular issues throughout the nineteenth century and well into the twentieth century. Nativists remained dedicated to the destruction of minority "enemies," who, directly or indirectly, menaced their image of the American way of life.

For women in the first half of the nineteenth century, the American way of life meant that although they formed one-half the population, they were relegated to the status of an underprivileged minority. They could not vote, hold public office, earn their livelihood without great difficulty, freely go to college, or choose a profession. These disabilities barred them from taking a substantial part in the nation's political and social life. Custom and practice brought over from England held that woman's only reputable vocation was marriage. But upon marriage the woman lost even the limited independence society allowed her. Her rights became merged with and subordinated to those of her husband. She had no legal, or even social, existence of her own.

The industrial revolution, by creating jobs for women in great numbers, gave them an opportunity for a limited independence and led them to demand more through a Women's Rights movement. This feminine activism, stimulated also by new educational opportunities not available to women in other countries, coincided with the broad reform movement of the 1830s and 1840s. The abolition movement became the most important of the reform issues and the area in which feminine enterprise carried weight: women supplied more than half the signatures on the great petitions that forced Congress to face the issue of slavery. The reform movement created new opportunities for women, stimulated in them a more enterprising spirit than in the past, and benefited them because of the tendency for one reform to lead to another.

In these decades American feminists made their position known and laid the foundation for later accomplishments. Leaders such as Angelina and Sarah Grimké spoke out publicly against slavery and for women's rights, and they wrote on the equality of the sexes. Such publicity led to the feminists' first organizational effort, a Women's Rights Convention in Seneca Falls, New York, in 1848. Called by Elizabeth Cady Stanton, who lived in that village, the convention denounced the history of mankind as "usurpatious on the part of man toward woman" and came out in favor of suffrage for women. It also led to women's conventions elsewhere.

Still, the women's movement remained provincial until the Civil War, when women, mostly in the North, gained new jobs and participated in various war activities. Many felt that their war services to the nation entitled them to vote. Since Congress would not be moved, women turned to the states, where slowly, mostly in the West, they gained the right to vote, a right which did not come on a national basis until 1920. Gradually, too, the states were the first to relax the legal disabilities imposed on women.

America's historians have seldom showed an awareness of women's disabilities or of how different their lives were from those of the men in their families. General histories usually say something about women's struggle to gain the vote or their slow but eventual entrance into the industrial labor market, but they rarely mention the social life of women or what they did to build the nation. Even at the hands of social historians women suffered from omission and neglect. Now this state of affairs has changed; scholars are producing important studies that tell us a great deal about how the neglected half of the population contributed to the building of the nation.

In the following selections three historians discuss minority problems in nineteenth-century America. Each group had its unique handicaps, but all shared the experience of the underdog in confrontation with the dominant, white, male society.

Dee Brown

"Their Manners Are Decorous and Praiseworthy"

This selection, taken from a best-selling book, traces the main theme of Indian-white relations in America—conflict. As everyone knows, the Europeans were the victors in the long struggle. They exterminated Indian peoples, destroyed Indian cultures, and dispossessed Indians of their lands. Whites advanced various theories to justify this bitter conquest, but Theodore Roosevelt put the matter simply, saying that "the settler and pioneer have at bottom had justice on their side; this great continent could not have been kept as nothing but a game preserve for squalid savages." This contempt for the Indian, as Dee Brown points out, stems from the first contact with whites; Columbus himself set the pattern. Indians had to conform to European standards, "adopt our ways," or be crushed, and even those who tried to conform were pushed aside by whites. Perhaps the Indian way of life was doomed, no matter what the Indian did, because of the white man's superior technology and desire for his land. Note that this piece is written with considerable sympathy for the Indian. It recounts briefly what has happened to him at the hands of whites since Columbus's time. [From Bury My Heart at Wounded Knee *by Dee Brown, pp. 1–13. Copyright © 1970 by Dee Brown. Reprinted by permission of Holt, Rinehart and Winston, Inc.]*

It began with Christopher Columbus, who gave the people the name *Indios*. Those Europeans, the white men, spoke in different dialects, and some pronounced the word *Indien*, or *Indianer*, or Indian. *Peaux-rouges*, or redskins, came later. As was the custom of the people when receiving strangers, the Tainos on the island of San Salvador generously presented Columbus and his men with gifts and treated them with honor.

"So tractable, so peaceable, are these people," Columbus wrote to the King and Queen of Spain, "that I swear to your Majesties there is not in the world a better nation. They love their neighbors as themselves, and their discourse is ever sweet and gentle, and accompanied with a smile; and though it is true that they are naked, yet their manners are decorous and praiseworthy."

All this, of course, was taken as a sign of weakness, if not heathenism, and Columbus being a righteous European was convinced the people should be "made to work, sow and do all that is necessary and to *adopt our ways*." Over the next four centuries (1492–1890) several million Europeans and their descendants undertook to enforce their ways upon the people of the New World.

Columbus kidnapped ten of his friendly Taino hosts and carried them off to Spain, where they could be introduced to the white man's ways. One of them died soon after arriving there, but not before he was baptized a Christian. The Spaniards were so pleased that they had made it possible for the first Indian to enter heaven that they hastened to spread the good news throughout the West Indies.

The Tainos and other Arawak people did not resist conversion to the Europeans' religion, but they did resist strongly when hordes of these bearded strangers began scouring their islands in search of gold and precious stones. The Spaniards looted and burned villages; they kidnapped hundreds of men, women, and children and shipped them to Europe to be sold as slaves. Arawak resistance brought on the use of guns and sabers, and whole tribes were destroyed, hundreds of thousands of people in less than a decade after Columbus set foot on the beach of San Salvador, October 12, 1492.

Communications between the tribes of the New World were slow, and news of the Europeans' barbarities rarely overtook the rapid spread of new conquests and settlements. Long before the English-speaking white men arrived in Virginia in 1607, however, the Powhatans had heard rumors about the civilizing techniques of the Spaniards. The Englishmen used subtler methods. To ensure peace long enough to establish a settlement at Jamestown, they put a golden crown upon the head of Wahunsonacook, dubbed him King Powhatan, and convinced him that he should put his people to work supplying the white settlers with food. Wahunsonacook vacillated between loyalty to his rebellious subjects and to the English, but after John Rolfe married his daughter, Pocahontas, he apparently decided that he was more English than Indian. After Wahunsonacook died, the Powhatans rose up in revenge to drive the Englishmen back into the sea from which they had come, but the Indians underestimated the power of English weapons. In a short time the eight thousand Powhatans were reduced to less than a thousand.

In Massachusetts the story began somewhat differently but ended virtually the same as in Virginia. After the Englishmen landed at Plymouth in 1620, most of them probably would have starved to death but for aid received from friendly natives of the New World. A Pemaquid named Samoset and three Wampanoags named Massasoit, Squanto, and Hobomah became self-appointed missionaries to the Pilgrims. All spoke some English, learned from explorers who had touched ashore in previous years. Squanto had been kidnapped by an English seaman who sold him into slavery in Spain, but he escaped through the aid of another Englishman and finally managed to return home. He and other Indians regarded the Plymouth colonists as helpless children; they shared corn with them from the tribal stores, showed them where and how to catch fish, and got them through the first winter. When spring came they gave the white men some seed corn and showed them how to plant and cultivate it.

For several years these Englishmen and their Indian neighbors lived in peace, but many more shiploads of white people continued coming ashore. The ring of axes and the crash of falling trees echoed up and down the coasts of the land which the white man now called New England. Settlements began crowding in upon each other. In 1625 some of the colonists asked Samoset to give them 12,000 additional acres of Pemaquid land. Samoset knew that land came from the Great Spirit, was as endless as the sky, and belonged to no man. To humor these strangers in their strange ways, however, he went through a ceremony of transferring the land and made his mark on a paper for them. It was the first deed of Indian land to English colonists.

Most of the other settlers, coming in by thousands now, did not bother to go through such a ceremony. By the time Massasoit, great chief of the Wampanoags, died in 1662 his people were being pushed back into the wilderness. His son Metacom foresaw doom for all Indians unless they united to resist the invaders. Although the New Englanders flattered Metacom by crowning him King Philip of Pokanoket, he devoted most of his time to forming alliances with the Narragansetts and other tribes in the region.

In 1675, after a series of arrogant actions by the colonists, King Philip led his Indian confederacy into a war meant to save the tribes from extinction. The Indians attacked fifty-two settlements, completely destroying twelve of them, but after months of fighting, the firepower of the colonists virtually exterminated the Wampanoags and Narragansetts. King Philip was killed and his head publicly exhibited at Plymouth for twenty years. Along with other captured Indian women and children, his wife and young son were sold into slavery in the West Indies.

When the Dutch came to Manhattan Island, Peter Minuit purchased it for sixty guilders in fishhooks and glass beads, but encouraged the Indians to remain and continue exchanging their valuable peltries for such trinkets. In 1641, Willem Kieft levied tribute upon the Mahicans and sent soldiers to Staten Island to punish the Raritans for offenses which had been committed not by them but by white settlers. The Raritans resisted arrest, and the soldiers killed four of them. When the Indians retaliated by killing four Dutchmen, Kieft ordered the massacre of two entire villages while the inhabitants slept. The Dutch soldiers ran their bayonets through men, women, and children, hacked their bodies to pieces, and then leveled the villages with fire.

For two more centuries these events were repeated again and again as the European colonists moved inland through the passes of the Alleghenies and down the westward-flowing rivers to the Great Waters (the Mississippi) and then up the Great Muddy (the Missouri).

The Five Nations of the Iroquois, mightiest and most advanced of all the eastern tribes, strove in vain for peace. After years of bloodshed to save their political independence, they finally went down to defeat. Some escaped to Canada, some fled westward, some lived out their lives in reservation confinement.

During the 1760's Pontiac of the Ottawas united tribes in the Great

Lakes country in hopes of driving the British back across the Alleghenies, but he failed. His major error was an alliance with French-speaking white men who withdrew aid from the *peaux-rouges* during the crucial siege of Detroit.

A generation later, Tecumseh of the Shawnees formed a great confederacy of Midwestern and southern tribes to protect their lands from invasion. The dream ended with Tecumseh's death in battle during the War of 1812.

Between 1795 and 1840 the Miamis fought battle after battle, and signed treaty after treaty, ceding their rich Ohio Valley lands until there was none left to cede.

When white settlers began streaming into the Illinois country after the War of 1812, the Sauks and Foxes fled across the Mississippi. A subordinate chief, Black Hawk, refused to retreat. He created an alliance with the Winnebagos, Pottawotamies, and Kickapoos, and declared war against the new settlements. A band of Winnebagos, who accepted a white soldier chief's bribe of twenty horses and a hundred dollars, betrayed Black Hawk and he was captured in 1832. He was taken East for imprisonment and display to the curious. After he died in 1838, the governor of the recently created Iowa Territory obtained Black Hawk's skeleton and kept it on view in his office.

In 1829, Andrew Jackson, who was called Sharp Knife by the Indians, took office as President of the United States. During his frontier career, Sharp Knife and his soldiers had slain thousands of Cherokees, Chickasaws, Choctaws, Creeks, and Seminoles, but these southern Indians were still numerous and clung stubbornly to their tribal lands, which had been assigned them forever by white men's treaties. In Sharp Knife's first message to his Congress, he recommended that all these Indians be removed westward beyond the Mississippi. "I suggest the propriety of setting apart an ample district west of the Mississippi . . . to be guaranteed to the Indian tribes, as long as they shall occupy it."

Although enactment of such law would only add to the long list of broken promises made to the eastern Indians, Sharp Knife was convinced that Indians and whites could not live together in peace and that his plan would make possible a final promise which never would be broken again. On May 28, 1830, Sharp Knife's recommendations became law.

Two years later he appointed a commissioner of Indian affairs to serve in the War Department and see that the new laws affecting Indians were properly carried out. And then on June 30, 1834, Congress passed *An Act to Regulate Trade and Intercourse with the Indian Tribes and to Preserve Peace on the Frontiers*. All that part of the United States west of the Mississippi "and not within the States of Missouri and Louisiana or the Territory of Arkansas" would be Indian country. No white persons would be permitted to trade in the Indian country without a license. No white traders of bad character would be permitted to reside in Indian country. No white persons would be permitted to settle in the Indian country. The military force of the United States would be employed in the apprehension of any white person who was found in violation of provisions of the act.

Before these laws could be put into effect, a new wave of white settlers swept westward and formed the territories of Wisconsin and Iowa. This made it necessary for the policy makers in Washington to shift the "permanent Indian frontier" from the Mississippi River to the 95th meridian. (This line ran from Lake of the Woods on what is now the Minnesota-Canada border, slicing southward through what are now the states of Minnesota and Iowa, and then along the western borders of Missouri, Arkansas, and Louisiana, to Galveston Bay, Texas.) To keep the Indians beyond the 95th meridian and to prevent unauthorized white men from crossing it, soldiers were garrisoned in a series of military posts that ran southward from Fort Snelling on the Mississippi River to Forts Atkinson and Leavenworth on the Missouri, Forts Gibson and Smith on the Arkansas, Fort Towson on the Red, and Fort Jesup in Louisiana.

More than three centuries had now passed since Christopher Columbus landed on San Salvador, more than two centuries since the English colonists came to Virginia and New England. In that time the friendly Tainos who welcomed Columbus ashore had been utterly obliterated. Long before the last of the Tainos died, their simple agricultural and handicraft culture was destroyed and replaced by cotton plantations worked by slaves. The white colonists chopped down the tropical forests to enlarge their fields; the cotton plants exhausted the soil; winds unbroken by a forest shield covered the fields with sand. When Columbus first saw the island he described it as "very big and very level and the trees very green . . . the whole of it so green that it is a pleasure to gaze upon." The Europeans who followed him there destroyed its vegetation and its inhabitants—human, animal, bird, and fish—and after turning it into a wasteland, they abandoned it.

On the mainland of America, the Wampanoags of Massasoit and King Philip had vanished, along with the Chesapeakes, the Chickahominys, and the Potomacs of the great Powhatan confederacy. (Only Pocahontas was remembered.) Scattered or reduced to remnants were the Pequots, Montauks, Nanticokes, Machapungas, Catawbas, Cheraws, Miamis, Hurons, Eries, Mohawks, Senecas, and Mohegans. (Only Uncas was remembered.) Their musical names remained forever fixed on the American land, but their bones were forgotten in a thousand burned villages or lost in forests fast disappearing before the axes of twenty million invaders. Already the once sweet-watered streams, most of which bore Indian names, were clouded with silt and the wastes of man; the very earth was being ravaged and squandered. To the Indians it seemed that these Europeans hated everything in nature—the living forests and their birds and beasts, the grassy glades, the water, the soil, and the air itself.

The decade following establishment of the "permanent Indian frontier" was a bad time for the eastern tribes. The great Cherokee nation
had survived more than a hundred years of the white man's wars, diseases, and whiskey, but now it was to be blotted out. Because the
Cherokees numbered several thousands, their removal to the West was
planned to be in gradual stages, but discovery of Appalachian gold
within their territory brought on a clamor for their immediate wholesale
exodus. During the autumn of 1838, General Winfield Scott's soldiers
rounded them up and concentrated them into camps. (A few hundred
escaped to the Smoky Mountains and many years later were given a small
reservation in North Carolina.) From the prison camps they were started
westward to Indian Territory. On the long winter trek, one of every four
Cherokees died from cold, hunger, or disease. They called the march
their "trail of tears." The Choctaws, Chickasaws, Creeks, and Seminoles
also gave up their homelands in the South. In the North, surviving
remnants of the Shawnees, Miamis, Ottawas, Hurons, Delawares, and
many other once mighty tribes walked or traveled by horseback and
wagon beyond the Mississippi, carrying their shabby goods, their rusty
farming tools, and bags of seed corn. All of them arrived as refugees, poor
relations, in the country of the proud and free Plains Indians.

Scarcely were the refugees settled behind the security of the "permanent Indian frontier" when soldiers began marching westward through
the Indian country. The white men of the United States—who talked so
much of peace but rarely seemed to practice it—were marching to war
with the white men who had conquered the Indians of Mexico. When the
war with Mexico ended in 1847, the United States took possession of a
vast expanse of territory reaching from Texas to California. All of it was
west of the "permanent Indian frontier."

In 1848 gold was discovered in California. Within a few months,
fortune-seeking easterners by the thousands were crossing the Indian
Territory. Indians who lived or hunted along the Santa Fe and Oregon
trails had grown accustomed to seeing an occasional wagon train licensed
for traders, trappers, or missionaries. Now suddenly the trails were filled
with wagons, and the wagons were filled with white people. Most of them
were bound for California gold, but some turned southwest for New
Mexico or northwest for the Oregon country.

To justify these breaches of the "permanent Indian frontier," the
policy makers in Washington invented Manifest Destiny, a term which
lifted land hunger to a lofty plane. The Europeans and their descendants
were ordained by destiny to rule all of America. They were the dominant
race and therefore responsible for the Indians—along with their lands,
their forests, and their mineral wealth. Only the New Englanders, who
had destroyed or driven out all their Indians, spoke against Manifest
Destiny.

In 1850, although none of the Modocs, Mohaves, Paiutes, Shastas,
Yumas, or a hundred other lesser-known tribes along the Pacific Coast

were consulted on the matter, California became the thirty-first state of the Union. In the mountains of Colorado gold was discovered, and new hordes of prospectors swarmed across the Plains. Two vast new territories were organized, Kansas and Nebraska, encompassing virtually all the country of the Plains tribes. In 1858 Minnesota became a state, its boundaries being extended a hundred miles beyond the 95th meridian, the "permanent Indian frontier."

And so only a quarter of a century after enactment of Sharp Knife Andrew Jackson's Indian Trade and Intercourse Act, white settlers had driven in both the north and south flanks of the 95th meridian line, and advance elements of white miners and traders had penetrated the center.

It was then, at the beginning of the 1860's, that the white men of the United States went to war with one another—the Bluecoats against the Graycoats, the great Civil War. In 1860 there were probably 300,000 Indians in the United States and Territories, most of them living west of the Mississippi. According to varying estimates, their numbers had been reduced by one-half to two-thirds since the arrival of the first settlers in Virginia and New England. The survivors were now pressed between expanding white populations on the East and along the Pacific coasts— more than thirty million Europeans and their descendants. If the remaining free tribes believed that the white man's Civil War would bring any respite from his pressures for territory, they were soon disillusioned.

The most numerous and powerful western tribe was the Sioux, or Dakota, which was separated into several subdivisions. The Santee Sioux lived in the woodlands of Minnesota, and for some years had been re-treating before the advance of settlements. Little Crow of the Mdew-kanton Santee, after being taken on a tour of eastern cities, was convinced that the power of the United States could not be resisted. He was reluctantly attempting to lead his tribe down the white man's road. Wabasha, another Santee leader, also had accepted the inevitable, but both he and Little Crow were determined to oppose any further sur-render of their lands.

Farther west on the Great Plains were the Teton Sioux, horse Indians all, and completely free. They were somewhat contemptuous of their woodland Santee cousins who had capitulated to the settlers. Most numerous and most confident of their ability to defend their territory were the Oglala Tetons. At the beginning of the white man's Civil War, their outstanding leader was Red Cloud, thirty-eight years old, a shrewd warrior chief. Still too young to be a warrior was Crazy Horse, an intelli-gent and fearless teenaged Oglala.

Among the Hunkpapas, a smaller division of the Teton Sioux, a young man in his mid-twenties had already won a reputation as a hunter and warrior. In tribal councils he advocated unyielding opposition to any intrusion by white men. He was Tatanka Yotanka, the Sitting Bull. He was mentor to an orphaned boy named Gall. Together with Crazy Horse of the Oglalas, they would make history sixteen years later in 1876.

Although he was not yet forty, Spotted Tail was already the chief spokesman for the Brulé Tetons, who lived on the far western plains. Spotted Tail was a handsome, smiling Indian who loved fine feasts and compliant women. He enjoyed his way of life and the land he lived upon, but was willing to compromise to avoid war.

Closely associated with the Teton Sioux were the Cheyennes. In the old days the Cheyennes had lived in the Minnesota country of the Santee Sioux, but gradually moved westward and acquired horses. Now the Northern Cheyennes shared the Powder River and the Bighorn country with the Sioux, frequently camping near them. Dull Knife, in his forties, was an outstanding leader of the Northern branch of the tribe. (To his own people Dull Knife was known as Morning Star, but the Sioux called him Dull Knife, and most contemporary accounts use that name.)

The Southern Cheyennes had drifted below the Platte River, establishing villages on the Colorado and Kansas plains. Black Kettle of the Southern branch had been a great warrior in his youth. In his late middle age, he was the acknowledged chief, but the younger men and the Hotamitaneos (Dog Soldiers) of the Southern Cheyennes were more inclined to follow leaders such as Tall Bull and Roman Nose, who were in their prime.

The Arapahos were old associates of the Cheyennes and lived in the same areas. Some remained with the Northern Cheyennes, others followed the Southern branch. Little Raven, in his forties, was at this time the best-known chief.

South of the Kansas-Nebraska buffalo ranges were the Kiowas. Some of the older Kiowas could remember the Black Hills, but the tribe had been pushed southward before the combined power of the Sioux, Cheyenne, and Arapaho. By 1860 the Kiowas had made their peace with the northern plains tribes and had become allies of the Comanches, whose southern plains they had entered. The Kiowas had several great leaders—an aging chief, Satank; two vigorous fighting men in their thirties, Satanta and Lone Wolf; and an intelligent statesman, Kicking Bird.

The Comanches, constantly on the move and divided into many small bands, lacked the leadership of their allies. Ten Bears, very old, was more a poet than a warrior chief. In 1860, half-breed Quanah Parker, who would lead the Comanches in a last great struggle to save their buffalo range, was not yet twenty years old.

In the arid Southwest were the Apaches, veterans of 250 years of guerrilla warfare with the Spaniards, who taught them the finer arts of torture and mutilation but never subdued them. Although few in number—probably not more than six thousand divided into several bands—their reputation as tenacious defenders of their harsh and pitiless land was already well established. Mangas Colorado, in his late sixties, had signed a treaty of friendship with the United States, but was already disillusioned by the influx of miners and soldiers into his territory. Cochise, his son-in-law, still believed he could get along with the white Americans. Victorio and Delshay distrusted the white intruders and gave them a wide berth. Nana, in his fifties but tough as rawhide, considered the English-speaking white men no different from the Spanish-speaking Mexicans he had been fighting all his life. Geronimo, in his twenties, had not yet proved himself.

The Navahos were related to the Apaches, but most Navahos had taken the Spanish white man's road and were raising sheep and goats, cultivating grain and fruit. As stockmen and weavers, some bands of the tribe had grown wealthy. Other Navahos continued as nomads, raiding their old enemies the Pueblos, the white settlers, or prosperous members of their own tribe. Manuelito, a stalwart mustachioed stock raiser, was head chief—chosen by an election of the Navahos held in 1855. In 1859, when a few wild Navahos raided United States citizens in their territory, the U.S. Army retaliated not by hunting down the culprits but by destroying the hogans and shooting all the livestock belonging to Manuelito and members of his band. By 1860, Manuelito and some Navaho followers were engaged in an undeclared war with the United States in northern New Mexico and Arizona.

In the Rockies north of the Apache and Navaho country were the Utes, an aggressive mountain tribe inclined to raid their more peaceful neighbors to the south. Ouray, their best-known leader, favored peace with white men even to the point of soldiering with them as mercenaries against other Indian tribes.

In the far West most of the tribes were too small, too divided, or too weak to offer much resistance. The Modocs of northern California and southern Oregon, numbering less than a thousand, fought guerrilla-fashion for their lands. Kintpuash, called Captain Jack by the California settlers, was only a young man in 1860; his ordeal as a leader would come a dozen years later.

Northwest of the Modocs, the Nez Percés had been living in peace with white men since Lewis and Clark passed through their territory in 1805. In 1855, one branch of the tribe ceded Nez Percé lands to the United States for settlement, and agreed to live within the confines of a large reservation. Other bands of the tribe continued to roam between the Blue Mountains of Oregon and the Bitterroots of Idaho. Because of the vastness of the Northwest country, the Nez Percés believed there would always be land enough for both white men and Indians to use as each saw fit. Heinmot Tooyalaket, later known as Chief Joseph, would have to make a fateful decision in 1877 between peace and war. In 1860 he was twenty years old, the son of a chief.

In the Nevada country of the Paiutes a future Messiah named Wovoka, who later would have a brief but powerful influence upon the Indians of the West, was only four years old in 1860.

During the following thirty years these leaders and many more would enter into history and legend. Their names would become as well known as those of the men who tried to destroy them. Most of them, young and old, would be driven into the ground long before the symbolic end of Indian freedom came at Wounded Knee in December, 1890. Now, a century later, in an age without heroes, they are perhaps the most heroic of all Americans.

David Brion Davis

Some Themes of Counter-Subversion: An Analysis of Anti-Masonic, Anti-Catholic, and Anti-Mormon Literature

Nativism is a strong, persistent theme within the patterns of American history. In this essay a talented intellectual historian analyzes nativism in the Jacksonian era as expressed through powerful and popular movements of counter-subversion against imaginary conspiracies. Although Masonry, Catholicism, and Mormonism differed markedly from each other, nativists saw in each group a similar danger—anti-Americanism. Each movement menaced the image Jacksonian America held of itself; each threatened the cult of the common man. Each was especially dangerous because its members had no outwardly distinguishing traits, such as color, and their loyalty was difficult to prove; each did not conform to nativists' standards of Americanism. In a society in which opportunity was expanding and tradition breaking down, according to Davis, nativists could overcome their own insecurities by attacking nonconformists and asserting their own sense of orthodoxy and unity. Other historians have explained nativism from different perspectives; they have related it to ethnic tensions, status rivalries, and economic cycles. Davis's psychological analysis adds depth to our understanding of the irrationalities of nativism. Note the nativists' concept of womanhood and the need to protect it against Catholic and Mormon corrupters. [From David Brion Davis, "Some Themes of Counter-Subversion: An Analysis of Anti-Masonic, Anti-Catholic, and Anti-Mormon Literature," Mississippi Valley Historical Review, XLVII (September 1960), 205–224.]

During the second quarter of the nineteenth century, when danger of foreign invasion appeared increasingly remote, Americans were told by various respected leaders that Freemasons had infiltrated the government and had seized control of the courts, that Mormons were undermining political and economic freedom in the West, and that Roman Catholic priests, receiving instructions from Rome, had made frightening progress in a plot to subject the nation to popish despotism. This fear of internal subversion was channeled into a number of powerful counter movements which attracted wide public support. The literature produced by these movements evoked images of a great American enemy that closely resembled traditional European stereotypes of conspiracy and subversion. In Europe, however, the idea of subversion implied a threat to the established order—to the king, the church, or the ruling aristocracy—rather than to ideals or a way of life. If free Americans borrowed their images of subversion from frightened kings and uneasy aristocrats, these images had to be shaped and blended to fit American conditions. The movements would have to come from the people, and the themes of counter-subversion would be likely to reflect their fears, prejudices, hopes, and perhaps even unconscious desires.

There are obvious dangers in treating such reactions against imagined subversion as part of a single tendency or spirit of an age. Anti-Catholicism was nourished by ethnic conflict and uneasiness over immigration in the expanding cities of the Northeast; anti-Mormonism arose largely from a contest for economic and political power between western settlers and a group that voluntarily withdrew from society and claimed the undivided allegiance of its members. Anti-Masonry, on the other hand, was directed against a group thoroughly integrated in American society and did not reflect a clear division of economic, religious, or political interests. Moreover, anti-Masonry gained power in the late 1820's and soon spent its energies as it became absorbed in national politics; anti-Catholicism reached its maximum force in national politics a full generation later; anti-Mormonism, though increasing in intensity in the 1850's, became an important national issue only after the Civil War. These movements seem even more widely separated when we note that Freemasonry was traditionally associated with anti-Catholicism and that Mormonism itself absorbed considerable anti-Masonic and anti-Catholic sentiment.

Despite such obvious differences, there were certain similarities in these campaigns against subversion. All three gained widespread support in the northeastern states within the space of a generation; anti-Masonry and anti-Catholicism resulted in the sudden emergence of separate political parties; and in 1856 the new Republican party explicitly condemned the Mormons' most controversial institution. The movements of counter-subversion differed markedly in historical origin, but as the image of an un-American conspiracy took form in the nativist press, in sensational exposés, in the countless fantasies of treason and mysterious criminality, the lines separating Mason, Catholic, and Mormon became almost indistinguishable.

The similar pattern of Masonic, Catholic, and Mormon subversion was frequently noticed by alarmist writers. The *Anti-Masonic Review* informed its readers in 1829 that whether one looked at Jesuitism or Freemasonry, "the organization, the power, and the secret operation, are the same; except that Freemasonry is much the more secret and complicated of the two." William Hogan, an ex-priest and vitriolic anti-Catholic, compared the menace of Catholicism with that of Mormonism. And many later anti-Mormon writers agreed with Josiah Strong that Brigham Young "out-popes the Roman" and described the Mormon hierarchy as being similar to the Catholic. It was probably not accidental that Samuel F. B. Morse analyzed the Catholic conspiracy in essentially the same terms his father had used in exposing the Society of the Illuminati, supposedly a radical branch of Freemasonry, or that writers of sensational fiction in the 1840's and 1850's depicted an atheistic and unprincipled Catholic Church obviously modeled on Charles Brockden Brown's earlier fictional version of the Illuminati.

If Masons, Catholics, and Mormons bore little resemblance to one another in actuality, as imagined enemies they merged into a nearly common stereotype. Behind specious professions of philanthropy or religious sentiment, nativists discerned a group of unscrupulous leaders plotting to subvert the American social order. Though rank-and-file members were not individually evil, they were blinded and corrupted by a persuasive ideology that justified treason and gross immorality in the interest of the subversive group. Trapped in the meshes of a machine-like organization, deluded by a false sense of loyalty and moral obligation, these dupes followed orders like professional soldiers and labored unknowingly to abolish free society, to enslave their fellow men, and to overthrow divine principles of law and justice. Should an occasional member free himself from bondage to superstition and fraudulent authority, he could still be disciplined by the threat of death or dreadful tortures. There were no limits to the ambitious designs of leaders equipped with such organizations. According to nativist prophets, they chose to subvert American society because control of America meant control of the world's destiny.

Some of these beliefs were common in earlier and later European interpretations of conspiracy. American images of Masonic, Catholic, and Mormon subversion were no doubt a compound of traditional myths concerning Jacobite agents, scheming Jesuits, and fanatical heretics, and of dark legends involving the Holy Vehm and Rosicrucians. What distinguished the stereotypes of Mason, Catholic, and Mormon was the way in which they were seen to embody those traits that were precise antitheses of American ideals. The subversive group was essentially an inverted image of Jacksonian democracy and the cult of the common man; as such it not only challenged the dominant values but stimulated those suppressed needs and yearnings that are unfulfilled in a mobile, rootless, and individualistic society. It was therefore both frightening and fascinating.

It is well known that expansion and material progress in the Jacksonian era evoked a fervid optimism and that nationalists became intoxicated with visions of America's millennial glory. The simultaneous growth of prosperity and social democracy seemed to prove that Providence would bless a nation that allowed her citizens maximum liberty. When each individual was left free to pursue happiness in his own way, unhampered by the tyranny of custom or special privilege, justice and well-being would inevitably emerge. But if a doctrine of laissez-faire individualism seemed to promise material expansion and prosperity, it also raised disturbing problems. As one early anti-Mormon writer expressed it: What was to prevent liberty and popular sovereignty from sweeping away "the old landmarks of Christendom, and the glorious old common law of our fathers"? How was the individual to preserve a sense of continuity with the past, or identify himself with a given cause or tradition? What, indeed, was to insure a common loyalty and a fundamental unity among the people?

Such questions acquired a special urgency as economic growth intensified mobility, destroyed old ways of life, and transformed traditional symbols of status and prestige. Though most Americans took pride in their material progress, they also expressed a yearning for reassurance and security, for unity in some cause transcending individual self-interest. This need for meaningful group activity was filled in part by religious revivals, reform movements, and a proliferation of fraternal orders and associations. In politics Americans tended to assume the posture of what Marvin Meyers has termed "venturesome conservatives," mitigating their acquisitive impulses by an appeal for unity against extraneous forces that allegedly threatened a noble heritage of republican ideals. Without abandoning a belief in progress through laissez-faire individualism, the Jacksonians achieved a sense of unity and righteousness by styling themselves as restorers of tradition. Perhaps no theme is so evident in the Jacksonian era as the strained attempt to provide America with a glorious heritage and a noble destiny. With only a loose and often ephemeral attachment to places and institutions, many Americans felt a compelling need to articulate their loyalties, to prove their faith, and to demonstrate their allegiance to certain ideals and institutions. By so doing they acquired a sense of self-identity and personal direction in an otherwise rootless and shifting environment.

But was abstract nationalism sufficient to reassure a nation strained by sectional conflict, divided by an increasing number of sects and associations, and perplexed by the unexpected consequences of rapid growth? One might desire to protect the Republic against her enemies, to preserve the glorious traditions of the Founders, and to help insure continued expansion and prosperity, but first it was necessary to discover an enemy by distinguishing subversion from simple diversity. If Freemasons seemed to predominate in the economic and political life of a given area, was one's joining them shrewd business judgment or a betrayal of republican tradition? Should Maryland citizens heed the warnings of anti-Masonic itinerants, or conclude that anti-Masonry was itself a conspiracy hatched by scheming Yankees? Were Roman Catholics plotting to destroy public schools and a free press, the twin guardians of American democracy, or were they exercising democratic rights of self-expression and self-protection? Did equality of opportunity and equality before the law mean that

Americans should accept the land claims of Mormons or tolerate as jurors men who "swear that they have wrought miracles and supernatural cures"? Or should one agree with the Reverend Finis Ewing that "the 'Mormons' are the common enemies of mankind and ought to be destroyed"?

Few men questioned traditional beliefs in freedom of conscience and the right of association. Yet what was to prevent "all the errors and worn out theories of the Old World, of schisms in the early Church, the monkish age and the rationalistic period," from flourishing in such salubrious air? Nativists often praised the work of benevolent societies, but they were disturbed by the thought that monstrous conspiracies might also "show kindness and patriotism, when it is necessary for their better concealment; and oftentimes do much good for the sole purpose of getting a better opportunity to do evil." When confronted by so many sects and associations, how was the patriot to distinguish the loyal from the disloyal? It was clear that mere disagreement over theology or economic policy was invalid as a test, since honest men disputed over the significance of baptism or the wisdom of protective tariffs. But neither could one rely on expressions of allegiance to common democratic principles, since subversives would cunningly profess to believe in freedom and toleration of dissent as long as they remained a powerless minority.

As nativists studied this troubling question, they discovered that most groups and denominations claimed only a partial loyalty from their members, freely subordinating themselves to the higher and more abstract demands of the Constitution, Christianity, and American public opinion. Moreover, they openly exposed their objects and activities to public scrutiny and exercised little discrimination in enlisting members. Some groups, however, dominated a larger portion of their members' lives, demanded unlimited allegiance as a condition of membership, and excluded certain activities from the gaze of a curious public.

Of all governments, said Richard Rush, ours was the one with most to fear from secret societies, since popular sovereignty by its very nature required perfect freedom of public inquiry and judgment. In a virtuous republic why should anyone fear publicity or desire to conceal activities, unless those activities were somehow contrary to the public interest? When no one could be quite sure what the public interest was, and when no one could take for granted a secure and well-defined place in the social order, it was most difficult to acknowledge legitimate spheres of privacy. Most Americans of the Jacksonian era appeared willing to tolerate diversity and even eccentricity, but when they saw themselves excluded and even barred from witnessing certain proceedings, they imagined a "mystic power" conspiring to enslave them.

Readers might be amused by the first exposures of Masonic ritual, since they learned that pompous and dignified citizens, who had once impressed non-Masons with allusions to high degrees and elaborate ceremonies, had in actuality been forced to stand blindfolded and clad in ridiculous garb, with a long rope noosed around their necks. But genuine anti-Masons were not content with simple ridicule. Since intelligent and distinguished men had been members of the fraternity, "it must have in its interior something more than the usual revelations of its mysteries declare." Surely leading citizens would not meet at night and undergo degrading and humiliating initiations just for the sake of novelty. The alleged murder of William Morgan raised an astonishing public furor because it supposedly revealed the inner secret of Freemasonry. Perverted by a false ideology, Masons had renounced all obligations to the general public, to the laws of the land, and even to the command of God. Hence they threatened not a particular party's program or a denomination's creed, but stood opposed to all justice, democracy, and religion.

The distinguishing mark of Masonic, Catholic, and Mormon conspiracies was a secrecy that cloaked the members' unconditional loyalty to an autonomous body. Since the organizations had corrupted the private moral judgment of their members, Americans could not rely on the ordinary forces of progress to spread truth and enlightenment among their ranks. Yet the affairs of such organizations were not outside the jurisdiction of democratic government, for no body politic could be asked to tolerate a power that was designed to destroy it. Once the true nature of subversive groups was thoroughly understood, the alternatives were as clear as life and death. How could democracy and Catholicism coexist when, as Edward Beecher warned, "The systems are diametrically opposed: one must and will exterminate the other"? Because Freemasons had so deeply penetrated state and national governments, only drastic remedies could restore the nation to its democratic purity. And later, Americans faced an "irrepressible conflict" with Mormonism, for it was said that either free institutions or Mormon despotism must ultimately annihilate the other.

We may well ask why nativists magnified the division between unpopular minorities and the American public, so that Masons, Catholics, and Mormons seemed so menacing that they could not be accorded the usual rights and privileges of a free society. Obviously the literature of counter-subversion reflected concrete rivalries and conflicts of interest between competing groups, but it is important to note that the subversive bore no racial or ethnic stigma and was not even accused of inherent depravity. Since group membership was a matter of intellectual and emotional loyalty, no *physical* barrier prevented a Mason, Catholic, or Mormon from apostatizing and joining the dominant in-group, providing always that he escaped assassination from his previous masters. This suggests that counter-subversion was more than a rationale for group rivalry and was related to the general problem of ideological unity and diversity in a free society. When a "system of delusion" insulated members of a group from the unifying and disciplining force of public opinion, there was no authority to command an allegiance to common principles. This was why oaths of loyalty assumed great importance for nativists. Though the ex-Catholic William Hogan stated repeatedly that Jesuit spies respected no oaths except those to the Church, he inconsistently told Masons and Odd Fellows that they could prevent infiltration by requiring new members to swear they were not Catholics. It was precisely the absence of distinguishing outward traits that made the enemy so dangerous, and true loyalty so difficult to prove.

When the images of different enemies conform to a similar pattern, it is highly probable that this pattern reflects important tensions within a given culture. The themes of nativist literature suggest that its authors simplified problems of personal insecurity and adjustment to bewildering social change by trying to unite Americans of diverse political, religious, and economic interests against a common enemy. Just as revivalists sought to stimulate Christian fellowship by awakening men to the horrors of sin, so nativists used apocalyptic images to ignite human passions, destroy selfish indifference, and join patriots in a cohesive brotherhood. Such themes were only faintly secularized. When God saw his "lov'd Columbia" imperiled by the hideous monster of Freemasonry, He realized that only a martyr's blood could rouse the hearts of the people and save them from bondage to the Prince of Darkness. By having God will Morgan's death, this anti-Mason showed he was more concerned with national virtue and unity than with Freemasonry, which was only a providential instrument for testing republican strength.

Similarly, for the anti-Catholic "this brilliant new world" was once "young and beautiful; it abounded in all the luxuries of nature; it promised all that was desirable to man." But the Roman Church, seeing "these irresistible temptations, thirsting with avarice and yearning for the reestablishment of her falling greatness, soon commenced pouring in among its unsuspecting people hoardes of Jesuits and other friars." If Americans were to continue their narrow pursuit of self-interest, oblivious to the "Popish colleges, and nunneries, and monastic institutions," indifferent to manifold signs of corruption and decay, how could the nation expect "that the moral breezes of heaven should breathe upon her, and restore to her again that strong and healthy constitution, which her ancestors have left to her sons"? The theme of an Adamic fall from paradise was horrifying, but it was used to inspire determined action and thus unity. If Methodists were "criminally indifferent" to the Mormon question, and if "avaricious merchants, soulless corporations, and a subsidized press" ignored Mormon iniquities, there was all the more reason that the *"will of the people* must prevail."

Without explicitly rejecting the philosophy of laissez-faire individualism, with its toleration of dissent and innovation, nativist literature conveyed a sense of common dedication to a noble cause and sacred tradition. Though the nation had begun with the blessings of God and with the noblest institutions known to man, the people had somehow become selfish and complacent, divided by petty disputes, and insensitive to signs of danger. In his sermons attacking such self-interest, such indifference to public concerns, and such a lack of devotion to common ideals and sentiments, the nativist revealed the true source of his anguish. Indeed, he seemed at times to recognize an almost beneficent side to subversive organizations, since they joined the nation in a glorious crusade and thus kept it from moral and social disintegration.

The exposure of subversion was a means of promoting unity, but it also served to clarify national values and provide the individual ego with a sense of high moral sanction and imputed righteousness. Nativists identified themselves repeatedly with a strangely incoherent tradition in which images of Pilgrims, Minute Men, Founding Fathers, and true Christians appeared in a confusing montage. Opposed to this heritage of stability and perfect integrity, to this society founded on the highest principles of divine and natural law, were organizations formed by the grossest frauds and impostures, and based on the wickedest impulses of human nature. Bitterly refuting Masonic claims to ancient tradition and Christian sanction, anti-Masons charged that the Order was of recent origin, that it was shaped by Jews, Jesuits, and French atheists as an engine for spreading infidelity, and that it was employed by kings and aristocrats to undermine republican institutions. If the illustrious Franklin and Washington had been duped by Masonry, this only proved how treacherous was its appeal and how subtly persuasive were its pretensions. Though the Catholic Church had an undeniable claim to tradition, nativists argued that it had originated in stupendous frauds and forgeries "in comparison with which the forgeries of Mormonism are completely thrown into the shade." Yet anti-Mormons saw an even more sinister conspiracy based on the "shrewd cunning" of Joseph Smith, who convinced gullible souls that he conversed with angels and received direct revelations from the Lord.

By emphasizing the fraudulent character of their opponents' claims, nativists sought to establish the legitimacy and just authority of American institutions. Masonic rituals, Roman Catholic sacraments, and Mormon revelations were preposterous hoaxes used to delude naïve or superstitious minds; but public schools, a free press, and jury trials were eternally valid prerequisites for a free and virtuous society.

Moreover, the finest values of an enlightened nation stood out in bold relief when contrasted with the corrupting tendencies of subversive groups. Perversion of the sexual instinct seemed inevitably to accompany religious error. Deprived of the tender affections of normal married love, shut off from the elevating sentiments of fatherhood, Catholic priests looked on women only as insensitive objects for the gratification of their frustrated desires. In similar fashion polygamy struck at the heart of a morality based on the inspiring influence of woman's affections: "It renders man coarse, tyrannical, brutal, and heartless. It deals death to all sentiments of true manhood. It enslaves and ruins woman. It crucifies every God-given feeling of her nature." Some anti-Mormons concluded that plural marriage could only have been established among foreigners who had never learned to respect women. But the more common explanation was that the false ideology of Mormonism had deadened the moral sense and liberated man's wild sexual impulse from the normal restraints of civilization. Such degradation of women and corruption of man served to highlight the importance of democratic marriage, a respect for women, and careful cultivation of the finer sensibilities.

But if nativist literature was a medium for articulating common values and exhorting individuals to transcend self-interest and join in a dedicated union against evil, it also performed a more subtle function. Why, we may ask, did nativist literature dwell so persistently on themes of brutal sadism and sexual immorality? Why did its authors describe sin in such minute details, endowing even the worst offenses of their enemies with a certain fascinating appeal?

Freemasons, it was said, could commit any crime and indulge any passion when "upon the square," and Catholics and Mormons were even less inhibited by internal moral restraints. Nativists expressed horror over this freedom from conscience and conventional morality, but they could not conceal a throbbing note of envy. What was it like to be a member of a cohesive brotherhood that casually abrogated the laws of God and man, enforcing unity and obedience with dark and mysterious powers? As nativists speculated on this question, they projected their own fears and desires into a fantasy of licentious orgies and fearful punishments.

Such a projection of forbidden desires can be seen in the exaggeration of the stereotyped enemy's powers, which made him appear at times as a virtual superman. Catholic and Mormon leaders, never hindered by conscience or respect for traditional morality, were curiously superior to ordinary Americans in cunning, in exercising power over others, and especially in captivating gullible women. It was an ancient theme of anti-Catholic literature that friars and priests were somehow more potent and sexually attractive than married laymen, and were thus astonishingly successful at seducing supposedly virtuous wives. Americans were cautioned repeatedly that no priest recognized Protestant marriages as valid, and might consider any wife legitimate prey. Furthermore, priests had access to the pornographic teachings of Dens and Liguori, sinister names that aroused the curiosity of anti-Catholics, and hence learned subtle techniques of seduction perfected over the centuries. Speaking with the authority of an ex-priest, William Hogan described the shocking result: "I have seen husbands unsuspiciously and hospitably entertaining the very priest who seduced their wives in the confessional, and was the parent of some of the children who sat at the same table with them, each of the wives unconscious of the other's guilt, and the husbands of both, not even suspecting them." Such blatant immorality was horrifying, but everyone was apparently happy in this domestic scene, and we may suspect that the image was not entirely repugnant to husbands who, despite their respect for the Lord's Commandments, occasionally coveted their neighbors' wives.

The literature of counter-subversion could also embody the somewhat different projective fantasies of women. Ann Eliza Young dramatized her seduction by the Prophet Brigham, whose almost superhuman powers enchanted her and paralyzed her will. Though she submitted finally only because her parents were in danger of being ruined by the Church, she clearly indicated that it was an exciting privilege to be pursued by a Great Man. When anti-Mormons claimed that Joseph Smith and other prominent Saints knew the mysteries of Animal Magnetism, or were endowed with the highest degree of "amativeness" in their phrenological makeup, this did not detract from their covert appeal. In a ridiculous fantasy written by Maria Ward, such alluring qualities were extended even to Mormon women. Many bold-hearted girls could doubtless identify themselves with Anna Bradish, a fearless Amazon of a creature, who rode like a man, killed without compunction, and had no pity for weak women who failed to look out for themselves. Tall, elegant, and "intellectual," Anna was attractive enough to arouse the insatiable desires of Brigham Young, though she ultimately rejected him and renounced Mormonism.

While nativists affirmed their faith in Protestant monogamy, they obviously took pleasure in imagining the variety of sexual experience supposedly available to their enemies. By picturing themselves exposed to similar temptations, they assumed they could know how priests and Mormons actually sinned. Imagine, said innumerable anti-Catholic writers, a beautiful young woman kneeling before an ardent young priest in a deserted room. As she confesses, he leans over, looking into her eyes, until their heads are nearly touching. Day after day she reveals to him her innermost secrets, secrets she would not think of unveiling to her parents, her dearest friends, or even her suitor. By skillful questioning the priest fills her mind with immodest and even sensual ideas, "until this wretch has worked up her passions to a tension almost snapping, and then becomes his easy prey." How could any man resist such provocative temptations, and how could any girl's virtue withstand such a test?

We should recall that this literature was written in a period of increasing anxiety and uncertainty over sexual values and the proper role of woman. As ministers and journalists pointed with alarm at the spread of prostitution, the incidence of divorce, and the lax and hypocritical morality of the growing cities, a discussion of licentious subversives offered a convenient means for the projection of guilt as well as desire. The sins of individuals, or of the nation as a whole, could be pushed off upon the shoulders of the enemy and there punished in righteous anger.

Specific instances of such projection are not difficult to find. John C. Bennett, whom the Mormons expelled from the Church as a result of his flagrant sexual immorality, invented the fantasy of "The Mormon Seraglio" which persisted in later anti-Mormon writings. According to Bennett, the Mormons maintained secret orders of beautiful prostitutes who were mostly reserved for various officials of the Church. He claimed, moreover, that any wife refusing to accept polygamy might be forced to join the lowest order and thus become available to any Mormon who desired her.

Another example of projection can be seen in the letters of a young lieutenant who stopped in Utah in 1854 on his way to California. Convinced that Mormon women could be easily seduced, the lieutenant wrote frankly of his amorous adventures with a married woman. "Everybody has got one," he wrote with obvious pride, "except the Colonel and Major. The Doctor has got three—mother and two daughters. The mother cooks for him and the daughters sleep with him." But though he described Utah as "a great country," the lieutenant waxed indignant over polygamy, which he condemned as self-righteously as any anti-Mormon minister: "To see one man openly parading half a dozen or more women to church . . . is the devil according to my ideas of morality, virtue and decency."

If the consciences of many Americans were troubled by the growth of red light districts in major cities, they could divert their attention to the "legalized brothels" called nunneries, for which no one was responsible but lecherous Catholic priests. If others were disturbed by the moral implications of divorce, they could point in horror at the Mormon elder who took his quota of wives all at once. The literature of counter-subversion could thus serve the double purpose of vicariously fulfilling repressed desires, and of releasing the tension and guilt arising from rapid social change and conflicting values.

Though the enemy's sexual freedom might at first seem enticing, it was always made repugnant in the end by associations with perversion or brutal cruelty. Both Catholics and Mormons were accused of practicing nearly every form of incest. The persistent emphasis on this theme might indicate deep-rooted feelings of fear and guilt, but it also helped demonstrate, on a more objective level, the loathsome consequences of unrestrained lust. Sheer brutality and a delight in human suffering were supposed to be the even more horrible results of sexual depravity. Masons disemboweled or slit the throats of their victims; Catholics cut unborn infants from their mothers' wombs and threw them to the dogs before their parents' eyes; Mormons raped and lashed recalcitrant women, or seared their mouths with red-hot irons. This obsession with details of sadism, which reached pathological proportions in much of the literature, showed a furious determination to purge the enemy of every admirable quality. The imagined enemy might serve at first as an outlet for forbidden desires, but nativist authors escaped from guilt by finally making him an agent of unmitigated aggression. In such a role the subversive seemed to deserve both righteous anger and the most terrible punishments.

The nativist escape from guilt was more clearly revealed in the themes of confession and conversion. For most American Protestants the crucial step in anyone's life was a profession of true faith resulting from a genuine religious experience. Only when a man became conscious of his inner guilt, when he struggled against the temptations of Satan, could he prepare his soul for the infusion of the regenerative spirit. Those most deeply involved in sin often made the most dramatic conversions. It is not surprising that conversion to nativism followed the same pattern, since nativists sought unity and moral certainty in the regenerative spirit of nationalism. Men who had been associated in some way with un-American conspiracies were not only capable of spectacular confessions of guilt, but were best equipped to expose the insidious work of supposedly harmless organizations. Even those who lacked such an exciting history of corruption usually made some confession of guilt, though it might involve only a previous indifference to subversive groups. Like ardent Christians, nativists searched in their own experiences for the meanings of sin, delusion, awakening to truth, and liberation from spiritual bondage. These personal confessions proved that one had recognized and conquered evil, and also served as ritual cleansings preparatory to full acceptance in a group of dedicated patriots.

Anti-Masons were perhaps the ones most given to confessions of guilt and most alert to subtle distinctions of loyalty and disloyalty. Many leaders of this movement, expressing guilt over their own "shameful experience and knowledge" of Masonry, felt a compelling obligation to exhort their former associates to "come out, and be separate from masonic abominations." Even when an anti-Mason could say with John Quincy Adams that "I am not, never was, and never shall be a Free-mason," he would often admit that he had once admired the Order, or had even considered applying for admission.

Since a willingness to sacrifice oneself was an unmistakable sign of loyalty and virtue, ex-Masons gloried in exaggerating the dangers they faced and the harm that their revelations supposedly inflicted on the enemy. In contrast to hardened Freemasons, who refused to answer questions in court concerning their fraternal associations, the seceders claimed to reveal the inmost secrets of the Order, and by so doing to risk property, reputation, and life. Once the ex-Mason had dared to speak the truth, his character would surely be maligned, his motives impugned, and his life threatened. But, he declared, even if he shared the fate of the illustrious Morgan, he would die knowing that he had done his duty.

Such self-dramatization reached extravagant heights in the ranting confessions of many apostate Catholics and Mormons. Maria Monk and her various imitators told of shocking encounters with sin in its most sensational forms, of bondage to vice and superstition, and of melodramatic escapes from popish despotism. A host of "ex-Mormon wives" described their gradual recognition of Mormon frauds and iniquities, the anguish and misery of plural marriage, and their breath-taking flights over deserts or mountains. The female apostate was especially vulnerable to vengeful retaliation, since she could easily be kidnapped by crafty priests and nuns, or dreadfully punished by Brigham Young's Destroying

Angels. At the very least, her reputation could be smirched by foul lies and insinuations. But her willingness to risk honor and life for the sake of her country and for the dignity of all womankind was eloquent proof of her redemption. What man could be assured of so noble a role?

The apostate's pose sometimes assumed paranoid dimensions. William Hogan warned that only the former priest could properly gauge the Catholic threat to American liberties and saw himself as providentially appointed to save his Protestant countrymen. "For twenty years," he wrote, "I have warned them of approaching danger, but their politicians were deaf, and their Protestant theologians remained religiously coiled up in fancied security, overrating their own powers and undervaluing that of Papists." Pursued by vengeful Jesuits, denounced and calumniated for alleged crimes, Hogan pictured himself single-handedly defending American freedom: "No one, before me, dared to encounter their scurrilous abuse. I resolved to silence them; and I have done so. The very mention of my name is a terror to them now." After surviving the worst of Catholic persecution, Hogan claimed to have at last aroused his countrymen and to have reduced the hierarchy to abject terror.

As the nativist searched for participation in a noble cause, for unity in a group sanctioned by tradition and authority, he professed a belief in democracy and equal rights. Yet in his very zeal for freedom he curiously assumed many of the characteristics of the imagined enemy. By condemning the subversive's fanatical allegiance to an ideology, he affirmed a similarly uncritical acceptance of a different ideology; by attacking the subversive's intolerance of dissent, he worked to eliminate dissent and diversity of opinion; by censuring the subversive for alleged licentiousness, he engaged in sensual fantasies; by criticizing the subversive's loyalty to an organization, he sought to prove his unconditional loyalty to the established order. The nativist moved even farther in the direction of his enemies when he formed tightly-knit societies and parties which were often secret and which subordinated the individual to the single purpose of the group. Though the nativists generally agreed that the worst evil of subversives was their subordination of means to ends, they themselves recommended the most radical means to purge the nation of troublesome groups and to enforce unquestioned loyalty to the state.

In his image of an evil group conspiring against the nation's welfare, and in his vision of a glorious millennium that was to dawn after the enemy's defeat, the nativist found satisfaction for many desires. His own interests became legitimate and dignified by fusion with the national interest, and various opponents became loosely associated with the un-American conspiracy. Thus Freemasonry in New York State was linked in the nativist mind with economic and political interests that were thought to discriminate against certain groups and regions; southerners imagined a union of abolitionists and Catholics to promote unrest and rebellion among slaves; gentile businessmen in Utah merged anti-Mormonism with plans for exploiting mines and lands.

Then too the nativist could style himself as a restorer of the past, as a defender of a stable order against disturbing changes, and at the same time proclaim his faith in future progress. By focusing his attention on the imaginary threat of a secret conspiracy, he found an outlet for many irrational impulses, yet professed his loyalty to the ideals of equal rights and government by law. He paid lip service to the doctrine of laissez-faire individualism, but preached selfless dedication to a transcendent cause. The imposing threat of subversion justified a group loyalty and subordination of the individual that would otherwise have been unacceptable. In a rootless environment shaken by bewildering social change the nativist found unity and meaning by conspiring against imaginary conspiracies.

Barbara Welter

The Cult of True Womanhood: 1820–1860

Although in most societies there has been a sexual division of labor that designated woman as child-rearer and homemaker, before the industrial revolution took hold in America men and women often worked side by side tilling the land and caring for the home. Then, as men trekked to factories, their work separated them from the home. Most women stayed at home doing "woman's work." That is where men wanted them to stay, believing that household chores were clearly woman's work and that man's work lay outside the home. In this essay, based on research in nineteenth-century periodicals, the author shows that woman stayed at home as a hostage for enduring values in a changing society while man worked at his job away from the home. What remained was not woman herself but the characteristics or ideals that nineteenth-century Americans shaped into a cult—that of True Womanhood. If a woman did not cultivate these virtues—piety, purity, submissiveness, and domesticity— she would, according to the cult, lose her femininity and cease to be a true woman. Note why, according to the author, the very perfection of this cult meant that it would destroy itself. [*From Barbara Welter, "The Cult of True Womanhood: 1820–1860," American Quarterly, XVIII (Spring 1966), 151–174.*]

The nineteenth-century American man was a busy builder of bridges and railroads, at work long hours in a materialistic society. The religious values of his forebears were neglected in practice if not in intent, and he occasionally felt some guilt that he had turned this new land, this temple of the chosen people, into one vast countinghouse. But he could salve his conscience by reflecting that he had left behind a hostage, not only to fortune, but to all the values which he held so dear and treated so lightly. Woman, in the cult of True Womanhood presented by the women's magazines, gift annuals and religious literature of the nineteenth century, was the hostage in the home. In a society where values changed frequently, where fortunes rose and fell with frightening rapidity, where social and economic mobility provided instability as well as hope, one thing at least remained the same—a true woman was a true woman, wherever she was found. If anyone, male or female, dared to tamper with the complex of virtues which made up True Womanhood, he was damned immediately as an enemy of God, of civilization and of the Republic. It was a fearful obligation, a solemn responsibility, which the nineteenth-century American woman had—to uphold the pillars of the temple with her frail white hand.

The attributes of True Womanhood, by which a woman judged herself and was judged by her husband, her neighbors and society could be divided into four cardinal virtues—piety, purity, submissiveness and domesticity. Put them all together and they spelled mother, daughter, sister, wife—woman. Without them, no matter whether there was fame, achievement or wealth, all was ashes. With them she was promised happiness and power.

Religion or piety was the core of woman's virtue, the source of her strength. Young men looking for a mate were cautioned to search first for piety, for if that were there, all else would follow. Religion belonged to woman by divine right, a gift of God and nature. This "peculiar susceptibility" to religion was given her for a reason: "the vestal flame of piety, lighted up by Heaven in the breast of woman" would throw its beams into the naughty world of men. So far would its candle power reach that the "Universe might be Enlightened, Improved, and Harmonized by WOMAN!!" She would be another, better Eve, working in cooperation with the Redeemer, bringing the world back "from its revolt and sin." The world would be reclaimed for God through her suffering, for "God increased the cares and sorrows of woman, that she might be sooner constrained to accept the terms of salvation." A popular poem by Mrs. Frances Osgood, "The Triumph of the Spiritual Over the Sensual," expressed just this sentiment, woman's purifying passionless love bringing an erring man back to Christ. . . .

One reason religion was valued was that it did not take a woman away from her "proper sphere," her home. Unlike participation in other societies or movements, church work would not make her less domestic or submissive, less a True Woman. In religious vineyards, said the *Young Ladies' Literary and Missionary Report*, "you may labor without the apprehension of detracting from the charms of feminine delicacy." Mrs. S. L. Dagg, writing from her chapter of the Society in Tuscaloosa, Alabama, was equally reassuring: "As no sensible woman will suffer her intellectual pursuits to clash with her domestic duties" she should concentrate on religious work "which promotes these very duties."

The women's seminaries aimed at aiding women to be religious, as well as accomplished. Mt. Holyoke's catalogue promised to make female education "a handmaid to the Gospel and an efficient auxiliary in the great task of renovating the world." The Young Ladies' Seminary at Bordentown, New Jersey, declared its most important function to be "the forming of a sound and virtuous character." In Keene, New Hampshire, the Seminary tried to instill a "consistent and useful character" in its students, to enable them in this life to be "a good friend, wife and mother" but more important, to qualify them for "the enjoyment of Celestial Happiness in the life to come." And Joseph M' D. Mathews, Principal of Oakland Female Seminary in Hillsborough, Ohio, believed that "female education should be preeminently religious."

If religion was so vital to a woman, irreligion was almost too awful to contemplate. Women were warned not to let their literary or intellectual pursuits take them away from God. Sarah Josepha Hale spoke darkly of those who, like Margaret Fuller, threw away the "One True Book" for others, open to error. Mrs. Hale used the unfortunate Miss Fuller as fateful proof that "the greater the intellectual force, the greater and more fatal the errors into which women fall who wander from the Rock of Salvation, Christ the Saviour. . . ."

Purity was as essential as piety to a young woman, its absence as unnatural and unfeminine. Without it she was, in fact, no woman at all, but a member of some lower order. A "fallen woman" was a "fallen angel," unworthy of the celestial company of her sex. To contemplate the loss of purity brought tears; to be guilty of such a crime, in the women's magazines at least, brought madness or death. Even the language of the flowers had bitter words for it: a dried white rose symbolized "Death Preferable to Loss of Innocence." The marriage night was the single great event of a woman's life, when she bestowed her greatest treasure upon her husband, and from that time on was completely dependent upon him, an empty vessel, without legal or emotional existence of her own.

Therefore all True Women were urged, in the strongest possible terms, to maintain their virtue. although men, being by nature more sensual than they, would try to assault it. Thomas Branagan admitted in *The Excellency of the Female Character Vindicated* that his sex would sin and sin again, they could not help it, but woman, stronger and purer, must not give in and let man "take liberties incompatible with her delicacy." "If you do," Branagan addressed his gentle reader, "you will be left in silent sadness to bewail your credulity, imbecility, duplicity, and premature prostitution."

Mrs. Eliza Farrar, in *The Young Lady's Friend,* gave practical logistics to avoid trouble: "Sit not with another in a place that is too narrow; read not out of the same book; let not your eagerness to see anything induce you to place your head close to another person's."

If such good advice was ignored the consequences were terrible and inexorable. In *Girlhood and Womanhood: Or Sketches of My Schoolmates,* by Mrs. A. J. Graves (a kind of mid-nineteenth-century *The Group*), the bad ends of a boarding school class of girls are scrupulously recorded. The worst end of all is reserved for "Amelia Dorrington: The Lost One." Amelia died in the almshouse "the wretched victim of depravity and intemperance" and all because her mother had let her be "high-spirited not prudent." These girlish high spirits had been misinterpreted by a young man, with disastrous results. Amelia's "thoughtless levity" was "followed by a total loss of virtuous principle" and Mrs. Graves editorializes that "the coldest reserve is more admirable in a woman a man wishes to make his wife, than the least approach to undue familiarity."

A popular and often-reprinted story by Fanny Forester told the sad tale of "Lucy Dutton." Lucy "with the seal of innocence upon her heart, and a rose-leaf on her cheek" came out of her vine-covered cottage and ran into a city slicker. "And Lucy was beautiful and trusting, and thoughtless: and he was gay, selfish and profligate. Needs the story to be told? . . . Nay, censor, Lucy was a child—consider how young, how very untaught—oh! her innocence was no match for the sophistry of a gay, city youth! Spring came and shame was stamped upon the cottage at the foot of the hill." The baby died; Lucy went mad at the funeral and finally died herself. "Poor, poor Lucy Dutton! The grave is a blessed couch and pillow to the wretched. Rest thee there, poor Lucy!" The frequency with which derangement follows loss of virtue suggests the exquisite sensibility of woman, and the possibility that, in the women's magazines at least, her intellect was geared to her hymen, not her brain.

If, however, a woman managed to withstand man's assaults on her virtue, she demonstrated her superiority and her power over him. Eliza Farnham, trying to prove this female superiority, concluded smugly that "the purity of women is the everlasting barrier against which the tides of man's sensual nature surge."

A story in *The Lady's Amaranth* illustrates this dominance. It is set, improbably, in Sicily, where two lovers, Bianca and Tebaldo, have been separated because her family insisted she marry a rich old man. By some strange circumstance the two are in a shipwreck and cast on a desert island, the only survivors. Even here, however, the rigid standards of True Womanhood prevail. Tebaldo unfortunately forgets himself slightly, so that Bianca must warn him: "We may not indeed gratify our fondness by caresses, but it is still something to bestow our kindest language, and looks and prayers, and all lawful and honest attentions on each other." Something, perhaps, but not enough, and Bianca must further remonstrate: "It is true that another man is my husband, but you are my guardian angel." When even that does not work she says in a voice of sweet reason, passive and proper to the end, that she wishes he wouldn't but "still, if you insist, I will become what you wish; but I beseech you to consider, ere that decision, that debasement which I must suffer in your esteem." This appeal to his own double standards holds the beast in him at bay. They are rescued, discover that the old husband is dead, and after "mourning a decent season" Bianca finally gives in, legally.

Men could be counted on to be grateful when women thus saved them from themselves. William Alcott, guiding young men in their relations with the opposite sex, told them that "Nothing is better calculated to preserve a young man from contamination of low pleasures and pursuits than frequent intercourse with the more refined and virtuous of the other sex." And he added, one assumes in equal innocence, that youths should "observe and learn to admire, that purity and ignorance of evil which is the characteristic of well-educated young ladies, and which, when we are near them, raises us above those sordid and sensual considerations which hold such sway over men in their intercourse with each other."

The Rev. Jonathan F. Stearns was also impressed by female chastity in the face of male passion, and warned woman never to compromise the source of her power: "Let her lay aside delicacy, and her influence over our sex is gone.". . .

Sometimes, however, a woman did not see the dangers to her treasure. In that case, they must be pointed out to her, usually by a male. In the nineteenth century any form of social change was tantamount to an attack on woman's virtue, if only it was correctly understood. For example, dress reform seemed innocuous enough and the bloomers worn by the lady of that name and her followers were certainly modest attire. Such was the reasoning only of the ignorant. In another issue of *The Ladies' Wreath* a young lady is represented in dialogue with her "Professor." The girl expresses admiration for the bloomer costume—it gives freedom of motion, is healthful and attractive. The "Professor" sets her straight. Trousers, he explains, are "only one of the many manifestations of that wild spirit of socialism and agrarian radicalism which is at present so rife in our land." The young lady recants immediately: "If this dress has any connexion with Fourierism or Socialism, or fanaticism in any shape whatever, I have no disposition to wear it at all . . . no true woman would so far compromise her delicacy as to espouse, however unwittingly, such a cause."

America could boast that her daughters were particularly innocent. In a poem on "The American Girl" the author wrote proudly:

> Her eye of light is the diamond bright,
> Her innocence the pearl,
> And these are ever the bridal gems
> That are worn by the American girl.

Lydia Maria Child, giving advice to mothers, aimed at preserving that spirit of innocence. She regretted that "want of confidence between mothers and daughters on delicate subjects" and suggested a woman tell her daughter a few facts when she reached the age of twelve to "set her mind at rest." Then Mrs. Child confidently hoped that a young lady's "instinctive modesty" would "prevent her from dwelling on the information until she was called upon to use it." In the same vein, a book of advice to the newly-married was titled *Whisper to a Bride.* As far as intimate information was concerned, there was no need to whisper, since the book contained none at all.

A masculine summary of this virtue was expressed in a poem, "Female Charms":

> I would have her as pure as the snow on the mount—
> As true as the smile that to infamy's given—
> As pure as the wave of the crystalline fount,
> Yet as warm in the heart as the sunlight of heaven.
> With a mind cultivated, not boastingly wise,
> I could gaze on such beauty, with exquisite bliss;
> With her heart on her lips and her soul in her eyes—
> What more could I wish in dear woman than this.

Man might, in fact, ask no more than this in woman, but she was beginning to ask more of herself, and in the asking was threatening the third powerful and necessary virtue, submission. Purity, considered as a moral imperative, set up a dilemma which was hard to resolve. Woman must preserve her virtue until marriage and marriage was necessary for her happiness. Yet marriage was, literally, an end to innocence. She was told not to question this dilemma, but simply to accept it.

Submission was perhaps the most feminine virtue expected of women. Men were supposed to be religious, although they rarely had time for it, and supposed to be pure, although it came awfully hard to them, but men were the movers, the doers, the actors. Women were the passive, submissive responders. The order of dialogue was, of course, fixed in Heaven. Man was "woman's superior by God's appointment, if not in intellectual dowry, at least by official decree." Therefore, as Charles Elliott argued in *The Ladies' Repository*, she should submit to him "for the sake of good order at least." In *The Ladies' Companion* a young wife was quoted approvingly as saying that she did not think woman should "feel and act for herself" because "When, next to God, her husband is not the tribunal to which her heart and intellect appeals—the golden bowl of affection is broken." Women were warned that if they tampered with this quality they tampered with the order of the Universe.

The Young Lady's Book summarized the necessity of the passive virtues in its readers' lives: "It is, however, certain, that in whatever situation of life a woman is placed from her cradle to her grave, a spirit of obedience and submission, pliability of temper, and humility of mind, are required from her."

Woman understood her position if she was the right kind of woman, a true woman. "She feels herself weak and timid. She needs a protector," declared George Burnap, in his lectures on *The Sphere and Duties of*

Woman. "She is in a measure dependent. She asks for wisdom, constancy, firmness, perseverance, and she is willing to repay it all by the surrender of the full treasure of her affections. Woman despises in man every thing like herself except a tender heart. It is enough that she is effeminate and weak; she does not want another like herself." Or put even more strongly by Mrs. Sandford: "A really sensible woman feels her dependence. She does what she can, but she is conscious of inferiority, and therefore grateful for support."

Mrs. Sigourney, however, assured young ladies that although they were separate, they were equal. This difference of the sexes did not imply inferiority, for it was part of that same order of Nature established by Him "who bids the oak brave the fury of the tempest, and the alpine flower lean its cheek on the bosom of eternal snows." Dr. Meigs had a different analogy to make the same point, contrasting the anatomy of the Apollo of the Belvedere (illustrating the male principle) with the Venus de Medici (illustrating the female principle). "Woman," said the physician, with a kind of clinical gallantry, "has a head almost too small for intellect but just big enough for love."

This love itself was to be passive and responsive. "Love, in the heart of a woman," wrote Mrs. Farrar, "should partake largely of the nature of gratitude. She should love, because she is already loved by one deserving her regard."

Woman was to work in silence, unseen, like Wordsworth's Lucy. Yet, "working like nature, in secret" her love goes forth to the world "to regulate its pulsation, and send forth from its heart, in pure and temperate flow, the life-giving current." She was to work only for pure affection, without thought of money or ambition. . . .

"True feminine genius," said Grace Greenwood (Sara Jane Clarke) "is ever timid, doubtful, and clingingly dependent; a perpetual childhood." And she advised literary ladies in an essay on "The Intellectual Woman"—"Don't trample on the flowers while longing for the stars." A wife who submerged her own talents to work for her husband was extolled as an example of a true woman. In *Women of Worth: A Book for Girls,* Mrs. Ann Flaxman, an artist of promise herself, was praised because she "devoted herself to sustain her husband's genius and aid him in his arduous career."

Caroline Gilman's advice to the bride aimed at establishing this proper order from the beginning of a marriage: "Oh, young and lovely bride, watch well the first moments when your will conflicts with his to whom God and society have given the control. Reverence his *wishes* even when you do not his *opinions*."

Mrs. Gilman's perfect wife in *Recollections of a Southern Matron* realizes that "the three golden threads with which domestic happiness is woven" are "to repress a harsh answer, to confess a fault, and to stop (right or wrong) in the midst of self-defense, in gentle submission." Woman could do this, hard though it was, because in her heart she knew

she was right and so could afford to be forgiving, even a trifle conde-
scending. "Men are not unreasonable," averred Mrs. Gilman. "Their
difficulties lie in not understanding the moral and physical nature of our
sex. They often wound through ignorance, and are surprised at having
offended." Wives were advised to do their best to reform men, but if they
couldn't, to give up gracefully. "If any habit of his annoyed me, I spoke
of it once or twice, calmly, then bore it quietly."

A wife should occupy herself "only with domestic affairs—wait till your
husband confides to you those of a high importance—and do not give
your advice until he asks for it," advised the *Lady's Token*. At all times
she should behave in a manner becoming a woman, who had "no arms
other than gentleness." Thus "if he is abusive, never retort." *A Young
Lady's Guide to the Harmonious Development of a Christian Character*
suggested that females should "become as little children" and "avoid a
controversial spirit." *The Mother's Assistant and Young Lady's Friend*
listed "Always Conciliate" as its first commandment in "Rules for Con-
jugal and Domestic Happiness." Small wonder that these same rules
ended with the succinct maxim: "Do not expect too much."

As mother, as well as wife, woman was required to submit to fortune.
In *Letters to Mothers* Mrs. Sigourney sighed: "To bear the evils and
sorrows which may be appointed us, with a patient mind, should be the
continual effort of our sex. . . . It seems, indeed, to be expected of us;
since the passive and enduring virtues are more immediately within our
province." Of these trials "the hardest was to bear the loss of children
with submission" but the indomitable Mrs. Sigourney found strength to
murmur to the bereaved mother: "The Lord loveth a cheerful giver."
The Ladies' Parlor Companion agreed thoroughly in "A Submissive
Mother," in which a mother who had already buried two children and
was nursing a dying baby saw her sole remaining child "probably scalded
to death. Handing over the infant to die in the arms of a friend, she
bowed in sweet submission to the double stroke." But the child "through
the goodness of God survived, and the mother learned to say 'Thy will
be done.' "

Woman then, in all her roles, accepted submission as her lot. It was a
lot she had not chosen or deserved. As *Godey's* said, "the lesson of submission is forced upon woman." Without comment or criticism the writer
affirms that "To suffer and to be silent under suffering seems the great
command she has to obey." George Burnap referred to a woman's life as
"a series of suppressed emotions." She was, as Emerson said, "more
vulnerable, more infirm, more mortal than man." The death of a beautiful woman, cherished in fiction, represented woman as the innocent
victim. suffering without sin, too pure and good for this world but too
weak and passive to resist its evil forces. The best refuge for such a
delicate creature was the warmth and safety of her home.

The true woman's place was unquestionably by her own fireside—as
daughter, sister, but most of all as wife and mother. Therefore domes-

ticity was among the virtues most prized by the women's magazines. "As society is constituted," wrote Mrs. S. E. Farley, on the "Domestic and Social Claims on Woman," "the true dignity and beauty of the female character seem to consist in a right understanding and faithful and cheerful performance of social and family duties." Sacred Scripture re-enforced social pressure: "St. Paul knew what was best for women when he advised them to be domestic," said Mrs. Sandford. "There is composure at home; there is something sedative in the duties which home involves. It affords security not only from the world, but from delusions and errors of every kind."

From her home woman performed her great task of bringing men back to God. *The Young Ladies' Class Book* was sure that "the domestic fireside is the great guardian of society against the excesses of human passions." *The Lady at Home* expressed its convictions in its very title and concluded that "even if we cannot reform the world in a moment, we can begin the work by reforming ourselves and our households—it is woman's mission. Let her not look away from her own little family circle for the means of producing moral and social reforms, but begin at home."

Home was supposed to be a cheerful place, so that brothers, husbands and sons would not go elsewhere in search of a good time. Woman was expected to dispense comfort and cheer. In writing the biography of Margaret Mercer (every inch a true woman) her biographer (male) notes: "She never forgot that it is the peculiar province of woman to minister to the comfort, and promote the happiness, first, of those most nearly allied to her, and then of those, who by the Providence of God are placed in a state of dependence upon her." Many other essays in the women's journals showed woman as comforter: "Woman, Man's Best Friend," "Woman, the Greatest Social Benefit," "Woman, A Being to Come Home To," "The Wife: Source of Comfort and the Spring of Joy."

One of the most important functions of woman as comforter was her role as nurse. Her own health was probably, although regrettably, delicate. Many homes had "little sufferers," those pale children who wasted away to saintly deaths. And there were enough other illnesses of youth and age, major and minor, to give the nineteenth-century American woman nursing experience. The sickroom called for the exercise of her higher qualities of patience, mercy and gentleness as well as for her housewifely arts. She could thus fulfill her dual feminine function—beauty and usefulness.

The cookbooks of the period offer formulas for gout cordials, ointment for sore nipples, hiccough and cough remedies, opening pills and refreshing drinks for fever, along with recipes for pound cake, jumbles, stewed calf head and currant wine. *The Ladies' New Book of Cookery* believed that "food prepared by the kind hand of a wife, mother, sister, friend" tasted better and had a "restorative power which money cannot purchase."

A chapter of *The Young Lady's Friend* was devoted to woman's privilege as "ministering spirit at the couch of the sick." Mrs. Farrar advised a soft voice, gentle and clean hands, and a cheerful smile. She also cautioned against an excess of female delicacy. That was all right for a young lady in the parlor, but not for bedside manners. Leeches, for example, were to be regarded as "a curious piece of mechanism . . . their ornamental stripes should recommend them even to the eye, and their valuable services to our feelings." And she went on calmly to discuss their use. Nor were women to shrink from medical terminology, since "If you cultivate right views of the wonderful structure of the body, you will be as willing to speak to a physician of the bowels as the brains of your patient."

Nursing the sick, particularly sick males, not only made a woman feel useful and accomplished, but increased her influence. In a piece of heavy-handed humor in *Godey's* a man confessed that some women were only happy when their husbands were ailing that they might have the joy of nursing him to recovery "thus gratifying their medical vanity and their love of power by making him more dependent upon them." In a similar vein a husband sometimes suspected his wife "almost wishes me dead—for the pleasure of being utterly inconsolable."

In the home women were not only the highest adornment of civilization, but they were supposed to keep busy at morally uplifting tasks. Fortunately most of housework, if looked at in true womanly fashion, could be regarded as uplifting. Mrs. Sigourney extolled its virtues: "The science of housekeeping affords exercise for the judgment and energy, ready recollection, and patient self-possession, that are the characteristics of a superior mind." According to Mrs. Farrar, making beds was good exercise, the repetitiveness of routine tasks inculcated patience and perseverance, and proper management of the home was a surprisingly complex art: "There is more to be learned about pouring out tea and coffee, than most young ladies are willing to believe." *Godey's* went so far as to suggest coyly in "Learning vs. Housewifery" that the two were complementary, not opposed: chemistry could be utilized in cooking, geometry in dividing cloth, and phrenology in discovering talent in children.

Women were to master every variety of needlework, for, as Mrs. Sigourney pointed out, "Needle-work, in all its forms of use, elegance, and ornament, has ever been the appropriate occupation of woman." Embroidery improved taste; knitting promoted serenity and economy. Other forms of artsy-craftsy activity for her leisure moments included painting on glass or velvet, Poonah work, tussy-mussy frames for her own needlepoint or water colors, stands for hyacinths, hair bracelets or baskets of feathers.

She was expected to have a special affinity for flowers. To the editors of *The Lady's Token* "A woman never appears more truly in her sphere, than when she divides her time between her domestic avocations and the culture of flowers." She could write letters, an activity particularly feminine since it had to do with the outpourings of the heart, or practice her drawingroom skills of singing and playing an instrument. She might even read.

Here she faced a bewildering array of advice. The female was dangerously addicted to novels, according to the literature of the period. She should avoid them, since they interfered with "serious piety." If she simply couldn't help herself and read them anyway, she should choose edifying ones from lists of morally acceptable authors. She should study history since it "showed the depravity of the human heart and the evil nature of sin." On the whole, "religious biography was best."

The women's magazines themselves could be read without any loss of concern for the home. *Godey's* promised the husband that he would find his wife "no less assiduous for his reception, or less sincere in welcoming his return" as a result of reading their magazine. *The Lily of the Valley* won its right to be admitted to the boudoir by confessing that it was "like its namesake humble and unostentatious, but it is yet pure, and, we trust, free from moral imperfections."

No matter what later authorities claimed, the nineteenth century knew that girls *could* be ruined by a book. The seduction stories regard "exciting and dangerous books" as contributory causes of disaster. The man without honorable intentions always provides the innocent maiden with such books as a prelude to his assault on her virtue. Books which attacked or seemed to attack woman's accepted place in society were regarded as equally dangerous. A reviewer of Harriet Martineau's *Society in America* wanted it kept out of the hands of American women. They were so susceptible to persuasion, with their "gentle yielding natures," that they might listen to "the bold ravings of the hard-featured of their own sex." The frightening result: "such reading will unsettle them for their true station and pursuits, and they will throw the world back again into confusion."

The debate over women's education posed the question of whether a "finished" education detracted from the practice of housewifely arts. Again it proved to be a case of semantics, for a true woman's education was never "finished" until she was instructed in the gentle science of homemaking. Helen Irving, writing on "Literary Women," made it very clear that if women invoked the muse, it was as a genie of the household lamp. "If the necessities of her position require these duties at her hands, she will perform them nonetheless cheerfully, that she knows herself capable of higher things." The literary woman must conform to the same standards as any other woman: "That her home shall be made a loving place of rest and joy and comfort for those who are dear to her, will be the first wish of every true woman's heart." Mrs. Ann Stephens told women who wrote to make sure they did not sacrifice one domestic duty. "As for genius, make it a domestic plant. Let its roots strike deep in your house. . . ."

The fear of "blue stockings" (the eighteenth-century male's term of derision for educated or literary women) need not persist for nineteenth-century American men. The magazines presented spurious dialogues in which bachelors were convinced of their fallacy in fearing educated wives. One such dialogue took place between a young man and his female cousin. Ernest deprecates learned ladies ("A *woman* is far more lovable than a *philosopher*") but Alice refutes him with the beautiful example of their Aunt Barbara who "although she *has* perpetrated the heinous crime of writing some half dozen folios" is still a model of "the spirit of feminine gentleness." His memory prodded, Ernest concedes that, by George, there was a woman: "When I last had a cold she not only made me a bottle of cough syrup, but when I complained of nothing new to read, set to work and wrote some twenty stanzas on consumption."

The magazines were filled with domestic tragedies in which spoiled young girls learned that when there was a hungry man to feed French and china painting were not helpful. According to these stories many a marriage is jeopardized because the wife has not learned to keep house. Harriet Beecher Stowe wrote a sprightly piece of personal experience for *Godey's,* ridiculing her own bad housekeeping as a bride. She used the same theme in a story, "The Only Daughter," in which the pampered beauty learns the facts of domestic life from a rather difficult source, her mother-in-law. Mrs. Hamilton tells Caroline in the sweetest way possible to shape up in the kitchen, reserving her rebuke for her son: "You are her husband—her guide—her protector—now see what you can do," she admonishes him. "Give her credit for every effort: treat her faults with tenderness; encourage and praise whenever you can, and depend upon it, you will see another woman in her." He is properly masterful, she properly domestic and in a few months Caroline is making lumpless gravy and keeping up with the darning. Domestic tranquillity has been restored and the young wife moralizes: "Bring up a girl to feel that she has a responsible part to bear in promoting the happiness of the family, and you make a reflecting being of her at once, and remove that lightness and frivolity of character which makes her shrink from graver studies." These stories end with the heroine drying her hands on her apron and vowing that *her* daughter will be properly educated, in piecrust as well as Poonah work.

The female seminaries were quick to defend themselves against any suspicion of interfering with the role which nature's God had assigned to women. They hoped to enlarge and deepen that role, but not to change its setting. At the Young Ladies' Seminary and Collegiate Institute in Monroe City, Michigan, the catalogue admitted few of its graduates would be likely "to fill the learned professions." Still, they were called to "other scenes of usefulness and honor." The average woman is to be "the presiding genius of love" in the home, where she is to "give a correct and elevated literary taste to her children, and to assume that influential station that she ought to possess as the companion of an educated man."

At Miss Pierce's famous school in Litchfield, the students were taught that they had "attained the perfection of their characters when they could combine their elegant accomplishments with a turn for solid domestic virtues." Mt. Holyoke paid pious tribute to domestic skills: "Let a young lady despise this branch of the duties of woman, and she despises the appointments of her existence." God, nature and the Bible "enjoin these duties on the sex, and she cannot violate them with impunity." Thus warned, the young lady would have to seek knowledge of these duties elsewhere, since it was not in the curriculum at Mt. Holyoke. "We would not take this privilege from the mother."

One reason for knowing her way around a kitchen was that America was "a land of precarious fortunes," as Lydia Maria Child pointed out in her book *The Frugal Housewife: Dedicated to Those Who Are Not Ashamed of Economy.* Mrs. Child's chapter "How to Endure Poverty" prescribed a combination of piety and knowledge—the kind of knowledge found in a true woman's education, "a thorough religious *useful* education." The woman who had servants today might tomorrow, because of a depression or panic, be forced to do her own work. If that happened she knew how to act, for she was to be the same cheerful consoler of her husband in their cottage as in their mansion.

An essay by Washington Irving, much quoted in the gift annuals, discussed the value of a wife in case of business reverses: "I have observed that a married man falling into misfortune is more apt to achieve his situation in the world than a single one . . . it is beautifully ordained by Providence that woman, who is the ornament of man in his happier hours, should be his stay and solace when smitten with sudden calamity."

A story titled simply but eloquently "The Wife" dealt with the quiet heroism of Ellen Graham during her husband's plunge from fortune to poverty. Ned Graham said of her: "Words are too poor to tell you what I owe to that noble woman. In our darkest seasons of adversity, she has been an angel of consolation—utterly forgetful of self and anxious only to comfort and sustain me." Of course she had a little help from "faithful Dinah who absolutely refused to leave her beloved mistress," but even so Ellen did no more than would be expected of any true woman.

Most of this advice was directed to woman as wife. Marriage was the proper state for the exercise of the domestic virtues. "True Love and a Happy Home," an essay in *The Young Ladies' Oasis,* might have been carved on every girl's hope chest. But although marriage was best, it was not absolutely necessary. The women's magazines tried to remove the stigma from being an "Old Maid." They advised no marriage at all rather than an unhappy one contracted out of selfish motives. Their stories showed maiden ladies as unselfish ministers to the sick, teachers of the young, or moral preceptors with their pens, beloved of the entire village. Usually the life of single blessedness resulted from the premature death of a fiancé, or was chosen through fidelity to some high mission. For example, in "Two Sisters," Mary devotes herself to Ellen and her abandoned children, giving up her own chance for marriage. "Her devotion to her sister's happiness has met its reward in the consciousness of having fulfilled a sacred duty." Very rarely, a "woman of genius" was absolved from the necessity of marriage, being so extraordinary that she did not need the security or status of being a wife. Most often, however, if girls proved "difficult," marriage and a family were regarded as a cure. The "sedative quality" of a home could be counted on to subdue even the most restless spirits.

George Burnap saw marriage as "that sphere for which woman was originally intended, and to which she is so exactly fitted to adorn and bless, as the wife, the mistress of a home, the solace, the aid, and the counsellor of that ONE, for whose sake alone the world is of any consequence to her." Samuel Miller preached a sermon on women: "How interesting and important are the duties devolved on females as WIVES . . . the counsellor and friend of the husband; who makes it her daily study to lighten his cares, to soothe his sorrows, and to augment his joys; who, like a guardian angel, watches over his interests, warns him against dangers, comforts him under trials; and by her pious, assiduous, and attractive deportment, constantly endeavors to render him more virtuous, more useful, more honourable, and more happy." A woman's whole interest should be focused on her husband, paying him "those numberless attentions to which the French give the title of *petits soins* and which the woman who loves knows so well how to pay . . . she should consider nothing as trivial which could win a smile of approbation from him."

Marriage was seen not only in terms of service but as an increase in authority for woman. Burnap concluded that marriage improves the female character "not only because it puts her under the best possible tuition, that of the affections, and affords scope to her active energies, but because it gives her higher aims, and a more dignified position." *The Lady's Amaranth* saw it as a balance of power: "The man bears rule over his wife's person and conduct. She bears rule over his inclinations: he governs by law; she by persuasion. . . . The empire of the woman is an empire of softness . . . her commands are caresses, her menaces are tears."

Woman should marry, but not for money. She should choose only the high road of true love and not truckle to the values of a materialistic society. A story,"Marrying for Money" (subtlety was not the strong point of the ladies' magazines), depicts Gertrude, the heroine, rueing the day she made her crass choice: "It is a terrible thing to live without love. . . . A woman who dares marry for aught but the purest affection, calls down the just judgments of heaven upon her head."

The corollary to marriage, with or without true love, was motherhood, which added another dimension to her usefulness and her prestige. It also anchored her even more firmly to the home. "My friend," wrote Mrs. Sigourney, "If in becoming a mother, you have reached the climax of your happiness, you have also taken a higher place in the scale of being

. . . you have gained an increase of power." The Rev. J. N. Danforth pleaded in *The Ladies' Casket,* "Oh, mother, acquit thyself well in thy humble sphere, for thou mayest affect the world." A true woman naturally loved her children; to suggest otherwise was monstrous.

America depended upon her mothers to raise up a whole generation of Christian statesmen who could say "all that I am I owe to my angel mother." The mothers must do the inculcating of virtue since the fathers, alas, were too busy chasing the dollar. Or as *The Ladies' Companion* put it more effusively, the father, "weary with the heat and burden of life's summer day, or trampling with unwilling foot the decaying leaves of life's autumn, has forgotten the sympathies of life's joyous springtime. . . . The acquisition of wealth, the advancement of his children in worldly honor—these are his self-imposed tasks." It was his wife who formed "the infant mind as yet untainted by contact with evil . . . like wax beneath the plastic hand of the mother."

The Ladies' Wreath offered a fifty-dollar prize to the woman who submitted the most convincing essay on "How May An American Woman Best Show Her Patriotism." The winner was Miss Elizabeth Wetherell who provided herself with a husband in her answer. The wife in the essay of course asked her husband's opinion. He tried a few jokes first—"Call her eldest son George Washington," "Don't speak French, speak American"—but then got down to telling her in sober prize-winning truth what women could do for their country. Voting was no asset, since that would result only in "a vast increase of confusion and expense without in the smallest degree affecting the result." Besides, continued this oracle, "looking down at their child," if "we were to go a step further and let the children vote, their first act would be to vote their mothers at home." There is no comment on this devastating male logic and he continues: "Most women would follow the lead of their fathers and husbands," and the few who would "fly off on a tangent from the circle of home influence would cancel each other out."

The wife responds dutifully: "I see all that. I never understood so well before." Encouraged by her quick womanly perception, the master of the house resolves the question—an American woman best shows her patriotism by staying at home, where she brings her influence to bear "upon the right side for the country's weal." That woman will instinctively choose the side of right he has no doubt. Besides her "natural refinement and closeness to God" she has the "blessed advantage of a quiet life" while man is exposed to conflict and evil. She stays home with "her Bible and a well-balanced mind" and raises her sons to be good Americans. The judges rejoiced in this conclusion and paid the prize money cheerfully, remarking "they deemed it cheap at the price."

If any woman asked for greater scope for her gifts the magazines were sharply critical. Such women were tampering with society, undermining civilization. Mary Wollstonecraft, Frances Wright and Harriet Martineau were condemned in the strongest possible language—they were read out of the sex. "They are only semi-women, mental hermaphrodites." The Rev. Harrington knew the women of America could not possibly approve of such perversions and went to some wives and mothers to ask if they did want a "wider sphere of interest" as these nonwomen claimed. The answer was reassuring. " 'NO!' they cried simultaneously. 'Let the men take care of politics, *we will take care of the children!'* " Again female discontent resulted only from a lack of understanding: women were not subservient, they were rather "chosen vessels." Looked at in this light the conclusion was inescapable: "Noble, sublime is the task of the American mother."

"Women's Rights" meant one thing to reformers, but quite another to the True Woman. She knew her rights,

> The right to love whom others scorn,
> The right to comfort and to mourn,
> The right to shed new joy on earth,
> The right to feel the soul's high worth . . .
> Such women's rights, and God will bless
> And crown their champions with success.

The American woman had her choice—she could define her rights in the way of the women's magazines and insure them by the practice of the requisite virtues, or she could go outside the home, seeking other rewards than love. It was a decision on which, she was told, everything in her world depended. "Yours it is to determine," the Rev. Mr. Stearns solemnly warned from the pulpit, "whether the beautiful order of society . . . shall continue as it has been" or whether "society shall break up and become a chaos of disjointed and unsightly elements." If she chose to listen to other voices than those of her proper mentors, sought other rooms than those of her home, she lost both her happiness and her power—"that almost magic power, which, in her proper sphere, she now wields over the destinies of the world."

But even while the women's magazines and related literature encouraged this ideal of the perfect woman, forces were at work in the nineteenth century which impelled woman herself to change, to play a more creative role in society. The movements for social reform, westward migration, missionary activity, utopian communities, industrialism, the Civil War—all called forth responses from woman which differed from those she was trained to believe were hers by nature and divine decree. The very perfection of True Womanhood, moreover, carried within itself the seeds of its own destruction. For if woman was so very little less than the angels, she should surely take a more active part in running the world, especially since men were making such a hash of things.

Real women often felt they did not live up to the ideal of True Womanhood: some of them blamed themselves, some challenged the standard, some tried to keep the virtues and enlarge the scope of womanhood. Somehow through this mixture of challenge and acceptance, of change and continuity, the True Woman evolved into the New Woman —a transformation as startling in its way as the abolition of slavery or the coming of the machine age. And yet the stereotype, the "mystique" if you will, of what woman was and ought to be persisted, bringing guilt and confusion in the midst of opportunity.

The women's magazines and related literature had feared this very dislocation of values and blurring of roles. By careful manipulation and interpretation they sought to convince woman that she had the best of both worlds—power and virtue—and that a stable order of society depended upon her maintaining her traditional place in it. To that end she was identified with everything that was beautiful and holy.

"Who Can Find a Valiant Woman?" was asked frequently from the pulpit and the editorial pages. There was only one place to look for her—at home. Clearly and confidently these authorities proclaimed the True Woman of the nineteenth century to be the Valiant Woman of the Bible, in whom the heart of her husband rejoiced and whose price was above rubies.

A slave auction, Richmond, Virginia. (Library of Congress)

13 Southern Nationalism

Many historians, when writing of the years 1830 to 1801, see the sectional issue, or the growing antagonism between North and South, as the central theme of this period of American history. This viewpoint is logical, for the sectional issue brought on a series of crises that jeopardized the Union. In this period, as had not been the case previously, majority opinion within the two sections appeared to crystallize on the opposite sides of political and social questions touching the nature of slavery as an institution, its status under the Constitution, the place of the Negro in American society, and the very nature of the federal government itself—essentially its powers and limitations as compared with those of the states.

Although each section had its special characteristics, there seems to be general agreement that the South, more than the North, was self-consciously developing distinctive features and attitudes—what some historians have called "Southern nationalism." Many historians dispute the existence of any genuine Southern nationalism but nonetheless concede that Southern society was more homogeneous and conservative, and less exposed to the ferment of new ideas, than was Northern. In short, the South contained social, economic, and cultural features that separated it from the rest of the Union.

This Southern feeling of separateness became acute in these years, it has been argued, because Southerners were drawn together to fend off danger or discriminations from the outside. They could not, for instance, escape the trends of population growth. They saw the North rapidly increasing in numbers, and it seemed inevitable that the Northerners would gain control of the federal government and make their will dominant in the handling of sensitive sectional issues. Many Southerners identified the basic interests of their section with slavery, and in these years Northerners—especially abolitionists—stepped up their attacks on slavery as an institution until their program took on the characteristics of a crusade against what some called the "cornerstone of Southern society."

Faced with a decline in power within the federal government, with attacks on their institutions, and with new perils to their sectional interests, Southerners, some historians have concluded, were driven to behave as if they belonged to a conscious minority seeking to defend itself against a ruthless majority. Many Southerners were convinced that their interests could be maintained only if something were done to arrest the growing power of the North—to keep the two sections in balance.

Northern critics, and some historians since, have argued that the South did not truly want a political balance, but sought dominance instead. It

369

was, they point out, controlled by a "slavocracy" that held a bloated and unjustified political power over national issues because of the three-fifths rule in the Constitution; this control trampled human rights, of whites as well as blacks; it held democratic government in contempt, it aggressively sought to expand slavery, and it demanded protection from the federal government for that expansion.

Regardless of the merits of these interpretations, it is clear that if balance and expansion were at issue, a third region, the West, was involved in the sectional rivalry. Each society—the free and the slave—desired control of the West, or at least to win it as an ally. The South looked upon free access to the Western territories as a constitutional and moral right, a necessary expansion to keep it from becoming a permanent political minority and an economic colony of the North. Numerous Northerners believed that slavery had no legal, constitutional, or moral right to expand, particularly into the Old Northwest, where it had been forbidden by the Ordinance of 1787.

Slavery was not the only issue in the West. Power, wealth, influence, and the future were at stake. A Southerner, writing in *De Bow's Review* in 1847, explained the rivalry in this way: "A contest has been going on between the North and South not limited to slavery or no slavery—to abolition or no abolition, nor to the politics of either whigs or democrats as such, but a contest for the wealth and commerce of the great valley of the Mississippi—a contest tendered by our Northern brethren, whether the growing commerce of the great West shall be thrown upon New Orleans or given to the Atlantic cities."

In this contest for the West, too, Southerners could foresee defeat. Before the sectional rivalries had reached the emotional intensity of the late 1840s and '50s, there had been something of a unity of interest between the farmers of the Old Northwest and the planters of the South. That unity was destroyed in these years, and the North and Middle West came to be welded into one economic and social pattern. The attitudes of these sections now became those of the majority and came to prevail as the national interest.

The South, now unmistakably a minority, clung tenaciously to the unique feature of its sectionalism, to the institution that brought its attitudes in conflict with those of the majority—to slavery. Despite conflicts over expansion, lands, and tariffs, neither the North nor the South would yield on the issue of slavery, because slavery had come to symbolize opposing values in each section; it had become the touchstone of Southern "nationalism," and hence of the sectional issue.

Selections in this chapter therefore analyze aspects of Southern society, or "nationalism," from three perspectives: the growth of sectionalism and the South's estrangement from the Northeast; the economics of slavery and the relationship between master and slave as the unique feature of Southern society; and an analysis of the special characteristics of Southern nationalism. In reading these selections, remember that some historians minimize slavery as an institution, as a fundamental source of conflict, or as a vital sectional issue, whereas others see it as the basic cause of the growing sectional rift.

Avery O. Craven   **Realignment of Sections**

Avery O. Craven has written extensively on the South as a section and on the conflict between North and South. His views and interpretations on this subject have marked him as a "revisionist"—that is, a historian who doubts that slavery lay at the center of the sectional issue and that the conflict between the sections was irrepressible. Basic in his thinking is the idea that the dissimilarities between the agrarian South and the industrial Northeast were not fundamental enough to make war inevitable. He believes that the sections had much in common and that the antagonism between them arose from unreasoning emotional attitudes in each section—attitudes aroused by extremist political agitators. In other words, he sees the growing sectional differences to be the result of psychological attitudes and not concrete interests.

In the selection that follows, Craven concentrates on the bonds that had tied the South and the Northwest together—blood, trade, agrarianism, and common attitudes on national issues—and he explains what sundered those ties and why these two sections began to drift apart in the 1840s. It is in this period, he maintains, that the South lost an ally, for ultimately the Northwest would realign itself with the Northeast. [Avery O. Craven, The Growth of Southern Nationalism, 1848–1861 *(Baton Rouge: Louisiana State University Press, 1953). Reprinted by permission.]*

The most alarming feature of developments in the 1840's was the growing cleavage between the Northwest and the South. These regions had long been tied together both physically and socially. Like the blood vessels of a human body, the Ohio-Mississippi River system had helped to bind the whole interior of the continent into organic unity. The streams that drained every state in the Old Northwest except Michigan rose well back in the interior and flowed southward, and the rivers of Kentucky and Tennessee, sometimes after strange wanderings, turned northward, also to empty their waters into the Ohio. Missouri, southeastern Iowa, and Minnesota were tied in from the west as the Mississippi gathered to itself the total flood and bore it on to the Gulf.

These rivers early had become the highways along which population moved. By way of the Watauga, the Nolichucky, the Clinch; down the

New and the Kanawha; through mountain gaps to the Kentucky, the Cumberland, and the Tennessee, ever reaching for the Ohio itself, the tall, angular men of the Piedmont South had pushed their way from the Carolinas and Virginia into the hilly, wooded sections of the great Northwest and made them their own. Until 1850 these men and their descendants exerted the predominant influence on the social and political ways of the section. From the kind of food they ate to the patterns worked into the quilts on their beds, they revealed their origins and the kinship they bore to the friends and neighbors they had left behind. Southern-born men were responsible for the county type of local government set up, for the prevalence of Quaker, Methodist, Baptist, and Presbyterian churches, and for the region's corn and hog economy. Southern-born men made both the effort to perpetuate some kind of forced labor for Negroes and the effort to prevent it. They were the men who, in different Northwestern states, denied the franchise to Negroes, drew up "black codes" for their regulation, and, even as late as 1848, forbade them to enter their territory. But they were also the men who published the first antislavery periodicals in the nation and laid the foundations of the underground railroad.

Nor did these immigrants to the Ohio Valley in its broadest extent differ from their fellow upland Southerners who turned south and west to carry cotton along the Gulf. That too was a movement of pioneers on to a frontier. It revealed all the characteristics of a typical American westward movement. There were distinct states in the advance. Trappers and traders led the way, and well before the Revolution great quantities of furs and skins found their way to market through Richmond and Charleston. Restless farmers followed the trappers' wake and crowded the Indians into bloody resistance but inevitable retreat. On the southern frontier the national policy of Indian removal to "permanent" reservations beyond the Mississippi was developed. In the battles against these Indians and the accomplishment of their removal from potential cotton fields Andrew Jackson won the undying affection of Western men.

These were cattle days on the Georgia frontier and later in Mississippi Territory—roundups and brandings, cowboys "mounted on low built, shaggy, but muscular and hardy horses . . . and armed with . aw hide whips . . . and sometimes with a catching rope or lasso. . . . They scour[ed] the wood . . . sometimes driving a herd of a thousand heads to the pen."

The mining rush was also present. A recent writer has told of the "gold fever" which raged in North Carolina in 1825. Travelers "heard scarce anything . . . except gold"; of "bankrupts . . . restored to affluence, and paupers turned to nabobs." "The prospector" became "a distinct race," and the population around the mines "agonized under the increased and increasing fever for gold." Prospectors rushed from diggings to diggings, boom towns rose and fell, and "the state of morals" became "deplorably bad." Mining days in North Carolina, Georgia, and Alabama differed little in character and temper from those on other frontiers.

The agricultural advance was also typical. The more or less unstable pioneer in the vanguard came as a rule from the Piedmont region, where he had been farming. He made a clearing but moved easily when fresher soils lured or when some more substantial emigrant offered a profit from the sale of his land. He raised his own food; his womenfolk made the family clothing; he had a small amount of livestock, and he might or might not raise a little cotton to sell to the outside world. If he had a slave or two, they were more nearly a part of his family than a separate working force. The more fortunate or more energetic might "make," as the saying was—enlarge their holdings and, planting cotton, become planters after the accepted Southern pattern. On the other hand, they might be still on the move when Texas offered its opportunities.

With hard times dogging the steps of planters in the older Atlantic coastal region and slaves becoming a burden to their owners, some planters early joined the trek to the new cotton kingdom to be. When the future was well assured, still others moved out with their establishments complete, purchased lands from those who had pioneered, and added a bit of maturity in capital, labor, and management to the economy of the region. They corresponded to the "timber barons" and the "cattle kings" of other frontiers, and they conformed to the free, individualistic, democratic social customs of their lesser neighbors, or they found themselves disliked and isolated.

In spirit and temper too the Lower South was strictly Western. "Everyone was over-optimistic." Speculation drove land prices and rates of interest to unheard-of levels. A New Orleans newspaper described the period after 1835 as one in which the people were "drunk with success. . . . The poor man of yesterday was worth his thousands today; the beggar of the morning retired to his straw pallet at night, burdened with the cares of a fortune acquired between the rising and the setting of the sun." A visitor to the Louisiana metropolis in 1833 wrote: "There is a hurry, a 'rush' among all classes of people here, that I have not seen in so great a degree, elsewhere. It looks almost like intrusion to detain any one upon matters unconnected with ordinary business-pursuits."

It was a personal world in which men settled their differences by direct methods and in which "gun-toting" was widely practiced. A Natchez citizen unblushingly complained of a sprained wrist and a dislocated thumb resulting from a hard fought battle with Daniel Hickey "whose Eyes by the Bye I completely closed." An Alabama paper listed the fines for fist fights at from five to ten dollars, fights with sticks at twice as much, those with dirks at from twenty to thirty dollars, and those with bowie knives or pistols at from thirty to fifty dollars. Reuben Davis admitted that the people of his neighborhood "drank hard, swore freely, and were utterly reckless of consequences when their passions were aroused," but he insisted that they were sober, reverent, and industrious. His version of the Mississippian's creed is as good a statement of the frontiersman's social attitudes as can be found for any West: "A man ought to fear God, and mind his own business. He should be respectful and courteous to all women; he should love his friends and hate his enemies. He should eat when he was hungry, drink when he was thirsty, dance when he was merry, vote for the candidate he liked best, and knock down any man who questioned his right to these privileges."

Religious expression was also of the frontier brand. The itinerant preacher usually pioneered the way for the different evangelical denominations. The wanderings and deeds of a Lorenzo Dow in Mississippi differed little in essential detail from those of a Peter Cartwright in Illinois. Both of these men would have agreed with the Georgian who a few years earlier insisted that "larnin' " made preachers "proud and worldly" and that Westerners wanted "none of your new-fangled, high flying preaching." Camp meetings flourished, and men and women "got religion" after desperate struggles with the Lord and an undue amount of noise. A contemporary description of how Methodism won its way would apply to all other denominations: "It lodged roughly, and it fared scantily. It tramped up muddy ridges, it swam or forded rivers to the waist; it slept on leaves or raw deer-skin, and pillowed its head on saddle-bags; it bivouacked among wolves or Indians . . . *but it throve.*"

To these common ties of blood and experiences between the men of the Northwest and the South were soon added those of trade. In early days stock and some other agricultural products had found a way back through the mountain gaps to the planters of the Old South. Now flat-boats loaded with the produce of Northern farms floated down the smaller streams to the main thoroughfares that led to New Orleans and the rising cotton kingdom. As early as 1825, from the upper portion of the Mississippi Valley, there had come to New Orleans "a hundred forty thousand barrels of flour, half that amount of corn, sixteen thousand barrels of pork, thirty thousand barrels of whiskey, and eighteen thousand hogs-heads of tobacco."

Even with the building of canals and railroads, which linked the Northwest with eastern seaboard cities, trade still flourished with the South. In 1844, for instance, "of nearly a million and a half bushels of corn exported," 90 per cent went South; of nearly eight hundred thousand barrels of pork and bacon, 81 per cent went South; and of a hundred thousand barrels of whisky some 95 per cent followed the same course. Only the bulk of wheat and wool found its way eastward.

It is, therefore, not surprising that up to the middle of the forties the "Mississippi Valley" as a whole was in general agreement on the larger national issues or that these farmers were also on the best of terms with those of the older South. The newer regions, in particular, favored liberal land policies for settlers, and men, both North and South, talked of the "natural right" to a share in the national domain. Senator John McKinley of Alabama, in 1830, spoke as enthusiastically for the squatters on the public lands as did Henry H. Sibley of Minnesota in 1852. Both refused to consider them "violators of the law" or "trespassers" but insisted that they were "meritorious individuals" who pioneered settlement and opened the wilderness to profits both for individuals and the government. Northwest and Southwest alike denounced the speculator, and both produced ardent advocates of homestead legislation and votes in Congress for its passage. On the other hand, the representatives of the older settlements of Ohio, Kentucky, and Tennessee stood together in opposition to the moves to reduce the price of lands in their neighborhoods. All spoke as Westerners and, in spite of local differences, generally accepted the position taken by Albert Gallatin Brown of Mississippi in support of "land to the homeless."

Nor did the upper and lower parts of the great valley differ as regions on the protective tariff issue. Democrats in both favored tariffs for revenue only, while Whigs, regardless of region, followed Henry Clay in support of protection. In the Northwest the Ohio Valley was usually the Democratic stronghold, but in the late thirties and early forties, the wheat growers of the Lakes region, in their drive to break the English corn laws and to open markets for their growing surplus, were free traders almost as ardent as the cotton producers in the Lower South. Even the stanch antislavery leaders of the region quickly saw the advantage to be gained for their cause by association with British antislavery leaders and joined their voices in support of free trade and more liberal land legislation.

The expansionist urge which brought the annexation of Texas and the demand for Oregon up to 54 degrees and 40 minutes found its main strength in a West that knew no division into North and South. Enthusiasm for the Mexican War was generally more intense here and volunteering to fight its battles more popular than in other parts of the nation but showed little variation from Indiana and Illinois to Mississippi and Louisiana. In spite of differences that may have been on the increase, the Valley, up to the outbreak of the Mexican War, showed few signs of serious cleavage.

Nor had John C. Calhoun, who now spoke more directly for the Old South, lost hopes of forming a close political alliance between the West and the South as a whole on which he might ride to the presidency. He urged the Western states to claim the public lands within their borders on grounds of state rights and offered, over and over again, his bill for the cession of lands to the states. He was willing to go so far in accepting a moderately protective tariff, in 1842, that even Robert Barnwell Rhett drew back in surprise. At the Memphis Convention of 1845, called to promote Western trade and internal improvements, he urged the right of the Federal government to take any steps necessary to increase the "safety and facility of commerce" on the Mississippi River. He frankly confessed the hope that this would remove all causes for alliance between the Northeast and the West.

The election of James K. Polk in 1844 had left much bitterness in its train and had intensified personal and group differences already existing. The twelve years of party rule under Andrew Jackson and Martin Van Buren had brought a sharp split in Democratic ranks. Jackson had quarreled with Calhoun, who had, in turn, made use of the nullification controversy and the question of receiving antislavery petitions in Congress to organize Southern resentment into a working bloc. Van Buren's efforts to establish the Independent Treasury and his decided leanings towards the Locofoco element in the party had alienated others and had led to the Whig victory in 1840. Calhoun had, in the meantime, returned to the fold but had done so with the very clear idea of engrafting a Southern position on the party and of winning the nomination for himself in 1844. Benton, Francis P. Blair, and others of the old Jackson group were as determined to renominate Van Buren and kept a firm hold on party machinery for that purpose. Calhoun was pushed aside, but the introduction of the Texas annexation issue into the campaign and Van Buren's refusal to accept it as a pressing measure led to his downfall and the quick turning to Polk as the man best suited to carry the party to victory on an expansionist program. He was strictly a "dark horse" candidate. His platform, favoring the annexation of Texas and the settlement of the Oregon boundary, represented the demands of the aggressive element.

Calhoun secured revenge for his failure by accepting the post of Secretary of State under President John Tyler and twisting the annexation of Texas into a step absolutely necessary for the protection of slavery. Both he and President Tyler accepted Polk's election in November as an ultimatum for immediate action and forthwith pressed annexation to completion. Van Buren, Benton, and Blair, on the other hand, could only sulk and complain. They gave Polk little support in his campaign. They were quite ready to criticize his administration at every opportunity.

Polk in office did not improve the situation by seeming to favor the New York group opposed to Van Buren in his appointments. His blunt dismissal of Blair and his *Globe* as the administration organ hurt even more. The ready acceptance of war with Mexico and the termination of the agreement for joint occupation of Oregon with England widened the opposition and gave it a sectional quality. In New England, upper New York, and Ohio the Mexican War, which had developed over Texas boundary differences, was viewed by many as a war of conquest and an effort to find new fields for the expansion of slavery. Opposition was open and ugly. Determination to check the further spread of slavery was widely expressed. Joshua R. Giddings, in Congress, took the lead but many Old Jacksonian Democrats began to show decided sympathy. Political parties were beginning to feel the stress and strain of the new day.

The impact of these events on the West was sharp and immediate. Ohio Whigs of strong antislavery convictions early expressed their fears and resentments. In May, 1844, Giddings called attention to the balance and rivalry between North and South, which had produced a deadlock in legislation. "But so equally balanced has been the political power," he said, ". . . that for five years past our lake commerce has been entirely abandoned; and such were the defects of the tariff, that for many years our revenues were unequal to the support of the government." He insisted that the annexation of Texas was urged "most obviously to enhance the price of human flesh in our slave-breeding States." He was convinced that the addition of Texas strength to the South would place the control of the "policy and destiny of this nation" in their hands.

"Are the liberty-loving Democrats of Pennsylvania ready to give up the tariff?" he asked. "Are the farmers of the West, of Ohio, Indiana, and Illinois, prepared to give up the sale of their beef, pork, and flour, in order to increase the profits of those who raise children for sale, and deal in the bodies of women? Are the free states prepared to suspend their harbor and river improvements for the purpose of establishing this slave-trade with Texas, and to perpetuate slavery therein?"

To Giddings, slavery had become the symbol of an interest hostile to his own. "Our Tariff," he said, "is as much an antislavery measure as the rejection of Texas. So is the subject of internal improvements and the distribution of the proceeds of the public Lands. The advocates of perpetual slavery oppose all of them, they regard them as opposed to the interests of slavery." He was soon convinced that the Northern people "literally" become the " 'hewers of wood and the drawers of water' to the slave-holding South."

So when Texas had been annexed and the Oregon boundary compromised, he talked of the Northern states being driven "to the alternative of abjectly surrendering up their political rights" or "of resuming their sovereignty as States." He was certain that Polk, as a slaveholder, had betrayed the Northern Democrats on Oregon and had violated the Constitutional "compact of 1787" in annexing Texas. He was sure of his Constitutional position, because the legislatures of several Northern states had passed resolutions "declaring that Congress possessed no constitutional power to annex a foreign government to this Union." With "the voice of these sovereign States to support" his position, he was as confident as South Carolina had been in the nullification days.

Senator Thomas Corwin, of the same state and the same party, viewed the war with Mexico as "wanton, unprovoked, *unnecessary,* and therefore, unjust." He saw it shot through with the slavery issue, and announced the "deeply-rooted determination" of men in the nonslaveholding states, from all parties, to check the further spread of that institution. He also recognized the perfectly natural determination of Southern men to carry their slaves into any territory won in part by the spending of their blood and treasure. Territory acquired by conquest from Mexico would, therefore, bring North and South into "collision on a point where neither . . . [would] yield." The "fires of internal war" would be lit; "the sister States of this Union" would be hurled "into the bottomless gulf of civil strife." As a patriot he would have none of it!

That some Southerners did not approve of the war with Mexico and were not in favor of seizing Mexican territory did not alter the case when there were others, especially in the Lower South, ready for the conquest and seizure not only of all Mexico but of Central America as well. The free North, said Giddings, was about to be "politically bound, hand and foot, and surrendered to the rule and government of a slave-holding oligarchy."

But it was Polk's handling of the Oregon question which stirred the Northwest most deeply. Hard times in the 1840's and the ever-present problem of satisfactory markets had engendered an emigration fever and brought dreams of rich markets to be found in far-off China and other lands of the East. The platform on which Polk had come into office asserted our "clear and unquestionable" title to "the whole of the territory of Oregon" and declared the "reoccupation of Oregon and the re-annexation of Texas" to be "great American measures." So, with Texas annexed and its boundaries maintained at the cost of a war, men of the Northwest reasonably understood that the granting of Polk's request for permission to notify England of the termination of joint occupation opened the way for some positive step in that direction. The delay in granting the request and the sharp opposition by Southern leaders to it had already raised suspicion of bad faith. Polk's stated willingness to submit to Congress any British offer of compromise on the 49 degree line and the perfectly clear linking of compromise with the reduction of the tariff incensed men of the Ohio Valley. Senator Edward A. Hannegan of Indiana spoke of the report "that for Oregon we can get free trade" and declared that as much as he loved free trade, it would never "be bought by me by the territory of my country." "A new and most profitable market" for Western wheat "for a surrender of ports and harbors on the Pacific" was not to be considered. He reminded his fellow congressmen that "Texas and Oregon were born at the same instant, nursed and cradled in the same cradle—The Baltimore Convention." He noted that there had not been "a moment's hesitation, until Texas was admitted; but the moment she was admitted, the peculiar friends of Texas turned, and were doing all they could to strangle Oregon!"

John Wentworth, Congressman and editor of the Chicago *Daily Democrat,* wanted to know from Southerners what had occurred since "the adjournment of the last Congress to make our title [to Oregon] good to only forty-nine degrees, when it was good to fifty-four degrees and forty minutes when the House passed the bill, at the last session?" He noted further that "Already have certain politicians and papers begun to predict the South, having used the West to get Texas, would now abandon it, and go against Oregon?" Stephen A. Douglas was equally sarcastic. He charged that "every little question" possible was seized upon "to postpone and prevent action" on Oregon; that men were terrified by it where they "had met the Texas question boldly and without shrinking, last year." So harsh was the criticism of these Western men that Calhoun felt impelled to explain his position by saying that Texas was a Western gain and that a difference in method was all that he had ever desired.

The effects, however, had already become apparent. Polk was soon recording in his diary that "Messrs. Hannegan, Semple, and Atchison have lashed themselves into a passion because two thirds of the Senate advised the acceptance of the British [*sic*] proposition for the adjustment of the Oregon question" and were voting with the Whigs on other measures, "Their course is that of spoiled children," he added.

Discussion of the tariff, which preceded the act of 1846, again aroused Western anger. Prices of all Western produce were low that year and surpluses great. The proposed tax on tea and coffee especially aroused feelings. Jacob Brinkerhoff of Ohio called it "a *sectional tax*"—one that was "wrong, unequal and unjust." All Western people—all free laborers—used tea and coffee, whereas "three million slave laborers" scarcely used them at all. "[You] ask us for a war tax upon tea and coffee to make Southern conquests," he concluded, "while Northern territory is given away by empires."

The fact that the Walker tariff finally passed the Senate only by the aid of the two new Texas members was not overlooked. Its sectional implications were too obvious.

Presidential veto of a river and harbor bill, which was primarily intended to aid shipping on the Great Lakes and other Western waters, was the final proof that Polk's administration, under Southern influence, was determined to thwart every Northwestern interest.

The "Democracy prefers to pay money for blowing out brains, rather than blowing up & getting round rocks, that impede the progress of the most efficient civilizer of our Barberous [*sic*] race—commerce," charged Corwin. "The lives and property of the freemen of the North, her free laborers, sailors, and those passing to and fro on her great Lakes and Rivers," echoed the Chicago *Daily Journal*, "are of no concern to the government. They live and labor in a portion of the country which is out of the pale of its care and protection. The lives of an hundred or two of hardy mariners, and a few millions of property are of no consequence in the eye of James K. Polk, when weighed against a Virginia abstraction, or that idol of the South, Negro slavery."

Everything added up to studied neglect, if not hostility. Slavery ruled and slavery cared only for its own interests. "Is it not strange that enlightened men of the South cannot be persuaded that our Lakes are something more than goose ponds?" asked the Chicago *Democrat*. "If we were *blessed* with the *glorious* institution of *slavery* this comprehension would not be so difficult!" Then the warning: "But let them beware! Let them take heed how they trifle with the West." "Hereafter the West must be respected, and her commerce must be protected as well as that of other portions of the Union; and the iron rod wielded over her by Southern despots must be broken. The Constitution was intended for the great West as well as for the South." "We must have these improvements," said Brinkerhoff, "and I tell you . . . we will have them, veto or no veto." "If no measures for the protection and improvement of anything North or West are to be suffered by our Southern masters," added the Chicago *Daily Journal*, "if we are to be down-trodden, and all our cherished interests crushed by them, a signal revolution will eventually ensue."

The Western answer was, indeed, not long in coming. On a hot August evening in 1846, David Wilmot, representative in Congress from a somewhat backward district in Pennsylvania, moved an amendment to an appropriation bill under consideration, to the effect that slavery should be forever prohibited in any territory acquired from Mexico. His proposal was to extend the Jeffersonian prohibition in the Northwest Ordinance to all such territory.

The reactions to this proposal were violent and destined to be enduring throughout the ensuing years. The proviso was quickly rejected, but it had so completely expressed the feelings and the impulses of Northern and Western men that it became their answer to every Southern demand which seemed to carry a sectional import. Wilmot had not acted alone. Brinkerhoff and other Western men had worked closely with him, and one of them would certainly have introduced a like proviso if Wilmot had not done so. The point is that the North, and especially the Northwest, felt itself abused and neglected. Southern influence, now symbolized by slavery, seemed to dominate, and Southern demands were granted while those of the North were neglected. The time had come to right the balance in national and party affairs. Resolutions in support poured in from Northern states, and speakers on the floors of Congress let it be known that there would be no further admission of slaveholding states to the Union and no further extension of slavery into any territory.

Calhoun, as has been seen, answered this uprising with a series of resolutions pointing out the grave danger to Southern interests in a move which would soon reduce his section to "a helpless minority" in all the affairs of government. He noted that the territories belonged "to the several States of this Union," and were held "as their joint and common property." He denied the right of Congress to pass any law or to do any act which discriminated between the states of the union or by which any one of them was denied full and equal opportunity to migrate to the territories "with their property." The Wilmot Proviso was thus a violation of the Constitution, a flagrant effort to weaken the South.

Others joined in Calhoun's protest and a few began to talk of the necessity for secession from the Union if such unfair and unsound procedures were permitted. The Richmond *Enquirer* spoke of the tocsin, "the firebell at night," which was sounding in Southern ears. "The madmen of the North and Northwest," it said, "have, we fear, cast the die, and numbered the days of this glorious Union." South Carolina meetings suggested that their representatives withdraw from Congress and come home. Robert Toombs of Georgia let it be known that "The South would remain in the Union on a ground of perfect equality . . . or they would not stay at all." Early the next year the Virginia legislature passed resolutions supporting Calhoun's position, threatening opposition to the last extremity; and the governor of Mississippi declared that the South would resist even to secession and civil war.

Calhoun had, by his attitude toward Oregon, lost his hold on the West and all hope of its further support. The South, for the same reason, had lost an ally and the Democratic party more of its unity. Whereas it hau seemed that Calhoun's efforts to unite South and West were about to succeed, now he was forced back to the near-hopeless task of securing a unified Southern bloc. He had, moreover, only the Constitution with which to protect his section. The Northwest was gone and with it all chances of the Democratic nomination of 1848. And what was more important, the Northwest was bitter and angry. It blamed Southern men and their influence with the administration for their plight. They were placing the blame for Southern and Democratic attitudes on slavery. The term "slave power" began to slip naturally into their talk. They were not yet ready to ally themselves with the Northeast. They were, however, well on their way towards an independent course that no longer took Southern friendships and support for granted.

Eugene D. Genovese # The Slave South: An Interpretation

In this piece, taken from a larger work, an acute historian who frequently probes the social and economic problems of the pre-Civil War South takes issue with two of the leading interpretations of the fundamental causes of the Civil War. Like historians of the earlier nationalist school, he contends that slavery rests at the core of the causes of the Civil War, and that given the differences between the North and South, the conflict was inevitable. But his thesis, based in large part upon economic arguments, is more sophisticated than that of older nationalist historians. He rejects the interpretations that say a special kind of capitalism or plantation agrarianism drove the South to secession. Instead, he maintains, slavery was the foundation of the South's economy and culture. This unique way of life, anchored in the relationship between white master and black slave, was the basic cause of sectional conflict. Note how Genovese uses his evidence and develops his arguments. Look for his analysis of capitalism and explanation of why the South did not fit within the definition of a true capitalist society. What, in the author's judgment, was the South's greatest economic weakness? What factor prevented the South from giving up slavery? [Copyright © 1961 by Eugene Genovese. From The Political Economy of Slavery *by Eugene Genovese, pp. 13–36. Reprinted by permission of Pantheon Books/A Division of Random House, Inc.]*

The Problem. The uniqueness of the antebellum South continues to challenge the imagination of Americans, who, despite persistent attempts, cannot divert their attention from slavery. Nor should they, for slavery provided the foundation on which the South rose and grew. The master-slave relationship permeated Southern life and influenced relationships among free men. A full history would have to treat the impact of the Negro slave and of slaveless as well as slaveholding whites, but a first approximation, necessarily concerned with essentials, must focus on the slaveholders, who most directly exercised power over men and events. The hegemony of the slaveholders, presupposing the social and economic preponderance of great slave plantations, determined the character of the South. These men rose to power in a region embedded in a capitalist country, and their social system emerged as part of a capitalist world. Yet, a nonslaveholding European past and a shared experience in a new republic notwithstanding, they imparted to Southern life a special social, economic, political, ideological, and psychological content.

To dissolve that special content into an ill-defined agrarianism or an elusive planter capitalism would mean to sacrifice concern with the essential for concern with the transitional and peripheral. Neither of the two leading interpretations, which for many years have contended in a hazy and unreal battle, offers consistent and plausible answers to recurring questions, especially those bearing on the origins of the War for Southern Independence. The first of these interpretations considers the antebellum South an agrarian society fighting against the encroachments of industrial capitalism; the second considers the slave plantation merely a form of capitalist enterprise and suggests that the material differences between Northern and Southern capitalism were more apparent than real. These two views, which one would think contradictory, sometimes combine in the thesis that the agrarian nature of planter capitalism, for some reason, made coexistence with industrial capitalism difficult.

The first view cannot explain why some agrarian societies give rise to industrialization and some do not. A prosperous agricultural hinterland has generally served as a basis for industrial development by providing a home market for manufactures and a source of capital accumulation, and the prosperity of farmers has largely depended on the growth of industrial centers as markets for foodstuffs. In a capitalist society agriculture is one industry, or one set of industries, among many, and its conflict with manufacturing is one of many competitive rivalries. There must have been something unusual about an agriculture that generated violent opposition to the agrarian West as well as the industrial Northeast.

The second view, which is the more widely held, emphasizes that the plantation system produced for a distant market, responded to supply and demand, invested capital in land and slaves, and operated with funds borrowed from banks and factors. This, the more sophisticated of the two interpretations, cannot begin to explain the origins of the conflict with the North and does violence to elementary facts of antebellum Southern history.

Slavery and the Expansion of Capitalism. The proponents of the idea of planter capitalism draw heavily, wittingly or not, on Lewis C. Gray's theory of the genesis of the plantation system. Gray defines the plantation as a "capitalistic type of agricultural organization in which a considerable number of unfree laborers were employed under a unified direction and control in the production of a staple crop." Gray considers the plantation system inseparably linked with the international development of capitalism. He notes the plantation's need for large outlays of capital, its strong tendency toward specialization in a single crop, and its commercialism and argues that these appeared with the industrial revolution.

In modern times the plantation often rose under bourgeois auspices to provide industry with cheap raw materials, but the consequences were not always harmonious with bourgeois society. Colonial expansion produced three sometimes overlapping patterns: (1) the capitalists of the advanced country simply invested in colonial land—as illustrated even today by the practice of the United Fruit Company in the Caribbean; (2) the colonial planters were largely subservient to the advanced countries—as illustrated by the British West Indies before the abolition of slavery; and (3) the planters were able to win independence and build a society under their own direction—as illustrated by the Southern United States.

In alliance with the North, the planter-dominated South broke away from England, and political conditions in the new republic allowed it considerable freedom for self-development. The plantation society that had begun as an appendage of British capitalism ended as a powerful, largely autonomous civilization with aristocratic pretensions and possibilities, although it remained tied to the capitalist world by bonds of commodity production. The essential element in this distinct civilization was the slaveholders' domination, made possible by their command of labor. Slavery provided the basis for a special Southern economic and social life, special problems and tensions, and special laws of development.

The Rationality and Irrationality of Slave Society. Slave economies normally manifest irrational tendencies that inhibit economic development and endanger social stability. Max Weber, among the many scholars who have discussed the problem, has noted four important irrational features. First, the master cannot adjust the size of his labor force in accordance with business fluctuations. In particular, efficiency cannot readily be attained through the manipulation of the labor force if sentiment, custom, or community pressure makes separation of families difficult. Second, the capital outlay is much greater and riskier for slave labor than for free. Third, the domination of society by a planter class increases the risk of political influence in the market. Fourth, the sources of cheap labor usually dry up rather quickly, and beyond a certain point costs become excessively burdensome. Weber's remarks could be extended.

Planters, for example, have little opportunity to select specifically trained workers for special tasks as they arise.

There are other telling features of this irrationality. Under capitalism the pressure of the competitive struggle and the bourgeois spirit of accumulation direct the greater part of profits back into production. The competitive side of Southern slavery produced a similar result, but one that was modified by the pronounced tendency to heavy consumption. Economic historians and sociologists have long noted the high propensity to consume among landed aristocracies. No doubt this difference has been one of degree. The greater part of slavery's profits also find their way back into production, but the method of reinvestment in the two systems is substantially different. Capitalism largely directs its profits into an expansion of plant and equipment, not labor; that is, economic progress is qualitative. Slavery, for economic reasons as well as for those of social prestige, directs its reinvestments along the same lines as the original investment—in slaves and land; that is, economic progress is quantitative.

In the South this weakness proved fatal for the slaveholders. They found themselves engaged in a growing conflict with Northern farmers and businessmen over such issues as tariffs, homesteads, internal improvements, and the decisive question of the balance of political power in the Union. The slow pace of their economic progress, in contrast to the long strides of their rivals to the north, threatened to undermine their political parity and result in a Southern defeat on all major issues of the day. The qualitative leaps in the Northern economy manifested themselves in a rapidly increasing population, an expanding productive plant, and growing political, ideological, and social boldness. The slaveholders' voice grew shriller and harsher as they contemplated impending disaster and sought solace in complaints of Northern aggression and exploitation.

Just as Southern slavery directed reinvestment along a path that led to economic stagnation, so too did it limit the volume of capital accumulated for investment of any kind. We need not reopen the tedious argument about the chronology of the plantation, the one-crop system, and slavery. While slavery existed, the South had to be bound to a plantation system and an agricultural economy based on a few crops. As a result, the South depended on Northern facilities, with inevitably mounting middlemen's charges. Less obvious was the capital drain occasioned by the importation of industrial goods. While the home market remained backward, Southern manufacturers had difficulty producing in sufficient quantities to keep costs and prices at levels competitive with Northerners. The attendant dependence on Northern and British imports intensified the outward flow of badly needed funds.

Most of the elements of irrationality were irrational only from a capitalist standpoint. The high propensity to consume luxuries, for example, has always been functional (socially if not economically rational) in aristocratic societies, for it has provided the ruling class with the facade necessary to control the middle and lower classes. Thomas R. Dew knew what he was doing when he defended the high personal expenditures of Southerners as proof of the superiority of the slave system. Few Southerners, even few slaveholders, could afford to spend lavishly and affect an aristocratic standard of living, but those few set the social tone for society. One wealthy planter with a great house and a reputation for living and entertaining on a grand scale could impress a whole community and keep before its humbler men the shining ideal of plantation magnificence. Consider Pascal's observation that the habit of seeing the king accompanied by guards, pomp, and all the paraphernalia designed to command respect and inspire awe will produce those reactions even when he appears alone and informally. In the popular mind he is assumed to be naturally an awe-inspiring being. In this manner, every dollar spent by the planters for elegant clothes, a college education for their children, or a lavish barbecue contributed to the political and social domination of their class. We may speak of the slave system's irrationality only in a strictly economic sense and then only to indicate the inability of the South to compete with Northern capitalism on the latter's grounds. The slaveholders, fighting for political power in an essentially capitalist Union, had to do just that.

Capitalist and Pseudo-Capitalist Features of the Slave Economy. The slave economy developed within, and was in a sense exploited by, the capitalist world market; consequently, slavery developed many ostensibly capitalist features, such as banking, commerce, and credit. These played a fundamentally different role in the South than in the North. Capitalism has absorbed and even encouraged many kinds of precapitalist social systems: serfdom, slavery, Oriental state enterprises, and others. It has introduced credit, finance, banking, and similar institutions where they did not previously exist. It is pointless to suggest that therefore nineteenth-century India and twentieth-century Saudi Arabia should be classified as capitalist countries. We need to analyze a few of the more important capitalist and pseudo-capitalist features of Southern slavery and especially to review the barriers to industrialization in order to appreciate the peculiar qualities of this remarkable and anachronistic society.

The defenders of the "planter-capitalism" thesis have noted the extensive commercial links between the plantation and the world market and the modest commercial bourgeoisie in the South and have concluded that there is no reason to predicate an antagonism between cotton producers and cotton merchants. However valid as a reply to the naive arguments of the proponents of the agrarianism-versus-industrialism thesis, this criticism has unjustifiably been twisted to suggest that the presence of commercial activity proves the predominance of capitalism in the South. Many precapitalist economic systems have had well-developed commercial relations, but if every commercial society is to be considered capitalist, the word loses all meaning. In general, commercial classes have supported the existing system of production. As Maurice Dobb observes, their fortunes are bound up with those of the dominant producers, and merchants are more likely to seek an extension of their middlemen's profits than to try to reshape the economic order.

We must concern ourselves primarily with capitalism as a social system, not merely with evidence of typically capitalistic economic practices. In the South extensive and complicated commercial relations with the world market permitted the growth of a small commercial bourgeoisie. The resultant fortunes flowed into slaveholding, which offered prestige and economic and social security in a planter-dominated society. Independent merchants found their businesses dependent on the patronage of the slaveholders. The merchants either became planters themselves or assumed a servile attitude toward the planters. The commercial bourgeoisie, such as it was, remained tied to the slaveholding interest, had little desire or opportunity to invest capital in industrial expansion, and adopted the prevailing aristocratic attitudes.

The Southern industrialists were in an analogous position, although one that was potentially subversive of the political power and ideological unity of the planters. The preponderance of planters and slaves in the countryside retarded the home market. The Southern yeomanry, unlike the Western, lacked the purchasing power to sustain rapid industrial development. The planters spent much of their money abroad for luxuries. The plantation market consisted primarily of the demand for cheap slave clothing and cheap agricultural implements for use or misuse by the slaves. Southern industrialism needed a sweeping agrarian revolution to provide it with cheap labor and a substantial rural market, but the Southern industrialists depended on the existing, limited, plantation market. Leading industrialists like William Gregg and Daniel Pratt were plantation-oriented and proslavery. They could hardly have been other.

The banking system of the South serves as an excellent illustration of an ostensibly capitalist institution that worked to augment the power of the planters and retard the development of the bourgeoisie. Southern banks functioned much as did those which the British introduced into Latin America, India, and Egypt during the nineteenth century. Although the British banks fostered dependence on British capital, they did not directly and willingly generate internal capitalist development. They were not sources of industrial capital but "large-scale clearing houses of mercantile finance vying in their interest charges with the local usurers."

The difference between the banking practices of the South and those of the West reflects the difference between slavery and agrarian capitalism. In the West, as in the Northeast, banks and credit facilities promoted a vigorous economic expansion. During the period of loose Western banking (1830–1844) credit flowed liberally into industrial development as well as into land purchases and internal improvements. Manufacturers and merchants dominated the boards of directors of

Western banks, and landowners played a minor role. Undoubtedly, many urban businessmen speculated in land and had special interests in underwriting agricultural exports, but they gave attention to building up agricultural processing industries and urban enterprises, which guaranteed the region a many-sided economy.

The slave states paid considerable attention to the development of a conservative, stable banking system, which could guarantee the movement of staple crops and the extension of credit to the planters. Southern banks were primarily designed to lend the planters money for outlays that were economically feasible and socially acceptable in a slave society: the movement of crops, the purchase of land and slaves, and little else.

Whenever Southerners pursued easy-credit policies, the damage done outweighed the advantages of increased production. This imbalance probably did not occur in the West, for easy credit made possible agricultural and industrial expansion of a diverse nature and, despite acute crises, established a firm basis for long-range prosperity. Easy credit in the South led to expansion of cotton production with concomitant overproduction and low prices; simultaneously, it increased the price of slaves.

Planters wanted their banks only to facilitate cotton shipments and maintain sound money. They purchased large quantities of foodstuffs from the West and, since they shipped little in return, had to pay in bank notes. For five years following the bank failures of 1837 the bank notes of New Orleans moved at a discount of from 10 to 25 per cent. This disaster could not be allowed to recur. Sound money and sound banking became the cries of the slaveholders as a class.

Southern banking tied the planters to the banks, but more important, tied the bankers to the plantations. The banks often found it necessary to add prominent planters to their boards of directors and were closely supervised by the planter-dominated state legislatures. In this relationship the bankers could not emerge as a middle-class counterweight to the planters but could merely serve as their auxiliaries.

The bankers of the free states also allied themselves closely with the dominant producers, but society and economy took on a bourgeois quality provided by the rising industrialists, the urban middle classes, and the farmers who increasingly depended on urban markets. The expansion of credit, which in the West financed manufacturing, mining, transportation, agricultural diversification, and the numerous branches of a capitalist economy, in the South bolstered the economic position of the planters, inhibited the rise of alternative industries, and guaranteed the extension and consolidation of the plantation system.

If for a moment we accept the designation of the planters as capitalists and the slave system as a form of capitalism, we are then confronted by a capitalist society that impeded the development of every normal feature of capitalism. The planters were not mere capitalists; they were precapitalist, quasi-aristocratic landowners who had to adjust their economy and ways of thinking to a capitalist world market. Their society, in its spirit and fundamental direction, represented the antithesis of capitalism, however many compromises it had to make. The fact of slave ownership is central to our problem. This seemingly formal question of whether the owners of the means of production command labor or purchase the labor power of free workers contains in itself the content of Southern life. The essential features of Southern particularity, as well as of Southern backwardness, can be traced to the relationship of master to slave.

The Barriers to Industrialization. If the planters were losing their economic and political cold war with Northern capitalism, the failure of the South to develop sufficient industry provided the most striking immediate cause. Its inability to develop adequate manufactures is usually attributed to the inefficiency of its labor force. No doubt slaves did not easily adjust to industrial employment, and the indirect effects of the slave system impeded the employment of whites. Slaves did work effectively in hemp, tobacco, iron, and cotton factories but only under socially dangerous conditions. They received a wide variety of privileges and approached an elite status. Planters generally appreciated the potentially subversive quality of these arrangements and looked askance at their extension.

Slavery concentrated economic and political power in the hands of a slaveholding class hostile to industrialism. The slaveholders feared a strong urban bourgeoisie, which might make common cause with its Northern counterpart. They feared a white urban working class of unpredictable social tendencies. In general, they distrusted the city and saw in it something incongruous with their local power and status arrangements. The small slaveholders, as well as the planters, resisted the assumption of a heavy tax burden to assist manufacturers, and as the South fell further behind the North in industrial development more state aid was required to help industry offset the Northern advantages of scale, efficiency, credit relations, and business reputation.

Slavery led to the rapid concentration of land and wealth and prevented the expansion of a Southern home market. Instead of providing a basis for industrial growth, the Southern countryside, economically dominated by a few large estates, provided only a limited market for industry. Data on the cotton textile factories almost always reveal that Southern producers aimed at supplying slaves with the cheapest and coarsest kind of cotton goods. Even so, local industry had to compete with Northern firms, which sometimes shipped direct and sometimes established Southern branches.

William Gregg, the South's foremost industrialist, understood the modest proportions of the Southern market and warned manufacturers against trying to produce exclusively for their local areas. His own company at Graniteville, South Carolina, produced fine cotton goods that sold much better in the North than in the South. Gregg was an unusually able man, and his success in selling to the North was a personal triumph. When he had to evaluate the general position of Southern manufacturers, he asserted that he was willing to stake his reputation on their ability to compete with Northerners in the production of *"coarse cotton fabrics."*

Some Southern businessmen, especially those in the border states, did good business in the North. Louisville tobacco and hemp manufacturers sold much of their output in Ohio. Some producers of iron and agricultural implements sold in nearby Northern cities. This kind of market was precarious. As Northern competitors rose and the market shrank, Southern producers had to rely on the narrow and undependable Southern market. Well before 1840 iron-manufacturing establishments in the Northwest provided local farmers with excellent markets for grain, vegetables, molasses, and work animals. During the antebellum period and after, the grain growers of America found their market at home. America's rapid industrial development offered farmers a magnificently expanding urban market, and not until much later did they come to depend to any important extent on exports.

To a small degree the South benefited in this way. By 1840 the tobacco-manufacturing industry began to absorb more tobacco than was being exported, and the South's few industrial centers provided markets for local grain and vegetable growers. Since the South could not undertake a general industrialization, few urban centers rose to provide substantial markets for farmers and planters. Southern grain growers, except for those close to the cities of the free states, had to be content with the market offered by planters who preferred to specialize in cotton or sugar and buy foodstuffs. The restricted rations of the slaves limited this market, which inadequate transportation further narrowed. It did not pay the planters to appropriate state funds to build a transportation system into the back country, and any measure to increase the economic strength of the back-country farmers seemed politically dangerous to the aristocracy of the Black Belt. The farmers of the back country remained isolated, self-sufficient, and politically, economically, and socially backward. Those grain-growing farmers who could compete with producers in the Upper South and the Northwest for the plantation market lived within the Black Belt. Since the planters did not have to buy from these local producers, the economic relationship greatly strengthened the political hand of the planters.

The General Features of Southern Agriculture. The South's greatest economic weakness was the low productivity of its labor force. The slaves worked indifferently. They could be made to work reasonably well under close supervision in the cotton fields, but the cost of supervising them in more than one or two operations at a time was prohibitive. Slavery prevented the significant technological progress that could have raised productivity substantially. Of greatest relevance, the impediments to technological progress damaged Southern agriculture, for improved implements and machines largely accounted for the big increases in crop yields per acre in the Northern states during the nineteenth century.

Slavery and the plantation system led to agricultural methods that depleted the soil. The frontier methods of the free states yielded similar results, but slavery forced the South into continued dependence upon exploitative methods after the frontier had passed further west. It prevented reclamation of worn-out lands. The plantations were much too large to fertilize easily. Lack of markets and poor care of animals by slaves made it impossible to accumulate sufficient manure. The low level of capital accumulation made the purchase of adequate quantities of commercial fertilizer unthinkable. Planters could not practice proper crop rotation, for the pressure of the credit system kept most available land in cotton, and the labor force could not easily be assigned to the required tasks without excessive costs of supervision. The general inefficiency of labor thwarted most attempts at improvement of agricultural methods.

The South, unable to feed itself, faced a series of dilemmas in its attempts to increase production of nonstaple crops and to improve its livestock. An inefficient labor force and the backward business practices of the dominant planters hurt. When planters did succeed in raising their own food, they also succeeded in depriving local livestock raisers and grain growers of their only markets. The planters had little capital with which to buy improved breeds and could not guarantee the care necessary to make such investments worth while. Livestock raisers also lacked the capital, and without adequate urban markets they could not make good use of the capital they had.

Thoughtful Southerners, deeply distressed by the condition of their agriculture, made a determined effort to remedy it. In Maryland and Virginia significant progress occurred in crop diversification and livestock improvement, but this progress was contingent on the sale of surplus slaves to the Lower South. These sales provided the income that offset agricultural losses and made possible investment in fertilizers, equipment, and livestock. The concomitant reduction in the size of the slave force facilitated supervision and increased labor productivity and versatility. Even so, the income from slave sales remained an important part of the gross income of the planters of the Upper South. The reform remained incomplete and could not free agriculture from the destructive effects of the continued reliance on slave labor.

The reform process had several contradictions, the most important of which was the dependence on slave sales. Surplus slaves could be sold only while gang-labor methods continued to be used in other areas. By the 1850s the deficiencies of slavery that had forced innovations in the Upper South were making themselves felt in the Lower South. Increasingly, planters in the Lower South explored the possibilities of reform. If the deterioration of agriculture in the Cotton Belt had proceeded much further, the planters would have had to stop buying slaves from Maryland and Virginia and look for markets for their own surplus slaves. Without the acquisition of fresh lands there could be no general reform of Southern agriculture. The Southern economy was moving steadily into an insoluble crisis.

The Ideology of the Master Class. The planters commanded Southern politics and set the tone of social life. Theirs was an aristocratic, antibourgeois spirit with values and mores emphasizing family and status, a strong code of honor, and aspirations to luxury, ease, and accomplishment. In the planters' community, paternalism provided the standard of human relationships, and politics and statecraft were the duties and responsibilities of gentlemen. The gentleman lived for politics, not, like the bourgeois politician, off politics.

The planter typically recoiled at the notions that profit should be the goal of life; that the approach to production and exchange should be internally rational and uncomplicated by social values; that thrift and hard work should be the great virtues; and that the test of the wholesomeness of a community should be the vigor with which its citizens expand the economy. The planter was no less acquisitive than the bourgeois, but an acquisitive spirit is compatible with values antithetical to capitalism. The aristocratic spirit of the planters absorbed acquisitiveness and directed it into channels that were socially desirable to a slave society: the accumulation of slaves and land and the achievement of military and political honors. Whereas in the North people followed the lure of business and money for their own sake, in the South specific forms of property carried the badges of honor, prestige, and power. Even the rough parvenu planters of the Southwestern frontier—the "Southern Yankees"—strove to accumulate wealth in the modes acceptable to plantation society. Only in their crudeness and naked avarice did they differ from the Virginia gentlemen. They were a generation removed from the refinement that follows accumulation.

Slavery established the basis of the planter's position and power. It measured his affluence, marked his status, and supplied leisure for social graces and aristocratic duties. The older bourgeoisie of New England in its own way struck an aristocratic pose, but its wealth was rooted in commercial and industrial enterprises that were being pushed into the background by the newer heavy industries arising in the West, where upstarts took advantage of the more lucrative ventures like the iron industry. In the South few such opportunities were opening. The parvenu differed from the established planter only in being cruder and perhaps sharper in his business dealings. The road to power lay through the plantation. The older aristocracy kept its leadership or made room for men following the same road. An aristocratic stance was no mere compensation for a decline in power; it was the soul and content of a rising power.

Many travelers commented on the difference in material conditions from one side of the Ohio River to the other, but the difference in sentiment was seen most clearly by Tocqueville. Writing before the slavery issue had inflamed the nation, he remarked that slavery was attacking the Union "indirectly in its manners." The Ohioan "was tormented by wealth," and would turn to any kind of enterprise or endeavor to make a fortune. The Kentuckian coveted wealth "much less than pleasure or excitement," and money had "lost a portion of its value in his eyes."

Achille Murat joined Tocqueville in admiration for Southern ways. Compared with Northerners, Southerners were frank, clever, charming, generous, and liberal. They paid a price for these advantages. As one Southerner put it, the North led the South in almost everything because the Yankees had quiet perseverance over the long haul, whereas the Southerners had talent and brilliance but no taste for sustained labor. Southern projects came with a flash and died just as suddenly. Despite such criticisms from within the ranks, the leaders of the South clung to their ideals, their faults, and their conviction of superiority. Farmers, said Edmund Ruffin, could not expect to achieve a cultural level above that of the "boors who reap rich harvests from the fat soil of Belgium." In the Northern states, he added with some justification, a farmer could rarely achieve the ease, culture, intellect, and refinement that slavery made possible. The prevailing attitude of the aristocratic South toward itself and its Northern rival was ably summed up by William Henry Holcombe of Natchez: "The Northerner loves to make money, the Southerner to spend it."

At their best, Southern ideals constituted a rejection of the crass, vulgar, inhumane elements of capitalist society. The slaveholders simply could not accept the idea that the cash nexus offered a permissible basis for human relations. Even the vulgar parvenu of the Southwest embraced the plantation myth and refused to make a virtue of necessity by glorifying the competitive side of slavery as civilization's highest achievement. The slaveholders generally, and the planters in particular, did identify their own ideals with the essence of civilization and, given their sense of honor, were prepared to defend them at any cost.

This civilization and its ideals were antinational in a double sense. The plantation offered virtually the only market for the small nonstaple-producing farmers and provided the center of necessary services for the small cotton growers. Thus, the paternalism of the planters toward their slaves was reinforced by the semipaternal relationship between the planters and their neighbors. The planters, in truth, grew into the closest thing to feudal lords imaginable in a nineteenth-century bourgeois republic. The planters' protestations of love for the Union were not so much a desire to use the Union to protect slavery as a strong commitment to localism as the highest form of liberty. They genuinely loved the Union so long as it alone among the great states of the world recognized that localism had a wide variety of rights. The Southerners' source of pride was not the Union, nor the nonexistent Southern nation; it was the plantation, which they raised to a political principle.

The Inner Reality of Slaveholding. The Southern slaveholder had "extraordinary force." In the eyes of an admirer his independence was "not as at the North, the effect of a conflict with the too stern pressure of society, but the legitimate outgrowth of a sturdy love of liberty." This independence, so distinctive in the slaveholders' psychology, divided them politically from agrarian Westerners as well as from urban Easterners. Commonly, both friendly and hostile contemporaries agreed that the Southerner appeared rash, unstable, often irrational, and that he turned away from bourgeois habits toward an aristocratic pose.

Americans, with a pronounced Jeffersonian bias, often attribute this spirit to agrarians of all types, although their judgment seems almost bizarre. A farmer may be called "independent" because he works for himself and owns property; like any grocer or tailor he functions as a petty bourgeois. In Jefferson's time, when agriculture had not yet been wholly subjected to the commanding influences of the market, the American farmer perhaps had a considerable amount of independence, if we choose to call self-sufficient isolation by that name, but in subsequent days he has had to depend on the market like any manufacturer, if not more so. Whereas manufacturers combine to protect their economic interests, such arrangements have proved much more difficult, and until recently almost impossible, to effect among farmers. In general, if we contrast farmers with urban capitalists, the latter emerge as relatively the more independent. The farmer yields constantly to the primacy of nature, to a direct, external force acting on him regardless of his personal worth; his independence is therefore rigorously circumscribed. The capitalist is limited by the force of the market, which operates indirectly and selectively. Many capitalists go under in a crisis, but some emerge stronger and surer of their own excellence. Those who survive the catastrophe do so (or so it seems) because of superior ability, strength, and management, not because of an Act of God.

The slaveholder, as distinct from the farmer, had a private source of character making and mythmaking—his slave. Most obviously, he had the habit of command, but there was more than despotic authority in this master-slave relationship. The slave stood interposed between his master and the object his master desired (that which was produced); thus, the master related to the object only mediately, through the slave. The slaveholder commanded the products of another's labor, but by the same process was forced into dependence upon this other.

Thoughtful Southerners such as Ruffin, Fitzhugh, and Hammond understood this dependence and saw it as arising from the general relationship of labor to capital, rather than from the specific relationship of master to slave. They did not grasp that the capitalist's dependence upon his laborers remains obscured by the process of exchange in the capitalist market. Although all commodities are products of social relationships and contain human labor, they face each other in the market not as the embodiment of human qualities but as things with a seemingly independent existence. Similarly, the laborer sells his labor-power in the way in which the capitalist sells his goods—by bringing it to market, where it is subject to the fluctuations of supply and demand. A "commodity fetishism" clouds the social relationship of labor to capital, and the worker and capitalist appear as mere observers of a process over which they have little control. Southerners correctly viewed the relationship as a general one of labor to capital but failed to realize that the capitalist's dependence on his laborers is hidden, whereas that of master on slave is naked. As a Mississippi planter noted:

I intend to be henceforth stingy as far as unnecessary expenditure—as a man should not squander what another accumulates with the exposure of health and the wearing out of the physical powers, and is not that the case with the man who needlessly parts with that which the negro by the hardest labor and often undergoing what we in like situation would call the greatest deprivation . . .

This simultaneous dependence and independence contributed to that peculiar combination of the admirable and the frightening in the slaveholder's nature: his strength, graciousness, and gentility; his impulsiveness, violence, and unsteadiness. The sense of independence and the habit of command developed his poise, grace, and dignity, but the less obvious sense of dependence on a despised other made him violently intolerant of anyone and anything threatening to expose the full nature of his relationship to his slave. Thus, he had a far deeper conservatism than that usually attributed to agrarians. His independence stood out as his most prized possession, but the instability of its base produced personal rashness and directed that rashness against any alteration in the status quo. Any attempt, no matter how well meaning, indirect, or harmless, to question the slave system appeared not only as an attack on his material interests but as an attack on his self-esteem at its most vulnerable point. To question either the morality or the practicality of slavery meant to expose the root of the slaveholder's dependence in independence.

The General Crisis of the Slave South. The South's slave civilization could not forever coexist with an increasingly hostile, powerful, and aggressive Northern capitalism. On the one hand, the special economic conditions arising from the dependence on slave labor bound the South, in a colonial manner, to the world market. The concentration of landholding and slaveholding prevented the rise of a prosperous yeomanry and of urban centers. The inability to build urban centers restricted the market for agricultural produce, weakened the rural producers, and dimmed hopes for agricultural diversification. On the other hand, the same concentration of wealth, the isolated, rural nature of the plantation system, the special psychology engendered by slave ownership, and the political opportunity presented by the separation from England, converged to give the South considerable political and social independence. This independence was primarily the contribution of the slaveholding class, and especially of the planters. Slavery, while it bound the South economically, granted it the privilege of developing an aristocratic tradition, a disciplined and cohesive ruling class, and a mythology of its own.

Aristocratic tradition and ideology intensified the South's attachment to economic backwardness. Paternalism and the habit of command made the slaveholders tough stock, determined to defend their Southern heritage. The more economically debilitating their way of life, the more they clung to it. It was this side of things—the political hegemony and aristocratic ideology of the ruling class—rather than economic factors that prevented the South from relinquishing slavery voluntarily.

As the free states stepped up their industrialization and as the westward movement assumed its remarkable momentum, the South's economic and political allies in the North were steadily isolated. Years of abolitionist and free-soil agitation bore fruit as the South's opposition to homesteads, tariffs, and internal improvements clashed more and more dangerously with the North's economic needs. To protect their institutions and to try to lessen their economic bondage, the slaveholders slid into violent collision with Northern interests and sentiments. The economic deficiencies of slavery threatened to undermine the planters' wealth and power. Such relief measures as cheap labor and more land for slave states (reopening the slave trade and territorial expansion) conflicted with Northern material needs, aspirations, and morality. The planters faced a steady deterioration of their political and social power. Even if the relative prosperity of the 1850s had continued indefinitely, the slave states would have been at the mercy of the free, which steadily forged ahead in population growth, capital accumulation, and economic development. Any economic slump threatened to bring with it an internal political disaster, for the slaveholders could not rely on their middle and lower classes to remain permanently loyal.

When we understand that the slave South developed neither a strange form of capitalism nor an undefinable agrarianism but a special civilization built on the relationship of master to slave, we expose the root of its conflict with the North. The internal contradictions in the South and the external conflict with the North placed the slaveholders hopelessly on the defensive with little to look forward to except slow strangulation. Their only hope lay in a bold stroke to complete their political independence and to use it to provide an expansionist solution for their economic and social problems. The ideology and psychology of the proud slaveholding class made surrender or resignation to gradual defeat unthinkable, for its fate, in its own eyes at least, was the fate of everything worth while in Western civilization.

John Hope Franklin   # Toward a
Unified South

John Hope Franklin, a distinguished black historian on the faculty of the University of Chicago, has written extensively on the history of Negroes in the United States. He has also examined a unique feature of the pre-Civil War South, those aspects that gave the section a reputation of being a land of violence. In the following selection from his book on the militant South, Franklin shows how the South as a region shifted away from the support of a strong army to champion local, sectional defenses. He traces the rise of regional sensitivity, pride, defensiveness, and intellectual independence that gave the South a sectional consciousness bordering on nationalism. Franklin argues that one can see the emergence of a Southern nationalism in the 1850 s. Note the kind of evidence he uses to support his argument. One of his themes, that the growth of Southern nationalism was matched by a rising willingness on the part of Southerners to use force to maintain their sectional institutions, has implications for understanding nationalism in general. [Reprinted by permission of the publishers from John Hope Franklin, The Militant South. *Cambridge, Mass.: The Belknap Press of Harvard University Press, Copyright 1956 by the President and Fellows of Harvard College.*]

As the South developed an intense interest in military matters and as it engaged in activities reflecting that interest, it did not, in the beginning, place any special emphasis on its sectional needs. The opinion prevailed that, with the dangers rising from the proximity of Indians and the presence of Negro slaves, military precautions should be taken in the interest of self-preservation. But there was no indication, for many years, that the section needed military strength to repel a Northern foe. As a matter of fact, early in the century, Southern leaders focused their attention on the task of strengthening national defenses. Between the close of the War in 1812 and the beginning of the conflict in 1861, the War Department was under Southern leadership a vast majority of the time; and many of these Southern Secretaries of War argued strongly for a program of greater national defense. In 1818, as Secretary of War, John Calhoun made an eloquent plea for a larger military establishment, while Joel R. Poinsett, also of South Carolina, did much to strengthen the nation's defenses during the Van Buren administration.

Down to the 1830's there was considerable public support in the South for a strong army. In 1821, the editor of the *Nashville Whig* was alarmed over the prospect of a reduction in federal army appropriations. He thought that, in view of the movements in Europe, it was especially shortsighted to "extinguish every spark of martial spirit" in the United States. The *Louisville Public Advertiser* was opposed to any reduction of appropriations, arguing that such a step would be in keeping with neither the character of the nation nor with its great and growing interest. Perhaps the most bitter opposition to the proposed reductions came from the editor of the Charleston *Courier*, who pointed out that to cut the army after the recent acquisition of Florida would reduce the country not only to the liability of insult but to something "more painful, the consciousness of imbecility." He then put a series of questions that reflected his deep appreciation for the whole complex of the military cult:

Is it nothing to impair, if not destroy that confidence in the government which induces high-minded men to leave the pursuits of civil life for the profession of arms? Is this no longer to be a profession in our republic, which men of genius may study with the desire of serving their country . . . Is military experience, valor, and fame so cheap that we may dispense with all we have, and expect to find it always in the market when we need it?

In the years that followed, various Southerners spoke out for a stronger military force. If none of them quite reached the vehemence of the Charleston editor in 1821 they, nevertheless, showed a real desire to maintain the defense machinery at a high level of efficiency. As late as 1845, "A Subaltern" wrote articles for the *Southern Literary Messenger* calling for a thorough reorganization of the army with a view to strengthening it. He decried the subordination of the commanding general to a civilian, the Secretary of War, and argued that it was a waste of training and talent to use West Point graduates in the Quartermaster and Commissary Departments as "corn, coal, or pork merchants."

Even in the final decade before the Civil War, there was some Southern support for a stronger federal army. In 1852, De Bow was distressed over what he termed the insufficiency of the army. Four years later the correspondent of a New Orleans newspaper said that the army on the western frontier was greatly neglected and all but abandoned. The most tragic aspect of the matter, from that reporter's view, was that the Northern bloc in the Congress was trading its support of the army bill for acquiescence "in its fanatical and treasonable designs against the Constitutional rights of the South and the continuance of our glorious and happy union." Since army reductions were associated with abolitionist schemes, small wonder that the South supported a stronger United States army as the intersectional feeling mounted. The willingness of some Southerners to continue such support is explained by the fact that between 1844 and 1861 every Secretary of War was a Southerner, one in whom the South could have faith.

Before 1850, however, the feeling had emerged that the South's principal interest in military affairs should be directed toward strengthening local defenses. An increasing sensitivity, born of its way of life and relationship to the rest of the country, fostered this redirection of the South's martial spirit toward self-preservation. Southern sensitivity to criticism increased substantially during the abolitionist crusade, and the reaction was most often resentment and pugnacity. It was this hypersensitivity that caused a Southerner like Edmund Ruffin to denounce his critics as "self-seekers" and "schemers" without even an examination of the merits of their criticism. It drove some to the use of the most abusive language and the adoption of the most desperate measures against all forms of criticism. When the editor of the *Illustrated London News* criticized Preston Brooks for attacking Charles Sumner in 1856, a Southern editor called the English writer a "coster-monger" and dared him to come into the Southern part of the United States.

Not only did the South react spontaneously and emotionally to what it regarded as unfair criticism, but it also argued that as a section it was treated unjustly by the rest of the country. It will be recalled that the feeling persisted that the federal government provided inadequate defenses against Indians on the south and southwestern frontier. It hardly seemed an accident, moreover, that "every establishment of the government, navyyards, armories, military schools, etc." had been erected "to the north of the Potomac or on its borders." In fact it appeared "as if the Southern States were considered unsuitable for any national establishment, and all must, of necessity, be located at the North."

Southerners came to feel that they were being deliberately mistreated. There was a record of exactions, they argued, by a ruthless majority of the hard earnings of the people of one section to build up overgrown monopolies in another; wasteful expenditures of the public treasury to create the necessity for high duties and depressive tariffs; and reckless expenditures for lighthouses, canals, and fortifications in one section, while the other was scarcely lighted, improved, or fortified. Past injustices were insignificant, one ardent Southerner contended in 1850, when compared with the effort to exclude Southern institutions from the Mexican cession despite the fact that the South contributed two-thirds of the forces in the Mexican War.

This sensitivity combined with a growing regional pride to produce a distemper that was capable of the most volatile reactions when the South was subjected to strains and stresses. The pride that was characteristic of the person became a trait of the section; and gone was any disposition to make concessions. Southern pride in its institutions and ways of life was transformed into a fierce intolerance of everything outside of and the most uncritical and slavish acceptance of everything within the sectional sanctuary. "I'll give you my notion of things," declared a sturdy, old up-country planter shortly before the war. "I go first for Greenville, then for Greenville District, then for the up-country, then for South Carolina, then for the South, then for the United States. . . ." A more articulate Southerner put a similar thought more cleverly when he said, "Our place in the union is provincial, and as such our peculiarities will have to be defended, excused, ridiculed, pardoned. We can take no pride in our national character, because we must feel that from our peculiar position we do not contribute to its formation."

It would follow that persons living in an atmosphere charged with sectional pride would be extremely critical of persons of other sections.

There was unconcealed delight when any Northern undertaking could be regarded as less than successful. In 1857, the *Daily Picayune* seemed joyous over the fact that less than one-third of the expected 12,800 citizen soldiers turned out for a military parade in New York City. When Thomas Nichols made the trip from New Orleans to Mobile by boat in 1857, he engaged a "fiery Southerner" in conversation. The latter was critical of every phase of Northern life and bitter in his denunciation of Northern policies. He was unwilling to trust any Northern leader and was convinced that if a Southern President was not elected in 1860 the Union would be gone forever.

This proclivity to criticize the North led Southerners to make disparaging remarks regarding the capacities of Northerners in such crucial pursuits as military activities. While one critic was willing to concede that they were vigorous and inventive, he insisted that Northerners were destitute of the capacity for control. And "while they evince no capacity to control, they are uncontrollable." In contrast the people of the South were the inheritors of a great tradition of command and ever remained masters of any situation in which they found themselves.

The way in which large numbers looked on the South with increasing devotion and fidelity did not augur well for the spirit of American nationalism in the land below the Potomac. Indeed, signs of a nascent Southern nationalism became more apparent in the 1840's and 1850's. Even a unionist like Henry W. Hilliard manifested this growing spirit. In the Alabama legislature in 1839, he decried the growing hostility between the sections. "Yet, sir," he hastened to add, "the South is my own, my native land—my home, and the birth-place of my children. Her people are my people; her hopes are my hopes; her interests are my interests."

Alexander Stephens was even more explicit, saying, in a speech in the Congress favoring the annexation of Texas, that he was "free from the influence of unjust prejudices and jealousies towards any part or section." Yet, he added, "I must confess that my feelings of attachment are most ardent towards that with which all my interests and associations are identified . . . The South is my home—my fatherland. There sleep the ashes of my sire and grandsires; there are my hopes and prospects; with her my fortunes are cast; her fate is my fate, and her destiny my destiny." The expression of such sentiments by responsible men like Hilliard and Stephens reflected the deep attachment to the South eclipsing any loyalty to the Union, which helped to crystallize the movement toward Southern nationalism.

The notion that the South was unique, that it had a case to present to the world, and that its future course would be decided in terms of its own peculiar interests became more widespread in the period between the outbreak of the Mexican War and the election of Abraham Lincoln. When the *Southern Quarterly Review* changed hands in 1847, the new editor promised faithfully that the magazine would seek to stimulate

Southern intellect and Southern learning. In addition, it would vigorously defend the peculiar forms of social life in the South for which the section was "arraigned before the bar of Christendom for alleged wrongdoing, oppression, and injustice."

This was in conformity with the growing sentiment for Southern intellectual independence. C. K. Marshall warned that if dissolution, "that sad catastrophe," should come, the South would not be as prepared as it should be to educate its own children. The real hope of the South lay in the development of a program for the education of Southern youth with Southern materials, he concluded. A New Orleans editor argued that the effect of intellectual independence on the political and mental health of the South could not fail to have a good effect:

Let us have independent thought. Push on the work. Stir up the apathetic. Wake up the dreamers. Shake off the incubus of mere party organization. Acknowledge fealty to nothing in party but principle . . . The fool is a slave to the past; the wise man understands the now, and equipping himself from the armory of the present, goes forth to meet the future. Push on the work.

In 1857 *De Bow's Review* felt that the South had achieved a measure of intellectual independence, an important step toward the realization of a Southern nation. "Twenty years ago," the editor said, "the South had no thought—no opinions of her own. Then she stood behind all christendom, admitted her social structure, her habits, her economy, and her industrial pursuits to be wrong, deplored them as a necessity, and begged pardon for their existence. Now she is about to lead the thought and direct the practices of christendom; for christendom sees and admits that she has acted a silly and suicidal art in abolishing African slavery—the South a wise and prudent one in retaining it." By that time Southerners could point with pride to various evidences of a growing sectional consciousness bordering on nationalism: academies, colleges, and universities were multiplying; literature was increasing; educational and commercial conventions were solidifying thought.

The relative absence of restlessness and lack of emigration seemed convincing proof to Southerners of the general prosperity of the section and the loyalty of its people. With a complacent air they pointed out that Northerners were to be found in every part of the hemisphere. While some regarded this continuous movement as evidence of an enterprizing character, their critical rivals preferred to think that such movement was "prompted by need and stimulated by the want of comfort at home."

Professional Southerners even objected to their fellows' visiting the North for short periods. In 1850, the reviewer of Charles Lanman's *Letters from the Allegheny Mountains* dubbed as "Soft-heads" those Southerners who saw nothing good in their home surroundings. He insisted that it was not necessary to visit the North during the summer, that such visitors were "born and wedded to a sort of provincial servility that finds nothing grateful but the foreign." Only a cholera epidemic in the North forced some Southerners to discover that they had delightful resorts in their own section, he concluded. The campaign to discourage Southerners from visiting in the North had met with some success. In 1858, a Southerner reported, with ill-concealed pleasure, that the springs and popular watering places of the Northern states were not as crowded with Southern families as they had been in previous years. Amid the South's own sublime mountain scenery, he said, "by the health-giving waters gushing out of the hillsides . . . they are gathering freshness and vigor, enjoying rustic pleasures and relaxation . . ."

If the South was to turn its back on the world, build its own nation, become intellectually self-sufficient, and satisfy itself in the exclusive enjoyment of its own resources, it was desirable to develop ways and manners peculiar to itself. That arch protagonist Fitzhugh summed it up when he insisted that Southerners should become national, "nay, provincial, and cease to be imitative cosmopolitans." William L. Yancey hoped that Southerners would cherish their peculiar ways. His aims, he declared, were to cast before the people of the South their great mass of wrongs, injuries, and insults. "One thing will catch our eye here and determine our hearts; another thing elsewhere; all united, may yet produce spirit enough to lead us forward, to call forth a Lexington, to fight a Bunker Hill, to drive the foe from the city of our rights."

The articulation of Southern aspirations by men like Fitzhugh and the leadership of men like Yancey contributed to the cohesion that bound the people of the South together in the struggle to achieve a measure of independence. Gradually, the geographic differences became unimportant, and the differences between the views represented by the moderate Jefferson Davis and the extremist Robert Toombs tended to disappear. The differences decreased in importance under the pressure of "outside interference," and the overriding conviction was that the dispute between the North and the South was infinitely greater than any internal conflicts that could be imagined. As one writer put it, "under the pressure of foreign insolence and outrage, the Southern states have been drawing closer the bonds of a common brotherhood, and developing in self-reliance, energy, courage, and all the resources of independent nationality. They are rapidly aspiring to the station which God designed that they should occupy and adorn."

That the North and South were drifting apart was a common view. Observers seemed to hope that, by discussion, they would make the rift more pronounced. In 1854, Henry C. Carey pointed out that differences between Northern and Southern thought were increasing daily, and "*must* eventually lead to separation." In May 1857, the leading article in *Russell's Magazine* was "Southern and Northern Civilization Contrasted," which said, "the philosophy of the North is a dead letter to us . . . We cannot live honestly in the Union, because we are perpetually aiming to square the maxims of an impracticable philosophy with the practice which nature and circumstances force upon us." In June 1860, the *Southern Literary Messenger* featured, "The Difference of Race Between Northern People and Southern People," which emphasized the differences in temperament, religion, mental capacities, and numerous other areas. A. Roane handled the problem for *De Bow's Review* in "The South, In the Union or Out of It." For him, one of the principal differences was the overwhelming military superiority of the South, which would ensure the achievement of political independence after separation.

It was important to give some attention to the military, for strength in arms is an important factor in any nationalist movement. This aspect could hardly be overlooked by a section whose people took such great pride in their military prowess. It is not without significance that the rise of military schools and the growing interest in the citizen soldiery coincided with the rise of Southern nationalism. If the interest in military affairs encouraged the movement for independence, the latter, in turn, stimulated the growth of the martial spirit.

The role of the military in the growth of nationalism was important, not only because of the promise of protection and defense that it gave but also because it provided the political symbolism required by the state. The psychological effect of this display of power and symbolism on the people was profound but difficult to measure. If the Southern confederacy was not to die a-borning, it had to understand this factor and to exploit it as it struggled to emerge.

The evidences of unity in the final decades before the Civil War are an impressive manifestation of the emergence of Southern nationalism. In 1848, during the controversy following the Mexican War, sixty-nine Southern members of Congress issued an address to their constituents urging "unity among ourselves." Within a few weeks, Florida served notice that she was ready to join other Southern states "for a defence of our rights, whether through a Southern convention or otherwise." In 1850, Mississippi warned that "the time has arrived when, if they hope to preserve their existence as equal members of the confederacy . . . they must prepare to act—to act with resolution, firmness and unity of purpose . . ."

Various organizations sprang into existence to facilitate the achievement of Southern unity and to assist in the defense of Southern rights. Among them were the numerous Southern Rights Associations, which appealed especially to the younger men. In 1851, a chapter was organized at the University of South Carolina, and its members urged other college students to do likewise. In May 1851, the Southern Rights Associations of South Carolina met at Charleston and talked freely of secession and of the state's right to establish adequate defense against the encroachments on its powers. Upon observing their inclination toward drastic action, Benjamin F. Perry said that the most prominent agitators were young men "panting for fame and military laurels."

In other states special conventions of Southern Rights Associations were held; their recommendations were similar to those of the South Carolina group. The commercial conventions, moreover, gave attention to the rights of the Southern states and, in doing so, contributed substantially to sectional unity. At the New Orleans Convention of 1855,

Captain Albert Pike of Arkansas offered a resolution condemning the North and calling for unified Southern action. He accused the non-slave-holding states of exhibiting an "utter want of fraternal spirit" and said that their conduct "not only fully warrants a union of the Southern states *within* the Constitution . . . but makes such a union an inexorable necessity . . ." The resolution then called on the Southern states to encourage those pursuits that would guarantee the self-sufficiency of the section when the break with the North came.

These disparate, independent efforts did not satisfy the vigorous champions of Southern rights. In 1848, William Yancey wrote a friend that the remedy for the South's plight was in "a diligent organization of her true men, for prompt resistance to the next aggression." No party, national or sectional, could save the South, he argued:

> But if we could do as our fathers did, organize Committees all over the cotton states . . . we shall fire the Southern heart—instruct the Southern mind—give courage to each other, and at the proper moment, by one organized concerted action, we can precipitate the cotton states into a revolution.

Ruffin had suggested the organization of a League of United Southerners to operate "by discussion, publication, and public speeches" on the public mind of the South. Taking the suggestion seriously, in the summer of 1858, Yancey organized the Montgomery League of United Southerners whose object was "to create a sound public opinion in the South on the subject of enforcing the rights of the South in the Union."

Within a year the League had many chapters. Its March 1859 statement called for "*firm, united, organized* defence . . . Organization is indispensable . . . it is only by associated and well-directed effort that great objects are accomplished. And we solemnly believe that it is only by a union of the true men of the South . . . that we can avert a fate, the most ignominious that ever befell a people." Southerners were urged to form associations, to put them into communication with each other, to hold conventions, and to do everything possible "to meet and repel the inroads of an insolent foe, who already vaunts his triumph, and claims your native South as a 'conquered province.' "

In an atmosphere of frenzied agitation such as that produced by the proclamations of the Southern Rights Associations, the commercial conventions, and the League of United Southerners, the people of the South were in no mood to meet the challenge of the North passively. Southerners almost invariably reacted to Northern criticism by hurling angry threats and defiances, as though these very acts strengthened the hand of the South. During the dispute over the admission of California in 1850, one Southern editor feared that war would follow California's admission as a free state, a war the South could not decline "without dishonor and disaster." He pointed out that the six states that opposed Clay's bill had half a million brave men with their own horses and rifles. "The liberties of these states were won by the sword—and if necessary by the sword they will be maintained."

John Brown symbolizes the wrath of the coming war in this detail from John Steuart Curry's mural in the Kansas State Capitol. (Architectural Services, State of Kansas)

14 Splintering Democracy

Many historians do not distinguish the causes of sectional conflict from those of secession, or from the causes of the Civil War itself. It is possible to do so, and some have tried. Within the broad theme of sectional conflict, therefore, the search for the war's specific causes has formed one of the most absorbing problems to engage the attention of the American historian. He has investigated, analyzed, interpreted, and reinterpreted the causes, and in the century since the war his interpretations have gone through several important stages.

Shortly after the fighting had ended, partisan writers of the North and South tried to justify the conduct of their own sides. Northerners advanced a clear, direct explanation. Slavery and disunion, they argued, were the fundamental causes. A ruthless slave power sought to rule or ruin, and Northerners had to fight to wipe out a national disgrace and to preserve the Union. This interpretation said, thus, that the war was morally justifiable and inevitable.

Southerners either dismissed or ignored the question of morality, blamed abolitionist fanaticism, or tried to explain the war's causes in less direct terms. Some argued that war came because the North had violated state sovereignty and because of conflicting interpretations of the Constitution. They attempted to show that the South fought to protect constitutional principles and hence was on the right side of the constitutional argument.

These partisan analyses were followed by what has been called the "nationalistic" interpretation. The writings of the Northern historian James Ford Rhodes are usually cited as examples of this interpretation. Rhodes said that "there was a single cause, slavery," but blamed neither North nor South for touching off the war. The nation, not the South, he insisted, was responsible for slavery. If all were at fault, then there was no way of fixing responsibility and no way in which the war could have been prevented. It was relatively easy to conclude, as a result, that the Civil War was unavoidable, and that no one could be blamed for it. "Everybody, in short," according to another upholder of this view, "was right; no one wrong."

The nationalistic interpretation was formless and intellectually unappealing to many historians, but the next interpretation to gain wide acceptance—based on the ideas of economic motivation, which became fashionable in the 1920s—offered greater appeal, in part at least because of its seemingly logical structure. Slavery and expansion, this interpretation pointed out, were economic as well as moral and legal problems. The true origins of the war, it stressed, lay in the clash of economic interests, in the efforts of Northern industrialists to seize power from the planter class that had long held it. There was no conflict of principle involved, the economic determinists held, no question of freedom locked in a battle against slavery, for the great moral and constitutional issues were raised merely to disguise economic self-interest in the sections. Idealism—the basis of the moral and legal arguments—was dismissed as a veneer hiding deeper causes. The travail of the nation thus became another of the great historical struggles for power between special interests—between business and agrarianism in this instance.

In the 1930s and '40s this analysis gave way to the "revisionist" interpretation, perhaps the most influential of all recent interpretations—one that made its way into the textbooks and the vocabulary of popular historical writing. One reason for its widespread influence, no doubt, was the fact that it was advanced or supported by some of the most respected scholars in the field of Civil War history. Essentially, the revisionists sought to revise the old view that slavery, a moral issue, was the fundamental cause and that the war was inevitable. In their view everyone was wrong and no one right.

The revisionists held that war was avoidable; that the crisis, in its various moral, economic, social, and political aspects, could have been resolved within the existing constitutional structure if it had not been for incompetent leadership—what one of the best-known revisionists, James G. Randall, called a "blundering generation." The revisionists have placed most of the blame, however, upon extremists, agitators, and fanatics—on Northern abolitionists and Southern fire-eaters, but more on the Northern reformers. They have rejected economic determinism and maintained that psychological factors and not the nature of the issues themselves brought on war.

To many historians, some of them not specialists in Civil War history, this was a disturbing interpretation. It could not be, they argued, that the bitter strife that led more than a half-million men to their graves was a useless struggle, that the freeing of humans from bondage was the result of blunders, that the sectional antagonism of several decades had no meaning, and that the cause of one side was as good as the other.

Beginning in the middle of the 1940s, these "moralist" historians launched a vigorous counterattack against the revisionists. This group went back to the earliest explanation for its basic interpretation. It insisted that morality, based on opposition to slavery, was the fundamental cause. In 1945 Arthur M. Schlesinger, Jr., summarized this position by saying that "the emotion which moved the North finally to battlefield and bloodshed was moral disgust with slavery." More than a decade later he insisted that by draining the moral content out of history the revisionists had "reduced the Civil War to an ignoble and wanton affair, an episode of passion and demagogy."

These new moralists also assailed the revisionists for blaming the war on fanatics, and for equating abolitionists with secessionists. "There is surely a difference," Oscar Handlin, Schlesinger's colleague at Harvard, wrote, "between being a fanatic for freedom and being a fanatic for slavery." The moralists thus rejected the idea that sectional crises, secession, and war were based on nothing more than unreasoning emotion. They also rejected the economic interpretation.

In effect the interpretations of the causes of the Civil War form a kind of cycle. They have traveled a circle from the early emphasis on slavery as the single cause to the moralist stress on degrading human bondage as the basic issue. The search for the essential cause will undoubtedly continue, for the modern historian accepts the obligation of explaining why a great democracy splintered. The student is also under an obligation. Since scholars cannot handle the matter of causation with either precision or substantial agreement, he should realize that the causes of war are complex and that often more than one interpretation can explain those causes. The selections that follow, while not offering a balance of revisionist and moralist interpretations, do show how complex historical interpretation is and how serious historians approach the problem of causation.

Charles A. Beard and Mary R. Beard

The Approach of the Irrepressible Conflict

Even though the ideas of the economic determinists were known before, it was not until Charles and Mary Beard, historians with a wide popular following, took the lead in interpreting the Civil War as an economic conflict that economic motivation gained an important place in the historiography of the war. The Beards were among the first to deny that slavery as a moral issue caused the war and to assert instead that the dominance of economic forces was responsible. In this selection they examine the attitudes prevalent before the war regarding the constitutionality of secession, and conclude that the conflict over the nature of the Union was based not on fundamental principles but on social interests. [Reprinted with permission of the publisher from The Rise of American Civilization *by Charles A. Beard and Mary R. Beard. Copyright 1927, 1930, 1933 by The Macmillan Company. Renewed 1955, 1958 by Mary Beard, 1963 by William Beard and Mary B. Vagts.]*

Had the economic systems of the North and South remained static or changed slowly without effecting immense dislocations in the social structure, the balance of power might have been maintained indefinitely by repeating the compensatory tactics of 1787, 1820. 1833, and 1850; keeping in this manner the inherent antagonisms within the bounds of diplomacy. But nothing was stable in the economy of the United States or in the moral sentiments associated with its diversities.

Within each section of the country, the necessities of the productive system were generating portentous results. The periphery of the industrial vortex of the Northeast was daily enlarging, agriculture in the Northwest was being steadily supplemented by manufacturing, and the area of virgin soil open to exploitation by planters was diminishing with rhythmic regularity—shifting with mechanical precision the weights which statesmen had to adjust in their efforts to maintain the equilibrium of peace. Within each of the three sections also occurred an increasing intensity of social concentration as railways, the telegraph, and the press made travel and communication cheap and almost instantaneous, facilitating the centripetal process that was drawing people of similar economic status and parallel opinions into coöperative activities. Finally the intellectual energies released by accumulating wealth and growing leisure—stimulated by the expansion of the reading public and the literary market—developed with deepened accuracy the word-patterns of the current social persuasions, contributing with galvanic effect to the consolidation of identical groupings. . . .

. . . The forces which produced the irrepressible conflict were very complex in nature and yet the momentous struggle has been so often reduced by historians to simple terms that a reëxamination of the traditional thesis has become one of the tasks of the modern age. On the part of northern writers it was long the fashion to declare that slavery was the cause of the conflict between the states. Such for example was the position taken by James Ford Rhodes and made the starting point of his monumental work.

Assuming for the moment that this assertion is correct in a general sense, it will be easily observed even on a superficial investigation that "slavery" was no simple, isolated phenomenon. In itself it was intricate and it had filaments through the whole body economic. It was a labor system, the basis of planting, and the foundation of the southern aristocracy. That artistocracy, in turn, owing to the nature of its economic operations, resorted to public policies that were opposed to capitalism, sought to dominate the federal government, and, with the help of free farmers also engaged in agriculture, did at last dominate it. In the course of that political conquest, all the plans of commerce and industry for federal protection and subvention were overborne. It took more than a finite eye to discern where slavery as an ethical question left off and economics—the struggle over the distribution of wealth—began.

On the other hand, the early historians of the southern school, chagrined by defeat and compelled to face the adverse judgment of brutal fact, made the "rights of states"—something nobler than economics or the enslavement of Negroes—the issue for which the Confederacy fought and bled. That too like slavery seems simple until subjected to a little scrutiny. What is a state? At bottom it is a majority or perhaps a mere plurality of persons engaged in the quest of something supposed to be beneficial, or at all events not injurious, to the pursuers. And what are rights? Abstract, intangible moral values having neither substance nor form? The party debates over the economic issues of the middle period answer with an emphatic negative. If the southern planters had been content to grant tariffs, bounties, subsidies, and preferences to northern commerce and industry, it is not probable that they would have been molested in their most imperious proclamations of sovereignty.

But their theories and their acts involved interests more ponderable than political rhetoric. They threatened the country with secession first in defying the tariff of abominations and when they did secede thirty years later it was in response to the victory of a tariff and homestead party that proposed nothing more dangerous to slavery itself than the mere exclusion of the institution from the territories. It took more than a finite eye to discern where their opposition to the economic system of Hamilton left off and their affection for the rights of states began. The modern reader tossed about in a contrariety of opinions can only take his bearings by examining a few indubitable realities.

With reference to the popular northern view of the conflict, there stands the stubborn fact that at no time during the long gathering of the storm did Garrison's abolition creed rise to the dignity of a first rate political issue in the North. Nobody but agitators, beneath the contempt of the towering statesmen of the age, ever dared to advocate it. No great political organization even gave it the most casual indorsement.

When the abolitionists launched the Liberty party in the campaign of 1844 to work for emancipation, as we have noted, the voters answered their plea for "the restoration of equality of political rights among men" in a manner that demonstrated the invincible opposition of the American people. Out of more than two and a half million ballots cast in the election, only sixty-five thousand were recorded in favor of the Liberty candidate. That was America's answer to the call for abolition; and the advocates of that policy never again ventured to appeal to the electorate by presenting candidates on such a radical platform.

No other party organized between that time and the clash of arms attempted to do more than demand the exclusion of slavery from the territories and not until the Democrats by repealing the Missouri Compromise threatened to extend slavery throughout the West did any party poll more than a handful of votes on that issue. It is true that Van Buren on a free-soil platform received nearly three hundred thousand votes in 1848 but that was evidently due to personal influence, because his successor on a similar ticket four years afterward dropped into an insignificant place.

Even the Republican party, in the campaign in 1856, coming hard on the act of defiance which swept away the Missouri compact, won little more than one-third the active voters to the cause of restricting the slavery area. When transformed after four more years into a homestead and high tariff party pledged merely to liberty in the territories, the Republicans polled a million votes fewer than the number cast for the opposing factions and rode into power on account of the divided ranks of the enemy. Such was the nation's reply to the anti-slavery agitation from the beginning of the disturbance until the cannon shot at Sumter opened a revolution.

Moreover not a single responsible statesman of the middle period committed himself to the doctrine of immediate and unconditional abolition to be achieved by independent political action. John Quincy Adams, ousted from the presidency by Jacksonian Democracy but returned to Washington as the Representative of a Massachusetts district in Congress, did declare that it was the duty of every free American to work directly for the abolition of slavery and with uncanny vision foresaw that the knot might be cut with the sword. But Adams was regarded by astute party managers as a foolish and embittered old man and his prophecy as a dangerous delusion.

Practical politicians who felt the iron hand of the planters at Washington—politicians who saw how deeply intertwined with the whole economic order the institution of slavery really was—could discover nothing tangible in immediate and unconditional abolition that appealed to reason or came within the range of common sense. Lincoln was emphatic in assuring the slaveholders that no Republican had ever been detected in any attempt to disturb them. "We must not interfere with the institution of slavery in the states where it exists," he urged, "because the Constitution forbids it and the general welfare does not require us to do so."

Since, therefore, the abolition of slavery never appeared in the platform of any great political party, since the only appeal ever made to the electorate on that issue was scornfully repulsed, since the spokesman of the Republicans emphatically declared that his party never intended to interfere with slavery in the states in any shape or form, it seems reasonable to assume that the institution of slavery was not the fundamental issue during the epoch preceding the bombardment of Fort Sumter.

Nor can it be truthfully said, as southern writers were fond of having it, that a tender and consistent regard for the rights of states and for a strict construction of the Constitution was the prime element in the dispute that long divided the country. As a matter of record, from the foundation of the republic, all factions were for high nationalism or low provincialism upon occasion according to their desires at the moment, according to turns in the balance of power. New England nullified federal law when her commerce was affected by the War of 1812 and came out stanchly for liberty and union, one and inseparable, now and forever, in 1833 when South Carolina attempted to nullify a tariff act. Not long afterward, the legislature of Massachusetts, dreading the overweening strength of the Southwest, protested warmly against the annexation of Texas and resolved that "such an act of admission would have no binding force whatever on the people of Massachusetts."

Equally willing to bend theory to practical considerations, the party of the slavocracy argued that the Constitution was to be strictly and narrowly construed whenever tariff and bank measures were up for debate; but no such piddling concept of the grand document was to be held when a bill providing for the prompt and efficient return of fugitive slaves was on the carpet. Less than twenty years after South Carolina prepared to resist by arms federal officers engaged in collecting customs duties, the champions of slavery and states' rights greeted with applause a fugitive slave law which flouted the precious limitations prescribed in the first ten Amendments to the Constitution—a law which provided for the use of all the powers of the national government to·assist masters in getting possession of their elusive property—which denied to the alleged slave, who might perchance be a freeman in spite of his color, the right to have a jury trial or even to testify in his own behalf. In other words, it was "constitutional" to employ the engines of the federal authority in catching slaves wherever they might be found in any northern community and to ignore utterly the elementary safeguards of liberty plainly and specifically imposed on Congress by language that admitted of no double interpretation.

On this very issue of personal liberty, historic positions on states' rights were again reversed. Following the example of South Carolina on the tariff, Wisconsin resisted the fugitive slave law as an invasion of her reserved rights—as a violation of the Constitution. Alarmed by this action, Chief Justice Taney answered the disobedient state in a ringing judicial decision announcing a high nationalism that would have delighted the heart of John Marshall, informing the recalcitrant Wisconsin that the Constitution and laws enacted under it were supreme; that the fugitive slave law was fully authorized by the Constitution; and that the Supreme Court was the final arbiter in all controversies over the respective powers of the states and the United States. "If such an arbiter had not been provided in our complicated system of government, internal tranquillity could not have been preserved and if such controversies were left to the arbitrament of physical force, our Government, State and National, would cease to be a government of laws, and revolution by force of arms would take the place of courts of justice and judicial decisions." No nullification here; no right of a state to judge for itself respecting infractions of the Constitution by the federal government; federal law is binding everywhere and the Supreme Court, a branch of the national government, is the final judge.

And in what language did Wisconsin reply? The legislature of the state, in a solemn resolution, declared that the decision of the Supreme Court of the United States in the case in question was in direct conflict with the Constitution. It vowed that the essential principles of the Kentucky doctrine of nullification were sound. Then it closed with the rebel fling: "that the several states . . . being sovereign and independent, have the unquestionable right to judge of its [the Constitution's] infraction and that a positive defiance by those sovereignties of all unauthorized acts done or attempted to be done under color of that instrument is the rightful remedy."

That was in 1859. Within two years, men who had voted for that resolution and cheered its adoption were marching off in martial array to vindicate on southern battlefields the supremacy of the Union and the sovereignty of the nation. By that fateful hour the southern politicians who had applauded Taney's declaration that the Supreme Court was the final arbiter in controversies between the states and the national government had come to the solemn conclusion that the states themselves were the arbiters. Such words and events being facts, there can be but one judgment in the court of history; namely, that major premises respecting the nature of the Constitution and deductions made logically from them with masterly eloquence were minor factors in the grand dispute as compared with the interests, desires, and passions that lay deep in the hearts and minds of the contestants.

Indeed, honorable men who held diametrically opposite views found warrant for each in the Constitution. All parties and all individuals, save the extreme abolitionists, protested in an unbroken chant their devotion to the national covenant and to the principles and memory of the inspired men who framed it. As the Bible was sometimes taken as a guide for theologians traveling in opposite directions, so the Constitution was the beacon that lighted the way of statesmen who differed utterly on the issues of the middle period. Again and again Calhoun declared that his one supreme object was to sustain the Constitution in its pristine purity of principle: "to turn back the government," as he said, "to where it commenced its operation in 1789 . . . to take a fresh start, a new departure, on the States Rights Republican tack, as was intended by the framers of the Constitution."

This was the eternal refrain of Calhoun's school. The bank, subsidies to shipping, protection for industries, the encouragement of business enterprise by public assistance were all departures from the Constitution and the intentions of its framers, all contrary to the fundamental compact of the land. This refrain reverberated through Democratic speeches in Congress, the platform of the party, and the official utterances of its statesmen. "The liberal principles embodied by Jefferson in the Declaration of Independence and sanctioned by the Constitution . . . have ever been cardinal principles in the Democratic faith"—such was the characteristic declaration of the elect in every platform after 1840. The Constitution warrants the peaceful secession of states by legal process—such was the answer of Jefferson Davis to those who charged him with raising the flag of revolution. Everything done by the Democratic party while in power was constitutional and finally, as a crowning act of grace, the Constitution gave approval to its own destruction and the dissolution of the Union.

It followed from this line of reasoning as night the day that the measures advanced by the Whigs and later by the Republicans were unconstitutional. In fact, Calhoun devoted the burden of a great speech in 1839 to showing how everything done by Hamilton and his school was a violation of the Constitution. Party manifestoes reiterated the pronouncements of party statesmen on this point. In their platform of 1840, the Democrats highly resolved that "the Constitution does not confer upon the general government the power . . . to carry on a general system of internal improvement . . . the Constitution does not confer authority upon the federal government, directly or indirectly, to assume the debts of the several states . . . Congress has no power to charter a United States Bank . . . Congress has no power, under the Constitution, to interfere with or control the domestic institutions of the several states." This declaration was repeated every four years substantially in the same form. After the Supreme Court announced in the Dred Scott case that Congress could not prohibit slavery in the territories, the Democratic party added that the doctrine "should be respected by all good citizens and enforced with promptness and fidelity by every branch of the general government."

In the best of all possible worlds everything substantial desired by the Democrats was authorized by the Constitution while everything substantial opposed by them was beyond the boundaries set by the venerable instrument. Hamilton, who helped to draft the Constitution, therefore, did not understand or interpret it correctly; whereas Jefferson, who was in Paris during its formation, was the infallible oracle on the intentions of its framers.

On the other hand, the Whigs and then the Republicans were equally prone to find protection under the ægis of the Constitution. Webster in his later years devoted long and eloquent speeches to showing that the Constitution contemplated a perpetual union and that nullification and secession were utterly proscribed by the principles of that instrument. He did not go as far as Calhoun. He did not declare free trade unconstitutional but he did find in the records of history evidence that "the main reason for the adoption of the Constitution" was to give "the general government the power to regulate commerce and trade." A protective tariff was therefore constitutional. Furthermore "it was no more the right than the duty" of Congress "but just discrimination to protect the labor of the American people." The provision of a uniform system of currency was also among "the chief objects" of the Fathers in framing the Constitution. A national bank was not imperatively commanded by the letter of the document but its spirit required Congress to stabilize and make sound the paper currency of the land. In fact Webster thought the Democrats themselves somewhat unconstitutional. "If by democracy," he said, "they mean a conscientious and stern adherence to the Constitution and the government, then I think they have very little claim to it."

In the endless and tangled debates on slavery, the orators of the age also paid the same sincere homage to the Constitution that they had paid when dealing with other economic matters. Southern statesmen on their side never wearied in pointing out the pro-slavery character of the covenant. That instrument, they said, recognized the slave trade by providing that the traffic should not be prohibited for twenty years and by leaving the issue open after that period had elapsed. It made slavery the basis of taxation and representation, "thus preferring and fostering it above all other property, by making it alone, of all property, an element of political power in the union, as well as a source of revenue to the federal government." The Constitution laid a binding obligation upon all states to return fugitive slaves to their masters upon claims made in due course. It guaranteed the states against domestic violence, not overlooking the possibilities of a servile revolt. "Power to abolish, circumscribe, or restrain slavery is withheld but power is granted and the duty is imposed on the federal government to protect and preserve it." The English language could hardly be more explicit.

All this was no accident; it was the outcome of design. "The framers of the Constitution were slave owners or the representatives of slave owners"; the Constitution was the result of a compromise between the North and the South in which slavery was specifically and zealously guarded and secured. Such were the canons of authenticity on the southern side.

This view of the Constitution contained so much sound historical truth that the opposition was forced to strain the imagination in its search for an answer. In an attempt to find lawful warrant for their creed in 1844, the abolitionists made a platform that became one of the prime curiosities in the annals of logic. They announced that the principles of the Declaration of Independence were embraced in the Constitution, that those principles proclaimed freedom, and that the provision of the Constitution relative to the return of fugitive slaves was itself null and void because forsooth common law holds any contract contrary to natural right and morality invalid.

Although the Republicans did not go that far in their defensive romancing, they also asserted, in their platform of 1860, that the principles of the Declaration of Independence were embodied in the Constitution and they claimed that neither Congress nor a state legislature could give legal existence to slavery in any territory of the United States. But there was one slip in this reasoning: the Supreme Court of the United States, with reference to the Dred Scott case, had read in the same oracle that Congress could not deprive any slave owner of his property in the territories and that the abolition of slavery there by Congress was null and void.

Nevertheless, the Republicans neatly evaded this condemnation of their doctrine, by calling it "a dangerous political heresy, at variance with the explicit provisions of that instrument itself, with contemporaneous exposition, and with legislative and judicial precedent." In short, the Republicans entered a dissenting opinion themselves; while it was hardly authentic constitutional law it made an effective appeal to voters—especially those fond of legal proprieties.

Even in their violent disagreement as to the nature of the Union, the contestants with equal fervor invoked the authority of the Constitution to show that secession was lawful or that the perpetuation of the Union was commanded as the case might be. With respect to this problem each party to the conflict had a theory which was finely and logically drawn from pertinent data and given the appearance of soundness by a process of skillful elision and emphasis.

Those who to-day look upon that dispute without rancor must admit that the secessionists had somewhat the better of the rhetorical side of the battle. Their scheme of historicity was simple. The thirteen colonies declared their independence as separate sovereignties; they were recognized by Great Britain in the treaty of peace as thirteen individual states; when they formed the Articles of Confederation they were careful to declare that "each state retains its sovereignty, freedom, and independence and every power, jurisdiction, and right, which is not by this Confederation expressly delegated to the United States in Congress assembled." These were undeniable facts. Then came the formation of the Constitution. The states elected delegates to the federal convention; the delegates revised the Articles of Confederation; the revision, known as the Constitution, was submitted for approval to the states and finally ratified by state conventions.

Q. E. D., ran the secessionist argument, the sovereign states that entered the compact can by lawful process withdraw from the Union just as sovereign nations may by their own act dissolve a treaty with other foreign powers.

There was, of course, some difficulty in discovering attributes of sovereignty in the new states carved out of the national domain by the surveyors' compass and chain and admitted to the Union under specific constitutional limitations—states that now outnumbered the original thirteen. But the slight hiatus in the argument, which arose from this incongruity, was bridged by the declaration that the subject territories when taken in under the roof were clothed with the sovereignty and independence of the original commonwealths.

The historical brief of those who maintained, on the other hand, that secession was illegal rested in part on an interpretation of the preamble of the Constitution, an interpretation advanced by Webster during his famous debate with Hayne. "It cannot be shown," he said, "that the Constitution is a compact between state governments. The Constitution itself, in its very front, refutes that idea; it declares that it is ordained and established by the people of the United States. . . . It even does not say that it is established by the people of the several states; but pronounces that it is established by the people of the United States in the aggregate." That is, the Constitution was not made by the states; it was made by a high collective sovereign towering above them—the people of the United States.

This fair argument, which seemed convincing on its face, was later demolished by reference to the journals of the Convention that drafted the Constitution. When the preamble was originally drawn, it ran: "We, the people of the states of New Hampshire, Massachusetts, &c., . . . do ordain and establish the following Constitution." But on second thought the framers realized that according to their own decree the new government was to be set up as soon as nine states had ratified the proposed instrument. It was obviously undesirable to enumerate the states of the Union in advance, for some of them might withhold their approval. Therefore the first draft was abandoned and the words "We the people of the United States" substituted. The facts of record accordingly exploded the whole thesis built on this sandy foundation.

This fallacy Lincoln was careful to avoid in his first inaugural address. Seeking a more secure historical basis for his faith, he pointed out that the Union was in fact older than the Constitution, older than the Declaration of Independence. It was formed, he said, by the Articles of Association framed in 1774 by the Continental Congress speaking in the name of revolutionary America. It was matured and continued in the Declaration of Independence which proclaimed "these United Colonies" to be free and independent states. It was sealed by the Articles of Confederation which pledged the thirteen commonwealths to a perpetual Union under that form of government; it was crowned by the Constitution designed to make the Union "more perfect."

Far more effective on the nationalist side was the argument derived through logical processes from the nature of the Constitution itself, by Webster, Lincoln, and the philosophers of their school. It ran in the following vein. The Constitution does not, by express provision or by implication, provide any method by which a state may withdraw from the Union; no such dissolution of the federation was contemplated by the men who drafted and ratified the covenant. The government established by it operates directly on the people, not on states; it is the government of the people, not of states. Moreover the Constitution proclaims to all the world that it and the laws and treaties made in pursuance of its terms, are the supreme law of the land and that the judges of the states are bound thereby, "anything in the constitution and laws of any state to the contrary notwithstanding." Finally, the Supreme Court of the United States is the ultimate arbiter in all controversies arising between the national government and the states. Chief Justice Marshall had proclaimed the doctrine in beating down the resistance of Virginia, Maryland, and Ohio to federal authority; Chief Justice Taney had proclaimed it in paralyzing the opposition of Wisconsin to the fugitive slave law. Such being the grand pledges and principles of the Constitution it followed, to use Lincoln's version, that no state could lawfully withdraw from the Union; secession was insurrectionary or revolutionary according to circumstances.

What now is the verdict of history on these verbal contests? Did the delegates at the Philadelphia convention of 1787 regard themselves as ambassadors of sovereign states entering into a mere treaty of alliance? Did they set down anywhere a pontifical judgment to the effect that any state might on its own motion withdraw from the Union after approving the Constitution? The answer to these questions is in the negative. Had they thought out a logical system of political theory such as Calhoun afterward announced with such precision? If so, they left no record of it to posterity.

What then was the Constitution? It was a plan of government designed to effect certain purposes, specific and general, framed by a small group of citizens, "informed by a conscious solidarity of interests," who, according to all available evidence, intended that government to be supreme over the states and enduring. They were not dominated by any logical scheme such as Calhoun evolved in defending his cause; they were engrossed in making, not breaking, a Union; they made no provision for, and if the testimony of their recorded debates be accepted as conclusive, did not contemplate the withdrawal of the states from the federation by any legal procedure. Surely it was not without significance that James Madison, the father of the Constitution, who lived tb see secession threatened in South Carolina, denounced in unmistakable terms the smooth and well-articulated word-pattern of Calhoun, condemning secession as utterly without support in the understandings of the men who made, ratified, and launched the Constitution.

But it may be said that the men of Philadelphia merely drafted the Constitution and that what counts in the premises is the opinions of the voters in the states, who through their delegates ratified the instrument. Did, then, the men who chose the delegates for the state ratifying conventions or the delegates themselves have clearly in mind a concept that made the great document in effect a mere treaty of alliance which could be legally denounced at will by any member? The records in the case give no affirmative answer. What most of them thought is a matter of pure conjecture. Were any of the states sovereign in fact at any time; that is, did any of them assume before the world the attributes and functions of a sovereign nation? Certainly not. Did the whole people in their collective capacity make the Constitution? To ask the question is to answer it; they did not.

When the modern student examines all the verbal disputes over the nature of the Union—the arguments employed by the parties which operated and opposed the federal government between the adoption of the Constitution and the opening of the Civil War—he can hardly do otherwise than conclude that the linguistic devices used first on one side and then on the other were not derived from inherently necessary concepts concerning the intimate essence of the federal system. The roots of the controversy lay elsewhere—in social groupings founded on differences in climate, soil, industries, and labor systems, in divergent social forces, rather than varying degrees of righteousness and wisdom, or what romantic historians call "the magnetism of great personalities."

The Disruption of American Democracy

Roy F. Nichols

In 1948, in a book that won the Pulitzer Prize, Roy F. Nichols published one of the last major expressions of the revisionist interpretation. Unlike other revisionists, such as Craven and Randall, he did not attempt to assess all the forces that caused the war. He confined himself to an institutional study, to an analysis of the sectional forces that broke up the Democratic party as a national political organization. Like other revisionists, he sees important clues in poverty-stricken statesmanship. In the following brief selection he explains how irresponsible politicians and hyperemotionalism brought on the Civil War. [Reprinted with permission of The Macmillan Company from The Disruption of American Democracy *by Roy F. Nichols. Copyright 1948 by The Macmillan Company.]*

The disruption of the American Democracy was complete in 1861. Secession had split the Republic, and the guns of civil war were thundering. The breakup of the Democratic party and the beginning of armed conflict were almost simultaneous; they were intimately related phenomena. The shattering of the party of Jackson was the bursting of a dike which unloosed an engulfing flood.

On the reasons for the Civil War there has been a vast amount of theorizing. Writers have been prone to select patterns—economic, cultural, political, racial, moral, and others—and to devise and emphasize theories in conformity with them. Long arguments as to whether the conflict was repressible or irrepressible, whether the war was inevitable or might have been avoided, have preoccupied historians. As they have unearthed more and more "causes," as they have introduced into the picture more and more elements, they have not altogether succeeded in answering the moot question: Why a civil war? Most of the principal "causes"—ideological differences, institutional differences, moral differences, cultural differences, sectional differences, physiographic differences —have existed in other times and places, without necessarily causing a war. Then why should they set the people of the United States to killing one another in 1861? This book, it is hoped, supplies some clues.

People fight under the stress of hyperemotionalism. When some compelling drive, whether it be ambition, fear, anger, or hunger, becomes supercharged, violence and bloodletting, thus far in human history, seem "inevitable." Now why was emotion in the United States in 1861 supercharged?

The basic reasons for this hyperemotionalism cannot be neatly formulated and weighted. Fundamentally the process was an illustration of what Machiavelli describes as the "confusion of a growing state." The population of the United States was rapidly multiplying, partly by natural increase and partly by foreign immigration, at the same time that it was arranging itself in rapidly changing patterns. Many Americans were creating new communities, others were crowding together into older urban centers. In old and new, change was continual, with a ceaseless moving out and coming in. The rate of growth, however, could not be uniform; for it was determined in large part by physiographical considerations and the Republic extended from the temperate into the semitropical zone. In the semitropical-to-temperate agricultural South, enterprise was less active, mobility less noticeable. In the northerly states, on the other hand, the variety of realized and potential wealth was greater, the stimulus from climate was sharper, the interest in projects of all sorts was more dynamic. There the vision of wealth and of the needs of the growing society continually inspired the creation of new and more powerful interests, under zealous and ambitious leaders.

So rapid and uneven a rate of social growth was bound to inflict upon Americans this "confusion of a growing state." Characteristic of it and dominant in it were pervasive, divisive, and cohesive attitudes which, as Whitman put it, were "significant of a grand upheaval of ideas and reconstruction of many things on new bases." The social confusion in itself was the great problem confronting statesmen and politicians. Turn where they would, they could not escape it; they themselves were confused by it, and yet they must wrestle with it.

The political system which was in the process of evolving reflected their predicament. They knew that they were operating a federal system, but they oversimplified their problem by believing that it was only a political federalism. They did not grasp the fact that it was a cultural federalism as well. Not only were they dealing with a political federation of states, they must understand this cultural federation of attitudes. The inability to understand contributed much to their failure to organize partisanship and to create political machinery which would be adequate to deal with the complexities of this cultural federation.

This lack of understanding was accompanied by a deep-seated enjoyment of political activity by Americans which proved dangerous. They gave themselves so many opportunities to gratify their desire for this sport. There were so many elections and such constant agitation. Contests were scheduled automatically by the calendar, at many different times and seasons; there were thirty-three independent state systems of election. Within each state the parties, despite their national names, were really independent, each a law unto itself, and none was subjected to much if any central direction; there were nearly eighty such party organizations. A great disruptive fact was the baneful influence of elections almost continuously in progress, of campaigns never over, and of political uproar endlessly arousing emotions. The system of the fathers might possibly bear within itself the seeds of its own destruction.

This constant agitation certainly furnishes one of the primary clues to why the war came. It raised to ever higher pitch the passion-rousing oratory of rivals. They egged one another on to make more and more exaggerated statements to a people pervasively romantic and protestant, isolated and confused. The men and women exhibiting these different attitudes were not isolated and separated by boundaries—they dwelt side by side, and the same person might be moved by more than one attitude at a time, or by different attitudes at different times. The emotional complex which was created by the variety of these attitudes, and the tension which their antagonisms bred, added confusion to that already provided by the chaotic electoral customs and poorly organized parties; the total precipitated a resort to arms. The baffling problem was not how to maintain a balance among states but how to preserve a balance among a number of emotional units or attitudes. It was this that proved beyond the political capacity of the time.

The Democratic party was not unaware of some of the danger. Its most enlightened leaders had sought to quiet such divisive attitudes as antislaveryism in the North and southernism in the South by encouraging such cohesive attitudes as nationalism. Unhappily they did not understand the pervasive romanticism and protestantism sufficiently to make use of them in strengthening the cohesive attitudes. No leader in the Democracy could find the formula. Buchanan, Douglas, the justices of the Supreme Court, Davis, Hammond, and Hunter all tried and failed. The Republicans, such as Lincoln and Seward, grasped the realities: a house so divided against itself could not stand; with such divisive attitudes in the ascendant and unchecked, the conflict was irrepressible.

Under the stimulus of constant agitation the leaders of the southern branch of the Democracy forbade the voters to elect a Republican President unless they wished him to preside over a shattered government. A number of voters sufficient to create a Republican majority in the Electoral College defied the prohibition. Then southerners, in a state of hyperemotion, moved by pride, self-interest, a sense of honor and fear, rushed to action; they were numerous enough and effective enough to force secession. They would flee the peril; in the spirit of 1776, they would organize a second American Revolution, this time against the tyranny not of a monarch but of "a mob." They would create a reformed confederacy free from corruption and centralization in which their social and economic institutions would be safe.

Also under the stimulus of constant agitation, the newly organized Republican administration decided to put down what it called the "Rebellion." Backed by an angered constituency including most northern Democrats, it determined to fight rather than permit the seceding states to break up a profitable partnership, a source of wealth and power, and an experiment in liberty and equality which Lincoln felt was the hope of the world. It undertook a "people's contest" to insure that "government of the people, by the people, for the people" should "not perish from the earth."

Thus war came when the American people for the first time refused to abide by a national election. The parties which had been promoting the cohesive attitudes had broken down, and their disorganization had permitted the new Republican organization to win through direct appeal to the divisive attitudes. The constant heat generated in the frequent elections brought an explosion. The social, economic, and cultural differences had been so used by the political operators as to produce secession and civil war.

War broke out because no means had been devised to curb the extravagant use of the divisive forces. Statesmanship seemed poverty-stricken. The work of the nationalists who sought to find a formula with which to overcome the divisive attitudes was vain. Too few even saw the need for the formula; they ran heedlessly down the path to disruption. The war was the product of the chaotic lack of system in ascertaining and directing the public will, a chaos exploited with little regard for the welfare of the general public by irresponsible and blind operators of local political machinery unchecked by any adequate central organization.

Finally, carrying the analysis even further, it may be postulated that the war came because of certain interests and activities characterized for convenience as the processes of human behavior, in which individual and general attitudes and emotional drives are constantly interacting—provoking and conditioning one another. At certain times and in certain circumstances, cooperative behavior predominates; but competitive behavior is seldom if ever absent, and when too vigorously aroused leads to a strife which ranges from argument to war. Indeed argument is itself a form of conflict short of war, more or less, and if pressed without checks and restraints easily passes over into war.

The American Democracy sought from 1850 to 1860 to keep in power by encouraging cooperative behavior. But, deeply affected by the shocks of the collisions occurring within the society in which it operated and of which it was a part, the party failed to overcome the divisive attitudes and was shattered. The disruption of the American Democracy eventuated in defeat, secession, and civil war.

David M. Potter

Why the Republicans Rejected Both Compromise and Secession

In March 1963, the Institute of American History at Stanford University sponsored a symposium on the crisis that brought on the Civil War. Distinguished scholars from various parts of the country debated the subject. David M. Potter, a former professor of history at Stanford and one of the most perceptive students of the Civil War and its causes, presented the following provocative interpretation. Note that Potter not only concerns himself with how Republicans rejected compromise and secession and faced war; he also considers matters of principle and the priorities that statesmen give to various alternatives in a time of crisis. Further, he analyzes the value of hindsight in trying to recreate and understand the crisis, concluding that the historian's supreme task is to see the past as did those who lived it. A critic, Professor Kenneth M. Stampp, argues instead that historians should look at the past "with all the wisdom and perspective that hindsight and experience can give us." Note how Potter applies his theory in this essay, especially as he analyzes how Abraham Lincoln and the Republicans were left with the choice for war and considers if they really had viable alternatives. [David M. Potter, "Why the Republicans Rejected Both Compromise and Secession," in George H. Knoles, ed., The Crisis of the Union, 1860–1861 *(Baton Rouge, Louisiana: Louisiana State University Press, 1965), pp. 90–106.]*

Historians have a habit of explaining the important decisions of the past in terms of principles. On this basis, it is easy to say that the Republicans rejected compromise because they were committed to the principle of antislavery and that they rejected secession because they were committed to the principle of union. But in the realities of the historical past, principles frequently come into conflict with other principles, and those who make decisions have to choose which principle shall take precedence. When principles thus conflict, as they frequently do, it is meaningless to show merely that a person or a group favors a given principle: the operative question is what priority they give to it. For instance, before the secession crisis arose, there were many Northerners who believed in both the principle of antislavery and the principle of union, but who differed in the priority which they would give to one or the other: William Lloyd Garrison gave the priority to antislavery and proclaimed that there should be "no union with slaveholders." Abraham Lincoln gave, or seemed to give, the priority to union and during the war wrote the famous letter to Horace Greeley in which he said: "My paramount object is to save the Union and it is not either to save or to destroy slavery. What I do about slavery and the colored race, I do because I believe it helps to save the Union, and what I forbear, I forbear because I do not believe it would help to save the Union." Lincoln was always precise to almost a unique degree in his statements, and it is interesting to note that he did not say that it was not his object to destroy slavery; what he said was that it was not his paramount object—he did not give it the highest priority.

To state this point in another way, if we made an analysis of the moderate Republicans and of the abolitionists solely in terms of their principles, we would hardly be able to distinguish between them, for both were committed to the principle of antislavery and to the principle of union. It was the diversity in the priorities which they gave to these two principles that made them distinctive from each other.

A recognition of the priorities, therefore, may in many cases serve a historian better than a recognition of principles. But while it is important to recognize which principle is, as Lincoln expressed it, paramount, it is no less important to take account of the fact that men do not like to sacrifice one principle for the sake of another and do not even like to recognize that a given situation may require a painful choice between principles. Thus, most Northern antislavery men wanted to solve the slavery question within the framework of union, rather than to reject the Union because it condoned slavery; correspondingly, most Northern Unionists wanted to save the Union while taking steps against slavery, rather than by closing their eyes to the slavery question.

In short, this means—and one could state it almost as an axiom—that men have a tendency to believe that their principles can be reconciled with one another, and that this belief is so strong that it inhibits their recognition of realistic alternatives in cases where the alternatives would involve a choice between cherished principles. This attitude has been clearly defined in the homely phrase that we all like to have our cake and eat it too.

Perhaps all this preliminary consideration of theory seems excessively abstract and you will feel that I ought to get on to the Republicans, the crisis, and the rejection of compromise and secession; but before I do, let me take one more step with my theory. If the participants in a historical situation tend to see the alternatives in that situation as less clear, less sharply focused than they really are, historians probably tend to see the alternatives as more clear, more evident, more sharply focused than they really were. We see the alternatives as clear because we have what we foolishly believe to be the advantage of hindsight—which is really a disadvantage in understanding how a situation seemed to the participants. We know, in short, that the Republicans did reject both compromise and secession (I will return to the details of this rejection later) and that the four-year conflict known as the Civil War eventuated. We therefore tend to think not only that conflict of some kind was the alternative to the acceptance of compromise or the acquiescence in secession, but actually that this particular war—with all its costs, its sacrifices, and its consequences—was the alternative. When men choose a course of action which had a given result, historians will tend to attribute to them not only the choice of the course, but even the choice of the result. Yet one needs only to state this tendency clearly in order to demonstrate the fallacy in it. Whatever choice anyone exercised in 1860–61, no one chose the American Civil War, because it lay behind the veil of the future; it did not exist as a choice.

Hindsight not only enables historians to define the alternatives in the deceptively clear terms of later events; it also gives them a deceptively clear criterion for evaluating the alternatives, which is in terms of later results. That is, we now know that the war did result in the preservation of the Union and in the abolition of chattel slavery. Accordingly, it is easy, with hindsight, to attribute to the participants not only a decision to accept the alternative of a war whose magnitude they could not know, but also to credit them with choosing results which they could not foresee. The war, as it developed, certainly might have ended in the quicker defeat of the Southern movement, in which case emancipation would apparently not have resulted; or it might have ended in the independence of the Southern Confederacy, in which case the Monday morning quarterbacks of the historical profession would have been in the position of saying that the rash choice of a violent and coercive course had destroyed the possibility of a harmonious, voluntary restoration of the Union—a restoration of the kind which William H. Seward was trying to bring about.

I suppose all this is only equivalent to saying that the supreme task of the historian, and the one of most superlative difficulty, is to see the past through the imperfect eyes of those who lived it and not with his own omniscient twenty-twenty vision. I am not suggesting that any of us can really do this, but only that it is what we must attempt.

What do we mean, specifically, by saying that the Republican party rejected compromise? Certain facts are reasonably familiar in this connection, and may be briefly recalled. In December, 1860, at the time when a number of secession conventions had been called in the Southern states but before any ordinances of secession had been adopted, various political leaders brought forward proposals to give assurances to the Southerners. The most prominent of these was the plan by Senator John J. Crittenden of Kentucky to place an amendment in the Constitution which would restore and extend the former Missouri Compromise line of 36° 30′, prohibiting slavery in Federal territory north of the line and sanctioning it south of the line. In a Senate committee, this proposal was defeated with five Republicans voting against it and none in favor of it, while the non-Republicans favored it six to two. On January 16, after four states had adopted ordinances of secession, an effort was made to get the Crittenden measure out of committee and on to the floor of the Senate. This effort was defeated by 25 votes against to 23 in favor. This was done on a strict party vote, all 25 of the votes to defeat being cast by Republicans. None of those in favor were Republicans. On March 2, after the secession of the lower South was complete, the Crittenden proposal was permitted to come to a vote. In the Senate, it was defeated 19 to 20. All 20 of the negative votes were Republican, not one of the affirmative votes was so. In the House, it was defeated 80 to 113. Not one of the 80 was a Republican, but 110 of the 113 were Republicans.

Another significant measure of the secession winter was a proposal to amend the Constitution to guarantee the institution of slavery in the states. This proposed amendment—ironically designated by the same number as the one which later freed the slaves—was actually adopted by Congress, in the House by a vote of 128 to 65, but with 44 Republicans in favor and 62 opposed; in the Senate by a vote of 24 to 12, but with 8 Republicans in favor and 12 opposed.

While opposing these measures, certain Republicans, including Charles Francis Adams, brought forward a bill to admit New Mexico to statehood without restrictions on slavery, and they regarded this as a compromise proposal. But this measure was tabled in the House, 115 to 71, with Republicans casting 76 votes to table and 26 to keep the bill alive. Thus, it can be said, without qualification, that between December and March, no piece of compromise legislation was ever supported by a majority of Republican votes, either in the Senate or the House, either in committee or on the floor. This, of course, does not mean either that they ought to have supported the measures in question, or that such measures would have satisfied the Southern states. It is my own belief that the balance between the secessionist and the non-secessionist forces was fairly close in all of the seceding states except South Carolina, and that the support of Congress for a compromise would have been enough to tip the balance. But the Crittenden measure would possibly have opened the way for Southern filibustering activities to enlarge the territorial area south of 36° 30′—at least this was apparently what Lincoln feared—and the "thirteenth" amendment would have saddled the country with slavery more or less permanently. When we say, then, that the Republicans rejected compromise, we should take care to mean no more than we say. They did, by their votes, cause the defeat of measures which would otherwise have been adopted by Congress, which were intended and generally regarded as compromise measures. In this sense, they rejected compromise.

When we say the Republican party rejected secession, the case is so clear that it hardly needs a recital of proof. It is true that at one stage of the crisis, many Republicans did talk about letting the slave states go. Horace Greeley wrote his famous, ambiguous, oft-quoted, and much misunderstood editorial saying that "if the cotton states shall become satisfied that they can do better out of the Union than in it, we insist on letting them go in peace." Later, when the situation at Fort Sumter had reached its highest tension, a number of Republicans, including Salmon P. Chase, Simon Cameron, Gideon Welles, and Caleb Smith, all in the cabinet, advised Lincoln to evacuate the fort rather than precipitate hostilities; but this hardly means that they would not have made the issue of union in some other way. Lincoln himself definitively rejected secession in his inaugural address when he declared: "No state upon its own mere motion, can lawfully get out of the Union. . . . I . . . consider that in view of the Constitution and the laws, the Union is unbroken; and to the extent of my ability I shall take care, as the Constitution itself expressly enjoins upon me, that the laws of the Union be faithfully executed in all the States." After the fall of Fort Sumter, he translated this affirmation into action by calling for 75,000 volunteers, and by preparing to use large-scale military measures to hold the South in the Union. The fact that no major figure in the North, either Republican or Democrat, ever proposed to acquiesce in the rending of the Union and that no proposal to do so was ever seriously advocated or voted upon in Congress, is evidence enough that the Republicans rejected secession even more decisively than they rejected compromise. They scarcely even felt the need to consider the question or to make an organized presentation of their reasons. It is true that some of them said that they would rather have disunion than compromise, but this was a way of saying how much they objected to compromise, and not how little they objected to separation. It was almost exactly equivalent to the expression, "Death rather than dishonor," which has never been understood to mean an acceptance of death, but rather an adamant rejection of dishonor.

Here, then, in briefest outline is the record of the Republican rejection of compromise and of secession. What we are concerned with, however, is not the mere fact of the rejection, but rather with its meaning. Why did the Republicans do this? What was their motivation? What did they think would follow from their decision? What did they believe the alternatives to be? Specifically, did this mean that the choice as they saw it was clear-cut, and that they conceived of themselves as opting in favor of war in a situation where they had a choice between secession and war? As I come to this question, I must revert to my comments earlier in this paper by pointing out again the tendency of historians to see the alternatives with preternatural clarity and the fallacy involved in attributing to the participants a capacity to define the alternatives in the same crystalline terms.

Peace or war? Compromise or conflict? Separation or coercion? These alternatives have such a plausible neatness, such a readiness in fitting the historian's pigeon holes, that it is vastly tempting to believe that they define the choices which people were actually making and not just the choices that we think they ought to have been making. We all know, today, that economists once fell into fallacies by postulating an economic man who behaved economically in the way economists thought he ought to behave. But even though we do know this, we are not as wary as we should be of the concept of what might be called an historical man who behaved historically in the way historians thought he ought to have behaved. It is very well for us, a hundred years later, to analyze the record and to say there were three alternatives, as distinct as the three sides of a triangle, namely compromise, voluntary separation, or war. Indeed this analysis may be correct. The error is not in our seeing it this way, but in our supposing that since we do see it in this way, the participants must have seen it in this way also.

Nothing can be more difficult—indeed impossible—than to reconstruct how a complex situation appeared to a varied lot of people, not one of whom saw or felt things in exactly the same way as any other one, a full century ago. But in the effort to approximate these realities as far as we can, it might be useful to begin by asking to what extent the choices of compromise, separation, or war had emerged as the possible alternatives in the minds of the citizens as they faced the crisis. Did they see the Crittenden proposals as embodying a possibility for compromise, and did a vote against these proposals mean an acceptance of the alternatives of war or separation? Did a policy which rejected both compromise and war indicate an acceptance of the alternative of voluntary separation? Did a decision to send food to Sumter and to keep the flag flying mean an acceptance of war? By hindsight, all of these indications appear plausible, and yet on close scrutiny, it may appear that not one of them is tenable in an unqualified way.

Did a vote against the Crittenden proposals indicate a rejection of the possibility of compromise? If Republicans voted against the Crittenden proposals, did this mean that they saw themselves as rejecting the principle of compromise and that they saw the possibilities thereby narrowed to a choice between voluntary separation or fierce, coercive war? If they repelled the idea of voluntary separation, did this imply that they were prepared to face a choice between political compromise or military coercion as the only means of saving the Union? If they urged the administration to send food to the besieged men in Sumter and to keep the flag flying there, did this mean that they had actually accepted the irrepressibility of the irrepressible conflict, and that they regarded peaceable alternatives as exhausted?

Although it makes the task of our analysis considerably more complex to say so, still it behooves us to face the music of confusion and to admit that not one of these acts was necessarily seen by the participants as narrowing the alternatives in the way which our after-the-fact analysis might indicate. To see the force of this reality, it is necessary to look at each of these contingencies in turn.

First, there is the case of those Republicans, including virtually all the Republican members in the Senate or the House, who refused to support the Crittenden proposals. To be sure, these men were accused of sacrificing the Union or of a callous indifference to the hazard of war; and to be sure, there were apparently some men like Zachariah Chandler who actually wanted war. (It was Chandler, you will recall, who said, "Without a little blood-letting, the Union will not be worth a rush.") But there were many who had grown to entertain sincere doubts as to whether the adoption of the Crittenden proposals, or the grant of any other concessions to the South, would actually bring permanent security to the Union. The danger to the Union lay, as they saw it, in the fact that powerful groups in many Southern states believed that any state had an unlimited right to withdraw from the Union and thus disrupt it. Southerners had fallen into the habit of asserting this right whenever they were much dissatisfied and declaring they would exercise it if their demands were not met. They had made such declarations between 1846 and 1850, when the Free-Soilers proposed to exclude slavery from the Mexican Cession. They had done so again in 1850 when they wanted a more stringent fugitive slave law. The threat of secession had been heard once more in 1856 when it appeared that the Republicans might elect a Free-Soiler to the presidency. One such occasion, concessions had been made: the Compromise of 1850 made it legally possible to take slaves to New Mexico; the Compromise also gave the slave owners a fugitive act that was too drastic for their own good; in 1856, timid Union-loving Whigs rallied to Buchanan and thus helped to avert the crisis that Frémont's election might have brought. Each such concession, of course, confirmed the Southern fire-eaters in their habit of demanding further concessions, and it strengthened their position with their constituents in the South by enabling them to come home at periodic intervals with new tribute that they had extorted from the Yankees. From the standpoint of a sincere Unionist, there was something self-defeating about getting the Union temporarily past a crisis by making concessions which strengthened the disunionist faction and perpetuated the tendency toward periodic crises. This was a point on which Republicans sometimes expressed themselves very emphatically. For instance, Schuyler Colfax, in 1859, wrote to his mother about conditions in Congress: "We are still just where we started six months ago," he said, "except that our Southern friends have dissolved the Union forty or fifty times since then." In the same vein, Carl Schurz ridiculed the threat of secession, while campaigning for Lincoln in 1860: "There had been two overt attempts at secession already," Schurz was reported as saying, "one the secession of the Southern students from the medical school at Philadelphia . . . the second upon the election of Speaker Pennington, when the South seceded from Congress, went out, took a drink, and then came back. The third attempt would be," he prophesied, "when Old Abe would be elected. They would then again secede and this time would take two drinks, but would·come back again." Schurz's analysis may have been good wit, but of course it was disastrously bad prophesy, and it had the fatal effect of preparing men systematically to misunderstand the signs of danger when these signs appeared. The first signs would be merely the first drink; confirmatory signs would be the second drink. James Buchanan recognized, as early as 1856, that men were beginning to underestimate the danger to the Union simply because it was chronic and they were too familiar with it: "We have so often cried wolf," he said, "that now, when the wolf is at the door it is difficult to make the people believe it." Abraham Lincoln provided a distinguished proof of Buchanan's point in August, 1860, when he wrote: "The people of the South have too much of good sense and good temper to attempt the ruin of the government rather than see it administered as it was administered by the men who made it. At least, so I hope and believe." As usual, Lincoln's statement was a gem of lucidity, even when it was unconsciously so. He hoped and believed. The wish was father to the thought.

The rejection of compromise, then, did not mean an acceptance of separation or war. On the contrary, to men who regarded the threat of secession as a form of political blackmail rather than a genuine indication of danger to the Union, it seemed that danger of disunion could be eliminated only by eliminating the disunionists, and this could never be accomplished by paying them off at regular intervals. The best hope of a peaceful union lay in a development of the strength of Southern Unionists, who would never gain the ascendancy so long as the secessionists could always get what they demanded. Viewed in this light, compromise might be detrimental to the cause of union; and rejection of compromise might be the best way to avoid the dangers of separation or of having to fight the disunionists.

If the rejection of compromise did not mean the acceptance of either separation or war, did the rejection of separation mean an acceptance of a choice between compromise and coercion as the remaining alternatives? This was the choice which history has seemed to indicate as the real option open to the country. But, though the unfolding of events may subsequently have demonstrated that these were the basic alternatives, one of the dominating facts about the Republicans in the winter of 1860–61 is that they rejected the idea of voluntary disunion and also rejected the idea of compromise, without any feeling that this narrowing of the spectrum would lead them to war. At this juncture, what may be called the illusion of the Southern Unionists played a vital part. Both Lincoln and Seward and many another Republican were convinced that secessionism was a superficial phenomenon. They believed that it did not represent the most fundamental impulses of the South, and that although the Southern Unionists had been silenced by the clamor of the secessionists a deep vein of Unionist feeling still survived in the South and could be rallied, once the Southern people realized that Lincoln was not an Illinois version of William Lloyd Garrison and that the secessionists had been misleading them. Lincoln and Seward became increasingly receptive to this view during the month before Lincoln's inauguration. Between December 20 and March 4, seven Southern states had held conventions, and each of these conventions had adopted an ordinance of secession. But on February 4, the secessionists were defeated in the election for the Virginia convention. Within four weeks thereafter, they were again defeated in Tennessee, where the people refused even to call a convention; in Arkansas, where the secessionist candidates for a state convention were defeated; in Missouri, where the people elected a convention so strongly anti-secessionist that it voted 89 to 1 against disunion; and in North Carolina, where anti-secessionist majorities were elected and it was voted that the convention should not meet.

It clearly looked as though the tide of secession had already turned. Certainly, at the time when Lincoln came to the presidency, the movement for a united South had failed. There were, altogether, fifteen slave states. Seven of these, from South Carolina, along the south Atlantic and Gulf coast to Texas, had seceded; but eight others, including Delaware, Kentucky, and Maryland, as well as the five that I have already named, were still in the Union and clearly intended to remain there. In these circumstances, the New York *Tribune* could speak of the Confederacy as a "heptarchy," and Seward could rejoice, as Henry Adams reported, that "this was only a temporary fever and now it has reached the climax and favorably passed it." The Southern Unionists were already asserting themselves, and faith in them was justified. Thus, on his way east from Springfield, Lincoln stated in a speech at Steubenville, Ohio, that "the devotion to the Constitution is equally great on both sides of the [Ohio] River." From this it seemed to follow that, as he also said on his trip, "there is no crisis but an artificial one. . . . Let it alone and it will go down of itself." Meanwhile, Seward had been saying, ever since December, that the Gulf states would try to secede, but that unless they received the backing of the border states, they would find their petty little combination untenable and would have to come back to the Union. Again we owe to Henry Adams the report that Seward said, "We shall keep the border states, and in three months or thereabouts, if we hold off, the Unionists and the disunionists will have their hands on each other's throats in the cotton states."

Today, our hindsight makes it difficult for us to understand this reliance upon Southern Unionism, since most of the unionism which existed was destroyed by the four years of war; and it was never what Seward and Lincoln believed it to be in any case. But it seemed quite real when five slave states in rapid succession decided against secession. Thus, in terms of our alternatives of compromise, separation, or war, it is interesting to see that an editorial in the New York *Tribune* on March 27, 1861, specifically examined the alternatives and specifically said that there were only three; but the three which it named were not the three we tend to perceive today. The fact that this editorial, rather closely resembling one in the New York *Times*, was probably inspired by the administration, gives it additional interest.

The *Tribune* began by saying that there were but three possible ways in which to meet the secession movement. One was "by prompt, resolute, unflinching resistance"—what I have been calling the alternative of war; the second was "by complete acquiescence in . . . secession"—that is, separation. But instead of naming compromise as the third alternative, the *Tribune* numbered as three "a Fabian policy, which concedes nothing, yet employs no force in support of resisted Federal authority, hoping to wear out the insurgent spirit and in due time re-establish the authority of the union in the revolted or seceded states by virtue of the returning sanity and loyalty of their own people." As the editorial continued, it explained the reasoning which lay behind the advocacy of this policy.

To war on the Seceders is to give to their yet vapory institutions the strong cement of blood—is to baptize their nationality in the mingled life-blood of friends and foes. But let them severely alone—allow them to wear out the military ardor of their adherents in fruitless drilling and marches, and to exhaust the patience of their fellow-citizens by the amount and frequency of their pecuniary exactions—and the fabric of their power will melt away like fog in the beams of a morning sun. Only give them rope, and they will speedily fulfill their destiny— the People, even of South Carolina, rejecting their sway as intolerable, and returning to the mild and paternal guardianship of the Union.

In behalf of this policy, it is urged that the Secessionists are a minority even in the seceded States; that they have grasped power by usurpation and retain it by terrorism; that they never dare submit the question of Union or Disunion fairly and squarely to the people, and always shun a popular vote when they can. In view of these facts, the Unionists of the South urge that the Government shall carry forebearance to the utmost, in the hope that the Nullifiers will soon be overwhelmed by the public sentiment of their own section, and driven with ignominy from power.

It seems reasonably clear that this editorial defined quite accurately the plan of action which Lincoln had announced in his inaugural. In that address, although affirming in general terms a claim of federal authority which, as the *Tribune* expressed it, conceded nothing, he made it quite clear that he would, as the *Tribune* also said, "employ no force" in the immediate situation. He specifically said he would not use force to deliver the mails—they would only be delivered unless repelled. He specifically said that federal marshals and judges would not be sent into areas where these functions had been vacated. "While the strict legal right may exist in the government to enforce the exercise of these offices, the attempt to do so would be so irritating that I deem it better to forego for the time the use of such offices." Without officials for enforcement, Lincoln's statement that he would uphold the law became purely a declaration of principle, with no operative or functional meaning. Finally, after having first written into his inaugural a statement that "all the power at my disposal will be used to reclaim the public property and places which have fallen," he struck this passage from the address as it was ultimately delivered. It was at about this time that Senator William P. Fessenden of Maine wrote that "Mr. Lincoln believed that gentleness and a conciliatory policy would prevent secession"—as if secession had not already occurred.

Finally, there is a question of whether even the decision to send supplies to Fort Sumter involved a clear acceptance of the alternative of war as well as a rejection of the alternatives of separation or compromise. Professor Stampp and Richard Current have both argued with considerable persuasiveness that Lincoln must have known that the Sumter expedition would bring war, since his informants from Charleston had warned him that such an expedition would be met with military force; and they have shown too that anyone with as much realism as Lincoln had in his makeup must have recognized that the chances for peace were slipping away. Yet I think their argument is more a reasoning from logic—that Lincoln must have seen the situation as we see it—and not an argument based primarily on expressions by Lincoln himself, showing that he had abandoned his belief in Southern Unionism and accepted the alternative of war. Indeed, insofar as we have expressions from him, he continued to believe in the strength of Southern Unionism. Even when he sent his war message to Congress on July 4, he said: "It may well be questioned whether there is today a majority of the legally qualified voters of any state, except perhaps South Carolina, in favor of disunion. There is much reason to believe that the Union men are in the majority in many, if not in every one of the so-called seceded states."

The crisis at Fort Sumter has possibly had almost too sharp a focus placed upon it by historians, and I do not want to dissect that question all over again in this paper. I will state briefly that, in my opinion, Lincoln pursued the most peaceful course that he believed was possible for him to pursue without openly abandoning the principle of union. That is, he assured the Confederates that food only would be sent into Fort Sumter, and nothing else would be done to strengthen the Union position unless the delivery of the food was resisted. While this may be construed, and has been construed, as a threat to make war if the food were not allowed, it can equally well be regarded as a promise that no reinforcement would be undertaken if the delivery of the food was permitted. Lincoln's critics, who accuse him of a covert policy to begin in an advantageous way a war which he now recognized to be inevitable, have never said what more peaceable course he could have followed that would have been consistent with his purpose to save the Union. Thus, they are in the anomalous position of saying that a man who followed the most peaceable course possible was still, somehow, a maker of war.

But as I suggested a moment ago, this focus upon Fort Sumter can perhaps be intensified too much. Even if Lincoln anticipated that there would be shooting at Sumter (and he must have known that there was a strong likelihood of it), what would this tell us about the choice of alternatives leading to the American Civil War? We may again revert to the somewhat arbitrary practice of answering this question in terms of the alternatives as they appear to us now. If the situation is viewed in this way, one would say we have three options neatly laid in a row: separation, compromise, war. If a man rejects any two of them, he is choosing the third; and since Lincoln and the Republicans rejected separation or compromise, this means that they exercised a choice for war. As a statement of the way in which the historical process narrows the field of possible action, this may be realistic; but for illumination of the behavior of men it seems to me very misleading. It assumes two things: first that choices are positive rather than negative; second that a choice of a course which leads to a particular result is in fact a choice of that result. Neither of these assumptions seems valid. What often happens is not that a given course is chosen because it is acceptable, but that given alternatives are rejected because they are regarded as totally unacceptable; thus one course remains which becomes the course followed, not because it was chosen, but because it was what was left.

When Lincoln ordered the Sumter expedition to sail, it was not because he wanted to do so; it was because he hated even worse the contingency of permitting the Sumter garrison to be starved into surrender. As he himself said, he had been committed to "the exhaustion of peaceful measures, before a resort to any stronger ones." But by mid-April at Sumter, the peaceful measures had all been exhausted; and the course that Lincoln followed was taken not because it was what he had chosen, but because it was what was left. That course resulted, as we now say, in the bombardment of Sumter, and the bombardment of Sumter was followed by four years of fighting which we call the Civil War. But even though the sending of the expedition led to events which in turn led on to war, it does not follow that the choice to send the expedition involved an acceptance of the alternative of war.

If deeds and consequences could be thus equated, our view of human nature would have to be more pessimistic than it is; and at the same time, our view of the future of humanity might perhaps be somewhat more optimistic. For it would imply that men have deliberately caused the succession of wars that have blotted the record of human history—certainly a harsh verdict to pronounce on humanity—and it would also imply that they have a certain measure of choice as to what forces of destruction they will release in the world—a proposition which would be comforting in the age of nuclear fission. But when we examine the situations of the past, how seldom does it appear that men defined the alternatives logically, chose the preferable alternative, and moved forward to the result that was intended? How often, on the other hand, do we find that they grope among the alternatives, avoiding whatever action is most positively or most immediately distasteful, and thus eliminate the alternatives until only one is left—at which point, as Lincoln said, it is necessary to have recourse to it since the other possibilities are exhausted or eliminated. In this sense, when the Republicans rejected both compromise and secession, thus narrowing the range of possibilities to include only the contingency of war, it was perhaps not because they really preferred the Civil War, with all its costs, to separation or to compromise, but because they could see the consequences of voting for compromise or the consequences of accepting separation more readily than they could see the consequences of following the rather indecisive course that ended in the bombardment of Fort Sumter. They did not know that it would end by leaving them with a war on their hands, any more than they knew it would cost the life of one soldier, either Rebel or Yank, for every six slaves who were freed and for every ten white Southerners who were held in the Union. When they rejected compromise, because they could not bear to make concessions to the fire-eaters, and rejected separation, because they could not bear to see the Union broken up, this does not mean that they accepted war or that they were able to bear the cost which this war would make them pay. It may really mean that they chose a course whose consequences they could not see in preference to courses whose consequences were easier to appraise.

Historians try to be rational beings and tend to write about history as if it were a rational process. Accordingly, they number the alternatives, and talk about choices and decisions, and equate decisions with what the decisions led to. But if we examine the record of modern wars, it would seem that the way people get into a war is seldom by choosing it; usually it is by choosing a course that leads to it—which is a different thing altogether. Although war seems terribly decisive, perhaps it requires less positive decision to get into wars than it does to avert them. For one can get into a war without in any way foreseeing it or imagining it, which is easy. But to avert war successfully, it has to be foreseen or imagined, which is quite difficult. If this is true, it means that the Republicans may have rejected separation and compromise not because they accepted the alternative, but precisely because they could not really visualize the alternative. When they took the steps that led them into a war, they did so not because they had decisively chosen the road to Appomattox or even the road to Manassas, in preference to the other paths; instead they did so precisely because they could not grasp the fearfully decisive consequences of the rather indecisive line of action which they followed in the months preceding their fateful rendezvous.

Charleston, South Carolina, 1865. Young blacks in the ruins, viewed through the porch of Circular Church. (Library of Congress)

15 Reconstruc-
tion

Anyone who attempts to arrive at a sound and unbiased interpretation of Reconstruction in the South in the twelve years following the War will encounter a challenge unlike those found in other areas of historical investigation. In this area, more than in others, judgments have been swayed by emotion and distorted by prejudice. This is true even of the constitutional and legal aspects of Reconstruction, where cold reason should prevail. A basic reason for the frequently emotional approach to the history and constitutional theory of Reconstruction is the question of race, or the place of the Negro in American society. This question stands defiantly at the core of interpretation.

Reconstruction was also affected by volcanic changes in economic life, but these changes, too, were affected by the new constitutional and social status of the Negro. Devastated by four years of fighting on its soil, the South had to rebuild its economy with free labor, and at the same time find a place for some four million newly freed Negroes who were guaranteed freedom by the Constitution. It was this racial and constitutional problem, entangled in political, economic, and social upheaval, that made Reconstruction more of a national than a sectional issue. It is also this problem that makes Reconstruction a major era in American history.

To the historians who first wrote on the subject at the beginning of the twentieth century, Reconstruction was an evil, an aberration, a temporary revolution that allowed power to slip into the hands of ignorant and inexperienced Negroes and unscrupulous carpetbaggers and scalawags. It was, in the words of a later historian, a "blackout of honest government." Briefly, this interpretation attempts to explain how and why vindictive radical Republicans in Congress trampled over the wishes of President Andrew Johnson, intimidated the Supreme Court, and with bayonets fastened corrupt Negro governments on the South. These governments were made up of incompetents and plunderers who debauched a proud but defenseless people. Such governments prevented a happy return of the Southern states to the Union and prohibited their quick, smooth readjustment to national life after the war. They drove the whites to desperate measures, usually into secret organizations such as the Knights of the White Camelia and the Ku Klux Klan, which retaliated against the Negro with terror and violence. Finally, this interpretation explains, proud Southerners were able to take advantage of Northern disgust with Radical reconstruction, "redeem" white supremacy, and restore unchallenged "home rule," which meant that the old aristocracy regained control of state and local government.

Out of this interpretation emerged the stereotypes that became an almost unquestioned part of the education of later generations of Americans. Textbooks in the schools of both North and South, movies—notably in such films as *The Birth of a Nation*—and novels helped spread the message. By definition, carpetbaggers and scalawags were wicked, Negroes ignorant and incompetent. The whole South, perhaps the nation as well, the stereotype held, was indebted to the "redeemers" of white supremacy.

Although there had been some protest earlier, it was not until the end of the 1930s that professional historians began to question this version of complex social upheaval, examine the forces of change in the South and in the whole nation with new intensity, and revise this traditional interpretation of Reconstruction. Obviously, the objectives and findings of revisionists vary, but as a whole their interpretations indicate that the so-called scalawags did not all come from the lower stratum of Southern society, and hence the struggle for power among the whites was not one between the unwashed on one side and the best elements of society on the other. The Negro, more than the white Southerner, was defenseless. Oftentimes the causes of difference between redeemers and radicals stemmed from rivalry over patronage and profit, and not from issues of race. Honesty and dishonesty, the revisionists say, were not the exclusive attributes of any one group, white or black. The state governments in the South under radical Reconstruction accomplished a number of praiseworthy social, political, and educational reforms. Furthermore, the revisionists insist, there is no convincing evidence to support the view that the radicals formed a unified and conspiratorial group committed to the overthrow of a venerated constitutional arrangement.

The revisionists have taken a more national view of Reconstruction than have the traditionalists. The traditionalists have seen a vindictive North trying to reshape a helpless South—an interpretation that is basically a continuation of the pre-war story of the clash of sections. Revisionists say this approach fails to explain the similarities in all sections, the evidence of corruption throughout the nation, and the hustling entrepreneurship found everywhere, even in the South. Recent scholarship shows that it was because of these forces, and not because of immediate congressional or presidential action, that reconstruction gradually came to an end.

It makes more sense, recent analysts have pointed out, to study Reconstruction by looking at the social conflict, the raw manipulation of power, the class friction, the racial antagonism, and the Negro trying to attain his constitutional guarantees. The traditional concepts of states' rights, agrarianism versus industrialism, and the clash of sections are by themselves inadequate tools.

Historians have yet to deal adequately with Reconstruction on a broad scale; they have yet to conquer the stereotypes still found in popular writing on this period. They might, as recent critics have insisted, recognize and analyze the racial motives in the Southerners who tried to thwart the radicals. They might find that in many instances the devotion to states' rights, to agrarian ideals, to constitutional principles, or to the Democratic party were rationalizations. It is difficult to escape the conclusion that Southerners refused to allow Negroes a share in government because they believed, probably sincerely, that institutions fashioned by the "superior" Anglo-Saxon race should not be contaminated by a race of "inferiors."

Reconstruction, in addition to being an episode in the decline of the power of the states, is part of the larger themes of suspended constitutional guarantees and race conflicts still critical today. Thus the story of Reconstruction, particularly in its constitutional and racial aspects, is modern. It belongs to the present as well as to the era following the Civil War. Although the South is the center of focus, Reconstruction is not just the story of Negro rule or merely a segment of Southern history. It was a national problem that the Constitution failed to meet on a national scale. We are still trying to cope with the effects of this failure.

The selections in this chapter are not meant to offer a balance of interpretations. Instead, they probe three important aspects of Reconstruction: its historical ideology, the political motives of Republicans, and the racial problems of the period. Each selection is an example of penetrating scholarship and of original critical thinking outside the traditional pattern.

Kenneth M. Stampp

The Tragic Legend of Reconstruction

Kenneth M. Stampp, a scholar at the University of California, Berkeley, who has written a political history of Reconstruction, feels that many of the popular notions about the era are distorted and untrue. As an intellectually committed revisionist who believes that those notions still influence social action, he considers it important to dispel them and to explain all aspects of the Reconstruction drama. In this selection from his history, he explains how revisionists differ from historians of the Dunning school, praises the radical reconstructionists, and discusses the mythology of Northern postwar brutality. Note what he has to say about the laws the radicals pushed through Congress and their subsequent significance in gaining federal protection for Negroes against legal and political discrimination. See also how he explains the radicals' later disillusionment with the progress of Reconstruction and how he feels racial bigotry has helped shape American attitudes toward Reconstruction. [From The Era of Reconstruction, 1865–1877, *by Kenneth M. Stampp. Copyright © 1965 by Kenneth M. Stampp. Reprinted by permission of Alfred A. Knopf, Inc.]*

In much serious history, as well as in a durable popular legend, two American epochs—the Civil War and the reconstruction that followed— bear an odd relationship to one another. The Civil War, though ad- mittedly a tragedy, is nevertheless often described as a glorious time of gallantry, noble self-sacrifice, and high idealism. Even historians who have considered the war "needless" and have condemned the politicians of the 1850's for blundering into it, once they passed the firing on Fort Sumter, have usually written with reverence about Civil War heroes—the martyred Lincoln, the Christlike Lee, the intrepid Stonewall Jackson, and many others in this galaxy of demigods.

Few, of course, are so innocent as not to know that the Civil War had its seamy side. One can hardly ignore the political opportunism, the graft and profiteering in the filling of war contracts, the military blundering and needless loss of lives, the horrors of army hospitals and prison camps, and the ugly depths as well as the nobility of human nature that the war exposed with a fine impartiality. These things cannot be ignored, but they can be, and frequently are, dismissed as something alien to the essence of the war years. What was real and fundamental was the idealism and the nobility of the two contending forces: the Yankees struggling to save the Union, dying to make men free; the Confederates fighting for great constitutional principles, defending their homes from invasion. Here, indeed, is one of the secrets of the spell the Civil War has cast: it involved high-minded Americans on both sides, and there was glory enough to go around. This, in fact, is the supreme synthesis of Civil War historiography and the great balm that has healed the nation's wounds: Yankees and Confederates alike fought bravely for what they believed to be just causes. There were few villains in the drama.

But when the historian reaches the year 1865, he must take leave of the war and turn to another epoch, reconstruction, when the task was, in Lincoln's words, "to bind up the nation's wounds" and "to do all which may achieve and cherish a just and lasting peace." How, until recently, reconstruction was portrayed in both history and legend, how sharply it was believed to contrast with the years of the Civil War, is evident in the terms that were used to identify it. Various historians have called this phase of American history "The Tragic Era," "The Dreadful Decade," "The Age of Hate," and "The Blackout of Honest Government." Recon- struction represented the ultimate shame of the American people—as one historian phrased it, "the nadir of national disgrace." It was the epoch that most Americans wanted to forget.

Claude Bowers, who divided his time between politics and history, has been the chief disseminator of the traditional picture of reconstruction, for his book, *The Tragic Era,* published in 1929, has attracted more readers than any other dealing with this period. For Bowers reconstruc- tion was a time of almost unrelieved sordidness in public and private life; whole regiments of villains march through his pages: the corrupt politicians who dominated the administration of Ulysses S. Grant; the crafty, scheming northern carpetbaggers who invaded the South after the war for political and economic plunder; the degraded and depraved southern scalawags who betrayed their own people and collaborated with the enemy; and the ignorant, barbarous, sensual Negroes who threatened to Africanize the South and destroy its Caucasian civilization.

Most of Bowers's key generalizations can be found in his preface. The years of reconstruction, he wrote, "were years of revolutionary turmoil, with the elemental passions predominant. . . . The prevailing note was one of tragedy. . . . Never have American public men in responsible positions, directing the destiny of the nation, been so brutal, hypocritical, and corrupt. The constitution was treated as a doormat on which politicians and army officers wiped their feet after wading in the muck. . . . The southern people literally were put to the torture . . . [by] rugged conspirators . . . [who] assumed the pose of philanthropists and patriots." The popularity of Bowers's book stems in part from the simplicity of his characters. None are etched in shades of gray; none are confronted with complex moral decisions. Like characters in a Victorian romance, the Republican leaders of the reconstruction era were evil through and through, and the helpless, innocent white men of the South were totally noble and pure.

If Bowers's prose is more vivid and his anger more intense, his general interpretation of reconstruction is only a slight exaggeration of a point of view shared by most serious American historians from the late nineteenth century until very recently. Writing in the 1890's, James Ford Rhodes, author of a multi-volumed history of the United States since the Compromise of 1850, branded the Republican scheme of reconstruction as "repressive" and "uncivilized," one that "pandered to the ignorant negroes, the knavish white natives and the vulturous adventurers who flock from the North." About the same time Professor John W. Burgess, of Columbia University, called reconstruction the "most soul-sickening spectacle that Americans had ever been called upon to behold." Early in the twentieth century Professor William A. Dunning, also of Columbia University, and a group of talented graduate students wrote a series of monographs that presented a crushing indictment of the Republican reconstruction program in the South—a series that made a deep and lasting impression on American historians. In the 1930's, Professor James G. Randall, of the University of Illinois, still writing in the spirit of the Dunningites, described the reconstruction era "as a time of party abuse, of corruption, of vindictive bigotry." "To use a modern phrase," wrote Randall, "government under Radical Republican rule in the South had become a kind of 'racket.'" As late as 1947, Professor E. Merton Coulter, of the University of Georgia, reminded critics of the traditional interpretation that no "amount of revision can write away the grievous mistakes made in this abnormal period of American history." Thus, from Rhodes and Burgess and Dunning to Randall and Coulter the central emphasis of most historical writing about reconstruction has been upon sordid motives and human depravity. Somehow, during the summer of 1865, the nobility and idealism of the war years had died.

A synopsis of the Dunning School's version of reconstruction would run something like this: Abraham Lincoln, while the Civil War was still in progress, turned his thoughts to the great problem of reconciliation; and, "with malice toward none and charity for all," this gentle and compassionate man devised a plan that would restore the South to the Union with minimum humiliation and maximum speed. But there had already emerged in Congress a faction of radical Republicans, sometimes called Jacobins or Vindictives, who sought to defeat Lincoln's generous program. Motivated by hatred of the South, by selfish political ambitions, and by crass economic interest, the radicals tried to make the process of reconstruction as humiliating, as difficult, and as prolonged as they possibly could. Until Lincoln's tragic death, they poured their scorn upon him—and then used his coffin as a political stump to arouse the passions of the northern electorate.

The second chapter of the Dunning version begins with Andrew Johnson's succession to the presidency. Johnson, the old Jacksonian Unionist from Tennessee, took advantage of the adjournment of Congress to put Lincoln's mild plan of reconstruction into operation, and it was a striking success. In the summer and fall of 1865, Southerners organized loyal state governments, showed a willingness to deal fairly with their former slaves, and in general accepted the outcome of the Civil War in good faith. In December, when Congress assembled, President Johnson reported that the process of reconstruction was nearly completed and that the old Union had been restored. But the radicals unfortunately had their own sinister purposes: they repudiated the governments Johnson had established in the South, refused to seat southern Senators and Representatives, and then directed their fury against the new President. After a year of bitter controversy and political stalemate, the radicals, resorting to shamefully demagogic tactics, won an overwhelming victory in the congressional elections of 1866.

Now, the third chapter and the final tragedy. Riding roughshod over presidential vetoes and federal courts, the radicals put the South under military occupation, gave the ballot to Negroes, and formed new southern state governments dominated by base and corrupt men, black and white. Not satisfied with reducing the South to political slavery and financial bankruptcy, the radicals even laid their obscene hands on the pure fabric of the federal Constitution. They impeached President Johnson and came within one vote of removing him from office, though they had no legal grounds for such action. Next, they elected Ulysses S. Grant President, and during his two administrations they indulged in such an orgy of corruption and so prostituted the civil service as to make Grantism an enduring symbol of political immorality.

The last chapter is the story of ultimate redemption. Decent southern white Democrats, their patience exhausted, organized to drive the Negroes, carpetbaggers, and scalawags from power, peacefully if possible, forcefully if necessary. One by one the southern states were redeemed, honesty and virtue triumphed, and the South's natural leaders returned to power. In the spring of 1877, the Tragic Era finally came to an end when President Hayes withdrew the federal troops from the South and restored home rule. But the legacy of radical reconstruction remained in the form of a solidly Democratic South and embittered relations between the races.

This point of view was rarely challenged until the 1930's, when a small group of revisionist historians began to give new life and a new direction to the study of reconstruction. The revisionists are a curious lot who sometimes quarrel with each other as much as they quarrel with the disciples of Dunning. At various times they have counted in their ranks Marxists of various degrees of orthodoxy, Negroes seeking historical vindication, skeptical white Southerners, and latter-day northern abolitionists. But among them are numerous scholars who have the wisdom to know that the history of an age is seldom simple and clear-cut, seldom without its tragic aspects, seldom without its redeeming virtues.

Few revisionists would claim that the Dunning interpretation of reconstruction is a pure fabrication. They recognize the shabby aspects of this era: the corruption was real, the failures obvious, the tragedy undeniable. Grant is not their idea of a model President, nor were the southern carpetbag governments worthy of their unqualified praise. They understand that the radical Republicans were not all selfless patriots, and that southern white men were not all Negro-hating rebels. In short, they have not turned history on its head, but rather, they recognize that much of what Dunning's disciples have said about reconstruction is true.

Revisionists, however, have discovered that the Dunningites overlooked a great deal, and they doubt that nobility and idealism suddenly died in 1865. They are neither surprised nor disillusioned to find that the Civil War, for all its nobility, revealed some of the ugliness of human nature as well. And they approach reconstruction with the confident expectation that here, too, every facet of human nature will be exposed. They are not satisfied with the two-dimensional characters that Dunning's disciples have painted.

What is perhaps most puzzling in the legend of reconstruction is the notion that the white people of the South were treated with unprecedented brutality, that their conquerors, in Bowers's colorful phrase, literally put them to the torture. How, in fact, *were* they treated after the failure of their rebellion against the authority of the federal government? The great mass of ordinary Southerners who voluntarily took up arms, or in other ways supported the Confederacy, were required simply to take an oath of allegiance to obtain pardon and to regain their right to vote and hold public office. But what of the Confederate leaders—the men who held high civil offices, often after resigning similar federal offices; the military leaders who had graduated from West Point and had resigned commissions in the United States Army to take commissions in the Confederate Army? Were there mass arrests, indictments for treason or conspiracy, trials and convictions, executions or imprisonments? Nothing of the sort. Officers of the Confederate Army were paroled and sent home with their men. After surrendering at Appomattox, General Lee bid farewell to his troops and rode home to live his remaining years undisturbed. Only one officer, a Captain Henry Wirtz, was arrested; and he was tried, convicted, and executed, not for treason or conspiracy, but for "war crimes." Wirtz's alleged offense, for which the evidence was rather flimsy, was the mistreatment of prisoners of war in the military prison at Andersonville, Georgia.

Of the Confederate civil officers, a handful were arrested at the close of the war, and there was talk for a time of trying a few for treason. But none, actually, was ever brought to trial, and all but Jefferson Davis were released within a few months. The former Confederate President was held in prison for nearly two years, but in 1867 he too was released. With a few exceptions, even the property of Confederate leaders was untouched, save, of course, for the emancipation of their slaves. Indeed, the only penalty imposed on most Confederate leaders was a temporary political disability provided in the Fourteenth Amendment. But in 1872 Congress pardoned all but a handful of Southerners; and soon former Confederate civil and military leaders were serving as state governors, as members of Congress, and even as Cabinet advisers of Presidents.

What, then, constituted the alleged brutality that white Southerners endured? First, the freeing of their slaves; second, the brief incarceration of a few Confederate leaders; third, a political disability imposed for a few years on most Confederate leaders; fourth, a relatively weak military occupation terminated in 1877; and, last, an attempt to extend the rights and privileges of citizenship to southern Negroes. Mistakes there were in the implementation of these measures—some of them serious—but brutality almost none. In fact, it can be said that rarely in history have the participants in an unsuccessful rebellion endured penalties as mild as those Congress imposed upon the people of the South, and particularly upon their leaders. After four years of bitter struggle costing hundreds of thousands of lives, the generosity of the federal government's terms was quite remarkable.

If northern brutality is a myth, the scandals of the Grant administration and the peculations of some of the southern reconstruction governments are sordid facts. Yet even here the Dunningites are guilty of distortion by exaggeration, by a lack of perspective, by superficial analysis, and by overemphasis. They make corruption a central theme of their narratives, but they overlook constructive accomplishments. They give insufficient attention to the men who transcended the greed of an age when, to be sure, self-serving politicians and irresponsible entrepreneurs were all too plentiful. Among these men were the humanitarians who organized Freedmen's Aid Societies to help four million southern Negroes make the difficult transition from slavery to freedom, and the missionaries and teachers who went into the South on slender budgets to build churches and schools for the freedmen. Under their auspices the Negroes first began to learn the responsibilities and obligations of freedom. Thus the training of Negroes for citizenship had its successful beginnings in the years of reconstruction.

In the nineteenth century most white Americans, North and South, had reservations about the Negro's potentialities—doubted that he had the innate intellectual capacity and moral fiber of the white man and assumed that after emancipation he would be relegated to an inferior caste. But some of the radical Republicans refused to believe that the Negroes were innately inferior and hoped passionately that they would confound their critics. The radicals then had little empirical evidence and no scientific evidence to support their belief—nothing, in fact, but faith. Their faith was derived mostly from their religion: all men, they said, are the sons of Adam and equal in the sight of God. And if Negroes are equal to white men in the sight of God, it is morally wrong for white men to withhold from Negroes the liberties and rights that white men enjoy. Here, surely, was a projection into the reconstruction era of the idealism of the abolitionist crusade and of the Civil War.

Radical idealism was in part responsible for two of the most momentous enactments of the reconstruction years: the Fourteenth Amendment to the federal Constitution which gave Negroes citizenship and promised them equal protection of the laws, and the Fifteenth Amendment which gave them the right to vote. The fact that these amendments could not have been adopted under any other circumstances, or at any other time, before or since, may suggest the crucial importance of the reconstruction era in American history. Indeed, without radical reconstruction, it would be impossible to this day for the federal government to protect Negroes from legal and political discrimination.

If all of this is true, or even part of it, why was the Dunning legend born, and why has it been so durable? Southerners, of course, have contributed much to the legend of reconstruction, but most Northerners have found the legend quite acceptable. Many of the historians who helped to create it were Northerners, among them James Ford Rhodes, William A. Dunning, Claude Bowers, and James G. Randall. Thus the legend cannot be explained simply in terms of a southern literary or historiographical conspiracy, satisfying as the legend has been to most white Southerners. What we need to know is why it also satisfies Northerners—how it became part of the intellectual baggage of so many northern historians. Why, in short, was there for so many years a kind of national, or inter-sectional, consensus that the Civil War was America's glory and reconstruction her disgrace?

The Civil War won its place in the hearts of the American people because, by the end of the nineteenth century, Northerners were willing to concede that Southerners had fought bravely for a cause that they believed to be just; whereas Southerners, with few exceptions, were willing to concede that the outcome of the war was probably best for all concerned. In an era of intense nationalism, both Northerners and Southerners agreed that the preservation of the federal Union was essential to the future power of the American people. Southerners could even say now that the abolition of slavery was one of the war's great blessings—not so much, they insisted, because slavery was an injustice to the Negroes but because it was a grievous burden upon the whites. By 1886, Henry W. Grady, the great Georgia editor and spokesman for a New South, could confess to a New York audience: "I am glad that the omniscient God held the balance of battle in His Almighty hand, and that human slavery was swept forever from American soil—the American Union saved from the wreck of war." Soon Union and Confederate veterans were holding joint reunions, exchanging anecdotes, and sharing their sentimental memories of those glorious war years. The Civil War thus took its position in the center of American folk mythology.

That the reconstruction era elicits neither pride nor sentimentality is due only in part to its moral delinquencies—remember, those of the Civil War years can be overlooked. It is also due to the white American's ambivalent attitude toward race and toward the steps that radical Republicans took to protect the Negroes. Southern white men accepted the Thirteenth Amendment to the Constitution, which abolished slavery, with a minimum of complaint, but they expected federal intervention to proceed no further than that. They assumed that the regulation of the freedmen would be left to the individual states; and clearly most of them intended to replace slavery with a caste system that would keep the Negroes perpetually subordinate to the whites. Negroes were to remain a dependent laboring class; they were to be governed by a separate code of laws; they were to play no active part in the South's political life; and they were to be segregated socially. When radical Republicans used federal power to interfere in these matters, the majority of southern white men formed a resistance movement to fight the radical-dominated state governments until they were overthrown, after which southern whites established a caste system in defiance of federal statutes and constitutional amendments. For many decades thereafter the federal government simply admitted defeat and acquiesced; but the South refused to forget or forgive those years of humiliation when Negroes came close to winning equality. In southern mythology, then, reconstruction was a horrid nightmare.

As for the majority of northern white men, it is hard to tell how deeply they were concerned about the welfare of the American Negro after the abolition of slavery. If one were to judge from the way they treated the small number of free Negroes who resided in the northern states, one might conclude that they were, at best, indifferent to the problem—and that a considerable number of them shared the racial attitudes of the South and preferred to keep Negroes in a subordinate caste. For a time after the Civil War the radical Republicans, who were always a minority group, persuaded the northern electorate that the ultimate purpose of southern white men was to rob the North of the fruits of victory and to re-establish slavery, and that federal intervention was therefore essential. In this manner radicals won approval of, or acquiescence in, their program to give civil rights and the ballot to southern Negroes. Popular support for the radical program waned rapidly, however, and by the middle of the 1870's it had all but vanished. In 1875 a Republican politician confessed that northern voters were tired of the "worn-out cry of 'southern outrages,'." and they wished that "the 'nigger' the 'everlasting nigger' were in—Africa." As Northerners ceased to worry about the possibility of another southern rebellion, they became increasingly receptive to criticism of radical reconstruction.

The eventual disintegration of the radical phalanx, those root-and-branch men who, for a time, seemed bent on engineering a sweeping reformation of southern society, was another important reason for the denigration of reconstruction in American historiography. To be sure, some of the radicals, especially those who had been abolitonists before the war, never lost faith in the Negro, and in the years after reconstruction they stood by him as he struggled to break the intellectual and psychological fetters he had brought with him out of slavery. Other radicals, however, lost interest in the cause—tired of reform and spent their declining years writing their memoirs. Still others retained their crusading zeal but became disenchanted with radical reconstruction and found other crusades more attractive: civil service reform, or tariff reform, or defense of the gold standard. In 1872 they repudiated Grant and joined the Liberal Republicans; in subsequent years they considered themselves to be political independents.

This latter group had been an important element in the original radical coalition. Most of them were respectable, middle-class people in comfortable economic circumstances, well educated and highly articulate, and acutely conscious of their obligation to perform disinterested public service. They had looked upon Senator Charles Sumner of Massachusetts as their political spokesman, and upon Edwin L. Godkin of the New York *Nation* as their editorial spokesman. Like most radicals they had believed that the Negro was what slavery had made him; give the Negro equal rights and he would be quickly transformed into an industrious and responsible citizen. With the radical reconstruction program fairly launched, they had looked forward to swift and dramatic results.

But reconstruction was not as orderly and the Negro's progress was not nearly as swift and dramatic as these reformers had seemed to expect. The first signs of doubt came soon after the radicals won control of reconstruction policy, when the *Nation* warned the Negroes that the government had already done all it could for them. They were now, said the *Nation,* "on the dusty and rugged highway of competition"; henceforth "the removal of white prejudice against the Negro depends almost entirely on the Negro himself." By 1870 this bellwether of the reformers viewed with alarm the disorders and irregularities in the states governed by Negroes and carpetbaggers; by 1871 it proclaimed: "The experiment has totally failed. . . . We owe it to human nature to say that worse governments have seldom been seen in a civilized country." And three years later, looking at South Carolina, the *Nation* pronounced the ultimate epithet: "This is . . . socialism." Among the former radicals associated with the *Nation* in these years of tragic disillusionment were three prewar abolitionists: Edmund Quincy of Massachusetts, James Miller McKim of Pennsylvania, and the Reverend O. B. Frothingham of New York.

Finally, in 1890, many years after the reconstruction governments had collapsed, the *Nation,* still accurately reflecting the state of mind of the disenchanted reformers, made a full confession of its past errors. "There is," said the *Nation,* "a rapidly growing sympathy at the North with Southern perplexity over the negro problem. . . . Even those who were not shocked by the carpet-bag experiment . . . are beginning to 'view with alarm' the political prospect created by the increase of the negro population, and by the continued inability of southern society to absorb or assimilate them in any sense, physical, social, or political. . . . The sudden admission to the suffrage of a million of the recently emancipated slaves belonging to the least civilized race in the world . . . was a great leap in the dark, the ultimate consequences of which no man now living can foresee. No nation has ever done this, or anything like this for the benefit of aliens of any race or creed. Who or what is . . . [the Negro] that we should put the interests of the 55,000,000 whites on this continent in peril for his sake?" Editor Godkin answered his own question in a letter to another one-time radical: "I do not see . . . how the negro is ever to be worked into a system of government for which you and I would have much respect."

Actually, neither the obvious shortcomings of reconstruction nor an objective view of the Negro's progress in the years after emancipation can wholly explain the disillusionment of so many former radicals. Rather, their changed attitude toward the Negro and the hostile historical interpretation of reconstruction that won their favor were in part the product of social trends that severely affected the old American middle classes with whom most of them were identified. These trends had their origin in the industrial revolution; they were evident in the early nineteenth century but were enormously accelerated after the Civil War. Their institutional symbols were the giant manufacturing and railroad corporations.

In the new age of industrial enterprise there seemed to be no place for the old families with their genteel culture and strong traditions of disinterested public service. On the one hand, they were overshadowed by new and powerful industrial capitalists whose economic strength brought with it vast political influence. Legislative bodies became arenas in which the political vassals of oil, steel, and railroad barons struggled for special favors, while the interests of the public—and the old middle classes liked to think of themselves as *the public*—counted for nothing. On the other hand, they were threatened by the immigrants who came to America to work in the mines and mills and on the railroads—Italians, Slavs, and Jews from Poland and Russia. The immigrants crowded into the tenements of eastern cities, responded to the friendly overtures of urban political bosses, and used their ballots to evict the old middle-class families from power. Here was a threat to the traditional America that these families had loved—and dominated—to that once vigorous American nationality that was Protestant, Anglo-Saxon, and pure. Henry James commented bitterly about the people he met on Boston Common during a stroll one Sunday afternoon: "No sound of English, in a single instance escaped their lips; the greater number spoke a rude form of Italian, the others some outland dialect unknown to me. . . . The types and faces bore them out; the people before me were gross aliens to a man, and they were in serene and triumphant possession."

Soon the new immigrant groups had become the victims of cruel racial stereotypes. Taken collectively it would appear that they were, among other things, innately inferior to the Anglo-Saxons in their intellectual and physical traits, dirty and immoral in their habits, inclined toward criminality, receptive to dangerous political beliefs, and shiftless and irresponsible.

In due time, those who repeated these stereotypes awoke to the realization that what they were saying was not really very original—that, as a matter of fact, these generalizations were *precisely* the ones that southern white men had been making about Negroes for years. And, in their extremity, the old middle classes of the North looked with new understanding upon the problems of the beleaguered white men of the South. Perhaps all along Southerners had understood the problem better than they. Here, then, was a crucial part of the intellectual climate in which the Dunning interpretation of reconstruction was written. It was written at a time when xenophobia had become almost a national disease, when the immigration restriction movement was getting into high gear, when numerous northern cities (among them Philadelphia and Chicago) were seriously considering the establishment of racially segregated schools, and when Negroes and immigrants were being lumped together in the category of unassimilable aliens.

Several other attitudes, prevalent in the late nineteenth century, encouraged an interpretation of reconstruction that condemned radical Republicans for meddling in southern race relations. The vogue of social Darwinism discouraged governmental intervention in behalf of Negroes as well as other underprivileged groups; it encouraged the belief that a solution to the race problem could only evolve slowly as the Negroes gradually improved themselves. A rising spirit of nationalism stimulated a desire for sectional reconciliation, and part of the price was a virtual abdication of federal responsibility for the protection of the Negro's civil and political rights. An outburst of imperialism manifested in the Spanish-American War and the annexation of the Hawaiian Islands, found one of its principal justifications in the notion that Anglo-Saxons were superior to other peoples, especially when it came to politics. In the words of Senator Albert J. Beveridge of Indiana: "God has not been preparing the English-speaking and Teutonic people for a thousand years for nothing but vain and idle self-admiration. No! He has made us the master organizers of the world to establish system where chaos reigns. . . . He has made us adepts in government that we may administer government among savages and senile peoples." What folly, then, to expect Italians and Slavs to behave like Anglo-Saxons—or to accept the sentimental doctrine that Negroes deserve to be given the same political rights as white men!

Finally, at this critical juncture, sociologists, anthropologists, and psychologists presented what they regarded as convincing evidence of innate racial traits—evidence indicating that Negroes were intellectually inferior to whites and had distinctive emotional characteristics. The social scientists thus supplied the racists of the late nineteenth and early twentieth centuries with something that ante-bellum pro-slavery writers had always lacked: a respectable scientific argument. When, in 1916, Madison Grant, an amateur cultural anthropologist, published *The Passing of the Great Race,* his racism was only a mild caricature of a point of view shared by numerous social scientists. Examining the history of the United States, Grant easily detected her tragic blunder:

Race consciousness . . . in the United States, down to and including the Mexican War, seems to have been very strongly developed among native Americans, and it still remains in full vigor today in the South, where the presence of a large negro population forces this question upon the daily attention of the whites. . . . In New England, however . . . there appeared early in the last century a wave of sentimentalism, which at that time took up the cause of the negro, and in so doing apparently destroyed, to a large extent, pride and consciousness of race in the North. The agitation over slavery was inimical to the Nordic race, because it thrust aside all national opposition to the intrusion of hordes of immigrants of inferior racial value, and prevented the fixing of a definite American type. . . . The native American by the middle of the nineteenth century was rapidly becoming a distinct type. . . . The Civil War, however, put a severe, perhaps fatal, check to the development and expansion of this splendid type, by destroying great numbers of the best breeding stock on both sides, and by breaking up the home ties of many more. If the war had not occurred these same men with their descendants would have populated the Western States instead of the racial nondescripts who are now flocking there.

In this social atmosphere, armed with the knowledge of race that the social scientists had given them, historians exposed the folly of radical reconstruction. At the turn of the century, James Ford Rhodes, that intimate friend of New England Brahmins, gave his verdict on Negro suffrage—one that the Dunningites would soon develop into the central assumption, the controlling generalization, of the reconstruction legend.

"No large policy in our country," concluded Rhodes, "has ever been so conspicuous a failure as that of forcing universal negro suffrage upon the South. . . . From the Republican policy came no real good to the negroes. Most of them developed no political capacity, and the few who raised themselves above the mass did not reach a high order of intelligence. . . . The negro's political activity is rarely of a nature to identify him with any movement on a high plane. . . . [He] has been politically a failure and he could not have been otherwise."

In the course of time the social scientists drastically revised their notions about race, and in recent years most of them have been striving to destroy the errors in whose creation their predecessors played so crucial a part. As ideas about race have changed, historians have become increasingly critical of the Dunning interpretation of reconstruction. These changes, together with a great deal of painstaking research, have produced the revisionist writing of the past generation. It is dangerous, of course, for a historian to label himself as a revisionist, for his ultimate and inevitable fate is one day to have his own revisions revised.

But that has never discouraged revisionists, and we may hope that it never will, especially those who have been rewriting the history of the reconstruction era. One need not be disturbed about the romantic nonsense that still fills the minds of many Americans about their Civil War. This folklore is essentially harmless. But the legend of reconstruction is another matter. It has had serious consequences, because it has exerted a powerful influence upon the political behavior of many white men, North and South.

C. Vann Woodward

The Political Legacy of Reconstruction

Here one of the foremost scholars of the South's history offers an interpretation of Reconstruction that has something in common with both traditional and revisionist schools and that differs with both. He does not find the Negro politicians in Reconstruction governments any more corrupt than whites, a view that varies from that of traditionalists. Recent revisionist studies also differ with Woodward's interpretation; they show the Northern business community as mixed in its support of radical Reconstruction. These studies also suggest that the motives of the radicals were much more idealistic than Woodward indicates. Still, Woodward's article presents a balanced analysis that is sound in its main theme and therefore has stood up well against the newer scholarship. Its clarity and graceful prose contribute to its persuasiveness. What, according to Wood-

*ward, are the important determinants for Negroes of the political legacy
of Reconstruction? Why does he believe that this First Reconstruction
was not a golden age for anyone?* [From C. Vann Woodward, "The Political Legacy of Reconstruction," Journal of Negro Education, *XXVI
(Winter 1957), 231–240.*]

Of all the revolutionary proposals that eventually received the sanction
of law in the upheaval of Reconstruction, the proposal to give the freedmen the unrestricted right to vote was the most difficult for contemporaries to accept, in the North as well as in the South. Emancipation itself
had been repeatedly disavowed as a war aim until the war was well under
way. Civil rights for freedmen was another cautiously advanced after-
thought. Enfranchisement came in belatedly a poor third, surreptitiously,
almost disingenuously advanced by its proponents, grudgingly accepted
by a North that moved under duress and the argument of necessity, and
greeted with gloomy forebodings of failure, if not disaster. These attitudes were widespread, and they were not confined to copperheads,
doughfaces, and mossback conservatives.

Representative of the skeptical and negative attitude of the time is the
following pronouncement: "When was it ever known that liberation
from bondage was accompanied by a recognition of political equality?
Chattels personal may be instantly translated from the auction-block into
freemen; but when were they ever taken at the same time to the ballot-
box, and invested with all political rights and immunities? According to
the laws of development and progress, it is not practicable. . . . Nor, if
the freed blacks were admitted to the polls by Presidential fiat, do I see
any permanent advantage likely to be secured by it; for, submitted to as a
necessity at the outset, as soon as the state was organized and left to
manage its own affairs, the white population, with their superior intelligence, wealth, and power, would unquestionably alter the franchise in
accordance with their prejudices, and exclude those thus summarily
brought to the polls. Coercion would gain nothing."

The author of these sentiments, written in 1864, was none other than
William Lloyd Garrison of the *Liberator,* the man who swore to be
"harsh as truth and uncompromising as death." Nor was he alone among
the abolitionists in these sentiments, for the radicals themselves were
divided on the matter of Negro suffrage. Even Senator Charles Sumner,
one of the earlier and most powerful advocates of placing the ballot in
the freedman's hands, was prepared in a Senate speech on February 5,
1866, to admit that educational qualifications for the suffrage would be
advisable. At that time, of course, educational restrictions, even a literacy
test fairly administered, would have limited the franchise to a small
minority of the freedmen. Horace Greeley of the New York *Tribune,* an
old friend of the slave, would "limit the voting privilege to the competent and deserving" and suggested such qualifications as ability to read
and write, payment of taxes, or establishment in a trade. General O. O.

Howard, head of the Freedmen's Bureau, hoped that the franchise would be limited "at least by an educational qualification." This far, of course, President Lincoln and President Johnson were prepared to go, and both in fact did unsuccessfully recommend to Southern states such franchise laws.

To go further than that in 1866 or even later was to incur grave political risks with Northern opinion, risks that even the most radical of Republicans were reluctant to assume. Only five states in the North, and those with a negligible percentage of colored population, provided for Negro franchise. In 1865 Wisconsin, Minnesota, and Connecticut all defeated proposals to allow the Negroes to vote, and the Nebraska constitution of 1866 confined suffrage to whites. New Jersey and Ohio in 1867 and Michigan and Pennsylvania in 1868 turned down proposals for Negro suffrage. Dr. W. E. B. Du Bois, who contends that in 1861 "probably not one white American in a hundred believed that Negroes could become an integral part of American democracy," concludes that even by 1868 "the country was not ready for Negro suffrage."

Yet Negro suffrage did come. It came very quickly. In fact by that time it had already come in the South. How it came and why are important determinants in the political legacy left the American Negro by Reconstruction.

Thaddeus Stevens, foremost champion of the freedmen, master of the Republican House majority, and leader of Radical Reconstruction, was advocating some extremely radical measures. He was quite ready to disfranchise Southern whites in great numbers and to confiscate great quantities of their land. "It is intended to revolutionize their feelings and principles," he declared. "This may startle feeble minds and shake weak nerves. So do all great improvements." To those who objected to humiliating the defeated foe he replied: "Why not? Do not they deserve humiliation? If they do not, who does? What criminal, what felon deserves it more?"

But for all his radicalism, Thaddeus Stevens was not yet prepared to enfranchise the Negro freedmen. For one thing, of course, he knew that public opinion would not support it and that the majority of his own party was against it. But apart from political reasons he had other doubts about the wisdom of the measure, some of them similar to those expressed by William Lloyd Garrison, Horace Greeley, General O. O. Howard, and for that matter—President Andrew Johnson. On this vital matter Stevens, contrary to his reputation, can be classified in this phase as a moderate or conservative. For one thing he doubted that the freedmen were prepared for intelligent voting. The conditions and laws of slavery, he said on December 18, 1865, "have prevented them from acquiring an education, understanding the commonest laws of contract, or of managing the ordinary business of life." The following month, on January 31, 1866, while urging a constitutional amendment basing representation in the House on the number of qualified voters in a state, Stevens actually expressed the hope that the Southern states would not immediately grant the freedmen suffrage and thereby increase Southern voting power in Congress. He assumed that the Negroes would fall under the political influence of their former masters. "I do not therefore want to grant them this privilege for some years. . . . four or five years hence, when the freedmen shall have been made free indeed, when they shall have become intelligent enough, and there are sufficient loyal men there to control the representation from those States." Negro voting would be safe enough. In fact at this time Stevens adopted a states rights position: "I hold that the States have the right, and always have had it, to fix the elective franchise within their own States."

Stevens' solution to the freedmen's suffrage problem was to force upon the Southern states the dilemma posed by the proposed Fourteenth Amendment. According to these terms the states would have to choose between excluding the freedmen from the ballot box and thus reduce their number of representatives to about forty-six, or on the other hand enfranchise them and thereby increase their representatives to about eighty-three, but run the grave risk of losing control to the Republican party. To ensure the adoption of the amendment, Stevens proposed that it be submitted only to the non-Southern states and declared adopted when approved by three-fourths of these states, exclusive of the South. This solution was rejected by his party, and the Southern states voted the amendment down when it was submitted to them along with the other states.

Still hesitant, still reluctant to accept immediate freedman's suffrage and impose it by force, Stevens temporized with still another proposal. This was contained in a bill he introduced on December 13, 1866 for the reconstruction of North Carolina. In this he proposed to restrict the ballot to those of both races who could read and write or who owned real estate assessed at a value of a hundred dollars or more. Loyal men who had voted before (white) were not to be disfranchised, but certain classes of Confederates were. There was at times, as Ralph Korngold has suggested, something of Lincoln's hesitant approach to emancipation about Stevens' approach to enfranchisement. Hesitation ceased, however, early in 1867, almost two years after the war. He now went the whole way of military rule, disfranchisement of large numbers of Southern whites, and immediate and universal Negro suffrage full scale Radical Reconstruction.

About the reasons for Thaddeus Stevens' conversion there will always be debate. A few facts stand out, however, with inescapable clarity. President Johnson's plan of reconstruction would have increased the Southern delegation in the House of Representatives by some thirteen members, since all the freedmen instead of three-fifths would be counted in apportionment. Without Negro ballots it was probable that all the additional seats plus all the rest of the seats of the eleven states, would be filled by Democrats and not Republicans. These same states would not only swell the opposition votes in Congress but the electoral votes in presidential contests. About thirty-seven of the Southern seats in the House would be accounted for by Negro population, who had no votes, and likely filled by sworn opponents of the party that took credit for Negro freedom. To ask an overwhelmingly Republican Congress—radical or conservative— to approve such a plan was to ask water to run uphill. Conservative Republicans were no more ready to commit political hara kiri than Radical Republicans.

"Another good reason is," said Stevens in support of his plan, "it would insure the ascendency of the Union [Republican] party. Do you avow the party purpose? exclaims some horror stricken demagogue. I do. For I believe, on my conscience, that on the continued ascendency of that party depends the safety of this great nation. If impartial [Negro] suffrage is excluded in the rebel States then every one of them is sure to send a solid rebel [Democratic] representation to Congress, and cast a solid rebel electoral vote. They, with their kindred Copperheads [Democrats] of the North, would always elect the President and control Congress."

Stevens' follower, Roscoe Conkling of New York was quite as blunt and more specific. "Shall one hundred and twenty-seven thousand white people in New York cast but one vote in this House and have but one voice here, while the same number of white people in Mississippi have three votes and three voices? Shall the death of slavery add two fifths to the entire power which slavery had when slavery was living? Shall one white man have as much share in the Government as three other white men merely because he lives where blacks out-number whites two to one? . . . No sir; not if I can help it."

In addition to "the party purpose" so frankly avowed by Stevens there was another purpose which was not frankly avowed. It was more often disavowed, concealed, deprecated. The power and significance of that purpose, however, have been established beyond question by the researches of Howard K. Beale in *The Critical Year*. This was the collective purpose of the business community which saw in the return of a disaffected and Democratic South a frightening menace to the economic order that had been established during the absence of the seceding states from the Union. On every delicate and disturbing economic issue of the day—currency, taxation, the National Bank, the national debt, the government bonds and their funding, the railroads and their financing, the regulation of corporations, government grants and subsidies to business, the protective tariff legislation—on one and all the business community recognized in the unreconstructed South an antagonist of long standing. In combination with traditional allies in West and North the South could upset the new order. Normally very conservative in politics, the Northern business community under these unusual circumstances put aside conservative habits and threw its support to radical Reconstruction.

Neither the party purpose, the business purpose, nor the two combined constituted a reputable justification with which to persuade the public to support a radical and unpopular program. But there was a purpose that *was* both reputable and persuasive—the philanthropic purpose, the argument that the freedmen needed the ballot to defend and protect their dearly bought freedom, their newly won civil rights, their welfare and livelihood. Of their philanthropic argument the Radicals could make a persuasive and cogent case. And it is undoubtedly true that some of the Radicals were motivated almost entirely by their idealism and their genuine concern for the rights and welfare of the freedmen. What is doubtful is that these were the effective or primary motives, or that they took priority over the pragmatic and materialistic motives of party advantage and sectional economic interests. It is clear at any rate that until the latter were aroused and marshalled the former made little progress. On the whole the skepticism of Secretary Gideon Welles would seem to be justified. "It is evident," he wrote in his diary, "that intense partisanship instead of philanthropy is the root of the movement."

The point of this is the incubus with which the Negro was burdened before he was ever awakened into political life. The operative and effective motives of his political genesis were extraneous to his own interests and calculated to serve other ends. If there ever came a time when those ends—party advantage and sectional business interests—were better served in some other way, even in a way destructive of the basic political rights of the race, then the political prospects of the Negro would darken. Another incubus was the strongly partisan identifications of his political origins. The major national party of opposition took no part in those origins, regarded them as wholly inimical to its interests, and consequently felt no real commitment to the movement nor to the preservation of its fruits. If there came a time when that party was in the ascendency, even locally, the political future of the Negro again would darken. To these evil portents should be added the strong resistance to Negro suffrage in the Northern states, the obvious reluctance and hesitance of Radical leaders to commit the party to that course, the grudging acquiescence of the North in the coercive use of it in the South, and the continued denial of suffrage to the Negro in the North. After enfranchisement was in full effect in the Southern states, the Republican party felt obliged to give specific promise to the people of the North that they would be left free to keep the Negro disfranchised in their own states. In the Republican platform of 1868 appeared the following: "The guaranty by Congress of equal suffrage to all loyal men at the South was demanded by every consideration of public safety, of gratitude, and of justice, and must be maintained; while the question of suffrage in all loyal [non-Southern] States properly belongs to the people of those States." Only after the presidential election was over and General Grant had won did the party dare bring forward the Fifteenth Amendment denying the right of any state to disfranchise the Negro, and not until 1870 was its ratification completed.

In the meantime a political revolution was under way in the Southern states, a revolution that is the first important chapter in the history of the Negro voter in America. The initial step under military government, after the destruction of the old civil governments, was the creation of the new electorate in 1867 and 1868. In all more than 703,000 Negroes and some 627,000 whites were registered as qualified voters, with the processes of disfranchisement and enfranchisement going on simultaneously. The number of whites disfranchised is unknown and unknowable, but it is evident from a comparison of population and registration figures that the number was rather large in some states. While only two states had a colored majority of population, five states were given a colored majority of registered voters. The male population of voting age in Louisiana in 1860 was 94,711 whites and 92,502 Negroes, but only 45,218 whites were registered as against 84,436 Negroes. Alabama's voting age population in 1860 was 113,871 whites and 92,404 Negroes, but only 61,295 whites were registered against 104,518 Negroes. While some states with white majorities in population were given colored majorities in their electorate, others had their white majorities drastically reduced, and the two states with a preponderance of Negroes in population, South Carolina and Mississippi, had overwhelming majorities of colored voters.

This new-born electorate of freedmen was plunged immediately into action by the election of delegates to constitutional conventions. They followed by electing legislative bodies, state and local officials, and by full scale and continuous participation in all phases and aspects of political life in a period that was abnormally active in a political way. To characterize the quality of the performance of this many people over a decade of time and in a multiplicity of activities with sweeping adjectives, "good" or "bad" or "indifferent," would be to indulge in empty generalities. That the mass of these people had less education, less experience in public affairs, and less property of all sorts than the white voters is obvious. As for the more intangible endowments of status and inner security that the psychologists stress, their relative impoverishment was appalling, unprecedented among American or any other known electorates. Their very appearance at the polls in mass, wearing the rags of slave days and bearing the ancient stigma of oppression, conjured up in conservative minds every gloomy prognostication of the fate of democracies from Aristotle to the Federalists. Not Athens, nor Rome, nor Paris at greatest turbulence had confronted their like. Here was the Federalist beast who would turn every garden into a pigsty. Here was old John Adams's shiftless and improvident Demos, pawn of demagogues and plutocrats and menace to all order. Here in the flesh was Hamilton's "turbulent and changing" mass who "seldom judge or determine right" and who made it necessary to give to "the rich and well born" that "distinct, permanent share in the government" which alone would insure stability. Here was the ultimate test of the democratic dogma in the most extreme form ever attempted.

The records left by that revolutionary experiment have been widely used to discredit both the experiment itself and democratic faith in general. Yet those records need not put democracy out of countenance, nor are they wholly devoid of comfort for those of that faith. No red glow of anarchy lit up the southern horizon as a consequence of the revolution, and the enfranchised freedman did not prove the unleashed beast of Federalist imagination. Moral pigsties undoubtedly developed, but they were oftener than not the creation of the other race, and more of them were to be found outside the South than within.

The new electorate of freedmen proved on the whole remarkably modest in their demands, unaggressive in their conduct, and deferential in their attitude. In no state did they hold place and power in anything approaching their actual numbers and voting strength. The possible exception was South Carolina, and there they held a majority of seats only in the lower house of the legislature. In the first legislature under the new constitution of Mississippi, the other state with a large Negro majority of population, Negro representatives constituted only two-sevenths of the membership of the House and an even smaller proportion of the Senate. Freedmen of that state almost never took advantage of their numbers to seize control in local government, for a Negro majority in a municipal government seems to have been unknown. There was only one Negro mayor of a city in the state and record of only twelve sheriffs. Only three Negroes were elected in the whole country to the Forty-first Congress, the first to which they were eligible, and there were never more than eight at one time out of a total of more than a hundred members from the Southern states. In view of the subordinate role and the few offices that the freedmen took, no state in the South could properly be said to have been under Negro rule or "domination" at any time.

Yet in varying numbers and different states Negroes occupied all the varieties of public office in existence, up to but not including the governorship. They served as policemen and supreme court justices, recorders of deeds and lieutenant-governors, sheriffs and prosecuting attorneys, justices of the peace and state superintendents of education, mayors and United States senators. Without doubt some of them made awkward efforts and a few of them cut some grotesque capers, but upon the crude stage of frontier democracy comic figures had appeared before this time, and none of them could have been taken for colored minstrels before 1868. In an age of low public morals the country over, some of the neophyte politicians were as guilty of corruption as the old hands, but the neophytes rarely seem to have got their fair share of graft.

In retrospect, one is more impressed with the success that a people of such meager resources and limited experience enjoyed in producing the number of sober, honest, and capable leaders and public servants they did. The appearance of some of this sort in every state is the main comfort the record provides to the democratic faith. They give the impression of people struggling conscientiously under desperate odds to live up to a test to which no other people had ever been subjected in all the long testing of the democratic theory. Their success varied from state to state. With regard to Mississippi the conclusions of Vernon Wharton are that: "Altogether, as governments go, that supplied by the Negro and white Republicans in Mississippi between 1870 and 1876 was not a bad government. Never, in states, counties, or towns, did the Negroes hold office in proportion to their numbers . . . The Negroes who held county offices were often ignorant, but under the control of white Democrats or Republicans they supplied a form of government which differed little from that in counties where they held no offices. The three who represented the state in Congress were above reproach. Those in the legislature sought no special advantages for their race, and in one of their very first acts they petitioned Congress to remove all political disabilities from the whites. With their white Republican colleagues, they gave to the state a government of greatly expanded functions at a cost that was low in comparison with that of almost any other state."

By the operation of a sort of historical color bar, the history of the Negro's political experience in Reconstruction has been studied too much in isolation and pictured as unique. There were unique features in that history, of course, but it does not constitute the only, nor the last, instance of the sudden enfranchisement of large numbers of politically inexperienced people. Nor does it support the stereotype of the Negro as the political tyro and neophyte of the western world, the laggard in the race for political maturity. After the Reconstruction episode was over, millions of people entered this country. Of the more than twelve million white immigrants who poured into the stream of American citizenship in the fifty years after 1880 from Southern and Eastern European countries, it is doubtful that more than a very small percentage had ever enjoyed any significant experience of direct political participation in the democratic sense. Their first taste of such experience came in the 1880's, 1890's, 1900's or later when they took out citizenship papers. Here were the real political neophytes of the American electorate. They greatly outnumbered the Negro population. They too were dominated by bosses and influenced by handouts and small favors. The record of the inexperience and naiveté and ineptitude of these erstwhile peasants in the big city slums is written in the history of corrupt city bosses, rings, and machines, a history that can match some of the darker chapters of Reconstruction government. The Mugwump reformers turned against them, as they turned against the Radical Republicans, because of the corruption associated with their regimes. Eventually the immigrants learned the ropes, gained experience and assurance, helped clean up some of the messes their inexperience had created, and gained acceptance as respected members of the body politic.

The immigrants had their own handicaps of language and prejudice to deal with. But they never had anything approaching the handicaps against which the Negro had to struggle to gain acceptance. The prejudices that the immigrants confronted were nothing like as powerful as the race prejudice with which the Negro had to cope. Nor was the white immigrant's enfranchisement accompanied by the disfranchisement of the ruling and propertied classes of the community in which he settled. Nor did the exercise of his franchise have to be protected by the bayonets of federal troops. Nor did the gaining of his political rights appear to old settlers as a penalty and punishment inflicted upon them, a deliberate humiliation of them by their conquerors. Nor were the political leaders of the immigrants ordinarily regarded by the old settlers as "carpet-baggers," intruders, and puppets of a hostile government sent to rule over them. Nor did the immigrants regard the old settlers as their former owners, any more than the old settlers looked upon the immigrants as their former slaves. The situation of the latest political neophytes was, after all, in many ways quite different from that of the neophytes of the seventies.

The time eventually came when the incubus of their political genesis returned to haunt the freedmen and destroy their future. That was the time when the two dominant operative motives of Radical Reconstruction, party advantage and sectional business interests, became inoperative; the time when it became apparent that those mighty ends could better be served by abandoning the experiment and leaving the freedmen to shift for themselves. The philanthropic motive was still operative, and in many minds still strong, but it was not enough without the support of the two powerful props of party advantage and sectional interests. The moment of collapse came at different times in different states, but the climax and consolidation of the decision came with the disputed presidential election of 1876 and the settlement that resolved it in the Compromise of 1877.

It would be neither fair nor accurate to place all the blame upon the North and its selfish interests. There had been plenty of willing cooperation on the part of Southern whites. They had used craft and guile, force and violence, economic pressure and physical terror, and all the subtle psychological devices of race prejudice and propaganda at their command. But the Southern whites were after all a minority, and not a strong minority at that. The North had not only numbers and power on its side, but the law and the Constitution as well. When the moment of crisis arrived, however, the old doubts and skepticism of the North returned, the doubts that had kept the Negro disfranchised in the North after freedman's suffrage had been imposed upon the South. After the Fifteenth Amendment was passed the North rapidly lost interest in the Negro voters. They were pushed out of the limelight by other interests, beset by prejudices, and neglected by politicians. The Northern Negro did not enjoy a fraction of the political success the Southern Negro enjoyed, as modest as that was. Reformers and Mugwumps of the North identified corruption with the Radical wing of the Republican party, lost interest in the Negro allies of the Radicals, and looked upon them as a means of perpetuating corrupt government all over the nation as well as in the South. In this mood they came to the conclusion that the Negro voter had been given a fair chance to prove his worth as a responsible citizen and that the experiment had proved a failure. This conclusion appeared in many places, most strangely perhaps in the columns of that old champion of the race, the New York *Tribune* (April 7, 1877) which declared that the Negroes had been given "ample opportunity to develop their own latent capacities," and had only succeeded in proving that "as a race they are idle, ignorant, and vicious."

The North's loss of faith in its own cause is reflected in many surprising places. One example must suffice. It is of special interest because it comes from the supreme official charged with enforcing the Fifteenth Amendment and guaranteeing to the freedmen their political rights, the President whose administration coincided with Radical Reconstruction and the whole great experiment, General U. S. Grant. According to Secretary Hamilton Fish's Diary, January 17, 1877: "He [Grant] says he opposed the Fifteenth Amendment and thinks it was a mistake, that it had done the Negro no good, and had been a hindrance to the South, and by no means a political advantage to the North."

During the present struggle for Negro rights, which might even be called the Second Reconstruction—though one of quite a different sort— I have noticed among Negro intellectuals at times a tendency to look back upon the First Reconstruction as if it were in some ways a sort of Golden Age. In this nostalgic view that period takes the shape of the race's finest hour, a time of heroic leaders and deeds, of high faith and firm resolution, a time of forthright and passionate action, with no bowing to compromises of "deliberate speed." I think I understand their feeling. Reconstruction will always have a special and powerful meaning for the Negro. It is undoubtedly a period full of rich and tragic and meaningful history, a period that has many meanings yet to yield. But I seriously doubt that it will ever serve satisfactorily as a Golden Age—for anybody. There is too much irony mixed with the tragedy for that.

William E. Burghardt Du Bois **Black Reconstruction**

As might be expected of members of a minority group whose professional aspirations have often been blocked by prejudice and lack of opportunity, Negro historians of eminence have been few. Those Negroes who have written on the history of Reconstruction have been criticized for writing from a minority point of view, for occasionally losing objectivity because of an intense concern with matters of race, and for sometimes allowing a persecution complex to intrude upon scholarship. What white historians frequently forget in making such criticisms is that the rules of their discipline are founded (1) on a majority point of view, (2) on principles of judgment that may be quite unfair to any minority, but especially to the Negro, and (3) on racial attitudes, unacceptable to non-whites, which have become so much a part of American historical writing that they are considered as hallmarks of objectivity.

One of the first to question these white-majority attitudes in Reconstruction history was William E. Burghardt Du Bois, a Negro historian and sociologist. He is considered one of the first revisionists. In his study of Reconstruction he boldly states that the racial question is central and that he interprets the period from the point of view of the Negro, refuting the charge of Negro corruption and incompetence. He also argues that the Negro carpetbag governments brought democracy, social legislation, and public schools, for both whites and Negroes, to the South. Part of his argument is presented in the following selections. [William E. Burghardt Du Bois, Black Reconstruction (New York: Harcourt, Brace and Co., 1935). Reprinted by permission.]

A great political scientist in one of the oldest and largest of American universities wrote and taught thousands of youths and readers that "There is no question, now, that Congress did a monstrous thing, and committed a great political error, if not a sin, in the creation of this new electorate. It was a great wrong to civilization to put the white race of the South under the domination of the Negro race. The claim that there is nothing in the color of the skin from the point of view of political ethics is a great sophism. A black skin means membership in a race of men which has never of itself succeeded in subjecting passion to reason; has never, therefore, created any civilization of any kind."

Here is the crux of all national discussion and study of Reconstruction. The problem is incontinently put beyond investigation and historic proof by the dictum of Judge Taney, Andrew Johnson, John Burgess and their confreres, that Negroes are not men and cannot be regarded and treated as such.

The student who would test this dictum by facts is faced by this set barrier. The whole history of Reconstruction has with few exceptions been written by passionate believers in the inferiority of the Negro. The whole body of facts concerning what the Negro actually said and did, how he worked, what he wanted, for whom he voted, is masked in such a cloud of charges, exaggeration and biased testimony, that most students have given up all attempt at new material or new evaluation of the old, and simply repeated perfunctorily all the current legends of black buffoons in legislature, golden spittoons for fieldhands, bribery and extravagance on an unheard-of scale, and the collapse of civilization until an outraged nation rose in wrath and ended the ridiculous travesty.

And yet there are certain quite well-known facts that are irreconcilable with this theory of history. Civilization did not collapse in the South in 1868–1876. The charge of industrial anarchy is faced by the fact that the cotton crop had recovered by 1870, five years after the war, and by 1876 the agricultural and even commercial and industrial rebirth of the South was in sight. The public debt was large; but measured in depreciated currency and estimated with regard to war losses, and the enlarged functions of a new society, it was not excessive. The legislation of this period was not bad, as is proven by the fact that it was retained for long periods after 1876, and much of it still stands.

One must admit that generalizations of this sort are liable to wide error, but surely they can justifiably be balanced against the extreme charges of a history written for purposes of propaganda. And above all, no history is accurate and no "political science" scientific that starts with the gratuitous assumption that the Negro race has been proven incapable of modern civilization. Such a dogma is simply the modern and American residue of a universal belief that most men are sub-normal and that civilization is the gift of the Chosen Few.

Since the beginning of time, most thinkers have believed that the vast majority of human beings are incorrigibly stupid and evil. The proportion of thinkers who believed this has naturally changed with historical evolution. In earliest times all men but the Chosen Few were impossible. Before the middle class of France revolted, only the Aristocracy of birth and knowledge could know and do. After the American experiment a considerable number of thinkers conceived that possibly most men had capabilities, except, of course, Negroes. Possibly never in human history before or since have so many men believed in the manhood of so many men as after the Battle of Port Hudson, when Negroes fought for Freedom.

All men know that by sheer weight of physical force, the mass of men must in the last resort become the arbiters of human action. But reason, skill, wealth, machines and power may for long periods enable the few to control the many. But to what end? The current theory of democracy is that dictatorship is a stopgap pending the work of universal education, equitable income, and strong character. But always the temptation is to use the stopgap for narrower ends, because intelligence, thrift and goodness seem so impossibly distant for most men. We rule by junta; we turn Fascist, because we do not believe in men; yet the basis of fact in this disbelief is incredibly narrow. We know perfectly well that most human beings have never had a decent human chance to be full men. Most of us may be convinced that even with opportunity the number of utter human failures would be vast; and yet remember that this assumption kept the ancestors of present white America long in slavery and degradation.

It is then one's moral duty to see that every human being, to the extent of his capacity, escapes ignorance, poverty and crime. With this high ideal held unswervingly in view, monarchy, oligarchy, dictatorships may rule; but the end will be the rule of All, if mayhap All or Most qualify. The only unforgivable sin is dictatorship for the benefit of Fools, Voluptuaries, gilded Satraps, Prostitutes and Idiots. The rule of the famished, unlettered, stinking mob is better than this and the only inevitable, logical and justifiable return. To escape from ultimate democracy is as impossible as it is for ignorant poverty and crime to rule forever.

The opportunity to study a great human experiment was present in Reconstruction, and its careful scientific investigation would have thrown a world of light on human development and democratic government. The material today, however, is unfortunately difficult to find. Little effort has been made to preserve the records of Negro effort and speeches, actions, work and wages, homes and families. Nearly all this has gone down beneath a mass of ridicule and caricature, deliberate omission and misstatement. No institution of learning has made any effort to explore or probe Reconstruction from the point of view of the laborer and most men have written to explain and excuse the former slaveholder, the planter, the landholder, and the capitalist. The loss today is irreparable, and this present study limps and gropes in darkness, lacking most essentials to a complete picture; and yet the writer is convinced that this is the story of a normal working class movement, successful to an unusual degree, despite all disappointment and failure. . . .

It was soon after the war that a white member of Johnson's restored Louisiana legislature passed one of the schools set up by the Freedmen's Bureau in New Orleans. The grounds were filled with children. He stopped and looked intently, and then asked, "Is this a school?" "Yes," was the reply. "What, for niggers?" "Evidently." He threw up his hands. "Well, well," he said, "I have seen many an absurdity in my lifetime, but *this is the climax!*"

If a poor, degraded, disadvantaged horde achieves sudden freedom and power, what could we ask of them in ten years? To develop some, but surely not all, necessary social leadership; to seek the right sort of leadership from other groups; to strive for increase of knowledge, so as to teach themselves wisdom and the rhythm of united effort.

This latter accomplishment crowns the work of Reconstruction. The advance of the Negro in education, helped by the Abolitionists, was phenomenal; but the greatest step was preparing his won teachers—the gift of New England to the black South.

If the Negro public school system had been sustained, guided and supported, the American Negro today would equal Denmark in literacy. As it is, he surpasses Spain and Italy, the Balkans and South America; and this is due to the Negro college, which despite determined effort to curtail the efficiency of the Negro public school, and despite a sustained and violent attack upon higher education for black folk, nevertheless, through white Northern philanthropy and black Southern contributions, survived and furnished teachers and leaders for the Negro race at the time of its greatest crisis.

The eagerness to learn among American Negroes was exceptional in the case of a poor and recently emancipated folk. Usually, with a protective psychology, such degraded masses regard ignorance as natural and necessary, or even exalt their own traditional wisdom and discipline over "book learning"; or they assume that knowledge is for higher beings, and not for the "likes of us."

American Negroes never acted thus. The very feeling of inferiority which slavery forced upon them fathered an intense desire to rise out of their condition by means of education. Of the 488,070 free Negroes in the United States in 1860, 32,629 were attending school, and only 91,736 were unable to read and write. In the slave states, there were 3,651 colored children attending schools supported by the free Negroes.

The mass of the slaves could have no education. The laws on this point were explicit and severe. There was teaching, here and there, by indulgent masters, or by clandestine Negro schools, but in the main, the laws were followed. All the slave states had such laws, and after the Nat Turner insurrection in Virginia, these laws were strengthened and more carefully enforced.

As late as May, 1862, Edward Stanley, whom Lincoln appointed Provisional Governor of North Carolina, sought to conciliate the white people when he stopped a Negro school at New Bern. He said that he had been sent there to restore the old order of things, and that the laws of North Carolina forbade the teaching of slaves to read and write; and he could not expect success in his undertaking if he encouraged the violation of the law.

At the time of the emancipation, not all Southern Negroes were illiterate. In South Carolina, a majority of the nearly 10,000 free Negroes could read and write, and perhaps 5% of the slaves. But illiteracy among the colored population was well over 95% in 1863, which meant that less than 150,000 of the four million slaves emancipated could read and write.

The first great mass movement for public education at the expense of the state, in the South, came from Negroes. Many leaders before the war had advocated general education, but few had been listened to. Schools for indigents and paupers were supported, here and there, and more or less spasmodically. Some states had elaborate plans, but they were not carried out. Public education for all at public expense was, in the South, a Negro idea.

Prior to the abolition of slavery, there was no general public educational system, properly speaking, in the Southern states, except perhaps, in North Carolina. In some populous centers, there were free schools; in some localities, academies and colleges, but for the most part, no adequate provision was made for the education even of the poorer whites. Emerging from their bondage, the

Negroes in the very beginning manifested the utmost eagerness for instruction, and their hunger was met by a corresponding readiness on the part of the people of the North to make provisions for it [American Freedmen's Union Commission].

The original state constitution of North Carolina, in 1775, provided for public education, but there was no appropriation for the schools, and the only direct result was the establishment of the state university. In 1825, a literary fund was established toward defraying the cost of the public schools. A school system was sketched in 1839, but without an executive head, and with small funds. In 1852, a Superintendent of Public Instruction was appointed. His work for a long time was confined to propaganda, and he especially noted the lack of any demand for public schools, and the feeling that such schools were simply for paupers.

Nevertheless, the work of the first superintendent, C. H. Wiley, was important as propaganda, but only as propaganda, because at the time of the war, "only here and there in the state is there a schoolhouse for whites of very inferior description, and with long distance between." There was no state support of schools. The burden of public education, such as it was, rested on local authorities.

In South Carolina, there was even less effort. In 1811, there was "An Act to Establish Free Schools Throughout the State." It provided for as many free schools in each election district as the district was entitled to representatives in the Lower House. After forty-four years of operation (1811–1855), Governor J. A. Adams pronounced the system a failure, saying of the handling of funds: "Great inequalities prevailed, and during twenty-seven years, returns were made in only five years; the small districts and parishes did not receive regular sums, and the amounts received, did not have proportion to the number of schools, or to the population; after 1815, the annual appropriation was $37,000 annually, nearly $1,500,000 in all, of which only $109,740 was accounted for."

In December, 1855, Governor Adams pleaded for the appointment of a Superintendent of Education. "Let us make at least this effort, and if the poor of the land are hopelessly doomed to ignorance, poverty, and crime, you will at least feel conscious of having done your duty." He was, of course, referring only to the whites, and did not himself seem to believe much in the educability of the poor.

In Virginia, Armstead reports that in 1851, less than one-half the poor white children were attending any schools, and those attended only eleven weeks in the year. "This pitiable result was obtained with a cost to the state of $69,000." Thomas Jefferson in the eighteenth century had evolved a school system for whites, with industrial schools for Negroes, "but there was bitter and successful opposition" and as Jefferson himself said, "Such a permissive scheme was doomed to failure from the very moment of its inception."

In Georgia, the constitution of 1777 had spoken of schools, but nothing was done. Some private academies were incorporated in 1783, and permission given the Governor to grant a thousand acres of free land for erection of free schools, but few if any grants were made. In 1815, $250,000 was appropriated, known as the Poor School Fund. Nothing further was done until the legislature of 1851, when something was added to this fund to pay tuition for the children of parents too poor to pay anything.

The whole fund for education as late as 1865 was only $23,355. Governor Brown urged a system of public schools before the war, but the legislature did nothing but make a small increase of the poor school fund.

In 1858, a movement was started in Atlanta looking toward the establishment of a system of free schools in Georgia. A. N. Wilson went to Rhode Island to look into the public school system there, and on his return, held several meetings, culminating in a meeting October 6, 1858, called by the mayor. The chairman appointed a committee, but some of the members of the committee took charge of the entire movement and blocked it. The original movers, seeing that they had lost control, withdrew, and the proposal fell through. The constitution of 1865 under the provisional government gave the legislature permission to appropriate money for the "promotion of learning and science," and "for the education of the people," and provided "for the resumption of the regular exercises of the University of Georgia."

In the first session of the legislature after the war, a bill to establish public schools was introduced, but postponed until late in 1866. By a vote of 62–58, in the House, and an equally close vote in the Senate, a bill to establish a system of public schools was squeezed through but only on condition that nothing was to be done until 1868. This proposal lapsed because of the Reconstruction Acts of 1867.

Thus although there had been much talk and some legislation on the subject, there had been "no regularly organized system of common schools supported by public taxation in Georgia prior to the Civil War."

Mississippi did lip service to the idea of public education in her earlier constitutions, but little tangible was accomplished. The Sixteenth Section fund given to the states by the Federal government for education, amounting to at least $15,000,000 in Mississippi, was totally mismanaged and lost, while tens of thousands of white children grew up in ignorance. Florida tried, about 1850, to obtain schools for whites, from taxes on certain sales of slaves, with small results.

Alabama and North Carolina had the best pre-war systems, due to the enthusiasm of certain teachers, but even here, there was no disposition among the planters to accept taxation for public education. Joel Riggs, comptroller of the state treasury in 1851, said: "Perhaps of all trust-funds, none has been so greatly mismanaged as the school-fund of Alabama."

The experience of the other Southern states shows similar neglect and indisposition to educate the poor whites.

The fact of the matter was that in the pre-war South, there were two insuperable obstacles to a free public school system. The first was the attitude of the owners of property. They did not propose under any circumstances to be taxed for the public education of the laboring class. They believed that laborers did not need education; that it made their exploitation more difficult; and that if any of them were really worth educating, they would somehow escape their condition by their own efforts.

The second obstacle was that the white laborers did not demand education, and saw no need of it, save in exceptional cases. They accepted without murmur their subordination to the slaveholders, and looked for escape from their condition only to the possibility of becoming slaveholders themselves. Education they regarded as a luxury connected with wealth.

It was only the other part of the laboring class, the black folk, who connected knowledge with power; who believed that education was the stepping-stone to wealth and respect, and that wealth, without education, was crippled. Perhaps the very fact that so many of them had seen the wealthy slaveholders at close range, and knew the extent of ignorance and inefficiency among them, led to that extraordinary mass demand on the part of the black laboring class for education. And it was this demand that was the effective force for the establishment of the public school in the South on a permanent basis, for all people and all classes.

If the planters opposed schools for poor whites, they all the more regarded Negro schools as absurd. The unalterable conviction of most white Southerners was that Negroes could not and would not learn, and thus their education involved an unjustifiable waste of private property for public disaster.

D. R. Grattan, a native Virginian, testified before the Reconstruction Committee in 1866: "They cannot educate themselves; they are not disposed to educate themselves."

In the face of this, listen to the words of Booker T. Washington: "Few people who were not right in the midst of the scenes can form any exact idea of the intense desire which the people of my race showed for education. It was a whole race trying to go to school. Few were too young, and none too old, to make the attempt to learn. As fast as any kind of teachers could be secured, not only were day-schools filled, but night-schools as well. The great ambition of the older people was to try to learn to read the Bible before they died. With this end in view, men and women who were fifty and seventy-five years old, would be found in the night-schools. Sunday-schools were formed soon after freedom, but the principal book studied in the Sunday-school was the spelling-book. Day-school, night-school, and Sunday-school were always crowded, and often many had to be turned away for want of room."

The first educational efforts came during the war, when the Negroes, refugees and soldiers were taught at various camps and places of refuge at their own pressing request. This was followed by the efforts of philanthropic societies. Schools were started among the Negroes of the peninsula of Virginia and of Port Royal, South Carolina, as soon as they were captured.

In Virginia, when Federal authority was established in the Southeast, the American Missionary Association asked to work among the freedmen and was welcomed by Governor Butler.

The first day-school was established on September 17, 1861, in the town of Hampton in a small brown house near the Seminary, a school formerly used by the whites. This school was taught by Mrs. Mary Peake under the auspices of the American Missionary Association. Mrs. Peake was a mulatto, whose father was an Englishman. She was born a free woman and received a fair education at her home in Alexandria. She wanted to help her race, and she had gone among the slaves during slavery to teach them to read and write. She held her school at Hampton, however, only until the next spring, when she died of consumption at the early age of 39. Her school was not only the first one at Hampton but the first of the kind in the South. Around the small school she began followed the other schools in the Hampton vicinity, all of which led to the Hampton Institute of today. . . .

It will be noted that in nearly all the Southern states there were continual and well-proven charges of peculation and misuse of public school funds. This was not a part of the general charge of stealing and graft, but was the fault of local county officials. In most cases, the leading white landholders, who took no part in the administration of the state, nevertheless kept their hands upon local taxation and assessments, and were determined that the impoverished property-holder should not be taxed for Negro education. By various methods, direct and indirect, they thus continually diverted the school funds, and this class of white people was primarily the one responsible for such dishonesty as there was in administration of local school funds. On the other hand, there were Negro and poor white officials, here and there, who were guilty of waste and theft.

During and after Reconstruction, diversion of school funds was common. In North Carolina, $136,076 was collected for education in 1870, but the Department of Education received only $38,931. In Louisiana $1,000,000 worth of bonds for the school fund were used to pay the expenses of the legislature in 1872. In Texas, a large part of the income and public lands which belonged to the education fund was lost. In 1870, the school funds in Georgia were partially used for other purposes, and in 1874, Alabama school funds were diverted. In Tennessee, from 1866–1869, only 47% of the school taxes were spent on schools.

In nearly every state, the question of mixed and separate schools was a matter of much debate and strong feeling. There was no doubt that the Negroes in general wanted mixed schools. They wanted the advantages of contact with white children, and they wanted to have this evidence and proof of their equality. In addition to this, they were strengthened in their stand by white Northern leaders, who pointed out the practical difficulty of two separate systems of schools, which must, to an extent, duplicate effort, and would certainly greatly increase cost. In many of the states, the matter was left in abeyance, and in some states, like Louisiana, mixed schools were established.

This raised a fury of opposition among the whites, but for reasons of economy and democracy it was obviously the best policy. The propaganda of race hatred made it eventually impossible, and the separate school systems so increased the cost of public education in the South that they resulted in the retardation of the whole system and eventually in making the Negro child bear the burden of the increased cost; so that even to this day throughout the South, the Negro child has from one-half to one-tenth as much spent on his education as the white child, and even then, the white child does not receive sufficient funds for a thorough elementary education.

Separation by race was prohibited in the Constitutions of South Carolina and Louisiana. In Atlanta, the Board of Education wanted mixed schools, but allowed separate schools when they were desired. The trustees of the Peabody Fund caused the dropping of a clause prohibiting separate schools in the original draft of the Federal Civil Rights Bill of 1875.

One Southern Congressman's speech represents the strength of this fear. "Woe be unto the political party which shall declare to the toiling yeoman, the honest laboring poor of this country, 'Your children are no better than a Negro's.' If you think so, you shall not practice on that opinion. We are the rulers; you are the servants! We know what is best for you and your children. We, the millionaires—we, who are paid out of your pockets, will take your money and will send our children to select high schools, to foreign lands, where no Negroes are, but you, you who are too poor to pay, shall send your ragged, hungry urchins to the common schools on such terms as we dictate, or keep them away to stray among the treacherous quick-sands and shoals of life; to wander on the streets and learn to syllable the alphabet of vice and crime, or stay at home, and like blind Samson, in mental darkness, tramp barefoot, the tread-mill of unceasing toil!"

In the Reconstruction constitutions, state taxation for schools was a new feature, unknown in the previous school laws of Alabama, Florida, Arkansas, Georgia, Mississippi, North Carolina, and South Carolina. The principle of direct taxation was undoubtedly the most important contribution of the Reconstruction regime to the public school movement in the South. It was perpetuated in all the revisions of these constitutions after 1876, except in Alabama. The victory of home rule in 1876 was followed by a period of hostility or at least indifference to public education. In 1879, in Virginia, $1,000,000 belonging to the school fund had been used for other purposes. In Georgia, the legislature of 1876 destroyed $350,000 worth of bonds belonging to the school fund. Tennessee, in 1869, abolished the general tax for school purposes, and the administrative system. The Alabama Constitution of 1875, instead of allocating one-fifth of the state revenue to education, which was the provision in the Constitution of 1868, substituted direct appropriation. In Arkansas, the income from land sales belonging to the school fund was used for other purposes. There were similar reductions of school revenue in Louisiana. In Texas, a voluntary county system was substituted for the state system in 1875 and 1876. The public school system of the South was helped by the gifts of the Peabody Fund in 1876 and 1879.

On account of the influences mentioned, it became common throughout the South, for all parties to pledge themselves to the cause of public schools. Yet, by some of those strange fatalities of history, the strongest of all influences for educational progress was the very one which during and just after the Reconstruction period undoubtedly checked the cause. That was the race issue. The movement to eliminate the Negro as a factor in politics involved an appeal to passion, to prejudice, and sometimes a misrepresentation of the part of the colored man in Southern progress [William K. Boyd].

It is fair to say that the Negro carpetbag governments established the public schools of the South. Although recent researches have shown many germs of a public school system in the South before the war, there can be no reasonable doubt that common school instruction in the South, in the modern sense of the term, was founded by the Freedmen's Bureau and missionary societies, and that the state public school system was formed mainly by Negro Reconstruction governments.

Dunning says: "Free public education existed in only a rudimentary and sporadic form in the South before the war, but the new constitutions provided generally for complete systems on advanced northern models."

Colonel Richard P. Hallowell adds: "The whites had always regarded the public school system of the North with contempt. The freedman introduced and established it, and it stands today a living testimony."

From the beginning of the public school system under Reconstruction, and after, the fight between local and state control and supervision has been bitter. Local control meant the control of property and racial particularism. It stood for reaction and prejudice; and wherever there was retrogression, particularly in Negro schools, it can be traced to the increased power of the county and district administrators. This accounts for the difficulties, corruption, and failures in Alabama and South Carolina, particularly, and in most of the other Southern states.

For the first success of the Negro schools, the South deserved little praise. From the beginning, most of the Southern states made the Negro schools just as bad as they dared to in the face of national public opinion, and every cent spent on them was taken from Negro rents and wages, and came back to the property-holders tenfold in increased opportunities for exploitation.

It is said, for instance, in one state: "There were to be free public schools. The blacks were to be the chief beneficiaries of the new system, but the whites would pay the taxes. Whites considered such education either useless or positively dangerous to society." Of free, self-sacrificing gifts for the sake of Negro uplift and intelligence, the vast majority of Southern white people contributed almost nothing.

In recent years under the influence of educational leaders like Atticus Haygood and James Dillard, the support of Negro education in some Southern states has become more enlightened and generous. This is particularly true in North Carolina, West Virginia, and Texas. Improvement over unusually bad conditions may be noted also in Louisiana, Virginia, and Delaware. The situation in South Carolina, Florida, Georgia, Alabama, and Mississippi is still reactionary and deplorable, while the improvement in Arkansas, Tennessee, and Kentucky is not great.

Finally, the movement that saved the Negro public school system was not enlightened Southern opinion, but rather that Northern philanthropy which at the very beginning of the Negro education movement contributed toward the establishment of Negro colleges. The reason for them at first was to supply the growing demand for teachers, and was also a concession to Southern prejudice, which so violently disliked the white teacher in the Negro school.

This led to the establishment by 1879 of eighty-four normal and high schools and sixteen colleges, with over twelve thousand students. But these institutions soon saw a higher mission. In the midst of reaction and disfranchisement, of poverty and growing caste, they became the centers of a training in leadership and ideals for the whole Negro race, and the only fine and natural field of contact between white and black culture.

The fathers of forty years ago anticipated the criticisms of later years as to the wisdom of colleges for the development of a backward race. So, they said, let it be granted that other lines of education are imperative; colleges also certainly are needed, and we must set the standards for the education of the race now! Thorough training, large knowledge, and the best culture possible are needed to invigorate, direct, purify, and broaden life; needed for the wise administration of citizenship, the duties of which are as sure to come as the sun is to shine, though today or tomorrow may be cloudy; needed to overcome narrowness, one-sidedness, and incompleteness [Augustus F. Beard].

Howard University and Freedman's Hospital are survivals of the Freedmen's Bureau. Howard University was chartered in 1867 and General O. O. Howard, head of the Freedmen's Bureau, was made its first president. Succeeding as presidents were W. W. Patton, J. E. Rankin, who wrote "God Be With You Until We Meet Again," and John Gordon, a lineal descendant of Jonathan Edwards. On its governing board have been Douglass, Langston and Bruce; it has the largest Negro medical center in the United States, and has furnished about half of the Negro lawyers.

Berea College was started by John G. Fee, a Kentuckian, who became an abolitionist. After the war, colored students were admitted, and a brother of the President of Oberlin was at the head of the school. For forty years, colored students attended Berea, but finally, in 1904, the institution was by law closed to Negroes.

Hampton Institute was founded by General S. C. Armstrong, near where the Negroes were first made "contraband of war," and where a colored woman founded the first colored school. Among its trustees were Mark Hopkins, Phillips Brooks, and John G. Whittier.

Atlanta University was founded by Edmund Ware in 1867. "To have gone on as President Ware did during those early years there must have been in his heart deathless love and pity for men who needed what he could give them—a faith in the gospel and eternal righteousness that never wavered, and a love for God that made work easy and suffering joy."

Add to this the picture of DeForrest at Talledega, Cravath at Fisk, and others at Biddle, Knoxville, New Orleans, and Central Tennessee. There were those two influential schools at the edge of the South, Lincoln in Pennsylvania, and Wilberforce in Ohio.

Nearly all of these educational leaders were either nominated by Howard, head of the Freedmen's Bureau, as in the case of General S. C. Armstrong, or received from him the most thorough-going cooperation. There is no greater tribute to the Freedmen's Bureau than this.

Propaganda has centered the attention of the world upon those Northerners who took part in the political reconstruction of the South, and particularly upon those who were charged with dishonesty, while of the history of this astonishing movement to plant the New England college in the South, and to give the Southern black man a leadership based on scholarship and character, almost nothing has been said. And yet this was the salvation of the South and the Negro. These "carpetbaggers" deserve to be remembered and honored. Without them there can be no doubt that the Negro would have rushed into revolt and vengeance and played into the hands of those determined to crush him. As it was, when reaction triumphed in 1876, there was already present a little group of trained leadership which grew by leaps and bounds until it gripped and held the mass of Negroes at the beginning of the twentieth century.

Had it not been for the Negro school and college, the Negro would, to all intents and purposes, have been driven back to slavery. His economic foothold in land and capital was too slight in ten years of turmoil to effect any defense or stability. His reconstruction leadership had come from Negroes educated in the North, and white politicians, capitalists and philanthropic teachers. The counter-revolution of 1876 drove most of these, save the teachers, away. But already, through establishing public schools and private colleges, and by organizing the Negro church, the Negro had acquired enough leadership and knowledge to thwart the worst designs of the new slave drivers. They avoided the mistake of trying to meet force by force. They bent to the storm of beating, lynching and murder, and kept their souls in spite of public and private insult of every description; they built an inner culture which the world recognizes in spite of the fact that it is still half-strangled and inarticulate.

Author Index